invitation to human communication

Second Edition

Cindy L. Griffin
Colorado State University

Jennifer Emerling Bone
Colorado State University

CENGAGE
Learning·

Australia • Brazil • Mexico • Singapore • United Kingdom • United States

CENGAGE
Learning®

**Invitation to Human Communication,
Second Edition**
Cindy L. Griffin, Jennifer Emerling Bone

Product Director: Monica Eckman

Product Manager: Kelli Strieby

Content Developer: Erin Bosco

Associate Content Developer: Karolina Kiwak

Product Assistant: Colin Solan

Marketing Manager: Sarah Seymour

Content Project Manager: Dan Saabye

Art Director: Marissa Falco

Manufacturing Planner: Doug Bertke

IP Analyst: Ann Hoffman

IP Project Manager: Betsy Hathaway

Production Service: MPS Limited

Compositor: MPS Limited

Text Designer: Joel Sadagursky

Cover Designer: Red Hangar Design

Cover Image: Jon Hicks/Corbis

For product information and technology assistance, contact us at
Cengage Learning Customer & Sales Support, 1-800-354-9706

For permission to use material from this text or product,
submit all requests online at **www.cengage.com/permissions**.
Further permissions questions can be emailed to
permissionrequest@cengage.com.

Library of Congress Control Number: 2015943722

Student Edition:

ISBN: 978-1-305-50282-6

Loose-leaf Edition:

ISBN: 978-1-305-65516-4

Cengage Learning
20 Channel Center Street
Boston, MA 02210
USA

Cengage Learning is a leading provider of customized learning solutions with employees residing in nearly 40 different countries and sales in more than 125 countries around the world. Find your local representative at **www.cengage.com**.

Cengage Learning products are represented in Canada by Nelson Education, Ltd.

To learn more about Cengage Learning Solutions, visit
www.cengage.com.

Purchase any of our products at your local college store or at our preferred online store **www.cengagebrain.com**.

Printed in Canada
Print Number: 01   Print Year: 2015

CONTENTS

4   LANGUAGE 74

5   LISTENING 96

PART II: INTERPERSONAL COMMUNICATION

6 UNDERSTANDING INTERPERSONAL COMMUNICATION 116

7 IMPROVING INTERPERSONAL COMMUNICATION 141

PART III: COMMUNICATION IN GROUPS

8 | FOUNDATIONS OF COMMUNICATION IN GROUPS AND TEAMS 165

PART IV: PUBLIC COMMUNICATION

10 | DEVELOPING YOUR SPEECH TOPIC AND PURPOSE 218

13 | INFORMATIVE SPEAKING 319

14 | PERSUASIVE SPEAKING 343

15 | INVITATIONAL SPEAKING 370

ACKNOWLEDGMENTS

Invitation to Human Communication results not only from our own collaboration as coauthors but also from the generous support, assistance, and guidance of many individuals. We extend our sincere and heartfelt thanks to Monica Eckman, product director, who supported this project from its inception and had the vision to see the positive and productive link between *Invitation to Human Communication* and the National Geographic Society and the courage to help us develop and nurture that link. Many thanks go to Nicole Morinon and Kelli Strieby, product managers, and to Erin Bosco, associate content developer, for her work ideas and expertise as we negotiated this innovative partnership and brought the book to its second edition. To Colin Solan, product assistant; Sarah Seymour, marketing manager; Dan Saabye, content project manager; Wesley Della Volla, NGL associate manager; Marissa Falco, senior art director; Edward Dionne, project manager; and S. M. Summerlight, copy editor—we thank you from the bottom of our hearts for all the work you have done to support, develop, and market this fundamentals of communication book.

Many thanks are also in order to all the reviewers of this edition: Kimberly Boren Dumas, Columbia College; Mary Gill, Buena Vista University–Storm Lake; Roxanne Heimann, University of Northern Iowa; Heather Heritage, Cedarville University; Yasmin Shenoy, University of Hartford; and Tanika Smith, Prince Georges Community College.

A warm thank you to the reviewers of the first edition: Shae Adkins, Lone Star College, North Harris; Todd Allen, Geneva College; Pete Bicak, Rockhurst College; John O. Burtis, University of Northern Iowa; Diane Carter, University of Idaho; Kathryn Coker, St. Charles Community College; Angela Gibson, Shelton State Community College; Cynthia Gordon, Syracuse University; Brent Kice, Frostburg State University; Darren Linvill, Clemson University; Yvette Lujan, Miami Dade College; Tami Olds, Northern Virginia Community College, Sandra Rath, Arizona State University; Adam Roth, University of Rhode Island; David K. Scott, Northeastern State University; Glynis Strause, Coastal Bend College; and Lisa Waite, Kent State University.

We also wish to thank Kristin Slattery, Special Instructor at Colorado State University, for her invaluable research assistance in the early stages of this project; and Dr. Andy Merolla, now at Baldwin Wallace University, our "go-to expert" for random questions, source clarifications, and general great humor in the first edition of this book; and Martha Mathews for providing a detailed review with helpful feedback for the second edition.

To our National Geographic Explorers, and to those at National Geographic who saw the powerful link between the work that National Geographic does and communication principles and practices, we extend our sincerest "Thank you." Thank you for reaching out to us; for sharing your innovative images, ideas, and practices with us; and for trusting us to showcase the important role communication plays in "inspiring people to care about the planet." The National Geographic stories told throughout the book and the tips shared with our readers illustrate the amazing potential each person has, working in teams and alone, to make a positive difference. We sincerely appreciate the time National Geographic Explorers T. H. Culhane, Barrington Irving, Mireya Mayor, Greg Anderson, David Harrison, Josh Thome, Aziz Abu Sarah, Alexandra Cousteau, Shabana Basij-Rasikh,

Sylvia Earle, Asher Jay, Wade Davis, Sol Guy, Becca Skinner, and Raghava KK, who took time to speak with us over the phone and to communicate with us via e-mail so they could share their important work and inspirational words and ideas with us. Each Explorer's inspiring story demonstrates the importance of communication and civic engagement and the compassion of the human heart to help the environment, animal species, and humankind.

Jennifer would like to thank several people for their support throughout the process of writing this book. To Cindy, a special thank you for your academic support, mentorship, and confidence in partnering on this project. I appreciate the many conversations that reinforced the importance of collaboration and respect for each other's ideas. I learned that friendship can be the foundation for amazing work. Your patience and honesty are admirable. Thank you! To Hilary Nye, thank you for your love and devotion to my family during the initial making of this book. A heartfelt thank you goes to my family for their continual support and encouragement. The many hours of research, writing, and editing were accomplished with unwavering love from my husband, Ryan Bone, and children, Miles and Alex Bone. From Cindy, a heartfelt thanks to Michael Harte, who offered me unending support, love, good humor, problem solving, and levity when it was most needed. To my family, Joe and Kari, the Webster-Wheeler clan, and Tracy, John, and Wendy, I offer my gratitude and deepest thanks. And to mom, and dad, I know you are up there watching and smiling. And finally to Jen, who had the courage to say, "Yes, I can do this with you," I say, "I couldn't have done this without you"—many, many thanks.

Cindy L. Griffin, Colorado State University
Jennifer Emerling Bone, Colorado State University

As professors of communication attempt to prepare their students for success in our increasingly complex, diverse, and interconnected world, materials that allow them to do so in meaningful, civil, and accessible ways become imperative. Because communication is central to the social, political, professional, and personal lives of our students, the Fundamentals of Communication course is poised to facilitate our students' success in these areas in important and powerful ways. *Invitation to Human Communication*, working in partnership with the National Geographic Society, acknowledges the complexity of today's world, the power of communication, and the necessity of teaching students the foundational skills they will need to both compete and succeed in this complex and exciting environment.

Because of our innovative alliance with National Geographic, *Invitation to Human Communication* is able to facilitate the teaching of foundational communication theories and skills in unique and groundbreaking ways. Our collaboration allows us not only to showcase the best of communication theories and practice but also to showcase and explore the ways that National Geographic Explorers and researchers use communication to carry out their work, develop professional and personal relationships with others, and share their discoveries and research with the larger public. The addition of inspiring and thought-provoking photos and interesting videos enhance the connection between National Geographic and the *Invitation to Human Communication* program. Social media links allow students to connect directly with the Explorers and learn about new discoveries, continuing the learning process well beyond the classroom.

Invitation to Human Communication also incorporates extensive research that illuminates practices and theories of civility, dialogue and deliberation, civic engagement, and ethical communication, which are central to a democratic society. This framing allows students to see that their own communication directly affects the quality of an interaction as well as the perpetuation of ethical and civil forms of interacting. Incorporating deliberative and invitational styles of communication, also central to a democratic society, allows students to link concepts and practices to the world around them and to understand the various ways communication assists us in exploring, understanding, and even respecting our differences. The end result is not necessarily agreement, as many of our National Geographic Explorers attest, but meaningful communication that assists us in making decisions that are informed and respectful of others.

The incorporation of case studies, a Communicating in the Workplace feature that focuses on the role of communication in our workplaces, and discussions related to the uses of technology, provide an additional venue for students to think critically about their styles of communication, their approaches to others, and the impact of technology on their communication. Students' exposure to technology is framed as learning to communicate effectively through and with technology rather than simply "using" technology. And our National Geographic Explorers help us teach our students about the important role of technology related to communication and effective and ethical communicative practices.

The framing of communication as foundational to our lives—and our partnership with National Geographic—runs consistently throughout the text. *Invitation to Human Communication* thus encourages students to make links between material read in the text, real-world examples and case studies, material presented by the instructor, and experiences they either have had or likely will have as they move beyond the fundamentals course and into their chosen professions.

Our approach, our case studies and feature boxes, and our National Geographic partnership allow instructors to incorporate and discuss contemporary as well as historical events and issues, illustrate the ways communication is at work in those issues, and then link those events back to the material taught in the course. Thus, the complexities of communication, teaching and learning, and human interactions in a variety of venues and contexts are recognized and valued. In addition, links between the material students are asked to learn and their own lives are made relevant and honored. As such, the fundamentals course becomes clearly connected to their future goals and daily practices. And students are equipped to communicate more effectively in a variety of situations, some of them already familiar, that they will likely encounter in their futures outside the classroom.

Invitation to Human Communication is divided into four sections.

We begin with material that explores the foundations of communication principles and practices. In this section, we explore the process of communication, perception, nonverbal and verbal communication, and listening. In the second section, we address interpersonal communication, its nature, and its scope, as well as ways to improve communication in interpersonal relationships. Working with the voices and experiences of our National Geographic Explorers, we frame these two sections to showcase the centrality of communication in our lives as well as the importance of civil and ethical communicative practices. We present not only the most recent and innovative research in these two sections but also the foundational scholarship that lays the framework for the study of communication. *Invitation to Human Communication* also incorporates discussions of the effects of technology on our interpersonal relationships throughout the first two sections. With this integration, students are reminded that the theories and ideas they are learning are not arbitrary or found only in a text but part of their everyday interactions. In this way, the role of communication in facing communication dilemmas and interpersonal challenges is emphasized.

In the third and fourth sections of *Invitation to Human Communication*, we continue our partnership with National Geographic. Part III explores communication in groups, and Part IV examines public speaking. These components of communication are also presented through the lenses of civil and ethical communication and civic engagement, as well as invitational conversations and dialogues. The materials in these two sections are presented in a skills-based manner, and this approach assists students in recognizing that they are learning skills that will help them attain success outside the classroom in their professional lives. We continue our partnership with National Geographic such that students can begin to see themselves as able to participate in both the larger public and professional dialogues that surround them. These dialogues are about complex issues that affect us all.

As a result of the framing of the text, students begin to recognize the importance of communication and to feel empowered to participate in contemporary conversations and dialogues. The impact of technology is also a key component of the final section of the book, and students are encouraged to understanding the benefits and dilemmas presented with the integration of technology into their speaking and work environments. The result of this coherent and real-world focus is that concepts that once seemed disconnected and linked only to the classroom become ideas and tools that help students succeed in both their personal and professional lives.

Features of *Invitation to Human Communication*

Features are an important part of any textbook, enticing students to read and learn the concepts. This text offers the following innovative pedagogical features.

National Geographic Partnership

Invitation to Human Communication is the only communication textbook to work collaboratively with National Geographic, highlighting the central role of communication in our work, social interactions, and personal lives. To this end, *Invitation to Human Communication* includes two unique features:

- **National Geographic Speaks** features Thomas Taha Rassam Culhane, Barrington Irving, Mireya Mayor, Gregory D. S. Anderson, K. David Harrison, Josh Thome, Aziz Abu Sarah, Alexandra Cousteau, Shabana Basij-Rasikh, Sylvia Earle, Asher Jay, Wade Davis, Sol Guy, Becca Skinner, and Raghava KK. These case studies, developed from interviews and research, showcase the importance and centrality of ethical and civil communication in the work of these nationally recognized Explorers, scientists, researchers, and activists. Questions at the end of each case study prompt students to reflect on the communication used by these Explorers and the ways in which a particular communication strategy might also become a part of their own skill set.
- **National Geographic Explorer Tips from National Geographic Explorers** Alexandra Cousteau, Thomas Taha Rassam Culhane, Mireya Mayor, and Aziz Abu Sarah. These tips are gathered through interviewing these nationally known researchers, Explorers, and scientists and are included in every chapter of the book.

Ethical Moments

Recognizing the crucial role of ethics in communication, *Invitation to Human Communication* includes additional feature boxes that highlight moments of communication that raise ethical questions and dilemmas. These ethical moments are

- Global Graffiti: Whose Space Is It?
- Awareness Campaign Versus the Environment and Safety
- What Are Appropriate Artifacts, Ambiguities, and Arguments?
- Free Speech and "You're Going to Hell"
- Listening to One Woman's Choice to Die With Dignity
- Terminating a Relationship: Facebook or Face to Face?
- When Anonymous Posts Turn From Helpful to Hurtful
- Can Maneuvers for Power Be Avoided?
- Who Can Be a Member of Our Team?
- Protecting Human Rights
- Anti-Drug Campaigns and Persuasion
- Social Commentary, YouTube Style
- When Must We Speak?

- Ribbon Campaigns and Awareness Bracelets
- What Are Good Reasons?

Questions are included at the end of each Ethical Moment box to prompt students to reflect on the ethical dilemma at play and the role of communication in addressing that dilemma.

Communicating in the Workplace

Understanding the role of communication in our workplaces is a necessary part of our students' education. As such, *Invitation to Human Communication* includes feature boxes that address contemporary dilemmas that relate to communication in the workplace. These include

- recognizing the top ten communication skills employers seek
- preparing for job interviews
- understanding nonverbal communication in the workplace
- composing professional e-mails
- working across different generations
- navigating romances in the workplace
- seeking mentors at work
- recognizing and reporting bullying
- keeping a new job
- preparing for the role of public speaking in our jobs
- interviewing successfully
- coping with communication anxiety
- managing rumors
- motivating employees
- appreciating the benefits of diversity in our workplaces.

Case Studies

To complement our National Geographic case studies, we've included additional explorations of important moments of communication for students to discuss and explore. These include

- Could There Be Noise in Those Tattoos?
- Women's Self-Esteem and the Media
- Leaders, Greetings, and Cultural Differences
- It Begins With the Phrase "That's So Gay"
- The Listening Project: What Does the World Think of America?
- The Consequences of Social-Media Blunders
- Cultural Representations and Stereotypes
- The Everest Peace Project: International Teamwork
- Food Not Bombs: Decision Making by Consensus
- Wangari Maathi, "I Had No Idea That Anyone Was Listening"
- Shakira, "I'm Going to Help These Kids"
- Language and the Music Industry
- Unheard Voices to the Rescue
- A Few Citizen Activists With Buckets
- Trespassers Welcome

Questions are included at the end of each case study so that students can explore the role of communication in these case studies and apply what they are reading to these important communication moments.

Practicing Human Communication

To learn effectively, students must go beyond reading and apply the concepts they are encountering for the first time. To assist with this learning, *Invitation to Human Communication* includes a hands-on feature that asks students to reflect on and apply the material they have just read. Practicing Human Communication boxes are included in every chapter and address such topics as ethnic and cultural backgrounds, stereotyping, flexibility, listening, stages of friendship, technology and conflict, reasoning, delivery, confidence during public speaking, and many more.

Writing Style

Invitation to Human Communication is written in an accessible and engaging writing style that draws students into the material and facilitates their exploration of ideas that may be familiar or new.

Practical Skills and Introduction to Theory

Invitation to Human Communication offers a skills-based approach and a careful introductory level framing of the research behind those skills. The text includes foundational and contemporary research so that the wide range of ideas and theories students explore are connected. Ideas build on or relate to one another throughout the text. This is done through the presentation of communication theory and skills in highly pragmatic ways, highlighting the foundations and strengths of the communication discipline, as well as linking communication theory and skills to civility, civic engagement, invitational communication, and ethical practices.

Review and Reflect

Our end-of-chapter summaries, questions that ask students to apply what they have read, and list of key terms and definitions are helpful mechanisms for student review and self-testing. These are included at the end each chapter and serve as excellent reviews for studying for exams or reviewing chapters before class.

Technology

Invitation to Human Communication highlights and explores the power of technology and media and their relationship to communication throughout the text. We pay careful and comprehensive attention to technology, presenting the most up-to-date research and examples so that students can explore the role of technology and media in their lives, and their effects on communication.

Videos, Web Links, and Other Interactive Media

MindTap marginal notes will link students to videos associated with National Geographic Explorers and topics of interest related to chapter content.

Resources Designed to Streamline Teaching and Facilitate Learning

MindTap Resources

MindTap®

Invitation to Human Communication 2nd edition features an outstanding array of online supplements to assist in making this course as meaningful and effective as possible. **Note:** For students to have access to the online resources for *Invitation to Human Communication* 2nd edition, they need to be ordered for the course—otherwise, students will not have access to them on the first day of class. These resources can be bundled with every new copy of the text or ordered separately. Students whose instructors do not order these resources as a package with the text may purchase them or access them at **cengagebrain.com.** *Contact your local Cengage Learning sales representative for more details.*

MindTap Speech for *Invitation to Human Communication* is a fully online, highly personalized learning experience that enhances learner engagement and improves outcomes while reducing instructor workload. By combining readings, multimedia, activities, and assessments into a singular Learning Path, MindTap guides students through their course with ease and engagement. Videos are available in the Speech Video Library so that students can better comprehend the key concepts of each chapter. Activities, powered by MindApps developed specifically for this discipline, guide students through the process of analyzing sample speeches, creating topics, building outlines, and practicing and presenting their speech. Instructors personalize the Learning Path by customizing Cengage Learning resources and adding their own content via apps that integrate into the MindTap framework seamlessly with any Learning Management System.

YouSeeU

With **YouSeeU**, students can upload video files of practice speeches or final performances, comment on their peers' speeches, and review their grades and instructor feedback. Instructors create courses and assignments, comment on and grade student speeches and allow peer review. Grades flow into a gradebook that allows instructors to easily manage their course from within MindTap. Grades can also be exported for use in learning-management systems. YouSeeU's flexibility lends itself to use in traditional, hybrid, and online courses.

Outline Builder

Outline Builder breaks down the speech preparation process into manageable steps and can help alleviate speech-related anxiety. The wizard-format provides relevant prompts and resources to guide students through the outlining process. Students are guided through topic definition, research and source citation, organizational structure outlining, and drafting note cards for speech day. The outline is assignable and gradable through MindTap.

Speech Video Library

Speech Video Library gives instructors the chance to share videos with students of real speeches that correspond to the topics in *Invitation to Human Communication.* Each speech activity provides a video of the speech; a full transcript so that viewers can read along; the speech outline—many in note card and full sentence form and evaluation questions so that students are guided through their assessment. While viewing each clip, students evaluate the speech or scenario by completing short answer questions and submitting their results directly to their instructor.

Additional MindTap Study Tools

 Flashcards a classic learning tool. Digitally reimagined, flashcards detect the chapter a student last opened, then shows cards for that chapter.

 Notebook Integrating Evernote technology, this app aggregates student annotations and notes into a single consolidated view.

 Flashnotes.com an online marketplace full of study guides, notes, flashcards, and video help created by students, for students.

 ReadSpeaker Text-to-speech technology offers varied reading styles and the option to select highlighted text to reinforce understanding.

 Merriam-Webster Dictionary enriches the learning experience and improves users' understanding of the English language.

 NetTutor® staffed with U.S.-based tutors and facilitated by a proprietary whiteboard created for online collaboration in education.

Sharing and Collaboration

 Google Docs Instructors and students share dynamically updated text documents, spreadsheets, presentations, and PDFs.

 Inline RSS Feed Send timely, valid feeds to students—within the Learning Path or as a separate reading—with the option to add remarks.

 Kaltura Simple video, audio and image uploading tools open a wealth of instructional, testing and engagement opportunities.

 Web Video Easily incorporate YouTube videos as a separate viewing activity within the Learning Path or directly within a reading assignment.

 ConnectYard MindApp social media platform that fosters communication among students and teachers without the need to "friend" or "follow" or join a social network.

Resources for Instructors

Invitation to Human Communication features a full suite of resources for instructors. These resources are available to qualified adopters, and ordering options for student supplements are flexible. Please consult your local Cengage Learning sales representative for more information, to evaluate examination copies of any of these instructor or student resources, or to request product demonstrations.

- The **Instructor' Resource Manual** provides a comprehensive teaching system. Included in the manual are sample syllabi, chapter outlines, in-class activities, and test questions for each chapter. All the Web Connect links and activities listed at the end of each chapter of the student edition are included in detail in the Instructor's Manual in the event that online access is unavailable or inconvenient. The Instructor's Manual is available through cengagebrain.com.

- **Cengage Learning Testing, powered by Cognero.** Accessible through cengage.com/login with your faculty account, this test bank contains multiple choice, true/false, and essay questions for each chapter. Cognero is a flexible, online system that allows you to author, edit, and manage test bank content. Create multiple test versions instantly and deliver through your LMS platform from wherever you may be. Cognero is compatible with Blackboard, Angel, Moodle, and Canvas LMS platforms.

Michael J. Harte

Cindy L. Griffin

is a professor of communication studies at Colorado State University. She received her PhD from Indiana University and has taught public speaking; civility; gender and communication; communication, language, and thought; contemporary theories of rhetoric; history of rhetorical theories; feminist theories of discourse; identity, voice and agency; and graduate seminars in women's studies. A proponent of civic engagement and civility in our communication and our lives, her research interests include developing the theory of invitational rhetoric, advancing theories that help communication scholars and students understand our complex identities, and exploring the relationships between civility, power, and rhetoric. She is the author of *Invitation to Public Speaking* (Cengage, 2015) and *Invitation to Public Speaking Handbook* (Cengage, 2011); coeditor of *Standing in the Intersections: Feminist Voices, Feminist Practices in Communication Studies* (with Karma Chávez, SUNY Press, 2013); coauthor of *Feminist Rhetorical Theories* (with Sonja Foss and Karen Foss; Waveland, 2006), and has published articles and book chapters that address identities, civility, feminisms and rhetorical and communication theories. She also served as the editor of *Women's Studies in Communication* from 2006 to 2010.

Elizabeth Emerling

Jennifer Emerling Bone

is a senior special assistant professor of communication studies at Colorado State University. She received her PhD from the University of Colorado at Boulder and has taught introduction to human communication, public speaking, gender and communication, theories of persuasion, argumentation, contemporary rhetorical criticism, rhetoric and social movements, contemporary public address, and the evolution of rhetoric. Seeking to understand how marginalized voices create public arguments, through her research, she examines how historical women used narratives and storytelling to change social and political attitudes about birth control. She has published in *Women's Studies in Communication* and *Western Journal of Communication* (with Cindy Griffin and T. M. Linda Scholz), has a coauthored chapter in *Contemplating Maternity in the Era of Choice: Explorations into Discourses of Reproduction* (edited by Sara Hayden and D. Lynn O'Brien Hallstein), and instructor's manuals and supplements for *Invitation to Public Speaking* (by Cindy Griffin). She also served as the basic course director at Colorado State University from 2010 through 2012.

The Communication Process

When we communicate civilly and ethically, we recognize the presence of others in our lives and around the world. How aware of other people are you when you communicate?

IN THIS CHAPTER YOU WILL LEARN TO:

- Explain what it means to communicate ethically and to communicate civilly.

- Describe how the process of communication requires mutual recognition of others and is an ongoing exchange of meaning.

- Explain five different types of communication and the contexts in which they are used.

- Distinguish between the linear, interactive, and transactional models of communication.

- Identify how the elements of flexibility, practice, and cognitive complexity influence competent communication.

- Summarize six reasons why we study communication.

When we communicate, we connect with, learn from, influence, and even disagree with other people. With every communication encounter, we choose the kind of messages we send and whether we will listen to someone else. We choose what feelings or ideas we will share, when to agree and disagree, when to explore and gather more information, and whether to pursue a relationship with another person. We even communicate with ourselves, talking to ourselves about jobs, friends, and family and how we want our futures to unfold. When we communicate, we bring our worldviews, ethics, and values to each exchange. And we expose ourselves to the worldviews, ethics, and values of other people.

bell hooks, a media scholar and cultural critic, explains that we need to practice understanding others. According to hooks, we need practice in listening to the logic of others (identifying the system, principles, and arguments that make up their worldviews) and in interacting with other people. She says we need this "practice of interaction" because people in our fast-paced and media-driven society have forgotten how to slow down and really listen to others and how to communicate their views carefully. To hooks, in the "practice of interaction" there is "an opportunity for mutual recognition"—an opportunity to listen to other people and to think carefully about the effects of our words and gestures on others. This is the opportunity for ethical and civil communication. The practice of interaction does not mean we always agree with others. Instead, we recognize the "presence of one another" (hooks, 1994).

This book invites you to learn about the foundations of human communication from an ethical and civil perspective. You will learn

- the definition of communication;
- how communication shapes our identities and worldviews;
- how to use communication in personal relationships, professional lives, and groups;
- the different contexts for and models of communication; and
- strategies and tips you can use to be a competent, civil, and ethical communicator.

Definition of Communication

The word *communication* refers to an activity at the center of our lives. Communication is so central that this era has been titled the Information Age. Communication scholars have found that college students spend 55 percent of their time listening, 17 percent reading, 16 percent speaking, and 11 percent writing (Emanuel et al., 2008) (see Figure 1.1). Communication research also finds that people in most workplaces spend between 50 percent and 80 percent of their day in communication-related activities (Klemmer & Snyder, 1972). Imagining a day without communication is difficult: no conversations with friends or family, no music or television, no internal dialogues. Communication is so central to our daily lives that we often take it for granted—we engage in communication constantly but rarely notice its presence. For psychologists and communication scholars, however, who we are and how we interpret the world around us are products and processes of communication.

In its simplest definition, communication is the human activity of creating and exchanging meaning. We can define **communication** as *the use of symbols by humans to create messages for other humans*. This definition involves several elements: it is symbolic, it is a process, it is human, and it is influenced by culture.

Civil and Ethical Communication

This book is not only about the choices we make as communicators but also about learning to communicate those choices ethically and civilly. When we make a choice to **communicate ethically**, we *consider the moral impact of our words, ideas, and views on other people*. When we choose to **communicate civilly**, we *make a decision to be open to hearing different views and perspectives, even though we may not agree with them*. Choosing civil and ethical communication does not require that we silence our own views or that we agree with everything another person says. Instead, ethical and civil communication means that we consider the impact of our words on other people before, during, and after we say them. It also means that we are willing to listen to other people and to consider what their words mean, even if we disagree with them.

Choosing to communicate civilly and ethically means choosing an interested, honest, and flexible approach to communication. It means we listen to views that are different from our own to try to *understand* those views. It also means we communicate our views in the same spirit—so that others can better understand us.

To **understand** a view or idea is *to gain knowledge of that view or idea*, to know it better and more fully and to recognize its logic. When we

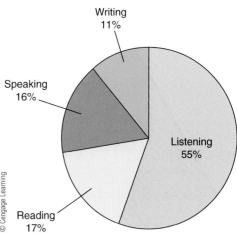

© Cengage Learning

Figure 1.1 *Time college students spend communicating*

communication
the use of symbols by humans to create messages for other humans.

communicating ethically
considering the moral impact of our words, ideas, and views on other people when we communicate.

communicating civilly
making a decision to be open to hearing different views and perspectives, even though we may not agree with them.

understand
to gain knowledge of a view or an idea.

Jodi Cobb/National Geographic Creative

Consider the amount of time you spend during a day communicating with others. How much of it is in person, and how much is via phone or computer?

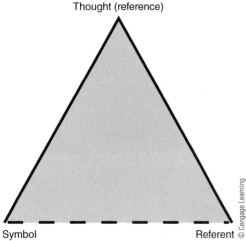

Thought (reference)

Symbol ---- Referent

© Cengage Learning

Figure 1.2 *Semantic triangle of meaning*

logic
system, principles, and arguments that make up a person's worldview.

symbol
word, gesture, sound, image, or object that stands for or represents something else.

semantic triangle of meaning
ways people use or hear a symbol or word and attach a meaning to it.

referent
concept or thing the symbol represents.

thought or reference
memory or past experiences people have with the words being communicated.

recognize the **logic** of someone else's views or ideas, we are identifying the *system, principles, and arguments that make up that person's worldview*. This approach to communication can help us share our experiences, thoughts, and ideas with families and friends, communities, and workplaces.

Communication Is Symbolic

When we communicate, we use symbols. A **symbol** is a *word, gesture, sound, image, or object that stands for or represents something else*. We use symbols because we would otherwise have to act out—or *dramatize*—everything we wished to share. This is because few words literally replicate the things we want to communicate. The closest we come to an actual replica of our meaning are words such as *bang, hiss,* and *woof*. These *onomatopoeic* words are vocal imitations or representations of the thing they symbolize—that is, they sound like the things they represent. The majority of our words, however, are not imitations of something else, they are symbols of them.

In 1923, C. K. Ogden and I. A. Richards created the **semantic triangle of meaning** to help us understand the symbolic nature of communication (Ogden & Richards, 1923). This representation illustrates the *ways people use or hear a symbol or word and attach a meaning to it*. It also illustrates the arbitrary or symbolic nature of this attachment. To understand this process, think of a triangle (Figure 1.2). On the left corner of the triangle is the symbol—the word or phrase spoken by the speaker. For example, when a person says "Hope," as Barack Obama did during his campaign for the presidency, or when someone says, "It's all good," after a mistake or difficult moment, then those words are the *symbols*. They represent the idea being communicated.

On the right corner of the triangle is the **referent**, the *concept or thing that the symbol represents*. In the Obama example, the referent is the actual desire or wish that something good will happen. The referent for "It's all good," however, could be from the 1999 album *It's All Good* by rapper M. C. Breed or from the desire to rise above whatever problem a person faces. Referents are the commonly held definitions of words, phrases, and even objects. These are sometimes called the *denotative definitions* of a word. They are *denotative* because we could find the referents by looking in a dictionary or asking a large group of people what a word or phrase means. The symbolic nature of communication begins to emerge because there is no direct connection between the word or phrase and the thing it represents. A wish for something good or the desire to rise above a problem could be called many other things. The word *hope* and the phrase "It's all good" are human inventions. People use them to name emotions or desires and not the actual things they suggest. To help explain this referential or arbitrary aspect of communication, Ogden and Richards used a broken line between the two sides of the triangle to show the indirect connection between the symbol and the referent.

The top of the triangle is the **thought** or **reference** associated with a symbol. This is the *memory or past experiences people have with the words* *being communicated*. We recall our own experiences when we hear words or phrases. The symbol *hope* and the phrase "It's all good" recall personalized and subjective interpretations, experiences, and memories for us. These may be successes or disappointments or even a like or dislike of a certain kind of music or commonly used phrase. These are called *connotative* definitions of a word because they are the personal meanings we have for words or phrases. Our connotative definitions of words are often more powerful than their denotative definitions. When we hear words and phrases, we usually know what they mean in the dictionary, but we also attach meaning beyond their denotative definitions based on our experiences.

The semantic triangle of meaning helps us understand that communication is symbolic for three reasons: (1) it helps us see that we use symbols to represent things and to express ourselves, (2) there may be common referents or meanings for those things (dictionary definitions), and (3) there also are highly individual referents for those symbols (connotative definitions). This symbolic aspect of communication helps make it interesting to study as well as challenging to use and sometimes understand.

Communication Is a Process

Although a single statement sometimes fails to get any reply, our statements are usually part of a larger and ongoing exchange. And even though we might produce a single word, sound, or gesture, we usually do it in response to something someone has said or done. We say that *communication is a process*, rather than an isolated act because civil and ethical communication makes us part of an ongoing exchange of meaning. When we first meet another person, our communication unfolds: we consider what we want to say, we say that thing, and we listen to the other person's response. If the exchange goes well, we continue the process, developing new messages and often new relationships or connections with the other person.

This process of communication also is present in larger familial, social, and professional contexts because we are often part of a larger ongoing conversation in these contexts. Kenneth Burke (1941/1973) describes this process of communication as follows:

> Imagine that you enter a parlor. You come late. When you arrive, others have long preceded you, and they are engaged in a lively discussion, a discussion too passionate for them to pause and tell you exactly what it is about. In fact, the discussion had already begun long before any of them got there, so that no one present is qualified to retrace for you all the steps that had gone before.
>
> You listen for a while, until you decide that you have caught the tenor of the argument; then you put in your oar. Someone answers; you answer them; another perspective is shared. The hour grows late; you must depart. And you do depart, with the discussion still vigorously in progress. (pp. 110–111)

As members of these larger groups, we step into, contribute to, and build on this ongoing communication process.

When we give feedback to others, we send messages to them about how receptive we are to their communication. Positive feedback signals that we like their messages, and negative feedback communicates the opposite. How clear do you think your feedback is when you communicate with others?

To be civil and ethical, the process of communication requires two things: *reciprocity* and *feedback*. **Reciprocity** is the *mutual exchange of symbols and meanings*, a process that represents our willingness to interact with other people rather than dominate a conversation. Although we may sometimes demand that someone do something or "give an order," most civil and ethical communication involves a mutual exchange between two or more people. **Feedback** refers to *the verbal and nonverbal signals we give to one another while we communicate*. When the people we are communicating with yawn, groan, look bored or angry, or laugh or smile, we are getting feedback—information that tells us a bit about how our messages are being received.

When we say communication is a process, we are saying (1) that it involves an exchange of meaning, however short or long; (2) that it requires a mutual recognition of others; and (3) that we recognize the ongoing and influential nature of our communication.

Communication Is Influenced by Culture

When he became the Anglican Archbishop of Cape Town, South Africa, in 1986, Desmond Mpilo Tutu, explained,

> We Africans speak about a concept difficult to render in English. We speak of *ubuntu* or *botho*. You know when it is there, and it is obvious when it is absent. It has to do with what it means to be truly human; it refers to gentleness, to compassion, to hospitality, to openness to others, to vulnerability, to being available for others and to know that you are bound up with them in the bundle of life, for a person is only a person through other persons. And so we search for this ultimate attribute and reject ethnicity and other such qualities as irrelevancies. A person is a person because he recognizes others as persons. (1994, p. 125)

Archbishop Tutu captures the power of culture: it influences what we see as valuable, how we think, and the ways we interact with others.

Like the word *communication*, the word *culture* has been defined in many ways because it also is influenced and shaped by many factors. **Culture** can be defined as the *learned patterns of perception, values, and behaviors shared by a group of people* (Martin & Nakayama, 2011). These patterns are often called *dynamic* because *they change over time* and shape how we see ourselves in relation to the world around us. This, in turn, influences how we communicate with ourselves and other people. In some cultures (Asian and Native American, for example), communication is characterized by an indirect style that is designed to produce and maintain harmony. Communication scholar Deborah Tannen calls U.S. American culture an "argument culture" that is characterized by direct and open disagreement and "winning" or being right (Tannen, 1998).

Because cultures have unique ways of explaining and organizing the world, when we communicate ethically and civilly, we try to

reciprocity
the mutual exchange of symbols and meanings.

feedback
verbal and nonverbal signals we give to one another while we communicate.

culture
learned patterns of perception, values, and behaviors shared by a group of people.

recognize these different worldviews and guard against **ethnocentrism**, or the *belief that our own cultural perspectives, norms, and ways of organizing society are superior to other cultures.* When we hold ethnocentric views, we see other cultures as odd, wrong, or deficient because they do not do things the way we do.

Lynn Johnson/National Geographic Creative

Cultural differences often cause people to argue with one another over their views of right and wrong, differences that can make communication complex and difficult. Do you think either person will win this argument? Why or why not?

Types of Communication

Communication is such a central part of our lives that it occurs in a variety of contexts. In a single day, we might watch television, talk with other people briefly or at length, solve problems in groups at work or in our communities, or share information in a formal setting such as giving a speech or Prezi presentation. Identifying the various contexts for communication helps us understand why and how we communicate, and it helps us study communication more effectively.

When people engage in **intrapersonal communication**, they are *communicating internally with their own selves.* Intrapersonal communication is the internal communication that goes on in our own heads, the mental processing of decisions we have to make, choices we have made, and even conversations we want to have or should have. Intrapersonal communication is sometimes called *self-talk*, and it can be both positive and negative or even civil and uncivil.

Interpersonal communication is *communication with other people that ranges from highly personal to highly impersonal.* This type of communication usually takes place in a dyad (two people) or small group (fewer than six people), but its defining characteristic is that it involves relationships. When we communicate interpersonally, we are establishing, maintaining, and disengaging from relationships with other people. We might communicate interpersonally in person or in a face-to-face setting, but we also communicate interpersonally by telephone, text message, e-mail, card or letter, or something similar. In interpersonal communication, it often is easier to be civil to those we like and uncivil to those we do not because it is easier to listen to and communicate with people who are similar to us. However, in interpersonal communication we sometimes communicate uncivilly with those people we care deeply about, especially when we are angry or when ending a relationship. Interpersonal communication is explored more fully in Chapters 6 and 7.

Group communication, sometimes called *small group communication,* occurs *when we interact with a small but organized collection of people.* In group communication, we usually have a focus or goal. Group communication takes place when we communicate as part of a team, study or work group, collective or committee, or even hobby, club, or political organization. We often are guided by rules or specific goals, and we may discuss strategies or plans that guide the interactions. Group communication may be formal or informal, and group members often assume certain roles such as team captain, recorder or note taker, or behind-the-scenes organizer. Group

ethnocentrism
belief that our own cultural perspectives, norms, and ways of organizing society are superior to other cultures.

intrapersonal communication
when people communicate internally with their own selves.

interpersonal communication
communication with other people that ranges from highly personal to highly impersonal.

group communication
interacting with a small but organized collection of people.

COMMUNICATING IN THE WORKPLACE

Top Ten Skills

The Association of American Colleges and Universities (2007) reports that "acquiring the right skills for a rapidly changing workplace" has more effect on your chances of getting a great job than your choice of major. To assist students, the association publishes "Top Ten Things Employers Look for in New College Graduates." The list includes the following:

1. Working well in teams
2. Using science and technology in real-world settings
3. Writing and speaking well
4. Thinking clearly about complex problems
5. Analyzing problems and developing solutions
6. Understanding our current global environment

7. Creativity and innovation
8. Applying skills in new settings
9. Understanding numbers and statistics
10. Strong ethics and integrity

Most of these skills require communication in teams, on projects, or sharing ideas and solutions. This chapter introduces many of those foundational skills. You can use your understanding of what communication is, the processes involved in communicating with others, the types of communication available to you, the different models for communication, and your awareness of communication competence to assist you not only in securing a job but also in keeping it and performing well.

communication also occurs face to face or via technology. The most effective and successful groups make civil and ethical communication a priority. However, when groups engage in *group think* or when they turn against one or more members, uncivil and unethical communication can take over. Group communication is explored more fully in Chapters 8 and 9.

Mass communication is *communication generated by media organizations that is designed to reach large audiences.* This type of communication is transmitted by television, the Internet, radio, print media, and the entertainment industry. It is one of the most prevalent forms of communication today. Mass communication is one of the few types of communication that fits the linear model of communication (discussed in the following sections) because it flows one way and is one of the few forms of communication that involves limited immediate feedback and reciprocity. Although the invitation to write, "call or e-mail us," or "vote now" does offer some exchange, media messages tend to be highly scripted and slow to respond to viewer input. Mass communication ranges from highly civil and ethical to highly uncivil and unethical, and because people and cultures are so diverse, the interpretation of what is civil and uncivil varies across groups and over time.

Public or presentational communication is communication in which *one person gives a speech to other people, most often in a public setting.* It differs from other forms of communication in many ways. First, our reasons for communicating in public speaking are unique. Sometimes we are asked to give a speech because we have knowledge or expertise on a topic. At other times, we want to give a public presentation because an issue is important to us. We may even be required to give a speech as part of our job or as a part of a formal ceremony. So public communication is characterized by particular reasons for speaking. Second, this form of communication occurs with a single person, a *speaker*, delivering a message to a group of people, an *audience*. In public communication, one person usually does more

mass communication
communication designed and generated by media organizations to reach large audiences.

public or presentational communication
when one person gives a speech to other people, most often in a public setting.

DAN WESTERGREN/National Geographic Creative

Aziz Abu Sarah,
Emerging Explorer and Cultural Educator

What types of communication do you enjoy most in your work and why? Are there cultural challenges that you have had to overcome as a communicator?

I talk about pretty tense things. I talk about being killed. I talk about war. I learned very early to use a little bit of humor. I spoke to a group in Northern Ireland, for example, and I remember coming in and seeing uneasiness, they're like, "Who is this guy?" Instead of starting my normal lecture, I started with a little bit of humor and slowly the same people who had their arms crossed were changed and much more open. I also use what I call *emotional communication*, which focuses on narratives and storytelling, and that's my favorite style. The bulk of the speaking that I do is persuasive. My goal is to persuade people. So when I tell a story, the goal is actually not just to tell the story, it's actually to move people from point A to B and try to show them a new alternative or a new narrative. In my case, we're talking about conflict. Many times I'm speaking to a group that disagrees with me. And the challenge I have to overcome is always to quickly turn that around and win that crowd back, which is very hard. So, that's where storytelling helps. When I think of our cultural divides, and the very different groups I speak with, I try to relate through listening to them and understanding their perspective, even when I personally have disagreements with them And, that's my own personal dilemma that I deal with. But I really believe that you can't make a change, and you can't have an effective conversation, if you're not willing to first listen and understand and show a respect to the person in front of you, regardless of how much you disagree. But you also have to make sure you are not losing your own values as you're doing that. And that's—that's the hardest dilemma I think I face on a personal level.

talking and others more listening. Sometimes, however, a speaker acts as a facilitator, or listener, inviting other people to communicate so that she or he can understand an issue more fully or gather information about a topic or problem. A third difference is that public speaking tends to be more formal than conversational, usually occurring on a stage or in a formal setting, sometimes using technology to support the ideas being presented. Finally, speeches have predetermined goals and are highly organized and practiced before they are given. Ethical and civil communication is important in public communication to ensure audience members get accurate and honest information that does not manipulate them or prey on their emotions. Public communication is discussed in Chapters 10 through 15.

 ## Models for Communication

Linear Model of Communication

Sometimes we can view communication as a one-way transmission of meaning. Although rare, people sometimes engage in this one-way model of communication. The linear model of communication (Figure 1.3) is

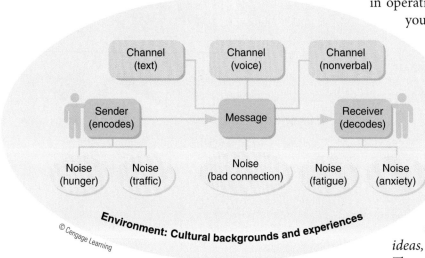

Channel (text) Channel (voice) Channel (nonverbal)

Sender (encodes) → Message → Receiver (decodes)

Noise (hunger) Noise (traffic) Noise (bad connection) Noise (fatigue) Noise (anxiety)

Environment: Cultural backgrounds and experiences

© Cengage Learning

Figure 1.3 *Linear model of communication*

encode

putting ideas, thoughts, and meanings into a message.

decode

interpreting or trying to understand what the sender is communicating.

channel

means by which ideas are communicated.

noise

things that interfere with the transmission and reception of a message.

external noises

distractions that exist around you—like sights and sounds that take your attention away from the message.

internal noises

thoughts and feelings we are experiencing.

semantic noise

interference that occurs when a speaker uses a word or phrase that is unfamiliar, confusing, offensive, or contradictory.

in operation when your boss appears in your doorway and says, "Finish the report by the end of the day," your manager sends an e-mail that announces "Tomorrow's meeting is at 3," or your professor writes on your paper, "Very nice, B+." In this model, there is a *sender* (your boss or professor) and a *receiver* (you). The sender **encodes** a message—she or he *puts ideas, thoughts, and meanings into a message.* The receiver **decodes** that message, which is to say, you *interpret or try to understand what the sender is communicating.*

The *means by which the message is transmitted or ideas are communicated* is called the **channel**. A channel can be many things—your boss's spoken words, your manager's written words, or your professor's comments on your paper, as well as a telephone, text message, Web page, song, card, or letter. The channel is important because how a message is sent affects the way it is received. In face-to-face communication, we can see a person's facial expression and hear his or her tone of voice. On a Web page, we are influenced by visual images and design features. When we know someone well, we can read the cues in their e-mails or text messages, but we can misunderstand an electronic message when we do not know the sender well.

Noise is also present in this linear model. **Noise** refers to *the things that interfere with the transmission and reception of a message.* Three kinds of noise disrupt communication: external noise, internal noise, and semantic noise. **External noises** are *distractions that exist around you—like sights and sounds that take your attention away from the message.* These could be loud motors, large crowds, bad phone connections, or other people who take your attention away from the message (children, classmates, or co-workers, for example), or poor lighting or sound systems. **Internal noises** are *thoughts and feelings we are experiencing.* Hunger and fatigue are two common physiological noises, but illness and injuries can also create this type of noise. Internal noise disrupts the sending or receiving of a message because we are distracted by our own physical needs or problems and cannot send or receive a message effectively.

Finally, **semantic noise** is the *interference that occurs when a speaker uses a word or phrase that is unfamiliar, confusing, offensive, or contradictory.* Technical or specialized language that is unfamiliar to a person outside that field of expertise creates semantic noise. For example, online marketers refer to a Web site's conversion rate optimization (CRO) to discuss the success of a call to action on a particular Web site, and day partying is the strategy of limiting ad displays to certain times of the day (Jantsch, 2012). Without this background information, a listener might experience confusion or semantic noise when hearing these terms.

The last component of the linear model of communication is the **environment** or *cultural backgrounds and experiences people bring to the exchange*. This part of the model refers to the location where the communication occurs (office, home, coffee shop, car) as well as the worldviews of those communicating—their cultural norms and values, individual experiences, and expectations. In the linear model, environment and cultural backgrounds can influence communication in obvious or subtle ways. When your boss tells you in front of several co-workers, "Finish that project," you get a different message than if he or she tells you the same thing in private. Similarly, if your cultural and familial background values humor, teasing, and verbal play but your receiver's cultural and familial background do not, then your message may be perceived as an insult rather than as a sign of fondness and closeness.

Most communication does not fall into the linear model because of communication's interactive nature. However, when we are in a hurry to get something done, when we want to send a quick message ("Meet me in front of the library at 9"), and even when we are angry, this model might best describe our communication. One-way communication can be civil or uncivil, but it is easy to interpret it as uncivil. When a sender makes no effort to listen to the receiver's response to the sender's message, he or she ignores bell hooks's call for recognizing the presence of another person, and the result is an uncivil interaction. But when a quick text message saves a person time ("Meet me at the library") or a boss's "Finish that project" saves that person's job, then the linear model of communication might show us especially civil communication.

Interactive Model of Communication

The interactive model of communication helps us understand communication interactions that are two-way (Figure 1.4). The model helps us understand how often communication is reciprocal and the role that feedback plays in communication. Recall that reciprocity is the *mutual exchange of symbols and meanings*. Feedback refers to the *verbal and nonverbal signals we give to one another while we communicate with them*. In the interactive model, symbols are exchanged between two people and feedback is present. When your friend sends a text message to meet at the library and you text back "I'm starving, can we meet at a coffee shop instead?" communication is reciprocal—you and your friend exchanged messages. When your boss stands in your doorway and says, "Finish that project by the end of the day," and you smile

environment
cultural backgrounds and experiences that people bring to the exchange.

Could There Be Noise in Those Tattoos?

A survey conducted by the Pew Research Center found that 36 percent of Americans eighteen to twenty-five, 40 percent of those twenty-six to forty, and 10 percent of those forty-one to sixty-four have at least one tattoo (Statistic Brain, 2013). Reports vary, but today, among the most popular tattoo designs are tribal, stars, crosses, angels, wings, butterflies, flowers, feathers, text, and fairies (Dennis G, 2014; Klegdord, 2014). As common as they are, what happens when all those tattoos enter the workplace? Individuals report that tattoos make them feel rebellious and sexy, but could they also be adding noise to our workplaces? Consider the history of tattoos before you answer.

According to the Smithsonian Institution's Web site, "Humans have marked their bodies with tattoos for thousands of years. These permanent designs—sometimes plain, sometimes elaborate, always personal—have served as amulets, status symbols, declarations of love, signs of religious beliefs, adornments, and even forms of punishment" (Lineberry, 2007a, 2007b). The earliest known examples of tattoos are found on the 5,200-year-old "Iceman" found along the Italian–Austrian border in 1991 and 4,000-year-old female Egyptian mummies. The Iceman's tattoos are thought to be the result of an effort to release pain, as they are found in random spots along his joints. The tattoos on the Egyptian mummies are believed to be artistic markers of status or permanent amulets designed to protect women during pregnancy. Ancient tattoos are thought to have marked status (high or low, depending on the era), and other tattoos were used to identify individuals as slaves.

Facial tattoos have been most commonly associated with the Maori of New Zealand and some Native American people such as the Cree. They were also found on the mummified bodies of six Greenland Inuit women who lived around 1475 A.D.

In the Maori culture, the head was considered the most important part of the body, with the face embellished by incredibly elaborate tattoos or "*moko*," which were regarded as marks of high status. Each tattoo design was unique to that individual and since it conveyed specific information about their status, rank, ancestry, and abilities, it has accurately been described as a form of ID card or passport, a kind of aesthetic bar code for the face (Lineberry, 2007a). However, tattoos as markers or conveyors of information have also been used by sailors so that their bodies could be easily identified should they drown, as a way for Nazi guards to identify prisoners of concentration camps, and as symbols of gang membership or activities.

Adam Radosavljevic/Shutterstock.com

Although the excessively tattooed body was once seen as deviant or lower class and was most commonly seen at fairs and circuses, according to communication scholar Mindy Fenske, today's tattoos are a form of "writing on the body" that communicates a challenge to notions of class, acceptability, and even what a body is for and can do. Today's tattooed bodies, Fenske argues, are a "performance of resistance" and often serve as visual statements about someone's identity and the body's ability to speak out about or for something (Fenske, 2004).

What Do You Think?

1. External noise is defined as *distractions that exist around you* and internal noise is defined as thoughts and feelings *we are experiencing*. Could the presence of individuals with obvious tattoos be creating noise in an environment in which tattoos are not the norm? What kind of external and internal noise might be present in such a workplace?

2. Semantic noise is the interference that occurs when a speaker uses a word or phrase that is unfamiliar, confusing, offensive, or contradictory. Although tattoos are not spoken words or phrases, they do communicate to others. What kinds of tattoos might be unfamiliar, confusing, offensive, or contradictory in a workplace?

3. Review the material you have read thus far in this chapter. Using this information, what skills might you use as a communicator in your workplace to reduce the noise that could be caused by tattoos?

and nod, not only is communication reciprocal, but you are also giving feedback. The feedback you are giving your boss is the nonverbal signal that she or he can count on you to finish.

The reciprocal exchange of meaning and the addition of feedback make the interactive model different from the linear model. Because of this model's reciprocity of communication, both senders and receivers are engaged in feedback and are responsible for considering the ethical or moral impact of their messages. Each communicating person must consider how her or his communication is being received, how it is affecting the other person, the kinds of signals (feedback) the other person is giving, and the degree of honesty and integrity of the communication.

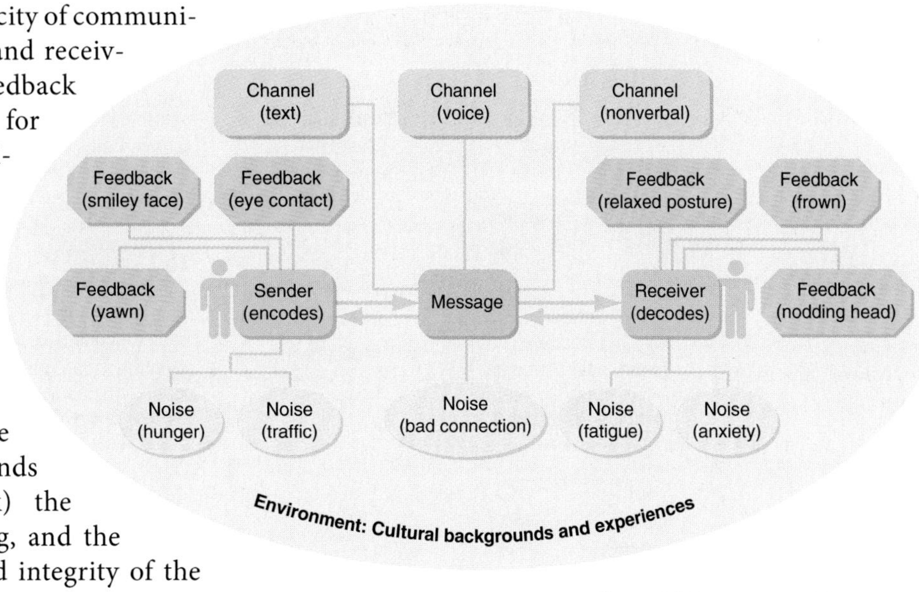

Figure 1.4 *Interactive model of communication*

Both communicators are also responsible for thinking about the civility or incivility of their messages and their willingness to hear ideas they might not agree with. When we are exposed to information we disagree with, we may be inclined to fall back into the linear model of communication and not respond. Shutting down an exchange can be a sign of incivility. When we continue to communicate in the spirit of "interaction," as bell hooks suggests, we decide to remain civil, listen to other people so that we can understand their messages and think carefully about the impact of our words and gestures on them. However, if the message another person sends is too difficult or uncomfortable to listen to, then the civil and ethical response is to communicate that message to the other person. When continuing a conversation would be uncivil or unethical, then ending it or changing the topic would be appropriate.

Transactional Model of Communication

The transactional model of communication reflects the ongoing and collaborative nature of communication (Figure 1.5). This model helps us see that communication is more than a single act or a single event. In the transactional model, the relationships between the individuals communicating are highlighted. This model also emphasizes the ongoing and fluid nature of communication.

PRACTICING HUMAN COMMUNICATION
What Are Your Ethnic and Cultural Backgrounds?

Do you know your family's ethnic and cultural identities? Do you see ways in which those backgrounds are part of your life today? Do holidays, food, and traditions reflect your ethnic and cultural heritages? Now consider the ethnic and cultural backgrounds of your friends or co-workers. Have you ever encountered different "environments" because of these different backgrounds? How have those differences affected your communication and relationships with others?

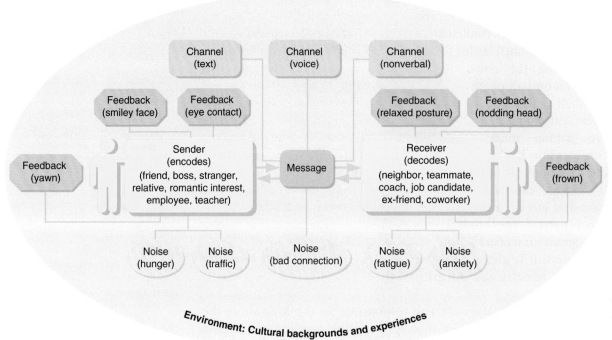

Figure 1.5 *Transactional model of communication*

© Cengage Learning

When we communicate with other people, we are in relationships with them. A relationship implies a connection. Sometimes that connection is brief and causal, but at other times it is long term and significant. When we are in a relationship with another person, we are involved with her or him. At work, this connection might take different forms. For example, we have bosses and co-workers, and we might be a manager or supervisor. Our connections to other people in our workplaces might be supportive and fun, but they might also be filled with power differences. You might be a manager, for example, and want and need your staff to behave in certain ways for the business to be successful. Or you might be the dishwasher in a restaurant and want or need those who bus tables to help you do your job faster by clearing dishes in a certain way. At home, our connections and transactions also may be rewarding or difficult. Whether we greet our family with smiles and hugs or repeatedly leave our shoes where others trip over them, our connections and power relationships are being communicated. These connections rely on transactions: on the ongoing exchange of communication. When people acknowledge the transactional nature of relationships, they also acknowledge the relationships they have with other people. When we see communication as a transaction, we recognize not only the power of communication to help us build healthy and positive relationships but also its power to affect other people's lives.

When we say communication is ongoing and fluid, we are saying that our relationships with other people usually are established and shaped over time. Although the length of a relationship can be a few moments (we assist a stranger with a door or a heavy box), they usually are developed over days, weeks, months, and years. In these long-term relationships, our communication shifts and changes because we have a past with these people, are developing histories with them, and are building a future. Thus, our communication is ongoing. When we first meet a person, for example, we have one style of communication. After we become familiar with that person, we know something of his or her background and preferences: our communication patterns and options change with this new information. When we know a person for years or even over the course of our lifetime, our communication choices continue to evolve and change. Through our communication, we develop a long history with this person. This history might be good or bad, but it still shows us that our communication with other people is ongoing, changing, and always a transaction: an exchange that involves two people existing in relationship to one another.

Communication as an Act of Civility

Recall that when we choose to communicate civilly, *we make a decision to be open to hearing different views and perspectives, even though we may not agree with them*. When we choose to communicate ethically, *we consider the moral impact of our words, ideas, and views on other people*. When we choose to communicate both civilly and ethically, we are choosing an interested, honest, and flexible approach to communication. The word *civility* comes from a root word meaning "to be a member of a household." In ancient Greece, *civility* referred to displays of temperance, justice, wisdom, and courage. Over time, the definition has changed only slightly; in the study of communication, **civility** has come to mean *expressing care and concern for others, the thoughtful use of words and language, and the flexibility to see the many sides of an issue.*

Choosing civil and ethical communication does not mean we silence our own views or agree with everything another person says. The models of communication share an additional component: communication is intertwined with civility. Law professor Stephen Carter explains civility in this way:

> The term *civility* is often translated as *politeness*, but it means something more. It suggests an approach to life, a way of carrying one's self and of relating to others—in short living in a way that is civilized. The word *civilité* shares with the words *civilized* and *civilization* (and the word *city*, for that matter) a common etymology, an Indo-European root meaning "member of the household." Of course: civility is what enables us to live together. To be civilized is to understand that we live in society as in a household, and that within that household, if we are to be moral people, our relationships with other people are governed by standards of behavior. (1998, p. 15)

civility
expressing care and concern for others, the thoughtful use of words and language, and the flexibility to see the many sides of an issue.

When we communicate with others, we are acknowledging that household, and we are acknowledging that we, like other people, are members of it. When we communicate with other people by e-mail, text message, or face-to-face interaction, we are acknowledging that we have a connection to other people. As Carter explains, in this increasingly interconnected and global world, it is important to recognize that we are "all passengers on the same train." Whether we are strangers or friends, we are traveling together.

Carter suggests that even when we do not agree with someone else, or perhaps do not even like them, we still have an obligation to practice civility in our communication. According to Carter, this sometimes demands and even requires "passionate disagreement." When we mask our differences in "politeness" or silence, we are not engaged in ethical communication with other people—instead, we are hiding our views from them. However, our "passionate disagreements" must be communicated civilly and ethically. Carter explains, "[W]e must not encourage gratuitous insult simply to drive the point home" (p. 23). We must not let our anger and frustration push us into saying something rude or insulting. Instead, we must ethically express our disagreements and differences "for the sake of our common journey with others, and out of love and respect for the very idea that there are others. When we are civil, we are not pretending to like those we actually despise; we are not pretending to hold any attitude toward them, except that we accept and value them as our equals" (p. 23). We are, as hooks explains, recognizing the presence of others and communicating in ways that open up possibilities for listening and exchange rather than shutting others down.

Our attempts at communicating civilly with others have limits, however. Communication scholars Brian Spitzberg and William Cupach (2007) describe what is now called "the dark side of communication." In this "dark side," individuals communicate in ways that are "dysfunctional, distorted, distressing, and destructive." This kind of communication "dallies with deviance, betrayal, transgression, and violation" (Spitzberg & Cupach, 2007, p. 5). The dark side of communication is highly uncivil: it is mean spirited, dishonest, manipulative, and abusive or humiliating. Examples of the dark side of communication are bullying, name-calling, harassing or humiliating exchanges, stonewalling (refusing to communicate), and lies about one's self or others. Spitzberg and Cupach's research tells us that this dark side of communication is common, and many people can easily recall dark communication encounters and relationships.

When we are faced with this negative and harmful communication, the role of civility is quite complex. Often the most civil thing we can do is to get out of or avoid the uncivil interaction. This is because allowing others to treat us poorly is not only harmful but also uncivil. Civility requires us to treat our own selves civilly and with respect. However, direct expressions of civility may have a role in our responses to communication from the dark side. To decide how to respond civilly, we

Global Graffiti: Whose Space Is It?

The film *Bomb It* (Reiss, 2007) is described as an "explosive . . . documentary" that "explores the most subversive and controversial art form currently shaping international youth culture: graffiti." Directed by Jon Reiss and filmed over several years, the award-winning documentary showcases the art of approximately two dozen street-graffiti artists from around the world, and it makes the argument that public space belongs to the public. In the film, artists argue that "Art is a weapon," that graffiti "represents life"—"It's energy, it's f—n' energy"—and that because it is on walls, in subways, and out in public, "It's alive, it's livin', it's communicatin' to you right now."

Reiss and those featured in *Bomb It* make the argument that graffiti artists are "not asking for the space" but "taking the space." They suggest that "people believe that they live in a public space that's neutral" but that in reality we have become so numb to billboards and storefronts that are ignorant to what we are really "being assaulted with." Graffiti disrupts that numbness. Advocates of graffiti argue that what many people may not realize is presented as "neutral to them" actually is "excluding a lot of people." Beyond disrupting this supposedly neutral space, graffiti artists argue that their art takes ugly spaces and makes them beautiful. It goes beyond "Hello, world, I'm here" and adorns public property in ways that are aesthetic, accessible, and even political.

Other people, however, consider graffiti a nuisance, an eyesore, and a crime to be eradicated. Graffiti may be painted over within minutes or hours after it is finished, and graffiti artists often land in jail. Graffiti artists respond that their work is the marketing of an idea or an image, a way to participate in the larger conversations that they and other everyday people have been excluded from. Graffiti art transforms a public space, taking control of the communication disseminated there, and gives voice to those we normally would not hear from.

What Do You Think?

1. What do public space and free speech mean to you? Does graffiti fall into the category of communication?

2. Is it uncivil to post graffiti on public buildings and spaces? Why or why not?

3. What model of communication does graffiti fit? Is it linear, interactive, transactional, or could it be a combination of these three? If you can fit graffiti into one of these models, does that help explain the powerful responses people have to graffiti? How so?

have to ask ourselves several questions: What are the consequences of treating those who are uncivil with civility? What options do we have to be civil? What are the limits of our willingness to respect those who are uncivil?

Communication and Competence

To be competent is to do something well or to meet some required standard. When we say someone is "competent," we are saying the person possesses a certain level of skill in an activity and understands and follows a particular set of rules or criteria for a task. A competent soccer player, for example, has a reasonable level of skill in running, kicking, and passing and can follow the rules of the game. But what does it take to be considered a competent communicator? The answers to this question are varied, but communication research suggests the competence requires three different elements: flexibility, practice, and cognitive complexity.

Communication Competence Requires Flexibility

Most of us know from our own experiences that effective communication is different in different situations. What is appropriate with a child is ineffective with your instructor. How you communicate with your friends when you are relaxed is different from your communication in a job interview. Sometimes an outgoing and lively personality is as effective as a quiet and reserved style. Our language choices shift with various situations, as do our nonverbal manners. And what one person can "get away with" in an interaction may be your biggest downfall. These examples tell us that to be competent in communication is to be flexible. In fact, flexibility is considered an essential part of communication competence.

With regard to communication, flexibility refers to three things about a person: (1) awareness that there are options in any communication situation, (2) willingness to adapt to a situation, and (3) **self-efficacy** or *belief that she or he can be flexible*. Communication research also finds that confidence has a direct relationship to flexibility. In two separate studies, Matthew Martin, Carolyn Anderson, and Sydney Staggers found that people who are flexible "have more confidence in their ability to communicate effectively, especially in new situations" (Martin & Anderson, 1998, pp. 1–9; Martin, Staggers & Anderson, 2011). Competent communicators thus adjust their styles to different people, situations, and forms of communication. They often blend a variety of styles to meet the environment and the feedback they receive. Competent communicators are able to adapt to different people, places, and needs, and they do so while staying ethical and civil to others and their own selves. And they possess a level of confidence that their communication efforts will be successful.

However, this notion of flexibility is one of the challenges of studying communication. The vast number of advice and self-help books for better leadership skills, sales techniques, relational advice, and even intrapersonal skills suggests that we are seeking "rules" for how to "best" communicate—formulas for communicating competently. The sheer number of such books, though, shows that no single rule applies. Competent communication changes from moment to moment, person to person, relationship to relationship, and situation to situation. The "first rule" of communication competency is to be flexible. And, although flexibility may be one of the biggest challenges in studying communication, it is one of the most intriguing and exciting aspects.

self-efficacy
a person's belief that she or he can be flexible.

Communication Competence Requires Practice

When we are babies, we listen to the communication going on around us. We also try out sounds, putting them together in ways that do not make sense to those who hear us. At some point, we manage to utter something that makes sense. If English is our first language, we sometimes say, "Ma-ma," "Da-da," or even "No-no" or "Uh-oh." We have practiced long enough to successfully send a message that someone understands. To be competent, however, we must continue practicing communication, regardless of how fluent we are in one or more languages. Research documents the ways we practice and learn to communicate as we mature. For example, our ability to successfully persuade others develops and improves over time. Susan Kline and Barbara Clinton (1998) studied the persuasive abilities of young children and found that older children (sixth grade) were better able to construct persuasive messages than younger children (second and fourth grades). Kline and Clinton's research, and the research of those before them, found that younger children use fewer and simpler arguments as they attempt to persuade, and they employ "pleading, sulking, threats, and simple requests." Older children use more actual arguments in their persuasive attempts, and they appeal to "compromises, advantage arguments, appeals to social norms, and moral obligation and discussions of the advantages and disadvantages of competing alternatives" (Kline & Clinton, 1998).

Personal experience probably tells you that the more you practice something (a speech or an interview), the better your actual performance usually is. Studying communication in a class such as the one you are taking now is a good way to practice your skills. And the more you communicate with others, the more you are exposed to differences, similarities, and a wide range of communication styles. You can use these interactions as models or templates, and they will inform the decisions you make about the best choices for communicating with others.

Communication Competence Requires Cognitive Complexity

Competent communicators not only are flexible and willing to practice their skills but also possess what is called **cognitive complexity**. Joseph Bieri (1955) first introduced the concept as the *capacity to make sense of social behavior in a multidimensional way*. A person high in cognitive complexity is able to simultaneously hold onto different and even conflicting definitions, perceptions, and explanations of an event without discomfort. A person low in cognitive complexity has difficulty doing so and struggles with ambiguity and contradictions (Domangue, 1978). Competent communicators, in short, are able to entertain different

PRACTICING HUMAN COMMUNICATION
What Is Flexibility?

Your boss asks you to come in on Saturday (a day you normally do not work). You had promised to take your seven-year-old nephew to get new school supplies. List the possible responses you could give your boss. List the possible responses you could give your young shopping partner. Which would you choose? Why? Compare your responses to those of your classmates. How many different options did you generate as a class? Do your options reflect the definition of flexibility previously offered?

cognitive complexity
capacity to make sense of social behavior in a multidimensional way.

speculations about an encounter: your instructor is short with you because you were rude to him or her, she or he is rushed or just had an unpleasant encounter with another student or is worried about something, is in a bad mood, is hungry, or is generally unhappy.

Cognitive complexity involves more than the ability to manage ambiguity. It requires that we be empathetic as well as able to monitor our own behaviors. **Empathy** is the *ability to see the world through another person's eyes and to understand his or her feelings and perspectives*. Empathy is sometimes confused with **sympathy**. When we feel sympathetic, we usually *feel sorry for or pity another*. When you are fired from a job, for example, some friends may feel sympathy for you—they feel sorrow or pity. Other friends feel empathy for you—they may have been fired before, too, and they know what it feels like to have that experience. They can "get into your shoes" and understand why and how you feel the way you do. We do not always have to share the same experiences to have empathy—in fact, it is almost impossible to have all of the same experiences as other people. Competent communicators make use of cognitive complexity, practice, and flexibility to take another's perspective and communicate with empathy.

Self-monitoring, or the *ability to observe your own behaviors and communication and to see how they are affecting others*, is a final component of cognitive complexity and competent communication (Snyder, 1974). People high in self-monitoring are well aware of social situations and watch themselves during an interaction. They give themselves feedback and make adjustments to their communication throughout the process to ensure their interaction goes well. Self-monitors say to themselves intrapersonally as they are talking, "I think my boss is receptive to my not coming in on Saturday," or "I think my boss is getting frustrated with me." Self-monitors say to themselves, "This isn't going well," or "He seems to understand what I'm saying" and, where necessary and appropriate, change their communication styles to better fit a situation (Mill, 1984). High self-monitors are more skilled at communication—they are aware of their impact and the emotional states of others, and they are better able to remember information. Low self-monitors, in contrast, overestimate their communication strengths and fail to recognize that communication may not be going well.

To determine whether or not you are a high or low self-monitor, consider how much you pay attention to the feedback of others when you communicate with them. Are you aware of the signals they are giving you? Do you adjust your message accordingly? The answers to these questions also raise questions of civility and ethics. Communication competence involves the ability not only to be flexible and to self-monitor but also to practice civility—listening to others in respectful ways, regardless of differences and disagreements. It also requires our attention to ethics. Are we adjusting our communication so that we can communicate more clearly and effectively or are we going against our principles and values to get what we want? Communication competence requires that we pay attention not only to what and how we say things but also to the ethical and civil impact of the things we do say.

empathy
ability to see the world through another person's eyes and to understand his or her feelings and perspectives.

sympathy
feeling sorry for or pitying another.

self-monitoring
ability to observe one's own behaviors and communication and to see how they are affecting others.

Why Study Communication?

Communication Is All Around Us

Even if this era were not called the Information Age, we can recognize the ever-present nature of communication. Communication is all around us; it helps us learn about the world, other people and cultures, and ourselves. We engage the world by talking, asking, watching, reading, and listening. Our identities are shaped by communication. We often find out what our choices are and how they will affect us and other people through communication. We make decisions, inform others of those decisions, and learn of theirs through communication. Indeed, communication is one of the most important and significant ways we move through the world. Because communication is all around us, it is easy to forget that we can study it and actually learn more about this complex and ever-present phenomenon.

Communication Is Irreversible

A second reason to study communication is that we cannot "take back" what we have said. Communication is irreversible. Because of this, knowing how to communicate effectively in a wide variety of contexts and with a wide variety of people becomes very important. Most of us can recall the moment we said something, followed by "I didn't mean it that way" because we confused, hurt, angered, or insulted someone. Once a message leaves our mouths, computers, phones, or the like, if someone receives that message, it is theirs—for better or worse. We can certainly backtrack, try to explain, apologize, or make amends, but the irreversible nature of communication is one very important reason for studying it.

Stephen Morris/Vetta/Getty Images

Can you think of a time you hit "Send" and then wished you could take it back? Were you able to fix the exchange? Was your solution civil and ethical?

Communication Is Always Evolving

Language and words are never static. Meanings shift and change over time, and new words are developed to name new events, processes, and ideas. In fact, the publisher Merriam-Webster recently announced the addition of more than 150 new entries to its *Collegiate Dictionary* (including such words as *hashtag, selfie, pho, turducken,* and *freegan*) (Merriam-Webster 2014). Cultures, traditions, social norms, and people are in a constant state of change, as well, affecting the ways we interact with one another. In addition, mediums for communication are always evolving: technology adds new options and dimensions to communication—e-mail, established in 1993, is just over twenty years old and smartphones, with all their communication options, change almost annually. People can communicate across continents in ways that were not possible just a few years ago, thanks to computer and satellite technologies. The rapidly changing nature of our world and the ways we are able to interact with other people is a third reason to study communication.

Thomas Taha Rassam Culhane, Explorer, Urban Planner and Blackstone Innovation Challenge Grantee: The Great Conversation

Courtesy of T.H. Culhane

Thomas Taha Rassam (T.H.) Culhane, urban planner and explorer for the National Geographic, states "We're taught that garbage is garbage," but, is it really? Cairo's Zabaleen people (literally, "garbage people") "view everything around them as useful for something." Culhane's work with the Zabaleen began when he watched mothers carry buckets back and forth and up and down stairs for seven hours just to secure water for their families. Wanting to understand firsthand what these families faced, Culhane and his wife moved into the poorest of neighborhoods in Cairo to experience the obstacles they faced. Culhane founded Solar C.³I.T.I.E.S. and worked with residents of the poorest neighborhoods in Cairo to install solar water heaters and biogas digesters in their homes.

Culhane describes Solar C.³I.T.I.E.S. as "not merely a clean power provider" but an organization that places group work and collaboration at its center. Solar C.³I.T.I.E.S. is "an idea generator," Culhane explains. "We realize the value of collective intelligence. These neighborhoods are filled with welders, plumbers, carpenters, and glassworkers. We bring capital and plans; they bring talent and creativity. We build these systems together from scratch."

Promoting the value of working together, Solar C.³I.T.I.E.S. also has reduced tensions between a primarily Coptic Christian community and an Islamic neighborhood. Culhane explains: "I knew if they could actually meet one another and connect on a project to solve common problems, they would overcome their differences. They immediately began sharing and building on each other's expertise. Now we're using the strengths of both Christianity and Islam to fight a common enemy: environmental degradation" (Culhane, 2011b).

Culhane is not satisfied with just developing options for solar power, however; he is also an advocate of what he refers to as "the Great Conversation." Our actions, Culhane explains, tell a story—but there is only one story, the story of "the Universe." This story "is a never-ending story, ever unfolding. When we learn to see our Earth . . . as a living thing, as a giant organism within that Universe, we can also learn to see our essential roles as parts of that planetary body. From an ecological point of view we can see that nobody is expendable." We all play different roles at different times, depending on our locations and our context, and what Culhane calls our "behavioral plasticity and flexibility." This plasticity and flexibility show us when to add our voice to the conversation, using the "appropriate voice at the appropriate time." When we tell our stories, Culhane explains, we become *interested* in our place in that story and *interesting* to others. What is more, according to Culhane, "today's globalized digital media platforms and technology have removed most of the barriers to entry! We can connect with each other across the globe via YouTube and Flickr and Facebook and MySpace and blogging and commenting and expand the great conversation to include our voices among the many" (Culhane, 2011a).

MindTap® Go to cengagebrain.com to access your MindTap for *Invitation to Human Communication* to view a video about T. H. Culhane.

WHAT DO YOU THINK?

1. Culhane suggests that there is "a Great Conversation" made up of stories that help us understand our place in the universe. Do you agree with Culhane that this Great Conversation exists? Why or why not?

2. Culhane talks about each of us having a story to tell and an important part in the Great Conversation. Consider your cultural background, family upbringing, and unique experiences. What might you share with others (as a story) that would add to this conversation and help us understand your part in the universe?

3. Share your stories with one another. As you listen, do you use the skills of cognitive flexibility, empathy, and self-monitoring? Explain how.

Communication and Careers

Businesses report that competent communicators are among their most valued employees. The variety of situations, people, and tasks we must understand, work with, and accomplish, however, make achieving communication competence feel almost impossible. People in the workplace must make sense of and generate communication in real time through virtual (i.e., electronic) means as well as face-to-face and written employment settings. As a result of information and communication technologies, people find themselves interacting with some individuals who are quite similar as well as those who are quite different from them. This "online mobility" creates opportunities for "networking instead of isolation," but it also requires that workers communicate their work, successes, dilemmas, and solutions across cultures and sometimes languages (Ferreira da Cruz, 2008). The importance of the information and ideas received and generated in our workplaces is a fourth reason to study communication.

Communication and Family

Studying communication can also help us build and maintain healthy relationships with our families. It can assist us in understanding parent and child interactions, the reasons we are attracted to someone else, the evolution of our romantic relationships, power dynamics, and what makes someone a good listener, among many other things. In almost every relationship, we communicate at both the content and relational levels. **Content messages** are *the actual things we say,* while **relational messages** are *the parts of the communication that give us information about how we are or are not connected to a person.* For example, if you say to a friend, with sincerity, "I'm happy to go with you to the doctor," you are communicating both content and connection or relationship. The content message is that you will go with your friend to the doctor. The relational message is that you value that person enough to assist him or her. When you change the tone or style of delivery, you may not change the content message, but you likely will change the relational message (you might feel pressured to help your friend, for example). Studying communication helps us learn how to communicate more clearly with our families and friends on both levels. And clearer communication helps us establish and maintain strong and rewarding relationships.

Communication and Self

Studying communication teaches us a great deal about ourselves. When we read about and practice different styles and techniques for communicating effectively, we learn about our own unique strengths and weaknesses. We can build on those strengths and try to eliminate or minimize our weaknesses. We also can learn where we are comfortable communicating—is it one on one? In groups? In front of large audiences? We can also find out where we might have some **communication apprehension** or *anxiety about communicating in any number of situations.* Almost everyone has some apprehension about communicating. Some people are anxious about job interviews or public speeches. Others become anxious when

content messages
the actual things we say.

relational messages
the parts of the communication that give us information about how we are or are not connected to another person.

communication apprehension
anxiety about speaking in any number of situations (interviews, speeches, etc.).

they need to ask for help or guidance. Many people become fearful when they decide to tell someone they like them and want to build a romantic relationship with them (or, conversely, do not like them and do not wish to see them again). So studying communication helps us understand not only what our own strengths and weaknesses are but also when we are likely to experience communication apprehension and how to work with that feeling (we will study communication apprehension more in Chapter 12).

Communication and Civic Engagement

A final reason to study communication is that we do not live in isolation from other people. As Stephen Carter noted, we live as members of communities. Because of our relationships to other people, our need to communicate with people who are sometimes quite similar and sometimes quite different from us, and the nature of democracy in the United States, we must engage other people and ideas so that we can make informed and sustainable decisions. The term **globalization** has become a familiar part of our everyday language and defines this increasingly interconnected way of life. It refers to the *processes through which local and regional ideas, products, and practices are transformed into worldwide ideas, products, and practices.*

Globalization helps us understand the importance of communication and civic engagement. **Civic engagement**, a term made popular by Thomas Ehrlich (2000), refers to *individual and collective actions designed to identify and address issues of public concern.* It does not refer to any particular political, religious, or social affiliation. It is a practice common to people around the world as they identify events and practices that benefit or harm (or both) their homes, workplaces, communities, states, countries, and continents. When we communicate about these issues, we are engaged civically: we recognize that what we do as individuals and collectives affects other people.

globalization
processes through which local and regional ideas, products, and practices are transformed into worldwide ideas, products, and practices.

civic engagement
individual and collective actions designed to identify and address issues of public concern.

Chapter Summary

Communication Can Be Defined as the Use of Symbols by Humans to Create Messages for Other Humans

- Communication is the use of symbols by humans to create messages for other humans.
- When we communicate civilly we make a decision to be open to hearing different views and perspectives, even though we may not agree with them.
- When we communicate ethically we consider the moral impact of our words, ideas, and views on other people.
- Communication is a symbolic process, which means that it consists of a symbol, a referent, and a thought

or a reference, and a reciprocal, a process that requires feedback.
- Communication is also influenced by culture.

The Five Types of Communication Are Intrapersonal, Interpersonal, Group, Mass, and Public Communication

- Three models describe the communication process: the linear model, the interactive model, and the transactional model.
- Each model contains the following components: sender, receiver, encoding, decoding, feedback, channel, noise, and environment.

Competent Communication Requires Flexibility, Practice and Cognitive Complexity; There Are Six Reasons to Study Communication

- Communication is inevitable, irreversible, and evolving. It influences careers, families, and self.

- In addition, it is important to recognize the effects of globalization and the importance of civic engagement as we communicate with others about issues that affect us all.

Key Concepts

channel (10)

civic engagement (24)

civility (15)

cognitive complexity (19)

communicating civilly (3)

communicating ethically (3)

communication (3)

communication apprehension (23)

content messages (23)

culture (6)

decode (10)

empathy (20)

encode (10)

environment (11)

ethnocentrism (7)

external noises (10)

feedback (6)

globalization (24)

group communication (7)

internal noises (10)

intrapersonal communication (7)

interpersonal communication (7)

logic (4)

mass communication (8)

noise (10)

public or presentational communication (8)

reciprocity (6)

referent (4)

relational messages (23)

self-efficacy (18)

self-monitoring (20)

semantic noise (10)

semantic triangle of meaning (4)

symbol (4)

sympathy (20)

thought or reference (4)

understand (3)

Invitation to Human Communication Online

MindTap Speech includes an interactive MindTap Reader and interactive learning tools, including National Geographic Explorer videos, student videos, quizzes, flashcards, and more. You can build your speech outline with Outline Builder and record, post, and watch videos with YouSeeU. Go to cengagebrain.com to access your MindTap for *Invitation to Human Communication* where these resources can be found.

MindTap®

Further Reflection and Discussion

1. Consider what you want to get out of this course. Do you want to learn more effective ways to communicate at work? Do you hope to improve relationships with friends or family?

2. Take a moment to create your own definition of communication. What does it include? Who does it involve? In what contexts does it take place? Now compare your definition of communication to the one offered in this chapter. What are the similarities and differences?

3. This chapter presented Deborah Tannen's notion of an argument culture. What is your perception of this culture? Have you been exposed to interpersonal communication as an argument? If the people engaged in this interaction were to communicate civilly, what specifically would change?

4. What does it mean to you to communicate civilly and ethically? Give an example of civil and ethical communication from your own life.

5. Think about the African concept of *ubuntu* or *botho* and explain ways in which this concept might be communicated when talking with someone you have just met.

6. Log on to Merriam-Webster's list of new words (http://merriam-webster.com/new-words/2014-update.htm) and select three words from that list. Now, using Richard's semantic triangle of meaning, draw three semantic triangles representing the meanings for each of those three words. What are the concepts and referents associated with these three words?

7. How might your own cultural backgrounds affect your views of other people who may not be share your background? If you think ethnocentrism might affect your styles of communication, how might you begin to change this?

8. This chapter talks about communication being irreversible. Are there times in your life when you said something that you wish you had not? Were you able to "reverse" that communication minimize the damage? How so?

9. Communication apprehension affects us all. In what contexts and situations are you most apprehensive? In what contexts and situations are you the least apprehensive? Can you identify why you are more comfortable in some communication situations than others? How do you think studying communication will help you with communication apprehension?

10. This chapter emphasizes the importance of communicating civilly with other people. Civility involves listening carefully to ideas and opinions that might be very different from your own. What topics or issues do you think you could listen civilly to? Which do you think you might have problems listening to? Consider these as possible speech topics for Chapters 13, 14, or 15.

Activities and Web Links

Visit cengagebrain.com to access the MindTap for *Invitation to Human Communication* where these activities and Web links can be found.

1. Visit the Web site for the National Communication Association. Search for the list of publications related to one of the topics covered in this chapter. Which publications interest you? What would you like to know more about? Go to *Web link 1.1*.

2. Watch this video that shows a person who is a low self-monitor. What do you suggest he do differently to achieve his goal in this communication? Go to *Web link 1.2*.

3. Personal report of communication apprehension. Take this self-test and determine whether you have any communication apprehension. Score your results and note in which areas you have apprehension: group discussion, meetings, interpersonal communication, public speaking. Go to *Web link 1.3*.

Communication, Perception, and the Self

IN THIS CHAPTER YOU WILL LEARN TO:

- Discuss the variety of conditions that shape perceptions and selective attention.

- Recognize the role standpoints play in shaping primary and secondary dimensions of our identities.

- Explain how family, culture, and communication influence our self-concepts.

- Discuss how communication shapes the development of self-esteem.

- Recognize the power that first impressions and stereotyping have in affecting perceptions of others.

- Identify how civil communication affects our perceptions, actions, and words on other people and cultures.

Ming Thein/mingthein/Flickr/Getty Images

Self concept is the perception of who we are and how we are similar to and different from others. What are your perceptions of who you are?

No place to call home, people called me "A Lost Boy," meaning a child with no parents (Orphan). I live on my own in hardship, using only my tears. No father, no mother. I have never known the benefits of having parents. I don't know how good the world is. I was born in war, grew in fear, and remained in despair. My life has been useless, all useless. Suffering is my daily life. (Rose, 2004)

These are the words of Jacob Deng Ding, a child from the second civil war in southern Sudan (1983–2005), which claimed more than 2 million lives and left thousands of children, mostly boys between the ages of five and fifteen, orphaned or displaced. Known as the "Lost Boys," these courageous boys embarked on a terrifying journey across Africa to Ethiopia, back to Sudan, and finally to refugee camps in Kenya. These young men lived in thatched roof huts or tents, had never used electricity, and were accustomed to bathing in water drawn from a nearby river. As part of a resettlement program, approximately 3,800 Lost Boys came to the United States. Upon arriving to the United States, the Lost Boys found that everything was different—from living in their first apartment, trying different foods like potato chips and donuts, and seeing Santa Claus for the first time (National Geographic Video, n.d.). Not all of the differences were enjoyable. One Sudanese later said, "When we came [to the United States] it was very confusing; we were afraid to walk around because of our color and because we feared we would be abducted" (Muhindi & Nyakato, 2002). According to the documentary *God Grew Tired of Us: Cultural Differences* (National Geographic Video, n.d.), the Sudanese men were used to greeting people on the streets as they walked at home in Sudan, and they were confused when U.S. citizens ignored them. The resettled Sudanese young men claimed that "everything is different" in America.

Sudanese refugees and Lost Boys sit together on June 18, 1992, at a camp inside Kenya. Some 17,000 boys were lured away from home to receive military training in camps that held 300,000 refugees during a six-year period. After reading about their experiences, can you think of some of the ways your perception of the world might be different from theirs?

Scott Peterson/Getty Images

Meanwhile, some Americans were also confused by practices of the young resettled Sudanese men. Another Sudanese man explained, "We went to church one Sunday, and we met people on the way who asked us why we were walking in a big group. They thought we were a gang. We answered by telling them that no, we are not a gang; to walk together is our nature. We are used to walking together from the time we lived in south Sudan, and we like to be with each other" (Muhindi & Nyakato, 2002). In addition, it made the group feel safe. The experiences of these Lost Boys illustrate the power of perception. How can the simple act of a group of men walking together lead to two completely different perceptions? How can greeting strangers in one country be so different in another?

In this chapter, we explore some of the reasons that different people interpret the same situation in different ways. First, we discuss how our five senses can influence the way we understand ourselves and our experiences. Then we examine how significant others in our lives and the surrounding environment can impact our self-concept and self-esteem. Finally, we explore how our experiences shape the way we perceive others.

MindTap®

Go to your MindTap for *Invitation to Human Communication* to view the stories of these Lost Boys and to get a sense of how different our perceptions can be.

 ## Definition of Perception

When we interact with others, we focus on more than just the words being spoken: we focus on the occasion or context surrounding the interaction and the way things look, feel, smell, taste, and sound. The combination of these elements shapes our perceptions. **Perception** is the *process of acquiring and interpreting information from sensory data.* Perception is what we see, hear, smell, taste, and touch during any interaction. Every interaction contains sensory information or data; to understand our experiences, we must organize all the data collected by our senses. We may choose to focus on some senses (like the way something smells or tastes) and not on others (such as the way it looks). Because we receive a considerable amount of sensory input each day, we give attention to and remember only particular parts of each situation. This means we *select* (consciously or unconsciously) which sensory information to focus on. *The process of consciously or unconsciously selecting sensory data to maintain our focus* is called **selective attention**. Selective attention helps explain the different perceptions between Americans and the Sudanese boys. Because perception is so important to understanding communication, we examine several different factors that shape our perceptions.

Process of Perception

The processes of perception and selective attention, or focusing on particular sensory data, are influenced by a variety of conditions. Among the factors that help determine what we pay attention to are intensity and size, repetition, contrast, and personal motivations.

perception
process of acquiring and interpreting information from sensory data.

selective attention
process of consciously or unconsciously selecting sensory data to maintain our focus.

Intensity and Size The intensity and size of a stimulus will capture our attention. A loud noise or sound of a screaming child, a bright flashing light on an ambulance or police car, or seeing the bright lights and billboards of Las Vegas for the first time are intense stimuli that are immediately noticed.

Repetition When a noise or message is continuous, we are likely to pay attention to it. For example, we may focus on the ticktock of a clock, on a phone number repeated several times in an infomercial, or on teachers repeating information multiple times (we are hoping you will pay attention and remember the information).

Contrast We tend to notice objects, sounds, or behaviors that are different from our expectations: unanticipated storm clouds rolling in, an overly lethargic pet, or seeing food from another culture for the first time.

Personal Motivations Our feelings or intentions also affect which sensory data get priority. If we intend to purchase a car, then we probably pay more attention to car advertisements than if we were not looking for a vehicle. If we visit a new city, we may pay close attention to street signs but ignore them when driving around a familiar neighborhood. If we want to do well on an upcoming exam, we may listen more carefully in class.

Understanding the process of perception helps explain why we notice and remember certain events and not others. But certain factors cause us to focus on certain sensory data but not on others, including our families, cultures, and technology. We explore those influences next.

Influences on Perception

Our families, cultures, and even technology influence the process of perception in important ways, shaping who we are and how we see the world around us. We now take a look at each of these factors.

Self and Family Our perception of ourselves and the world around us is influenced by the roles we assume or are expected to take on in our families. A role is "the part an individual plays in a group" (DeVito, 1986, p. 269). In our families, roles include a variety of possibilities: sons and daughters, sisters and brothers, parents and children, youngest or oldest, responsible or forgetful, comedian or drama queen, and more. Perceptions about who we are get communicated through verbal and nonverbal feedback. A father might introduce one of his children this way—"This is my son; he's our risk taker"—but another by saying, "This is our youngest, the baby in the family." These roles are described verbally and communicate expectations that the individual is expected to fulfill. A mother might reinforce these roles verbally and nonverbally by hesitating to let the younger one explore while encouraging the "risk taker" to do so, and even rewarding both for fulfilling their roles.

PRACTICING HUMAN COMMUNICATION
What Kind of Perceptions Do You Have?

Recall the activities, events, or observations you made from last Sunday. What details can you remember? Now analyze the process of your perception. Which of the four categories listed in this section explain your ability to remember? What are the main reasons you notice and remember information? Do you tend to rely on the same factors for recalling most events in your life?

Although our roles evolve and change as we grow, our initial perceptions of who we are become defined early by the family unit. If your family continuously comments on your athletic ability, then you may begin to see yourself as athletic. However, outside individuals may also influence your perception of yourself. If your teacher tells you that your academic work is not good enough to qualify you as "gifted and talented" or to progress to the next grade, then you may believe that you are not intelligent. Researchers call this influence the **looking-glass self**, and it describes *the way other people's perceptions of us defines our own perceptions of ourselves* (Cooley, 1968). The looking-glass self begins early and is primarily influenced by family members, but it also is affected by our teachers, friends, coaches, and neighbors. And these messages influence how we later see the world. So, in the preceding example, the risk taker might see new opportunities as an adventure, whereas the baby of the family might see them as challenges and obstacles to be avoided.

Self and Culture Culture also influences the way we perceive ourselves and the world around us. What we see, hear, smell, taste, and touch are often determined, influenced, or guided by the cultures in which we live (Singer, 1982). Cognitive psychologist Richard Nisbett has explored this influence, noting that people we describe as coming from Eastern cultures (Chinese, Koreans, and Japanese) and Western cultures (Europeans, Canadians, and U.S. Americans) differ in how they perceive objects and situations. He claims that people from Eastern cultures focus attention on backgrounds, group objects according to thematic relationships, and usually see both sides of an argument. People from Western cultures, on the other hand, focus directly on objects, group in taxonomies, and tend to reject one side of an argument (Nisbett, 2000). Hence, our culture shapes which sensory data are observed and how they are interpreted.

The speed at which tasks are accomplished is also bound by cultural influences. In many cultures, getting things done quickly is valued. Instant messaging and texting can produce immediate feedback, fast-food restaurants can produce meals in minutes, and overnight delivery services can have packages on doorsteps by the next or even the same day. Fast service is not a priority in other cultures. In Central America, Mexico, and Spain, for example, people enjoy a more leisurely pace of life, and taking time to relax and enjoy life at a slower pace is a more typical cultural experience. So, although it is tempting to think that all humans organize their perceptions similarly, culture influences and helps explain differences in perceptions of time, appointments, and the overall pace by which tasks are completed.

Perception and Technology Technology and media also affect our perceptions. The sound from our computers indicating we have new e-mail, the vibration of our smartphones letting us know that someone is calling or texting, the bright letters flashing on our televisions with breaking news stories, and advertisements popping up on our devices—all of these show what some person or organization wants us to look at.

looking-glass self
the way other people's perceptions of us define our own perceptions of ourselves.

The staggering number of advertisements an average person is exposed to each day (as many as 5,000 every day) means there are plenty of requests and opportunities for us to pay attention to and organize certain sensory data (Story, 2007). These data, however, are already highly organized. Colors, images, words, and sounds are strategically placed in every advertisement to draw our attention to certain things and encourage us to accept a message or purchase an item. Beyond family or cultural influences, technology challenges us to sort through messages about who we are or can be, consider what the looking glass of technology is reflecting back to us, and ponder these influences more and more carefully and thoughtfully.

Our families, culture, and media, as well as the factors that influence perception, shape the way we experience and interpret situations. However, as individuals, we also bring an important component called a *standpoint* to the process of perception. We explore standpoints and identity and their influence on perception next.

Perception, Identity, and Standpoint

Identity refers to the *social categories that we and others identify as important characteristics of who we are.* Although many social categories exist— "Latina," "female," "college student," "middle child," "punk," "nerd," and "girly girl"—they only become part of our identity if we accept or associate with them. Identities are what make us unique. Researchers Loden and Rosener (1991) explain that our identities have primary and secondary dimensions. **Primary dimensions** are *based on identity traits that we are born with and are a significant part of who we are.* Primary dimensions of our identity might include our race, gender, social class, sexual orientation, physical abilities, and ethnicity. **Secondary dimensions** are *identities that we acquire, develop, or discard throughout our lives.* Examples of secondary dimensions include educational level, career choice, and relationship status. Both dimensions of our identities shape our perceptions, but research suggests that our primary identities might hold more influence than the secondary dimensions because our primary identities tend to be more stable (Ting-Toomey, 1999).

As noted, both primary and secondary identities shape what is often called our *standpoints.* A **standpoint** is *the perspectives from which a person views and evaluates society.* Standpoints are influenced by the different aspects of our identities, or the complex combination of traits that make up our self. Each person's identity is unique and slightly different from others. One person may describe herself as "heterosexual, female, Asian American, adopted, and an only child." Another might describe himself as "gay, male, Caucasian, youngest of six, and Texan." A third might choose "young male from Sudan who lost his entire family when he was a small boy" to best describe his complex identity. These identities, complex and different, influence not only how a person perceives events and experiences but also how others perceive them. The different parts of these identities make up a person's standpoint, or the perspective from which she or he sees and experiences the world.

Standpoints help to explain how the perception of who we are exists in relationship to others and how this relationship is based on social, political, cultural, and economic power systems (Hartstock, 1999).

We often have different standpoints, depending on our identities. What are your primary and secondary identities? How do they influence your standpoints?

identity
social categories that we and others identify as important characteristics of who we are.

primary dimensions
identity traits that we are born with and are significant parts of who we are.

secondary dimensions
identities that we acquire, develop, or discard throughout our lives.

standpoint
the perspectives from which a person views and evaluates society.

Standpoints help us see that different identities are weighted differently in our society. For example, although "heterosexual, White, college-educated male" may be highly ranked in U.S. culture, "gay" or even "Sudanese" affect rankings in ways that "heterosexual" or "White" do not. Similarly, although the identity of "heterosexual" holds a high ranking in the United States, "Asian American," "female," and even "relocated to the United States from Sudan" change that ranking slightly. And the identities of "only child," "adopted," or "youngest of six" affect how a person sees the world, as do "homeless" and "orphaned." Like the example of the Lost Boys that opened this chapter, the identities we find salient, the ones we describe as important to us, shape our perceptions. Our standpoints, as well as the primary and secondary dimensions of our identity, help explain our differences, our relationships to others, and the ways in which social, political, and economic systems affect our perceptions.

The process of perception is complex, and the ways we communicate are influenced by what we perceive and how others perceive us. Understanding these processes and influences helps us communicate more clearly with others and appreciate our uniqueness and similarities.

Perceiving Our Self

The perception of who we are influences the way we behave in our personal relationships, at work, and in society. The answers to the question "Who am I?" constitute our **self-concept**, or the *perception of who we are and what makes us unique as well as similar to others* (Hormouth, 1990). Our self-concept is based on many characteristics, including our physical appearance, talents, intellect, popularity, age, professional status, fears, and beliefs (Piers & Harris, 1996). Some aspects remain stable, others change throughout our lives, and some may be more important or significant than others. Turning eighteen and being eligible to join a political party and vote, graduating from college and obtaining employment, and committing to a relationship are changes we experience over time and may help define our self-concept. In addition to these characteristics, our families, culture, and society affect our understanding of who we are.

Self-Concept and Family
Family members help shape our self-concept, particularly as children. Parents, siblings, and other relatives rely on verbal and nonverbal forms of communication to convey messages about who we are. **Labels**, or the *words used to describe ourselves and others*, are an important component of this influence. Andie, a five-year-old girl, may believe she is "shy, musically talented, and pretty" based on the way her family talks to and about her. Her sister, Georgia, however, sees herself as "outgoing, athletic, and a tomboy" based on the way her family labels her. Our self-concept also can be filled with positive or negative characteristics. A child growing up in a negative environment may be labeled a "problem child," whereas a child growing up in a positive environment with the same behaviors might be labeled "high spirited." Labels have a powerful influence on our self-concept. Positive labels can enhance our self-concept and self-esteem, and

self-concept
perception of who we are and what makes us unique as well as similar to others.

labels
words used to describe ourselves and others.

What messages were communicated to you by family members that shaped your self-concept?

negative labels can be detrimental to our perceptions of who we are as a person.

Self-Concept and Culture

Culture also shapes our understanding of our self-concept. Particular cultural norms and social rules affect the way we think about ourselves, behave in public and in private, and respond toward others. The United States is said to be an individualistic culture that values free enterprise and freedom of speech, religious freedom, and democracy. These cultural norms shape our perceptions of who we are; in the United States, our self-concepts are shaped by the belief that we should be independent and self-sufficient. Our self-concepts also are shaped by U.S. views of religion and how religious practices are carried out. In addition, the United States' commitment to the freedom of speech shapes our views about our ability to speak out, write letters to public officials, and even tolerate hostile or hateful speech. Other cultures influence self-concepts differently. In some cultures, open conflict or speaking out publicly against the government is discouraged or even dangerous. The way religions are practiced may be quite different from the U.S. practices of Christianity, Catholicism, and Judaism. Who can attend school, what can be studied, and for how long even varies from culture to culture. These cultural factors affect a person's self-concept or response to "Who am I?" in powerful and subtle ways.

The way a culture views a person's race and ethnicity can also influence their self-concept. Within the United States, labels for a person's race and ethnicity have changed over time (Bahk & Jandt, 2004). For example, the labels for people of African descent have evolved as social and political norms shifted and individuals renegotiated their identities according to these shifts. These different labels include African, colored, Negro, Afro-American, Black, African American, and Black American (Orbe & Drummond, 2009). Similarly, the label "White" has also changed. Until the early 1900s, people of Irish, Eastern European, and Italian heritage, for example, were not considered "White." These "umbrella terms" of "Black" and "White" often do not allow for key distinctions within large and heterogeneous groups. Orbe and Drummond interviewed more than 100 individuals to explore how labels for race and ethnicity influence identity. In response to the question, "Who am I?" one respondent explained why the umbrella term "Black" is not always sufficient:

> I really didn't have a problem with it [the label of Black] in the beginning. . . . Then as I started to, I guess, I wouldn't say differentiate myself but started to understand my ethnic background. I'm Haitian as well. My parents are from Haiti. I felt like just classifying people or people from outside of the [United States], who are of Black origin, in this big category wasn't accurate. We are Black, but you know there is more to us than just being Black. We are Black Caribbean, Black African, Black American. . . . (p. 449)

At age 13, surfer Bethany Hamilton lost her arm in a shark attack while surfing off Kauai's North Shore in Hawaii. Losing her arm did not stop her from surfing. She told an ESPN interviewer, "For me, losing my arm was definitely worth it. I can still surf. I get to inspire people who don't have hope in life. . . . I'm just really glad that I can do something bigger than just live my life for myself" (Huckshorn, 2009).

So, the way a culture labels racial and ethnic groups may shape the way a person understands her or his self-concept. Yet those labels and who they describe change over time as cultural norms shift and as individuals' concepts of themselves adjust to those shifts.

Self-Concept and Communication

We receive all kinds of messages about who we are from family members, teachers, neighbors, friends, co-workers, and members of organizations or clubs in which we belong. **Symbolic interactionism** describes this influence and is the *process of understanding our sense of self based on other's observations, judgments, and evaluations of our behavior* (Mead, 1934). When similar messages about who we are get repeated by significant others in our lives, we begin to understand what makes us similar to and different from others. When friends, teachers, and neighbors comment on our artistic abilities, we are likely to believe we have a talent. When friends, co-workers, and significant others tell us we are generous, we may believe we are kind.

Our self-concept is shaped by the language used to define us as individuals. When we internalize labels or comments made about who we are and then *act in accordance with these expectations*, we are engaging in a **self-fulfilling prophecy**. When a child is labeled "clumsy," she may internalize this message and see herself as awkward and ungraceful. If a child is labeled the "class clown," he may see himself as funny and continue to make jokes during class. Although some labels may be accurate for a particular

symbolic interactionism
process of understanding our sense of self based on other's observations, judgments, and evaluations of our behavior.

self-fulfilling prophecy
to act in accordance with expectations.

David Gregerson/Sport Studio Photos/Getty Images

Barrington Irving, Emerging Explorer, Pilot, Educator: Challenging Others People's Perceptions

Raised in a low-income neighborhood in Miami, Barrington Irving's life changed when he met a pilot who asked him if he had ever considered becoming a pilot. Irving explains, at the age of fifteen, "I didn't think I was smart enough; but the next day he gave me a chance to sit in the cockpit of the commercial airplane he flew, and just like that I was hooked. There are probably millions of kids out there like me who find science and exploration amazing, but lack the confidence or opportunity to take the next step." Convinced he wanted to become a pilot, Irving turned down a football scholarship to the University of Florida in favor of flight school, which he paid for by washing airplanes. After obtaining his pilot's license, he had another dream to pursue: to fly solo around the world. To sponsor his dream, Irving approached various manufacturers asking them to donate parts for an airplane he wanted to build; more than fifty companies rejected him before he found some who would help. With no weather radar, no deicing system, and only $30 in his pocket, he took flight: "I like to do things people say I can't do." At age twenty-three, Irving became the youngest person and first African American ever to fly solo around the world.

Following his historic flight, Irving decided to help other young people achieve their dreams. "I was determined to give back with my time, knowledge, and experience." He founded a nonprofit organization, Experience Aviation, intended to increase the number of students in aviation, as well as other math and science-related careers. Irving uses examples of his own life to inspire students. After landing his record-breaking flight at age 23, he said, "Everyone told me what I couldn't do. They said I was too young, that I didn't have enough money, experience, strength, or knowledge. They told me it would take forever and I'd never come home. Well . . . guess what?" Now, when Irving speaks to students who "aren't sure what they want to do with their lives," he tries to inspire them to have a dream, and to have the confidence to believe they can fulfill that dream. He says, "No matter what the challenge the only one who can stop you is you."

WHAT DO YOU THINK?

1. What do you think Irving's primary and secondary perceptions of himself are? How are they similar and or different to your own primary and secondary perceptions?

2. What labels do you believe Irving would use to describe himself?

3. Consider the concept of symbolic interactionism. How could Irving's life have been different if he listened to the people who said he could not accomplish his dream?

time in our life, we often grow and develop in ways that reshape these expectations. If Erin is labeled a "shy child," she may feel afraid in unfamiliar social settings. However, Erin may outgrow this fear and eventually become an outspoken and confident person later in life. Other labels may never be valid at all. If a child is told he will never succeed in college (even though he could), he may adopt a destructive self-fulfilling prophecy by choosing to not enroll in college classes. However, he may also overcome this label, avoiding the self-fulfilling prophecy, and find the self-esteem he needs to succeed. In the next section, we look at how self-esteem can help us avoid the negative prophecies we hear from others.

Self-Esteem

Our **self-esteem** consists of *how we feel about ourselves based on perceptions of our own strengths and weaknesses*. Our self-esteem reflects our view of our own value or worth: it is the high or low regard we give to our selves. If we like ourselves and value who we are, then we are said to have high self-esteem. If we do not see ourselves as valued or worthy or do not like who are, then we are said to have low self-esteem. Self-esteem can and often does fluctuate over time. On days you are feeling good about yourself because things have gone well (you got that job offer you worked hard for) or when you feel good about what you accomplished throughout the day (you did well on an exam), you may have high self-esteem. On the other hand, if you receive a failing grade on an assignment that you spent a great deal of time on, or if you are the only one on a team who does not play well during a game, then you may have a day of lower self-esteem. But how can you be sure you have a healthy self-esteem rather than an overinflated one? In the next sections we discuss ways to assess and enhance your esteem as well as the role communication plays in both.

Assessing Our Self-Esteem We can assess our self-esteem in a few ways. One way is to listen to other people's assessments of who we are. Do other people praise us or criticize us? Do they label us positively or negatively? What kind of worth or value do they assign us? The influence of their communication is called **reflected appraisal**, *the process of developing an image of who we are based on the way others describe us*. Regardless of whether the appraisals are accurate or not, the impact is powerful. If we have received predominantly negative messages about ourselves, we might suffer from low self-esteem. However, if we have received predominantly positive messages, we might also suffer from an overinflated self-esteem.

As you consider the messages others have communicated to you and the value or worth assigned to those messages, keep in mind the concept of self-fulfilling prophecy and the impact it can have on our views of our selves. You will also want to consider the effect of gender on self-esteem. Decades of research have determined that boys' and girls' self-esteems develop differently. Adolescent girls experience a significant drop in their self-esteem as they attend middle and high school. Adolescent boys may see a slight drop but nothing as profound as lowering of self-esteem seen in girls at that same age (Kilbourne, 1999). The differences are attributed to many factors, including messages from media, teachers, and parents;

self-esteem
how we feel about ourselves based on perceptions of our own strengths and weaknesses.

reflected appraisal
the process of developing an image of who we are based on the way others describe us.

athletic and extracurricular opportunities; social pressures; and even messages about physical appearance and development. In addition, even though girls fare far worse than boys during this time, research is beginning to suggest that boys' self-esteem regarding academic potential is lower than girls' during this same period (Kimmell, 2008).

A second way to assess your self-esteem is through the process of social comparison. When we use **social comparison**, *we compare ourselves with another in order to determine our value or worth in relationship to that other person*. Although social comparisons can be helpful in assessing our own value or worth, they also can backfire and lower our self-esteem. Consider the following example.

Etine is a highly creative writer and poet. She likes to take long walks and loves quiet evenings, but she is not interested in or good at team sports such as soccer and basketball. She is tall (5'11") and has a healthy body, fitting into the appropriate weight category for her height and bone structure.

Courtesy of Erin Foley

Erin Foley, Ph.D., talks about social comparison in her speeches to college sorority sisters. Foley encourages her audience to live a "strong life" by paying attention to and enhancing their own self-esteem.

Marlena is tall, like Etine, and also has a healthy body. She loves basketball and soccer and is quite good at both. She is not one to sit still, so writing is difficult for her. She would much rather watch a good movie with friends or go to a concert than read a book or take a walk.

Etine and Marlena can use social comparison positively or negatively. Used positively, Etine might say, "Marlena and I are both tall and healthy—and this is a good thing. Marlena is good at sports and in busy social settings, and I am better at quiet, creative activities. Together we make a great team." Used negatively, however, Marlena might say, "Etine and I are both too tall for women and not thin enough. I'm too much of a tomboy, and Etine is much better at the right sort of feminine activities than I am. I'm a failure at writing, and I'm too undisciplined—I waste my time with all these social activities."

Etine has used social comparison in a positive way, whereas Marlena has used it in a negative way. When we compare ourselves to others and find that we are lacking in some or all aspects, then we lower our self-esteem. If we compare ourselves to others and come away with a healthy balance, we are using social comparison more productively.

A final way to assess your self-esteem is to consider the role culture and society play in influencing the worth or value we place on our self. Psychologists suggest that individuals with strong ties to their racial or ethnic groups have higher self-esteem than do those who do not identify strongly with a group or are uncertain about their identification (Phinney, Cantu, & Kurtz, 1997; Umaña-Taylor, 2004). Individuals who have a negative view of their ethnic or racial membership also experience lower self-esteem. But these psychologists also discovered that even if the larger culture or society views the ethnic or racial category negatively, an individual who views it positively and identifies with it strongly maintains high self-esteem.

social comparison

comparing ourselves with another in order to determine our value or worth in relationship to that other person.

When people have high self-esteem, they have a positive appraisal of their worth and who they are as persons. Having high self-esteem can determine certain personality traits and even be an indicator of success. For example, people with high self-esteem tend to be extraverted, conscientious, emotionally stable, better at conflict resolution, and open to new experiences (Bechtoldt, Carsten, Dreu, Nijstad, & Zapf, 2010; Robins, Trzesniewski, Potter, & Gosling, 2001). In addition, someone who possesses high self-esteem may be more independent, optimistic, and self-directed. By contrast, those who possess low self-esteem may be more pessimistic, insecure, lonely, and depressed (Mruk, 1999). If you have low self-esteem, then there are ways to begin to raise it. Similarly, if your self-esteem is too high, there might be ways to find a better balance.

Enhancing or Maintaining Our Self-Esteem Self-esteem is important for building healthy relationships, performing well in school and extracurricular activities, and for maintaining self-worth. The desire for high self-esteem begins at an early age. As children hear they are talented, smart, funny, or kind (and believe these things to be true), their self-esteem is likely to increase. If children are told the opposite—that they are not talented or smart—then they may adopt low self-esteem. The desire for praise does not end with childhood. A recent study of college students found that receiving a compliment or earning a good grade to enhance self-esteem was more important than drinking alcohol, getting a paycheck, eating a favorite food, or seeing a best friend (Salamon, 2011). But we do not always receive compliments, and sometimes exams do not go well for us. There are ways we can improve or manage our self-esteem: get involved, move forward, make friends, exercise, and connect with our families.

Get Involved People who are involved in their families and communities, volunteer their time, and even attend social or community events (book clubs, fund-raising events, etc.) report improved self-esteem. "'Engaged' individuals" report benefits to their "physical and psychological health," improved self-confidence and self-esteem, and a "sense of personal empowerment" and better social relationships. But too much engagement can overtax us and leave us feeling fatigued (Attree, French, Milton, Poval, Whitehead, & Popay, 2011).

Move Forward In *Boost Your Self-Esteem*, John Caunt suggests that people need to sort out and then move past experiences that have damaged their self-esteem. Caunt suggests ten ways to "put yourself in the driver's seat" and move beyond emotional hurts and traumas that have led to lower self-esteem. Among his suggestions are identifying the excess baggage we carry around, moving beyond blaming others, finding positive outcomes from difficult experiences, and rewarding yourself for letting go of the negative experiences (Caunt, 2003). When we move beyond what is making us feel poorly about ourselves, we can begin to develop a positive view of ourselves.

Make Friends Sometimes a person's self-esteem may be low because of illness, injury, or loneliness. In "Cool Friends," Kath MacDonald and Alison Greggans discovered that individuals with health problems—in this case, cystic fibrosis—had improved self-esteem as a result of a "befriending" program. Those who were befriended felt more important and improved their social skills, and the befriending was described as a positive process by all parties involved. In addition, Jennifer Thomas and Kimberly Daubman report that for both boys and girls, friendship played an important role in achieving and maintaining positive self-esteem (MacDonald & Greggans, 2010; Thomas & Daubman, 2001). The role of friends is also important for lesbian, gay, bisexual, and transgendered individuals, who report that support networks other than family play a major role in the development of positive self-esteem (Wilson, Zeng, & Blackburn, 2011).

Exercise Decades of research suggest a positive correlation between healthy self-esteem and exercise (Holland & Andre, 1994; Taylor, 1995; Wilkins, Boland, & Albinson, 1991). Intuitively, we know that we often feel better about ourselves after we work out or engage in some form of exercise. However, Jo Barton and Jules Pretty suggest that "green" exercise—that is, exercise done outside in nature—goes even further in improving self-esteem. Barton and Pretty argue that "acute exposure to green exercise" positively affects the self-esteem of both women and men (Barton & Pretty, 2010).

Family Our families play a crucial role in our self-esteem. When individuals report receiving the guidance and positive support of one parent, their self-esteem tends to be strong; when they receive positive guidance and support from two parents, it is even higher (Bulanda & Majumdar, 2009). Studies also show that when our families are involved in our lives in positive ways, both males and females are less likely to engage in delinquent behaviors, take fewer sexual risks, and engage in less risky substance-abuse behaviors. For Latinas, who have higher rates of suicide attempts than their White and African American peers, *familism*, or the positive involvement of family, appears to reduce the risk of suicide attempts (Kuhlberg, Peña, & Zayas, 2011; Paterson, Buser, & Westburg, 2010).

Having a healthy self-esteem is important to leading a healthy life, but someone with too much self-esteem—a "big ego"— can be difficult to work or socialize with.

Self-Esteem and the Media

Messages communicated through media affect our self-esteem, but this effect may not always be positive. In her video *Killing Us Softly IV*, Jean Kilbourne argues that the only image young girls see in the media today are tall, slim, and busty White or light-skinned women (Jhally & Kilbourne, 2010). Because many girls' self-esteem is directly related to body image, the pervasiveness of an unachievable ideal beauty standard and extreme thinness can prove deadly. Girls are constantly exposed to messages that say only thin girls

Our perceptions of the ideal male or female body change over time. The image of Batman in the 1980s is very different from his image today. Some young men who do not meet the current standard for the perfect male body suffer lower self-esteem.

Moviestore collection/Alamy

AF archive/Alamy

Women's Self-Esteem and the Media

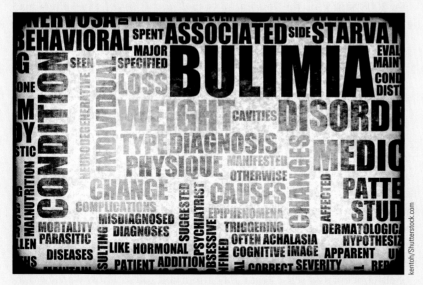

kentoh/Shutterstock.com

and "What the scale says is the most important thing";

- approximately 43 percent provided specific instructions on concealing eating disorders; and

- approximately 33 percent of sites did include information about recovery or treatment, though only 13 percent of sites contained an overt statement that eating disorders are a problem.

Many people are outraged at the availability of content that promotes eating disorders and online advice and images. Letters have been written to YouTube demanding that thinspiration videos be banned on the grounds that they promote eating disorders.

Eating disorders are epidemic in the United States. A recent study by Harris Interactive found the percentage of girls who believe they must be thin rose from 48 percent in 2000 to 60 percent in 2006 (Zaslow, 2009). *Wall Street Journal* reporter Jeffrey Zaslow tracked girls and dieting for more than three decades. He argued that "self-starvation in girls can be triggered by media images, including Internet sites promoting anorexia and bulimia as lifestyle choices" (Zaslow, 2009). He noted that the pitch lines used to lure young women such as "Nothing tastes as good as thin feels" and "Thirty hours food-free sounds like heaven" are promoting an unhealthy (and potentially deadly) fascination with starvation.

Finding support groups that encourage anorexia and bulimia are now just a click away. The new catchphrase for so-called pro-ana (pro-anorexia) Web sites is called "thinspiration," which means using exceptionally thin female models as role models and inspiration to diet, binge, purge,

or starve. Thinspiration videos, blogs, and tweets are available for young girls to encourage this distorted motivation to be thin. Borzekowski, Schenk, Wilson, and Peebles (2010), researchers at The Johns Hopkins Bloomberg School of Public Health, examined the content and messages of 180 Web sites that advocated for eating disorders and concluded the following:

- 91 percent of sites were open to the public;

- 85 percent of sites featured thinspiration material (e.g., photographs of extremely thin models and celebrities);

- 79 percent had interactive features such as calorie and body-mass-index (BMI) calculators;

- approximately 16 percent had a "creed" or "oath to Ana," such as the "Thin Commandments," or ten rules for eating disorders—"Thou shall not eat without feeling guilty," "Thou shall not eat fattening food without punishing oneself afterward,"

What Do You Think?

1. What labels, aspects of symbolic interactionism, and self-fulfilling prophecies influence the perception that self-starvation is a worthy goal for young women? Make a list of these influences and sort them by "label," "symbolic interactionism," and "self-fulfilling prophecy."

2. Do you believe regulations are necessary to limit or ban pro-anorexia Web sites and videos? Would regulations be civil or uncivil? Explain why.

3. What are some alternatives to these catchphrases and Web sites that draw young women in to the thinspiration craze? Create several catchphrases and locate online videos, blogs, and Web sites that create a healthy image and dialogue around weight and normal body sizes, altering the perception that unhealthy thinness is the desired goal.

are desirable, yet only 5 percent of the U.S. population genetically has the body type consistent with popular media depictions.

Young men also are susceptible to lower self-esteem after viewing images of muscular men on television and in advertisements and sports. Even action figures and superhero costumes now contain six-pack abs and large biceps. However, research suggests that men's perception of what women desire as the ideal chest size for men is larger than what women actually report as desirable. And men experience lower self-esteem than women when they do not achieve their desired chest size (Tantleff-Dunn, 2001).

A 2008 study in the *Journal of Social and Clinical Psychology* also determined that

> both men and women are affected by exposure to idealized images in the mass media, which is often associated with negative feelings and thoughts about their bodies. This suggests that the use of muscular male models or skinny female models in the mass media is potentially damning to "everybody." (Barlett, Vowels, & Saucier, 2008, p. 306)

Media can and do affect our self-esteem in positive ways, however. Independent films, documentaries, YouTube videos, blogs, Facebook posts, and a variety of organizational Web sites allow individuals to create their own images, narratives, and stories to poke fun at social norms and codes and challenge unhealthy standards, as well as share experiences. They provide venues to educate ourselves, communicate with others who are seeking to break out of constricting images of masculinity and femininity, and try out new ways of being and living.

Self-concept and self-esteem play important roles in how we view ourselves and what makes us unique. The way we internalize labels, access our strengths and weaknesses, and respond to others' appraisals of us influence our feelings about who we are, and these are reflected in our communications with ourselves and others. We have learned what influences our perceptions of ourselves, so now let us look at how we perceive others.

Perceiving Others

First impressions significantly affect how we perceive others. In this section, we look at how to check the accuracy of our first impressions. Note, too, that we are also influenced by stereotypes when we form perceptions of other people. Because these broad generalizations can be ill informed, in this section we examine first impressions and then take a close look at stereotypes.

The Power of First Impressions

When meeting someone for the first time, we form an impression more quickly than we might imagine. Some research suggests that initial opinions—"first impressions"—are formed within as few as three seconds of meeting someone (Sterling, 2006). Other research indicates that some impressions are even faster. Princeton psychologists Janine Willis and Alexander Todorov (2006) claim that an impression of a stranger's trustworthiness and attractiveness is formed from her or his facial appearance in just one-tenth of a second. Although these impressions may not be completely accurate, they are certainly powerful. First impressions often determine the future success of the relationship and play an important role in how the relationship evolves. If two people determine an immediate liking for each other, then the

Job Interviews

First impressions are an important part of the job-interviewing experience. As you prepare for a job or internship interview, consider the type of first impression you would like to make. According to the *US News and World Report*, interviewers notice the following seven things about a job candidate. You can use them to your advantage.

1. **Arrival Time**: Try to arrive 10 minutes before the scheduled interview time. Never arrive late, or even excessively early, to a job interview.
2. **Attire**: Look the part. If you are unable to observe the dress code beforehand, call the front desk and ask about the dress code policy. Try to wear something slightly better.
3. **Nonverbal Communication**: Pay attention to your posture and movement. Try to look comfortable but not overly relaxed. Avoid fidgeting.
4. **Verbal Communication**: Pay attention to the speed and tone of speech from the interviewer, then try to match her or his verbal communication style.

5. **Preparedness**: Research the company and the position for which you have applied. Be familiar with the company's overall mission. Practice responses to some of the more commonly asked interview questions ahead of time.
6. **Enthusiasm**: Demonstrate enthusiasm and excitement for the possibility of working with the company. Showcase your ability to work well with others.
7. **Qualifications**: Be prepared to explain your skills and expertise. Do not forget to match your skills to the responsibilities of the position.

Because first impressions are so important, use the communication skills you learn in this chapter to help you manage them. Prospective employers are paying close attention to the people they interview, and your ability to present a confident, organized, and qualified first impression can help you get and keep that job.

relationship will likely continue over time. If the immediate impression is that one person is "cool toward the other," then it is unlikely the relationship will grow (Sunnafrank & Ramierz, 2004). Initial impressions can have a significant impact on long-term development of a relationship.

Unfortunately, first impressions can be determined by extraneous or atypical circumstances. Have you ever met someone while you were experiencing tremendous emotional, psychological, or physical stress? Perhaps you stayed up all night studying for a final, or maybe you learned that a grandparent recently died. You likely exhibited behaviors that are not consistent with your usual demeanor. Yet meeting someone when you are extremely stressed can create an inaccurate impression of you. For these reasons, recognize that our first impressions of others also may be perceptual errors. To help avoid committing these errors, engage in **perception checking,** which means that *we consider a series of statements or questions to confirm (or challenge) our perceptions of others and their behaviors.* Three types of statements can help us determine the accuracy of our evaluations:

1. Describe the verbal and nonverbal behavior observed.

2. Provide two possible interpretations for the behavior.

3. Seek clarification of or an explanation for the behavior.

Here is how perception checking works. After your roommate failed to meet you before class, you approach her and begin by saying, "When I noticed that you were not waiting for me before class" (the behavior), "I thought that you might have forgotten to do so" (first interpretation) "or perhaps you were mad at me" (second interpretation). "Why weren't you outside the building today?" (seek clarification).

perception checking
when we consider a series of statements or questions to confirm (or challenge) our perceptions of others and their behaviors.

Bil Zelman

Alexandra Cousteau
Emerging Explorer and Social Environment Advocate

Can you describe an experience in which perceptions of others played a significant role? For example, the impact of a first impression, or issues of stereotyping? How did this perception impact your effectiveness as a communicator?

I'm a young woman in a male-dominated legacy that includes my grandfather, my father, my brother, and my uncle and cousin, so it is always somewhat surprising when other people see a young blond girl who goes out at the field for seven months a year and does everything that the men of the family do. Sometimes when I go somewhere with my brother people think I'm his wife because we have same name.

On the other hand, I receive a lot of fan mail from women from all over the world. Women from places like Pakistan, India, and Bolivia write me letters saying, "You're such a role model for me." I realize that these women are watching and taking notes, and I hope that they feel empowered by the choices that I've made.

I tell young women, "Don't be afraid to have a big idea, and don't be afraid to go after it. If you fail, keep going because that failure will help you get up." I have had failures of my own, and I'm always happy in retrospect that I had these failures because they have taught me so much about how to get where I want to go. It is just a matter of knowing yourself, knowing what you want, and never giving up (Cousteau, 2012).

When using perception checking to understand a person's behavior, try not to suggest interpretations that might make others feel defensive (e.g., "You always forget and you don't care about our friendship" will probably make your roommate defensive). Offering interpretations should not sound like accusations but as heartfelt attempts to understand the other person. Perception checking can be a valuable skill in maintaining healthy relationships with friends and romantic partners.

Understanding Stereotypes

When we make assumptions about others based on initial impressions, incomplete information, or oversimplified assumptions, we may resort to stereotyping. A **stereotype** is a *broad generalization about a group of people based on limited exposure to an individual or small number of members of that particular group.* When we categorize people based on demographic characteristics such as age, sex, race, political or religious affiliation, occupation, socioeconomic backgrounds, or sexual orientation, we tend to rely on stereotypes. For instance, believing that all African Americans are good at sports, employees on Wall Street do not care about those working on Main Street, fraternity brothers only care about partying, or all gay men are fashionable are all

stereotype
broad generalization about a group of people based on limited exposure to an individual or small number of members of that particular group.

examples of stereotypes. In contrast to generalizations, stereotypes are the result of a limited and often incorrect assessment of a group. Although stereotypes can help predict certain actions or behaviors (employees on Wall Street do not work on Main Street), they also can lead to prejudice and discrimination (not all Wall Street employees are heartless).

When a stereotype consists of a negative evaluation of others (women are not intelligent enough to run a company, for example), then conscious or unconscious forms of discrimination may occur (a woman may not be promoted to CEO). Therefore, it is important to remember that not all members of a group are alike. When we talk about a demographic trait or use language that indicates that an entire group "is" or "does" something—women *are*, lesbians *will*, Mormons *believe*, men *will not*, or politicians *do not*, for example—then we tend to assume that *all* members of the group are alike. Unfortunately, this viewpoint does not account for the differences and uniqueness of individuals. To avoid stereotyping, we need to realize that members of a similar group or demographic category are still unique individuals with different life experiences and worldviews.

Managing Impressions

Sociologist Erving Goffman explains that people are actors who create impressions of who they are by behaving differently in different types of situations. According to Goffman, individuals attempt to manage others' impressions by modifying their behaviors, appearance, and manners (Trevino, 2003). He calls this **identity management**, which is *the process of altering our own behaviors to shape others' impressions of who we are*. Goffman uses the term *face* to describe each individual's socially approved and presenting self. The process of **facework** consists of the *verbal and nonverbal strategies used to present different faces to others*. Think of facework as similar to putting on different faces for different social situations. You may have one face or identity for communicating with family members, another face for the workplace, a third for hanging out with friends, another as a student attending class, and a final face for your romantic relationship. Although each face shares common features with others, there is something unique about each identity given the social situation. Putting on faces is part of identity management. We may continue to wear the faces that are rewarded and discard the ones that solicit negative reactions from others.

The ways we manage our identity—*self-monitoring*—may be conscious or unconscious. **High self-monitors** are *individuals who are*

PRACTICING HUMAN COMMUNICATION
Experiencing Stereotyping

Think about a situation in which someone made a biased judgment about you or someone you know based on age, skin color, clothing, sex, sexuality, political affiliation, religious affiliation, ability or disability, socioeconomic status, or some other quality or attribute. Explain how you knew that stereotyping was occurring. What assumptions, words, or actions resulted from these stereotypes? How can communicating civilly help reduce stereotyping others?

identity management
process of altering our own behaviors in order to shape others' impressions of who we are.

facework
verbal and nonverbal strategies used to present different faces to others.

high self-monitors
individuals who are acutely aware of their self-expressions and identity management behavior.

When we label someone "two-faced," we are making a negative assessment of that person. However, most of us do quite a bit of impression management and facework every day. What is the difference between being two-faced and engaging in impression management?

acutely aware of their self-expressions and identity management behavior (Snyder, 1979). High self-monitors adjust and respond to the social cues in the surrounding environment. They work at "behaving appropriately" for every situation and are skilled at reading other people's nonverbal cues. You could say they wear many faces. Because of their desire to respond appropriately to each situation, high self-monitors may conceal their true internal feelings (such as feeling ill or having opinions that strongly differ from those being expressed) by continuing to present themselves in ways expected of them. High self-monitors may be referred to as "chameleons" because they "present the right image for the right audience."

Low self-monitors are more willing to respond the way they truly feel in most social situations. **Low self-monitors** *communicate without paying much attention to how others are responding to their messages.* Low self-monitors pay less attention to other peoples' nonverbal cues and instead show more consistency between their own feelings and behaviors. They are more forthcoming about their true thoughts, feelings, and desires regardless of the social context surrounding the situation. They wear only a few faces, and you usually know their true feelings and where they stand on issues, regardless of who they are with.

High and low self-monitoring are simply different approaches to the way we interact with others. From a self-monitoring perspective, high self-monitors can adjust their behaviors to meet the demands of different situations. They may ask, "Who does this situation want me to be, and how can I be that person?" (Snyder, 1979). Low self-monitors usually demonstrate behavior that is consistent with their inner feelings, attitudes, and beliefs (Mehra, Kilduff, & Brass, 2001). They may ask, "Who am I, and how can I be me in this situation?" (Snyder, 1979). Martin Kilduff, a professor of management at the University of Cambridge, explains that high self-monitors may be better at managing conflict or difficult workplace circumstances (Toegel, Anand, & Kilduff, 2007). Because high self-monitors pay more attention to nonverbal cues and are sensitive toward other peoples' needs, they are more likely to successfully mediate or manage difficult situations. Low self-monitors, however, may contribute positively to discussions of complex issues where a range of opinions are sought because they are more willing to directly express who they are and how they feel.

Civility, Social Justice, and Perception

The power of first impressions, stereotypes, limited exposure to diverse groups or individuals, and culture undoubtedly affect perception and civility. Consider the following examples.

Alexandra Wallace, a student at the University of California at Los Angeles (UCLA), received national attention and criticism after posting a three-minute video rant against Asians. Wallace complained about

low self-monitors
people who communicate without paying much attention to how others are responding to their messages.

Awareness Campaign Versus the Environment and Safety

ITAR-TASS Photo Agency/Alamy

In the summer of 2014, the ALS Ice Bucket Challenge became a social media phenomenon, sparking old and young around the world to participate in the activity of dumping ice water on their heads. Although this challenge had been used previously to raise awareness of other devastating diseases, it was not until Pete Frates and friend Pat Quinn, both diagnosed with amyotrophic lateral sclerosis (ALS), began posting about the challenge that the challenge went viral. Not surprisingly, the ice bucket challenge significantly increased public awareness of ALS or Lou Gehrig's disease, a progressive neurodegenerative disease that affects nerve cells in the brain and spinal cord (ALS Association, n.d.). The ALS Association reported surprise at the amount of attention the challenge brought to the disease. In just a few months, people posted more than 1.2 million Facebook videos showing themselves completing the challenge, and the ALS Association received $150 million dollars in donations.

Although the many positive effects this campaign brought to the ALS Association cannot be denied, there were critics. One of the most compelling criticisms is the amount of water consumed: more than 5 million gallons of water (Samenow, 2014). Many places in the United States face severe drought conditions, and many nations around the world struggle with access to clean water. Blogger Michael Rowley explains the concern:

We are blessed to live in the United States. We have resources at our fingertips that many people throughout the world can only dream of. We use them freely and often times without thought. I applaud the amount of support and resources that were shared with the Ice Bucket Challenge. It captured the imagination, the inner "daredevil" in us, and the philanthropic pulse in our hearts. . . . Day after day I watched links to videos and talked to participants. (Rowley, 2014)

Rowley says each time he watched a video link or talked to those who participated in the ice bucket challenge, he was reminded of nations around the world like Haiti that have no access to clean water. Men, women, and children must walk miles to access small amounts of water that must then be filtered before it can be consumed. Beyond the consumption of water, however, is the fact that some people have been seriously injured and even killed in their efforts to help with the challenge (Fox31 News, 2014).

The successes that come with campaigns such as the Ice Bucket Challenge are legitimate and powerful, yet should we also make an effort to balance the importance of raising awareness for a cause with a sensitivity to the lack of a resource such as clean water around the world? In addition, what are the risks we ask individuals to take as they attempt to support these campaigns—both to themselves and others?

What Do You Think?

1. What aspects of the Ice Bucket Challenge can be considered civil and ethical? What aspects of the campaign might be considered problematic? Explain why.

2. Social media are fundamental to the exposure the Ice Bucket Challenge received. Are there any ethical or civil implications to using social media to increase public awareness of causes? What might those implications be?

3. How might campaigns like the Ice Bucket Challenge play into a person's attempts at identity management, either positively or negatively?

Asian students sitting in the library talking on their cell phones to family members about the devastating tsunami that struck Japan. Sitting in front of her laptop camera, Wallace stated, "The problem is these hordes of Asian people that UCLA accepts into our school every single year, which is fine . . . but if you're going to come to UCLA, then use American manners" (Lovett, 2011). She then mimicked the people she spoke against. Wallace's video caused many debates about ethnocentrism, stereotyping, and racial discrimination. In fact, shortly after the video was viewed by more than 100,000 people, and after receiving death threats, Wallace withdrew from UCLA. Meanwhile, UCLA's chancellor posted a video response claiming Wallace's opinions were not the opinions of the UCLA community and called for more "civil discourse."

In Detroit, Michigan, a federal investigation followed allegations that Arab Americans and Muslims were inappropriately questioned about their religion, groped, and physically searched in "invasive and humiliating" ways at U.S. border crossings. Those who were searched described the events as "a form of sexual harassment." Chris Ortman, spokesperson for the Department of Homeland Security (DHS) said, "The DHS does not tolerate religious discrimination or abusive questioning—period" (Brand-Williams, 2011).

In France, a 2011 law banned women from wearing burqas in public and imposed fines if they do. Police are to escort women wearing burqas to "a police station" and ask them "to remove the veil there for identification." According to one British newspaper, *The Guardian*, Rachid Nekkaz, a property dealer in France who is Muslim, is asking women to continue to wear the veil, "if they so desire," and states that "the street is the universal home of freedom and nobody should challenge that so long as these [women] are not impinging on anyone else's freedom" ("France Begins Ban on Niquab and Burqa," 2011).

In each case, stereotypes, perceptions, and attitudes reduce civil discourse and potentially lead to acts of discrimination and violence. Recall from Chapter 1 that when we decide to communicate civilly, we *make a decision to be open to hearing different views and perspectives, even though we may not agree with them.* Choosing civil communication does not require that we silence our own views or that we agree with everything another person says or does. Instead, civil communication means that we consider the impact of our perceptions, actions, and words on other people as we interact with them or even speak about them. Civil perception means that we understand stereotypes, engage in perception checking, and become aware of our first impressions. It means that we understand that our assumptions about others are shaped by our culture, our own experiences, and the media. To ensure our perceptions do not cause harm to others, we can monitor our tendency to stereotype, recognize ethnocentric acts (or the belief that one cultural perspective, norms, and ways of organizing are superior to others), and engage in perception checking to help increase civil discourse and action.

Even though burqas are the cultural dress norm for women in several countries, they have been banned and critiqued, as well as defended, as acceptable dress. As a class, discuss what you think might be possible civil approaches to understanding the various perceptions of women wearing burqas.

Chapter Summary

How Is Perception Defined?

- Perceptions are determined by what we see, hear, smell, taste, and touch.
- The intensity, size, repetition, contrast, and personal motivations that are part of many communication interactions help shape our perception of those interactions.

A Combination of Elements Shapes Our Perceptions of Our Self

- Families, culture, and technology affect the way we see ourselves—that is, our self-concept.
- Labels, cultural norms, and social rules have a powerful influence on our self-concept.
- Our self-esteem is influenced by reflected appraisals, social comparisons, and popular media.

Our Perceptions of Others Are Formed Quickly

- Perception checking can help ensure that we have formed appropriate evaluations of others.

- Categorizing people based on demographic characteristics may result in stereotyping.
- The process of identity management, including facework and self-monitoring, can shape other's impressions of who we are.

Civil Perception Means That We Make a Decision to Be Open to Hearing Different Views and Perceptions, Even Though We May Not Agree with Them

- First impressions, stereotypes, and limited exposure to diverse groups and cultures can negatively affect our perceptions.
- Civil perception means that we understand stereotypes, engage in perception checking, and become aware of our first impressions.

Key Concepts

facework (45)

high self-monitors (45)

identity (32)

identity management (45)

labels (33)

looking-glass self (31)

low self-monitors (46)

perception (29)

perception checking (43)

primary dimensions (32)

reflected appraisal (37)

secondary dimensions (32)

selective attention (29)

self-concept (33)

self-esteem (37)

self-fulfilling prophecy (35)

social comparison (38)

standpoint (32)

stereotype (44)

symbolic interactionism (35)

Invitation to Human Communication Online

MindTap Speech includes an interactive MindTap Reader and interactive learning tools including National Geographic Explorer videos, student videos, quizzes, flashcards, and more. You can build your speech outline with Outline Builder and record, post, and watch videos with YouSeeU. Go to cengagebrain.com to access your MindTap for *Invitation to Human Communication* to access these resources.

MindTap®

Further Reflection and Discussion

1. Consider your cultural background. In what ways does that background influence your perception of others or your experiences? Does it encourage you to hold a particular view of time or to organize experiences in specific ways? Explain how.

2. Make a list of your various identities (male, Christian, employed, etc.). In what ways do these identities serve as the foundation of your standpoint? How does this standpoint influence your perceptions? Now imagine your identities were different (female, atheist, unemployed, etc.). How might your perceptions change?

3. The looking-glass self explains how other people's perceptions of who we are affect our own perceptions of our selves. Identify individuals in your life who have been in the role of looking glass. Do you agree with their perceptions of you? Why or why not?

4. Make a list of the specific ways your family, culture, technology, and media have shaped your perceptions of the world. Compare this list to the list of someone in the class. How are they similar and different?

5. What first impressions do you think you make? Make a list of how you think others perceive you when you first meet them. Introduce yourself to someone in your class you do not know well. Compare your lists with one another. Do they match? Are their stereotypes in either of your lists? Discuss your findings with one another and then as a class.

6. This chapter explained that enhancing and maintaining self-esteem is determined by the ability to be involved, move forward, make friends, exercise, and receive family support. Discuss, as a class, how being a college student encourages or discourages you from engaging in these important activities.

7. Who do you know personally who has high self-esteem? People with high self-esteem tend to be extraverted, conscientious, emotionally stable, better at dealing with conflict, and open to new experiences. Which of these attributes do you possess? Which ones do you want to develop?

8. Think about ways in which you may alter your behavior to management your identity. You may have one face or identity for communicating with family members, another for the workplace or for hanging out with friends, and one for romantic relationships. What is unique about each identity in yourself? What are you "managing" by changing your face for each type of communication?

9. Consider the information in this chapter about the French controversy over allowing women to wear burqas on the street. Is this civil and just? What is the reason France initiated this policy? Do you agree that "the street is the universal home of freedom"? If you agree, are there any exceptions? If you disagree, explain your viewpoint. How does perception play a role in this controversy? Are fines or lessons in French citizenship a civil and just response to women wearing burqas? Explain the points of view of both the French government and those who oppose this idea.

10. Consider the many campaigns that exist to raise awareness about issues or diseases. Which of these do you find interesting, informative, or even problematic? Make a list of these campaigns and consider using one of them as a topic for a speech you might give in this class.

Activities and Web Links

Visit cengagebrain.com to access the MindTap for *Invitation to Human Communication* where these activities and web links can be found.

1. Read this brief *New York Times* article: "Anywhere an Eye Can See, It's Likely to See an Ad." Go to *Weblink 2.1*. Look at the photographs at the beginning of the article. Would you be influenced to buy the eggs with advertisements printed on them? Do you see yourself reflected in any advertisements? If not, what advertisements would you like to see that reflect your identity and values? How might these advertisements influence people's perceptions about the company that supplies the eggs or the doctor's office with the advertisement?

2. Read this article online: "For College Students, Praise May Trump Sex and Money." What do you think about the five-year-old wearing the "I'm a winner!" sticker? Was it an effective way for the teacher to raise her students' self-esteem? What other methods may help to boost their self-esteem? What activities have boosted your self-esteem? Go to *Weblink 2.2*.

3. Practicing public speaking through role playing. Review the concept of facework, then select three people you interact with on a semiregular basis. For example, choose a friend, a teacher, a neighbor, or a family member. Now consider how you would describe what you last weekend to each person. Next, role play with the class. Present the story of your weekend as if you were telling your friend, then as if you were telling your grandmother or telling your teacher. Do you share different details with each one? Do you use different expressions and nonverbal communication behaviors? As a class, discuss the different types of facework used for different audiences.

3

IN THIS CHAPTER YOU WILL LEARN TO:

- Discuss how culture and gender shape nonverbal communication codes.

- Explain how nonverbal communication can reveal our liking and disliking of others, our positions of status and power in society, and our responsiveness toward others.

- Identify the six ways that nonverbal communication works in conjunction with verbal communication.

- Describe the different types of visual codes for nonverbal communication.

- Explain how auditory codes of nonverbal communication reveal information about the speaker.

- Summarize the five types of nonverbal communication that we cannot see.

Nonverbal Communication

Jasper Cole/Blend {RM}/Corbis

We use nonverbal communication to convey meaning without words. What are some of the nonverbal communication codes displayed in this photograph?

Children learn the basics of nonverbal communication at a young age (Boone & Sunningham, 1998). They learn to interpret the meaning of certain facial expressions such as smiling or frowning. They understand when their parent's vocal cues indicate they are excited, happy, or angry. Children also learn to follow hand signals that indicate which direction to move (a father points to a ball that has rolled behind a chair). But this nonverbal communication does not stop there: all of us continue to use and interpret it throughout our lives. In fact, nonverbal communication tells us a lot about the meaning of a message. In this chapter, we examine the characteristics of nonverbal communication and how gender, culture, verbal communication, and other factors affect it. Then we look at how to become more aware of nonverbal communication in order to become a more effective communicator.

Characteristics of Nonverbal Communication

We use nonverbal forms of communication every day. For example, when you raise your hand in class, your teacher recognizes that you want to ask a question. **Nonverbal communication** is *the process of conveying meaning without speaking*. Nonverbal communication not only consists of wordless vocalizations such as "Shhh" and "Uh-huh" but also gestures, facial expressions, body movements, and even the items around us convey meaning. We rely on nonverbal communication to help us understand the meaning of a message. In fact, studies indicate that between 65 percent and 93 percent of the total meaning of a message is determined by nonverbal signals (Birdwhistell, 1970; Hickson, Stacks, & Moore, 2004; Mehrabian, 1981).

This chapter explores the complex components of nonverbal communication. You will learn that your ability to understand nonverbal codes may be determined by your culture, gender, and even age. We examine how relationships affect our nonverbal communication and the different forms, or codes, we use to communicate nonverbally. We also will explore the relationship between nonverbal and verbal communication. In the following sections, we examine each of these characteristics of nonverbal communication, as well as the influence of technology on our nonverbal messages.

Nonverbal Communication Is Influenced by Culture

Have you ever felt uncomfortable when someone stood too close to you and occupied your personal space? Have you ever traveled and found it challenging to communicate with someone from a different culture because you were unfamiliar with their nonverbal customs? The

nonverbal communication
the process of conveying meaning without using the spoken word.

Leaders, Greetings, and Cultural Differences

President Barack Obama's nonverbal greeting practices with several foreign leaders set off several controversies. Photographers captured Obama bowing to foreign leaders, including Emperor Akihito of Japan, King Abdullah of Saudi Arabia, Queen Elizabeth of England, Ukrainian president Viktor Yushchenko, and Chinese president Hu Jintao. Bowing is an expression of respect in many Asian and Middle Eastern cultures. Hence, some national and international viewers interpreted Obama's gesture as a sign of civility and respect for other cultures and customs. Supporters viewed the president's bows as acknowledging the worth of other world leaders and communicating respect for their traditional forms of greeting. Critics, however, were outraged at the sight of then President Obama bowing to other leaders and believed that he displayed weakness and submission to other cultures. In short, they argued that his bowing was an act of incivility to the American people—communicating that the United States was inferior to other countries.

Charles Dharapak/AP/Corbis

What Do You Think?

1. What are the customary protocols and practices for greeting one another in the United States? In what ways do these practices and protocols differ by age, gender, economic status, and professional position?
2. People in many Asian and Middle Eastern cultures bow their heads when greeting. Do you believe the president of the United States should follow traditional greeting practices of the country in which he is visiting, or should he always greet dignitaries and world leaders using the U.S. custom of a firm handshake?
3. In addition to bowing or shaking hands, what other ways do different cultures greet one another?

meaning associated with different forms of nonverbal communication varies from culture to culture. For example, although many North Americans view "time as money" and expect things to start and finish "on time," other cultures have a more relaxed attitude about and a different sense of time. This can lead to a communication gap that is based in a nonverbal understanding of what it means to be "on time." If a North American plans to meet a friend for lunch at noon, it is common for him or her to become fidgety if the friend has not arrived by 12:10 or 12:20. Other cultures hold different perspectives on time. Many Latin American and Middle Eastern cultures value their relationships and interactions with others more than they value the amount of time they have to spend with others. Because of this, they will not abruptly end a conversation to rush to their next appointment; instead, they would remain and talk even though they might be late to that appointment (Ting-Toomey, 1997).

The use and meaning of personal space and displays of emotions also vary among cultures. Many Americans converse with acquaintances or strangers while standing 4 to 12 feet away from that person.

Germans also tend to create more distance between themselves and others (Hall & Hall, 1990). People from the Middle East tend to stand much closer (Hall, 1969) as do people from South American countries (Lewis, 1999). Generally, people residing in individualistic cultures tend to require more space than those residing in collectivist cultures. Andersen (2003) suggests this may be because those living in collectivist cultures tend to "work, play, live and sleep in close proximity to one another" (p. 239).

Although many emotions—happiness, anger, disgust, fear, surprise, and sadness—are considered "universal" (Ekman, Sorenson, & Friesen, 1969), there are differences in the rules for when it is appropriate to display these emotions. For example, open expressions of anger, disgust, and contempt are considered inappropriate in collectivistic cultures such as Japan because they are seen as threats to interpersonal harmony (Matsumoto, 1989; Safdar et al., 2009; Smith & Bond, 1994).

Cultural differences in nonverbal communication may be subtle or quite significant. You probably interact with people from a variety of cultural backgrounds already and will continue to do so as you enter new work environments and social situations. You will read more about similarities and differences between cultures and nonverbal communication throughout this chapter.

Nonverbal Communication Is Influenced by Gender

Men and women perform and interpret nonverbal communication in different ways. For example, women tend to be more responsive communicators than men. They tend to smile and gesture more often, maintain more eye contact, sit and stand closer to others, and include more emotion in their facial expressions than do men. For their part, men tend to take up more space with their bodies, lean forward in conversations, speak louder, and hold onto the "talk stage" longer than women do (Burgoon, Guerrero, & Floyd, 2010; Wood, 2013). The reasons for these differences are complex, and most scholars believe they come from our different gender socializations that occur when people are still children.

enciktat/Shutterstock.com

What types of nonverbal communication do you see being expressed as these women share a meal together? Are these nonverbal communication styles similar to your own or different? How so?

Multiple tests studying the ability to interpret nonverbal communication confirm that females typically score higher than males in decoding nonverbal cues (Hall, 1984; McClure, 2000). Beginning in grade school, girls begin decoding nonverbal cues at a higher success rate (an average of 2 percent better) than their male counterparts and continue doing so through adulthood. Because these differences are important to communication, the influence of gender on nonverbal communication is discussed throughout this chapter.

Nonverbal Communication Is Relational

Nonverbal communication also conveys our view of ourselves and how we feel about others. We create a particular image about who we are based on our personal appearance, facial expressions, body language, and use of time and space. We can also show how we feel about others based on the way we greet another person, how closely we stand or sit by another person, and what forms of touch we use, if any. Communication scholars who study nonverbal communication claim there are three dimensions of relationships that are expressed through our use of nonverbal messages: our liking and disliking of others, our positions of status and power in society, and our responsiveness toward others (Keeley & Hart, 1994; Mehrabian, 1971).

Nonverbal behaviors can communicate whether we feel good or bad about another person. **Liking** can be determined by *our body orientation, facial expression, use of touch,* and *proximity.* Standing or sitting face to face, leaning toward another person, being in close physical proximity, smiling, and making direct eye contact are all expressions of liking. Nonverbal behaviors that indicate liking also vary between genders and cultures.

Nonverbal messages are ambiguous. Consider the many possible messages these children are communicating. Are there additional nonverbal cues they could use to clarify their intent?

iStockphoto.com/RichLegg

An individual's status and power in society can also be determined through the use of nonverbal behaviors. Those in high-status positions tend to consume more space (have larger offices and houses), move into others' spaces more often, and use gestures and touch to exert control (Leathers, 1986). University presidents, company CEOs, and school principals tend to have the largest offices on campus and are more likely to enter the offices or spaces of teachers or subordinates than vice versa.

Finally, we communicate our interest or **responsiveness** to other people through nonverbal behaviors. *Displaying positive facial expressions, posture, and gestures* can indicate high levels of responsiveness. Remember that different cultures may express responsiveness in different ways. People in Western cultures tend to use eye contact to show interest, and they may look away, turn their body away, or physically move away to display disinterest. In other cultures such as Japan and some Native American cultures, direct eye contact is a sign of disrespect or even rudeness and can be seen as an invasion of another person's personal space.

Nonverbal Communication Is Ambiguous

Even though different cultures assign different meanings to nonverbal communication, different meanings also may be associated with the same

liking
using our body orientation, facial expression, use of touch, or proximity to communicate our feelings about another person.

responsiveness
displaying positive facial expressions, posture, and gestures.

MARK THIESSEN/National Geographic

Mireya Mayor
Emerging Explorer, Primatologist, and Conservationist

In your work as an explorer, are there times when you are conscious of these various types of nonverbal communication? Do you adjust your nonverbal style in different situations and contexts? Can you give an example of how?

I've led many, many expeditions, and most of the teams are primarily, if not all, male. And so because I'm a woman, I have to communicate in a more authoritative manner at times. But also when I'm dealing with people in the local community or village, and even sometimes in particular the women, I have to change my nonverbal style in order to not seem intimidating. In some of the places that I have worked, for example, it is not appropriate for women's legs to be exposed. So if I'm in a place where one mode of dressing is inappropriate, then clearly I'm not going to choose that type because it is almost like you're immediately setting up a barricade for effective communication.

When I was in Mexico for a town meeting in a rural area, the women were not allowed inside the hall for the meeting. And the entire meeting was actually about me. There were all these discussions about whether or not I would be allowed inside, and I found myself being very conscious of the way that I was dressed and the way that I carried myself. Because in that situation the more gender neutral I appeared, the more comfortable the men were in allowing me in.

display of nonverbal communication within a particular culture. This can make decoding nonverbal behavior challenging. For example, smiling and crying can have multiple meanings. You may smile to indicate happiness, to greet customers in your workplace, or because you want to conceal a more private emotion. You may cry as a way to express an intense feeling of joy or to show pain, sadness, guilt, or even frustration. Paying attention to the context surrounding the nonverbal behavior can provide the information we need to help us interpret nonverbal messages.

In addition, our moods and age also influence our ability to understand nonverbal behavior. We often interpret how others are feeling based on our own mood. When we feel happy, we tend to see that same emotion in others' facial expressions; this is true of sadness as well. When we feel frustrated, angry, or sad, we tend to see others displaying that same emotion (Niedenthal, Halberstadt, Margolin, & Innes-Ker, 2000). Our age also affects our success in decoding nonverbal cues. Our ability to decode nonverbal behavior improves as we grow older from age five and into our twenties and thirties (Harrigan, 1984; Markhan & Adams, 1992; Nowicki & Duke, 1994). As we continue to age, however, our ability to decode nonverbal communication may decline. Studies comparing the ability to decode nonverbal communication with age reported that older adults judge facial expressions and body cues less accurately and are also less able to identify levels of emotional intensity (Lieberman, Rigo, & Campain, 1988; Montepare, Koff, Zaitchik, & Albert, 1999; Thompson, Aidinejad, & Ponte, 2001).

In summary, nonverbal communication is ambiguous, and many factors affect our ability to understand the meaning behind nonverbal behaviors. Our culture, gender, relationships, and age all influence how we interpret nonverbal messages. Although understanding nonverbal communication can be challenging, it is not impossible to interpret this form of communication accurately. Learning about cultural and gender differences, along with the different forms of nonverbal communication, can improve your ability to better understand the meaning behind many messages.

Nonverbal Communication Is Related to Verbal Communication

Nonverbal and verbal forms of communication usually work together to send a message. There are six ways that nonverbal communication works in conjunction with verbal communication to create a message: repetition, emphasis, complementation, contradiction, substitution, and regulation. As such, nonverbal communication can serve varied and important functions (Afifi, 2007; Burgoon & Bacue, 2003).

Repetition consists of *using the nonverbal signals that reproduce what is said verbally*. For example, when you turn your head from side to side while saying "No," you are using repetition. **Emblems** are *gestures that can be translated into words*, and they help to repeat spoken language. When you move your index finger side to side as you tell your friend "No," you repeat the "No" that is stated orally with an emblem.

Emphasis consists of *using nonverbal cues that strengthen what is stated verbally*. A person who yells, "I'm so angry," while waving a fist in the air or hitting it against a table has emphasized his or her verbal statement.

Complementation occurs when *the nonverbal signal elaborates or expands the meaning of the verbal message*. An **illustrator** is a *nonverbal behavior that reinforces spoken words*. A child who says, "I'm tired," as his eyes begin to close displays complementary forms of communication.

Contradiction exists *when verbal and nonverbal forms of communication conflict with one another*. A person who says, "Everything is okay," while her face shows frustration or anger is revealing contradictory nonverbal cues and verbal messages. When contradiction exists, we typically believe the nonverbal cues more than the verbal message.

Substitution occurs *when we rely on nonverbal codes instead of verbal ones*. You are using substitution when you give a high five instead of saying, "Great job!" or shrug your shoulders without speaking to indicate that you are unsure of something.

Regulation is *the process of controlling conversations and interactions with others*. Looking at a clock or watch or grabbing your backpack are

---

repetition
using the nonverbal signals that reproduce what is said verbally.

emblems
gestures that can be translated into words.

emphasis
using nonverbal cues that strengthen what is stated verbally.

complementation
when the nonverbal signal elaborates or expands the meaning of the verbal message.

illustrator
nonverbal behavior that reinforces spoken words.

contradiction
when verbal and nonverbal forms of communication conflict with one another.

substitution
when we rely on nonverbal codes instead of verbal ones.

regulation
the process of controlling conversations and interactions with others.

Courtesy of Cindy Griffin

A coach is displaying emphasis by embracing his player while congratulating him verbally. What other types of behaviors can demonstrate the nonverbal form of emphasis?

examples of regulators that are used to control interaction with another and close a conversation. Making eye contact with another member of a group who has not contributed to its discussion may encourage that person to join the conversation.

Although these six components help explain how nonverbal and verbal communication relate to one another, the two modes of communication also have differences. As you have learned, nonverbal communication tends to be more ambiguous and have more options for communicating (e.g., posture, gestures, facial expressions, vocal cues) than verbal communication does. Nonverbal communication is also frequently unintentional, whereas verbal communication is usually deliberate. A yawning person probably is not intentionally revealing fatigue or boredom, but these are the typical meanings we associate with this nonverbal behavior.

Thus far, you have read how culture, gender, and relationships affect your ability to interpret nonverbal messages and that nonverbal cues are often ambiguous. You have also learned about the similarities and differences between verbal and nonverbal forms of communication. Now we will look at the different types, or codes, of nonverbal communication.

Types of Nonverbal Communication

Nonverbal codes of communication convey meaning through three interlocking systems: the visual, auditory, and invisible communication systems (Leathers, 1997). Communication scholar Dale Leathers offers the following scheme to explain these interlocking systems. The **visual communication system** includes *the codes of kinesics, proxemics, and artifacts*. The **auditory communication system** consists of *paralanguage*. The **invisible communication system** consists of *chronemics, olfactics, and haptics*. Although these codes intertwine and function together to create meaning, we discuss them here individually.

Visual Codes of Nonverbal Communication

Visual codes of nonverbal communication include the types of nonverbal communication that we can see: body movements (kinesics), the use of space (proxemics), and personal objects such as clothing or jewelry (artifacts).

Kinesics *The study of body movements such as gestures, posture, eye contact, and facial expressions* is called **kinesics**. Our body movements can communicate a great deal. In your classrooms, for example, notice students who sit upright and look directly at the professor. Others may be leaning back in their chairs and looking at their cell phones. Some might be frowning as they take notes. Do you have different interpretations of these variations in posture, eye contact, and facial expressions? Do you believe one student is more engaged in the lecture than another? We cannot always make accurate interpretations based on body movements alone, of course. Some students may look away from the professor while

Simone van den Berg/Shutterstock.com

Our bodies often send powerful messages to others about how we are feeling. Consider your own body and your kinesic expressions. What messages are you communicating to others at this moment?

visual communication system
includes the codes of kinesics, proxemics, and artifacts.

auditory communication system
paralanguage

invisible communication system
chronemics, olfactics, and haptics

kinesics
the study of bodily movements such as gestures, posture, eye contact, and facial expressions.

thinking about the course material, and others may learn better when seated in a more comfortable, relaxed position. The better you know a person, the better you can interpret her or his nonverbal communication.

Body movements such as posture, gestures, and eye contact can also indicate when we are willing to interact with others. When we make direct eye contact and offer a smile, we tend to signal that we are open to interacting with another. If our arms are crossed in front of our body and we have a stern expression on our face, we may be signaling disinterest or contempt. Kinesics also involve **affect displays**, or *nonverbal movements that indicate how we feel*. Facial expressions reveal how someone is feeling, and body orientation indicates the intensity of those feelings (Ekman & Friesen, 1967). For example, facial expressions can indicate disappointment, confusion, hope, or happiness. Consider the actions of sports fans: jumping in the air while smiling and clapping sends a very different message than jumping up with a scowl and pointing fingers at the referee.

Finally, kinesics involves **adaptors**, which are *gestures we use to manage our emotions*. For example, when we feel nervous, we may use adaptors to control our nervousness. We may tap our feet, twirl our hair, bite our nails, or even hold on tightly to a security object (Ekman & Friesen, 1969). As our anxiety increases, we tend to use adaptors more frequently (Burgoon et al., 2010).

Gestures and body movements (whether intentional or unintentional) communicate our thoughts and feelings. In addition, we have to consider cultural meanings of different gestures because of the many variations there are across cultures (Axtell, 2007). The thumbs-up gesture is often associated with something positive in the United States, but it is considered an obscene gesture in the Middle East and Australia. In the United States, the two-finger V sign can mean victory or peace, but it is considered a sexual insult in Great Britain if the palm faces the sender while the fingers form a V. Although it is usually interpreted as positive in the United States, waving your hand is perceived as an insult in Nigeria and Greece.

Gender also influences how frequently particular body movements are displayed. For example, you have read that women tend to smile more, but they also tilt their head when speaking or listening, and they take up less space than men do (e.g., they cross their legs when sitting, and they keep their arms close to their bodies). In addition, socioeconomic status, race, and ethnicity also influence how particular facial expressions are displayed. In the United States, Caucasian women, especially from middle-class families, tend to smile more than African American women (Eakins & Eakins, 1988; Halberstadt & Saitta, 1987). Japanese women typically avoid smiling in formal settings because it often indicates a lack of seriousness (Dresser, 1996). Being aware of these differences can help you communicate more effectively with people from different cultures and walks of life.

oliveromg/Shutterstock.com

People often use adaptors to control their feelings, especially when they do not want others to know they are hurt or upset. When you are hurt or upset, what sort of adaptors do you use to manage your emotions?

affect displays

nonverbal movements that indicate how we feel.

adaptors

gestures we use to manage our emotions.

Proxemics Proxemics refers to *the use of space*: how much of it we take up, how it is arranged, and whose space it is. The way we use space may tell us something about the relationship we have with other people. According to Edward T. Hall (1959), U.S. Americans use four distinct spatial spheres to communicate their relationships to others. Each sphere indicates the distance deemed most appropriate for various types of relationships:

- *Intimate distance* (0 to 18 inches) is usually reserved for close friends or romantic partners. This distance is often used for displaying physical and psychological intimacy.

- *Personal distance* (18 inches to 4 feet) is the space we use when conversing with friends and acquaintances. The range of personal distance can vary, depending on the relationship. Close friends are often allowed closer distances than new acquaintances. You may feel uncomfortable when someone you have just met violates your personal distance and stands too close to you.

- *Social distance* (4 to 12 feet) is the appropriate distance for many U.S. American business interactions. Impersonal or informal business practices, such as buying something (e.g., a car or an article of clothing), usually occur between 4 feet and 7 feet. Formal business situations, such as job interviews or performance evaluations, can take place with as much as 12 feet between two individuals.

- *Public distance* (12 to 25 feet) is appropriate for public ceremonies, lectures, concerts, and political rallies. When a large audience is present, a speaker often uses public distance (and appears on a stage or platform) in order to be seen by all audience members (Hall, 1959).

The use of space also indicates power and status. For example, those who have power and status in society tend to enter the spaces of those with less power but not vice versa. Because more men still have more power in U.S. culture, this typically means that men enter the space of women more

Yuri Arcurs/Shutterstock.com

These businesspeople are using social space to communicate their relationship to one another. Take a moment to look around you. What does your use of space communicate about your relationship to those near you?

proxemics
the use of space.

frequently. In addition, those with power and status also occupy larger spaces. Individuals who earn high salaries tend to live in larger houses, drive larger vehicles, and vacation at greater distances than those who earn lower salaries.

Finally, gender may influence who occupies particular spaces or rooms within the home. Did your father or stepfather occupy the same chair every night at the dinner table? Did your mother, sister, or grandmother use more closet and bathroom space? Did your mother refer to the kitchen as "my kitchen" or your father claim the basement or garage to be "his space"? Particular rooms such as kitchens, bathrooms, and closets are occupied most often by mothers and daughters. Garages, recliners, and even the backyard barbeque often are considered men's spaces.

Artifacts **Artifacts** are the *personal objects we use to communicate something about ourselves.* Clothing, jewelry, toys, and other personal accessories all reveal information about our identities and interests. Clothing in particular is considered an important factor in making a first impression. The way a person dresses communicates information about gender, age, socioeconomic status, mood, group affiliation, interests, and values. Positive first impressions are most often created when the person being judged is wearing similar clothing to the person making the observation (Reid, Lancuba, & Murrow, 1997). In addition, an occupation can be revealed by certain styles of dress. For example, police officers, firefighters, and military personnel have distinctive uniforms. Similarly, an artifact such as a backpack may communicate that a person is a student rather than a business executive.

Consider what types of clothing you wear. What do they say about you? Do you own T-shirts with messages that express your attitudes, beliefs, political affiliation, or hobbies? Many artifacts reveal our likes and dislikes. Sports memorabilia signify our favorite sports teams. T-shirts, buttons, and bumper stickers disclose our political, religious, and cultural beliefs. In fact, because clothing and artifacts can reveal differences in socioeconomic status, group affiliation, and belief systems, many schools now enforce strict dress codes and school uniform policies.

People often choose clothing, hairstyles, and other accessories to communicate their identities or personal styles. Examine your own dress. What are you trying to communicate about yourself by the way you are dressed today?

Ksenia Perminova/Shutterstock.com

Many people in the United States put enormous value on personal appearance and invest considerable time and money striving to achieve cultural standards of beauty. **Personal appearance** consists of *specific aspects of appearance, including facial features, skin color, hair color, length, and style, and body type.* Women and men invest in coloring their hair, tanning, dieting, exercising, and even plastic surgery to meet ideal cultural standards for beauty and attractiveness. Studies support the belief that changes in hair color, makeup, weight, and dress improve ratings for female's attractiveness and desired personality (Graham & Jauhar, 1982; Hammermesh & Biddle, 1994; Loureiro, Sachsida, & Cardoso de Medonça, 2011). Personal appearance and beauty standards, however, are not universal. Although the cultural ideal for American women is thinness,

artifacts
the personal objects we use to communicate something about ourselves.

personal appearance
specific aspects of our appearance including facial features; skin color; hair color, length, and style; and body type.

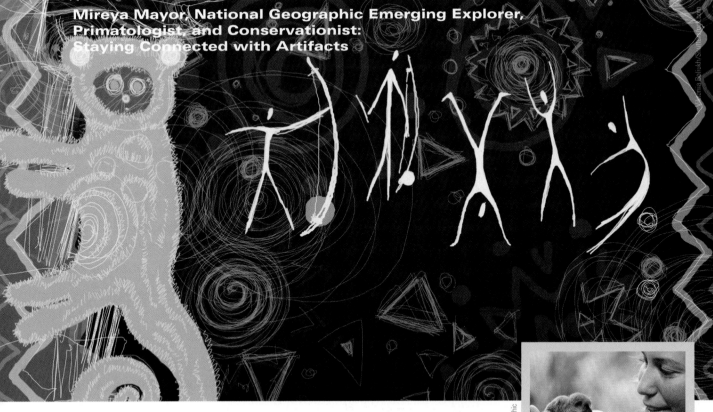

Mireya Mayor, National Geographic Emerging Explorer, Primatologist, and Conservationist: Staying Connected with Artifacts

Mireya Mayor is a primatologist and National Geographic correspondent. One of Mayor's most notable accomplishments occurred in a remote part of Madagascar, where more than sixty species of lemurs live, but where at least fifteen lemur species have become extinct. In 2000, Mayor and her team discovered a new lemur species—microcebus, or mouse lemur. Fitting in the palm of her hand, this tiny and rare creature inspired Mayor to take her findings directly to the prime minister of Madagascar. Mayor was able to convince the prime minister to declare the region a national park in order to protect and conserve the remaining 10 percent of the island's original vast forests and ultimately protect the lemurs. Today, Mayor continues to travel to Madagascar and other regions around the world to study endangered species and to help preserve the forests (Mayor, 2011).

After her first two daughters were born, Mayor was invited by TV producer Mark Burnett to join the cast of *Expedition Africa*. She initially struggled with the decision of staying at home or venturing back out into the field. With the help of her mother, Mayor realized that being an explorer is not what she does—it is who she is—so she agreed to go on the expedition to Africa. While Mayor was away, her husband, Roland Wolff, and her mother cared for her children.

For Mayor, the toughest part of being in the field is not the mosquitoes or snakes or living in wet clothes or even the starving. The toughest part is being away from her family. Mayor's traveling is tough on her children, too. She tries to help them cope by making a countdown calendar with photos of her in the jungle, and she leaves behind scrapbooks of photos for her children to look at while she is away. Sometimes, Mayor says, she is lucky enough to have a satellite phone connection so she can talk to them from the jungle. Still, being away for weeks with little opportunity to communicate is challenging. Mayor's husband still leaves little notes in Mayor's backpack for her to find throughout her journey. In the end, Mayor knows that her work is important. Not only is she helping to save endangered plants and forests, but also "I want my children to know that as women, they can do whatever they dream as long as they believe in themselves. More than anything it is my responsibility to instill in my daughters the knowledge that they can have a family and everything else too" (Mayor, 2011, p. 297–298).

WHAT DO YOU THINK?

1. Consider several of the possible professions you plan to enter. How might the information in this chapter on nonverbal communication help you communicate?

2. As you consider relocating for school or a job, how might you use technology to stay in touch with other people?

3. What cultural and co-cultural differences have you encountered in your education, work, or community? How have you used nonverbal communication to communicate more clearly across those differences?

63

What Are Appropriate Artifacts, Ambiguities, and Arguments?

Dearborn High School in Detroit, Michigan, received national attention when nine students of Arabic descent arrived at school wearing sweatshirts that referenced the September 11, 2001, attacks on the World Trade Center in New York City. The group of students from the class of 2011 wore sweatshirts with the number "11" representing the twin towers, the school's thunderbird mascot flying directly toward the numerals, and the slogan "You Can't Bring Us Down" at the bottom. Many teachers, staff members, and other students believed the image on the sweatshirt represented animosity toward Americans. Yet the nine students involved in the incident told school officials that they were simply showing pride for their class of 2011. Hiab Mussad, one of the students wearing the sweatshirt, stated that the public was overreacting. He claimed, "We just wanted to show our support (to our class)." Clearly, the image was ambiguous because multiple meanings were derived from the sweatshirt design. Although several angry parents called on school officials to suspend the group, school administrators eventually determined that the incident was a matter of "kids not thinking, not realizing the consequences of something they thought was pretty innocent." No disciplinary action was taken against the students (Lawrence, 2010).

The T-shirt worn by these students raises questions about the ambiguity of messages on articles of clothing.

What Do You Think?

1. Do you believe these students had the right to wear sweatshirts with a message pertaining to September 11? Why or why not?

2. Are there messages (or symbols) on clothing that should be banned from public schools or the workplace? Why do you think so?

3. Should individuals have the right to express their beliefs, group affiliations, or political and cultural views via artifacts in any setting they wish? Why or why not?

---

traditional African cultures equate full-figured bodies as being healthy, prosperous, and wealthy (Villaros, 1994).

The codes of kinesics, proxemics, and artifacts are visible forms of nonverbal communication that can convey information about one's thoughts, feelings, and identities. In addition to visual forms of nonverbal communication, we learn information about people through auditory codes.

Auditory Codes of Nonverbal Communication

Are you able to answer the phone and identify callers just by the way they say "Hello" and before they even identify themselves (without checking caller ID first)? Can you hear several of your roommates or family members talking in the hallway and identify who is speaking at any particular moment? If you answered "Yes" to either question, you probably relied on paralinguistic cues. **Paralinguistics** refers to *the vocal aspects of nonverbal communication such as rate, volume, pitch, and emphasis.* Paralinguistics consists of language that is oral but not verbal. We often identify the person on the phone or in the hallway because of the way they sound, not necessarily by the words they say. One study indicated that the utterance of a single sentence was enough for co-workers to identify between eight and ten of their colleagues with more than 97 percent accuracy (Van Lancker, Kreiman, & Emmorey, 1985). Accuracy rates, however, drop significantly when someone has not heard a particular voice for several months.

paralinguistics
the vocal aspects of nonverbal communication, such as rate, volume, pitch, and emphasis.

Vocal cues are *aspects of the human voice that create rhythm or musical flow*. Vocal cues consist of the following:

rate—the speed at which we speak;

volume—the loudness of a speaker's voice;

pitch—the highness or lowness of a speaker's voice;

inflection—the manipulation of pitch to create certain meanings or moods;

pauses—hesitations and brief silences in speech conversation;

pronunciation—saying a word correctly according to accepted standards of a language;

articulation—the physical process of producing specific speech sounds in order to make language intelligible; and

dialect—the pattern of speech shared among ethnic groups or people from specific geographical locations.

These qualities help us recognize particular voices. For example, consider the different vocal qualities of politicians. George W. Bush, Barack Obama, Hilary Clinton, and Sarah Palin have distinct vocal cues, and we can identify which one is speaking almost immediately. In addition to the vocal cues listed, some speakers use **vocalized pauses** or include *filler words or sounds such as "er," "um," and "uh"* in their speech. And some may speak in a **monotone** voice, which means they *lack variation in their rate, pitch, and volume* as they speak.

Vocal cues can also convey different feelings or emotions. Multiple studies indicate that most of us are highly accurate in determining another person's emotions simply by listening to his or her vocal expression (Chartrand & Bargh, 1999; Davitz, 1964; Pittman & Scherer, 1993). In addition, vocal cues often reveal information about a speaker such as age, gender, and even height. High-pitched voices are often linked to someone who is younger, female, and shorter (Kramer, 1963). Women's voices tend to be more variable and expressive than men's. Advanced age also changes some speech patterns. Seniors tend to slow down their speech rate and incorporate more vocalized pauses (Hummert, Mazloff, & Henry, 1999).

Silence **Silence**, or *the lack of vocal sound*, is another powerful form of nonverbal communication. Silence is a lengthened pause and can convey a variety of meanings. To determine the meaning of silence, look carefully at the communicator, the environment, the timing of the silence, the cultural norms, and other verbal and nonverbal messages surrounding the silence. For example, silence can indicate respect for an environment such as a church, library, hospital, or funeral. When a speaker includes silence in a speech, it may mean she wants to draw attention to the ideas previously conveyed, is thinking about what to discuss next, or has simply forgotten what she wanted to say. When a listener remains silent, it may indicate he is showing respect, empathy, agreement, or even disagreement with the speaker. Therefore, you must examine the context surrounding the silence to best interpret its meaning.

vocal cues
aspects of the human voice that create rhythm or musical flow.

vocalized pauses
the use of filler words or sounds such as *"er," "um,"* and *"uh."*

monotone
lack of variation in a speaker's rate, pitch, and volume.

silence
the lack of vocal sound.

Nonverbal Cues

Effective nonverbal communication can play an important role in job placement and career advancement. According to Darlene Price, a communication consultant for executives and business professionals, "[a]mong the top traits employers look for when hiring or promoting a candidate for management are confidence, professionalism, and enthusiasm. Expressing these and other leadership traits requires sending the right nonverbal cues." According to *Forbes* magazine, eight nonverbal communication behaviors can help communicate confidence and leadership effectiveness (Smith, 2013).

1. **Eye contact.** Eye contact is your primary tool for establishing nonverbal connections with others. To communicate confidence, look directly at someone for several seconds before looking away.
2. **A confident handshake.** In business, the handshake is often the only appropriate expression of touch, so having a good one is critical. Price states, "A good handshake consists of a full and firm handclasp with palms embraced web to web. Shake up and down once or twice, coupled with a sincere smile and eye contact. Avoid the extremes of either a weak limp handshake or an aggressive bone-crushing one. . . . Treat men and women with equal respect when shaking hands. Gender makes no difference, and either may initiate the handshake."
3. **Effective gestures.** A gesture is any physical movement that helps express an idea, opinion or emotion. "Strive to punctuate your words with movement that is natural, lively, purposeful and spontaneous," Price says. "Avoid common distracting mannerisms such as finger-pointing, fidgeting, scratching, tapping, playing with hair, wringing hands, and twisting a ring."
4. **Dressing the part.** For both men and women, clothing speaks volumes in the workplace, Price says. "Make sure 'business casual' is not 'business careless.' Choose high quality, well-tailored garments that convey professionalism. Avoid showy accessories, busy patterns, tight garments and revealing necklines."
5. **Authoritative posture and presence.** Whether standing or sitting, imagine a string gently pulling your head and spine toward the ceiling. Price explains: "When you stand up tall and straight, you send a message of self-assurance, authority and energy."
6. **Appropriate facial expressions.** Pay attention to what your face is communicating. Price shares, "Because your facial expressions are closely tied to emotion, they are often involuntary and unconscious. To show you're paying attention while listening, hold a very slight smile, nod occasionally, and maintain good eye contact."
7. **Appropriate voice tone.** If you have ever heard, "It's not what you said, it's how you said it," then it is time to consider *paralanguage*. This, Price says, refers to "voice tone, pacing, pausing, volume, inflection, pitch and articulation." The tone of our voice "is critically important because it conveys emotional meaning, attitude and impact."
8. **Responding to others' nonverbal cues.** By responding appropriately to others' cues, you not only convey confidence in yourself but also show a high level of empathy, sensitivity and care for them, which builds trust. Price says, "Listen with your eyes. Their nonverbal cues can tell you when they have a question, want to say something, agree or disagree, need a break, require more explanation, or have an emotional response."

Using paralinguistics, we are able to identify voices, make assumptions about others' feelings and emotions, and determine a speaker's characteristics. In addition to these auditory nonverbal communications, invisible forms of communication—chronemics, olfactics, haptics, and environmental factors—also create meaning.

Invisible Codes of Nonverbal Communication

Invisible communication includes types of nonverbal communication that we cannot see: perceptions of time, the sense of smell, the use of touch, environmental factors, and technology.

Chronemics Temporal communication, or **chronemics**, refers to *how humans organize and structure time and the messages conveyed as a result of this organization*. Time dictates when we eat, sleep, go to school, or go to work. Many people in the United States view time as something tangible. North Americans tend to use phrases such as "You should be on time," "New technology will save us time," or "You need time to yourself." You may count the days until a favorite holiday arrives or watch the clock to determine when class is over. Our watches, computers, and cell phones can be programmed to remind us when the time has arrived to be some

chronemics
how humans organize and structure time and the messages conveyed as a result of this organization.

place or meet a particular deadline. Individuals view the use of time differently, depending on whether they are from a monochronic or polychronic culture (Hall, 1959). People from **monochronic cultures** *carefully schedule tasks, complete them one by one, and follow strict agendas.* Monochronic individuals place tremendous value and priority on work-related objectives and view time as a rigid structure. The United States and Germany are two examples of monochronic cultures. **Polychronic cultures** *work on several tasks at once and view time as flexible.* People from polychronic cultures value relationships with others over work-related tasks. Italy and Brazil are two cultures that are primarily polychronic.

Our personalities and status also help determine how we organize time. Individuals with relaxed attitudes may arrive late to events, whereas highly structured or task-oriented individuals may make it a priority to arrive on time. High-status professional positions, including physicians and politicians, may be able to arrive late to appointments, but patients and political aides are expected to show up at specific times.

Olfactics **Olfactics** is *the use of our sense of smell to gather information.* Although we have long known that animals use smell to obtain information such as the presence of predators or prey, study of the human olfactory system began only recently. Like most other forms of nonverbal communication, the reliance on smell is cultural. Because odors convey meaning, they are an important part of our daily lives (Waskul & Vannini, 2008), yet Americans rely less on their sense of smell than they do on sight and hearing. Many Americans will rely primarily on smell when an odor is uncharacteristically strong or unique. This may help explain why Americans invest so much money in soaps, deodorants, perfumes, mouthwashes, breath mints, lotions, scented candles, and air fresheners to create pleasant but artificial scents.

Gender also plays a role in how olfactory senses are used. While olfactory senses help both men and women perceive the attractiveness of other persons, men and women use olfactory senses differently when choosing a mate. For example, women tend to rely more heavily on olfactory senses when choosing partners, whereas men rely less on scent and more on visual appeal when choosing their sexual partner (Havlicek et al., 2008).

Other cultures also view odor differently. Kate Fox, the director of the Social Issues Research Center, reports that many non-Western cultures historically valued or had a heightened awareness of the sense of smell. Here are a few examples:

- In India, the traditional affectionate greeting—equivalent to the Western hug or kiss—was to smell someone's head. An ancient Indian text declares, "I will smell thee on the head; that is the greatest sign of tender love" (Fox, 2010, p. 28).
- In Arab countries, breathing on people as you speak to them signals friendship and goodwill—and to "deny" someone your breath smell conveys a shameful avoidance of involvement.
- Among the Amazonian Desana, all members of a tribal group were believed to share a similar odor. Marriage was only allowed

monochronic cultures
cultures in which people carefully schedule tasks, complete them one by one, and follow strict agendas.

polychronic cultures
cultures in which people take on several tasks at once and view time as flexible.

olfactics
use of our sense of smell to gather information.

Can you recall being touched as a small child? In what ways could early touch have influenced your development or even attitudes toward touch?

OLJ Studio/Shutterstock.com

between persons of different odors, which required that spouses be chosen from other tribal groups.

In addition to human odors, environmental odors may influence various bodily responses. Certain smells may trigger positive or negative memories. Even if some memories have faded, a particular scent can cause an individual to recall more details of that memory (Morrin, Krisha, & Lwin, 2011). For example, certain scents may remind you of your grandparent's house, your first car, or a favorite vacation spot. On the other hand, the scent of a doctor's office or cologne of someone you do not like may elicit negative emotions and memories.

Haptics **Haptics** refers to *the study of communicating via touch*. Research indicates the importance of touch in creating physically and psychologically healthy infants and children (Field, 2002). Infants and children who are given plenty of physical stimulation have higher IQs than those who receive less physical touch at a young age, and maternal touch is shown to reduce the stress levels of infants (Feldman, Singer, Zagoory, 2009; Yarrow, 1963). Touch is also important in maintaining relationships later in life. The amount of touch provided in a relationship may vary, depending on the stage of the relationship and sex of the initiator. Andersen and Guerrero (1994) reported that married couples touch with the greatest frequency and casual daters touch the least. In more long-lasting and serious relationships, women tend to initiate touch more often than men, and they are more likely to initiate touch after marriage. Men, however, are more likely to initiate touch during the beginning stages of relationship development (Andersen & Guerrero, 1994).

Several categories of touch help distinguish relationships. Givens (2005) reports that most of the categories seem natural and are rarely noticed until a discrepancy occurs between the relationship type and form of touch. The following categories are listed in order from least intimate to most intimate (Heslin & Alper, 1983):

- **Functional** or **professional touch** is *the least intimate* and *includes touch by others according to their professional position*. This includes touch by physicians, hairstylists, tattoo artists, and other professions who require a certain degree of physical contact to do their jobs.

- **Social** or **polite touch** occurs as *part of an initial interaction, greeting, or informal ritual*. This includes the handshake in the United States and hugging and kissing in many European countries when greeting acquaintances.

- **Friendship** or **warmth touch** conveys *a sense of closeness and caring between individuals*. Friends hugging, holding hands, or linking arms together are examples of friendship touch. A pat on the back or resting a hand on one's shoulder can convey warmth and support.

haptics
the study of communicating via touch.

functional or professional touch
the least intimate touch, including touch by others according to their professional position.

social or polite touch
part of an initial interaction, greeting, or informal ritual.

friendship or warmth touch
a sense of closeness and caring between individuals.

- **Love** or **intimacy touch** typically *occurs between family members or romantic partners*. Extended hugs between relatives, kissing between romantic partners, and a child sitting on a parent's lap are examples of love or intimacy touch.

- **Sexual arousal touch** describes *the type of touching that conveys sexual meaning and stimulation*. Some forms of kissing and stroking are examples of sexual arousal touching.

Touching members of the royal family is often considered a breach of England's protocol. Do you think James should have observed the traditional codes of haptics? Why do you think so?

The form of touch considered most appropriate for a particular situation is often determined by the relationship level and type. The amount and kind of touch also varies between men and women. In the United States, women are expected to give gentle hugs, hold and comfort children, and reach out softly to someone in need. Men, by contrast, are expected to give vigorous pats on the back, shake a hand rather than gently hug someone, and engage in roughhousing with other men and even children (Derlega, Lewis, Harrison, Winstead, & Costanza, 1989).

Touch also conveys varied meanings across cultures. Although many North American societies are considered contact cultures, others are not. For example, touch between nonfamily members is often viewed negatively. Children in many Muslim cultures are taught not to touch members of the opposite sex (Dresser, 2005). The rules for haptics may also differ according to culture, power, and status. In 2014, NBA player LeBron James posed for a photograph with Prince William and his wife, Kate, the Duchess of Cambridge. James placed his arm around Kate for the photographs, a gesture that Britons immediately considered a breach of protocol. Commoners are not supposed to touch members of the royal family. The official Web site for the monarchy claimed "there are no obligatory codes of behavior for meeting the Queen or a member of the Royal Family, but many people wish to observe the traditional forms" (British Monarchy, 2014).

Environmental Factors **Environmental factors** consist of *surroundings that influence how we think, feel, and behave as we communicate with others*. In what is considered a foundational study, Abraham Maslow and N. L. Mintz (1956) confirmed the important role environment plays in our reactions to a given situation. Color and sound are two ways in which environment influences human behavior.

Colors are important in creating certain moods. Within the first ninety seconds of meeting someone or seeing a product, a person has

love or intimacy touch
touch between family members or romantic partners.

sexual arousal touch
the type of touching that conveys sexual meaning and stimulation.

environmental factors
surroundings that influence how we think, feel, and behave as we communicate with others.

formed a judgment. Research suggests that approximately 62 percent to 90 percent of that assessment is based on color (Singh, 2006). The influence of color and environment is so powerful that restaurants rely on environmental factors to influence customers' eating behavior. They may paint walls blue to ease stress and tension and create a calming atmosphere in which customers will linger and perhaps order dessert or after-dinner drinks. However, restaurants also know that too much blue can suppress appetites and lead customers to order less to eat and drink (Kido, 2000). Red, on the other hand, is believed to stimulate appetite and increase metabolism, so many restaurants, especially fast-food restaurants, choose red as their primary color.

Restaurants also use music to create particular effects. Fast-paced music can actually speed up eating. The effect is so powerful that researchers found that customers spend an average of 45 minutes eating when the background music was fast-paced or rock 'n' roll music but 56 minutes when the background music was slower (Prochnik, 2010, p. 100).

Technology Technology has become an important and familiar means for establishing and maintaining relationships, and communication scholars are now studying the communication patterns and styles of text-based messages. Because many interactions occur through the use of electronic devices, many of our familiar nonverbal cues are absent (tone, pitch, volume, pace, eye contact, expression, and the like), and text-based messages are easily misunderstood. In fact, facial expressions are such an important part of understanding verbal messages that Internet and cell-phone users often rely on what are now called **emoticons**, or *typed characters that are used to convey feelings*. Emoticons can emphasize or clarify one's feelings, regulate a communication interaction, or soften a negative tone—just as smiles and frowns do in face-to-face interactions (Derks, Bos, & von Grumbkow, 2008). Particular emotions such as happiness and sadness can be conveyed via smiling or frowning faces. Other emoticons are used to represent certain facial expressions such as a wink—;)—or vocal qualities such as getting LOUDER! Abbreviations can represent other nonverbal behaviors, including LOL (laughing out loud) or H&K (hugs and kisses). Using emoticons in text-based messages can help visually communicate the nonverbal messages that are absent when we communicate electronically. However, it is important to consider the amount and appropriateness of using emoticons, especially in business and professional interactions. Currently, there is some disagreement over the use of emoticons in workplace communication. Bill Lancaster, a lecturer in communication at Northeastern University in Boston, blames emoticons in part for "the degradation of writing skills—grammar, syntax, sentence structure, even penmanship—that come with digital technology" (DiNardo, 2011). He believes that "language, used properly, is clear on its own." British journalist Maria McErlane agrees. She is "deeply offended" by the use of the symbols and finds the use of emoticons "lazy." She states, "To use a little

emoticons
typed characters used to convey feelings.

picture with sunglasses on it to let you know how you're feeling is beyond ridiculous" (DiNardo, 2011).

Martha Heller, president of Heller Search Associates, a search firm for technology executives for *Fortune* 500 companies, and Columbia University professor Lisa M. Bates disagree. Heller likes to include a smiley or wink to signify that her previous comment was intended as a joke. Bates has also embraced the smiley, albeit "sparingly and strategically," because it "can take the edge off and avoid misunderstanding" (DiNardo, 2011). The differences in opinions over using emoticons in business and professional interactions indicate the importance of understanding how they are perceived in your own workplace. Do not assume that emoticons are appropriate and will be understood and appreciated.

Each of these codes of nonverbal communication—visual, auditory, and invisible—works with the others to contribute to the strength, clarity, and perception of our messages. Understanding their purpose and effects can help us communicate more effectively with others.

Chapter Summary

Nonverbal Communication Is the Process of Communicating Using Our Bodies, Faces, and Nonword Vocalizations

- A majority of what we understand about a message is determined by nonverbal forms of communicating.
- Culture, gender, and interpersonal relationships all influence how we communicate and interpret nonverbal behaviors.
- Nonverbal communication is ambiguous.
- Nonverbal communication works in conjunction with verbal communication in six ways: to repeat, to emphasize, to complement, to contradict, to substitute, and to regulate.
- Emblems, illustrators, and regulators are nonverbal behaviors that repeat or reinforce spoken words.

We Communicate Visually Through the Nonverbal Acts of Kinesics, Proxemics, and Artifacts

- Our posture, gestures, body movements, and eye contact all send messages about our willingness to interact with others.
- Affect displays help convey how we feel.
- The use of space provides signals about interpersonal relationships, gender, power, and status.

- Personal artifacts and appearance can reveal information about our identities and interests.
- Auditory communication consists of the way we communicate orally without uttering words.
- Vocal cues convey feelings and emotions.
- Paralinguistics affect our ability to identify voices, make inferences about others' feelings and emotions, and determine characteristics about a speaker.

We Can Communicate Without the Use of Sight and Sound

- The way we structure time differs between monochronic and polychronic cultures.
- Our sense of smell is viewed differently among different cultures.
- The form of touch considered most appropriate for a particular situation is often determined by the relationship level and type.
- Environmental factors can influence moods and reactions to particular events.
- When using technology to communicate with others, emoticons help reveal our emotions behind the message.

Key Concepts

adaptors (60)	functional or professional touch (68)	personal appearance (62)
affect displays (60)	haptics (68)	polychronic cultures (67)
artifacts (62)	illustrator (58)	proxemics (61)
auditory communication system (59)	invisible communication system (59)	regulation (58)
chronemics (66)	kinesics (59)	repetition (58)
complementation (58)	liking (56)	responsiveness (56)
contradiction (58)	love or intimacy touch (69)	sexual arousal touch (69)
emblems (58)	monochronic cultures (67)	silence (65)
emoticons (70)	monotone (65)	social or polite touch (68)
emphasis (58)	nonverbal communication (53)	substitution (58)
environmental factors (69)	olfactics (67)	visual communication system (59)
friendship or warmth touch (68)	paralinguistics (64)	vocal cues (65)
		vocalized pauses (65)

Invitation to Human Communication Online

MindTap Speech includes an interactive MindTap Reader and interactive learning tools including National Geographic Explorer videos, student videos, quizzes, flashcards, and more. You can build your speech outline with Outline Builder and record, post, and watch videos with YouSeeU. Go to cengagebrain.com to access your MindTap for *Invitation to Human Communication* for access to these resources.

MindTap®

Further Reflection and Discussion

1. In what situations might you want to adapt your nonverbal skills to be less gender specific and to communicate more strength (if you are female) and more emotion (if you are male)?

2. Discuss the nonverbal communication that tells you when, for example, someone is the life of the party, someone is shy in social situations, or someone is trying to deceive you.

3. Observe how physical space is occupied in your school library, who has more power? Less power? What aspects of the environment are giving you this information?

4. Consider your personal artifacts. What do they represent about you? Do you own T-shirts or hats or have tattoos that contain messages that express your attitudes, beliefs, political affiliation, or hobbies? What artifacts appear in your living room or bedroom? What do they suggest about you? Discuss these artifacts with the class.

5. Discuss how you communicate emotions when chatting online or in a text message with a friend. Do you ever have trouble communicating your tone or feeling?

6. Do you feel it is appropriate to use emoticons and text language when communicating to co-workers or supervisors? Why or why not?

7. Have you traveled to a different culture and experiences differences in nonverbal communication? If so, how did you adjust your own nonverbal

behaviors? Which aspects of nonverbal communication seemed to be the most different from U.S. American culture?

8. Spend the day observing how others use nonverbal communication in conjunction with their verbal communication. Which of the six ways discussed in the chapter did you see used most frequently?

9. Spend the day observing your own use of space. At what times, and with whom, do you use personal distance? Social distance? Public distance? Did you notice anyone violate the norms for proxemics that are typical for U.S. American culture?

10. Using children's books, practice your public speaking skills by reading a section of the book while focusing on vocal cues and kinesics. Try to change your rate, pitch, inflection, and volume while reading. Also, incorporate different types of gestures and facial expressions to correspond with the story.

Activities and Web Links

Visit cengagebrain.com to access the MindTap for *Invitation to Human Communication* where these activities and Web links can be found.

1. Watch this video about the TV show *Lie to Me*. Ask a friend to guess what emotion your facial expression and body language are revealing. Include anger, sadness, contempt, joy, fear, excitement, fake happiness (fake smile), and other emotions. Go to *Weblink 3.1*.

2. **Exploring International Nonverbal Communication**. Test your ability to "read" samples of real nonverbal communication. Take the quiz "A World of Gestures" to see if you can identify the meaning of these gestures from around the world. Go to *Weblink 3.2*.

3. **Kismet: A Humanoid Robot with Emotions**. Kismet is a robot that can interact and cooperate with people. Kismet's goal is to enter into natural and intuitive social interaction with a human caregiver and to learn from the caregiver, a process that is reminiscent of parent–infant exchanges. Kismet perceives natural social cues from visual and auditory channels and delivers social signals to the human through gaze direction, facial expression, and body posture. Look at Kismet's expressions and see if you can figure out what changes in the face can be attributed to each emotion. Go to *Weblink 3.3*.

4. Discusses the differences in nonverbal communication between men and women in both the United States and Brazil. Go to *Weblink 3.4*.

4

IN THIS CHAPTER YOU WILL LEARN TO:

- Recognize the three primary rules that govern language.

- Describe the different ways language is ambiguous.

- Explain how cultures and co-cultures influence our ability to communicate with and understand one another.

- Discuss the ways gender shapes the way we use language.

- Define the two ways that the meaning of messages affect interpersonal and small group communication.

- Explain why speakers need to consider civility and incivility when creating messages for various audiences.

Language

GORDON WILTSIE/National Geographic Creative

Language, and the meanings it conveys, can be confusing. If you encountered these signs while driving, what would you do? How would you explain your choices to a police officer?

How many people have you talked to in the past week? You probably talked to more than you realize: family members, friends, teachers, bosses, co-workers, roommates, store clerks, and more. You probably communicated face to face, over the phone, by e-mail and texting, and maybe in a blog. Was anything you said interpreted in a way you did not intend? Maybe your communication made someone angry or confused, made someone laugh, or even caused you extra work? Each day we rely on language to communicate with others. Sometimes our messages are understood exactly as we want, and other times miscommunication is the result.

In this chapter, we discuss language's most common characteristics. First, we discuss the nature of language. Then we turn our focus to examples of how language affects interpersonal relationships, group effectiveness, and public-speaking success. Finally, we focus on the connections between language, civility, and social justice.

The Nature of Language: Rules, Culture, Gender, and Technology

In this section, we learn three primary rules that govern language. Next we look at the ways in which language is ambiguous—that is, the way it causes potential confusion or misunderstanding between communicators. Then we explore how language is influenced by gender, culture, and technology.

Language Is Governed by Rules

Language consists of the use of *a collection of symbols or words to communicate with others*. To communicate effectively, we must follow three primary rules of language use. First, we must learn the basics of **phonology**, or *the study of how sounds are used to communicate meaning*. Each language has its own basic sound units, or *phonemes*; these include vowels, consonants, and diphthongs (the combination of two vowels that operate as one sound). The English language has twenty-four consonant sounds, twelve vowel sounds, and eight diphthongs. To be competent in a language, speakers need to learn the phonological rules that govern the language because some words have different pronunciations that will change the meaning of a word. For example, *content* has two different phonological rules. Are you content (satisfied) with the content (material) of the course? The first *content* is used as an adverb to ask how a person is feeling about something. The second *content* acts as a noun that refers to the topics covered in the course. Phonological rules (rules for pronunciation) help speakers communicate clearly and successfully—and these rules often prove challenging for someone who is just learning to speak a new language.

language
a collection of symbols or words used to communicate with others

phonology
the study of how sounds are used to communicate meaning.

The second rule of language refers to *syntax*, or how symbols (words) are arranged to create meaning. **Syntax** refers to *the rules that govern word order*. Our meanings often depend on the order in which our words appear. The following two examples illustrate how meaning is altered by a rearranged word order:

The exam is tomorrow.

Is the exam tomorrow?

Understanding the correct order of words helps us communicate clearly and effectively. If you speak more than one language, then you know that each language has its own rules for syntax. Improper syntax can create confusion—and possibly some humor for listeners or readers. For example, the following headline in the *Spartanburg* (South Carolina) *Herald-Journal* probably confused some readers and made others laugh: "Sisters Reunite After 18 Years in Checkout Line" ("Sisters," 1983). No, the sisters were not standing in the checkout line for eighteen years, but the syntax suggested that possibility.

Now read the following two examples of syntax and see if you notice *what* is misleading in each statement:

Poor syntax: "For those of you who parked your car in the pay lot and don't know it, there's a free parking lot located a block away."

Poor syntax: "There's a bag of groceries on the table that needs to go in the refrigerator."

The first example suggests the drivers did not know they parked their cars. The second indicates that the table needs to go in the refrigerator. Now look at how the following examples of proper syntax and how their meanings are clear.

Proper syntax: "For those of you who parked in the pay lot because you did not know there was free parking, the free lot is located a block away."

Proper syntax: "The bag of groceries on the table needs to go in the refrigerator."

When we use proper syntax or sentence structure, we communicate more clearly.

The final rule that effective communicators understand about language relates to **semantics**, or *the meaning of specific words*. When a teacher asks students to use a pencil on their exams, they know that a "pencil" is a particular type of writing utensil. However, if the teacher asks students to queue up for a pencil, they might not know that a "queue" is a line we wait in to receive something. When we communicate successfully, we are using the "right" word to convey an idea. The word means the same, or something similar, for those who are involved in the act of communicating. However, it is easy to misunderstand someone based on multiple meanings of some words. Have you ever been told that your work is "fine" or that your ideas are "interesting"? Were you unsure about what the feedback really meant? We may be confused because these words are ambiguous and can be interpreted in different ways.

syntax
the rules that govern word order.

semantics
the meaning of specific words.

Language Is Ambiguous

Friends often argue over the meaning of a word. This is because words are symbols, and their meaning is determined by the people involved in the act of communicating. Remember from Chapter 1 that there are two different ways we can interpret the meaning of language: **denotative meanings** are *the literal, or commonly accepted, meanings of a word*, and **connotative meanings** are *the meanings we associate with particular words based on our experiences, understanding, or opinions of the word*. Understanding the difference between denotative and connotative meanings may help reduce confusion over the use of a term. For example, the word *freedom* is used frequently in the United States to mean our ability to act, think, or speak without external restraints (denotative definition). However, the term *freedom* may represent different meanings based on our cultural background, country of origin, sex, class, race, or occupation. In Egypt and Iraq, for example, many people are struggling to assert their rights and find opportunities. The word *freedom* means quite different things to them than it does here in the United States, a country with a long history of "freedoms" that are taken for granted: voting, religious expression, public protest, education, and the like. Because language can be ambiguous and meanings can differ between individuals, we communicate more effectively when we clarify the meaning of ambiguous terms.

The idea that language is ambiguous is illustrated nicely by Ogden and Richards's semantic triangle of meaning (1923). This model illustrates the relationship between a word (*symbol*), the common definition it represents (*referent*), and the individual thoughts or reactions the symbol provokes (*reference*). Chapter 1 described how the semantic triangle helps us understand that language is symbolic—that is, beyond the dictionary definition, there often is no direct correlation between the word used to describe something and the thing itself. The word *bang* sounds like the thing it represents, but the word *door* has no direct connection to the solid wood slab "banging" in the wind. Moreover, our associations with words can be highly individual—like the examples of *freedom* and even *door*. Some may hear a banging door and think of freedom and escape, but others might think only of an irritating noise.

Wesley Bocxe/Photo Researchers/Getty Images

Baghdad, Iraq—April 9, 2003. Iraqis celebrate the end of the Saddam Hussein regime while standing atop a huge statue of the dictator that was toppled by a U.S. Marine recovery tank in Baghdad's Firdos Square. Some citizens even vented their anger against the dictator. How might the word *freedom* differ in meaning for one of the Iraqis in this photo than it might for a U.S. citizen?

PRACTICING HUMAN COMMUNICATION
Denotation and Connotation

On a sheet of paper, write down the following words: *space, mug, school, home, religion,* and *relationship.* Then write down both denotative and connotative definitions associated with each word. Share your definitions with a partner and identify similarities and differences in your denotative and connotative definitions. Discuss why it is likely that there were differences in the connotative understanding of the words.

denotative meanings
the literal or commonly accepted meaning of a word.

connotative meanings
the meanings we associate with particular words based on our experiences, understanding, or opinions of the word.

NATIONAL GEOGRAPHIC EXPLORER TIP ↗

T. H. Culhane
Emerging Explorer and Urban Planner

Courtesy of Chris Rainier

In your work as an explorer, have there been times where ambiguity or culture have affected clear communication? Can you give an example of when the ambiguous nature of language or cultural differences affected your communication and ability to understand others?

For the first week of what was a three-week expedition in Indonesia, we made little progress and couldn't understand why people were treating us civilly but not offering us any information. And some of the key scientists said, "You see what the problem is—they don't trust you. They believe that you're not here for knowledge of plants, but for gold or diamonds or oil or other minerals like the other people who have come in and lied to them in the past." And so there was tremendous mistrust. We did not know how we were going to get around this until one day sitting in the chief's hut trying very delicately to explain our motives and our backgrounds and establish our credentials which we thought we had done well enough up front. The chief saw me looking at a guitar that was at the far side of his hut. He said, "Play me a song." So he hands me the guitar and I sing the song "Burung Kakak Tua," which is a traditional Indonesian song, but I did it in sort of an Elvis hippy, hippy shake. The chief did not crack a smile at all; he just watched. And then when I finished it, I actually put down the guitar, and he pointed his finger at me and said, "Tomorrow you will perform in the village square celebration." Then he turned to the other scientists and he said, "You will perform with him." And one of the British scientists said, "I used to play drums in a high school band. I suppose I could play drums." One of the women said, "Well, I don't suppose you have a flute?" And he said, "Yes, there will be a reed flute."

The next day, they had a little stage built, and they had their own band playing and we got up and sang. The crowd went crazy and asked for more. Then we performed the next day at a village wedding. And then the chief said, "The next night there is another festival, and you will perform there." They still wouldn't speak about science at all. And finally the third day he invited us to his hut, and he said, "You have proven yourselves. Now we can trust you, so we are willing to take you anywhere, tell you anything, and get you everything you need to know."

And it dawned on me that you have to really insert yourself in the culture: celebrate together, eat together, honor each other's traditions—and then you can get to work. That is how I approach most of my work around the world. I find those cultural common points and work with them first. It is a give–give, win–win situation. For me, it turns into using music as one of the primary bridges to doing scientific research.

Because people associate their own experiences, emotions, or memories with particular words, speakers need to consider their audience's thoughts—their *references*—when communicating with others.

Equivocal Words Language is also ambiguous because many words have more than one commonly accepted or dictionary definition. **Equivocal words** are *words that have more than one meaning*. According to

equivocal words
words that have more than one meaning.

dictionary.com, the word *court* can mean a "place where justice is administered" or "an area open to the sky and mostly or entirely surrounded by buildings, walls, etc."; or "a smooth, level, quadrangle on which to play tennis, basketball, etc."; or "to seek another's love." The English language has numerous words with more than one meaning, and new words are created every year to represent new objects, experiences, and technologies. *Apple* is considered a piece of fruit or a brand of computers and other electronic devices. A *tweeter* has historically been defined as a type of loudspeaker that produces high-frequency sound. In 2009, though, *tweeter* emerged as one who uses the social Web site Twitter. As more equivocal terms enter our vocabularies, the greater the likelihood of confusion. But understanding the context surrounding a conversation or providing a quick definition can help reduce those misunderstandings.

When you hear the word *fraternity*, what do you think of? Does the photo match your connotative definition? Why or why not?

Slang and Jargon Slang is *informal nonstandard vocabulary used by members of a co-culture or group who have similar interests, goals, or life experiences.* Members of sports teams and clubs often use slang to establish their membership. Skiers, for example, often use "powder days" to refer to skiing on fresh snow. Slang can also communicate informal relationships between people. Addressing another person as "dude" is a form of slang often used by close friends. The use of slang usually indicates in-group membership. College students may use "hooking up" to describe an intimate encounter with another person. It may be appropriate for teenagers to say "peace out" when leaving friends, but they would likely find it strange, even embarrassing, if their parents used the same phrase.

Jargon refers to *technical language used by professional groups.* Scientists, technicians, educators, and physicians all incorporate jargon when communicating with other members of the same profession. Educators may discuss *tracking* systems where students are grouped according to ability. Members of online communities may describe people who post comments that are offensive or designed to upset readers as *trolls.* Jargon is also used in sports and hobbies. Skateboarders call a no-handed, aerial skateboarding trick an *ollie.* Like slang, jargon can create confusion for individuals who are not familiar with the language of a particular profession, and sometimes people use jargon or slang to signal their membership in a group.

slang
informal nonstandard vocabulary used by members of a co-culture or group who have similar interests, goals, or life experiences.

jargon
technical language used by professional groups.

Skateboarders use jargon to describe particular tricks. What jargon do you use when talking about particular hobbies or activities?

An **acronym**, or *the first letters or initials of terms that form a word*, can also be part of jargon. Medical professionals often use the term "CAT scan" to refer to a *computerized axial tomography scan*. Groups and clubs may also use acronyms to describe their professional titles or identities. The acronym EMT stands for "emergency medical technician," and LGBTQQI stands for "lesbian, gay, bisexual, transgendered, queer, questioning, and intersexed."

Jargon is easily understood by members of the same group or profession, but it is often confusing for individuals outside the group. To avoid unnecessary confusion, provide a quick definition, demonstration, or explanation of any unfamiliar term or acronym you are using.

Euphemisms and Doublespeak Language also makes it possible for us to make something unpleasant sound pleasant or to disguise its actual meaning. **Euphemisms** are *polite terms or more socially acceptable ways to describe something that someone may find unpleasant*. To say you are going to the "ladies room" instead of the "bathroom" or that you are "in between jobs" instead of "unemployed" are common euphemisms. Even though they are often considered polite forms of language, euphemisms may be confusing for listeners if the implied meaning is misunderstood. Being "in between jobs" may sound like a choice rather than an undesirable decision someone made for us.

Doublespeak is closely related to euphemisms. Whereas euphemisms attempt to make something sound more pleasant, **doublespeak** is *language used to purposefully disguise the actual meaning of something*. The phrase "friendly fire" is used by the military to describe the inadvertent firing toward one's own group or allies. When companies say they will be "outsourcing," they are using doublespeak for "laying off workers" or "taking business away from American cities and potentially American workers." Doublespeak can be misleading because the new term disguises what is actually occurring, making it seem less harmful or more benign than it actually is.

Language Is Influenced by Cultures and Co-Cultures

Considering that language consists of a set of symbols used to represent human experiences, people with different life experiences define the world in different ways. As such, culture plays an important role in our ability to communicate with and understand one another. Some cultures use feminine and masculine nouns and pronouns to define words. For example, the word *bridge* in German is *brücke*, a feminine noun. When asked to provide three words that describe a bridge shown

acronym
the first letters or initials of terms that form a word.

euphemism
polite terms or more socially acceptable ways to describe something that someone may find unpleasant.

doublespeak
language used to purposefully disguise the actual meaning of something.

in a photograph, German speakers most often used words such as *elegant*, *fragile*, and *beautiful*. In Spanish, the word for *bridge* is *puente*, a masculine noun. When Spanish speakers were asked the same question, they responded that the bridge appeared "strong," "dangerous," and "big." A similar result was found for the word *key*. The German word for key (*keil*) is masculine, whereas the word for key in Spanish (*llave*) is feminine. When German speakers were asked to describe a key, they used words such as *hard*, *heavy*, and *useful*. On the other hand, Spanish speakers described a key as *little*, *intricate*, and *golden* (Krulwich, 2009). Because many languages define words as feminine or masculine, the meanings people assign to the word correspond to its perceived gender.

Individuals who live in the same country or share the same culture may also use language differently. In the United States, different regions use different words for the same concept. For example, do you ask for a *pop*, a *soda*, or a *coke* when asking for a carbonated soft drink? Typically, people from the upper Midwest use the term *pop*, people from the West say *soda*, and residents in the South say *coke*.

Regionalisms are *words or phrases common to particular geographical regions*. New York City residents often refer to *upstate* as the geographical region just north of the city (often referring to Westchester County), but this term can be confusing for nonnative New Yorkers. When looking at a map of New York State, it is clear that nearly three hundred miles exist between Westchester County and Clinton County, the state's northernmost county, so *upstate* to nonnative New Yorkers often means something different than it does for those native to the state.

The geographical region in which we live can also dictate informal phrases used to relate to others. These differences are called **colloquialisms**, which are *words and phrases used in relaxed, informal conversations*. The different types of colloquialisms that exist between cultures can be quite prominent. Consider different greetings and salutations used throughout the United States and abroad. In the United States, the phrase "How y'all doin'?" is an informal greeting commonly used by those living in southern states. "G'day" is often used as an informal greeting in Australia, and "Cheerio" is a common way to say good-bye in English-speaking European countries. These phrases are considered colloquialisms because they are common, informal words used by members of a particular region; however, these words and phrases can easily be replaced by more formal language. Someone living in Texas may decide to not say "y'all" and use a more formal phrase when speaking to members of Congress or to a room full of CEOs.

Whether you are speaking to people from different cultures in your own hometown or online, traveling to another state, or heading abroad, it is important to consider cultural differences in language. Learning some of the colloquialisms common to different cultures shows respect and awareness for cultural differences. This **cultural competence** is *the ability to relate appropriately to members from a different culture*. In addition, becoming aware of your own use of colloquialisms, regionalisms, slang, jargon, euphemisms, and doublespeak is important. To avoid creating an awkward moment of confusion or misunderstanding, try to limit words and

regionalism
words or phrases common to particular geographical regions.

colloquialism
words and phrases used in relaxed, informal conversations.

cultural competence
the ability to relate appropriately to members from a different culture.

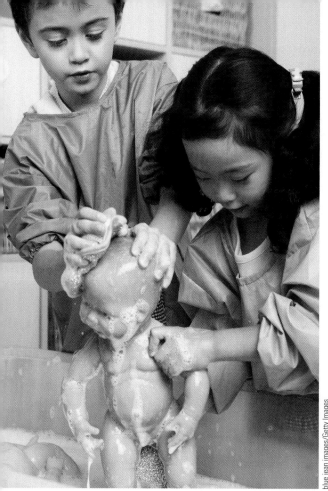

Children play a variety of games as they grow up, and those games teach them certain communication skills. How do you think the games you played as a child have influenced your communication today?

blue jean images/Getty Images

phrases that are ambiguous, difficult to interpret, or open to more than one definition. Linguist Gregory Anderson (2015) that there are certain taboos that can be learned before traveling to a different culture or region, but sometimes the best way to understand cultural differences is to immerse into a culture and carefully observe the nuances taking place. Understanding differences in cultural backgrounds and language is the first step to ensuring the successful transmission of information.

Language Is Influenced by Gender

Although males and females are more similar than different, our genders can and do influence the ways we use language and the word choices we prefer. In this section, we explore some of the ways that gender influences language and the ways these influences affect our communication.

Games and Gender As young children, the games we played taught us how to communicate in important ways (Maltz & Borker, 1982). Games such as kickball, king of the hill, and four square taught us a communication style that is more competitive and instrumental. Playing house, playing school, and playing with dolls requires language that is cooperative and inclusive. Although both boys and girls engage in competitive games and imaginary play as children, there are notable differences in the frequency and type of games played by each sex (Leaper, 1996; Martin, Fabes, Evans, & Wyman, 2000; Wood, 2013). Different games teach different communicative skills. For example, highly competitive games have a clear objective: to win. These games typically require a larger group of children with limited discussion. When communicating, talk is instrumental: children negotiate their positions and strategize how to win. On the other hand, imaginary play such as house requires communication that is cooperative and inclusive. House roles are created, and a great deal of talk is needed to continue the play as children negotiate and define their roles and relationships to others in the game. The lessons learned from communicating through play continue to be part of our language style as we grow older.

Communication Styles and Gender If we carry the lessons learned from childhood play forward, we bring a certain style of communication with us. Scholars now agree that adult women's speech is often labeled as feminine. This speech style tends to incorporate language that is supportive, expressive, personal, and disclosing (Mulac, Bradac, & Gibbons, 2001; Wood, 2011). Researchers sometimes call this *rapport talk* to refer to the bonds and relationships that are built and shared as a result of the communication (Tannen, 2007). Rapport talk consists of sharing personal information, asking questions about another's well-being, inviting others to participate in the conversation, and sharing information that builds and maintains relationships—something girls learn to do during childhood play. According to linguist Deborah Tannen, "[f]or women and girls, talk is the glue that holds a relationship together. Their best friend is the one they tell everything to. Spending an evening at home with a spouse is when this kind of talk comes into its own" (Tannen, 2007).

Men also bring the lessons learned from childhood play into adulthood. In contrast to women's styles of speech, men's verbal speech style is often labeled masculine and is characterized as instrumental, competitive, and assertive (Mulac et al., 2001; Wood, 2011). Also known as *report talk*, this style of speech is direct and used to accomplish something such as giving instructions or solving a problem. For example, Carlos and Alex are working together on a class project, and Carlos tells Alex, "Our project is due next Tuesday. You work on the written assignment and I will prepare the oral presentation. Meet me on Sunday night and we'll go over our assignment." Carlos is using report talk to communicate with Alex about the class project. Notice that Carlos did not ask Alex how he was feeling about the assignment expectations or what Alex's weekend plans involved outside of finishing the project. Carlos is using report talk, which is described as straight to the point to get things done.

Communication Topics and Gender Research also suggests that men and women often communicate about different topics and for different lengths of time (Holmes, 2006; Tannen, 2001; Wood, 2000). Female friends tend to discuss more personal topics such as family, friendships, and intimate relationships; health and reproductive matters; and issues related to personal appearance. Men are more likely to converse with one another about current events, sports, business, and dating. When men and women get together, however, they both tend to discuss work–life issues and events occurring in popular culture.

Interruptions, Discussions, and Gender Who do you believe interrupts conversations more often—men or women? Some people may be surprised, but men interrupt conversations more often than women, especially when they are speaking with other men. In same-sex groups, men interrupt one another often and use more directives to begin their statements (Mulac, Wiemann, Widenmann, & Gibson, 1988). Studies also indicate that in mixed-sex dyads and large groups, men will speak for longer periods than women will. Linguist Marjorie Swacker observed an academic conference and studied conversational patterns. She concluded that women presented 40 percent of the papers and made up 42 percent of audiences—but only accounted for 27 percent of the questions asked (as cited in Tannen, 2001). In addition, Swacker concluded that women's questions averaged half as long to ask as men's

PRACTICING HUMAN COMMUNICATION
Gender

Make a list of games you played as a child. Identify the type of communication (cooperative or instrumental) associated with each game. Now create a class list of games played and tally how many men and women played each one. Discuss whether any games are divided along gender lines and what this teaches us about learning to communicate with others.

questions, twenty-seven to fifty-two seconds. Swacker determined that this is because men tended to preface their questions by making statements first, asked more than one question, and then responded to the speaker's comments with a follow-up question or an additional comment (Roth Walsh, 1997).

Conversation and Gender Studies also reveal that conversational length differs between members of large and small groups and when members are of the same sex. When groups are small, women typically talk more than their male counterparts do. In addition, speech patterns are different in same-sex conversations. When women are speaking with other women, they tend to ask more questions, include more personal pronouns, and engage in what Leaper and Ayres call "affiliative speech," which includes agreeing with or acknowledging others' comments (Leaper & Ayres, 2007). In addition, men and women in some regions around the world have their own, unique way of speaking. Until recently, for example, the Chukchi people in the northeastern part of Siberia had different ways of pronouncing words, depending on whether they were spoken by a woman or a man (Anderson, 2015).

Although there are distinct differences between men's and women's communication styles, several studies suggest that men and women usually communicate in ways that are more alike than different (Canary & Hause, 1993; Pennebaker, Mehl, & Niederhoffer, 2003). Research shows that men and women are beginning to use both report and rapport speaking styles, and speaking styles may be influenced more by our occupations and social environments than by gender. For example, preschool teachers, nurses, and social workers are often encouraged to use supportive and cooperative language. Politicians, lawyers, and executives are typically trained to speak in direct and assertive ways. As women continue to train for careers traditionally held by men and as men work in service-related positions and raise children, we will likely see more examples of individuals shifting between communication styles. This style of communication is called *androgynous*, and **androgynous communicators** are *individuals who are adept at using different speech styles, depending on the situation.* Examples might be the father who uses rapport talk with his children and report talk at work and the college student who uses rapport talk when socializing with friends but report talk while working on group projects.

Language Is Influenced by Technology

Our increasing reliance on and time spent with technology is shaping the way we use language to communicate. The Internet, cell phones, smartphones, and tablets have increased our ability to communicate with others while also altering the type of language we use to communicate. We now look at each type of technology.

The Internet Because of the Internet, we have access to social-networking sites such as Facebook, LinkedIn, Instagram, Tumblr, and Google+, each of which allows people to communicate easily with family, friends, and

androgynous communicators
individuals who are adept at using different speech styles, depending on the situation.

even strangers. People can also display their thoughts, stories, interests, and ideas on blogs, personal Web pages, and Twitter. Professional sites such as LinkedIn allow us to post professional profiles and distribute them widely and quickly.

Before the Internet was widely used, communication researchers believed that personal information was disclosed only after trust was established in a relationship. We now know that the Internet provides a space in which the intimate details of people's personal lives are disclosed quickly and to large numbers of receivers—and without the trust base that researchers previously thought was central to self-disclosure. Even our screen names and usernames create messages and carry meaning for the user. Consider what your screen name implies. Although some users may find usernames humorous, employers may be hesitant to hire someone with an e-mail address beginning with something like CrackBaby91.

What we communicate to others and how we use language also has changed as a result of these new media. Twitter, for example, limits messages to 140 characters. This limited space encourages users to invent acronyms and use word fragments instead of spelling complete words and sentences and fully developed thoughts. Both tweets and texting, the result of advancements in media technology, create avenues for new words to enter the English language. For example, the online version of *Oxford Dictionary of English OED* adds about 1,000 new entries to its dictionary every year. *OED*'s print dictionary added thirty-nine new words or terms in 2010, eight of which pertained to new media. Among these were *social media, tweetup, microblogging,* and *defriend* ("New words in the OED," n.d.). In 2013, the OED Online added more words related to new media, among these are *BYOD* (bring your own device), *defriend, digital detox, live blog, mouseover, phablet, selfie, TLDR* (too long, didn't read), and *unfriend* (Oxford Dictionaries: Language Matters, 2013).

Advantages and Disadvantages In addition to creating language to represent new technology, rumors via new media circulate rapidly. One hacker group, Script Kiddies, broke into several Twitter accounts to report false information. On the tenth anniversary of the September 11, 2001, terrorist attacks, the group hacked into NBC News's Twitter account and posted false information about a plane hijacking at Ground Zero. Hackers also gained access to foxnews.com Twitter feed and sent several false reports that President Obama had been shot. Tweeting false reports can certainly have serious implications. According to a Twitter study by pearanalytics (2009), most information posted on Twitter is considered "pointless babble" about oneself or one's relationship status with others. Although most of what we write may, in fact, be meaningless and trivial, we still should carefully consider both the message and the intended receiver. Once sent, most messages cannot be retracted or deleted.

But technology is not all bad: it can also provide important relational outcomes. Communicating via technology can help maintain friendships and enhance perceptions of social value and belonging. As social networks keep track of how many "friends" we have and as instant

What to Put in an E-mail

Electronic communication is considered the lifeblood of a functioning organization, with e-mail cited as the preferred channel for communicating with others in the workplace (Guffey & Loewy, 2011). Estimates suggest that more than 200 billion e-mail messages are sent each day, which means that workplace communicators (as well as college students) need to think carefully about constructing their e-mail, especially messages sent to co-workers and supervisors. Remember, e-mails are permanent, searchable, and read as either professional or problematic. To help you stay professional in the workplace, here are four basic rules to follow:

1. **Create an informative subject line.** The subject line should include a quick summary of the e-mail content. Avoid using one-word headings such as "Important" or "Help" as it may trigger spam filters. Phrases like "Two Changes to Our Agenda" or "Meeting Postponed to Thursday" work best.
2. **Greeting.** Begin your message with a greeting and name for the intended recipient. Providing the recipient's name ensures the correct person is receiving the e-mail. If you are not sure how to address the recipient, the formal title of Mr. or Ms. is always acceptable.
3. **Body.** Each e-mail should generally discuss only one topic. Avoid making the e-mail too long; it is best to compile your message in fewer than three screens. Use standard caps and lowercase characters (using all uppercase letters feels like shouting, and all lowercase letters appear unprofessional).
4. **Closing and Signature.** While including a complimentary closing such as "Respectfully" or "Many Thanks" is optional, providing your name is mandatory. Be sure you include full contact information as part of your signature.

messaging allows us to connect to others in real time, technology users often report high levels of satisfaction from using technology to communicate. In fact, when technology becomes unavailable (even momentarily), users can become frustrated, angry, and even panicky. BlackBerry experienced several worldwide system shutdowns that temporarily kept users from accessing e-mail and Internet services, leading some users to blog "Never Again Blackberry" to show their frustration over temporary system glitches and the importance of this medium in their lives (Austin & Robins, 2009).

 ## Language and Interpersonal Communication

When we communicate in our interpersonal relationships, the meanings of messages are often interpreted in two distinct ways because every verbal statement has two dimensions: the content dimension and the relational dimension (Watzalwick, Beavin, & Jackson, 1967). Remember from Chapter 1 that content messages are the actual things we say and relational messages are the parts of the communication that give us information about how we are or are not connected to a person. Usually, the type of interpersonal relationship we have with another person will help determine the relational meaning behind the message. With our close friends, a simple "Hey" as a greeting might signal familiarity and warmth, but with a supervisor that same "Hey" could signal disrespect or a lack of professionalism.

But what happens to the content and relational aspects of interpersonal messages when two people have been separated over an extended period of time? Because of long separations, military families have to find ways to maintain relationships while one (or both) partners are deployed.

In *Relationship Maintenance During Military Deployment: Perspectives of Wives of Deployed U.S. Soldiers* (see Web links at the end of chapter for a link to the video), communication scholar Andy Merolla shows how couples communicated during deployment. After interviewing several dozen women whose husbands were deployed, Merolla discovered ten common communication strategies that helped couples maintain their relationships over long separations. Although each mode had its own set of restrictions (e.g., time limits for telephone calls and lack of privacy when communicating via Webcams), women reported using similar strategies when communicating via different modes of communication. Four common strategies were debriefing talk, topic avoidance, affection and intimacy, and future planning.

Families often use technology to communicate with one another across long distances, and when they are separated for long periods of time. What do you think are some positive aspects to this type of connection? Can you identify any possible negative aspects?

Debriefing Talk

Reporting the events and news from the day (content messages) can create a sense of normalcy for a couple (relational messages). One interviewee reported that the first thing she and her husband discuss on the phone is "what's been going on since we last spoke—work, house, cars, bills, et cetera" (Merolla, 2010).

Topic Avoidance

Because of the limited time allowed for communication and concern for the deployed spouse's situation abroad (relational message), negative topics (content message) are often not discussed.

Affection and Intimacy

Verbally expressing affection by stating "I love you" or making kissing noises (content message) are two ways couples maintain their relationship (relational message).

Future Planning

Couples reported talking about future plans (content messages) that help create hopeful attitudes during periods of uncertainty, as well as increase relational commitment (relational messages).

What is or is not talked about is an important part of maintaining long-distance relationships, especially with military families. Understanding both content and relational messages can help mitigate some of the hardships experienced when one partner is deployed for a long time. What we say and how we say it can make a difference in our interpersonal relationships.

Language and Small Group Communication

Language is an important part of successful group communication. Because groups form from a shared purpose or goal, group members must be able to communicate effectively with one another. Have you ever been

National Geographic Explorer Gregory D. S. Anderson: Language Hot Spots

MARK THIESSEN/National Geographic Creative

Dr. Gregory D. S. Anderson is a linguist and the co-founder of the Living Tongues Institute for Endangered Languages, a not-for-profit organization that documents, revitalizes, and preserves some of the world's vanishing languages. Dr. Anderson has worked in the field with speakers of languages in Siberia (Russia), Kyrgyzstan, Nigeria, India, Bolivia, Australia, Paraguay, Papua New Guinea, and the United States. In the image above, Dr. Anderson (and fellow linguist Dr. K. David Harrison) work with Ichiro John, a Mwoakillese elder, on Mwoakilloa Atoll, Federated States of Micronesia. More than 40 percent of the world's approximate 7,000 languages are currently at risk of becoming extinct. Anderson helped create a language hotspot map to showcase areas around the world with high linguistic diversity as well as high levels of linguistic endangerment. Cameroon, a country in west-central Africa, is an example of a region with a high level of linguistic diversity: more than 275 indigenous languages are spoken there. Dr. Anderson says it is important to document and preserve Cameroon's indigenous languages now because many are unlikely to survive the twenty-first century (Anderson, 2010–2013).

The United States also has many language hotspots. Oklahoma and California are two states of particular interest. The Winnemem Wintu people who live outside of Redding, California, were working to preserve their cultural and linguistic identity when a house fire in 2008 destroyed a large portion of the materials necessary to help their revitalization efforts. They have been struggling ever since to preserve their language. Their leaders contacted Dr. Anderson to seek his assistance with their efforts. With help from the Enduring Voices project, Dr. Anderson and his team delivered a Language Technology Kit to the Winnemem Wintu and trained them to use audio and video recorders to help record and preserve their language. Projects like these can help promote global awareness and expose the language extinction crisis around the world (Enduring Voices, 2009).

WHAT DO YOU THINK?

1. How important is the preservation of a language? What would losing your native language feel like to you and your family?

2. Do you speak more than one language? If so, what are some of the differences in those languages? What do these differences tell you about the languages and the cultures they come from?

3. Does Dr. Anderson need to consider cultural competence when he interacts with different cultures around the world? How might he display his cultural competence as he works to preserve languages?

assigned a group project in which members preferred to communicate via e-mail instead of face to face? Did you feel that your communication was just as effective online as it would have been meeting in person? As our lives continue to be filled with a variety of responsibilities and commitments, and as our society continues to rely more and more on mediated communication, we need to understand how technology can enhance rather than diminish the productivity and quality of group communication.

In "E-Mail Is Easy to Write (and to Misread)," Daniel Goleman (2007) describes how easy it is for e-mail messages to be misinterpreted. He explains that face-to-face communication allows group members to interpret what others say from their tone, facial expressions, and body language. Because typed words do not convey the same emotional contexts provided by in-person communication, e-mail increases the likelihood of conflict and miscommunication. However, people who know each other well are less likely to misinterpret online communication because they are familiar with the communication context. But what happens when virtual groups have a task to complete and group members do not know one another? Clay Shirky, at New York University's interactive telecommunications program, believes that groups can be more successful if their members spend time meeting face to face. Once members become familiar with one another and begin discussing ways to accomplish their intended goal, future e-mail correspondences are more effective (Goleman, 2007). With more options for conducting online virtual meetings via video-streaming programs, face-to-face communication is now a relatively easy and inexpensive way for groups to communicate. Companies like IBM, Cisco Systems, Hewlett-Packard, and Hilton Worldwide increasingly rely on virtual events and get-togethers. In fact, approximately 60 percent of professional employees work in virtual teams (Kanawattanachai & Yoo, 2002), yet research indicates that groups report higher levels of work satisfaction when they used face-to-face interaction at least 10 percent of the time and computer-mediated communication less than 90 percent of the time (Johnson, Bettenhuasen, & Gibbons, 2009). Knowing this, it may be important for groups to spend some time meeting in person or through a video-streaming program such as Skype or FaceTime.

Language and Public Speaking

Politicians, musicians, cartoonists, radio personalities, and the like face situations in which their speeches, song lyrics, or print or video images are constantly scrutinized. What we communicate publicly can cost us our jobs, negatively affect our goals, or harm others. When we share our messages with the larger public, we want to be sure our communication is not plagiarized or offensive.

Plagiarism
Plagiarism can occur in almost every medium of communication, including public speeches, books, Web site content, song lyrics, and

cartoons. Critics accused Senator Paul Rand of plagiarism in several of his political speeches as well as in a book he wrote (Blake, 2013). According to a 2011 Associated Press Report, Rand plagiarized exact words and content from Wikipedia as well as a 2003 study conducted by the Heritage Foundation. Rand admitted he was occasionally "sloppy" in his work but claimed he cited the Heritage Foundation in his end notes. In 2015, Robin Thicke and Pharrell Williams were charged with violating copyright laws for their hit song "Blurred Lines," which the court determined to have "extrinsic and intrinsic similarities" to Marvin Gaye's 1977 single "Got to Give It Up." Gaye's children wrote in an open letter:

> Instead of licensing our father's song and giving him the appropriate songwriter credit, Robin Thicke and Pharrell Williams released "Blurred Lines" and then filed a preemptive lawsuit against us, forcing us into court. They sought to quickly affirm that their song was "starkly different," than "Got to Give It Up." The Judge denied their motion for Summary Judgement, and a jury was charged with determining the "extrinsic and intrinsic similarities" of the songs. . . . Mr. Thicke and Mr. Williams certainly have a right to be inspired by "Got to Give It Up" but as the jury ruled, they did not have the right to use it without permission as a blueprint for a track they were constructing. (Spanos, 2015)

However, no formal charges were ever made or definitive conclusions reached. Finally, Alan Gardner writing for *The Daily Cartoonist*, accused cartoonist David Simpson of copying a cartoon by the late Jeff MacNelly. The cartoon appeared to be a replica "to the point of tracing and re-drawing it for publication in the *Urban Tulsa* weekly publication" (Spurgeon, 2011). Simpson apologized, resigned from his position at the *Urban Tulsa*, and later lost his Oklahoma Cartoonist Hall of Fame honor (Gardner 2011a, 2011b). Plagiarizing the words or images of another is highly unethical. It not only denies other people the recognition they deserve but also misrepresents the skills and talents of the person doing the plagiarizing. Plagiarizing can call into question or significantly reduce someone's credibility. So, as you consider the speeches you will give publicly or the posts you might share on the Internet, make sure you are not plagiarizing the work of others.

Hate Speech

Some radio hosts and deejays have been known to make controversial on-air statements. Radio personalities Rush Limbaugh, Howard Stern, and Don Imus know just how powerful language can be, especially if their language is perceived as hateful. DJ Cipha Sounds (whose real name is Luiz Diaz) found himself in the hot seat for making insulting comments about Haitian women. While speaking on the air at Hot97, Sounds joked, "The reason I'm HIV negative is because

ETHICAL MOMENT

Free Speech and "You're Going to Hell"

The late minister Fred Phelps of the Westboro Baptist Church in Topeka, Kansas, gained notoriety for his public demonstrations in the last few years of his life. Beginning in the 1990s, members of his church publicly demonstrated against what they considered to be American "sins" such as homosexuality and adultery. On March 10, 2006, Phelps led a protest at the military funeral of "Matthew Snyder, who had been killed by an improvised explosive device (IED) while serving in Iraq" (Congressional Digest Corp., 2010). The protestors held signs condemning the United States, the Catholic Church, and the U.S. military (Congressional Digest Corp., 2010, p. 30). The church's signs featured slogans such as "God Loves IED's" and "Thank God for Dead Troops." Shirley Phelps-Roper, a spokesperson for the church, which has no affiliation with mainstream Baptists, explained: "Our goal is to help the nation connect the dots. You turn this nation over to the fags, and our soldiers come home in body bags" (Harris, 2006).

Snyder's father sued the church for defamation and was initially awarded millions of dollars in punitive damages. Westboro Baptist appealed, and the U.S. Fourth Circuit Court ruled that the protest speech was protected by the First Amendment. Ever since protesting at Snyder's funeral, Westboro Baptist members picketed hundreds of military funerals while carrying signs saying "Thank God for Dead Soldiers," "You're Going to Hell," and "God Hates Fags" (Burke, 2010). In addition, the church expanded its activities to include protests at nonmilitary funerals, other public events such as theater productions and graduation ceremonies, the U.S. Holocaust Museum in Baltimore, and the victims of a devastating tornado in Oklahoma. Even after Fred Phelps died in March 2014 of natural causes, Westboro Baptist members have continued to visit hundreds more cities and picketed more than 44,000 events. A picket has been scheduled for nearly every day of the week.

In addition to protesting in person at public events, the church's Web site contains derogatory comments about the deceased. After the death of Elizabeth Edwards, wife of former presidential candidate John Edwards, the Westboro Church's Web site stated that she "rode the talk show circuit spewing blasphemy" and "defied God, so she died, and went to hell. Suck it up!" (Westboro Baptist Church, 2010). Is this hate speech that should be stopped, or is the Westboro Baptist Church simply exercising its First Amendment rights? What constitutes hateful speech, personal opinion, or protected speech? Supreme Court Justice Stephen Breyer questions the lack of legal guidelines for posting personal attacks on the Internet. And the public also is at a loss not only about how to protect free speech but also about how to protect individuals.

Even without laws that prohibit such public protests and online personal attacks, several groups have formed to counterprotest Westboro's picketing. Two groups, the Patriot Riders and Line of Love, have attended funerals to protest in a different way. The Patriot Guard Riders attend funerals, but only at the request of the families of the deceased. This organization of approximately 10,000 members, both hawks and doves, forms a protective shield with motorcycles and American flags around grieving families, protecting the family from seeing and hearing the church protestors. When speaking of the group's presence at the funeral of a soldier killed by a roadside bomb in Iraq, Richard Wilbur, state captain of the group's Indiana chapter, summed up the Riders' purpose: to afford families some privacy and to honor what the soldiers died for—the right to protest. The Riders recognize the irony in the situation—that the members of the Westboro Baptist Church are also exercising their right to protest—but they feel their own methods show respect but the Westboro Baptists' methods do not. As Kurt Mayer, a founding member of the Patriot Guard Riders, explains, "We show families in grieving communities that America still cares" (Harper, 2006; Harris, 2006; Simmons, 2007).

Line of Love organized after learning of Westboro's planned protest at Elizabeth Edwards's funeral. The group appeared at her funeral to act as a human shield and provide a barrier between Westboro members and the funeral attendees. The Line of Love antiprotesters carried signs that read "Hope" and "Friend" while chanting "Love, not hate."

These examples illustrate the power of language, issues of social justice, and civility in both our content and relational messages to others. The Westboro members, the Patriot Guard Riders, and the Line of Love participants all believe there are specific rights and protections for public speech. Each group interprets these rights differently, however. Where do you stand on the issue?

What Do You Think?

1. What does free speech mean to you? Should speech that communicates uncivil ideas be protected as free speech or should it be restricted? Why do you think as you do?

2. Do you think the members of the Westboro Baptist Church are ethical and civil in their actions and words? Why or why not?

3. Are there events in which protesting should be banned?

I don't mess with Haitian girls." What Sounds claims he intended as a joke turned into an immediate suspension. After the station was flooded with phone calls from enraged listeners, the station's management announced that Sounds would undertake sensitivity training and that the station would work directly with the community to increase HIV awareness (Boyle, 2010). Still, many listeners called for Sounds to be fired.

Hate speech is now getting more attention on college campuses. Most recently, in March 2015, fraternity members of the Sigma Alpha Epsilon house at the University of Oklahoma received national attention for their use of hate speech after a video surfaced showing students on a bus clapping and pumping their fists while singing a song apparently learned a few years earlier at a national fraternity retreat. The most offensive lyrics were "There will never be a n****r SAE. You can hang him from a tree, but he can never sign with me" (McLaughlin, 2015). As a result, university president David Boren banned the fraternity from campus and expelled two students who could be identified in the video.

In 2011, the phrase "All N*****s Must Die" was written on the wall of a dormitory at Williams College. The hateful message spurred an investigation by the Williamstown Police Department and the college's administration. Two days later, the college president cancelled all classes and activities and asked the community to unite and begin the process of healing from the "horrible racist attack" (Vitchers, 2011).

Hate speech often portrays others as inferior and is an extreme form of uncivil and unethical language. Although some people may find the hateful words of radio personalities funny or dismiss racist graffiti as insignificant, this language has a serious negative affect on the individuals who are attacked. It also diminishes the public dialogue, preventing people from examining ideas and issues carefully, ethically, and with civility.

Because of the increasingly public nature of spoken and written words, speakers need to consider carefully the impact of their messages on their audiences and be careful to maintain the highest of ethical standards. With planning and practice, we can become successful public speakers who are adept at choosing the right words for the public-speaking audience and occasion. For more tips and information on creating an effective speech, see Part V (Chapters 10 through 15).

Language and Civility

Throughout this text, you are asked to consider the role of civil communication in our interactions with other people. To be sure, most of us honor and respect our nation's commitment to free speech, and we recognize the value of hearing the widest range of views on various issues as possible. However, as students of communication, we also want to consider both the civil and uncivil parts of our language and the call

It Begins With the Phrase "That's So Gay"

Gay teenagers in the United States probably face more challenges than other teenagers, especially during their middle and high school years. In 2010, five teenagers committed suicide within three weeks after being taunted, harassed, and shamed for their allegedly gay orientation. These deaths occurred all across the country. Fourteen-year old Jamey Rodemeyer took his own life after claiming he could not handle the verbal harassment he was getting at school and online. Many other teens were beaten because of assumptions people were making about their sexuality. If we look more closely at the situations leading up to these suicides and assaults, we can see just how powerful language can be. Perhaps it begins with the phrase "That's so gay." This common phrase is used by young and old alike to represent something as profoundly unacceptable in some fundamental way.

Some people believe the expression "That's so gay" has no real meaning, but others disagree. Freshman student Rebekah Rice discovered just how hurtful the phrase can be. After being teased for her Mormon background and asked if she had multiple moms, Rebekah replied, "That's so gay." She later found herself in the high school principal's office for using the phrase, and a note was placed in her permanent file. Rebekah's parents sued the school for violating her First Amendment rights. Rebekah herself claimed that she did not mean to intentionally insult gay people. Instead, she claims that she meant that asking her if she had multiple moms was "so stupid—that's so silly—that's so dumb" ("That's So Gay" 2007). Although Rebekah and her parents believe she was unfairly punished for using a phrase that is widely used by her peers, school officials took a different position. They argued that a strict

stand against hurtful language was needed after two boys were paid to beat up a gay student the previous year.

Teenagers are not the only ones to use the phrase. The movie *The Dilemma* was heavily criticized for using the phrase to make fun of an electric car. After Universal Pictures pulled the scene from the trailer and substituted a scene without the use of the term *gay*, director Ron Howard decided to keep the joke in the movie. When asked why he chose to keep the joke, Howard replied, "Our lead character . . . has a mouth that sometimes gets him into trouble, and he definitely flirts with the line of what's okay to say. He tried to do what's right but sometimes falls short. Who can't relate to that?" (Howard, 2010). Other celebrities have also been publicly ridiculed for making antigay remarks. Tracy Morgan, for example, claimed during a comedy routine that homosexuality is a choice and that he would kill his son if his son came out as gay. Morgan later issued a public apology and claimed his humor was not meant to hurt anyone (Hughes, 2011).

Shannon Gilreath, a law professor at Wake Forest University, disagrees. "Physical violence begins with bullying, name-calling and homophobic remarks. When nothing happens to someone [for making slurs], it escalates to violence" (Petrow, 2009). Judy Shepard knows all too well the violence that can result from homophobia. Two men beat her son, Matthew, to death for being gay. Judy Shepard is now an advocate for LGBTQ people and makes the following plea:

> Our young people deserve better than to go to schools where they are treated this way. We have to make schools a safe place for our youth to prepare for their futures, not be confronted with threats, intimidation

or routine disrespect. Quite simply, we are calling one more time for all Americans to stand up and speak out against taunting, invasion of privacy, violence and discrimination against these youth by their peers, and asking everyone in a position of authority in their schools and communities to step forward and provide safe spaces and support services for LGBT youth or those who are simply targeted for discrimination because others assume they are gay. (Shepard, 2010)

Shepard is one of many public figures now educating audiences about the powerful impact of uncivil language. She and others like her argue that we have the power to shape and alter the meaning of words; we also have the ability to stop using language that can be considered hateful or derogatory.

What Do You Think?

1. Make a list of phrases such as "That's so gay" that have been banned from schools or workplaces or that cast people in negative, unflattering, or demeaning ways. What groups of individuals might be harmed by these phrases? How might they be harmed? If you think that these phrases have little meaning, explain why.

2. If language is as powerful as Judy Shepard and others argue, what are some other terms and phrases we might use to replace the derogatory ones we currently use?

3. How might we begin to educate others on offensive speech? How can we respond when we hear our friends using hate speech?

---

for free speech. We want to be mindful of the language we use as we address others and to always consider whether our cultural commitment to saying whatever we want whenever we want also means that we must accept uncivil moments. As you have read in this chapter, our language is a powerful tool, and the ways we use language affects others, clarifies or confuses our messages, and communicates who we are and what we value. Consider the following case study and how civility and incivility play a role in your own communication.

Chapter Summary

The Nature of Language

- Language is governed by rules.
- Phonological, syntactic, and semantic rules help us to communicate effectively.
- Slang, jargon, euphemisms, and doublespeak can create confusion for listeners who are unfamiliar with the terms.
- Differences in cultural and co-cultural language can create difficulty in communicating effectively with one another.
- Gender can affect the way we communicate. Men and women often talk about different topics and use different strategies to communicate.
- Technology also influences our language choices. The ease and accessibility of communicating via the Internet, cell phones, and smartphones have affected the way we communicate.

Language and Interpersonal Communication

- The type of interpersonal relationship we have with another person will help determine the content and relational meanings of a message.

- Content and relational messages can be an important part in maintaining long-distance relationships.

Language and Small Group Communication

- Groups can be more successful when members spend some time meeting face to face.
- Virtual meetings via video-streaming programs now make face-to-face group communication relatively easy.

Language and Public Speaking

- Speakers need to carefully consider the effects of their messages on audiences.
- To maintain the highest ethical standards, speakers need to avoid plagiarism and hate speech.

Language and Civility

- Language can be used civilly and uncivilly to express our views. Competent communicators consider the civil and uncivil aspects of the language they use.

Key Concepts

acronym (80)

androgynous communicators (84)

colloquialisms (81)

connotative meanings (77)

cultural competence (81)

denotative meanings (77)

doublespeak (80)

equivocal words (78)

euphemisms (80)

jargon (79)

language (75)

phonology (75)

regionalisms (81)

semantics (76)

slang (79)

syntax (76)

Invitation to Human Communication Online

MindTap Speech includes an interactive MindTap Reader and interactive learning tools including National Geographic Explorer videos, student videos, quizzes, flashcards, and more. You can build your speech outline with Outline Builder and record, post, and watch videos with YouSeeU. Go to cengagebrain.com to access your MindTap for *Invitation to Human Communication* for access to these resources.

MindTap®

Further Reflection and Discussion

1. Can you think of an example of an incident in which you were talking with someone and heard him or her say the words in the wrong order and therefore did not say what he or she wanted to say? Did you correct this person? Why or why not?

2. Think of a word that has several definitions and share the word and its meanings with classmates. Compare the different definitions you shared. How similar or different are they?

3. What are some common slang words you and your friends use? Ask your parents what slang words they used when they were your age. Do you know what those words mean?

4. What words can you think of that make something sound unpleasant? Create euphemisms to make those words sound more appealing.

5. Give an example of a strategy you have noticed women (more than men) using to communicate. Now give an example of a strategy you notice men (more than women) use. What are the differences? What would happen if men used the strategies more commonly used by women and vice versa?

6. What games did you play growing up? What type of communication was necessary to play the game successfully? Do you continue to use those styles of communication today?

7. Observe different groups communicating with one another. For example, observe men communicating with other men, women communicating with women, and men and women communicating with one another. Pay attention to who speaks the longest, what topics are discussed, and who interrupts the most. Do your observations support the theories presented in this chapter? Discuss what you observed.

8. What type of technology or social-media site do you use the most to communicate with family and friends? In what ways has this technology helped or hurt your relationships?

9. Write five sentences in which you intentionally use poor syntax. Now, switch papers with a classmate and rewrite each sentence using proper syntax. Which sentences do you think communicate most clearly? Discuss why.

10. Prepare a speech about the damage hate speech can do, including three major arguments to support your thesis. Next, prepare a speech on the right to use hate speech, including three major arguments supporting that thesis.

Activities and Web Links

Visit cengagebrain.com to access the MindTap for *Invitation to Human Communication* where these activities and Web links can be found.

1. Watch this video clip from an episode of the television show *Friends*. What does it reveal about the difference in how men and women communicate? Are there things that the men in this clip should learn from how the women communicate? What might the women learn? Go to *Web link 4.1*.

2. Read this list of items for e-mail etiquette. Do you agree with all of the items on the list? Choose five that you feel are the most important and explain why. What does this list say about how technology has affected our communication? Go to *Web link 4.2*.

3. Boys and girls often learn what are "appropriate" toys for them based on their packaging, labels, and placement in stores. Listen to the girl in the video challenging the gender bias of toys. What toys do you believe are designed specifically for boys? What toys do you believe are designed for girls? How can manufacturers make gender-neutral toys? Go to *Web link 4.3*.

5

IN THIS CHAPTER YOU WILL LEARN TO:

- Explain the five reasons why listening can be beneficial.

- Understand why listening and hearing are different.

- Describe the different types of external and internal interference that hinder our ability to openly receive messages.

- Explain the different types of listening styles and how each is suited for different types of interactions.

- Summarize the four most common types of speaker interference.

- Discuss ways to listen critically and civilly to new ideas and information.

Listening

Jason Edwards/National Geographic

When we listen, we have the opportunity to learn something new and express value for another. In what ways will you be listening to others today?

The day after Thanksgiving is often called Black Friday because retailers finally become profitable for the year by opening early, starting holiday promotional sales, and offering customers their best deals. However, thanks to Dave Isay, founder of National Public Radio's StoryCorps, people are now being encouraged to do something other than shop on Black Friday: they are encouraged to "listen." Isay asks Americans to take an hour out of their day to record an interview and listen to the stories of a loved one. In fact, Isay believes so strongly in the value of listening that he created the National Day of Listening. Tens of thousands of Americans have participated by listening to the stories of their families, friends, and community members. Research shows that we actually spend a good portion of every day listening. During an average day of communicating, we spend 55 percent of the time listening followed by speaking (17 percent), reading (16 percent), and writing (11 percent) (Emanuel et al., 2008). You may be surprised to learn, however, that most people retain little of what they hear.

In this chapter, we explore why listening is important, why our listening sometimes fails, and how to listen carefully, critically, and ethically. Learning the importance of listening effectively and communicating clearly can improve our relationships with others and teach us about ourselves.

Why Listening Is Important

Until now, you may not have considered the importance of effective listening. However, there are five important reasons why being "good" at listening can benefit us and our communities: listening helps confirm others, helps us understand, helps us learn, promotes civic engagement, and promotes social justice.

Listening Helps Confirm Others

Communication is a central component of building and maintaining relationships with others. For communication to be successful, we must first be willing to truly listen to others. *Listening in order to recognize, acknowledge, and express value for another person* is the process of **confirming**. The process of confirming lets others know that you are paying attention and acknowledging their message.

Listening Helps Us Understand

When we pay close attention to a message, we want to *understand* what someone is attempting to communicate. The goal of understanding a message provides us the opportunity to ask questions that seek clarification or more information.

confirming
listening in order to recognize, acknowledge, and express value for another person.

NATIONAL GEOGRAPHIC EXPLORER TIP ↗

DAN WESTERGREN/National Geographic Creative

Aziz Abu Sarah,
Emerging Explorer and Cultural Educator

Tell us about an experience where active listening made a difference in one of your speaking engagements. For example, did someone in the audience tell a story that you listened to that changed your thinking or how you made your next presentation?

When we speak to groups or individuals, the most important thing is to be able to listen—and not only to listen to the words. We have to listen to what is behind the words. We use active listening because there's an emotional component to what people are saying. So we listen to why they are upset, why they're angry, why they're ashamed, why they're sad or happy about what was just shared. And by doing that we avoid a lot of fights and unproductive conversations.

For example, when I was speaking in an Israeli classroom just a couple months after a suicide bombing had happened, I was speaking with an Israeli partner of mine. We told our stories and how we should try to overcome anger, bitterness, and hatred and begin to work together. But one of the students was very, very angry. And he interrupted us throughout the speech and was pretty verbally violent. And so we stopped, and we asked him to tell us what was bothering him. And eventually he shared that his uncle was in a suicide bombing just a couple months earlier, and he was very angry, and he had never met a Palestinian before. I was the first Palestinian he had met, and all his anger just came at me. He shared how he was just waiting to get a chance for revenge. But we started this conversation, and it ended up going on for a couple of hours, and we just listened. We listened to his position, and we learned where he was coming from, and we heard his pain. I think he needed somebody from the other side to yell at. And for me, that was fine. I think he needed to get all his emotions out, because after that we ended up having a very productive conversation. And at the end of our conversation, he said that he—although he was confused because he had a chance to say everything he wanted to say and because we listened—he was not as angry as he was earlier. And without us listening to the emotions and the pain, I think that would have been impossible to get to that point.

Listening Helps Us Learn

When we listen, we have the ability to learn important information. We may discover more about the likes and dislikes of our friends and family members, how to master a new skill, or the positions held by political candidates during an election campaign. In each situation, the process of listening allows us to grow as individuals because we learn new things.

Listening Promotes Civic Engagement

Listening can provide us the information we need to identify and address issues of public concern. When we listen, we can make informed decisions about the positions we hold on contentious issues, candidates we support for public or political office, and practices that may benefit or harm our families, workplaces, communities, states, countries, and continents.

The Listening Project: What Does the World Think of America?

How well do you think you can listen to what others think of you? Asking the question, "What do you think of America?" four "listeners" traveled to fourteen different countries to hear the answers. Carrie Lennox (seventh-grade history teacher), Bob Roeglin (corrections), Bao Phe (spoken word artist and poet), and Han Shan (trainer of grassroots youth activists) traveled around the globe to ask common people "What's wrong" and "What's right with America?" They made a commitment to be curious and listen to the answers. The result was the documentary and award-winning film *The Listening Project* (2008).

The producers of the film explain: "We had our own very strong feelings about the Unites States and its place in the world. How do you set that aside? How do you set aside your own personal views and really try to go out and very objectively talk to people and be able to really listen" to views you might not agree with? But the producers and the "listeners" made that commitment.

Here is a little of what they heard, when they asked, "When I say 'America' or 'American,' what's the first thing that pops into your head?"

"There is a Japanese saying: To criticize is to help . . ."

"America really influences the world . . ."

"America is what gives to you with one hand and then takes away with both."

"I love America, and I hate America."

"Most Americans don't understand how we live where we live and what is going on. We are not a terrorist people."

"In America, there is a sense that if you've got drive and ambition, you can make it."

"America's role always been to try and make peace."

"You have always been so much involved with wars."

"The Greeks and the Romans—America should learn from history."

"The world is one, one, two, three: there we all are."

"Does it really make you so happy to drive home in your Beemer and go out again in your Lexis?"

"There is a saying: 'God has given you two ears and one mouth to listen more than speak.'"

Source: The Listening Project documentary (http://thelisteningprojectfilm.com/).

What Do You Think?

1. What listening skills do you think *The Listening Project* listeners might have used to really listen to the people they spoke with?
2. Have you been in a situation in which you listened to things you agreed with and did not agree with? What listening strategies did you use?
3. If you could go around and ask people a question with a commitment to hearing answers you might not agree with, what would that question be?

Listening allows us to be more fully engaged with our communities, organizations, and political concerns.

Listening Promotes Social Justice

Listening can provide the means to create social change. When we listen to stories of injustice such as cases of homelessness, poverty, hunger, discrimination, or bullying, we have the ability to recognize how we can act to improve the lives of those who are experiencing hardship or injustice. When we confirm, learn, understand, and engage with others, our listening helps us sort out complex ethical, moral, and social issues that affect the people we live and work with, as well as those we may not come in direct contact with. David Harrison, a linguist who travels internationally to interview and record vanishing languages, explains that listening to the stories of indigenous people has helped him better understand their perspective of having their resources controlled and their property rights denied.

After listening to a ten-minute oral presentation, the average person understands and retains only 50 percent of the information presented. Forty-eight hours after the presentation, those same listeners only remember 25 percent of the information (Steil, Barker, &Watson 1993). Imagine that you could improve your listening skills. You would be able to participate in the public dialogue of your communities on topics you had learned about in school, work, and through news media. You would acknowledge value for another person's ideas by paying attention to their presentations. You might even improve your grades by recalling more information on exams. In fact, research shows that effective listening can lead to more positive teacher–student relationships (Wolvin & Coakley, 2000).

Facts About Listening

You may have heard that listening and hearing are not the same thing. Did you know that listening is not a natural process? It takes effort and understanding to listen effectively.

Listening Is Not the Same as Hearing

Although some people believe hearing and listening are the same thing, the two processes are actually quite different. **Hearing** refers to the *vibrations of sound waves on our eardrums and the resulting impulses that travel to the brain*. Hearing is a passive process. Assuming a person does not have a hearing impairment or an object blocking the eardrum, sound waves will automatically transmit to the brain. We hear many sounds and noises throughout the day without paying much attention to them. We may hear the sound of an air conditioner turning on, a car driving down the street, or people murmuring in the distance. We typically pay little attention to these sounds. **Listening**, on the other hand, *is the process of giving thoughtful attention to another person's words and understanding what we hear*. This occurs when we focus on a teacher's presentation, pay attention to our friend confiding in us, or attempt to understand the messages delivered through the media.

Listening Is Not a Natural Process

Many people believe listening is a natural process, something that occurs without a great deal of effort. However, the process of listening is more complex than the act of physically receiving messages. The act of listening actually requires effort. Notice that the definition of listening contains the phrase "giving thoughtful attention" to another. The act of listening is an active but not necessarily natural process. When listening, we must focus, attempt to understand, and respond to what others are saying.

Listening Is Influenced by Culture

Our ability to listen effectively also depends on our culture. In literate cultures, like the United States, information is written down, recorded, and stored. Therefore, the need to listen carefully to and remember information may become secondary to writing and storing the information. Harrison (2015b) claims "we have lost our ability to memorize simple things like phone numbers now that we can store those numbers in our phones." Oral cultures, on the other hand, rely solely on the ability to listen effectively in order to pass information from generation to generation. Listening becomes the only way to access language. In oral cultures, it is not uncommon for storytellers to memorize 10,000 lines. Harrison reminds us that our own worldview is culturally filtered until we try to access the world through a different cultural filter or a different language.

hearing
vibrations of sound waves on our eardrums; the impulses then travel to the brain.

listening
process of giving thoughtful attention to another person's words and understanding what you hear.

Why We Sometimes Fail to Listen

Think about recent situations in which you were expected to listen. Were you willing to confirm some people but not others? Similarly, were you able to understand some speakers but not able to follow others? Michael Nichols, a listening researcher, claims that "listening is so basic that we take it for granted." Yet, listening requires that we "pay attention, take an interest, care about, take to heart, validate, acknowledge . . . and appreciate" (Nichols, 2009, p. 12).

We often fail at listening for many reasons. **Listening interference** is *anything that stops or hinders a listener from receiving a message.* Although interference can be external to the listener (such as noises that capture our attention or visual distractions), there are also many forms of internal interference (distracting thoughts or feelings) that keep us from openly receiving a message. We explore the most common of kinds of interference here.

Pseudolistening

Pseudolistening occurs *when listeners act like they are listening or pretend to be paying close attention to the message.* Pseudolisteners appear to be focused on the speaker. They make eye contact, provide nonverbal feedback such as nodding in agreement or smiling at the appropriate times, and genuinely seem interested in the message; however, pseudolisteners are actually distracted by other thoughts. Internally, these listeners are thinking of other things (or not thinking much at all) instead of actually focusing on the speaker's message. Pseudolistening occurs when listeners are bored, disinterested, or preoccupied with other thoughts.

Selective Listening

Selective listening occurs *when listeners only pay attention to particular parts or sections of a message.* Selective listeners may tune out commercials or only pay attention to those parts of a longer message that seem most interesting to them. They may turn the radio on only to listen closely to the weather report or road conditions. In class, selective listeners may perk up and pay close attention after a teacher says, "Be sure to write this down," or "This will likely be on the test," and then tune out again after they get the information. When listening to a lengthy speech such as the State of the Union address, selective listeners may only listen to the parts of the speech that directly and immediately affect their lives and selectively tune out other parts.

Defensive Listening

Defensive listeners *perceive a message as a personal attack or form of criticism.* A person who listens defensively makes the judgment that the speaker does not like or respect him or her.

listening interference
anything that stops or hinders a listener from receiving a message.

pseudolistening
when listeners act like they are listening or pretend to be paying close attention to the message.

selective listening
when listeners only pay attention to particular parts or sections of a message.

Listening requires effort on the part of the listener. What signs are these two people giving that indicate they are actively listening to one another?

Golden Pixels LLC/Shutterstock.com

Employees of Different Generations Working Together

Generation Y (born in the 1980s and 1990s) consists of approximately 71 million young people who are tapped into technology and media and have now entered the workforce. This means that three generations—baby boomers (born 1946–1964), Generation X (born 1965–1980), and Generation Y—are working together (Belkin, 2007). Each generation brings different values and expectations to the workplace, and these differences may be the cause of workplace conflict. According to a report by Lee Hecht Harrison (n.d.), more than 60 percent of employers say they experience tension between employees of different generations. Although the differences in expectations are neither right nor wrong, they illustrate some of the challenges that multiple generations face when working together.

To help reduce potential workplace conflict, members of each generation do the following:

1. **Learn what each generation values in the workplace.** For example, baby boomers may be more conservative, have a strong work ethic, and value discipline. Members of Generation Y are continuously connected to technology, accustomed to instant feedback, and comfortable with virtual problem solving. Recognizing what each generation of workers values can help improve communication and team building.

2. **Respect the contribution and skills exhibited by each generation.** Harrison found that more than 70 percent of older employees are dismissive of younger workers' abilities. And nearly half of employers say that younger employees are dismissive of the abilities of their older co-workers. Acknowledging the different contributions made by each generation can help improve employee relationships.

3. **Listen to co-workers.** In the workplace, listening is used three times more often than speaking and four to five times more often than reading or writing (Grognet & Van Duzer, 2002–2003), so it is important that employees listen effectively and ethically to their co-workers. When we really listen to what others have to say, we can begin to understand their viewpoint more fully, reduce workplace differences, and show civility to our colleagues.

What listening behaviors do these students exhibit? What type of listeners would you describe them as?

Ariel Skelley/Blend Images/Getty Images

defensive listener
listener who perceives a message as a personal attack or a form of criticism.

ambushing
listening carefully to information in order to attack what the speaker has to say.

insulated listener
listener who purposefully avoids listening to specific pieces of information.

Defensive listeners also assume there are negative motives behind the communication act. A student who is worried about his grade in class may listen defensively when a teacher asks about absences or reasons for late assignments. A teenager may listen defensively when parents ask questions about her day, hearing the questions as expressions of mistrust rather than curiosity or interest. Defensive listeners assume others are being mean spirited, even when that is not the speaker's intention, and they hear comments and questions as challenges or demonstrations of a lack of respect.

Ambushing

Ambushing is *listening carefully to information in order to attack what the speaker has to say.* When prosecutors cross-examine witnesses in court, they often use ambushes to attack what a witness has said. Politicians may ambush during a debate when they listen to an opponent and then attack his or her arguments. In our interpersonal relationships, we sometimes listen to those we are in a conflict with to find ways to attack their reasons or arguments rather than understand them.

Insulated Listening

Insulated listening is *purposefully avoiding listening to specific pieces of information.* It is the opposite of selective listening: instead of listening to key parts of information, insulated listeners will ignore any undesirable topic that arises. For example, when a parent explains the reasons a teenager needs a curfew or when a roommate provides several reasons why making a chore chart can help keep the apartment clean and the division of labor fair, the teenager or roommate may decide she or he does not want to listen to the explanations and insulates her- or himself by ignoring those reasons.

Insensitive Listening

An **insensitive listener** *pays attention to the content or literal meaning of the message but not the relationship level of the meaning.* When listeners fail to acknowledge the relationship level or other subtle meanings in a message, they are insensitive to others' feelings about the topic. For example, Ivy tells her professor that she will be missing two weeks of class because her mother is having major surgery and needs additional help at home. Hoping for a sympathetic response, Ivy is surprised when her professor states that the absences will not be excused and she should plan to e-mail the assignments so they will not be graded as late. Ivy feels the professor is insensitive by not showing concern for her new responsibility at home and her mother's well-being.

Technology provides us the opportunity to learn about different cultures. In what ways can technology help or hinder our ability to listen to and learn about others?

Jack Daulton/Enduring Voices Project/National Geographic Creativity

Stage Hogging

Stage hogging occurs *when people make the conversation about themselves instead of showing interest in the person who is talking.* Stage hogging can occur in two ways. First, it occurs when a person redirects the conversation back to him- or herself. For example, when you share with a friend your dismay at having your hours cut at work and are hoping for sympathy and even solutions to cope with smaller paychecks, your friend is stage hogging if she laments the fact that she never has enough money to do the things she wants and does not respond to your concerns. Stage hogging also happens when a person interrupts another to focus attention back on her- or himself. For example, Stan wants to share what happened at last night's hockey game with Omar. Stan begins his story only to find that Omar interrupts to tell him about all the outstanding hockey games he has been to, hogging the stage and never making time for Stan to finish his story. Stage hogging can negatively affect relationships because the person who began to share something feels his or her opinions are not being heard or validated.

Technology

Although technology can open up avenues for listening to others, when it surrounds us we can easily fail to listen. The amount of new technology available has changed the way we listen to others (Bentley, 2000). Text messaging during class or at work, surfing the Internet with our laptops instead of listening to a spouse or co-worker, participating in multiple online chat discussions at the same time, or walking across campus with our earphones on can prevent us from listening to others. This can have serious negative consequences: we miss important information, fail to hear what others are

insensitive listener
listener who pays attention to the content or literal meaning of the message but not the relationship level of the meaning.

stage hogging
when people make the conversation about themselves instead of showing interest in the person who is talking.

Bob Pool/Getty Images

Many people "listen" best by seeing something in order to understand it. Others understand best when they hear something explained. What mode of listening suits you best?

saying to us, ignore friends who might be trying to get our attention, or even fail to hear important sounds, such as sirens, trains, or horns.

Differences in Listening Styles

Consider the following examples:

- Loretta loved her geology class. She was excited to spend class time touching and examining samples of rocks and minerals as her professor lectured. On field trips, she eagerly stood in front of the group, exploring the different soils and formations with her hands. When she studied for an exam, she could visualize the soil, rock, or mineral and remember its content and formation process.

- Phillip is a nutrition major. He enjoys learning about different nutrients that help the body grow and develop. Although Phillip's nutrition courses require him to read several textbooks on the subject, Phillip learns best when he hears his professor discuss the information in detail. When Phillip tells his parents what he is learning at school, he often repeats much of the information he has heard in class.

- Sierra was an art history major. She enjoyed taking art history courses from the professors in the department who showed examples of the different artists' work. Sierra knew that without actually seeing the artwork, she would struggle to understand the different periods and their artists. For Sierra, seeing was the easiest way to learn.

The students described here "listen" in different ways. Loretta is an **experiential listener**. She *learns best when she can touch, explore, and participate in what is being described.* She is the type of person who often says, "Let me try that," in order to learn the material. In the second example, Phillip is the "explain it to me" person. He is an **auditory listener** because he *needs to hear verbal descriptions and explanations.* Even if he reads the textbook, he understands the material better after hearing the professor talk about it. In the final example, Sierra *needs to see something to understand it* because she is a **visual listener**. Visual listeners often use the phrase "Show me" in order to fully comprehend new information (Kolb, 1984; Sims & Sims, 1995).

Jack Daulton and Roz Ho elicit and record Pingelapese words with Leilani Welley-Biza. What styles of listening are these people displaying? Are they people-oriented, content-oriented, action-oriented, or time-oriented listeners? What cues give you this sense?

Our senses can determine how we best listen and comprehend information: some of us prefer to touch, others to listen, and still others to see in order to listen best. In addition to learning and listening through stimulating our senses, we also may listen for specific types of information. These *listening styles* depend on the context surrounding the act of listening.

Listening Styles

Each of us has an individual **listening style** or *preferred approach to understanding a message.* Some of us listen to enhance the quality of a relationship, but others may listen to obtain as much information and detail as possible before making an informed decision. Researchers have identified four primary listening styles, which we explore in the following paragraphs (Johnson, Weaver, Watson, & Barker, 2000).

A **people-oriented listener** is *concerned about other people's feelings and emotions as well as the quality of the interpersonal relationship.* Individuals who use a people-oriented listening style can "read" others' emotions, so they focus on the emotional and relational aspects of the message. Listeners adopting this style tend to notice peoples' moods, understand the emotional meaning of a message, and display empathy toward other people. Although people-oriented listeners tend to be less apprehensive about communicating in groups and interpersonal situations, they may lose their ability to critically reflect on the information presented (Chesebro, 1999; Johnston et al., 2000; Sargent, Weaver, & Kiewitz, 1997).

Content-oriented listeners *pay close attention to the facts and details of a message.* Content listeners obtain as much information as possible about an issue. They excel at understanding and analyzing various positions on a topic. They take time to collect information, giving priority to expert opinions and other credible resources. They ask pointed questions, dismiss unreliable facts, and explore as many perspectives and points of view as they can. Content-oriented individuals often play the role of devil's advocate as a way to obtain information and explore different viewpoints, thus taking time before coming to a conclusion. There are many advantages to this approach, but it also can create an environment that seems

experiential listener
listener who learns best by touching, exploring, and participating in what is being described.

auditory listener
listener who needs to hear verbal descriptions and explanations.

visual listener
listener who needs to see something in order to understand it.

listening style
preferred approach to understanding a message.

people-oriented listener
listener who is concerned about the feelings and emotions of other people as well as the quality of interpersonal relationships.

content-oriented listener
listener who pays close attention to the facts and details of a message.

PRACTICING HUMAN COMMUNICATION

How Can You Listen More Effectively?

Take a few minutes to evaluate your listening skills.

1. Describe when you felt the most engaged with a face-to-face conversation this week. What was engaging about the conversation? Did you or the other person exhibit active listening?

2. At what point in the face-to-face communication did you feel most distant from what was happening? Explain the type of interference you were experiencing or other reasons why you felt distanced.

3. Consider what your responses indicate about your listening style and preferences. Also notice what types of interference may hinder your ability to listen. Now consider what you can do to listen more effectively in face-to-face communication (Brookfield, 1995).

disruptive, hostile, or even threatening to others if not used carefully.

Unlike content-oriented listeners who enjoy taking their time to learn about multiple perspectives on a topic, **action-oriented listeners** *want speakers to provide clear, detailed, and straight-to-the-point information.* Action-oriented listeners want to take care of business and are listening specifically for the information necessary to accomplish a task. They may grow impatient if a speaker includes nonessential information, digresses, or follows a tangent. Action-oriented listening can be an important part of getting a task completed, but these listeners may also avoid acknowledging important emotional concerns or cues of the message.

Time-oriented listeners *view time as a commodity and do not want to have it wasted.* These listeners, similar to action-oriented listeners, *want speakers to be clear, succinct, and to the point.* However, unlike action-oriented listeners, time-oriented listeners may set time guidelines for conversations or use particular behaviors to indicate their desire to end an interaction. Time-oriented listeners may verbalize that they only have "10 minutes to meet," may constantly check their watches, or may even abruptly end conversations. This listening style can be quite effective in meeting deadlines, but it can also make speakers feel uncomfortable or insulted if they feel rushed to deliver their message.

Although most of us have a distinct listening style, or at least two strong listening preferences, it is important to consider which listening style is best suited for different types of interactions. Because the four listening styles each have distinct advantages and disadvantages, one may be more appropriate than another for the context of a specific communication act. For example, you may be an action-oriented listener in class when an instructor is explaining a new assignment and then become a people-oriented listener when your roommate reveals that her romantic relationship just ended. If you were to approach the roommate's breakup with a time- or action-oriented approach, then you might unintentionally hurt her feelings. Similarly, if you approach your instructor's explanation from a people-oriented style, you may cause considerable confusion or even humor in the discussion.

 ## Speaker Interference

As you have learned, listeners have difficulty understanding and remembering information presented to them for many reasons. Listener interference and listening styles are two of them. However, sometimes

action-oriented listener
listener who wants speakers to provide clear, detailed, and straight-to-the-point information.

time-oriented listener
listener who views time as a commodity and does not want to have it wasted and wants speakers to be clear, succinct, and to the point.

listeners have difficulty listening to a message because of speaker interference. To understand listening and how to minimize speaker interference, whether we are listeners or speakers, we will now explore the four most common types of speaker interference.

Interference Caused by Information

Sometimes we simply stop paying attention to a message. Perhaps the speaker talked for a long time without taking a break, the information was too technical to understand, or you were bored with the simplicity of the message. Communication that is drawn out, overly complicated, or too simple can create interference. When we experience interference from the information itself, we are likely to just give up listening. There are three types of information interference: message overload, message complexity, and message simplicity.

How much time do you spend communicating with others during the average day?

Message Overload Klemmer and Snyder's classic study (1972) indicates that we spend an average of 70 percent of our day in some form of communication: attending meetings or class, talking or texting on the phone, reading or listening to the news. Today's college students spend a large portion of their day attending classes and listening to professors present information for fifty minutes, seventy-five minutes, or even two-and-a-half hours. Yet research indicates that adult learners are unable to stay focused for more than fifteen to twenty minutes at a time—so we often are subjected to message overload (Johnstone & Percival, 1976; Middendork & Kalish, 1996).

In addition to listening to information presented in class, students are often required to conduct their own research to complete assignments. But sometimes our initial research into a subject yields hundreds or thousands of results for our keyword search, and we have to deal with yet another form of information overload. Then we consume many messages outside of our responsibilities as students. We communicate at work, likely have the television turned on while we are at home, listen to the radio in the car, surf the Web, or pay attention to our cell phones for incoming messages all day. Most of the time, we simply cannot absorb this much information throughout our day. As our attention shifts between various messages, our ability to listen effectively decreases (Wallis, 2006).

Message Complexity When information is presented that is too complicated for us to understand, we likely give up on listening. Imagine the following scenario.

You walk into a biology class and the professor says, "Axonal signals transiently activate the expression of the transcription factor Oct6 in Schwann cells that will form myelin, and cyclic adenosine monophosphate can mimic axonal contact in vitro" ("Understanding Scientific Jargon," n.d.). Undoubtedly, you already feel behind on the material and consider dropping the class.

When messages are too complex for us to understand, we may decide to focus our attention elsewhere. When this happens, we can jeopardize our education, friendships, or ability to learn. On the other hand, speakers should take into account audience knowledge on the subject. At times, defining terms, providing examples, or showing visual representations of the information can help listeners stay focused.

Message Simplicity When information is too simple for the audience, listeners may become bored and stop listening. Consider the following examples:

- Martin was asked to deliver an informative speech in class, and he chose to present a speech titled "How to Make a Peanut Butter and Jelly Sandwich."

- Jacki was asked to coach the women's varsity basketball team and began the first practice by explaining the different positions on the court.

- Jorge was invited to speak to a group of computer scientists and informed them about the history of computers.

In each of these situations, the messages were too simple for the audience. When listeners already possess the information, they can become bored or easily distracted. As speakers, we need to make sure our information is appropriate for our audience and neither too complex nor too simplistic.

Interference Caused by Language

Interference can also be caused by language that is unclear. Language that is too formal, too casual, too noninclusive, or too cluttered makes it easy for listening to fail.

Too Formal As discussed in Chapter 4, jargon refers to *technical language used by professional groups.* It can be confusing for listeners who do not know what a particular word or acronym means. Imagine listening as your doctor tells you that "if you experience pain in your upper quadrant then you can take medicine PRN." When language is too formal, the message becomes difficult to understand.

Too Casual If language is too casual, it also can be difficult to listen to. It is easy to fall into our familiar, everyday language patterns, which may be too casual for our audience. One common way for language to be too casual is the use of slang or *informal nonstandard language.* A teenager telling her parents that the "band raised the roof with one totally sick song after another" and a student saying, "She was hotting me up," as a way to describe someone interfering in his business are clearly using slang that is confusing to some people. When our language is too casual, people may not be able to follow the ideas we are communicating or may feel uncomfortable.

Noninclusive Language Listening can break down when you use *noninclusive* language or language that refers only to certain groups of people. When people hear language that excludes those who are not in the "in-group," they may be offended and tune out. Common examples of noninclusive language are *chairman, mailman,* and *policeman* (inclusive language would be *chair, mail carrier,* and *police officer*). **Spotlighting** or the *practice of highlighting a person's race, ethnicity, sex, sexual orientation, or physical disability* also can be a form of noninclusive language. When we spotlight, we describe a friend as an "Asian American friend," a professor as a "gay professor," or a neighbor as a "disabled neighbor." Spotlighting is often used by members of the dominant

spotlighting
practice of highlighting a person's race, ethnicity, sex, sexual orientation, or physical disability.

culture to mark differences as being atypical or unusual; most of the time, marking difference is intended to mean that something is surprising or abnormal.

Sometimes, however, including cultural differences is important. When talking about pay equity in the workplace, it is important to recognize that Asian American women earn approximately 88 percent of what white men earn, whereas African American women earn approximately 70 percent and Latina women approximately 61 percent of what white men make (Villeneuve, 2012; White House, 2012). In this example, spotlighting illustrates important racial and cultural differences.

When you avoid spotlighting while using culturally inclusive and gender-inclusive language, you communicate that you are aware of diversity. Use language that is respectful of the diverse people you are speaking with; this will make listening easier for everyone.

Verbal Clutter Sometimes we have difficulty listening when people use **verbal clutter** or *extra words in sentences that do not add meaning*. Although listeners can mentally process more words per minute than speakers can speak (on average, a speaker speaks at a rate of 125 to 175 words per minute, but an active listener can process between 350 and 450 words per minute), verbal clutter impedes listening because listeners have to process words that are unnecessary or redundant (Wolvin & Coakly, 1996). Examples of verbal clutter include words and phrases such as *like, um, you know*, and *stuff like that*. These commonly used words and phrases distract listeners and add no useful meaning.

Similarly, verbal clutter also consists of loading our speech with adjectives and adverbs. Consider the following cluttered sentences and their uncluttered alternatives:

Cluttered: "Good, effective writers use carefully selected, well-planned, and detailed descriptions and stories to vividly portray images and ideas."

Uncluttered: "Effective writers use vivid stories to present their ideas."

The uncluttered example is easier to listen to and understand. To reduce clutter in our communication, we can ask ourselves, do the words we use help develop our ideas or make more work for the listener? How many of our words are redundant?

Interference Caused by Differences

Differences between a listener and a speaker can also cause interference with listening. Although we are all similar in many ways, no two people exactly match in appearance, mannerism, values, or background. When we confront differences, we may want to place value on or see those differences on a hierarchy. When we interpret differences as "right" or "wrong," "good" or "bad," we will have trouble focusing on the message. Four types of differences are common: speech style, appearance, values, and background and occupation.

Speech Style Accents, tonal and rhythmic qualities, stuttering, and speech patterns of nonnative speakers can affect our ability to listen.

verbal clutter
extra words in sentences that do not add meaning.

When we are unfamiliar with these styles, we may have a difficult time paying attention to the message.

Appearance Styles of dress, height, weight, hair color and style, body adornment, and even mannerisms can affect listening behaviors. When a person's appearance captures our attention, we may not be closely listening to the message.

Values When a listener holds values that differ from the speaker, listening can be difficult. If listeners are convinced that their values are right or best, then they often have trouble listening to understand why someone holds a different position.

Background and Occupation Differences in race, ethnicity, religion, education, occupation, upbringing, and economic status can affect our listening. If we hold assumptions or make judgments about people based on their backgrounds and occupations, we may forget to be open to listening to their experiences.

As listeners, we need to remember that *difference* simply means *different*. When we refrain from focusing on differences and remember to be open enough to listen to others, we can overcome interference caused by differences.

Interference Caused by Technology

The amount of technology constantly available to us can create interference. When a cell phone rings during class; a sporting event is broadcast on television, radio, or the Internet; or a new message is posted to our social media accounts, our attention can quickly turn from the person we are talking with to the technology. Today approximately 94 percent of college students and 75 percent of middle- and high-school students own cell phones (Burns & Lohenry, 2010; Reavy, 2008). With so many people carrying, talking, and texting on their phones, cell-phone etiquette has become an important topic of conversation. Shari Burns and Kevin Lohenry (2010) investigated cell-phone use in class and discovered that 73 percent of respondents admitted that their cell phones rang during class, and 84 percent of faculty claimed cell phones are a source of distraction during class time. Cell phones not only distract us as listeners but also distract others around us.

How to Listen Effectively

When we improve our listening skills, we increase the amount of information we comprehend and retain. To listen effectively, we must first overcome obstacles that interfere with our listening. A **careful listener** *overcomes listener interference in order to listen effectively to another person's message*. To reduce interference, try the following strategies:

- **Eliminate distractions**. Distractions may be external (auditory or visual distractions) or internal (distracting thoughts or feelings). Turn off your cell phone and commit yourself to focusing your

careful listener
listener who overcomes listener interference in order to listen effectively to another person's message.

K. David Harrison, National Geographic Explorer: "Let's Listen While We Still Can"

K. David Harrison is a linguist and leading specialist in the study of endangered languages. In addition to acting as co-leader of the Enduring Voices project with National Geographic Fellow Gregory Anderson, Harrison co-stars in the 2008 documentary film *The Linguists*. This film has been screened at the Sundance Film Festival and on college campuses across the United States. *The Linguists* is described as

> a fantastic little film that follows professors David Harrison and Gregory Anderson as they crisscross the globe on a mission to document languages on the verge of extinction. From the depths of Siberia to the high reaches of Bolivia, the pair is relentless in their goal, displaying a remarkable patience for interviewing deaf nonagenarians who are frequently the only surviving speakers [of a language]. . . . A two-man mission to document the world's endangered tongues becomes a fleet-footed study of human communication and its limitless structural and functional possibilities. (Harrison, 2015a)

Harrison believes there are many reasons to preserve vanishing languages. Most of the world's languages do not use writing; instead, they rely on their oral languages. Oral societies use cognitive skills and memory techniques to store information, and we can learn a lot by listening to them (Harrison, 2015a). These languages teach us how "ancestors calculated accurately the passing of seasons without clocks or calendars. How humans adapted to hostile environments, from the Artic to Amazonia" (Harrison, 2010). Yet preserving languages requires work. Designated "last speaker" of the Chemehuevi tribe of Arizona, Johnny Hill, Jr., says many children of his tribe claim they want to learn the language, "but when it comes time to do the work, nobody comes around." This leaves Hill feeling linguistically isolated. "There's nobody left to talk to, all the elders have passed on, so I talk to myself . . . that's just how it is" (Harrison, 2010).

Harrison and his team are willing to do the work of helping to preserve dying languages because they believe it to be the most consequential social trend for coming decades because "what they know—which we've forgotten or never knew—may some day save us." Harrison and Anderson are listening. Harrison says, "We hear their voices, now muted, sharing knowledge in 7,000 different ways of speaking. Let's listen while we still can" (Harrison, 2010).

WHAT DO YOU THINK?

1. What types of interference caused by differences do you believe Harrison faces when interviewing last speakers?

2. Explain how important listening effectively is for Harrison and his team.

3. What types of listening styles would be most valuable when listening to last speakers record their language?

111

attention on the person communicating. Avoid thinking of anything other than what the person is saying.

- **Use effective communication**. Although you may have the urge to interrupt and focus the conversation on yourself, avoid the tendency to dominate the discussion. Instead, ask questions that will help clarify information or demonstrate your understanding.

- **Offer feedback**. Providing appropriate and timely feedback is another important strategy for effective listening. Providing nonverbal feedback such as nodding your head in agreement, smiling at the right moment, and using direct body orientation (facing those who are speaking, maintaining a relaxed, alert, and open body position) can help ensure you are listening carefully to the speaker. In addition, offering verbal feedback can show others you are listening carefully to their message.

- **Paraphrase**. Restate the essence, or summary, of a person's message in your own words and then ask if you have summarized his or her ideas correctly. **Paraphrasing** helps to determine if you have understood the meaning of the message, and it shows the speaker you have been listening carefully.

- **Ask for clarification**. When you do not understand someone because of language, style, message complexity, or the like, respectfully ask for clarification.

How to Listen Critically

To listen critically means that you assess the strengths and weaknesses of someone's information. Listening critically does not mean that you immediately judge the person or message or listen to find fault with a message. Rather, a **critical listener** *listens for the accuracy of content and the implications of a message*. This means remaining open to new ideas, listening carefully to areas of disagreement, and considering how someone else's ideas affect oneself and one's community.

Guidelines for Critical Listening When we listen critically, we avoid making quick decisions about what is good or bad, right or wrong. Instead, we ask people appropriate questions about their ideas so we can more fully understand a message and explore areas of agreement or disagreement. To begin, we need to assess a person's credibility to decide if she or he has the authority to present information on the subject. Next, we need to analyze whether arguments presented were supported by sound evidence. Finally, we need to determine what effect a message has on our own lives or the lives of others:

- Does the person have the experience, expertise, or ability to access accurate information on the subject? Does he or she have a personal stake in the outcome leading to possible bias on the topic?

- How fully has the person developed an idea? Is the information based mostly on fact or on opinion? Where did the information come from? Is the information recent?

paraphrasing
restating the essence, or summary, of a person's message in your own words.

critical listener
listener who listens for accuracy of content and the implications of a message.

Listening to One Woman's Choice to Die With Dignity

Brittany Maynard had people across the United States listening to her story. At age twenty-nine, Maynard was diagnosed with stage 3 glioblastoma, a terminal brain cancer that causes excruciating pain before death. After carefully considering her diagnosis and prognosis, Maynard and her husband decided to move to Oregon in order to lawfully fulfill her wish to die with dignity.

Maynard's story is an important one for the public to listen to. Glioblastoma causes the brain to swell, ultimately leading to seizures, painful headaches, and the gradual loss of bodily functions. After Brittney began experiencing pain and seizures, she made a decision that she considered the only humane option provided to the terminally ill. Oregon is one of a small handful of states that allow terminally ill patients to take drugs to end their lives as long as patients meet certain criteria: they must be mentally competent to administer the drugs themselves, and two doctors must agree that patients have a terminal illness that will result in death within six months.

After making her decision, Maynard posted a YouTube video explaining her decision. More than 15 million viewers watched the video, and countless more followed her story on Facebook. Many people find Oregon's Death with Dignity Act a comforting option that can prevent needless suffering, but not all citizens agree with it. Opponents of assisted suicide mourned Maynard's death, and they criticized the manner in which her illness and death became the focus of a new media campaign to force legislators to make assisted suicide part of their political agenda. Other opponents argue that people with disabilities and the elderly may feel coerced into making the decision. The differences of opinion on the topic of dying with dignity are clear reminders of the importance of listening.

What Do You Think?

1. How might people-oriented and content-oriented listeners respond to Maynard's story?

2. Explain how interference caused by differences in values create opposing arguments for the Die with Dignity Act.

3. Why is the process of listening civilly important to the discussion of dying with dignity?

- How does the information fit with what you know to be true? What information is new? What are the implications of the message for you and your community?

Listening critically means that we ask a series of questions to determine someone's credibility, the quality of the material provided, and the implications for the ideas presented. When we are committed to asking questions first, we are less likely to judge a person's ideas before we listen to the complete message.

How to Listen Civilly

A **civil listener** is open to hearing different views and perspectives, even when there is disagreement. Listening civilly does not mean that we have to agree with someone, be persuaded that she or he is correct, or remain silent about our own views. Instead, when we listen civilly we consider views that are different from our own and try to understand those views. When we understand a viewpoint more fully, we can engage in productive conversations about disagreements in our relationships, workplace differences, community challenges, or global concerns.

When we listen civilly, we compare and contrast our beliefs and values with others. By fully listening to other perspectives, we may gain a clearer sense of who we are and what we believe. We may be able to learn about and participate in the discussion of local, state, national, and international issues.

civil listener
listener who is open to hearing different views and perspectives, even when there is disagreement.

Chapter Summary

Listening Is Important for Several Reasons

- Listening allows us to confirm others, understand a message, and learn something new.
- Listening also provides us the opportunity to become engaged citizens and possibly work toward improving our communities, relationships, and workplaces.

It Is Important to Understand the Misconceptions about Listening

- The idea that listening is a natural process is not accurate; it takes effort to listen.
- The belief that listening and hearing are the same is also a misconception. Hearing is the physiological process that takes place when sound waves travel in our eardrums; listening is paying close attention to another's words.

We Sometimes Fail to Listen for Three Primary Reasons

- Differences in listening styles and preferences (experiential listeners, auditory listeners, visual listeners, people-oriented listeners, content-oriented listeners, action-oriented listeners, and time-oriented listeners) can impede our ability to understand others.
- There are many types of listener interference that hinder our ability to understand a message fully: pseudolistening, selective listening, defensive listening, ambushing, insulated listening, insensitive listening, stage hogging, and technology.
- Failing to listen can also be caused by speaker interference because of information, language, differences, and technology.

There Are Several Ways to Improve Our Listening

- To listen effectively, we must overcome obstacles that interfere with our ability to listen to others.
- To listen critically, we need to assess the strengths and weaknesses of a person's message.
- To listen civilly, we need to remain open to new ideas and information, even when we may disagree with those ideas.

Key Concepts

action-oriented listener (106)

ambushing (102)

auditory listener (105)

careful listener (110)

civil listener (113)

confirming (97)

content-oriented listener (105)

critical listener (111)

defensive listener (102)

experiential listener (105)

hearing (100)

insensitive listener (103)

insulated listener (102)

listening (100)

listening interference (101)

listening style (105)

paraphrasing (111)

people-oriented listener (105)

pseudolistening (101)

selective listening (101)

spotlighting (108)

stage hogging (103)

time-oriented listener (106)

verbal clutter (109)

visual listener (105)

Invitation to Human Communication Online

MindTap Speech includes an interactive eBook and interactive learning tools including National Geographic Explorer videos, student videos, quizzes, flashcards, and more. You can build your speech outline with Outline Builder and record, post, and watch videos with YouSeeU. Go to cengagebrain.com to access your MindTap for *Invitation to Human Communication* where these resources can be found.

MindTap®

Further Reflection and Discussion

1. Do you ever hold more than one conversation at a time—for example, texting with a friend while also chatting online? Discuss experiences where you were able to listen well or not well in this situation. What is lost when holding two conversations at once? What might be gained?

2. Make a list of cell phone etiquette dos and don'ts. Compare them with others in your class and discuss the lists. Can you come to a consensus?

3. Think of a recent experience where your listening failed. What styles were you using? Was there speaker interference? How do you explain why your listening was ineffective?

4. Pay attention to your own listening behaviors in different situations. What types of confirming behaviors do you use to let others know you have been paying attention to them? What confirming behaviors do they use to acknowledge your message?

5. What types of listening interference do you experience the most while sitting in class? How can you work to overcome this type of interference?

6. Have a friend describe what he or she did this past weekend. Then, paraphrase the description. How accurate were you? What listening skills might you use to improve your paraphrasing?

7. Can you think of situations when it is better to listen more carefully than critically? Describe those situation and explain why listening carefully is more productive than listening critically.

8. Watch the news over the course of a week or more. What type of spotlighting do you hear in the news? Now listen to your friends and family for a week or more. What type of spotlighting do they use? What are the effects of this spotlighting?

9. Bring to class a newspaper editorial, opinion piece, or letter to the editor. Identify the verbal clutter that these authors have included. Now rewrite the sentences by removing the clutter. Which is easier to read and understand? Why?

10. Think of a time when interference caused miscommunication or conflict between you or someone. Now present a short speech in which you share with the class that miscommunication. Include a description of the setting, the events that took place, the reason(s) the interference occurred, and what you learned from the experience.

Activities and Web Links

Visit cengagebrain.com to access the MindTap for *Invitation to Human Communication* where these activities and web links can be found.

1. Watch this brief humorous video that depicts three people in a listening situation. What listening style does each person use? What types of interference do you notice? Go to *Web link 5.1*.

2. Watch this video clip that demonstrates self-centered listening. Now write a brief paragraph explaining what the self-centered listener might have said to show she was a skilled listener and communicator. Go to *Web link 5.2*.

3. Make a list of all the jargon used in your workplace or in your college major. For examples of jargon, go to *Web link 5.3*.

6

IN THIS CHAPTER
YOU WILL LEARN TO:

- Understand how relationships are unique, involve commitment, and are based on rules.

- Describe how relationships with family members, friends, and romantic partners evolve over time.

- Explain the two models that help explain self-disclosure in our interpersonal relationships.

- Discuss how technology can positively and negatively affect our relationships with others.

- Examine the effects of gender on relationships with family members, friends, romantic partners, and co-workers.

- Identify how different types of cultures view and communicate about relationships.

Understanding Interpersonal Communication

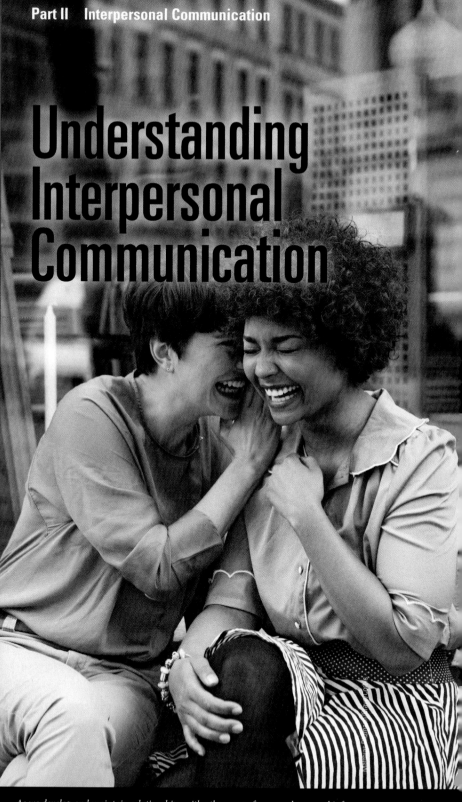

As we develop and maintain relationships with others, we often reveal personal information about ourselves. What personal information have you recently shared with another person?

The relationships we have with others are often the most rewarding parts of our lives. Because relationships are so important, this chapter discusses the components that influence them. We begin by defining the characteristics and types of interpersonal relationships. We then explain how relationships develop and deteriorate. Finally, we look at how technology, gender, and culture influence these relationships.

Characteristics of Interpersonal Relationships

Communication is the foundation for interpersonal relationships. We communicate with friends, family members, colleagues, or romantic partners to build and maintain relationships. We ask questions, share personal information, solve problems, and engage in small talk to sustain relationships we consider significant to us. But just because we communicate with another person does not necessarily mean we have a relationship with that person. **Interpersonal relationships** *involve a personal connection established with another person through the intentional use of communication.* These relationships are unique, require commitment, and are based on implicit or explicit rules. We now look at what this actually means for people who want rich relationships.

Interpersonal Relationships Are Unique

Every human being is different. We look, talk, and behave in distinctive ways. Because of this, every interpersonal relationship is unique. You likely have friendships with many people, and each one has particular patterns that make it unlike the others. You may share one kind of joke with one friend and a different kind with another. You may reveal certain information about yourself with your roommate but different information with a classmate. The way we interact with others is often determined by the type of interpersonal relationship (e.g., friend, co-worker, family member, or significant other), the context surrounding the interactions, and the predetermined norms and routines created by those in the relationship. For these reasons, every interpersonal relationship is unique.

Monkey Business Images/Shutterstock.com

Our relationships with family and friends can be profoundly meaningful. If you have an older or younger person in your life who is important to you, what makes that person unique?

interpersonal relationship
relationship that involves the establishment of a personal connection with another person through the intentional use of communication.

The Consequences of Social-Media Blunders

Does what we say and how we say it matter? Consider three examples.

After calling her students "arrogant and snobby" and posting "I'm so not looking forward to another year at Cohasset School," Dr. June Talvitie-Siple, a supervisor of the high school's math and science program, lost her job ("H.S. Teacher Loses Job Over Facebook Posting," 2010). Parents and students of this Massachusetts school found the postings online even though Talvitie-Siple thought she had posted them using her private setting on Facebook. The resulting furor led her to resign. Students suggested that although she was a great teacher, she clearly did not understand the Internet and that "if you are in a professional position, maybe you shouldn't be putting what you really feel about your job or whatever on Facebook." Parents replied, "It's horrid. Who says that about children you are teaching; children you are raising that you are a role model for?" Talvitie-Siple said in an interview that she was referring "to the political situation in the school, which she called very stressful,' and she said she thought she was only blowing off steam with friends in private" (Collins, 2010).

Three prison guards in Nebraska lost their jobs when Caleb Bartel's Facebook page said, "When you work in a prison, a good day is getting to smash an inmate's face into the ground. For me, today was a very good day" ("Facebook Post Prompts Prison Probe," 2010). The Nebraska Department of Corrections launched an investigation into Bartel and two other guards, Shawn Paulson and Derek Dickey, who had posted approving comments. All three guards lost their jobs. Former Nebraska State Senator Ernie Chambers described the posting as bringing "a cloud of negativity over the penitentiary." The state corrections department investigation "found that at least one of the guards used force on the day that the comment was posted, though there was no evidence of abuse."

In 2012, Yuri Wright, a high school football player was ranked fortieth on the ESPNU 150, was being recruited by Big Ten, PAC-12, ACC, and Big East colleges. Then Wright's dream of a football scholarship nearly ended after his sexually graphic and racial Twitter posts went public. Wright was expelled from his Catholic high school, and universities such as Michigan and Notre Dame stopped recruiting him. Wright had been warned. His high school football coach, Greg Toal, stated Wright "was told on numerous occasions not to be Twittering" and that there would be consequences for his choices ("Recruit Yuri Wright Expelled for Tweets," 2012).

Situations such as these raise interesting questions about communication and its effects. When individuals make claims or statements that are aired or become publicly known, there can be serious consequences: people lose their jobs and their credibility, they may lose scholarships and be expelled, and other people are often hurt and insulted. Television, radio, and other media outlets such as Facebook, Instagram, and Twitter make the mass distribution of our communication easy, fast, and accessible. Unlike previous generations, individuals today must monitor their public and private communication carefully; when they do not, they stand to lose a great deal.

What Do You Think?

1. Do you think there should be consequences for posting claims and images that are insulting to individuals or groups of people? Why or why not?

2. Evaluate your social-media sites. Would you want your employer to have access to everything you have posted? If you are interviewing for a job, what messages might your social-media postings say about you?

3. When an employee makes a comment using social media and the comment is posted using privacy settings, should the person be punished for the communication by losing his or her job? Or should the employee receive a warning, something like a "two strikes" warning, before being fired or forced to resign? Why or why not?

Interpersonal Relationships Require Commitment

Consider the different relationships that are important to you. Do you have a friend you socialize with on a daily or weekly basis? Do you regularly call a parent or sibling to check in? Do you have a co-worker you socialize with after work? Each of these relationships requires a degree of commitment, and these commitments are often (but not always) a choice. Some of us may choose to maintain a long-distance relationship with a friend or romantic partner. Some may choose to discuss an ongoing health issue with a close relative or friend. Others may choose to call a grandparent every Sunday or attend office hours regularly to chat with a favorite professor. On the other hand, you may decide to let a friendship dissipate or even not make friends with a neighbor. Although some commitments may be required by our families, professors, or supervisors (when they assign us to work in groups), most interpersonal relationships would not exist without a degree of voluntary commitment.

Deciding to commit to a relationship in some small or large way is one characteristic that defines our interpersonal relationships.

Interpersonal Relationships Are Built Around Rules

Interpersonal relationships function by their own set of rules. These rules are typically implicit, meaning we do not always talk openly about them, but they are a necessary part of every interpersonal relationship. Many rules are established by cultural norms and practices: it is appropriate for a husband to kiss his wife good-bye; it is not appropriate for her physician to do so. Rules are also created by the context surrounding the relationship: your boss expects you to discuss your work with her; the server at the restaurant does not. Finally, rules are determined by those involved in the relationship: you expect your best friend to call every week, but you do not expect the same from your ex-boyfriend or -girlfriend. Relationships continue to thrive only as long as we follow the established relationship rules. Violating these rules can lead to a relationship deteriorating or ending. No longer calling a friend on a regular basis may lead to some deterioration in the friendship. Acting dishonestly in a relationship with a romantic partner could end the relationship entirely. The rules that are established in each relationship help make the relationship unique, and these are often rules that show one's commitment to the relationship.

 ## Types of Interpersonal Relationships

Take a moment to consider your most important interpersonal relationships. If they are with family members, friends, co-workers, or romantic partners, then you fit the norm: our most significant interpersonal relationships come from these four major parts of our lives. Because they are so significant, we discuss them in the following sections.

Family

Over the past few decades, family structures have changed, resulting in more diversity in today's families. Now 58 percent of children live with both biological parents; approximately four in ten children do not (U.S. Census Bureau, 2013a). We consider these family structures next.

Family Arrangements Although there are many ways to define a family, communication scholars Kathleen Galvin, Carma Bylund, and Bernard Brommel (2003) define **family** as "*a network of people who live together over long periods of time bound by ties of marriage, blood, or commitment, legal or otherwise who consider themselves as family and who share a significant history and anticipated future of functioning in a family friendship.*" Today, we see many different types of family living arrangements, so we explore those here.

Communication scholar Mary Ann Fitzpatrick (2003) classified three primary types of relationships among married and cohabiting couples: interdependent couples, independent couples, and separate couples.

There are three primary types of relationships for married and cohabitating couples. What type of relationship do you expect to have with a romantic partner? Will it be one of the three primary types, or will you blend styles?

family

network of people who live together over long periods of time bound by ties of marriage, blood, or commitment, legal or otherwise, who consider themselves as family and share a significant history and anticipated future of functioning in a family relationship.

Interdependent Couples This traditional category consists of couples who are highly involved with one another without much distinction from one another. The **interdependent couple** *shares traditional views of marriage and family life, activities, and interests.*

Independent Couples **Independent couples** *hold less traditional views of family roles and expectations.* They are less dependent on one another and seek some autonomy in their activities.

Separate Couples **Separate couples** *are extremely autonomous.* Both people in the relationship allow the other his or her own time and space to enjoy activities.

Fitzpatrick realizes that not all married or cohabiting couples only fit into one category and that some couples blend styles. She claims that the most common form of blending styles is the separate-traditional style. In this type of relationship, one person, typically the wife or woman, holds a traditional view of marriage while the husband or man seeks more independence. Couples themselves determine which type of relationship best suits their interpersonal and individual needs.

Marriage and family do not have universal meanings. Even though the U.S. Supreme Court recently legalized gay marriages, in the United Stated and a few other countries, for example, there is an ongoing debate about who has the right to marry. The U.S. Census Bureau (2013b) estimates that approximately 250,000 same-sex couples identify themselves as being married and that more than 700,000 unmarried same-sex households also exist. In a story that aired on National Public Radio (2009), University of California demographer Gary Gates explained that same-sex couples often look a lot like opposite-sex married couples. They also are likely to have children and own their own homes.

The concept of family is also in transition, and many families consist of single parents raising children (see Figure 6.1). According to the U.S. Census Bureau (2013a), approximately 32 percent of children in the United States live with a single parent, and nearly 75 percent of those single parents are mothers. Children are also being raised by single fathers and even grandparents. Regardless of their structures, families tend to evolve as children grow and the makeup of a family changes. This is especially true for military families. For example, U.S. Army Major Daniel Kearney and his wife, Lauren, discuss the struggles that they and other military families have faced when a partner or parent is deployed for an extended length of time ("Military Life," n.d.). It can be difficult for these families to reconnect with one another and adjust and readjust to day-to-day routines.

interdependent couple
couple who shares traditional views of marriage and family life, activities , and interests.

independent couple
couple who holds less traditional views of family roles and expectations.

separate couple
couple who is extremely autonomous.

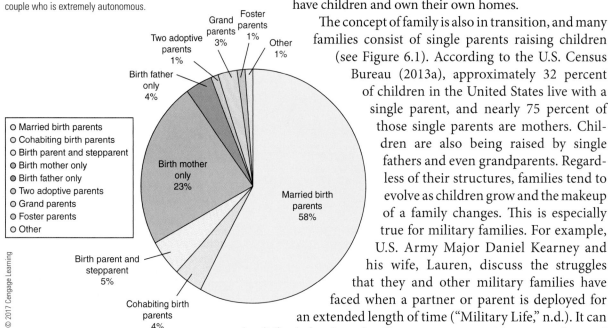

© 2017 Cengage Learning

- ○ Married birth parents
- ○ Cohabiting birth parents
- ○ Birth parent and stepparent
- ◉ Birth mother only
- ◉ Birth father only
- ○ Two adoptive parents
- ○ Grand parents
- ○ Foster parents
- ○ Other

Married birth parents 58%

Birth mother only 23%

Birth parent and stepparent 5%

Cohabiting birth parents 4%

Birth father only 4%

Two adoptive parents 1%

Grand parents 3%

Foster parents 1%

Other 1%

Figure 6.1 *Family* living arrangements of U.S. children, *2014*

Friendships

Recall your first days as a college student. You arrived at campus, met your roommate, attended orientation, and began taking classes. You likely interacted with many other students for the first time. Some may have become close friends, but others have not. Have you ever wondered what makes a friendship grow and develop? Interpersonal communication scholar Bill Rawlins (1981) developed the following six-stage model of friendship to help explain the stages of our friendships:

1. role-limited interaction,
2. friendly relations,
3. moves toward friendship,
4. nascent friendship,
5. stabilized friendship, and
6. waning friendship.

What is the makeup of your family and the families of your friends? With family demographics changing so rapidly, what do you imagine your family will look like in ten years?

Although not every friendship follows each developmental stage, you likely have friendships that have progressed more or less according to Rawlins's model (Mongeau & Henningsen, 2008). As you read about each stage, consider your own friendships and whether they followed the stages in sequence.

Stage One: Role-Limited Interaction In this stage, we encounter people for the first time. We may greet a cashier at a store, interact with other students in a classroom, introduce ourselves to a new neighbor, or seek out new friendships online. Whether we choose to meet new acquaintances or are put into situations that require us to interact with others, we tend to limit the amount of personal information we share when we first meet others. When we communicate in the **role-limited interaction** stage, we typically *engage in small talk and share only minimal amounts of information*. This stage can feel awkward, especially for people who experience communication apprehension when meeting others for the first time.

Stage Two: Friendly Relations The second stage of development focuses on the exchange of friendly conversation. The **friendly relations** stage *allows each person to determine whether common interests exist*. If enough interest and commonality are present, then the friendship moves forward. If not, the relationship is limited by the constraints of the situation. For example, you may speak pleasantly to classmates or co-workers but not extend the friendship beyond the classroom or work environment.

Stage Three: Moves Toward Friendship When friendships reach the stage of **moving toward friendship**, we *begin to self-disclose in small amounts*. Because we are continuing to discover common interests and whether we want to spend more time with another, we behave according to roles

role-limited interaction
engaging in small talk and sharing only minimal amounts of information.

friendly relations
situation that allows each person to determine whether common interests exist.

moves toward friendship
when people begin to self-disclose in small amounts.

determined by our culture and social environment. We may choose to interact outside the original social context. This happens when students decide to meet outside of class for social purposes, or when co-workers get together before or after work hours. These gatherings often occur in public settings where others are present. Because friends enjoy interacting and can come and go as they please, many friendships remain in this stage.

Stage Four: Nascent Friendship Once people consider themselves as friends, they have reached the **nascent friendship** stage—the stage in which the friendship blossoms. This is the point at which *we interact on a personal level, choose to participate in a range of activities with another, and let down our guard when it comes to communicating.* Friends work out their own distinct communication and behavioral rules. Patterns and routines begin to emerge. Friends may meet to work out together regularly, have lunch several times a week or month, or hear new musicians at the local coffee shop on open mike nights.

Stage Five: Stabilized Friendship Trust is the characteristic that distinguishes the fifth stage of friendship development. Once friendships have reached the **stabilized friendship** stage, *trust has been established, allowing friends to communicate fully, share private information, and establish additional relationship rules.* Friends understand one another's personality and behavioral traits. Moreover, certain expectations for the friendship (often unspoken) exist. For example, friends may begin to expect a certain level of interaction and self-disclosure. The high level of interaction and amount of self-disclosure is what distinguishes this relationship as close and best friends.

nascent friendship
time when people interact on a personal level, choose to participate in a range of activities with another, and let down their guard in communication.

stabilized friendship
when trust has been established, allowing friends to communicate fully, share private information, and establish additional relationship rules.

waning friendship
friendship that experiences a breach in trust, less quality or quantity of time spent together, or a violation in relational expectations.

PRACTICING HUMAN COMMUNICATION

Can You Recognize the Stages of Friendship?

Next to each stage of friendship in the following list, give an example of communication in that stage of friendship with someone who is now a close friend. For example, in a role-limited relationship, you may have first met your friend in a college class and engaged in small talk about the teacher and the course. For the last stage, you might need to use someone you are no longer in touch with.

Stage	Example of Communication
1. Role-limited, small talk	
2. Friendly relations, common interests determined	
3. Move toward friendship, begin to self-disclose, meet outside class or work	
4. Nascent, let down guard, interact more personally	
5. Stabilized, trust established communicate fully have relationship rules	
6. Waning, a breach of trust or someone who moved away and you see each other less	

Stage Six: Waning Friendship Friendships may wane slowly over time or end abruptly, depending on the reasons for the deterioration. **Waning friendships** *experience a breach in trust, decrease in quality or quantity of time spent together, or a violation in relational expectations.* Once friendships reach the waning stage, communication begins to be more strategic and less spontaneous. If we perceive the breach in trust or relational rules to be unintentional, then we may choose to continue the friendship with the hope that trust can be reestablished in the future. If we perceive the violation of trust or relational rules to be intentional, then we may choose to end the friendship. Many people have friendships that fall under all of these categories. This is because growing and developing friendships tend to shift categories, depending on the level of communication, self-disclosure, and

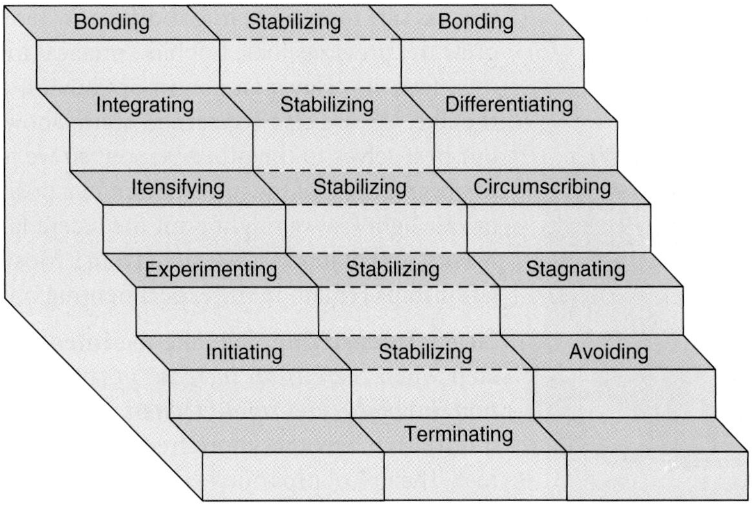
Bonding
Stabilizing
Bonding
Integrating
Stabilizing
Differentiating
Itensifying
Stabilizing
Circumscribing
Experimenting
Stabilizing
Stagnating
Initiating
Stabilizing
Avoiding
Terminating
© 2017 Cengage Learning

Figure 6.2 *Mark Knapp's relational stages model*

trust that exists. But what about a friendship that has developed into a romantic relationship? Because romantic relationships are important parts of our interpersonal relationships, we discuss those next.

Romantic Partners

Romantic relationships evolve much like friendships. This is because, like friendships, the quality and quantity of interactions, relational rules and expectations, and trust are necessary parts of our romantic partnerships. However, just as there are different kinds of friendships, there are also different models for romantic relationships. One of the more popular models that explains how relationships develop and deteriorate was developed by communication scholar Mark Knapp (Knapp, 1978, 1984; Knapp & Daly, 2010). Although not all romantic relationships develop or deteriorate following these stages, many do. Knapp's model uses a staircase metaphor to illustrate an upward climb toward commitment and a downward descent toward dissolution. Both staircases have five steps or phases. Notice the similarities between the development of friendships as discussed by Rawlins and the development of romantic relationships as described by Knapp.

The Staircase Up: Climbing Toward Commitment The five steps leading toward commitment are initiating, experimenting, intensifying, integrating, and bonding. Keep in mind that, although Knapp uses the step metaphor, these are actually phases in romantic relationships.

Step 1 **Initiating.** The first step of initiating is similar to Rawlins's role-limited stage of friendship. The **initiation step** *involves the first set of interactions made between people.* Communication consists mostly of initial greetings and additional information to fit the situation. For example, introducing ourselves to your best friend's new housemate or to a new co-worker initiates a relationship. At this time, our communication tends to be pleasant and provides little self-disclosure.

initiation step
step involving the first set of interactions made between people.

Step 2 **Experimenting.** In the **experimenting step**, *small talk is used to learn more about the other person and to help present a likable self-image.* Our communication continues to be polite, and we tend to

experimenting step
step when small talk is used to learn more about the other person and to help present a likable self-image.

What phase of the relationship might this couple be in? What do you think the next step might be for this couple?

discuss safe topics. We might discuss where we grew up, previous jobs, hobbies, musical interests, favorite television shows or movies, and the like. We are also concerned about showing our best selves to the other person, so we tend to present most of the information in a positive or safe light (so we might omit the recent family feud or that job we were fired from). Most relationships remain in the experimenting phase.

Step 3 Intensifying. We take the **intensifying step** when *there is an increase in communication, intimacy, and connectedness.* Verbal communication becomes more frequent and informal. The use of pronouns *we* and *us* signal that the relationship is developing. In the intensifying phase, we hear ourselves and our partner say things such as "We are going to Chicago this weekend," "We ate at Jay's last night," or "Do you think we should go to this party?" We may develop nicknames for one another or even shortened phrases that mean something to both people in the relationship but not to outsiders.

Step 4 Integrating. The **integrating step** *consists of two individuals merging their social circles and organizing their daily activities around each other.* In this phase, couples may begin to mirror one another in styles of dress, language, and activity choices. They may have a special place, song, or symbol that is "their own," and they may share the same friends and social activities and even grocery shop together or organize car-repair or doctor appointments so that one person can help out or support the other.

Step 5 Bonding. The **bonding step** occurs *when the couple commits to the relationship.* This commitment is usually conscious and intentional in this phase, and it may take the form of exchanging items that mark the relationship as official (rings or other jewelry and markers of togetherness, for example), cohabitation, or participating in a ceremony (e.g., civil union ceremony, marriage) to publicly or privately formalize the commitment.

Once a couple reaches the bonding phase, they usually engage in strategies to maintain the relationship. This is called **relational maintenance**; it is the *process of keeping a relationship together through the use of mundane activities.* These maintenance strategies are important; without routine maintenance, relationships often deteriorate. Of course, each relationship has its own unique maintenance strategies, However, scholars have studied relational maintenance strategies in both heterosexual and gay couples and identified certain routine communicative behaviors that help stabilize a relationship (Alberts, Yoshimura, Rabbi, & Loschiavo, 2005; Canary & Stafford, 1994; Haas & Stafford, 1998; Kurdek, 2005). These common maintenance strategies are (1) dividing household tasks evenly, (2) spending time with the other's friends and family, (3) using humor and cheerful communication, and (4) being open through self-disclosure.

intensifying step
step when there is an increase in communication, intimacy, and connectedness.

integrating step
step consisting of two individuals merging their social circles and organizing their daily activities around each other.

bonding step
step that occurs when a couple commits to their relationship.

relational maintenance
process of keeping a relationship together through the use of mundane activities.

Romance at Work?

According to a recent Harris Poll, nearly two in five U.S. workers (38 percent) have dated or will date someone working for the same company ("Thirty-Eight Percent," 2014). This may not be surprising because work is where we spend so much of our time. In fact, of those who date someone from the office, nearly one-third end up marrying that person ("Thirty-Eight Percent," 2014). So does that mean we should be seeking relationships with co-workers? What are the potential drawbacks to office romances? Many companies have strict policies regarding office romances, so you should always check the company handbook. If your company allows a relationship, then consider the following:

- **Weigh the pros and cons of starting an office relationship**. Not all office romances are successful, and some can have negative consequences such as being denied a promotion, being forced to relocate to a different department, or even being fired.

- **Avoid a relationship with someone you report to or who reports directly to you**. If you are seeing someone romantically, subordinates and supervisors may have a hard time being objective in completing performance evaluations, promotions, and raise requests. When promotions are granted, others may question whether the decision was fair. It may be best for one person to switch positions within the company to avoid a direct subordinate–supervisor relationship.

- **Keep public displays of affection out of the office**. You are at work to get a job done; wait until after work to pursue behaviors specific to your personal relationship. In other words, keep your work life separate from your home life.

- **Allow time for the relationship to develop before telling colleagues**. If you are following company policy and the relationship is not with someone to whom you directly report, then it may be best to avoid telling co-workers for awhile. Take time to get to know each other first. This way, you can be sure the relationship is not temporary. And when you are ready to reveal the relationship, always tell your boss first.

- **Be cautious of your posts.** What you say on your social-media accounts can reveal your relationship. Be sure you are ready to talk openly about your relationship before referring to it on social media.

Although relational maintenance is a necessary part in continuing the relationship, not all relationships survive. When relationships come to an end, Knapp suggests that they follow a five-step descent down the ladder toward deterioration.

The Staircase Down: Descending Toward Deterioration Knapp describes five steps that relationships take when they begin to deteriorate: differentiating, circumscribing, stagnating, avoiding, and terminating. Similar to the staircase up, the steps along the staircase down represent phases of romantic relationships.

Step 1 **Differentiating**. In the **differentiating step** *couples begin to spend time on their own interests in order to express their individuality and separate from their partner.* Although spending time on one's own activities and interests is a healthy way to sustain self-identity, differentiating exists when couples consciously engage in separate activities or focus on separate interests in order to distance themselves from the other person. In this early phase, couples might say, "I just need some time apart to get my head straight," or "I think I'll go to Chicago by myself this weekend."

Step 2 **Circumscribing**. When couples take the **circumscribing step**, *they begin communicating less frequently, share less personal information, and spend shorter amounts of time together.* The couple may continue to appear in public or attend gatherings with friends, but private interactions and time spent together have decreased. The *we* and *us* language common in the intensifying stage changes back to *I* and *me* language, and the couple begins to share fewer details of their days and how they feel about those details. As the relationship continues on its downward spiral toward dissolution, the couple may argue more or

differentiating step
when individuals in a couple begin to spend time on their own interests in order to express their individuality and separate from their partner.

circumscribing step
when couples begin communicating less frequently, share less personal information, and spend shorter amounts of time together.

This couple appears to be in the stagnating phase of their relationship. What advice could you give them as they work to rebuild their relationship or to continue to move toward its termination?

simply not want to share what is important with each other.

Step 3 **Stagnating**. The **stagnating step** *consists of minimal interaction or shared activities*. The couple has now reached a point at which they anticipate time together and communication to be unpleasant. Because self-disclosure is minimal in this phase, couples likely have grown apart and feel distant from one another. Couples may begin revealing relationship details and struggles with close friends and admitting that the relationship has deteriorated.

Step 4 **Avoiding**. In the **avoiding step**, *couples attempt to stay away from one another*. To accomplish this, couples may change their work schedules, sleep in separate bedrooms, or participate in more activities outside the home environment. Some couples may choose a temporary or trial separation. Communication often turns negative in this phase as each person blames the other for the relationship's problems and failures.

Step 5 **Terminating**. The final step in the dissolution of a romantic relationship is the **terminating step**. This occurs when *the couple makes their separation final*. One person may choose to move out or relocate to another city. If the couple is married, divorce proceedings begin. Friends and family are now aware the relationship has terminated. Important items are divided up, and the couple no longer exists as a romantic unit. Communication in this phase typically continues to place blame on the other person while also focusing on the future and exciting new possibilities.

Knapp explains that progression through the steps of deterioration is not always linear way. A couple's behavior may indicate one phase (an individual moves out of the house for a trial separation, representing the avoiding stage), but the couple may continue to talk regularly and go on occasional dates together. Furthermore, not all relationships develop or decline as suggested previously. Many relationships decline before reaching the bonding phase. Other relationships dissolve in a more mutually pleasant way than described in the stagnating phase. And many relationships are able to stop the descent and climb back up the ladder of commitment and stay together. Because a relationship begins a descent does not mean it will ultimately end. Two people can rebuild their commitment to one another, especially if they are aware of Knapp's ladder metaphor and use their communication skills to establish and maintain the kind of relationship they want with one another.

Understanding Self-Disclosure

As we sustain our families, forge friendships, become romantically involved, or converse with co-workers, we share information about ourselves with others. The more we trust another person, the more likely

stagnating step
when couples have minimal interaction or shared activities.

avoiding step
when couples attempt to stay away from each other.

terminating step
when individuals in a couple make their separation final.

Terminating a Relationship: Facebook or Face to Face?

Ilana Gershon, author of the book *The Breakup 2.0: Disconnecting over New Media* (2010), explains that virtual breakups are becoming more common everyday. Gershon tells the story of a college student named Leslie who experienced an online breakup:

> Leslie checked her Facebook profile late one day and discovered that she was suddenly single. Her now ex-boyfriend had met someone new, and she learned this through the ubiquitous news feed that presented her personal rejection like a breaking news story. When he changed his Facebook profile, he also changed hers as well—they were no longer announced as a couple. Their friends received the news before she had.

Gershon claims that although most people believe people should break up face to face, social media and technology provide different options for ending relationships. Gershon explains that "texting, instant messaging, Facebook, e-mail, Twitter . . . [are] now widely seen as acceptable" for announcing the termination of a relationship (Gershon, 2010; Vlahakis, 2010). In addition, a study by the American Academy of Matrimonial Lawyers found that one of every five divorcing couples blame Facebook for the demise of their marriage. Couples now use Facebook to do their detective work: "A Facebook status update, a

140-character Twitter post, or a confessional entry on a blog all leave behind a pretty much permanent digital trail that can be used in court in case of a divorce" (Stevens, 2011).

Author James Weaver, however, is skeptical that Facebook is to blame for so many divorces. In a blog posting by Benjamin Stevens, Weaver says, "Sure, social media makes it easier to connect with old flames and strike up new relationships, but divorces and infidelity have been around for all of human history, whereas social media is less than a decade old. Truth is that people cause divorces, not social media" (Stevens, 2011).

What Do You Think?

1. If you were to end a relationship with someone, would you use social media rather than face-to-face communication? Why or why not?

2. What are the ethical implications of using social media to announce the breakup of a relationship? Whose interests or feelings should take priority? What guidelines would you follow?

3. What are the ethical implications of posting and retrieving personal information from social-media venues such as Facebook and Twitter? What impact might Facebook or Twitter have on causing relationships to end?

we are to reveal information that is personal. When we share information about ourselves, we are engaged in self-disclosure. **Self-disclosure** is *the intentional sharing of personal information that would not otherwise be known to others*. We can understand self-disclosure in many ways, but two models in particular help explain self-disclosure in our interpersonal relationships: self-disclosure as an onion and self-disclosure as a window.

Self-Disclosure Is Like an Onion

Self-disclosure varies in breadth and depth, depending on the relationship. For example, we may reveal limited information about ourselves with an acquaintance but a great deal of personal information with our close friends. We may talk about one or two topics while sitting next to someone on an airplane but an endless number of topics with our siblings. The **social-penetration theory** *describes the variation in breadth and depth of self-disclosure in relationships* (Altman & Taylor, 1973; Petronino, 2002). According to this theory, self-disclosure involves the degree of **breadth** or *the range of topics discussed* and **depth** or *how personal the information disclosed*. For example, you may announce to your co-workers that you recently went on a date (little depth), but you may provide details about that date to close friends (more depth). In addition, we may only discuss work-related issues with our boss (little breadth) but talk about problems

self-disclosure
intentional sharing of personal information that would not otherwise be known to others.

social-penetration theory
describes the variation in breadth and depth of self-disclosure in a relationship.

breadth
the range of topics discussed in self-disclosure.

depth
how personal the information is in self-disclosure.

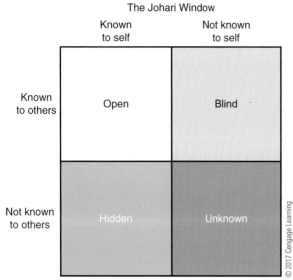

The Johari Window

	Known to self	Not known to self
Known to others	Open	Blind
Not known to others	Hidden	Unknown

© 2017 Cengage Learning

Figure 6.3 *The Johari window*

at work, family concerns, personal opinions on political issues, and our life goals with our romantic partner (more breadth). In the initial stages of building a relationship, the breadth may be high, but the depth is typically low until trust is established. This theory sees self-disclosure as similar to peeling an onion: as a relationship becomes more intimate, the depth of disclosure tends to increase, so we continually peel off the layers of the onion to reveal more and more of ourselves.

Self-Disclosure Is Like a Window

The Johari window is a model for self-disclosure that helps us understand ourselves and the reasons we might or might not disclose to others. This model shows us divided into four windows labeled *open*, *blind*, *hidden*, and *unknown* (Figure 6.3). Each window represents something personal about us. For example, the **open window** is *information about yourself that is already known by you and others*. The window may consist of your likes and dislikes, relationship or family status, hometown, occupation, and any other information you are aware of and have freely disclosed. The **blind window** is *information that others know about you but that you are unaware of*. The blind window may consist of some your personality traits (you are more picky than you realize or more courageous than you thought) or talents (you are highly empathetic, an excellent artist, or a natural comedian) that others realize you possess but that you are unaware of. We can learn about this blind window by listening to and getting feedback from others. The **hidden window** consists of *information that you know about yourself but are not willing to share with others*. The hidden window may consist of some of our past experiences, personal problems, or aspects of our identity (e.g., political affiliation, sexual orientation, religious affiliation, or age) that we choose for various reasons to not disclose. The **unknown window** is *information that is yet to be discovered by you and others*. The window may consist of hidden talents, passions, fears, or diseases we have yet to discover. Understanding self-disclosure as a window helps us see that the size of each window varies, depending on the relationship. In one relationship where we may not feel safe, we likely will have a large hidden window. In a relationship in which we are getting to know someone and coming to trust them, our open window may grow in size rapidly. And if we are resistant to feedback from others, our blind window might stay large for some time. Remember, too, that the sizes of these windows are rarely static: they shift as our relationships grow and develop.

Self-disclosure is important to relationships for two reasons. First, when we disclose to others, we gain a deeper understanding of ourselves. When we share our opinions on community issues, our relationship triumphs and failures, our ambitions and fears, we gain a better sense

open window
information about yourself that is already known by you and others.

blind window
information that others know about you but that you are not aware of.

hidden window
information that you understand about yourself but are not willing to share with others.

unknown window
information about yourself that is yet to be discovered by you and others.

of who we are as individuals. We learn what makes us unique and what commonalities we have with others. When that disclosure is reciprocated, we learn about the other person as well. Second, self-disclosure can improve the quality of our relationships. When we discuss our thoughts and feelings, difficult challenges, and even our successes and hopes, we learn about the ways we are similar and different—and that we are not the only ones to face adversity or to have hopes and dreams, that we can trust and respect others. But self-disclosure can be complicated, so we will discuss some of the guidelines for such disclosure next.

Guidelines for Self-Disclosure When we enter a relationship, we usually have expectations about self-disclosure. When we share information about ourselves, we expect others to share information in return. When self-disclosure is reciprocated, we view the relationship more favorably. On the other hand, we tend to feel uncomfortable in situations where someone self-discloses a lot of personal information early in the relationship or when someone self-discloses a lot, but we feel less favorable toward them. Several guidelines can help us understand these complex moments before we decide to share personal information with others.

Self-Disclosure Should Be Appropriate to the Relationship You are already aware that there is a certain degree of breadth and depth to our self-disclosure. This helps us understand that there are levels of appropriateness associated with revealing personal information to others. With acquaintances or co-workers, sharing small amounts of personal information across a range of topics is appropriate. With our romantic partners or close friends, sharing more intimate details across this range of topics is expected. Generally speaking, begin with small amounts of self-disclosure and increase the levels of breadth and depth as the relationship progresses and trust is established.

Match the Breadth and Depth of Disclosure Provided to You This rule is known as the *norm of reciprocity*, and it governs the process of sharing personal information with others. Relationships that incorporate similar amounts of self-disclosure are preferred. When someone reveals too much personal information, we begin to feel uncomfortable. One sign of revealing too much personal information too soon occurs when one person begins sharing less information or reverting back to previous "safe" topics. Paying attention to the norm of reciprocity can indicate important information about the relationship.

Pay Attention to the Purpose of the Self-Disclosure We have a great deal of private information we can choose to share or withhold from others. It is important to identify the reasons we choose to share particular information about ourselves. We may reveal our sexual history to our romantic partner as a way to establish trust in a sexual relationship. However, sharing this information in the locker room or with friends in a social setting serves quite a different purpose. This self-disclosure can be intended as a boast of our experiences or past commitments.

Self-disclosure is meant to enhance the quality of relationships rather than negatively affect them. Therefore, our most important and meaningful disclosures should be reserved for the relationships that are most important and special to us.

Relationships and our communication in them are affected by a variety of factors. The type of relationship we are experiencing, the level or developmental stage of the relationship, and degree of self-disclosure can shape the quality of and communication in the relationship. In the next section we explore how technology, gender, and culture also affect our interpersonal relationships.

Technology and Interpersonal Relationships

For several decades, communication scholars have studied the association between technology and interpersonal relationships. At first, scholars believed the increased time spent using mediated channels led to an increase in individual isolation, decrease in relationship quality, and unwillingness to participate in one's community (Finholt & Sproull, 1990; Putnam, 1995; Shah, McLeod, & Yoon, 2001; Sproull & Kiesler, 1986). There was a growing concern that increasing amounts of time spent on the Internet negatively affected the time spent with family and friends (Nie & Hillygus, 2002). More recent studies, however, have indicated just the opposite. The University of Southern California's Annenberg School of Communication and Journalism's annual study of Internet use reports that approximately 68 percent of Internet users between ages nineteen and thirty-five rank social media as "important and very important" for maintaining relationships, and more than 50 percent all other age groups agreed (USC Annenberg School, 2011). Be careful, though. Other studies indicate that too many "friends" on social media can actually reduce the feelings of connection we have with others (Tom Tong, Van Der Heide, Langwell, & Waither, 2008).

We know that media have changed the way relationships form and evolve over time. Texting and tweeting make it possible to communicate in real time with others, and romantic partners prefer texting as a way to stay connected when they are apart (Pettigrew, 2009). Blogging helps us engage in political and civic discourse, and social-networking sites allow new friendships to form and old friendships to stay active. The rapid growth in technology leaves communication scholars scrambling to understand how new forms of technology affect our personal relationships. We will now look at ways that technology positively affects our relationships with others and the ways it might also have negative effects.

Relationships and Computer-Mediated Communication

Computer-mediated communication (CMC) is *the exchange of messages transmitted between two or more people using a digital electronic device.* According to the Pew Research Center's Internet and

computer-mediated communication (CMC)
the exchange of messages transmitted between two or more people using a digital electronic device.

NATIONAL GEOGRAPHIC EXPLORER TIP ↗

Courtesy of Chris Rainier

T. H. Culhane
Explorer and Urban Planner

How does technology affect your ability to maintain long-distance working relationships?

I should just tell you that when I first joined Facebook back in, I guess it was 2007, I joined because I was a Harvard student and we knew about its potential. Then my lead professor at UCLA encouraged all his students to use it, and we were supposed to use it to further the research that we were doing. The people that I was communicating with on this tool became early adopters in Egypt and then in other parts of Africa and the Middle East. I have friends over in Indonesia and Guatemala who also saw Facebook as a tool for important things, which I think is why Egypt used it for a social revolution.

We now have Web 2.0 and social media to maintain our interpersonal connections. I use those tools to connect with friends in the Okavanga Delta or from Nigeria or Tanzania. We are all on our Facebook groups, and we are very active using Google Plus and YouTube. We make YouTube videos for each other, we've linked to other YouTube videos, and we've linked to Web sites. We sometimes chat. It doesn't matter whether they are in a small village or if they are in a slum or they are in a city, if they have access to a kiosk occasionally and the Internet, we can communicate. Integrating technologies can be an important part of maintaining relationships and continuing the work toward industrial ecology solutions for cooperative cities.

American Life Project, approximately 74 percent of adults over age eighteen in the United States use the Internet (Rainie, 2010). Nearly 72 percent of Americans use social-media sites like Facebook, Twitter, and Instagram, making it easy to connect with others throughout the day (Pew Research Internet Project, 2015). Facebook, the largest online social-media site, is used by 1.3 billion people worldwide (Facebook Statistics, 2015).

Most communication via the Internet is text based and either asynchronous or synchronous. **Asynchronous** means that the *messages are sent but not received at the same time.* This occurs when we post a message on our blog that is not immediately read or when we send a text to a cell phone that is turned off. E-mail, text messaging, blogs, and social-media postings are often asynchronous because the receiver typically does not receive the message immediately. **Synchronous** messages are *messages that are received in real time.* This happens when we communicate in chat rooms or send instant messages back and forth. Many forms of CMC can be asynchronous or synchronous, depending on whether the individuals are using the electronic device at the same time. Video sites such as FaceTime, Skype, and WebEx are synchronous tools that are becoming popular for maintaining long-distance working and romantic relationships. The one commonality between asynchronous and synchronous messages is that many CMC users engage in

asynchronous
message that is sent but not received at the same time.

synchronous
message that is received in real time.

hyperpersonal communication—that is, *communication that occurs when individuals express themselves more freely in a mediated channel than in a face-to-face interaction.* As such, technology has become not only a way to stay connected to others but also a relational maintenance strategy for interpersonal relationships.

Although many people complain that too much time spent texting or on Facebook detracts from real-time interactions with peers, research suggests something quite different. In 2007, media studies scholars Nicole Ellison, Charles Steinfield, and Cliff Lampe studied students at Michigan State University. These researchers wanted to know what the benefits of using Facebook might be for college students, and what they found was quite interesting. They discovered that new students use Facebook to stay connected with their friends from high school, which helped them feel less alone in their first year and minimized the "friendsickness" that came from missing old friends. They also discovered that for shy students struggling with self-esteem and feeling disconnected from the campus, Facebook boosted their self-esteem and confidence, helped make new friends, and made them feel more at home and involved in their school. Finally, they found that Facebook not only helped students at all grade levels maintain the friends they had before coming to college but also helped them make and strengthen new friendships with other students in their dorms and classes (Ellison et al., 2007).

Many individuals, bloggers, students, and activists agree that social-networking sites revolutionize how we create and maintain friendships and also affect politics, learning, work, and activism. Social networks make it possible for huge numbers of people to contact one another quickly and continuously. This means that information and ideas are shared and spread rapidly and immediately. Although this is a positive aspect of social networking, it also has a downside. Josh Thome (2015), producer of *4REAL*, says, "While technology can be an incredible tool it is crucial for people to come together. Nothing can beat the power of that. I can release a film online but it will have must less impact than a theater full of people experiencing it together. While computer and communication technologies can keep us connected they can also keep us apart."

In addition, studies show that many teens are disclosing too much personal information and putting themselves at risk with these social networks (Figure 6.4). The Pew Research Center reports 94 percent of teenagers include photos of themselves, 76 percent share their school names, 23 percent list their cell phone numbers, and 16 percent set up their profiles to automatically include their physical locations (Madden et al., 2013). Tracy Mooney, one of the researchers who conducted the survey, explains, "Online, there's a sense of trust and anonymity, so kids let their guard down. . . . Kids would never hand out their name and address to a stranger in the real world, so it's alarming to see how many kids do that very thing online" (Schwartz, 2010). Young adults between eighteen and twenty-nine, however, seem to be more savvy about privacy. Research from the Internet and the

hyperpersonal communication
communication that occurs when individuals express themselves more freely in a mediated channel than in a face-to-face interaction.

Josh Thome, Emerging Explorer and New Media Cultural Storyteller

Josh Thome and childhood friend Sol Guy (featured in Chapter 13) want you to hear a story. It is about a trio in South Africa whose hit song is credited with lowering the AIDS rate in their region, about a baby who was left in a box and eventually grew up to run a medical clinic for thousands of people in a slum of East Africa, and about a boy who survived Liberia's brutal civil war, exposed the training of child soldiers, and now builds orphanages and playgrounds for the next generation (Guy and Thome, 2015). These are just some of the stories featured on the television show *4REAL*.

Thome expanded what started as a high school environmental club into an international movement of youth engaged in social change. While attending a Global Leadership Jam in 2000, Thome was inspired by the stories being told by the thirty outstanding young leaders from around the world. He began developing a series about young people creating social change, and a couple years into the project reconnected with his childhood friend Sol Guy. The two coproduced the televesion show *4REAL* from that point on.

As the two describe it, *4REAL* "spans the globe—from the slums of Nairobi, to the Amazon forest, to the drug-ravaged Lower East Side of Vancouver and a block party in post-conflict Liberia—viewers get a raw and authentic view of life through the eyes of residents, community leaders and the visiting celebrities" (Guy & Thome, 2015). Celebrities such as Cameron Diaz, Joaquin Phoenix, Mos Def, and K'naan have traveled with Thome and Sol, creating an instant connection with young viewers.

Thome and Guy share the stories of people who are using music, art, culture, and school programs to inspire youth. The intersection of popular culture with social change has had enormous influences on youth involvement. As Thome writes, "The core of my interest in getting young people involved in social change today is basically my inspiration to see what our human potential is" (Thome, 2015). In fact, Thome knows today's young people are already making a difference. The statistics from the United Nations 2014 Millennium Development Goals reports reveals the following:

- Since 1990, extreme poverty in the world has been reduced by half.
- Between 2000 and 2010, the the percentage of people without access to improved drinking water sources was also reduced by half.
- Between 2000 and 2012, gender parity in primary education was achieved in almost every developing region.
- Between 2000 and 2014, political participation continued to increase globally, with forty-six countries having 30 percent or more female members of parliaments in at least one chamber.
- The proportion of undernourished people in developing regions decreased from 24 percent in 1992 to 14 percent in 2013.
- The mortality rate for children under age five dropped almost 50 percent between 1990 and 2012.
- Maternal mortality dropped 45 percent between 1990 and 2013.

Thome believes humanity is "capable of taking on some of the world's greatest challenges when we prioritize them" (Thome, 2015). As Thome continues to forge relationships with members of different cultures, he reminds us that building trust with others is "as simple as making a connection. We're ultimately not that different" (Thome, 2015). When developing relationships with members of a different culture, Thome is reminded of an aboriginal activists group's key belief: "If you have come here to help me, you are wasting your time. But if you come because your liberation is bound up with mine, then let us work together" (Thome, 2015).

WHAT DO YOU THINK?

1. In addition to Web sites, concerts, and videos, how else can technology inspire today's youth to participate in social change?

2. Why is understanding the concepts of breadth and depth of self-disclosure important when Thome and Guy are talking with community leaders and members?

3. Because interpersonal relationships are built around rules, how can someone traveling to another culture better understand its rules for developing and maintaining friendships?

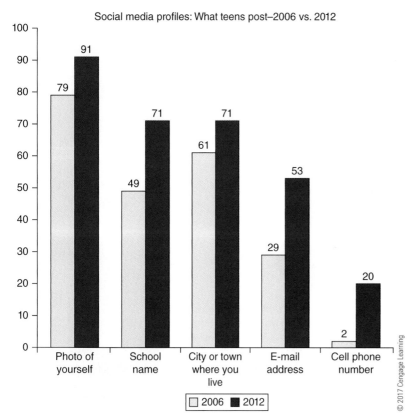

Social media profiles: What teens post–2006 vs. 2012

© 2017 Cengage Learning

Figure 6.4 *Social Media Profiles*

American Life Project indicates that 44 percent of young adult social-media users limit their personal information online, and 71 percent of eighteen- to twenty-nine-year-old social-networking users have tightened their privacy settings (Eiler, 2010).

Computer-mediated communication is an important part of our interpersonal relationships. From making new friends, to meeting romantic partners, and staying in touch over long distances, CMC provides the tools necessary to build and maintain strong relationships. Yet it also can negatively affect our professional and personal lives. Because of the ever-increasing forms of CMC, we need to understand this powerful tool for communicating and its effect on human relationships.

Gender and Interpersonal Relationships

Have you ever wondered why women are expected to talk more openly about their relationships than men or why men are expected to fix things around the house? Our sex and gender affect the way we experience our relationships. **Sex** refers to *our biological and genetic characteristics.* This consists of the chromosomal pattern that distinguishes whether we are biologically male, female or intersexed (possessing both female and male biological and genetic characteristics). **Gender**, on the other hand, is socially constructed and *refers to society's use of verbal and nonverbal symbols to express masculinity and femininity.* Communication scholar Julia Wood explains that gender "is neither innate nor necessarily stable. It is defined by society and expressed by individuals as they interact with others and media in their society" (2013, pp. 20–21). In the United States, we consider masculine men to be strong, ambitious, successful, and rational thinkers who are emotionally controlled (Wood, 2013). On the other hand, to be feminine typically means that someone is physically attractive, emotionally expressive, nurturing, and caring (Spence & Buckner, 2000). Gender, however, is a fluid concept and varies across cultures and co-cultures, over time, and between relationships. Today, many of these traditional definitions of masculinity and femininity are being challenged, even though families, society, and media emphasize traditional understandings of gender. We explore these factors next.

sex
biological and genetic characteristics.

gender
society's use of verbal and nonverbal symbols to express masculinity and femininity.

Gender and Family

Our families are enormously influential in teaching us how to perform gender. Families are usually the first group of people who model and teach us about gender roles and expectations. The term **gender role** is "commonly *used to refer to feminine and masculine social expectations in a family based on a person's sex*" (DeFrancisco & Palczewski, 2007, p. 154). According to Allen and Walker (2000), "there is no better predictor of the division of household labor than gender" (p. 7).

How was work divided in your household? Who was responsible for cooking, cleaning, and child care? Who was more likely to fix broken items, maintain vehicles, and do yard work (Canary & Wahba, 2006)? Did your family designate certain spaces in the house as "belonging to" a mother or father? Although gender roles are slowly changing, mothers still tend to occupy the kitchen, closet, and bathroom spaces, whereas fathers tend to claim the basement, the easy chair, and the garage as their spaces. Same-sex couples often reject these gendered divisions of labor and space (Peplau & Beals, 2004). Instead, many divide labor based on ability, interest, and the common goal of sharing responsibility for household labor and child care.

Many fathers are taking a more active role in the lives of their children than ever before. What roles did your parents and caregivers take during your childhood, and what roles do you expect to take on as you begin a family of your own?

The roles we are socialized into or that we take on consciously affect how we communicate with others. If we have a fluid view of gender roles, we likely will adopt the same-sex-couple approach, and our communication will be concerned more with discussing who is best at and likes a task. If we subscribe to more rigid or traditional views of gender roles, however, then our communication will likely focus on keeping those roles in place and not stepping into someone else's "role."

Gender and Friendships

Gender also affects the type and quality of our friendships. Research indicates that women's friendships are often based on communication and self-disclosure. Many women are socialized from a young age to engage in expressive and supportive communication. They typically talk about their feelings, daily lives, and personal struggles. This type of communication allows women to feel closely connected with one another. Men also create and maintain close friendships with others, but instead of building friendships via communication their friendships center around shared activities, such as playing or watching sports or video games or working on projects (Wright, 1982). These gendered differences in friendship formation are also carried into cross-sexed friendships. Although both men and women enjoy cross-sexed friendships, they do so for different reasons. Men typically receive more social and emotional support from their female friends and feel more comfortable expressing themselves emotionally

gender role
used to refer to feminine and masculine social expectations in a family based on a person's sex.

Some of the traditional roles expected of each person in a romantic relationship are changing. What roles are expected of you in your romantic relationships?

without being criticized for violating perceived societal expectations for masculine behavior. Women tend to engage in more competitive activities with male friends and value men's instrumental behavior. In addition, women report that men offer a more "objective viewpoint" than their same-sex friendships (Monsour, 2002).

Gender and Romantic Relationships

If you want to date someone, who is responsible for making the first move? Once you manage to get that date, who pays? And when problems happen in a relationship, who is in charge of handling the emotional aspects of that problem? Although traditional norms for dating and relationships are changing, men still are expected to initiate dates and physical intimacy and women are expected to perform relationship maintenance (Laner & Ventrone, 2000). Men continue to be the primary breadwinners whereas women assume responsibility for domestic labor and child care (only 22 percent of women earn more money than their husbands) (Fry & Cohn, 2010). However, these tendencies are beginning to shift. Studies show that both women and men appreciate partners who not only have professional lives but also assume domestic responsibilities, engage in expressive communication, and do things for and with their partners (Cancian & Oliker, 2000). Meanwhile, more and more men want to and are becoming more involved in raising their children.

Gender influences how we experience and communicate in our interpersonal relationships. The ways we negotiate our first meetings, our dates, our time together—in short, our romantic relationships—are often determined by society's expectations for gender. Sexuality plays into these scripts as well: heterosexual couples tend to follow more traditional roles and expectations, gay men tend to be more emotionally expressive than straight men (but less than heterosexual and lesbian women), and lesbian couples tend to rank the highest of all groups for emotional expressiveness and relationship maintenance (Biblarz & Savci, 2010; Downing & Goldberg, 2010; Goldberg & Perry-Jenkins, 2007). In addition to learning how we perform gender based on our interpersonal relationships, our culture also affects the way we experience our relationships.

 ## Culture and Interpersonal Relationships

Interpersonal relationships are influenced by the culture in which they reside. **Culture** is defined as *the learned patterns of perception, values, and behaviors, shared by a group of people* (Martin & Nakayama, 2004). Perhaps you have traveled to another country and noticed differences in communication styles, dress, behaviors, or lifestyles. Some of these

culture
the learned patterns of perception, values, and behaviors, shared by a group of people.

differences may be based on the type of culture you were visiting. **Individualistic cultures** such as those in North America and northern Europe believe individual autonomy and independence is important. Individuals are expected to *make their own decisions, take responsibility for their actions, and be self-sufficient.* **Collectivist cultures** such as those in Latin America and Asia emphasize the needs of the group. *Collectivist cultures value relationships and harmony with others; therefore, the individual's needs are subordinate to the group's needs.*

When different cultures perceive different goals for relationships, it is not surprising that there are also differences in how members of a given culture communicate with one another. **Low-context cultures** *emphasize direct and literal communication.* For example, in the United States, straightforward, honest, and detailed information is valued. People tend to say what they mean and mean what they say. By contrast, **high-context cultures** often avoid confrontation and use the context surrounding the communicative act and nonverbal cues to determine the meaning of the message. High-context cultures, which are common in many Eastern cultures, may use *less straightforward and more indirect communication.* Therefore, people must "read between the lines" to understand what another is actually saying. For example, instead of answering a question using "yes" or "no," members of high-context cultural groups may respond by saying, "Let me get back to you." Cultures are not necessarily high context or low context in an isolated and absolute way; rather, contexts exist on a continuum with some cultures being higher or lower than others.

To maintain a successful relationship with members of different cultures, it is important that we understand the differences in communication styles and behavioral practices. Learning about the history, values, and practices from other cultures is the first step toward building and maintaining our intercultural relationships. You will read more about how culture affects working in groups and teams in Chapter 8 and 9.

individualistic culture
culture in which individuals make their own decisions, take responsibility for their actions, and are self-sufficient.

collectivist culture
culture that values relationships and harmony with others.

low-context culture
culture in which people emphasize direct and literal communication.

high-context culture
culture in which people use less straightforward and more indirect communication.

Chapter Summary

Interpersonal Relationships Consist of Personal Connections Made with Others Through the Intentional Use of Communication

- The way we interact with others is often determined by the type of interpersonal relationship, therefore making every interpersonal relationship unique.
- Relationships require a certain degree of commitment.
- Interpersonal relationships function by their own set of rules as determined by those involved in the relationship.
- There are different types of interpersonal relationships, including families, friendships, and romantic partners.

Families Consist of a Network of People Who Are Bound Together by Ties of Marriage or Blood or Through Commitment to Another

- Married or cohabiting couples may have relationships that are interdependent, independent, separate, or a combination of relationship types.
- There is no universal definition of family in the United States.
- Family relationships tend to evolve and shift over time.

Friendships Tend to Go Through Stages as They Develop Over Time

- Friendships go through six stages as they form, develop, and dissolve: (1) role-limited interaction, (2) friendly relations, (3) moves toward friendship, (4) nascent friendship, (5) stabilized friendship, and (6) waning friendship.
- Friendships grow and develop depending on the level of communication, self-disclosure, and trust that exists.

Romantic Relationships May Develop Similarly to Friendships

- The five steps that occur as the romantic relationship develops toward commitment include initiating, experimenting, intensifying, integrating, and bonding.
- Relational maintenance, or everyday mundane activities, can help keep a relationship together.
- Relationships go through five steps or stages when they begin to deteriorate: differentiating, circumscribing, stagnating, avoiding, and terminating.

Self-Disclosure Can Be an Important Part of Relationship Development and Maintenance

- Self-disclosure involves the degree of breadth and depth of oneself as shared with another person.
- Self-disclosure allows us to gain a better understanding of our thoughts and opinions, improves the quality of our relationships, and provides us the opportunity to discover new things about ourselves.
- It is important to carefully consider the appropriateness and purpose of self-disclosure before sharing personal information with others.

Technology Has Changed the Way Relationships Form and Evolve Over Time

- Most communication via the Internet is text based and is either asynchronous or synchronous.
- Internet users often use hyperpersonal communication to maintain interpersonal relationships.
- Computer-mediated communication has the potential to negatively affect personal and professional lives, so users should be cautious about posting personal information, photos, and videos.

Sex and Gender Affect the Way We View Relationships

- The family is usually the first source of information to teach us about gender roles and expectations.
- Women's friendships are often based on their ability to communicate and self-disclose, whereas men tend to build friendships around shared activities.
- Gender may affect women and men differently in the workplace. For example, women continue to earn less than their male counterparts.
- Heterosexual romantic relationships continue to uphold many traditional gender roles. For example, many men are still expected to initiate dates and physical intimacy, whereas women are expected to perform relationship maintenance.

Culture Influences Interpersonal Relationships

- Individualistic and collectivist cultures approach relationship goals differently.
- Low-context cultures emphasize direct communication and tend to mean what they say.
- High-context cultures use less direct communication and rely more on nonverbal communication and context surrounding the communication act.
- Successful relationships between members of different cultures requires an understanding of each culture's difference in communication styles and behavioral practices.

Key Concepts

Invitation to Human Communication Online

MindTap Speech includes an interactive MindTap Reader and interactive learning tools, including National Geographic Explorer videos, student videos, quizzes, flash cards, and more. You can build your speech outline with Outline Builder and record, post, and watch videos with YouSeeU. Go to cengagebrain.com to access your MindTap for *Invitation to Human Communication* where these resources can be found.

MindTap®

Further Reflection and Discussion

1. Think about married couples in your family: parents, aunts and uncles, cousins. Which couples have inter-dependent relationships? Independent? Separate? A combined type? Explain how each couple exhibits that type of relationship.

2. What are some activities or actions that indicate a relationship is in the initiating stage? What are some activities that indicate the experimenting, intensifying, integrating, and bonding stages?

3. Discuss how you know when it is appropriate to disclose personal information about yourself in a relationship with a friend, family member, or romantic partner.

4. In romantic relationships, who is expected to initiate dates? Who is expected to maintain the relationship? Discuss how these roles may be between same-sex and heterosexual relationships and what advantages or disadvantages there might be.

5. What is your experience with gender roles in the home? Discuss this with one or more of your parents or grandparents. Do they represent gender equity? Are gender roles generational?

6. What personal information do you share about yourself in a friendship with a same-sex friend? How do you make this decision?

7. Do you believe social media should be used to announce a breakup? Why or why not?

8. In what ways does the use of Facebook, Instagram, and Twitter positively affect college students? In what ways do social-media accounts negatively affect college students?

9. To demonstrate the different stages of a friendship, write a one-minute speech that includes the information you share about yourself in stage one of a friendship, the role-limited interaction stage. Then write a one-minute speech including the information you would share in stage three, where the friendship continues to develop. How much more information is revealed in stage three?

10. Prepare and deliver a speech informing the class on how social media has somehow made a difference in your life.

Activities and Web Links

Visit cengagebrain.com to access the MindTap for *Invitation to Human Communication* where these activities and web links can be found.

1. Read the article and watch the video about Zach Wahls defending the right to same-sex marriage. Does this change your opinion on the issue? What is your definition of a family? Think critically about the arguments on the other side of the issue—that is, those who disagree with you. What are their arguments? How do you respond civilly? Find a credible online newspaper or magazine article that supports each side of the debate. What arguments are given? Are they presented civilly? Go to *Weblink 6.1*.

2. Read this article on how social-media blunders can affect interpersonal relationships at work, at home, and even in the government. Search the Internet for other Twitter or Facebook blunders and devise a policy to present your supervisor at work on how employees can avoid making blunders and what actions to take if they make such a mistake. Go to *Weblink 6.2*.

Improving Interpersonal Communication

Interpersonal Relationships
and Conflict

The Nature of Conflict

Creating a Positive Interpersonal
Communication Climate

Civility in Interpersonal Conflict

Challenges in Interpersonal
Relationships

IN THIS CHAPTER YOU
WILL LEARN TO:

- Discuss the reasons for
  interpersonal conflict.

- Explain how our perceived goals
  influence the different ways we
  handle conflict.

- Identify how our gender roles and
  our cultural norms shape how we
  manage conflict.

- Describe the three ways
  technology and conflict are
  intertwined.

- Discuss the four possible
  outcomes for conflict resolution.

- Explain how interpersonal
  communication climates and
  civility can help us manage
  conflict.

xPACIFICA/Terra/Corbis

Computer-mediated communication (CMC) allows us the ability to maintain relationships over periods of geographic separation. How many relationships are you maintaining via the use of CMC?

C onflict. Few people like it, but it is common in interpersonal relationships. Did you have a recent disagreement with someone in your family or with a friend or co-worker? How did you react? Did your heart beat faster when you raised your voice? Did you walk away from the situation? Or did you respond using a calm voice? When people are in close relationships with family members, roommates, friends, or romantic partners, there is an increased opportunity to disagree (Lloyd & Cate, 1985). According to researchers Ritu Kaushal and Catherine Kwantes (2006), whether conflict "occurs in the form of a difference of opinion, harsh words, or a form of direct action taken to resolve competing goals, it has the potential to exist in the many domains of our lives" (p. 580). Kaushal and Kwantes contend that our increasingly busy lifestyles have meant less time for ourselves and the people around us, leaving a precarious balance between work, family, and everything in between. This increased sense of urgency has left many of us scrambling and without the time we need to speak with family members, friends, and co-workers. We often do not have time to communicate our needs, to clarify the motivations and intentions behind our behaviors, or to understand the needs and motivations of others. This increases the potential for misperception and miscommunication, two of the negative aspects of conflict (Kaushal & Kwantes, 2006).

Understanding the reasons for interpersonal conflict and appropriate ways to handle conflict improves our interpersonal relationships. In this chapter, we discuss the nature of conflict, reasons for interpersonal conflict, and strategies for successfully managing conflict situations.

Interpersonal Relationships and Conflict

Although some people try to avoid engaging in conflict because they believe it signals the end of a relationship, having an honest discussion about differences can actually be healthy for a relationship. In fact, healthy conflict is a natural part of most interpersonal relationships. Conflict acknowledges that those involved are in close relationships, are connected to one another, and have feelings for one another. Those feelings might be love, friendship, or even jealousy or anger. **Interpersonal conflict** occurs *when two interdependent parties express*

interpersonal conflict
when two interdependent parties express different opinions, goals, or interests.

different opinions, goals, or interests. When those goals or interests clash, they come into conflict and a struggle or battle occurs. Because there are many ways people react to conflict, we explore the nature of conflict next.

Although most people do not like conflict, it can be an important part of a relationship. Think of the last conflict you had with someone. Were you more concerned for yourself or for the other person?

The Nature of Conflict

When people are in conflict, the root cause is often incompatibility (e.g., two people wanting different things) or perceived scarcity of rewards (e.g., time and money). Friends may disagree over personal needs. Romantic partners may disagree about where to purchase a home. Parents may disagree on the best approach to raising a child. Roommates may disagree about who is responsible for certain chores around the apartment. Co-workers may disagree about how to complete a project. Although some people choose to ignore the conflict in hopes that the conflict will go away, other people may rush in to engage in a heated argument with the goal of "winning" or achieving their goals.

Our responses to conflict can be distinguished by two dimensions: (1) concern for self and (2) concern for others. When people express **concern for self**, *they seek to satisfy their own desires and needs through direct and assertive communication.* In contrast, *when we attempt to get along with and satisfy the other's needs using cooperative communication,* we are said to be showing **concern for others**. Consider the following two scenarios:

Concern for self: Marissa and Manuel (sister and brother) are in conflict over who gets how much space and time in their shared bathroom. Marissa, expressing concern for herself, wants one uninterrupted hour every morning and to leave her "stuff" on the counters, floors, and so on. Manuel also wants an hour of uninterrupted time at the same hour that Marissa wants, and he also does not feel the need to clean up after himself. Both are expressing concern for self; as you can imagine, the conflict remains heated and unresolved.

Concern for others: Marissa and Manuel (sister and brother) share a bathroom, and both have jobs that require professional dress and appearance. Both have to be at work at the same time, and they have to travel the same distance to their jobs. They also do not want to take time every morning to clean up their messes. After conversation, they agree on the following compromise. They will alternate mornings so that one person gets the bathroom from 5:30 to 6:30 and the other from 6:30 to 7:30. To help contain their messes, they set up shelves and baskets so that they each can dump their stuff in the assigned spots. They show concern for one another in deciding to alternate "early mornings," and they agree to try the solution for one month and then check with each other to see how the arrangement is working.

Research suggests that beyond our concerns for self and others are five conflict styles that depend on our perceived goals and help to explain the

concern for self
when individuals seek to satisfy their own desires and needs through direct and assertive communication.

concern for others
when individuals attempt to get along with and satisfy another's needs using cooperative communication.

different ways we handle conflict (Thomas & Kilmann, 2007): competing, accommodating, avoiding, compromising, and collaborating.

Competing. People who use a competing style seek to control the interaction. They are more concerned with their own goals than the goals of the other person. People who compete want to "win" any argument.

Accommodating. People who use an accommodating style are more concerned for others than they are for themselves, so they will yield to others, passively accepting others' decisions, and neglect to make their own needs a priority.

Avoiding. The avoiding style occurs when someone chooses to physically or psychologically withdraw from conflict. People who use the avoiding style tend to believe that "if we don't talk about it, maybe the problem will go away." Other behaviors include denying a conflict exists, avoiding particular topics, or remaining silent about a conflict.

Compromising. The compromising style emphasizes cooperation. When people compromise, each person is willing to give up something to reach an agreement. This is often referred to as "meeting someone halfway."

Collaborating. The collaborating style focuses on cooperative problem solving in order to satisfy everyone's goals and needs. People who use a collaborative style are concerned not only for themselves but also for others. Establishing open lines of communication and seeking and sharing information will help those involved reach a solution in which everyone "wins."

How we choose to respond to conflict may also depend on our family of origin—or what we learned from those who took care of us when we were growing up. Recent studies suggest that people use styles of managing conflict that were learned in their family of origin (Taylor & Segrin, 2010). If our caregivers avoided conflict, then we might model that same strategy. If they fought heatedly or showed concern for one another, we are likely to adopt those styles as adults. In addition to the relationship type, our reactions to conflict may also be determined by gender and culture.

Gender and Conflict

In Chapter 4, you learned that language is influenced by gender; in Chapters 8 and 9 you will read about gender in group communication and how it can affect leadership. But how might our gender play a role in interpersonal conflict? We know that boys and girls are encouraged early on to use language differently and strategically. On one hand, girls typically learn to communicate in order to be cooperative and inclusive. They may be encouraged to "play nice." This can result in girls using avoiding or accommodating conflict styles that minimize conflict and help maintain relationships. On the other hand, boys may be encouraged to use competitive language. When boys assert themselves to establish the rules of a game or achieve some desired result, they may resort to using a competing style to manage conflict. We carry these language styles and

Conflict can be affected by our gender roles. What types of communication would you expect from these two women engaged in conflict? Does your style of conflict conform to gender expectations?

practices into adulthood, and these styles as well as our learned gender roles influence how we manage conflict. Remember, though, that gender influences (not determines) our language styles, and our other master statuses also shape our communication.

Gender roles, *the social expectations for how males and females should behave*, have also been linked to conflict styles. Strongly sex-typed individuals (those who strongly identify as masculine or feminine) may be constrained by stereotypical behaviors associated with their gender. This means that these individuals may manage conflict in ways that are perceived as appropriate for their gender (Bern & Lenney, 1976). For example, masculine gender roles often are associated with competing styles (so highly gender-identified males might use the win–lose approach to conflict), while avoiding behaviors are more consistent with feminine gender roles (so highly gender-identified females might use accommodating or avoiding styles of conflict) (Brower, Mitchell, & Weber, 2002). Individuals perceived as **androgynous**, meaning they *display both masculine and feminine behaviors*, are more likely to adopt compromising styles. So, the communication styles and gender-role behaviors we learn as children for managing conflict often are carried into adulthood.

gender roles
the social expectations for how males and females should behave.

androgynous
displaying both masculine and feminine traits or behaviors.

NATIONAL GEOGRAPHIC SPEAKS

Aziz Abu Sarah, National Geographic Explorer and Cultural Educator: Throwing Stones

Have you ever felt animosity toward someone or even a group of people that you had little or no actual interaction with? Have you ever had a neighbor you rarely spoke to yet did not particularly care for? Did your high school have a rival school? Did you or any of your classmates pull pranks against students at this rival school? If you answered yes to any of these questions, you have something in common with Aziz Abu Sarah.

Aziz Abu Sarah was born in Jerusalem. He was only nine years old when he watched Israeli soldiers storm into his home and arrest his eighteen-year-old brother, Tayseer, for allegedly throwing stones at Israeli cars. Tayseer was kept without a trial, interrogated, and beaten for fifteen days until he was finally coerced into admitting he had thrown the stones. Tayseer was held for eleven months, beaten repeatedly, and finally died within weeks of being released from prison. Aziz describes the pain he felt for losing his closest brother and how angry and bitter he felt toward Israelis. He wanted someone to be held responsible for his brother's death. He wanted revenge.

Aziz spent his adolescence and teenage years writing angry articles for a youth magazine. He describes how he used his "pain to spread hatred against the other side." Aziz refused to learn Hebrew because it was considered the "enemy's language." However, he knew that to attend college or obtain a good job, he would have to put his anger aside and study Hebrew. So he attended an institute that taught Hebrew to Jewish newcomers to Israel. Aziz recalls, "It was the first time I had sat in a room of Jews who were not superior to me. It was the first time I had seen faces different from the soldiers at checkpoints. Those soldiers had taken my brother; these students were the same as me. My understanding of the Jewish people started to collapse after just a few weeks of the Ulpan. I found myself confused, thinking 'How can they be normal human beings just like me?'"

Aziz soon discovered that he had a few things in common with his Jewish classmates, and he eventually formed friendships with them. Aziz believes, "As humans, we try to rationalize our hatred. In our minds we demonize the enemy, and discredit their humanity. This is the lie that fires the conflict between Israel and Palestine." Aziz now works as a lecturer and speaks in churches, synagogues, and mosques on the subject of Israeli-Palestinian conflict, peace, reconciliation, and interfaith dialogue. Aziz has won numerous awards for his work in the Israeli–Palestinian peace movement (Sarah, 2009).

WHAT DO YOU THINK?

1. In what ways does Aziz's story illustrate concern for self and concern for others?

2. How does a civil approach to handling conflict help explain Aziz's ability to resolve his feelings toward the Israeli people?

3. Consider a conflict you have had. What conflict strategies discussed in this chapter would work to resolve this conflict?

MindTap® Go to cengagebrain.com to access your MindTap for *Invitation to Human Communication* to view a video about Aziz Abu Sarah.

Culture and Conflict

Our conflict-management styles also are influenced by culture. As we become more aware of and connected to individuals from other countries, scholars are working to understand how cultural norms and practices influence conflict. Social psychologist Geert Hofstede (1986) explains that in Asian cultures, which are predominately collective in nature, people tend to value harmony and relationships with others. Many people from Asian cultures believe in the importance of studying and working hard to prepare for their future. On the other hand, many Western cultures (including the United States) value independence and autonomy. Rather than focusing on the future, individuals from these cultures tend to be more focused on immediate gratification. The differences between collectivist and individualist can influence communication patterns and conflict-resolution strategies. For example, people residing in collectivist cultures may tend to avoid expressing direct opinions about their own motivations and personal goals. In contrast, individualist cultures often use more direct and explicit language to convey personal thoughts and motivations and to handle conflict (Hall & Hall, 1989). Leung and Lind (1986) examined how American and Chinese people responded to conflict and concluded that Americans had a stronger preference for using adversarial resolution strategies, and Chinese individuals preferred nonadversarial or cooperative strategies. More recently, Holt and DeVore (2005) concluded that members of collectivist cultures tend to rely on more passive strategies such as the avoiding strategy to manage conflict.

But a person's cultural background influences more than just how conflict is managed. Culture influences which goals are considered incompatible, why such goals are seen as incompatible, how someone responds to incompatible goals, and whether the outcome is perceived as satisfactory or not. The nature of conflict itself thus varies across cultures. What one culture may address as an incompatible goal may not be acknowledged at all in another culture (Kaushal & Kwantes, 2006).

Conflict occurs for many social and personal reasons, and this means that the same conflict scenario may be handled differently across different cultures. For example, "disagreeing with a parent may be entirely acceptable in Canada and not at all condoned in Africa" (Kaushal & Kwantes, 2006, p. 581). Psychologists Kwantes and Kaushal also remind us that it is important to acknowledge both cultural and personality factors when trying to predict how someone will respond to conflict situations (2006, p. 581). For example, self-monitoring, regardless of the culture an individual is from, can affect the way conflict is managed. High self-monitors, those who emphasize "concern for others," are more likely to resolve conflict by using collaborative and compromising strategies. In contrast, low self-monitors often display less concern for others' needs and will likely resort to using the competing or avoiding resolution strategies (Warech, Smither, Reilly, Millsap, & Reilly, 1998). (For additional information on self-monitoring, see Chapter 2.) Although cultural practices and norms do affect how conflict is managed, they are just some of many factors in how disputes get resolved. Technology, which is explored next, also affects conflicts and their resolution.

Cultural Representations and Stereotypes

In 2013, administrators at California Polytechnic State University—San Luis Obispo launched a "cultural insensitivity and sexism" investigation into a Thanksgiving fraternity—sorority party with the theme of "Colonial Bros and Nava-hos" that 75 to 100 students allegedly attended. Male students reportedly donned colonial-era outfits, and female students dressed as sexy, scantily clad Native American women. After Native American students and faculty complained, Jennifer Rose Denetdale, associate professor of American Studies at the University of New Mexico and Navajo herself, condemned the party theme in an *Indian Country* op-ed:

> To invoke "Colonial Bros," then, is to refer to one of the most darkest moments in American history and certainly for the Navajo people, it is a reference to one of the most brutal, humiliating, and devastating experiences under American colonialism. To refer to the scantily clad women who came as "Nava-Hos" is to not only diminish the Navajo people as whole, because the term connotes "whore" and "prostitute" and suggests that Navajo women were sexually

available to the white soldiers; it says that it is not possible to rape or sexually assault Navajo women, because they are inherently rapable. "Colonial Bros and Nava-Hos" is also a slander on Navajo women who have survived rape and sexual assault that was a part of conquest. (Denetdale, 2013)

Cal Poly SLO president Jeffrey Armstong denounced the event in an e-mail to the entire student body: "Let us be clear, events like these have no place in the Cal Poly community and are not reflective of the principles of The Mustang Way. Obviously, this was not a university-sponsored event." Many campus and community members agreed that the event was in poor taste, but some students reported finding nothing wrong with the theme. A poll taken by the *Mustang News*, the campus newspaper, included a few of the students' reactions:

> "Personally, I don't think it was meant to be racist. . . . It's unfair. We are taught that Thanksgiving is Pilgrims and Indians."

> "There are a lot more offensive themes out there, especially during Halloween."

> "I think people are too sensitive these days. Not saying that the theme was not inappropriate, but there is so much more injustice in the world going on right now than a stupid frat party."

> "I think the action taken is too severe due to the fact that the sorority and fraternity made a bad decision, but I don't think they were purposefully targeting these groups." (Dries, 2013)

What Do You Think?

1. Do you think it's appropriate to use stereotypes and potentially offensive representations of cultures as themes for parties or costumes for Halloween? Why or why not?
2. Do you think the First Amendment's free speech rights provide protections for groups to host such parties?
3. Should the university be involved in investigating events that display cultural insensitivity but are hosted off campus? Why or why not?

Technology and Conflict

Today, many of us stay continuously connected to and communicating with families, friends, and co-workers using some form of electronic technology such as tablets, cell phones, and smartphones. As we spend more time using technology to interact, complete group projects, solicit feedback, and comment on our daily lives, it is no surprise that technology is also providing ways for us to create as well as resolve conflict. Let us look at three ways technology and conflict are intertwined: technology as a source of conflict, culture and technology, and technology and international conflict.

Technology as a Source of Conflict Information and communication technology (ICT) actually may be a source of conflict. This is because a "digital generation gap" often exists between children and their parents and grandparents. For many young and savvy ICT users, conflict occurs with parents or grandparents who know little about more advanced forms of technology. A study examining U.S. teenagers and their parents' interactions over technology use revealed that when parents or grandparents were unfamiliar with technology's capabilities, they would encourage older siblings or relatives to monitor the technology use of the youngest users. This often caused conflict between family members. Lynn Schofield Clark explains that "extended families were often a source of additional supervision" (2009, p. 397). One young woman reported that her aunt monitored her social-media use and would often tell her grandparents about her activities. Other teenagers believe their parents were "snooping" into their private lives by checking their social-networking sites (Clark, 2009).

No matter which family member monitored a teenager's online activity, conflict took place over how much privacy a teenager should have online from his or her parents. Schofield Clark concluded that teenagers and their parents used different strategies to address the knowledge gap. Although some parents used a competing strategy and imposed authoritarian rules to regulate the amount of time spent and the type of content posted on Internet sites, other parents took a different approach by talking with their children and asking questions about their online participation. Regardless of how knowledgeable parents are about digital technology, they can "retain a positive relationship with, and even an authoritative role in, their teens' lives, when they expressed trust and respect for their teenage children and the ways in which they chose to engage in practices in the digital realm" (Clark, 2009, p. 403).

Monkey Business Images/Getty Images

Parents often monitor the amount of time their children spend on their computers, as well as the sites they are visiting. Even though it can create conflict, do you think this is an effective way to parent? Why or why not?

Technology can also create interpersonal conflicts when friends post hurtful messages known as *flames*, or verbal attacks on others, to their social-media accounts. **Flaming** is *the uninhibited expression of hostility such as swearing, name-calling, ridicule, and insults toward another person, his or her character, religion, race, intelligence, and physical or mental ability* (Kayany, 1998). If you are the target of flaming, it may be tempting to respond with similarly hurtful language, but you can try to resolve the conflict by establishing a dialogue with the person. Ask for information that led to the sender's assumptions or conclusions or acknowledge the claims made and then respectfully state an alternative perspective.

Technology and Culture Cultural influences also affect the ways technology contributes to conflict. Research examining how students from collectivist and individualist cultures engaged in potential conflict in their online discussion forums illustrated a few of these cultural differences. When comparing students from Hong Kong with U.S. students

flaming

uninhibited expression of hostility such as swearing, name-calling, ridicule, and insults directed toward another person, his or her character, religion, race, intelligence, and physical or mental ability.

participating in threaded discussion forums, the amount of disagreement as well as the way in which students disagreed was different. Take a look at some of the responses to the topic of global warming:

Students from Hong Kong

> "I can see your point, but I think global warming is the most important thing that we have to pay attention to."

> "Someone expressed that the factories need to control their pollutants, but I wanted to point out that without many of the factories and their way of production we would lack many resources."

> "Therefore, ozone depletion is a serious problem, too. Do you think so?"

> "Can you suggest other methods to protect our world?"

Students from the United States

> "I have to disagree with some of the assumptions that you have made about global warming, which you clearly based off of this one article alone."

> "She said that the air quality is improving. I was wondering where she learned this. It is completely wrong."

> "It helps out the wildlife, plant life, and us. Anyway those are my feelings on this discussion."

> "I strongly doubt that anyone is willing to give up their cars. End of story." (Seo, Miller, Schmidt, & Sowa, 2008)

Notice that the students from Hong Kong avoided using the words *disagree* or *wrong* and encouraged participation by inviting others to respond. On the other hand, the U.S. students were more direct and straightforward when they disagreed, and they rarely encouraged further discussion. The Hong Kong students' posts indicated little explicit disagreement. Meanwhile, the U.S. students' posts often directly confronted one another when disagreeing. So, although technology is present for students from both countries, disagreements are handled differently.

Technology and International Conflict Computer-mediated communication (CMC) can provide support and outlets for those living in regions that experience war. For example, Twitter accounts, Facebook, YouTube, and other social-media and video sites allow people who are experiencing conflict to communicate their stories to people around the world. In 2012, Malala Yousafzai's story went viral on social-media accounts worldwide after this teenager survived an assassination attempt by the Taliban. Malala's determination to receive an education despite Taliban objections to the education of females began in 2008 when Malala started writing an anonymous blog about her life as a Pakistani schoolgirl. Malala posted her first blog entry at age eleven. In it, she wrote, "I had a terrible dream yesterday with military helicopters and the [Taliban]. . . . I was afraid going to school because the [Taliban] had issued an edict banning all girls from attending schools" (BBC News, 2009).

ETHICAL MOMENT

When Anonymous Posts Turn From Helpful to Hurtful

Today's teenagers and young adults are now posting their own secrets, telling other people's secrets, starting rumors, and even issuing threats on anonymous message boards using every type of smart device. Whisper, an anonymous mobile social network, helps people share secrets they otherwise would not tell. Viewers are allowed to "like" or comment on the whispers, and because no profiles are created, there is no way to track a secret back to its poster. Because Whisper has a zero-tolerance policy toward bullying, users feel it is a safe outlet and often admit the social network helped them "stop self-harming behaviors" or even saved their lives. With more than 4 million users, the app has received nearly 3 billion page views with hundreds of thousands of whispers uploaded each day (Fox, 2013)

But not all anonymous Web sites and apps are as helpful as Whisper. Yik Yak, a popular application used by college students across the United States, allows users to post anonymous bulletin-board messages that are then received by anyone using the device within a 1.5-mile radius. Although Yik Yak may have been intended to help create a sense of community with others in close proximity, it is often used to post "violent and racist 'yaks' without any foreseeable risk" (Hoffman, 2015). For example, one Eastern Michigan University professor reported being harassed on Yik Yak. To help minimize abuse of the app, Yik Yak now prevents yakkers from publishing full names and has placed so-called geo-fences around elementary and secondary schools to prevent their students from accessing the app. Although filters have been helpful, some observers argue that it is not enough. University of Delaware president Patrick T. Harker criticized the entire student body after derogatory yaks were posted about rival school students of color. Both University of Delaware and Delaware State University students were offended by the yaks, yet the yakkers went unpunished because the company protected them and their identities (Hoffman, 2015).

What Do You Think?

1. What anonymous Web sites and social-media applications are you familiar with? Do you think these sites are helpful or hurtful?

2. Do you think applications such as Yik Yak should be allowed near college campuses? Why or why not?

3. What type of restrictions, if any, do you think should be placed on Web sites and applications that allow anonymous posting?

After blogging to share her story, Malala began appearing in documentaries and on television news programs to publicly advocate for female education. One day on her way home from school, a masked gunman boarded the bus she was riding, asked Malala to identify herself, and then shot her. Miraculously, Malala survived the assassination attempt. Her story received worldwide media coverage and created international campaigns supporting the right for girls everywhere to be educated.

Today, technology is still helping to keep this international issue in the spotlight. Information on Malala's activism can be found on many YouTube videos, Instagram, Facebook accounts, Twitter accounts, and eBooks. In addition, Malala's story has encouraged teachers around the world to educate students about how to use technology to promote positive social change. Darcy Addo (2014), a teacher affiliated with The Virtual Voice, a Florida virtual school blog, believes everyone has a story to tell:

> Each day I speak to my Social Media students about their passion projects; we talk about how they can use their voice to create positive social change. . . . Our students—and all kids, really—care about social issues and want to make a difference in the world and in their community. "Issues" are relative, and we are blessed beyond measure not to have the concerns that Malala and many

THE NATURE OF CONFLICT | **151**

JONATHAN NACKSTRAND/Getty Images

Press conferences generate news about events that are timely and relevant. What types of situations are most appropriate for holding a press conference? How might press conferences be used to increase cultural awareness and understanding?

oppressed women in many parts of the world do, but our students do have their own issues and concerns. They want to stop bullying, promote kindness, and create safe havens for victimized kids. They want to promote pet adoption, have canned food drives, and work toward creating equality for various communities.

When used during times of international conflict, technology can help people understand stories of conflict, hope, activism, and change.

However, computer-mediated communication can also be used to help increase cultural awareness, understanding, and appreciation. As our world continues to become more interconnected, we will continue to see CMC's effects on our ability to communicate effectively and to resolve differences across the globe. In the next section, we explore some of the most common and most effective ways to manage conflict in our interpersonal relationships.

Managing Conflict

Managing conflict can be difficult, especially when the individuals involved are determined to have their goals met. We look at four possible outcomes for conflict: win–lose, lose–lose, compromise, and win–win.

Win–Lose The win–lose conflict-resolution outcome occurs when one person succeeds at accomplishing the desired goal at the expense of the other person. This means that one person essentially "wins" and the other "loses." Typically, this outcome is based on positions of power, access to resources, and even voting. Take a look at the following win–lose scenarios:

> Charlene learns from her supervisor that her work hours will be cut in half and that she will lose her company's health-insurance benefits. Charlene speaks to human resources and asks to be kept at forty hours per week so she can retain her health-care benefits. She is told that her hours and her benefits will be cut. The supervisor won; Charlene lost.

> Nine-year-old Timmy wants to stay up past his usual bedtime, but his mother disagrees and forces him to go to bed at his usual time. Timmy's mother achieves her goal of getting Timmy to bed on time, and Timmy loses his attempt to stay up late.

> Jassim runs for public office in his hometown. He campaigns for several months and learns on election night that he lost the election to his rival. Jassim's opponent won, and Jassim lost.

The first two examples illustrate how positions of authority can determine the outcome of a conflict situation. The third example reveals how a democratic process, or competition decided by a vote, can create a *win–lose* situation. At times, the win–lose scenario is unavoidable. For example, sporting events and elections are designed to have clear winners. At other times, the winner may not actually gain much; this is called a *lose–lose* strategy.

Lose–Lose In a lose–lose conflict-managing strategy, neither party is content with the outcome. Take, for example, Charlene's work situation. The company Charlene works for is facing a financial crisis, making it difficult to pay Charlene a full-time salary and benefits; however, the workload for the company has remained the same. Charlene's supervisor now has to assume more responsibility; therefore, both Charlene and her supervisor lose something in the resolution. Charlene is now being paid less, and her supervisor is now expected to work more. Moreover, the company still is having a difficult time paying its expenses. In this situation, no one is likely to feel content with the outcome. When both parties are unsatisfied with the outcome, it is important to consider whether another resolution such as a compromise is possible.

Compromise When two parties compromise, both are willing to give up part of their desired outcomes. Consider Timmy's request to stay up past his 8 P.M. bedtime. On Friday night, he asks to stay up until 9 P.M. Although his mother wants him to go to bed at his usual time to prepare for a busy Saturday filled with activities and errands, she decides to allow him to stay up until 8:30 P.M. In this situation, Timmy and his mother both achieved part of their initial goals.

If Charlene is able to compromise with her company to cut her hours to part-time but allow her to keep her benefits, then Charlene and her company each gain part of their desired goal. Charlene promises to not leave (forcing the company to bear the burden of finding another part-time employee or making other employees take on additional responsibilities), and Charlene keeps her health insurance.

Sometimes compromise can make those involved feel satisfied that part of their desired goal was achieved. However, sometimes compromise can produce a sense of uneasiness, especially if the compromises concern important values and beliefs. For instance, if Jassim adjusts his political platform so that he will be more appealing to voters but those changes go against his values, he may win but has created an uneasy and perhaps unethical path for himself in office.

Win–Win Ideally, everyone involved in a conflict will be satisfied with the solution. However, it can be extremely difficult to find a solution that everyone believes accomplishes their desired goals. Communication and conflict-management scholar Linda Putnam describes important steps that can be taken to help resolve conflict situations and produce win–win outcomes.

PRACTICING HUMAN COMMUNICATION
How Have Technologies Contributed to Conflict?

Can you think of a time when technology escalated or helped resolve a conflict in your life? Now pair up with a classmate and generate examples of how technology might have contributed to the escalation of interpersonal conflict. How were these conflicts resolved? Could technology also have helped deescalate the conflict? How so?

This mother and daughter have achieved a win–win. By agreeing to share computer time, the mother is confident that her daughter uses her online time more productively and safely. The daughter wins because she is allowed more time on the computer. Think of a recent conflict that ended in a win–win. What strategies were used to achieve that result?

Although we use the technique in many types of situations, Putnam explains that **framing**, *the way people use language to define a conflict situation* (Putnam, 2010), can help create a productive communication climate that allows parties to find an agreeable solution. When we frame a conflict, we describe it in a particular way, and this causes us to see it in a particular light. Framing has three steps that can shape the conflict-resolution process:

1. *Name the conflict.* Those involved in the conflict need to give it a name and agree on the labels and language choices used to describe the conflict. This might include introducing a new label, term, or description for the conflict situation. For example, are two people "at war," "at each other's throats," or "struggling to understand different perspectives"? Using different labels to name the conflict can help move the conflict toward resolution.

2. *Consider ways to redefine and shift the blame in the dispute.* Putnam describes this as "shifting the level of abstraction, or location, of the conflict." When the blame or cause of a conflict moves away from a person and becomes about a policy, institutional decision, or some other external force, individuals will likely feel less defensive and more focused on a solution. Although this is often hard to do when we are in an argument with a friend or someone close to us, Putnam urges us to consider how the issue can be moved from "specific to general, part to whole, individual to system level, or vice versa" (Putnam, 2010, p. 329). So, in an interpersonal conflict, rather than accuse the other person of always being late and not caring about you, redefining suggests that you talk about how showing up on time communicates respect and value for you.

3. *Employ the use of systematic questioning.* The third step in this win–win approach is to ask critical questions that can help each party understand the other's needs and goals. Avoid using loaded or leading questions. Leading questions might be "Don't you think that it would be better for you to help out with the chores?" and "Isn't it true that I am the one who always completes the month-end reports for work?" Instead, Putnam suggests that individuals use story questions or systematic questioning. Story questions provide some background to the concern or complaint and allow parties to expand the conflict definition and discuss other details involved in the conflict situation. For example, "I am feeling overwhelmed with my responsibilities at work and at home. I feel as though I can't keep up with it all. Do you think you could help with some of

framing
the way people use language to define a conflict situation.

the chores this week?" The statement shares the story behind the request. Providing information (the story) for how you are feeling and why you may be feeling a certain way gives context to the other person and helps her or him feel less attacked by the request.

Systematic questioning, which involves asking for the reasons something might be happening, is a second approach. In this next example, the systematic question helps the individuals in the conflict determine the motivation behind the issue causing the conflict: "I seem to be the one who turns in the month-end reports each month. Is there a reason you haven't attempted to complete one of these reports?" Using systematic questioning (rather than leading questions) helps two people explore the history and background related to the conflict and can provide additional context for the conflict. "I'm so glad you asked, I don't understand these forms at all and was embarrassed to ask for help" and "I didn't realize we had to do these monthly—no one told me that" are two possible win–win responses to the systematic question previously asked.

Asking questions can sometimes cause additional frustration for those involved in the conflict; therefore, timing is important in this step. Asking questions is ideal when both parties are feeling defensive and losing hope that an amenable solution will be reached. Used correctly, story or systematic questions rather than leading or attacking questions can move a conflict toward helping, rather than inhibiting, the process of reaching an agreeable resolution.

 ## Creating a Positive Interpersonal Communication Climate

Communication climates *set the tone for interpersonal relationships.* These climates can either create a conflict situation or help resolve one. When disconfirming statements are used, a negative climate is established. A **disconfirming statement** is one that *rejects or invalidates another person's statements.* For example, telling someone that her ideas are dumb or that he would never be able to make the team, pass a class, or get a job creates a negative communication climate. Disconfirming statements often use "you" language: "Your idea is terrible." "You never take responsibility for your schoolwork." "You aren't very good at basketball." We can also disconfirm others by ignoring them. When Marcos says, "I'm going out for a while, do you need anything at the store?" and gets no response from his partner, he is being disconfirmed. His partner is creating a negative environment by failing to acknowledge Marcos.

Confirming statements can help us build healthy communication climates and manage conflict productively. **Confirming statements** *validate other people by recognizing them, acknowledging their ideas and feelings, and approving or supporting their ideas.* One way to initiate a confirming statement is to use "I" language: "I really like that idea" or "I think you have a chance at making the team." These confirming statements recognize the ideas and talents of another person and show support for him or her. Confirming statements, however, may not always be appropriate. For example, if someone has chosen

communication climates
climates that set the tone for interpersonal relationships.

disconfirming statement
statement that rejects or invalidates another person's statements.

confirming statements
statements that validate other people by recognizing them, acknowledging their ideas and feelings, and approving or supporting their ideas.

to do something harmful, unethical, or unlawful, then it would be inappropriate to agree with those choices. Talking about why you choose to not go along with such decisions is a better option. And lying to another person is also inappropriate. When your roommate says, "I really like this shirt for the job interview—what do you think?" and it actually looks unprofessional, you can ask what the roommate likes about it and offer some other, more professional options rather than support the original choice.

Although managing conflict can be challenging for most of us, conflict can be resolved with practice and effort, open and respectful communication, and a desire to understand the needs of others. We now turn our attention to some of the external challenges individuals face as they manage their interpersonal relationships.

Civility in Interpersonal Conflict

Civility, as you read in earlier chapters, calls to mind not simply "good manners" but the reality of the "common journey" we share with others. When we participate in interpersonal relationships, we are, as law professor Stephen Carter states, "traveling on the same train" with other people. According to Carter, civility—which involves being willing to listen to others and to give them the chance to explain their reasons, ideas, views, and goals—makes "the ride tolerable" (1998, p. 15). Although U.S. American culture is often known for its many incivilities (road rage, cyberbullying, domestic abuse, interpersonal violence, and even marital infidelity), we do not have to bring these models into our interpersonal relationships. But how do we behave civilly in a conflict, especially one in which there are profound disagreements? Consider the scenario of Grace and Lisbeth and the steps that follow.

Grace and Lisbeth, friends for ten years, are furious with one another. Grace just broke up with her partner of three years, and Lisbeth shares with Grace that she now is dating that person. Grace feels a strong desire to lash out at Lisbeth in order to make her feel badly about her decision. Lisbeth feels defensive and confused—she really likes this person, but she also values Grace's friendship enormously. How might these two work through the conflict civilly?

> Step 1 Grace and Lisbeth find a neutral and safe place to communicate with one another. This might include help from a third party such as a counselor or therapist to help them talk though the issues. Although both are feeling angry and uncertain, they decide to meet at a quiet and neutral place like a coffee shop.

> Step 2 They agree on several civil ground rules. They agree to not interrupt or accuse one another, to be honest, to use "story" and "systematic" questions, and to listen and try to understand the other person even though they both really want to defend themselves.

> Step 3 After Grace explains how hurt and betrayed she feels, she tells Lisbeth, "I thought our friendship was one of trust and value, but I feel really hurt and betrayed. I don't understand how you

could date my ex, when you know how devastated I was when we broke up." Lisbeth listens without interrupting, even though she wants to defend herself as Grace talks, and she honestly tries to understand her friend.

Step 4 Lisbeth explains her actions. She shares that she has been attracted to Grace's ex for a long time, and she explains how difficult it was to see the two of them together. Because she listened to Grace in step 3 and tried to understand Grace's position (rather than defend herself), she has a better idea of how hurt Grace is. She says, "I didn't really think about how hurt you would be; I only thought about my feelings. I should have talked with you about my attraction, right?" Because Grace felt like Lisbeth really listened to her when she shared her feelings and anger, she is more able to put down her defensive side and try to understand Lisbeth's own feelings.

Step 5 Although hurt feelings remain and the conflict is not yet resolved, Grace and Lisbeth are now able to talk about their long friendship, some of the competitive and jealous feelings they have had, and some of the ways they have taken each other for granted. They give one another the opportunity to explain, without interruption, and they create feelings of reciprocity and that each person is valued and listened to.

Step 6 Neither really knows how to resolve the conflict yet. Grace still feels upset, and Lisbeth still really cares for Grace as well as her ex-partner. Lisbeth is able to apologize for not talking to Grace first, and Grace is able to apologize for making it hard for Lisbeth to do so. They agree to meet again in a week and to try to talk more about a possible resolution to the conflict that will work for both of them.

Although the conflict is not resolved, this civil approach lets the two continue to work out issues—as opposed to Grace saying, "I hate you! How could you betray me like this? You're a lying, cheating little #%*!!!" and Lisbeth saying, "I'm a #%*!!!/ You #*@&!!—you only think about yourself and what you want! I introduced the two of you, and look what I get for it!? I'm out of here and good riddance."

In summary, a civil approach to conflict involves six steps:

1. Find a neutral place to talk.
2. Establish ground rules that promote civil communication.
3. Share feelings and experiences using story questions and systematic questions without interrupting.
4. Listen to understand the other person rather than defend yourself.
5. Create new awareness and understandings of one another.
6. Agree to continue the conversation after some time has passed rather than force a resolution immediately (Bone, Griffin, & Scholz, 2008; Ratcliff, 2005).

Although not always successful, this approach to conflict can and does prevent unnecessary hurt and the selfish expression of anger. When both parties are willing, working through conflict civilly can be a powerful and productive communication tool.

Challenges in Interpersonal Relationships

Many pressures can challenge our interpersonal relationships. Three external challenges to interpersonal relationships are distance, difference, and interpersonal violence. We discuss each one of these in the following sections.

Distance

The number of interpersonal relationships that face geographical separations has been steadily increasing over the past few years. Although there are different understandings of what constitutes a long-distance relationship, such as the actual distance and duration of the separation, it is important to recognize how relationships can continue to thrive even in times of physical separation. Friends, family members, and spouses live apart from one another for many reasons. Attending college, military deployment, occupational needs, and dual-career marriages all add to geographical separation or distance in a relationship. Traditional understandings of long-distance relationships suggested that distance would eventually result in a deterioration of the relationship, but more recent research suggests that long-distance relationships can and often do thrive during times of separation.

Research on long-distance relationships has focused heavily on the importance of the face-to-face communication used to maintain the relationships (Dainton & Aylor, 2001; Gerstel & Gross, 1984). For this reason, it is easy to understand how previous scholarship concluded that many long-distance relationships do not survive lengthy periods

Most people have at least one close long-distance friendship. How do you deal with long-distance relationships with family and friends? What role does CMC have in maintaining those relationships?

Mireya Mayor
Emerging Explorer, Primatologist, and Conservationist

What strategies do you use to help maintain the relationship with your kids, particularly when you're separated for long periods?

I have four girls, and in many situations, I don't have a way of communicating with them because I don't have access to the Internet or a phone. And in many cases, I can't even send a letter. So I make a poster with a calendar on it, and I put a picture of me at home with them at the beginning of the calendar. The calendar tracks each day and tells them where I'll be—in the jungle, or flying, that sort of thing. Then at the end I have a picture of me at home with them. So they get a sense of time and place because sometimes I'm gone for six weeks at a time without any sort of communication whatsoever. I'll also create a little photo album and leave that with them to open up when they miss me.

As far as with the adults in my life, there are times where I do have access to a satellite phone, so the communication is infrequent but possible. And then, of course, there's letters, but also the journals that I keep. My journals are open access. I write in them at the end of every day, so that when I get home, the adults in my life can read them and "catch up" with me and where I've been. In fact, I wrote my book based on the journals that I kept while I was on these expeditions.

You know, we take for granted the fact that we have endless options for communicating, whether it is text or Twitter or Facebook or the telephone, or e-mail. There are just so many ways in which you can communicate with somebody. But in the line of work that I'm in, those are all completely removed. And so you do have to think of other ways, and while they're not as instantaneous as we are used to, they still tell your story.

of separation. However, the ability to communicate with friends (and maintain friendships) over great distances is now easier than ever. Advancements in computer-mediated communication such as Webcams allow long-distance partners to communicate face to face. In addition, texting, instant messaging, and communicating via social-media sites can provide daily updates on the happenings and whereabouts of friends, family members, and romantic partners that were previously impossible. Happily, the use of CMC can help a relationship remain strong even through times of geographical separation.

Most individuals have at least one close long-distance friendship; 82 percent of college students report that they keep in contact with a long-distance friend at least once per week (Johnson et al., 2004). Whereas distance was once believed to cause friends to be less committed to the friendship, a recent study revealed that 81 percent of long-distance friends report an increasing level of commitment to their friendship (Johnson, Becker, Craig, Gilchrist, & Haigh, 2009).

Growing numbers of intimate relationships also face the potential challenges of geographical separation. Recent statistics indicate that more than 4 million relationships maintained by college students are long distance (Statistic Brain, 2015). But how do these relationships stay healthy and

The Power of a Mentor

One of the most common pieces of advice employees hear when they start a new job is to find a good mentor. A mentor is someone who possesses a similar workplace trajectory and can provide support for overcoming challenges, advice for completing tasks, and networking connections that can help with career advancement. Many relationships with mentors focus primarily on work-related issues, but some mentoring relationships can develop into lifelong friendships. A successful relationship between a mentor and mentee, however, does not happen overnight. "In order to take advantage of the many benefits of mentorship, you must first ask someone for his or her guidance . . . even if you believe you've found the perfect mentor, that person may not be interested" (Fallon, 2014). Forming a successful mentor–mentee relationship is a mutual process that requires a certain type of chemistry between two people.

Sharon Straus studied mentor–mentee relationships and found that good mentors were honest and trustworthy as well as active listeners who focused on the issues identified by the mentee. In addition, some of the best mentors "have access to a network of colleagues and collaborators who can open doors for their mentees, help jump-start these protégés' careers, or just explain how the system works" (Fallon, 2014).

Straus also identifies some of the challenges of a mentoring relationship. One of the biggest for both mentors and mentees, she says, is a lack of time. Effective mentors recognize this challenge and attempt to overcome it by relying on e-mail and phone contact as a way to improve accessibility (Fallon, 2014).

The quality of a mentor–mentee relationship is determined not only by the mentor but also by the mentee. Research shows that she or he must also work to make the relationship a success. Mentees must first find the right mentor who fits their professional goals. Noam Kostucki and Lujie Chen, authors of *Seek to Keep: How to Find the Best Mentors and Keep Them* (2014), outlined four steps for asking someone to become a mentors:

1. **Identify potential mentors.** Create a list of people who have at least one characteristic that makes them potential mentors. For instance, they may have previously worked in your position or now have your ideal job. Prioritize the list and place the ones you are closest to and feel the most natural connection with at the top.
2. **Research your top mentors.** Learn everything you can about the top few candidates on your list by visiting their Web sites, reading articles or books they have written, and following their social-media accounts.
3. **Make contact.** Reach out to the top people on your list, set up meetings, and tell them what you want to talk about. For example, you might want to learn how they got the type of job they have or hear about their experience in your industry. Ask them for specific amounts of time to talk over the phone, to meet for coffee, or to have lunch.
4. **Repeat the process.** Continue reaching out to potential mentors. If necessary, keep adding to your list.

Once a colleague has agreed (formally or informally) to serve as a mentor, mentees have a responsibility to help maintain a productive and successful relationship. Mentees should be active listeners, be open to feedback, be respectful of their mentor's time, and be willing to take their mentors' advice seriously. Although mentees do not have to accept every word, ignoring most of the advice will make the relationship fruitless. Straus's research also found that effective mentorships produce more productive employees who are promoted more quickly and are more likely to stay in their workplaces. "These results, she says, show the importance of positive mentoring" (Brooks, 2012).

---

productive? Interpersonal communication scholars suggests that long-distance romantic relationships thrive when those involved do three things: (1) engage in positive self-presentation, (2) avoid conflict during face-to-face interactions, and (3) engage in romantic idealization of the partner and the relationship (Merolla, 2010; Stafford & Merolla, 2007).

The not-so-good news is that long-distance relationships may experience additional conflict and tension when both partners reunite and are in the same location. In fact, one-third of reunited relationships terminate within three months of becoming geographically close (Stafford, Merolla, & Castle, 2006). Regardless of whether those involved in an interpersonal relationship are geographically separated or close in proximity, communication, face to face or otherwise, is an important component in maintaining such relationships.

Difference

Sex, gendered norms, and cultural differences all play a role in our ability to successfully maintain interpersonal relationships. Communication scholars have investigated differences that exist between same-sex and cross-sex friendships and report that female friends are often preferred over male friends (by both males and females) when people need emotional support. This is because females tend to provide more social and emotional support than do males (Kunkel & Burleson, 1998). Men and women rate affective, supportive communication skills as more important than instrumental, or more direct and competitive, communication skills—and these are the skills women tend to have. Women are socialized to attend to others' emotions to a greater extent than men are, and this helps to explain why both men and women report greater satisfaction with friends who communicate more affectively. However, cross-sex friendships do provide unique benefits for women: women report appreciation for men's instrumentally oriented skills (Holstrom, 2009), and men's friendships with other men are highly valued, providing them with friends to do things with.

Cultural differences also present challenges for interpersonal relationships. For example, the cultural distinction of individualism and collectivism helps to explain potential challenges for cross-cultural interpersonal relationships. Recall that although individualistic cultures rely on direct communication, many collectivist cultures place value on indirect and polite forms of communication. As such, tensions may result from different communication styles used in cross-cultural relationships. When a culture relies more on "indirect and nonverbal information to reduce uncertainty in personal relationships . . . direct communication" can put people "in awkward situations and hurt the existing relationship and harmony" (Zhang, Merolla, & Lin, 2009). If someone from one culture is less likely to self-disclose information, then building a sense of trust and openness can be difficult for the person whose culture values disclosure (Zhang et al., 2009). Understanding cultural variations can help reduce potential conflict, and learning about differences in cultural norms can help minimize conflict in cross-cultural relationships.

Interpersonal Violence

According to the National Coalition Against Domestic Violence (n.d.), domestic violence, which is now known as **intimate partner violence**, is *"the willful intimidation, physical assault, battery, sexual assault, . . . or other abusive behavior perpetrated by an intimate partner against another"* (p. 1). See also Figure 7.1.

The NCADV states that domestic violence occurs in all cultures regardless of age, economic status, race, religion, nationality, or educational background (NCADV, n.d., p. 1). However, the prevalence of interpersonal violence against women is astounding. The coalition has estimated that 85 percent of all domestic violence victims are women. In the United States alone,

- a woman is assaulted every nine seconds,

- females ages twenty to twenty-four are at the greatest risk of non-fatal intimate partner violence, and

- an average of more than three women are murdered by their husbands or boyfriends every single day (Domestic Violence Statistics, n.d.).

intimate partner violence
willful intimidation, physical assault, battery, sexual assault, or other abusive behavior perpetrated by an intimate partner against another.

Figure 7.1 *Domestic violence*
Source: Original figure created by Domestic Abuse Intervention Project, Duluth, MN, from http://www.ncadv.org/files/DomesticViolenceFactSheet(National).pdf

VIOLENCE

physical   sexual

COERCION AND THREATS: Making and/or carrying out threats to do something to hurt her. Threatening to leave her, commit suicide, or report her to welfare. Making her drop charges. Making her do illegal things.

INTIMIDATION: Making her afraid by using looks, actions, and gestures. Smashing things. Destroying her property. Abusing pets. Displaying weapons.

MALE PRIVILEGE: Treating her like a servant: making all the big decisions, acting like the "master of the castle," being the one to define men's and women's roles.

EMOTIONAL ABUSE: Putting her down. Making her feel bad about herself. Calling her names. Making her think she's crazy. Playing mind games. Humiliating her. Making her feel guilty.

POWER AND CONTROL

ECONOMIC ABUSE: Preventing her from getting or keeping a job. Making her ask for money. Giving her an allowance. Taking her money. Not letting her know about or have access to family income.

ISOLATION: Controlling what she does, who she sees and talks to, what she reads, and where she goes. Limiting her outside involvement. Using jealousy to justify actions.

USING CHILDREN: Making her feel guilty about the children. Using the children to relay messages. Using visitation to harass her. Threatening to take the children away.

MINIMIZING, DENYING, AND BLAMING: Making light of the abuse and not taking her concerns about it seriously. Saying the abuse didn't happen. Shifting responsibility for abusive behaviour. Saying she caused it.

physical   sexual

VIOLENCE

But scholars are also beginning to question the "real numbers" related to interpersonal violence inflicted on men: bell hooks (2004); Abby Ferber, Christina Jimenez, Andrea Herrera, and Dena Samuels (2008); and Michael Kimmel (2011) are beginning to suspect that the rate of male-on-male interpersonal violence (in the workplace, in friendships, on athletic teams, and in social settings such as bars and parties) may be underreported and understudied, and they are beginning to turn their attention to this aspect of violence as well.

The causes of interpersonal violence are complex and can be difficult to understand. Experts agree that interpersonal violence occurs because of some combination of cultural values, gender socialization, family approaches to conflict, the prevalence of violent images and stories in our media, and an individual's unique approach to conflict and relationships. There are no direct causal links, but we do know that hypermasculine individuals are more likely to inflict violence on their partners and even their children and pets. Furthermore, threats of death or harm as well as a lack of economic resources or options out of violent relationships often keep individuals stuck in them.

Chapter Summary

Conflict Is a Natural Part of Interpersonal Relationships

- Conflict occurs because of incompatibility or the perceived scarcity of rewards.
- Our response to conflict is often determined by our concern for self and by our concern for others.

Gender Shapes the Way Conflict Is Handled

- Because boys and girls are encouraged to use language differently for strategic purposes, they often handle conflict differently.
- Gender roles have also been linked to conflict styles.
- Androgynous individuals are more likely to adopt flexible and compromising conflict-resolution styles.

Conflict-Management Styles Are Also Influenced by Culture

- The differences between collectivist and individualistic can influence communication patterns and conflict-resolution strategies.
- Collectivist cultures tend to avoid expressing direct opinions and personal goals.
- Individualist cultures tend to use more direct and explicit language to convey personal thoughts and motivations.
- Because conflict occurs for many social and personal reasons, the same conflict scenario may be handled differently across different cultures.
- Self-monitoring can affect the way conflict is managed.

Technology Provides a Means by Which Conflict Can Be Created and Resolved

- Technology may be a source of conflict because of a digital generation gap.
- Collectivist and individualistic cultures may handle online conflict differently.
- Computer-mediated conflict (CMC) may provide support and outlets for those who live in areas of conflict or who are separated from families and friends.

Managing Conflict

- Conflict resolution has four possible outcomes: win–win, lose–lose, win–lose, and compromise.
- Framing the conflict is an important step in finding a suitable solution.
- Creating a positive communication climate by using confirming statements can help manage conflict.
- Approaching conflict civilly can be a productive communication tool to resolving it.

Several External Pressures Can Create Challenges for Interpersonal Relationships

- Geographic separation can be challenging for interpersonal relationships.
- Sex, gendered norms, cultural differences, and interpersonal violence all play a role in our ability to successfully maintain interpersonal relationships

Key Concepts

androgynous (145)

communication climates (155)

concern for others (143)

concern for self (143)

confirming statements (155)

disconfirming statement (155)

flaming (149)

framing (154)

gender roles (145)

interpersonal conflict (142)

intimate partner violence (161)

Invitation to Human Communication Online

MindTap Speech includes an interactive MindTap Reader and interactive learning tools including National Geographic Explorer videos, student videos, quizzes, flash cards, and more. You can build your speech outline with Outline Builder and record, post, and watch videos with YouSeeU. Go to cengagebrain.com to access your MindTap for *Invitation to Human Communication* where these resources are located.

MindTap®

Further Reflection and Discussion

1. What is your style for managing conflict? Why do you think this style is constructive? Are there changes you want to make?

2. Using the information in this chapter, identify one way you could change your approach to conflict management.

3. Have you experienced a "digital generation gap" in your family's understanding of technology use? How did you manage the gap?

4. What are some ways to maintain a positive relationship (romance, family, or friend) over a long distance? Are there actions you can take to improve the relationship that go beyond using computer-mediated communication?

5. What examples of flaming have you observed on social-media sites? Were these justified statements? What strategies can a recipient of a flame use to turn a hostile statement into a civil conversation?

6. Recall a conflict you had with someone in which the outcome was a win–lose. What strategies could have been used to change the outcome to a compromise?

Would you have been happier with this new outcome? Why or why not?

7. Have you experienced a conversation where another person made disconfirming statements to you? How did it make you feel? How could the person have changed the disconfirming statement into a confirming statement?

8. Identify a time you were in conflict with someone of the opposite sex. Was the conflict managed in ways that are perceived to be appropriate for each gender? Why or why not? Were you satisfied with the outcome? Why or why not?

9. What stories have you read on social-media sites that pertain to social or political issues? What did you learn? Did your opinions change as a result of what you read?

10. Your roommate just announced that her fourteen-year-old brother is coming to stay in your apartment during finals week. You are concerned about the limited space available for an additional person as well as having a quiet space to study. Prepare a one-minute speech that reflects a concern-for-self response. Next, prepare a one-minute speech that reflects a concern-for-others response.

Activities and Web Links

Visit cengagebrain.com to access the MindTap for *Invitation to Human Communication* where these activities and Web links can be found.

1. Search online for National Geographic explorer Ken Banks and information on how he helped provide cell phones to solve conflicts in other parts of the world. How can technology help resolve conflicts? Think globally. *Go to Web link 7.1.*

2. Visit the Web site for the National Coalition Against Domestic Violence. Click on "Resources" and choose an article or fact sheet to read. What did you find out that you did not know before? How would you advise a friend in trouble to approach this interpersonal conflict? Go to *Web link 7.2.*

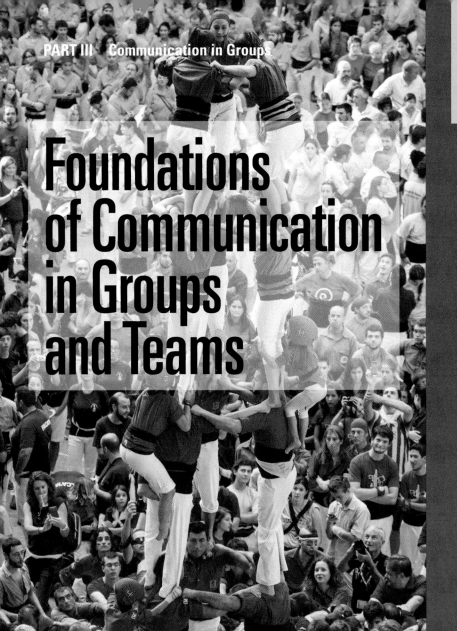

Foundations of Communication in Groups and Teams

Groups and teams come together for both work and play. How many groups and teams are you a part of and what do you and the other members accomplish when you are together?

8

Definition of Groups and Teams

Types of Groups and Teams

Roles in Groups and Teams

Leadership in Groups and Teams

Gender and Leadership

Culture and Leadership

Bullying in Groups and Teams

Technology in Groups and Teams

IN THIS CHAPTER YOU WILL LEARN TO:

- Explain the different features of groups and teams.

- Differentiate between the four most common types of groups and teams.

- Describe the variety of roles for members of groups and teams.

- Discuss the variety of leadership styles.

- Summarize the impact of gender, culture, and bullying on group communication.

- Determine the impact that technology has on group and team time and civility.

Our workplaces, classrooms, and social lives remind us that we regularly find ourselves collaborating with others. In this chapter, we explore the different features of small groups and teams, the different types of groups and teams, and their strengths and weaknesses. We also discuss the different styles of leadership, the role of gender, culture, and bullying in leading and the impact of technology as we work in groups and teams. By the end of the chapter, you will have a better understanding of the fundamentals of groups and teamwork as well as the benefits and nuances of working in groups and teams.

Definition of Groups and Teams

A **group** can be defined as a *small number of people who belong together, share something in common, or are assigned a similar task*. A group is distinct in that the people in it have a shared purpose or goal that brings them together. That shared purpose or goal keeps them together as they work to accomplish a common task. Groups might last only a few moments (a group of individuals who move a stalled car out of an intersection, for example) or they can last for years (a group of cancer survivors, for example). Although they share similarities, groups are slightly different from teams, which have a competitive element to them. **Teams** are *collections of individuals who come together to attempt to win something, to set a record, or to be the best at some task or event*. Both groups and teams share similar features, however, so let us look at what those might be.

Features of Groups and Teams

Size Small groups are usually a minimum of three to a maximum of fifteen people. Teams can be as small as three individuals but are often more than fifteen people. Athletic teams, for example, can consist of dozens of members, whereas a research team focused on winning a contract or developing a product might have twenty or more individuals helping to achieve those goals. When a group or team is small, its members are more visible and usually have more responsibility. When a group or team is larger, some of its members may be less visible or have more limited responsibilities. Athletic or research teams, for instance, usually have first-string members or those individuals who get more attention and

group

small number of people who belong together, share something in common, or are assigned to a similar task.

team

collection of individuals who come together to attempt to win something, to set a record, or be the best at some task or event.

have more responsibility, second- or third-string members or those who contribute important work but do not get the attention or recognition that first-string members do. When groups and teams are small, communication often is faster and more immediate. When a team or group is large, communication may take more time as dozens of members respond to requests or weigh in on various issues and conversations.

Small teams and groups often have incredible cohesion. If you are a member of a small team such as this crewing team, what unifies you?

Cohesion Cohesiveness is "the *degree of mutual interest among members" of a group* (Littlejohn & Foss, 2007). In a cohesive group or team, members are unified and have a shared identification with the group's purpose. Group cohesion can be positive because "it brings the members together and enhances" the interpersonal relationships within the group. However, Irving Janis and his associates identified a phenomenon they labeled *groupthink* to describe the negative aspects of group cohesion. According to Janis, **group think** is a *"mode of thinking that people engage in when they are deeply involved in a cohesive in-group, when the members' strivings for unanimity override their motivation to realistically appraise alternative courses of action"* (1972, p. 9). Groupthink occurs when members begin to think too much alike and avoid or silence disagreements. It also takes place when a group focuses more on cohesiveness and goodwill among its members than on fully exploring issues or raising questions that might lead to conflict or differences of opinion.

Although it is tempting to think that a small group of people will be highly cohesive and a larger group will be less likely to fall into groupthink, that is not always the case. When a group of any size follows the "Don't rock the boat" mentality of groupthink, it is placing cohesion and agreement over critically evaluating a situation and exploring many different approaches to that solution. Working in groups and teams requires a degree of cohesion—members need to feel they are working toward a common goal—but too much can be dangerous and cause a group to fall into groupthink.

Power Communication scholars today would agree that when a collection of individuals are communicating with one another, relationships of power exist (Foucault, 1972). Researchers also believe power can be

PRACTICING HUMAN COMMUNICATION
Speaking Up

Imagine you are working with a group of students to complete a class project. At the first meeting, the other students quickly decide on a project idea and begin dividing up the work. You are concerned that the other members rushed to a decision without discussing other ideas. Consider how you will respond. Now discuss as a class ways to handle and respond to groupthink.

cohesiveness
degree of mutual interest among members of a group.

group think
mode of thinking that people engage in when they are deeply involved in a cohesive in-group, when the members' striving for unanimity override their motivation to realistically appraise alternative courses of action.

defined in various ways. When individuals work together in groups or teams, two types of power can occur: *power over* and *power with*. **Power over** can be defined as *the ability to control others and dictate the course of events* (as in police officers or judges, controlling bosses, or even demanding coaches or parents). When individuals have this type of power in a group or team, they often control resources and have the ability to punish or reward others in the team or group.

Communication scholars have explored some of the bases of this authoritative form of power and have identified the five following foundations or sources people draw from when they interact with others:

> **Legitimate power:** the ability to control or influence others because of the formal position one holds in the group.

> **Coercive power:** the ability to punish those who do not meet demands or follow the rules set by the group.

> **Reward power:** the ability to give others what they seek or will benefit from for meeting the demands of the group or following the rules set by the group.

> **Referent power:** the ability to influence others because of an association with or respect for the people who hold power in the group.

> **Expert power:** the ability to influence others because of some skill, knowledge base, or set of experiences (French & Raven, 1968).

When someone has power over others, communication usually flows from the person on top down to those lower on the hierarchy. This type of communication can be quite linear: those with power give directions, and those without power follow those directions. Although too much power over others can be a negative thing, this type of communication is not always bad. In some groups and teams, military and emergency service workers, athletic teams involved in strenuous and serious competition, and even those dealing with crisis situations in the workplace or community, we often respect and need "powerful leaders who act decisively" and with clarity (Castells, 2009; Johnson, 2009, p. 8). We sometimes need individuals to take charge and lead others through a challenging or difficult situation. However, too much power over others can "have a corrosive effect on those who possess it," causing those with power over others to use that power unethically and irresponsibly (Johnson, 2009, p. 8).

The second type of power—**power with** or *reciprocal power* or *dialogic power* (Bakhtin, 1979/1993; Darlington & Mulvaney, 2002; Starhawk, 1990)—can also be present in teams and groups. Power with is *"the power of a strong individual in a group of equals, the power not to command, but to suggest and be listened to, to begin something and see it happen"* (Albrecht & Brewer, 1990; Starhawk, 1990, p. 10). Famous individuals who model power with are Mohandas Gandhi, Jane Goodall, Mother Teresa, and Nelson Mandela. These individuals worked with others, listened carefully to them, inspired them, and treated other people in respectful and egalitarian ways as they led movements and worked for particular causes. Less-famous individuals working in teams

power over
ability to control others and dictate the course of events.

legitimate power
ability to control or influence others because of the formal position one holds in the group.

coercive power
ability to punish those who do not meet demands or follow the rules set by the group.

reward power
ability to give others what they seek or will benefit from for meeting the demands of the group or following the rules set by the group.

referent power
ability to influence others because of an association with or respect for the people who hold power in the group.

expert power
ability to influence others because of some skill, knowledge base, or set of experience.

power with
power of a strong individual in a group of equals, the power not to command, but to suggest and be listened to, to begin something and see it happen.

Can Maneuvers for Power Be Avoided?

Ethical communication is an "explicit system" of individual and group "responsibilities and rights." According to organizational communication scholar Karen Ashcraft (2001), ethical communication "mandates authentic expression, declaring the group's right to know individual agendas. It asserts the group's duty to make room for all voices, affirming the individual's right to be heard." It also addresses conflict promptly, directly, and with "mutual accountability." Ethical communication is grounded in *open communication* that recognizes that hostility, hidden agendas, and misinformation block progress for a group and can inhibit change. Seven principles follow this commitment to open communication. Read these principles and then consider the questions at the end of the list.

1. *Different perspectives enrich the group process, and every member's views are important.* Rather than supporting conformity or the superiority of one or two voices over others, the goal of the group's communication is to find a mutual and acceptable balance among equal voices.

2. *Silencing others is a power-over maneuver.* Silencing others discourages true consensus and decreases long-term commitment to the group's goals and decisions. Communication within the group should promote individual expression and a feeling of being heard.

3. *Communication should create a climate in which opposing views can be raised.* Group members should feel free to express and negotiate their positions openly. Even though an individual might hold a decidedly different view, she or he should not feel alone.

4. *Group members should address each situation as directly as possible.* Individuals in the group are responsible for communicating clearly and directly with one another. Members of the group will not "tell tales" or spread rumors about others, and they will address issues directly with the person or people involved.

5. *Conflict does not always have to be engaged, but it has to be named openly and clearly.* Hiding or avoiding conflict creates negative environments and encourages negative communication, which can damage individuals. Each member of a group is responsible for "naming what is going on" when conflict arises.

6. *Personal relationships affect the whole group.* Individual relationships have an effect on the whole group. They are sources of affiliation, power, and conflict.

7. *The means are the ends.* How we communicate with others defines the product or outcome of the communication. How we communicate with others expresses our values, commitments, and relationship to the group and its goals.

What Do You Think?

1. Do you think you could practice ethical communication as it was just described? Why or why not?

2. Can you think of times when you or someone you know practiced ethical communication? Describe those situations.

3. Consider principle three—creating climates in which opposing views can be shared. How might a workplace, group, or team create this kind of climate?

or groups display power with when they model these same respectful and inspiring behaviors. These people often are the captains of teams, community leaders, and heads of projects at work. Using power with, their communication takes on a reciprocal, back-and-forth, and interactive pattern, with ideas being shared freely and openly as people work toward a common goal.

Interaction To be considered a group or team, members must also interact with one another for a period of time. These interactions are both verbal and nonverbal, and they can take place in person or electronically. Although we sometimes work independently within a group or team—gathering information or perfecting a skill, for example—our independent work becomes a part of the team when we share it with other members. We can interact with other group and team members verbally, sharing our message in person or via Internet or text message. And we can interact with them nonverbally, using gestures

Firefighters train together regularly so that when fires erupt, they work together safely, efficiently, and effectively as a team.

Courtesy of Wellington Fire Protection District

and expressions and even showcasing our skills on the playing field or during a workout.

In today's workplace and in our social networks, it is common to be a part of a **virtual group**, *a group of individuals who have never met one another in person but who communicate regularly through electronic means.* Although early research on virtual communication in groups expressed hope that many of the power dynamics present in face-to-face teams and groups would be eliminated, we now know that this is not so—group members find ways to assert their power and negotiate status electronically as well as in person (O'Sullivan & Flanagin, n.d.; Reid & Hammersley, 2000).

Norms Groups and teams also conform to certain group norms. **Norms** are *patterns of behavior that are expected of individuals and seen as correct or even necessary in specific situations.* In groups and teams, norms can be as simple as setting an "away" message on your e-mail when you will be out of the office for several days or scheduling a vacation during the off-season if you are a member of an athletic team. Norms also can be complicated, though, and involve determining who to invite to a work-related function, how to dress for particular occasions, whom to ask first for assistance with a problem, and even how and when to share a problem or dilemma with others in the group. Group norms are learned, and newcomers to a group try to learn those norms quickly in order to become productive members of a group. When group norms are violated, a group or team either must revisit those norms to determine whether they still are committed to that norm or try to instruct the

virtual group
group of individuals who have never met one another in person but who communicate regularly through electronic means.

norms
patterns of behavior that are expected of individuals and seen as correct or even necessary in specific situations.

person who violated that norm in the "expected" and "correct" behavior (Reid & Hammersley, 2000).

 ## Types of Groups and Teams

Groups can take on a variety of purposes or functions, depending on their goals. The most common types of groups are social, learning, task, and growth or therapy groups.

Social Groups **Social groups** are *formal or informal groups of individuals who gather to meet the personal, communal, and collective needs of people.* As you read in Chapter 6, today's social groups and networks can be established online via Facebook, LinkedIn, Twitter, and other social media, as well as face to face through churches, clubs, and neighborhoods. Facebook is the most popular source of online social networking. The Pew Research Center reports "fully [71 percent] of online adults use Facebook" (Duggan, Ellison, Lampe, Lenhart, & Madden, 2015). There is little difference in the percentage of males using Facebook as compared to females (66 percent to 71 percent, respectively) (Duggan et al., 2015). Even when divided by age group, adult online users always top 50 percent using Facebook, regardless of their age.

Total Online Adult Population	Percent Who Use Facebook (%)
Ages 18–29	87
30–49	73
50–64	63
65+	56

LinkedIn is increasingly popular as a professional networking site, especially among college graduates: 28 percent of adult online users are hosting accounts (Duggan et al., 2015). Twitter is another popular social networking site and is used by 23 percent of the adult online population. Twitter accounts that contain links to Web pages and include discussions rather than updates of personal information are extremely popular. Thousands of people now share information on politics, the law, technology, the workplace, and other topics. Hashtags allow individuals to connect and share information on political, social, and professional topics. For example, professionals can share reliable information on their area of expertise. Financial expert Jean Chatzky (@JeanChatzky) provides money-saving tips to followers, and Emily Goodhand of Reading University (@CopyrightGirl) provides advice on Twitter for those who have copyright questions (Green, 2011). Many college classes now incorporate Twitter as a way to get students involved. University of Texas at Dallas professors Monica Rankin and David Perry use Twitter to promote student engagement. Professor Rankin, who teaches a class with more than ninety students, provides the opportunity to become more involved in class discussion by setting up a class Twitter account. Rankin invites students to post messages and ask questions during class, which are then displayed on a large screen. Rankin discovered the practice

social groups
formal or informal groups of individuals who gather to meet the personal, communal, and collective needs of people.

Alexandra Cousteau: The Internet and Water

Steve McCulloch/National Geographic Creative

Bil Zelman

Take a sip of water—what do you taste and see? To Alexandra Cousteau, daughter of Philippe and Jan Cousteau, and granddaughter of the legendary Jacques Cousteau, "Water is life." We must redefine our relationships to it and our decisions around it. Cousteau established the Blue Legacy initiative, and she and her team are in the process working with people around the world to "help shape society's dialogue to include water as one of the defining issues of our century." Cousteau and her team are also combining the technologies developed in her grandfather's era with new media opportunities to create platforms for individuals concerned about the environment to speak out about water. And she is undertaking an exploration of many of the world's most precious water ecosystems to chronicle their connectivity and link to our own survival.

Cousteau and her team travel around the world telling the story of our water systems and their centrality to sustaining life on this planet. This story includes the Ganges River in India, "the cultural and spiritual lifeblood" of a nation. The Ganges provides water and spiritual cleansing to more than 400 million people, yet it is literally toxic. More than 400 tannery factories along the river pump more than 20 million liters of waste every day, not to mention raw sewage, into this most sacred of rivers. The story continues in Botswana, where, in a land that is mostly desert, she continues to explore the interconnected nature of water. In an interview with Onkokame Kitso Mokaila, Botswanian minister of the environment, wildlife, and tourism, Cousteau asks how Botswana, a land-locked country, views water as its most precious commodity. Mokaila responds: "All living things require water, whether you are in agriculture, tourism, or wildlife. . . . You have to treat it as gold." Cousteau and her team continue their work and their story as they travel to the Middle East, Mississippi, and Cambodia (forty-five major water sources in all) chronicling "the interconnectivity of water . . . what it means to live in a world where water is our most precious resource" (Boyes, 2011).

To tell her story, Cousteau relies on the most recent Internet technologies. And even though her father and grandfather were pushing the edge of technological advances, Cousteau explains that where the *Calypso* carried a crew of thirty people in the field for months and sent film back to Los Angeles for development, today she is able to work for three months in the field with a crew of only seven and post her stories immediately. She sees this as truly engaging people and as a truly interactive experience. Working with others and media in this way is very exciting for Cousteau. "From a communication standpoint, to be able to engage people through their networks and give them stories to talk about and start conversations around is one of our greatest opportunities" for change. Where 50,000 people see a movie in a theater, "I can reach 50,000 people in a day and maybe in an hour with this next expedition" (Cousteau, 2009, 2011, 2012).

Cousteau works as a member of a team, yet she presents information on panels and at symposiums and even narrates videos and interviews individuals who are working in environmental preservation.

MindTap® Go to cengagebrain.com to access your MindTap for *Invitation to Human Communication* to view a video about Alexandra Cousteau.

WHAT DO YOU THINK?

1. Alexandra Cousteau's family has a legacy of credibility from her grandfather's work, as well as the work her mother and father did, in oceanography. How might this legacy help or hinder Cousteau's work?

2. What kinds of power do you think this gives Alexandra Cousteau? What kinds of power do you think she is most comfortable using as she works with her team of explorers?

3. Although technology can be used for uncivil and unethical ends, Cousteau uses technology to capture and disseminate her story. What are the civil aspects of her use of technology?

If you could tweet about the power of working in groups, what might that tweet be?

encourages more student participation. Professor Perry uses Twitter to keep students engaged in the course outside of class time. Perry reports that students stay engaged by discussing world events that relate to the course on their Twitter account. Business professor Elaine Young believes Twitter is about creating connection with others and building professional networks (Minors, 2010).

Even though many of us use social-media networking because it is a powerful way to maintain a social group, research shows that "face-to-face time makes us happier than relying solely on social media to communicate." Researchers surveyed between 500 and 1,000 people in sixteen different countries and discovered that 40 percent reported "catching up with loved ones after work was the happiest time of their day." Only 5 percent said "they were happiest when connecting online with friends," and only 2 percent said "the first text message of the day made them joyful" (Fahmy, 2010).

Task Groups Sometimes called *problem-solving groups*, **task groups** *are formed when individuals want to take on a job or solve an issue that is affecting them or those around them.* Missionary groups, Mothers Against Drunk Driving (MADD), and People for the Ethical Treatment of Animals (PETA) are examples of task groups. When task groups form to address an issue, the issue or problem can be close to home or something taking place in another city, state, or even country. When task or problem-solving groups are working at their best, they usually follow several stages or steps:

>   identifying the problem,
>
>   gathering information about the problem,
>
>   analyzing the information and the problem,

task groups

problem-solving groups formed when individuals want to take on a job or solve an issue that is affecting them or those around them.

The Everest Peace Project: International Teamwork

For sixty days, people who were supposed to hate each other actually worked together "under incredibly difficult circumstances (rain, sleet, snow, hurricane force winds—at an elevation that passenger jets fly!)." The diverse members of Our Everest Climb for Peace literally put themselves and their lives in one another's hands, as well as their tents, and made history doing so. The climbers came from five major religious traditions—Hinduism, Islam, Judaism, Christianity, and Buddhism—as well as atheism and included individuals from two nations at war for decades: Palestine and Israel. Their mission was to work together as a team to climb one of the world's most spectacular and difficult mountains—Mt. Everest—and to inspire others. Working as a team, the climbers wanted to show that "people from diverse cultural backgrounds and faiths can unite together as friends and accomplish incredible things."

The climb received the endorsement of the Dalai Lama, who wrote that the project not only documents "a spectacular climb of the world's tallest mountain" but also shows how "people from different faiths and cultures" can work "successfully as a team to accomplish their goal. It reinforces my strong belief that if we adopt the right approach and make a determined effort, cooperation, trust, and understanding can always be established for a true and worthy cause."

But members of the Everest Peace Project did not put their commitment to teamwork to rest once they reached the top of the world. At the summit, one of the Israeli climbers, Dudu Yifrah, raised a "sewn together Israeli–Palestinian flag" and "dedicated his climb to his newfound brother and climbing partner, Ali Bushnaq," from Palestine. Lance Trumbull, the founder of Our Everest Climb for Peace, described it as "a magical moment, perhaps the greatest moment" of his life. After descending, the two Israeli and Palestinian climbers kept their historical friendship and efforts at teamwork alive. Despite how difficult it is to cross borders or even to communicate via telephone, they "meet at least once a year to climb" and "now consider themselves lifelong friends" (Everest Peace Project, 2009; Mesterhazy, 2008).

What Do You Think?

1. Review the types of groups discussed in this chapter. What type of group is the Everest Peace Project?
2. What kinds of communication do you think members of this climbing group used to bridge their vast cultural and religious differences as they climbed Mt. Everest? Do you think they used power with or power over? Why?
3. How do you think culture affected their communication styles and practices? How might they have worked across these differences?

suggesting possible solutions,

considering the implications of those solutions,

reaching a decision about the best solution, and

implementing that solution (Dewey, 1910).

Task groups also must consider the **ethics** of their problem-solving efforts, which can be defined as the *moral standards behind the decisions and how they affect others*. In considering the ethical component of a problem, a task group must take into account the diversity of perspectives it actually has considered, whether or not the actual voices of those affected by the problem and the possible solutions have been solicited and listened to, and any hidden or unintended consequences of the solution to the group. Without this kind of ethical consideration, task groups may be creating more problems than they solve or causing harms they did not intend to cause as they implement a solution.

Learning Groups **Learning groups** function to *teach members a new skill or to provide them with new information*. Study groups and classes are common examples of this type of group. Learning groups often have explicit agendas, and when you join or start a learning group you will want to learn or state that agenda clearly. This will help you decide if the learning group is right for you to join, and it helps those who might

ethics
moral standards behind decisions and how they affect others.

learning groups
groups that offer members a new skill or provide members with new information.

be thinking about joining the group in making that same decision. Although an agenda may be stated explicitly, sometimes learning groups also have **hidden agendas** or *unspoken goals and visions for the group that can get in the way of progress or take a group in a direction other than the one it has explicitly stated.* When hidden agendas take over, they can detract "from the real work at hand. Even a discussion that seems to be centered on substantial issues may, at a deeper level, concern issues of power, prestige, and other personal needs" (Kets de Vries, 2001, p. 189). You can sometimes spot a hidden agenda when your efforts to raise an issue or solve a problem are met with resistance or when the issue is tabled or reframed so that it does not address the original issue you raised.

Growth and Therapy Groups **Growth groups**, or *therapy groups, are groups whose goals are to help individuals cope with issues, recover from a crisis or trauma, or resolve personal concerns.* The group's common goal is to assist others in healing or resolving issues. In growth and therapy groups, self-expression, support, analysis, exploration, and conversation about the issues being addressed are the primary focus. Growth and therapy groups often are led by an experienced counselor or therapist, and they can bring different individuals together who are facing a similar crisis (cancer, for example) or an entire family or several families struggling with a common problem (such as alcoholism). Growth and therapy groups can last for years, or they can form for a shorter time and disband once the situation is resolved or even when it becomes apparent that group support is no longer productive or helpful (Davison, Pennebaker, & Dickerson, 2000; Goodwin et al., 2001; Kelly et al., 1993).

 ## Roles in Groups and Teams

Every group and team has formal and informal roles. A **role** is *an expected and defined pattern of behavior carried out by an individual or individuals.* **Formal roles** are those that are *clearly defined and assigned*—team captain, meeting facilitator, and notetaker, for example. Formal roles help a group function smoothly, and they provide order and predictability for the members of a group. **Informal roles** are those *roles that are not formally assigned to individuals in the group*, and they usually are not talked about directly or even acknowledged by the group. These informal roles, sometimes called *functional roles*, are as important as the formal ones, but they also can be a source of group conflict. This is because they can remain unrecognized and unappreciated, even though people are doing important work, or because individuals compete for these informal roles in order to receive rewards or praise. Table 8.1 shows the most common informal, functional, and dysfunctional roles in groups.

Emergence of Roles

Although formal roles in groups are usually assigned (notetaker or facilitator, for example), the informal roles listed in Table 8.1 usually develop without direct communication among group members. Instead of assigning these roles, people tend to gravitate toward them. In most

hidden agendas
unspoken goals and visions for the group that a can get in the way of progress or take a group in a direction other than the one it has explicitly stated.

growth group
group whose goals are to help individuals cope with issues, recover from a crisis or trauma, or resolve personal concerns; also known as a *therapy group.*

role
expected and defined pattern of behavior carried out by an individual or individuals.

formal role
role that is clearly defined and assigned.

informal role
role that is not formally assigned to individuals in the group.

TABLE 8.1 INFORMAL ROLES

Task Roles

Information giver	Provides information to the group
Information seeker	Requests information be provided
Opinion giver	States preferences about what group should do or think
Opinion seeker	Seeks the preferences and thoughts of others in the group
Starter	Gets the group going on tasks, discussions, brainstorming, etc.
Direction giver	Tells others how and when a task should be done
Summarizer	Reviews the discussion and sums up ideas and issues
Diagnoser	Identifies potential and real problems
Energizer	Gets the group excited and moving forward
Gatekeeper	Monitors and controls the process and individual input
Reality tester	Checks to see if the tasks and goals are realistic and feasible

Relational Roles

Participation encourager	Makes sure all voices are heard and recognized
Harmonizer	Works to reduce conflicts and disagreements
Tension reliever	Provides humor to relax and lighten the mood
Evaluator of emotional climate	Assesses how others might be feeling; shares own feelings with group
Praise giver	Encourages others and expresses approval
Empathic listener	Listens to others for clarification and without evaluation

Dysfunctional Roles

Blocker	Rejects ideas, refuses to cooperate, takes a negative stand on all issues
Attacker	Aggressive toward others, challenges and attacks people and ideas
Recognition seeker	Seeks acknowledgment and praise, exaggerates accomplishments
Joker	Uses humor to avoid productive conversation and participation
Withdrawer	Remains aloof, daydreams, engages in side conversations
Cynic	Skeptical of all options; voices inevitable failure of group efforts

Source: Adapted from Frey (1999, 2003), Putnam and Stohl (1990), and Wilson and Hanna (1986).

groups, you will notice that certain people regularly ask for additional information or block a conversation or decision, others look out for the emotional tone of meetings or offer praise or are aggressive toward others, and still others remain aloof or are jokers with each project assigned to the group. In groups that are functioning well, individuals will rotate in and out of both formal and informal roles. Different individuals will take on the role of facilitator, notetaker, energizer, starter, opinion giver, or information seeker, for example, at various stages in a project or even as the group works on different projects together.

Role-Related Problems and Solutions

Most groups experience minor struggles and problems related to the roles individuals adopt in the group. This might happen when there is a bid for a role and one person feels it is necessary to compete for a role at the expense of others. For example, a member of the group might want to be the sole evaluator or diagnoser and will not allow anyone else to occupy that role. Occasionally, role-related problems are severe enough for the group to disband, but usually these problems can be overcome. In this section, we look at three of the most common role-related problems groups face and the ways in which groups can successfully overcome those problems and work together productively.

One of the first problems that groups might face is individuals competing for both formal and informal roles. This happens when several people see themselves as the formal leader of the group or when more than one person competes for an informal role such as the direction giver. A second problem can arise when there is a shortage of people to fill roles. In this situation, no one wants to be the notetaker, for example, or none of the group members takes on the informal role of analyzer. Finally, problems can arise when individuals become too attached to their roles and insist on performing them when they are unnecessary. This can happen when the emotional evaluator continually shares emotions or constantly checks in on the emotions of others or when the joker insists on cracking jokes at every opportunity. Although these problems can disrupt the work of the group, Table 8.2 illustrates several ways to solve them.

Strengths of Groups and Teams

Working in a team or group can have many advantages. Working as a team, individuals

share different knowledge bases and experiences;

contribute different skill sets and expertise;

work collaboratively to create new ideas, products, and solutions;

praise and reward one another;

identify and troubleshoot problems together;

help one another accomplish a task; and

develop an identity and a sense of belonging.

TABLE 8.2 SOLUTIONS TO ROLE-RELATED PROBLEMS	
Identify the roles that people are competing for.	If they are formal roles, dialogue with the group to determine who should fill each role. If they are informal roles, communicate as a group about those roles as well, naming the function and contributions of each role as well as the dysfunction of some of them. Identify the group norms for productive and professional behaviors as members take on different formal and informal roles.
Identify the roles that no one is filling.	If they are formal roles, develop a plan for filling the important ones and talk about those that might not be necessary for that particular task and eliminate them. If they are informal roles, dialogue as a group about those and decide whether to move some of the informal roles to the status of formal. The group might decide, for example, that the gatekeeper role is especially important if there is considerable disagreement or energy around a project. Turn those important informal roles into formal ones.
Check to be sure that roles are being rotated.	Discuss with the group the importance of rotating both formal and informal group roles. Communicate about the value of each role, as well as the problems caused by the dysfunctional roles. Pay attention to who typically assumes a role; perhaps assign someone to monitor roles and ensure their rotation.
Discuss with the group strategies for avoiding the dysfunctional roles.	If the group is just forming, talk about strategies for identifying dysfunctional roles and for stopping them if they happen. If the group has been together for some time, hold a meeting to discuss productive roles, unproductive roles, and how to manage them so that the group can work effectively. Make sure all of the members of the group share their perspectives and are heard during this conversation. This will help the group identify and understand why the dysfunctional roles are happening and how to minimize them.

© Cengage Learning

PRACTICING HUMAN COMMUNICATION
What Kind of Groups Are You In?

Consider the interactions you have had with coworkers, students, roommates, teammates, and other groups in which you participate. Write down what the purpose and goals of the groups were or are (e.g., social, task, learning, or growth and therapy). Next, determine whether the roles in the group were formal or informal. What problems arose, and how did those problems get addressed? Finally, share your list of groups, roles, and problems with a partner and discuss how well each group communicated and how communication could be more effective.

When groups are working well together, these strengths and advantages provide individuals a sense of well-being and collective purpose. With many people working together productively on a task, a group often can accomplish a good deal more than a single individual working alone. In short, when groups and teams function well, there can be considerable positive payoffs for the individuals involved as well as the solutions and ideas they develop.

Limitations of Groups and Teams

Working in groups and teams can have limitations, though, and it is important to recognize not only the strengths of group work but also the limitations. Working as a team, individuals must

> make time to communicate with one another,
>
> make the time to process information together,
>
> support those individuals who need more time to develop a skill or idea,
>
> focus on group goals rather than individual advancement and promotion, and
>
> be willing to resolve conflicts civilly and ethically.

Although these limitations are not insurmountable, taking the time to work with others in a busy world can sometimes feel like a burden. Sometimes we do not want to put aside our differences for the good of the group goal, or we simply do not support a direction the group is moving in. Being patient with others as they develop a new skill or explore an idea also can be frustrating when we are in a rush to move forward. When you find yourself working in a group, it is important to consider the strengths and weaknesses of group work. Regardless of whether the group is functioning well or struggling, recognizing that there are both strengths and limitations of working in a group will help you remain a productive member of the group.

Leadership in Groups and Teams

The success of groups and teams often depends on the individuals working within those groups and teams. When people emerge as leaders or are asked to lead groups and teams, they take on unique roles. In this section, we explore the definition of a leader, different leadership styles, and the role of gender, culture, and bullying in leading groups and teams.

Leadership Defined

Although we are familiar with the term *leader,* and most of us can easily recognize a "good leader" or have studied "great leaders," we seldom take time to explore the definition of this term or the specific communication practices that go with leadership. Some scholars say leadership is in the eye of the beholder or that "I know a good leader when I see one," but others have spent decades systematically outlining the aspects of leadership and the differences between leading, ruling, and managing (Western, 2008). Most research suggests that to lead is to "guide others"; to "be the head of an organization," event, or activity; and to possess "charisma" and "vision." In addition, leaders believe that they are capable of changing things. They tend to be optimistic and positive thinkers, and they are responsive and caring toward others. Because leadership is somewhat subjective, it does require that the "followers" perceive the individual to be a leader and to have "exceptional qualities" (Fairhurst, 2001; Popper, 2005). So, a **leader** can be defined as *someone who guides or directs a group or activity with vision, charisma, and care.* This person is perceived to do these things—that is, to be a leader—by those in the group.

Alex Macnaughton/REX/Newscom

Animal rights activists often use public protests to advocate for the rights of animals and against using them to test products. Use Karen Ashcraft's ideas for ethical communication to assess the effectiveness of this approach to resolve differences.

Leaders, rulers, and managers play different roles. Rulers often "force people to act" because they hold power or control over people and resources. Managers organize or control processes and people in order to make sure things run smoothly, and they do so usually because they are hired or asked to coordinate and oversee things. In contrast, leaders help construct and carry out the larger vision of the organization. They also work with individuals, and this causes them to "want to act" because people feel involved in the decisions and respected by or important to the process (Popper, 2005; Western, 2008). Leaders operate without force or coercion, and they develop relationships of respect and mutual support with the people they communicate with.

Not all leaders produce positive outcomes, and we can think of individuals such as Adolph Hitler or religious cult leaders who lead individuals in ways that caused them to harm others and themselves. Because leaders can cause individuals to "want to act" in negative as well as positive ways, we explore four of the most common styles of leadership and the ways they can produce positive outcomes: authoritarian, democratic, laissez-faire, and transformative.

Leadership Styles

Authoritarian Leadership An authoritarian leader is a leader who functions a little like the stern parent or person in charge. Although **authoritarian leaders** often possess vision and charisma, they *tell others*

leader
someone who guides or directs a group or activity with vision, charisma, and care.

authoritarian leader
leader who tells others what to do, gives orders, and makes the final decisions regarding how to act or what to do next.

Jeff Bezos, the founder and CEO of Amazon.com, is known as both easy going and extraordinarily attentive to details. He turned Amazon.com from a startup business housed in his garage into the worlds largest Internet retailer. As you read about the various leadership styles in this section, identify those you think he likely used to inspire his employees and build his company.

what to do, give orders, and make the final decisions regarding how to act or what to do next. Authoritarian leaders can sometimes act like rulers, failing to listen to others or take them into consideration. They sometimes issue orders and demand that others do what they want. However, the best authoritarian leaders have the larger vision of the organization or event in mind, and they function well in highly structured organizations such as the military and police and fire services or for short periods of time when decisions must be made quickly and without extensive discussion.

The late Raymond Downey, deputy chief of New York City's fire department, is remembered as an effective leader who exemplified the best of authoritarian leadership in emergency circumstances he often found himself and his firefighters in. He is remembered as "one of the world's leading authorities on specialized rescue," and he lost his life on September 11, 2001, attempting to save others after the attacks on the World Trade Center. Even though he led others in an environment in which decisions must be made quickly and by the person in command, Downey always kept the larger mission or vision of the fire service in mind, and he possessed incredible charisma (Halverson, Murphy, & Riggio, 2004). He worked actively as a mentor and teacher to his staff and is described as "incredibly humble yet incredibly knowledgeable. Chief Downey never missed an opportunity to pass on what he knew to the younger members of the service and exercised a magnificent understanding of human character and soul" (Sargent, 2006, pp. xv–xvii).

Authoritarian leadership can spiral out of control, with individuals attempting to rule or dictate rather than lead. But, as the example of

Chief Downey suggests, individuals can lead effectively with this style during periods of stress or when decisions must be made quickly and orders must be delivered clearly and carried out safely.

Democratic Leadership Democratic leaders favor dialogue, discussion, and deliberation with members of the group before making decisions or issuing plans of action. **Democratic leaders** embrace three principles: *the distribution of responsibility among the group members, a desire to empower all members of the group, and a willingness to assist in decision making.* Democratic leaders spread responsibilities, tasks, and opportunities across the membership, giving those involved a sense of involvement and personal "buy in." They empower group members by giving them the opportunity to develop skills, learn new things, and challenge themselves. The result is an increase in self-esteem for members of the group. Finally, democratic leaders facilitate the decision-making process by describing procedures and processes, encouraging discussion and participation, and monitoring the process to be certain individuals are involved, engaged, and establishing and maintaining positive and healthy relationships (Gastil, 1994).

Democratic leadership is highly effective when a group has ample time to discuss an issue and gather additional information and when individuals can learn to trust and respect one another (or when they already hold one another in high regard). It also is effective when no clear course of action is obvious or when issues are highly complex and affect many individuals or entities. Democratic leadership can fail, however, when a group is unwilling to openly discuss or deliberate, when there is a high level of mistrust or animosity among group members, or when group members do not understand the process of or value in discussing ideas and sharing information. In the right settings, democratic leadership can be extremely successful, but it does take a skilled and confident leader to manage lively discussion, share responsibilities, and empower all members of a group.

Laissez-Faire Leadership Usually described as a "hands-off" leader, a **laissez-faire leader** can be described as one who *offers little or no guidance and allows individuals to make all decisions themselves, giving them as much freedom as possible* (Lewin, Lippitt, & White, 1939). The laissez-faire leader is available for brainstorming, troubleshooting, resources, and conversation, but under this style of leadership, group members are given total freedom to make decisions and plan courses of action on their own. This style of leadership can be especially effective "in situations where group members are highly skilled, motivated, and capable of working on their own" (Cherry, n.d.). It can be ineffective, however, when members of a group are less experienced or have trouble setting and achieving deadlines because communication can become competitive, deadlines overlooked or postponed, and team members fail to receive clear guidance or leaders (Eagly, Johannesen-Schmidt, & van Engen, 2003; Skogstad, Ståle, Torsheim, Aasland, & Hetland, 2007).

Transformative Leadership A **transformative leader** is one who exhibits leadership that *creates significant change in the life of people and organizations.* Transformative leadership depends on a person leading by example

democratic leader
one who distributes responsibility among the group members and shows a desire to empower all members of the group and a willingness to assist in decision making.

laissez-faire leader
one who offers little or no guidance and allows individuals to make all decisions themselves, giving them as much freedom as possible.

transformative leader
one who creates significant change in the life of people and organizations.

Nelson Mandela was recognized around the world as a transformational leader who inspired a nation of people to work toward ending apartheid. Can you think of other transformational leaders, well known or lesser known, who inspired individuals and transformed lives? What communication traits did they display?

and modeling behaviors, values, and ideas that inspire others to accomplish great things. In the 1970s and 1980s, James MacGregor Burns and Barnard M. Bass determined that transformational leaders are characterized by the following traits:

- their influence on others;

- the level of trust, admiration, loyalty, and respect the group feels for the leader;

- the display of charisma, intellectual stimulation, and consideration for each individual from the leader; and

- the willingness of group members to work harder than expected for something greater than their own self-gain (Bass, 1985; Burns, 1978; Popper, 2005).

Nelson Mandela is often described as an example of a transformational leader. After spending almost three decades in a South African prison, many of those years in isolation or hard labor, Mandela was released at age 71. He was widely admired and idolized because he rarely used the word *I* in his speeches and presentations, and he stated repeatedly that he "was simply the servant of the public"—someone who sought a greater good from his years in prison instead of personal revenge or benefit. Mandela inspired generations of people to work for a cause larger than themselves—the righting of a terrible imbalance of power—and his leadership modeled the kind of transformation that South Africa eventually accomplished (Popper, 2005). Table 8.3 summarizes the four types of leadership discussed here and their effectiveness and ineffectiveness.

Gender and Leadership

The gender of an individual significantly influences a group's perception of that leader. Studies show that when women and men display the same leadership traits with regard to authoritarian, democratic, and laissez-faire styles, they are perceived differently. For those styles, men are seen as focused and competent (authoritarian); confident, flexible, and in touch with the process (democratic); and willing to trust others to get the job done (laissez-faire). When women display authoritarian, democratic, or laissez-faire leadership styles, groups are more likely to evaluate them as bossy and demanding (authoritarian), too ineffective and wishy-washy (democratic), and as too soft or incompetent (laissez-faire) (Barbuto, Fritz, Matkin, & Marx, 2007; Druskat, 1994; Eagly et al., 2003; Jamieson, 1995). In addition, men are more likely to assume the role of leader, whereas

TABLE 8.3 EFFECTIVE AND INEFFECTIVE TRAITS OF LEADERSHIP

Leadership Style	Effective	Ineffective
Authoritarian leadership tells others what to do, gives orders, and makes the final decisions regarding how to act or what to do next.	When decisions must be made quickly; when leader holds a vision of the greater good; in highly structured situations.	When leader becomes too dogmatic and authoritarian; fails to listen to others; fails to consider needs of others.
Democratic leadership is characterized by the distribution of responsibility among the group members, a desire to empower all members of the group, and a willingness to assist in decision making.	When ample time to discuss issues; when issues are complex; when procedures and trust for discussion issues can be established.	When a high level of mistrust exists; when members do not understand procedures; when members do not see value in discussion ideas.
Laissez-faire leadership offers little or no guidance and allows individuals to make all decisions themselves, giving them as much freedom as possible.	When group members are highly skilled; when individuals do not need guidance and are good at setting and meeting deadlines.	When group members are inexperienced; when members have trouble setting and meeting deadlines.
Transformative leadership creates significant change in the lives of people and organizations by inspiring and motivating others to work harder than expected for a cause bigger than themselves.	When the leader can put aside own needs or desires; when issues are larger than individual group members; when leader displays consideration for individuals.	When leader puts own needs above others; when leader fails to inspire; when no intellectual stimulation exists; when leader fails to consider the needs of individuals.

© Cengage Learning

women are more likely to emerge as the "social leader" who "contributes to morale and good interpersonal relations" (Barbuto et al., 2007, p. 72).

With regard to transformational leadership styles, research indicates that both women and men are perceived as competent leaders and groups perceive that competence as a balancing of both masculine and feminine traits. So, as transformational leaders, both women and men display a balance of gender traits: the masculine traits of authoritativeness and confidence and the feminine traits of being friendly, kind, and considerate of others (Barbuto et al., 2007). In fact, Eagly et al.'s (2003) research identified women as using a transformational leadership style more often than do men. They believe this is because the transformational leadership style may give women "a means of overcoming the dilemma of role incongruity—namely, that conforming to their gender role can impede their ability to meet the requirements of their leader role" (Eagly et al., 2003, p. 573). In addition, psychology professor Vanessa Urch Druskat at Boston University argues that this transformational style of leadership likely will become increasingly common and important as "unstable social and economic times and rapidly changing organizational environments increase the need for able, transformational leaders" (Druskat, 1994, p. 99).

🗨 Culture and Leadership

The Internet, travel and tourism, foreign industry, and the internationalization of banking and investment all contribute to what scholars are labeling the "globalization of business." According to Robert J. House, professor of management at the University of Pennsylvania, "the increasing connection among countries and the globalization of corporations does not mean that cultural differences are disappearing or diminishing. On the contrary, as economic borders come down, cultural barriers could go up" (House, Hanges, Javidan, Dorfman, & Gupta,

MindTap®

Go to cengagebrain.com to access the MindTap for *Invitation to Human Communication* to view a video about the rising world population.

Aziz Abu Sarah,
Emerging Explorer and Cultural Educator

Have you ever faced issues of gender or culture when leading a group? How did you respond? How did the group respond?

I often find myself in situations where I am put in a team or even put in a leadership position because of my ethnicity. And I have been in situations where I was taken out because of ethnicity. So if it's one of those situations where [if] there is a need for an Arab and I have the qualifications, then it's "Oh, you're an Arab, okay well we'll put you in." Sometimes they'll exclude because of your ethnicity: I have applied for something where I was told that I didn't get it because of my ethnicity.

In my work now, I think the trick is learning different cultural styles of communication. I come from a culture where interrupting is normal and everybody says what they think at the moment. Well, in the United States, for example, you can't do that, so I have to adjust and remember what is correct in other cultures. I have to adjust my communication style for each country. And I have to ask questions about what is appropriate. For example, in Spain I had to ask what certain hand gestures meant because I know there are differences internationally, and I don't want to use those gestures that could be offensive. I have to understand cultural differences.

But even with gender, for example, handshakes are important. Sometimes I can shake a woman's hand, and sometimes I can't. And if I did shake a woman's hand in a country where that is not acceptable, I could really offend people. So, although it's acceptable for your own culture and maybe you disagree with the fact that a woman isn't allowed to shake your hand, you still have to respect that cultural practice if you're going to communicate effectively. It takes time to learn and to understand important cultural difference—but you have to if you want to be effective.

2004, p. 4). Professor House is one of the founding members of Global Leadership and Organizational Effectiveness (GLOBE), which comprises "170 social scientists and management scholars from sixty-one cultures throughout the world." Since the late 1990s, GLOBE has been working to understand the relationships between culture and leadership. GLOBE researchers have found that "selected cultural differences strongly influence" the ways in which people think about leaders and the norms they have "concerning the status, influence, and privileges granted to leaders" (House et al., n.d., p. 2). The traits that are influenced by cultural differences are uncertainty avoidance, power and assertiveness, collectivism, gender egalitarianism, and humane orientation.

- **Uncertainty avoidance** is the *extent to which members of an organization or society strive to avoid uncertainty by relying on social norms, rituals, and bureaucratic practices to alleviate the unpredictability of future events.*

- **Power and assertiveness** measure the *degree to which members of an organization or society expect and agree that power should be unequally shared or that individual assertiveness is valued.*

uncertainty avoidance
extent to which members of an organization or society strive to avoid uncertainty by relying on social norms, rituals, and bureaucratic practices to alleviate the unpredictability of future events.

power and assertiveness
measure of the degree to which members of an organization or society expect and agree that power should be unequally shared or that individual assertiveness is valued.

- **Collectivism** is the *degree to which organizational, societal, and family practices encourage and reward collective distribution of resources and collective action as well as the degree to which they express pride and loyalty.*

- **Gender egalitarianism** is the *extent to which an organization or a society minimizes gender-role differences.*

- **Humane orientation** is the *degree to which individuals in organizations or societies encourage and reward individuals for being fair, altruistic, friendly, generous, caring, and kind to others* (House et al., n.d., pp. 24–26).

GLOBE scholars also have explored such individual leadership traits as charisma, self-protection, other and team orientation, ability and willingness to delegate, decisiveness, and modesty. It is no surprise that cultural influences on leadership are profound and a culture's values are highly interconnected with the culture's view of effective and ineffective leadership. For example, Americans, Arabs, Asians, Britons, Eastern Europeans, French, Germans, Latin Americans, and Russians tend to romanticize the concept of leadership and consider leadership in both political and organizational arenas to be important. In these cultures, leaders are commemorated with statues, names of major avenues or boulevards, and names of buildings. Many people of the Netherlands, Scandinavia, and the German-speaking areas of Switzerland are skeptical about leaders and the concept of leadership out of fear they will accumulate and abuse power. In these countries, it is difficult to find leaders who have been publicly commemorated (House et al., 2004, p. 5).

How do we communicate effectively as leaders interacting with other cultures given the complexity of cultures, language differences, and the range of value systems and religious beliefs we will encounter? GLOBE researchers acknowledge that more studies are necessary to help us understand how to communicate effectively across cultures, and they urge the following:

- acknowledge and appreciate cultural differences,

- stay flexible as you respond to those differences,

- respond positively to values that may be drastically different from your own,

- be open to the ideals and opinions of others, and

- recognize that what your culture values (directness and frankness, for example) may be offensive to members of another culture.

Bullying in Groups and Teams

Reports of cyberbullying, school shootings, road rage, and single individuals acting out in hostile ways toward others remind us that there are uncivil people in too many aspects of our lives. Unfortunately, those in positions of leadership can be among this group of uncivil

collectivism
degree to which organizational, societal, and family practices encourage and reward collective distribution of resources and collective action as well as the degree to which they express pride and loyalty.

gender egalitarianism
extent to which an organization or society minimizes gender-role differences.

humane orientation
degree to which individuals in organizations or societies encourage and reward individuals for being fair, altruistic, friendly, generous, caring, and kind to others.

people. Called "mobbing" in the United Kingdom, U.S. workers recognize this leadership incivility as "bullying" and "workplace hostility" (Davenport, Schwartz, & Elliot, 2005). The Workplace Bullying Institute defines bullying as a systematic campaign of interpersonal destruction that jeopardizes someone's health, career, and job (Namie & Namie, 2011). The Washington State Department of Labor and Industries (2011) defines **bullying** as *"repeated, unreasonable actions of individuals (or a group) directed towards an employee (or a group of employees), which are intended to intimidate, degrade, humiliate, or undermine; or which create a risk to the health or safety of the employee(s)."*

Since the 1970s, organizations have been asked to recognize and respond to incidences of workplace sexual harassment and discrimination based on sexual orientation, health, physical ability, and racism. Fortunately, laws are in place that were designed to prevent these uncivil acts from occurring or to keep them from happening repeatedly. Workplace bullying, however, has yet to be identified as a legal category. According to the Washington State Department of Labor and Industries, studies show that bullying is present in almost 35 percent of workplaces; 41 percent of workers reported being bullied in 2010. Somewhere between 13 million and 53 million U.S. employees have experienced such hostility.

Bullying is different from aggression in that it is a repeated and systematic action. Examples of workplace bullying include repeated

> unwarranted or invalid criticism,
>
> blame without factual justification,
>
> being treated differently than the rest of your work group,
>
> being sworn at,
>
> exclusion or social isolation,
>
> being shouted at or humiliated,
>
> excessive monitoring or micromanaging,
>
> being given unrealistic work or deadlines, and
>
> being denied work you are qualified to accomplish (Davenport et al., 2005).

This ongoing pattern of incivility usually occurs between a superior and a subordinate (a boss bullying an employee, for example), but it can also occur between peers. Bullying is also slightly gendered: 60 percent of all bullies are men, but if a woman is doing the bullying, she will likely target another woman (71 percent of their targets are women).

Stopping this kind of leadership incivility is complex because most businesses have yet to recognize its severity in terms of loss of worker productivity, worker morale, and even loss of income from absences, stress-related illnesses, and hiring and training new employees when the bullied worker quits. In addition, bullies tend to be "close to powerful people in the organization and carefully target less powerful" people. However, New

bullying
repeated unreasonable actions of individuals or a group directed toward an individual or another group that are intended to intimidate, degrade, humiliate, or undermine; actions that threaten the health or safety of individuals or group.

corepics VOF/Shutterstock.com

York and at least sixteen other states are considering so-called healthy workplace bills (one version of this bill passed the New York state senate in 2010) that would make it possible for workers to "sue for physical, psychological, or economic harm due to abusive treatment on the job" (Cohen, 2010). And some organizations are adopting policies to address workplace bullying. The Commission of Occupational Safety and Health in Western Australia is taking the lead in this effort, and the state of Washington's recommended version of this policy appears in Table 8.4.

Students often are assigned group projects. Can you recall one experience where group members worked well together and one where it did not? What were the strengths and limitations of those groups?

 Technology in Groups and Teams

In *Digital Freedom: How Much Can You Handle?* (2008), Narian Batra asks two questions: "How much freedom do you need?" and "How much privacy do you need?" Batra suggests that the explosion of technology over the past several decades means that individuals must consider questions and issues of surveillance, intellectual property, and the ways in which technologies shape each moment of our working (and social) lives. Batra calls attention to what he calls the "boundlessness of the Internet" and "its impact upon human expression, privacy, and social controls" (Batra, 2008, p. 1). But what does this mean for our work as members of groups and teams?

TABLE 8.4 WASHINGTON'S HEALTHY WORKPLACE POLICY

Company X considers workplace bullying unacceptable and will not tolerate it under any circumstances. Workplace bullying is behavior that harms, intimidates, offends, degrades, or humiliates an employee, possibly in front of other employees, clients, or customers.

Workplace bullying may cause the loss of trained and talented employees, reduce productivity and morale and create legal risks.

Company X believes all employees should be able to work in an environment free of bullying. Managers and supervisors must ensure employees are not bullied.

Company X has grievance and investigation procedures to deal with workplace bullying. Any reports of workplace bullying will be treated seriously and investigated promptly, confidentially, and impartially.

Company X encourages all employees to report workplace bullying. Managers and supervisors must ensure that employees who make complaints or witnesses are not victimized.

Disciplinary action will be taken against anyone who bullies a co-employee. Discipline may involve a warning, transfer, counseling, demotion, or dismissal, depending on the circumstances.

The contact person for bullying at this workplace is:

Name: _____

Phone Number: _____

Source: http://www.lni.wa.gov/Safety/Research/Files/Bully.pdf.

Do You Have a Bully at Work?

In "How to Handle a Workplace Bully," Jennifer Alsever (2009) argues that every company, no matter how large or small, has at least one bully. According to Alsever, the the signs of a bully in the office include

- complaints of screaming, tantrums, public humiliation, sabotage, and verbal abuse;
- subtle signs such as a person always taking credit for the accomplishments of others;
- someone dominating meetings with sarcasm, insults, and interruptions;
- people refusing to speak at meetings or displaying signs of stress and tension; and
- inappropriate nonverbal behaviors when others are talking such as doodling, rolling eyes, squeaking chairs, and sighing heavily or obviously shifting in a seat.

Also watch out for mobbing, or a group of people ganging up on a single individual. This might take the form of hostile humor that is explained away as "just teasing," ostracizing an employee by repeatedly "forgetting" to put someone on the e-mail list or on a listserv, or repeatedly "forgetting" to extend invitations to a social gathering.

What do we do about bullies? Gary Namie and Ruth Namie of the Workplace Bullying Institute suggest the following:

- Do not ignore the bullying because it will only get worse.
- When an employee complains, talk directly to the bully.
- Communicate specific facts and details to the bully: "Saying 'You're an idiot,' even as a joke, is uncivil and not tolerated here." Or "When Joe speaks at meetings, you roll your eyes. It's rude and needs to stop." And "Claire has asked many times to be added to the electronic mailing list. Leaving her off is unprofessional. Add her name to the list now."

- Target the behavior and not the person. Tell the bully the behavior must stop rather than attack the person.
- Create a policy for civility in the workplace and make employment contingent on following that policy.

However uncivil workplace bullying may be, it is also expensive and toxic to the workplace environment. Although employers often fear that a bully might retaliate by filing a grievance or lawsuit, as Gary Namie and Ruth Namie observe, "[t]he truth is that it is costlier to fail to act than it is to pursue solutions. Bullies are undermining legitimate business processes and harming people in secret. It's time to examine the real costs of unwanted turnover, absenteeism, lawsuit or complaint settlements, workers comp, and disability claims. The bully is expensive" (Namie & Namie, 2014).

Technology and Time

No one can dispute the fact that the infusion of technology into the workplace saves us time. We can retrieve and transmit information quickly and efficiently, and we can connect instantly with individuals who are not physically nearby. Because of technology, we can do many parts of our work faster than ever before. Indeed, we have saved others and ourselves considerable time. Yet with so much information available to us, the ability to connect with so many people so quickly, and the fact that we can take technology with us wherever we are, we sometimes find ourselves spending inordinate amounts of time working through technology. We research and retrieve, communicate constantly with others, write and rewrite documents and reports, compile images and graphs, and create our own videos and Web sites—and we can do all this from our offices, homes, cars, bus stops, taxis, waiting rooms, coffee shops, restaurants, grocery stores, health clubs, sporting events, and many other places. It is no wonder that we sometimes feel that technology is all that there is or that we do.

In groups, technology can present many of the following time-related dilemmas (Kiesler & Sproull, 1992):

Too much time spent responding to inquiries by others.

Too much time spent sending inquiries to others.

Missed messages causing delays or misunderstandings.

Time spent avoiding sending responses to messages sent by others.

Repetitive information from the "Reply All" or "Forward" functions on e-mail.

Overly lengthy conversations held on electronic mailing lists and in chat rooms.

Virtual meetings leaving us feeling dissatisfied with or disconnected from other members of a group.

Virtual meetings scheduled with people working in different time zones.

Mountains of information available on the Internet must be sorted through.

Mountains of documents sent to us by others must be worked through and sorted.

So, although technology can be a tremendous benefit, it can also demand many hours of our days and weeks as we communicate with other members of our groups and teams. As Batra suggests, the tremendous freedom we gain with technology also comes at a price: our time.

Technology and Civility

Similar to technology and its effects on our time in groups and teams, technology also has affected our level of civility with others. Technology helps us reach out and connect professionally, positively, and respectfully with others. We can receive a message from someone and take time to sort out what and why that person might be asking us to take on a new job or solve a problem for them. We can acknowledge the speed with which a person responds to our questions and concerns, and we sometimes communicate more effectively when we are using e-mail, offering more detail or context in a difficult or complex situation or checking and verifying facts and opinions before we reply to others. However, the technology coin also has its uncivil side. With technology, we can engage in the following uncivil behaviors. We may, for instance,

expect immediate replies to our inquiries,

forward messages and texts that make others look bad,

distribute photos that cast others in an unprofessional light,

misrepresent others by using images and e-mail messages inappropriately,

engage in cyberbullying,

gain access to other peoples' private information via hacking or surveillance,

take credit for the ideas generated by members of the group, and

plagiarize information from the Internet.

As groups work together via technology, conversations about protocols, boundaries, and respect can help them practice civility rather than incivility. Although accidents do happen—for example, we might

TABLE 8.5 TECHNOLOGY GUIDES

Discuss how much interaction will take place via technology:

Identify whether the group is a virtual work group or the members will also meet face to face.

Determine how much and what kind of communication will take place electronically and in person (meetings in person or information shared electronically).

Discuss timelines for working electronically:

Establish reasonable timelines for responding to electronic inquiries (2 hours, 24 hours, 2 days).

Establish exemptions for these timelines (emergencies that delay a response or increase the need for an urgent response).

Establish protocols for electronic mailing lists and chat rooms (how many, how many postings are expected, how often they should be read).

Discuss protocols for sharing information:

Establish guidelines for forwarding messages (never; only when given permission; all messages sent can be forwarded to others).

Establish guidelines for length and number of attachments (different projects will require different kinds of information, so be clear about reasonable workload management).

Establish frameworks for giving people credit for the work they do:

Determine whether reports will be written and authored collaboratively or by one person (the contact person, first author, or responsible party or parties).

Identify ways to give all those involved credit for their contributions (list names by amount of work done alphabetically, by seniority, or by some other format).

Discuss plagiarism and how to avoid it (define what the group means by plagiarism; establish practices that record who and where information and ideas come from).

Establish guidelines for civility:

Define civility and share examples of what it is and is not (acknowledging others for their good work would be civil; discrediting individuals or damaging their reputation would be uncivil).

Identify what kinds of information are private and what information can be made public (determine whether you can share good news and bad news with other members of the group, for example).

Set standards for electronic styles of communication (how formal and informal messages can be and when formality or informality is expected).

Rotate meetings when different time zones are a part of the group (alternating early mornings and late afternoon or evenings).

© Cengage Learning

mistakenly forward a message we were not supposed to or expect a quick reply when a slow one is coming—there are several guidelines groups can implement to help them manage time and civility with regard to technology. Because electronic communication does not allow for the cues we get when we are communicating with group members face to face, guidelines such as these can help a group work together productively and avoid unnecessary conflict or misunderstandings (Table 8.5).

Chapter Summary

A Group Is a Small Number of People Who Belong Together, Share Something in Common, or Are Assigned a Similar Task

- Teams come together to attempt to win something, to set a record, or to be the best at a task or event.
- The features of groups and teams include size, cohesion, and several types of power (legitimate, coercive, reward, referent, and expert). Reciprocal power dynamics are called *power with*.
- The most common types of groups are social, learning, task, and growth or therapy.

- Working in a team or group has advantages that include but are not limited to sharing knowledge and skills, creating new products or solutions, troubleshooting problems, and accomplishing a task. Disadvantages include difficulty making time to communicate or process information together, focusing on group goals, and being willing to resolve conflicts civilly and ethically.
- Groups and teams use technology to communicate efficiently and with civility. Deadlines and protocols are important for success, as well as giving credit to people for their work and establishing guidelines for civility.

In Every Group and Team, the Members Take on Formal or Informal Roles

- Formal roles are clearly defined and assigned. Informal roles usually are not talked about directly and include a variety of task, relational, and dysfunctional roles.
- Most groups and teams experience role-related problems such as competition for certain roles, not enough members to fill the roles, or becoming overly attached to a role. Strategies to solve these problems include identifying certain roles, rotating roles, and avoiding dysfunctional roles.

A Leader Guides or Directs a Group or Activity with Vision, Charisma, and Care

- There are four types of leaders: authoritarian, democratic, laissez-faire, and transformative.
- Women and men are perceived differently even when they display the same leadership styles.
- When women display authoritarian leadership styles, they are perceived as bossy and demanding. When they display democratic styles, they are seen as too ineffective and wishy-washy. When they exhibit laissez-faire styles, they are seen as too soft or incompetent.

- Although both women and men are effective leaders, men are more likely to assume the role of leader, and women are more likely to emerge as the social leader who contributes to higher morale and good interpersonal relations.

Certain Cultural Differences Strongly Influence the Ways People Think About Leaders

- Influential factors include uncertainty avoidance, power and assertiveness, collectivism, gender, and a humane orientation.

Bullying Can Significantly Affect Leaders and the Members of a Group or Team

- Bullying is the repeated, unreasonable actions of individuals that are directed toward an employee and are intended to intimidate, degrade, humiliate, or undermine a person.
- Bullying creates a hostile environment and presents a risk to the health or safety of the employee being bullied.

Technology Can Affect the Members of Groups and Teams

- Some technologies actually increase the amount of time groups and teams spend on issues.
- Technology can lead to incivilities as members of a groups or team work together.

Key Concepts

authoritarian leader (179)

bullying (186)

coercive power (168)

cohesiveness (167)

collectivism (185)

democratic leader (181)

ethics (174)

expert power (168)

formal role (175)

gender egalitarianism (185)

group (166)

groupthink (167)

growth group (175)

hidden agendas (175)

humane orientation (185)

informal role (175)

laissez-faire leader (181)

leader (179)

learning groups (174)

legitimate power (168)

norms (170)

power and assertiveness (184)

power over (168)

power with (168)

referent power (168)

reward power (168)

role (175)

social groups (171)

task groups (173)

team (166)

transformative leader (181)

uncertainty avoidance (184)

virtual group (170)

Invitation to Human Communication Online

MindTap Speech includes an interactive MindTap Reader and interactive learning tools including National Geographic Explorer videos, student videos, quizzes, flash cards, and more. You can build your speech outline with Outline Builder and record, post, and watch videos with YouSeeU. Go to cengagebrain.com to access your MindTap for *Invitation to Human Communication* where these resources are located.

MindTap®

Further Reflection and Discussion

1. Make a list of the groups and teams you are a part of. Can you divide them into social, learning, task, and growth or therapy groups?

2. Evaluate the features of the groups you listed in question 1. Are they large or small? Are they cohesive? How is power distributed, used, or managed in these groups?

3. What roles did you take on in these groups? Was there competition for certain roles? If so, how was that handled by the members of the group?

4. What types of technology did these groups use to communicate? Evaluate the strengths and weaknesses of this technology in accomplishing the group's goals.

5. Have you ever experienced groupthink? What was the group? How would you describe the cohesive in-group and the drive to be united?

6. What alternative actions may have benefited the group if the groupthink attitude had not been present? Who was silenced in the group? What differing opinions did not come to light?

7. Think about different historical figures (presidents, civil rights leaders, and so on) who have each of these kinds of power: coercive power, reward power, referent power, and expert power. Explain how each historical figure exhibited the characteristics of that type of power.

8. Consider the impact of culture and gender on the leaders you have worked with. In what ways did culture and gender influence the communication of the leaders?

9. Now consider the ways that culture and gender influenced the members of the group and their communication with those leaders. What were those influences? How did they affect the communication of the members of the group?

10. Batra's book *Digital Freedom: How Much Can You Handle?* asks two questions: "How much freedom do you need?" and "How much privacy do you need?" Develop a short speech to give to the class (2–3 minutes) in which you raise those questions with your audience. How could you develop each question into an interesting speech for your classmates?

Activities and Web Links

Visit cengagebrain.com to access the MindTap for *Invitation to Human Communication* where these activities and web links can be found.

1. Read the article "Face-to-Face Time Makes Us Happier Than Facebook" (Fahmy, 2010). Do you agree with this article? Explain your viewpoint. Go to *Web link 8.1*.

2. Watch this video clip from the movie *Twelve Angry Men*. How does it exhibit groupthink? What pressures are being used in the group to change the mind of the group member who disagrees with the majority of the group? Go to *Web link 8.2*.

3. Watch this brief video clip, "Think Different." How many of the transformative leaders do you recognize? Write down their names. Choose one and explain how this person led by example and modeled and created significant change in the life of people and organizations (do some research if you need more information). Go to *Web link 8.3*.

4. Visit this Web site and read about the three women who won the Nobel Peace Prize in 2011. What leadership qualities do these women share? Go to *Web link 8.4*.

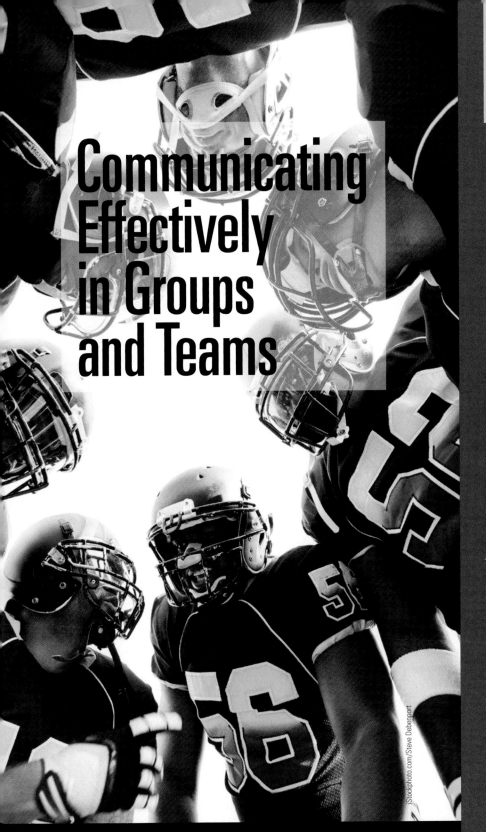

Communicating Effectively in Groups and Teams

Athletic teams sometimes work so well together that they set records, win tournaments, or become difficult to defeat. What makes an athletic team this successful? What role does communication play in this success?

9

IN THIS CHAPTER YOU WILL LEARN TO:

- Work productively in groups and teams.

- Identify the five stages of group and teamwork

- Explain the six-step reflective-thinking method for problem solving and decision making in groups.

- Recognize the role and various outcomes of conflict in groups and teams.

- Distinguish between five common types of presentations given by a group or team.

- Organize meetings and group discussions.

- Give presentations as members of a group or team.

n Chapter 8 you read about the different types of groups and teams, the roles people take on as they work in groups and teams, and some of the strengths and weaknesses of working in groups and teams. You also considered the different types and styles of leadership, as well as the power of technology in working in groups and teams. In this chapter, you will learn about group processes that affect communication in groups and teams. You will read about how groups and teams work productively, the stages of group and teamwork, and some of the decision-making processes used by groups and teams. You also will read about conflict, problem solving, and organizing meetings and making presentations in groups.

Working Productively in Groups and Teams

What makes groups and teams function well? Why does one group seem to achieve its goals with ease and even pleasure, whereas another group takes forever to reach a decision and only after a great deal of disagreement and even hostility? Some groups and teams work well together, and we will explore some of the reasons for this positive interaction.

How Groups Function

A group or team works well when its members understand how they are to operate, what they are to do, and the job they are to perform. Communication scholars Randy Hirokawa, Dennis Gouran, Kelly Julian, Geoff Leatham, Kathleen Propp, and Abran Salazar explored the kinds of mistakes groups often make and concluded that problems and breakdowns occurred largely as a result of faulty communication (Hirokawa & Salazar, 1999; Salazar, Hirokawa, Propp, Julian, & Leatham, 1994). These scholars take a functional approach to group communication, suggesting that communication functions in particular ways: to share information, explore issues, identify errors and problems, clarify thinking, and even persuade. Hirokawa and his colleagues suggest that groups that work effectively take several things into account as they try to solve problems or reach their goals. Successful groups identify group goals, identify appropriate group structure, identify ways to gather and evaluate information, identify ways to consider options, and maintain a civil approach.

Identify Group Goals Determine the reason the group is a group, the tasks it hopes to or is expected to accomplish, and the timelines for doing so.

Is the goal realistic and can it be accomplished, or is it too ambitious and something that cannot be achieved in the time allowed? Does the group have the resources it needs to accomplish the goal? Is everyone clear about the goal and the timelines?

Identify Appropriate Group Structure Determine what role each member will assume (Chapter 8). Determine how the group will operate: Will it meet via e-mail? In person? How often will it meet? How will discussions be managed? Will there be subcommittees, and how will information be shared (in writing, orally, or in Google documents)? How often are updates expected? How much time are people given to respond to e-mails and message boards? Is everyone clear about the structure? Does the structure need to be put in writing?

Identify Ways to Gather and Evaluate Information Identify the best sources of information and begin collecting it. Share information with group members. Assess and evaluate that information. Does the group need additional information? Are more questions raised?

Identify Ways to Consider Options Develop and formulate answers and plans of action that will satisfy the group's goals. Determine the pros and cons of each solution or option. Identify who is affected by the option. Select or identify the best option or solution.

Maintain a Civil Approach Recall that civility is "giving the world a chance to explain itself" and that decisions that are made affect individuals outside the group and the organization. Take stock of whose voices and perspectives were and were not included in the group's process. Can everyone's voices be included? Have different and even dissenting voices been listened to? Even if a decision or option is selected that goes against these voices, can the decision take into account the different views—is there a way to minimize the harm or damage a decision might cause to others?

iStockphoto.com/DaveBolton

Large groups often break into smaller groups to brainstorm solutions to problems. Can you identify the strengths and weaknesses of this step in problem solving?

PRACTICING HUMAN COMMUNICATION
Working Together

Practice working productively in a group. Imagine you are organizing a program to help the pets of homeless people receive food and veterinary treatment in your city.

1. Group goals: What are some reasonable goals? What resources will be needed?

2. Group structure: Will the group meet in person or via e-mail or both? Will committees be needed?

3. Gather and evaluate information. What additional information is needed?

4. Identify ways to consider options. What are some problems that might be encountered? What are the pros and cons of some of the solutions to the problems?

5. Maintain civility. What strategies might you use to ensure that all voices are heard?

For centuries, families and communities have worked together to run farms as well as other businesses. Are you part of a family- or community-run business? How well does each member work with others?

These five elements of group work should help a group work together productively and positively. One additional facet of working in groups and teams is important to consider as you attempt to work productively with other people: the stages most teams and groups go through.

Stages of Group Work and Teamwork

Groups and teams evolve through several stages as they meet to discuss and work through tasks and dilemmas. Understanding the evolution or stages of group processes can help you communicate more effectively, so we explore those stages here (Fisher, 1970; Forsyth, 1990; Miller, 2006; Reid & Hammersley, 2000).

Orientation Stage

Members of a group get to know one another. They are hesitant to share their views on the issue or problem, and they offer ideas and suggestions tentatively and cautiously. There is little disagreement.

Conflict Stage

Members express their views openly and often with a great deal of investment, and they defend their views strongly. Disagreements may become personal, but even the most intense conflict may help sort out stronger and weaker ideas and solutions.

Josef Mohyla/Getty Images

Emergence Stage

Some ideas begin to emerge as better solutions to the problem than others. Disagreements lessen, and consensus begins to form. Communication becomes more respectful, polite, and cooperative.

Reinforcement Stage

A decision is made and members of the group support that decision; disagreements and concerns are not voiced; group members work toward harmony and consensus.

Dissolution Stage

The group's job is accomplished, and members part ways. They may feel a sense of loss, even if they knew the group's work would end. Sometimes a group ends abruptly (funding is pulled or resources dissolve, for example, or the members just cannot get along). Members might also leave suddenly (illness, anger, or unworkable disagreements) or by giving timely notice (retirements or a change of jobs, for example).

Most groups pass through these five stages, and if a group exists over a long period of time, accomplishing many jobs or tasks, it will cycle through these stages again and again. Groups and teams must also manage specific kinds of relationships to work together effectively, so we look at those relationships and how they might be managed productively next.

Managing Relationships in Groups and Teams

Working with other people can be both rewarding and challenging. To help groups get the most out of their time together, pay attention to how discussions are managed, whether there are pressures to conform to "what the group wants," and whether there is information overload.

Manage Participation Groups and teams work most effectively when everyone feels comfortable participating. Many groups find a structure that satisfies the styles of its members, allowing individuals to participate equally and comfortably. This may be Robert's Rules of Order or some other structure (everyone speaks one time before someone can speak again, for example). But sometimes, even with the best of efforts, some individuals take over and participate far more than is equitable or productive. When that happens, try the following:

1. Determine who is speaking most often or for the longest amount of time. Is this based on rank, expertise, investment in the issue, or something else? Set up a structure for discussion to make the discussion more equitable. This might include setting time limits for speaking or requiring that ideas be submitted in writing before the discussion begins.

2. Pay attention to groupthink. Set up a structure that disrupts this process. This might include asking one or two people to voice disagreements or play devil's advocate. Or ask everyone to present one idea or solution not yet mentioned, even if they do not support that idea or solution.

Avoid Pressures to Conform When people work in groups, they often feel a good deal of pressure to "go along with the crowd." Occasionally, one person's personality is so charismatic and strong that group members feel compelled to follow that person's lead. At other times, a group of individuals might gain control of resources or might begin bullying behaviors. This, too, can cause individuals to go along even if they do not agree or support the ideas or solutions. To avoid this pressure, try the following:

1. Rotate group tasks, assignments, and roles. Distribute work evenly and do not assume that the person with the "most personality" is the best leader or that the quietest member is the best notetaker. Rotate these tasks and others among the group to help prevent some individuals from taking over and others being silenced.

2. Develop a healthy workplace bill or an antibullying policy. Ideally, group members will work together to develop the policy, but it may be necessary to bring in someone from the outside to help.

Prevent Information Overload As groups gather information, individuals may feel as though they must understand all the data they find. This can cause members to do any of several things, including withdraw, become resentful, or even decide there is no workable solution. To prevent information overload, try the following:

1. Divide the gathered information among group members and ask individuals to study and then present that information to the group. This helps members feel invested in the solution, and it shares the workload of understanding the problem and its possible solutions evenly.

2. Bring in an expert or resource from outside the group to help explain complex or emotionally charged ideas or arguments. This prevents one person from within the group from becoming the "know-it-all" or the target of hostility. It also creates a safe place for group members to ask questions and explore ideas without threatening or insulting one another.

Decision Making in Groups and Teams

One of the most widely used methods to solve problems and come to a decision is the **reflective-thinking method**, which was developed by philosopher John Dewey. This *six-step method is used to structure a problem-solving and decision-making discussion.* The name of this method highlights the importance of using a thoughtful and reflective process that involves taking a careful, systematic approach to a problem. The six steps of this model are the following:

1. Identify the problem.

2. Analyze the problem.

3. Suggest possible solutions.

4. Consider the implications of the solutions.

5. Reach a decision about the best solution.

6. Implement the solution.

We now look at these steps in more detail.

reflective-thinking method
six-step method for structuring a problem-solving and decision-making discussion.

Bil Zelman

Alexandra Cousteau,
Emerging Explorer and Social Environment Advocate

Are there specific decision-making strategies that you employ in your work? Can you tell us why they are effective?

My team and I are very strict with regard to personal integrity. We are always very courteous to the local community and respectful—we don't leave behind a mess. That's incredibly important to me. When it comes to how we tackle problems or projects, we listen to each other's ideas and work things out collaboratively. And I think the most important thing that I've learned is to be strategic rather than opportunistic. I have a strategy for what we want to accomplish. The projects that are meaningful and part of the strategy, that are helping us move forward with how we shape the conversation, are ones we take on. If they don't match up to those requirements, then we send our regrets.

Identify the Problem

The first step of the reflective-thinking model is problem identification. In this stage of the decision-making process, group participants identify the nature of the problem, its extent, who is affected by it, and the impact on those affected. Groups often do considerable research and may use an invitational approach (see Chapter 15) at this stage to be sure that they have identified all aspects of the problem they have been asked to solve. Once the group identifies the problem, it moves on to the next step of the model—problem analysis.

Analyze the Problem

It might be natural to jump to a discussion of solutions to the problems that have been identified. Instead, effective group communication starts by discussing why the problem exists. Much like a physician who must diagnose a patient's illness, the reflective thinker must understand the causes of the problem before moving on to discussing solutions. Besides helping the group arrive at a more reasoned solution, this step helps the group present its findings more successfully. At this stage, you will want to continue to use an open, invitational approach to ensure as full an understanding of the problem as possible. After group members have thought carefully about the reasons the problem exists, they can move on to suggesting solutions.

Suggest Possible Solutions

A popular method used by groups at this stage of the problem-analysis process is **brainstorming**, the *process of generating ideas randomly and uncritically without attention to logic, connections, or relevance*. When groups brainstorm, they suggest as many ideas as they can think of without judging those ideas. After the group has listed as many ideas as possible, members can do two things. They can go through the list and eliminate those ideas that are not suitable until just a few options remain. Or the group may rank a longer list of options and then choose the solution that has the most support.

Groups often brainstorm ideas as they consider the impact of the solutions to a problem. Computers can help groups identify potential affects. Can you recall a time when you used your computer to help your group solve a problem?

Monkey Business Images/Shutterstock.com

brainstorming

process of generating ideas randomly and uncritically without attention to logic, connections, or relevance.

When groups work together for a period of time, they can fall prey to groupthink or one person may continually take charge. How might groups and teams avoid this groupthink or takeover when it happens? How might they civilly respond to it if it does happen?

A potential pitfall for groups as they generate solutions is *groupthink* (discussed previously), which occurs when the group conforms to a single frame of mind and chooses a solution without fully and objectively examining other possible solutions. Groups that fall victim to groupthink often are under tight timelines, are pressured by leaders, or are afraid to question each other's ideas. They also tend to get along well and favor consensus over conflict. Groupthink can be avoided by having a group member play the role of devil's advocate who questions the decisions made or ideas offered, removing the group's leader from discussions, or taking time to fully evaluate each solution.

Consider the Implications of the Solutions

After a group has arrived at potential solutions, it studies the implications of those solutions. The discussion in the group should avoid immediately enacting a single solution and instead take time to fully examine its disadvantages or impact on others. This requires a good deal of discussion about cause and effect to allow the group to explore the full implications of each solution that is identified as feasible.

Reach a Decision About the Best Solution

Groups may use several methods to reach a decision about the best solution. For example, if the group has time and resources to implement a pilot study, it can study the effects of the decision over time. Groups can also use reasoning to choose the solution that has the fewest detrimental effects. Groups can also use a consensus model for deciding on the solution, which requires all members to agree on a single best solution. Or it can use a simple voting process, with the majority of group members supporting a single solution over others.

Implement the Solution

Although Dewey's reflective-thinking model originally had five steps, researchers now often include a sixth step: implementing the solution. In this stage, the group determines how to carry out what it has decided. It is important for the group to consider who will be responsible for the different parts of the solution and when the solution should be implemented. Although it is not a part of Dewey's model, groups often return to step one to assess whether or not there are any new problems they need to address as a result of the process they have just completed.

When you work in groups, you will be faced with a variety of problems to solve and issues to sort through. The six-step problem-solving process can help your group arrive at a solution that will actually solve the problem and benefit everyone involved.

Managing Technology Technology can contribute positively to group work, but it also can contribute to difficult group dynamics. When working together, groups tend to experience two types of stresses that can be magnified by technology: relational and task. **Relational stress** *occurs*

relational stress

stress that occurs when there are interpersonal incompatibilities among group members based on differences in their personalities, communication styles, attitudes, and preferences.

Shabana Basij-Rasikh, Educator and Explorer: Create the Best Educated Leadership

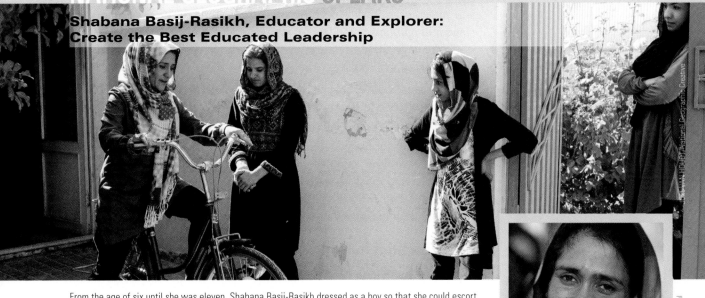

JOEL VAN HOUDT/National Geographic Creative

From the age of six until she was eleven, Shabana Basij-Rasikh dressed as a boy so that she could escort her sister, who was too old to go out in public alone, to a secret school in Afghanistan. Knowing that they would likely be killed if they were caught, the two girls disguised their books as groceries, took a different route each day to the secret school, and shared a small living-room-turned-schoolroom with 100 other girls. They knew that everyone there—teachers, students, and even the families who saw their education as so important—was at risk of death. Under Taliban rule, it was illegal for girls to receive an education. Basij-Rasikh recounts, "[F]rom time-to-time, the school would suddenly be canceled for a week because Taliban were suspicious. We always wondered what they knew about us. Were we being followed? Do they know where we live? We were scared, but still school was where we wanted to be."

Basij-Rasikh considers herself lucky because she grew up "in a family where education was prized and daughters were treasured." She describes her grandfather as an "extraordinary man for his time." He was disowned by his own father for educating his daughters. Basij-Rasikh's father was the first in his family to receive an education, and despite "the Taliban, despite the risks, Basij-Rasikh explains, to her father, "there was greater risk in not educating his children." He supported the education of his daughters, and she says, "During Taliban years I remember I would get so frustrated by our life and always being scared and not seeing a future. I would want to quit, but my father, he would say, 'Listen, my daughter, you can lose everything you own in your life. Your money can be stolen. You can be forced to leave your home during a war, but the thing that will always remain is [your education], and if we have to sell our blood to pay your school fees, we will, so do you still not want to continue?'"

Basij-Rasikh states: "I was raised in a country that has been destroyed by decades of war. Fewer than six percent of women my age have made it beyond high school, and had my family not been so committed to my education, I would be one of them." Because of this support, she attended high school and college in the United States and graduated from Middlebury College in Vermont. At the age of eighteen, she cofounded School of Leadership Afghanistan (SOLA), and established HELA, "a nonprofit organization to empower Afghan women through education." She returned to Kabul after graduation to "turn SOLA, into the nation's first boarding school for girls." However, Basij-Rasikh shares that it is still dangerous for girls to go to school and that without their fathers they likely would not go. One of her students and her father, walking home from school, narrowly missed being killed by a bomb, a bomb that exploded minutes after they passed. Basij-Rasikh says, "As he arrived home the phone rang, a voice warning him that if he sent his daughter back to school, they would try again. 'Kill me now, if you wish,' he said, 'but I will not ruin my daughter's future because of your old and backward ideas.'"

Because of SOLA, young women now can take college preparatory courses and "enter universities worldwide." More than this, however, the 3 million young girls who now receive an education "return to substantive careers in Afghanistan," and become the "first women to enter certain fields." Basij-Rasikh shares her belief that "The most effective antidote to the Taliban is to create the best educated leadership generation in Afghanistan's history" (Basij-Rasikh, 2012; National Geographic Society, 2014).

WHAT DO YOU THINK?

1. Basij-Rasikh and her family, and families like them, face an incredibly difficult problem: going against Taliban rule and educating girls. Could the strategies for problem solving discussed in this chapter be helpful in understanding this serious of a problem? Why or why not?

2. Many families in Afghanistan send their daughters to school and avoid the pressures to conform that the Taliban try to enforce. How do these families avoid such pressures and what kind of commitment does it take for them to do so?

3. Consider the material in Chapter 8 on leadership, what kind of leader do you think Basij-Rasikh is and what kind of leaders does she hope these young women will become?

when there are interpersonal incompatibilities among group members based on differences in their personalities, communication styles, attitudes, and preferences. **Task stress**, on the other hand, *consists of contrasting views and opinions among group members regarding the tasks at hand.*

To manage these pressures as you work via electronically mediated communication (EMC), try the following:

1. Because nonverbal cues cannot be read via EMC, make sure group members add them to their messages and take time to clarify if a message seems to be leading to conflict.

2. Using technology rather than face-to-face communication often increases the number of ideas and suggestions, and the ideas generated must be sorted, organized, and read by all the members of the group. So try setting a limit to the number of messages, the length of messages, and even guidelines for the content of messages.

Conflict in Groups and Teams

At some point, conflict is a part of almost every group or team. However uncomfortable conflict makes most of us, when handled productively, it can help produce a positive outcome. But when conflict is handled poorly, it can lead to a group's demise. As discussed in Chapter 7, there are negative and positive approaches to handling conflict. Possible outcomes are avoidance, accommodation, competition, compromise, and workplace democracy.

Avoidance

Usually unproductive, the **avoidance** style *occurs when individuals will not address the conflict or acknowledge its existence.* "It's all good," "Not now," and "I'm not talking about this with you" are examples of avoidance. Although an individual may have good reasons for avoiding conflict (possible job loss or becoming the target of bullying, for example), this style rarely leads to productive resolution.

Accommodation

With the **accommodation** style, *an individual "resolves" the conflict by doing what she or he is asked.* At times, the style is successful—for example, "I'll go with your idea this time, and you'll support mine next time." Too often, however, it leaves one individual feeling used and unappreciated. When Franklin agrees to meet at a time that is inconvenient for him just to avoid conflict, the other group members feel great about the decision, but his needs must be accommodated in other ways to prevent him from feeling alienated and used. This requires the practice of **reciprocity**, or *actions that demonstrate interdependence or mutual respect*—for example, *when people who help you later need help, you return the favor* (Forsyth, 1990).

Competition

The **competition** style of conflict management is present *when one individual makes sure that her or his needs are met—but with complete disregard for the needs of the other members of a group.* This is a win–lose style of conflict: in a group, one member (or a small group of individuals) walks away happy, but others are frustrated, angry, and feel as if their

Who Can Be a Member of Our Team?

Consider the following events:

When Nick Zamora's mom and her partner were kicked out of a Boy Scout troop meeting for being lesbians, Nick left the troop as well. Troop 152 told Nick he could stay, but his moms could not. Nick, a member of the troop for eight years, and close to becoming an Eagle Scout, replied, "Until the Boy Scouts change their policies, I'm done with them.... My moms are my family, and my family is everything to me. If the Boy Scouts can't accept my family for who they are, then the rank of Eagle Scout means nothing to me" (Reagan, 2015).

When the women's basketball team at Narbonne High School wore "unapproved uniforms" with "breast cancer awareness colors" in a playoff game, they almost had to forfeit their win. Changes in uniform colors must be approved, according to official rules, if a team wishes to wear "hues beyond the school's official colors." The team wore the uniforms in support of the Kay Yow Cancer Fund, a fund run by the Women's Basketball Coaches Association and "named in memory of former North Carolina State Women's basketball coach who died in 2009." Although officials reinstated the team, its coach was suspended, and the team was placed on probation for a year (Dowd, 2015).

When Lincoln Middle School cheerleader Desire Andrews became the target of heckling and jeers, her squad, as well as the school's basketball team, stood up in support of her. Desire has Down syndrome, and when the team realized "members of the crowd were making fun" of her, "three players went into the crowd during a time out with a simple message: 'Don't mess with her.'" The squad, the team, and Desire's father were upset. Desire, however, seemed more concerned by her father's anger than the heckling. So, her father explains, "she threw her hands around me and made me look at her face and said, 'Papa, it's OK. I still love them even if they don't like me'" (Chappell, 2015).

What Do You Think?

1. How was conflict resolved in each of these examples? Would you describe it as effective or not?

2. Select one of these cases and use Dewey's reflective thinking method for making decisions to see if you would make the same choices as Nick, the basketball officials, and the members of the basketball team who supported Desire.

3. Consider the approaches to conflict in groups and teams. What approach seems to describe each example? How ethical do you think those approaches were?

own needs have been sacrificed or ignored. Although competition is appropriate in many parts of life, in groups or teams, internal competition can cause a group to fall apart or become unproductive and unhealthy.

Compromise

Commonly referred to as a *win–win approach*, when conflict is handled in the spirit of compromise, all parties involved should feel respected and valued. In a **compromise**, *the needs of every group member are considered and met*—at least some of the time in the life of the group. In the spirit of compromise, meeting times are rotated so that they are convenient (or inconvenient) for all members of the group, both the best and worst assignments are shared among all group members, and individuals check in with one another regularly to be sure that the compromises continue to be win–win and not lose–lose for some.

Workplace Democracy

Many communication scholars now advocate and study *workplace democracy*, a concept that describes ways in which groups work together productively and positively and thus avoid many of the pitfalls previously described. **Workplace democracy** is described as a *system of governance that truly values individuals' goals and feelings*. This system also values the objectives of the organization, but it brings the individual and the organization together "by encouraging individual contributions to important organizational choices"

compromise
a style of managing conflict in which the needs of every member of the group are considered and met.

workplace democracy
system of governance that truly values individuals' goals and feelings.

(Miller, 2006, p. 184). According to the National Coalition for Dialogue and Deliberation (n.d.), workplace democracy requires deliberation:

> The ancient Greeks called *deliberation* the talk we use to teach ourselves before we act. Deliberation is the kind of reasoning and talking we do when a difficult decision has to be made, a great deal is at stake, and there are competing options or approaches we might take. At the heart of deliberation is weighing possible actions and decisions carefully by examining their costs and consequences in light of what is most valuable to us. Deliberation can take place in any kind of conversation—including dialogue, debate, and discussion.

In the context of groups within organizations, workplace democracy and deliberation rely on three things: (1) shared values among the members of a group, (2) organizational structures that support cooperation and encourage individual participation, and (3) fostering the development of individual talents and resources and then making appropriate use of them. Although complex, workplace democracy can be a successful approach to working within a group when the members

- take time to identify the values they share as well as the values of the organization,

- establish structures and practices that welcome and encourage participation and cooperation, and

- identify the talents of each member of the group and then use those talents positively and productively.

Problem Solving in Groups and Teams

One of the most important functions of a group is to make a decision about an issue, project, or course of action. This usually happens after conversation, careful exploration and analysis, and a consideration of the implications of the final choices. Here we explore three of the most common ways groups make decisions: consensus, voting, and authority rule.

Consensus

Consensus is a *general or widespread agreement among all the members of a group.* When groups reach a decision by consensus, they have determined that all members agree on a particular course of action. To reach a consensus, groups usually spend considerable time exploring an issue as well as the possible alternatives that could solve or address the issue. When an issue or problem is complex or when the impact of a decision is quite profound, consensus can be a perfect method of making a decision. Pay cuts, reductions or increases in services, protocols for granting awards or privileges, and job qualifications are good examples. When decisions are of such magnitude and a group wants to be sure that all members agree with the decision, then consensus is a way to achieve it.

Consensus can be hard to reach, however, and groups will want to be sure that they are not falling prey to two potential problems: groupthink and ultimatums. When groups are fairly cohesive or when there is pressure to conform, a group may think that it has consensus, when in fact it

consensus

general or widespread agreement among all the members of a group.

Food Not Bombs

CASE STUDY

Food Not Bombs: Decision Making by Consensus

Committed to the equal distribution of food worldwide, consensus, and self-empowerment, Food Not Bombs began in Cambridge, Massachusetts, in 1980. Currently, groups of individuals are working in hundreds of autonomous Food Not Bombs chapters "sharing free vegetarian food with hungry people and protesting war and poverty" (Food Not Bombs, n.d.). As the group's Web site explains, "Food Not Bombs is not a charity. This energetic grassroots movement is active throughout the Americas, Europe, Africa, the Middle East, Asia, and Australia. Food Not Bombs is organizing for . . . peace," and for "thirty years the movement has worked to end hunger and has supported actions to stop the globalization of the economy, restrictions to the movements of people, end exploitation and the destruction of the Earth" (Food Not Bombs, n.d.).

With so many members, why would a group like this want to reach decisions by consensus? According to Food Not Bombs, "[v]oting is a win or lose model in which people are more concerned about the numbers it takes to win a majority than they are in the issue itself. Consensus, on the other hand, is a process of synthesis, bringing together diverse elements and blending them into a decision which is acceptable to the entire group. . . . Each person's ideas are valued and become part of the decision." Working with a consensus model of decision making allows everyone to participate in a discussion, and this creates an environment in which trust and the valuing of all group members are of utmost importance. In addition, Food Not Bombs believes that when a consensus model is used, people are more committed to the final decision and its outcome.

Food Not Bombs suggests that a proposal is stronger when everyone works together to create the best possible decision for the group. The group explains that any "idea can be considered, but only those ideas which everyone thinks are in the best interests of the group are adopted." Although there are many models for reaching a decision by consensus, for Food Not Bombs, "[i]t is most important . . . that whatever process you use is clear, consistent, and able to be easily taught and learned so that all can participate fully." Groups also want to recognize that leaders are important, but we can avoid having power "concentrated in the hands of a few entrenched leaders" by developing leadership skills in every member of the group. "This can be accomplished by holding skill-building trainings and by encouraging and

supporting people to be self-empowered, especially those who are generally reserved." The benefits are many, according to Food Not Bombs: cultivating leadership skills in all group members "helps the group become more democratic and helps individuals feel more satisfied and, therefore, less likely to burn out or fade away" (Food Not Bombs, n.d.).

What Do You Think?

1. Explain what you think is meant by "Voting is a win or lose model in which people are more concerned about the numbers it takes to win a majority than they are in the issue itself." Could consensus be used instead of voting for local matters such as voting to give more tax money to the schools or voting to reduce levels of pollutants from local factories?

2. Have you ever tried to reach consensus in a group? What difficulties arose? What communication strategies worked well to address those difficulties?

3. Describe a problem you currently face in a group. What models for reaching a decision could you use to solve this problem? Given the makeup of the group, which models do you think would be most effective? Why?

has failed to fully explore issues, differences of opinion, and varying perspectives; in reality, it has engaged in groupthink. Although a decision is made, a group usually discovers later that there is dissension and dissatisfaction among its members or that members made a poor decision because they failed to fully explore all the options. When this happens, the group either has to revisit the decision or attempt to function with considerable disharmony and a poorly made decision.

Attempts at consensus also can lead to ultimatums. These occur when a member tries to block a decision by delivering a threat or demand. Ultimatums usually are communicated in a quid pro quo fashion: "If you do X, then I'll do Y." A group member may threaten to quit, to never agree to another decision again, to expose sensitive information, or to breach confidentiality. When members of a group feel isolated and backed into a corner by the overall group's attempts at consensus, they may resort to ultimatums to try to get their way. To preempt ultimatums if your group has decided to make a decision by consensus, set clear ground rules for discussion that do not allow any member to use ultimatums (Alderton & Frey, 1986; Frey, 2003; Keyton & Stalworth, 2003; Oetzel & Ting-Toomey, 2006; Poole & Garner, 2006; Seibold & Myers, 1986).

Voting

Groups can also come to a decision through voting. When a group makes a decision by vote, it can decide to go with two-thirds majority or a simple majority, which means that more than 50 percent of its members must vote in favor of the decision. A two-thirds majority vote means that at least two-thirds of the members must cast their vote in favor of the decision. Sometimes, groups simply need to know that more than half of their members support a decision (to postpone the vote until the group can gather more information on an issue, for example). But there are other times a group needs to know that a significant majority of its members support a decision (for example, to elect someone as the spokesperson for the group), so it will rely on a two-thirds majority vote. If a group decides to use the simple majority vote, it needs to remember that if it gets only 51 percent of its members to support a decision, then 49 percent do not—and those members may be extremely unhappy with a decision. Similarly, if it requires a two-thirds majority, the group also needs to consider that one-third of its members do not support the decision. In both cases, it is inaccurate and even uncivil to act as if the full group is 100 percent in support of a decision.

Authority Rule

When a group makes a decision by **authority rule**, it is *allowing the leader or head of the group to make the final choice.* When decisions are made this way, three things usually are happening. First, a group may not have time to meet, gather information, and then discuss a decision, so it will turn the choice over to a selected leader or authority. Second, a group may not need to meet and gather and then process information. This happens when the choice being made is a simple one that does not involve extensive work or deliberation. Third, the group trusts its leader to have the expertise and best interests of the group at heart to make a credible and ethical decision. Under this third condition, the person in authority needs to be certain she or he actually has the full support and trust of the group and should check in with other group members regularly to share decisions made, to gather information before making new decisions, and to stay connected and in touch with the members of the group.

Reaching decisions by consensus, voting, and authority rule all have a legitimate place in groups and teams. When you find yourself working in a group or team, take time to decide which option might work best for different situations. Be sure to communicate with other members of the group about the decision-making model that will work best for a situation, and recognize that all models have their strengths and weaknesses.

authority rule
allowing the leader or head of a group to make the final choice.

Asking Questions

Effective group work relies on asking good questions. Although asking questions feels intuitive and something that we should not have to learn, research shows the following:

- The most important part of a question is listening to the answers.

- You should understand your reasons for asking the question.

- Do not ask too many questions.

- Rather than think about the next question you will ask, be sure to listen to the answers to the ones you already have asked (Reid & Hammersley, 2000).

Members of a group can ask several types of questions: closed, open, affective, probing, and leading. These questions are discussed as follows, and each type can be use for both positive and negative reasons.

Closed Questions Often *described as "yes or no" questions,* **closed questions** *limit the kind of answers a person can give.* "Are we ready to begin?" "Did you ask him for more information?" "Do we need more time to think about this?" and "Do you think we should meet again?" are examples of closed questions. Closed questions can be useful when a group needs a quick answer, must take a poll of where the group is at on an issue, or needs to determine the next course of action. Too many closed questions can be awkward, however, so try to mix them with open questions.

Open Questions **Open questions** *give people freedom to answer in a range of ways.* In groups, open questions help with brainstorming, evaluating ideas and solutions, and avoiding groupthink. Open questions are framed so that individuals can share what they think about an issue or a problem: "What do we think about David's idea?" "What haven't we discussed?" "Who has other ideas about this problem that we need to hear?" and "Who is affected by this decision?" Open questions generate ideas and help people share what they are worried or excited about. Too many open questions, however, can lead a group offtrack, so try to balance open questions with closed questions as you sort through issues and solutions.

Affective Questions **Affective questions** *acknowledge that people have feelings as well as ideas—and that those feelings are important to share.* Affective questions can be both closed and open: "Are we happy about this choice?" "How do we feel about this decision?" and "I'm hearing some frustration with this discussion—can anyone elaborate on why?" are examples. A group can get too tied up with emotions, however, or focus on a single person's emotional state, so affective questions should be a part of the group discussion but not dominate the process.

Probing Questions **Probing questions** *help people talk more about an idea or a feeling.* They open up a space for more discussion on a topic. Examples of probing questions are "We seem stuck on this one issue— why is that so?" "I'm hearing only the positive aspects of this solution— are there negative outcomes we need to consider?" "Lisa, you've been very

---

closed questions
yes or no questions that limit the kind of answers a person can give.

open questions
questions that give people the freedom to answer in a range of ways.

affective questions
questions that acknowledge that people have feelings as well as ideas that are important to share.

probing questions
questions that help people talk more about an idea or feeling.

quiet during the conversation—is there something you want to add?" Probing questions can put people on the spot, asking them to become involved in a discussion when they might have good reasons not to, so use them carefully. If a person responds with "No, nothing to add," it is probably best to double-check that response privately rather than publicly.

Leading Questions Leading questions *urge people to respond in a particular way*. They set the stage for agreement or disagreement and do not always result in an honest answer or encourage productive conversation. A leading question that seeks agreement might be, "She's an amazing resource and an expert in this area. Don't you agree?" or "I think that's a wonderful solution—who wouldn't?" Examples of leading questions that seek disagreement are "That feels unethical to me, but I guess that's the approach you want to take, right?" or "I think we are making a huge mistake, but when have my ideas ever mattered?" Leading questions force a response, but they also might not add productively to the discussion, so use them carefully, if at all.

Culture and Communication in Groups and Teams

As our teams and groups become more international and diverse, they consist of individuals with different backgrounds, cultures, and ways of working with one another. Scholars agree that there are five major ways that a culture affects its individuals, and by culture they refer not only to national and ethnic cultures but also to regional and even community or business cultures. The five ways in which cultures can present challenges are discussed in the following sections as well as how those differences might affect us as we communicate in groups and teams (Hofstede, 2010; Stohl, 2001).

Collectivism and Individualism

A culture values collectivism when it promotes interdependence, community, and loyalty to the group, family, or community. A culture values individualism when it promotes independence, self-reliance, and looking out for one's own self (recall that you learned about collectivistic and individualistic cultures in Chapter 6).

How This Affects Groups and Teams Individualistic members of a group will be more likely to look out for their own needs, whereas collectivist members will look out for the needs of the whole group. Individualistic members work well independently; collectivistic members work well collaboratively.

Equality and Inequality

A culture that values equality will work to ensure that all members are cared for and treated equally, whereas a culture that sees inequalities as an accepted part of life will be comfortable with some of its members having more than others. This is sometimes referred to as *power distance*, or the degree to which members of a culture are comfortable with differences in power.

How This Affects Groups and Teams Individuals from cultures that value equality and sameness will be less likely to be comfortable with power hierarchies and the benefits given to those higher up in the

leading questions
questions that urge people to respond in a particular way.

hierarchy. They also may be less comfortable following a decision made by authority and more likely to be comfortable with consensus forms of decision making. Individuals from cultures that accept or see inequality as inevitable will follow leaders and authorities with more ease. They also will work to earn authority so that they can be higher on the hierarchy.

Uncertainty and Change

Cultures that value uncertainty and change are comfortable with risk, ambiguity, and even indecision. Cultures that value certainty and stability are more comfortable with strong convictions, clear expectations, and firm protocols for working together.

How This Affects Groups and Teams Individuals from cultures that value uncertainty will be more comfortable with flexible norms and rules and fluid processes for working together and solving problems. Individuals from cultures that value certainty will be happier with clear rules and norms and clearly defined rules for working together, making decisions, and solving problems.

Task and Social Orientation

Cultures that value task orientation are cultures that focus on training, learning the latest methods and technologies, and on "getting the job done." Task-oriented cultures value efficiency and saving time by doing a job well or accomplishing a task quickly. Cultures that value social orientation are cultures that put relationships before tasks and will work to avoid hurting people just to finish a job quickly.

How This Affects Groups and Teams Socially oriented members of a group or team will focus on creating a welcoming and friendly atmosphere, and they will monitor the feelings and undercurrents of group members and dynamics. They may slow down a group decision to ensure that the relationships in the group stay healthy. Task-oriented members of a group will push to get a job done and seek efficiency in making decisions. They may push a decision forward at the expense of group satisfaction.

Short- and Long-Term Orientation

Cultures with a short-term orientation look for immediate benefits or payoffs from a group's efforts and work. Short-term orientations encourage members to focus on the most pressing issue or the most obvious and direct advantage to a process or decision. Cultures that have a long-term orientation are willing to put off immediate gratification for rewards that come much later down the road. Long-term orientations encourage group members to consider what may happen later or what the consequences of a decision may be weeks or years from the time the decision is made.

How This Affects Groups and Teams Individuals from cultures with long-term orientations encourage a group to focus beyond the immediate and take a more visionary, interconnected, or even sustainable view of a process or decision. Individuals from cultures with a short-term orientation are quick to get a job done, and they

Blend Images/Ariel Skelley/Getty Images

Virtual meetings are common in today's online and global working environment. What are some of the advantages of this type of meeting? Can you identify any disadvantages, and how you might minimize them as you meet virtually?

encourage a group to focus on narrower goals and actions that lead to immediate decisions and solutions to issues.

Meetings and Group Discussions

One of the most time-consuming aspects of group work is meeting with other members of the group. Because members of a group usually have busy schedules and responsibilities outside their group tasks, organizing and planning for meetings is important. There are two venues for meetings: real time and virtual. When a group meets in **real time**, its members are *in a room together and can speak in the moment with one another without needing computers, phones, or the like.* **Virtual meetings** *take place via electronic means such as Skype, GChat, teleconferencing, or other electronic media that can bring people together across distances.* Real-time meetings offer group members the advantage of being able to clearly see all individuals who are attending and monitoring nonverbal cues. Virtual meetings eliminate the need for long days of travel to get to meetings, and they are easier to schedule when people work off-site or in different time zones, or when they simply have demanding and full work schedules.

Facilitating Group and Team Meetings

Regardless of the venue, productive meetings take planning and structure. Let us look at some of the components of planning meetings.

Determine the Goals for the Meeting Groups need a reason to gather, and depending on where the group is in its process, the reasons for meeting will vary. If the group is newly formed, its members might set an initial meeting with a goal of getting to know one another and understanding the job or reason for coming together. If the group is beyond the orienting stage, its members might meet to share information, assess or evaluate information or options, come to a final decision, or even bring a project to its conclusion. If the group is in the middle of intense conflict, its members might meet with a facilitator to help work through the conflict. If it needs more information, the group might meet with an outside resource. Whatever the reason, it is important to clearly answer the question, "Why are we going to meet?" Because it is important not to waste people's time, determine the reason you are bringing the group together before you set a meeting.

Organize the Agenda The next step is to develop the agenda for the meeting. An **agenda** is *a formal and organized outline of the items you*

real time
when people in a room together can speak and hear one another in the moment without needing computers, phones, or the like.

virtual meetings
meetings that take place via electronic means such as Skype or teleconferencing or other electronic media that can bring people together across distances.

agenda
formal and organized outline of items to address in order to meet the goals of a meeting.

want to cover in order to meet the goals of the meeting. To run effectively, meetings need a plan or structure, so take time to set out the agenda and assign time limits to each item on that agenda. Computer programs such as those at Office.com can provide templates for agendas.

Most agendas include the time, place, relevant contact information, and a list of business items to be covered. Depending on the goals for the meeting, you will want to organize your items accordingly. You may have one lengthy issue to cover, for example, but several small items that can be handled quickly. If so, take care of those small items first and then turn to the bigger item. However, you may have a series of small items that need discussion and delegation, and you might want to discuss each of them and then decide who will take responsibility for them after all tasks have been explained. Or you may be calling a meeting to vote on several matters, hear reports from members of the group, or set forth a plan of action for the next several weeks.

Once you determine the goals for the meeting, carefully map out how the group will accomplish those goals the most productively. You might have headings such as "Old Business," "Reports," "Action Items," and "Discussion Items" on the agenda. Carefully think about assigning a time frame for each item so that those who are attending the meeting can plan their reports and comments to match the agenda. Finally, distribute the agenda before the meeting whenever possible. This will give everyone in the group time to prepare and think about the goals for the meeting and how they can best help the group meet those goals.

Manage the Meeting Meetings run most effectively when one person is in charge. That person usually is the group leader or the person who establishes the agenda for the meeting, but that person can be appointed or the job of facilitator can even rotate. Before you begin the meeting, make sure the rules for conducting the meeting are clear—this might require rules for governing who may speak, for how long, and how often; how decisions will be made; and how votes will be taken. Many groups have an established procedure for conducting meetings that is easy for new group members to pick up as they attend a few meetings. The following is a general procedure for conducting a meeting:

- Begin the meeting by establishing the facilitator and appointing someone or asking a volunteer to take minutes or notes of the meeting.

- Open the meeting by stating what is to be discussed and what the group should try to accomplish by the end of the meeting.

- Begin with the first agenda item. If group members have been asked to present information to the group, ask them to do so now.

- Open the meeting to discussion, facilitating the conversation so that the group stays focused.

- Use the skills you have learned in this chapter to help you communicate effectively, manage the discussion, work with conflict, avoid groupthink, and gather information.

Keeping That New Job

According to the PRSA jobcenter, employees need to prove their commitment to a new job, as well as their "fit" with a company in just nine weeks. Employers not only quickly evaluate a new employee's skill set but also consider how compatible the person is with the culture of the workplace and how well they collaborate with co-workers. Rookies make six common mistakes (Creative Group, n.d.). Fortunately, there are ways to avoid them.

1. **Clarify expectations.** Within the first few days, new employees should meet with their managers to learn the priorities of their jobs, how they will be evaluated, and how they should communicate with bosses and co-workers. Get an overview of the "big picture": how does your job fit into the larger goals and visions of the company? Request "continual feedback" so you can make sure you are performing up to expectations.
2. **Watch others.** Learn and observe from your co-workers. Pay attention to their habits and communication styles and how they collaborate with others.
3. **Be enthusiastic.** Even if the job is not your dream job, keep a positive and upbeat attitude. Your enthusiasm will put you in a better light for a future promotion—or help you move to the job you really want.
4. **Make friends.** Take time to get to know your co-workers and socialize a bit with them. Take an interest in them and ask about tips for success. Introduce yourself to project managers and people you will be working closely with or reporting to. These people can help you learn the expectations and culture of your new job.
5. **Mind your meeting manners.** At those first meetings, pay attention to the communication styles, leaders, group roles, and culture and climate of the organization. Notice whether people take notes, bring laptops, follow agendas, speak out, or are quiet. Once you know the culture of meetings, take steps to follow that culture so you fit in.
6. **Wait to suggest change.** Unless you have been hired to change an organization, do not suggest changes until you have built relationships and established trust. Rookie employees need to earn the trust and respect of their co-workers and bosses. Take note of things that might be improved but wait until you are a trusted member of the team before you suggest changes.

- When the group has concluded its discussion, summarize the main points that were raised.
- Specify how the group should follow up on the meeting, assign any tasks that need to be accomplished, and set a time for the next meeting.

Follow-Up Communication After the meeting, provide copies of the minutes to group members. The minutes of a meeting should clearly identify what the group discussed and any action taken by the group. Be sure to identify group members who are responsible for certain tasks and assignments. Remind the group of timelines and the date for the next meeting.

 ## Presentations in Groups and Teams

Members of a group often have to report on the decisions they have made, make recommendations, or share the information they have gathered and compiled with other entities. These presentations can take several forms, and the most common are oral reports, panel discussions, symposiums, team presentations, and online forums.

Oral Reports

Oral reports *are presentations given by one or two of the group members who present a group's findings, conclusions, or proposals to other members of the group or to a larger audience.* When you present an oral report, use the skills you will learn in Chapters 10 to 15 for giving a speech. Remember to prepare your general purpose, specific purpose, and thesis statement. Outline your main points and select your pattern of organization. Be sure to prepare an introduction that catches your audience's attention, reveals the topic of your report, establishes your credibility, and previews your main points. Include connectives between the major sections of your report and write a conclusion that reinforces your thesis statement and brings your presentation to a close.

When you give an oral report, remember that you either are speaking to other members of your group who may be familiar with the issues under consideration or to outside audiences who may be less familiar but are highly invested in the issue. Be sure to consider your audience carefully, the amount of time you have for the presentation, and whether or not you will have technology to help you present your information. Carefully considering these factors will help you design and deliver a successful oral report.

Panel Discussions

A **panel discussion** is a *structured discussion among group members and facilitated by a moderator that takes place in front of an audience.* When you are part of a panel discussion, you share your ideas not only with other members of your group but also with a larger audience. A panel discussion typically begins with brief opening statements by each panelist followed by an informal discussion among panelists about their ideas. A moderator, who may be a member of the panel, facilitates the discussion. Usually, the discussion becomes more focused as group members learn from each other and the audience. Occasionally, the moderator or panel members may wrap up the discussion and summarize what has been said, but just as often the discussion ends without resolution or summary. Because the goal of the panel discussion is to react to the ideas of another person, it is an ideal setting for invitational communication (Chapter 15). Group members can present their current thinking on a topic, learn from each other and the audience, and refine their ideas for future decision making.

When you are part of a panel discussion, prepare your opening remarks beforehand, thinking of your speech as a short informative speech that previews what you hope to discuss during the session. Then view your participation in the discussion as a series of short speeches in which you develop a particular idea, invite others to understand your perspective, explore an issue with the other panel members, or encourage others to adopt your views. If you can, work closely with other members of your group to be sure that you are not duplicating information and that you are presenting the full spectrum of information your group has gathered.

oral reports
presentations given by one or two of the group members who present a group's findings, conclusions, or proposals to other members of the group or to a larger audience.

panel discussion
structured discussion among group members and facilitated by a moderator that takes place in front of an audience.

Symposiums

A **symposium** is a *public discussion in which several people each give speeches on different aspects of the same topic.* Unlike panel discussions, which usually feature short opening statements by the participants, symposium speakers usually have fully prepared speeches that are formally presented. At a symposium, either the speakers are experts in a particular subject area or a topic may be divided into different areas so the audience can learn about many aspects of a single topic. If you are part of a symposium, a moderator usually introduces each speaker and his or her topic and facilitates audience questions and comments if appropriate. Symposiums usually feature three to five speakers, with each person speaking for ten to fifteen minutes. Typically, a symposium session lasts anywhere from one to two hours, with the time divided between the participants and audience questions.

If you are part of a symposium, follow the procedures for giving your speech outlined in Chapters 10 to 15. You probably will find that you use a manuscript for this presentation or that your speaking outline is quite detailed. Remember to stay within your time limits so other speakers can present their speeches and to make sure there is enough time for the question-and-answer session. Typically, a moderator will time the speeches and give signals to the speakers as their time reaches the end. Be sure to practice your presentations before you give the speech and anticipate questions from the audience so you can formulate your answers. Again, work with your group before the symposium to ensure a fair and comprehensive presentation of information.

Team Presentations

A **team presentation** consists of *several individual members of a group, with each presenting a different speech on a single topic.* For instance, you might make a team presentation with other members of your group so you can present a proposal for a new program or product you have developed as a team. Each speech is formal, with speakers addressing different parts of the proposal or product and each speaker using similar delivery styles. The individual speeches in team presentations follow each other without interruption. To make sure the presentation flows smoothly, team presentations usually have one group member acting as the moderator.

If you give a team presentation, it should be well organized using one of the organizational patterns that will be discussed in Chapter 10. Ask each group member to give a speech on a single main point, with one member presenting the introduction and conclusion. This person usually is the moderator, who may introduce each speaker and his or her topic. Team presentations are common in groups that work in businesses, as well as grassroots or community organizations that want to present proposals to city councils or other government entities. Team presentations are highly collaborative projects, so make sure that your group has given itself enough time to work together to develop the presentation and then for each member to practice those presentations before you deliver them.

symposium
public discussion in which several people each give speeches on different aspects of the same topic.

team presentation
when several individual members of a group each present a different speech on a single topic.

Online Forums

Today's workplace also lends itself to online group presentations and discussions. **Forums** *occur when messages or topics are posted online and individuals have an opportunity to post their individual responses and ideas to those original messages.* Forums are an excellent way for members of a group to present their ideas to a select audience and then receive feedback and input from that audience about those ideas. Typically, online forums have a moderator who is in charge of posting the original information, organizing the categories or topics to be discussed (which become known as *threads*), and setting the time constraints for the discussion. Group members will be in charge of setting rules for the discussion, determining if and when individuals might be asked to leave the discussion, and compiling a summary of the various threads and subthreads from the forum (Bulletin Community Forum FAQ, n.d.; Cong, Wang, Lin, Song, & Sun, 2008; Internet and Environmental Education, 2010; Jansenn & Kies, 2005; "What Is an 'Internet Forum'?" n.d.).

forums
occur when messages or topics are posted online and individuals have an opportunity to post their individual responses and ideas to those original messages.

Chapter Summary

To Work Effectively in Groups, Begin by Identifying Group Goals, Determining Appropriate Group Structure, Gathering and Evaluating Information, Providing Options, and Maintaining a Civil Approach

- To work effectively, understand the stages through which groups typically go: orientation, conflict, emergence, reinforcement, and dissolution.
- Effective group work and teamwork also involve managing participation, avoiding pressures to conform, and preventing information overload.
- All groups experience conflict as their members work together. The communication styles that contribute to conflict productively and unproductively are avoidance, accommodation, competition, compromise, and workplace democracy.

The Reflective-Thinking Method Is a Method for Solving Problems and Decision Making in Groups

- This method includes identifying and analyzing the problem, suggesting and considering solutions, reaching a decision, and implementing the solution.

When You Solve Problems in Groups and Teams, Use Consensus, Voting, or Authority Rule

- To solve problems or manage discussions in groups, use closed questions, open questions, affective questions, probing questions, and leading questions.

Culture Affects the Members of a Group

- Members from individualistic cultures may work independently and look out for their needs; members from collectivistic cultures may look out for the needs of the group.
- Members from cultures that value equity are less comfortable with power hierarchies; members from cultures that accept inequities are more comfortable with hierarchy and authority.
- Members from cultures that value uncertainty and change are comfortable with flexible norms and rules and fluid processes; members from cultures that value stability will be happier with clear rules and norms for working together.
- Members from cultures that value social orientation will focus on creating a welcoming atmosphere and may take more time making a decision; members from a culture that values task orientation may make a decision quickly at the expense of group satisfaction.
- Members from cultures that value long-term orientations may take a more visionary focus; members from cultures that value short-term orientations encourage a more immediate decision and action.

Meetings Can Occur in Both Real Time and Virtual Time

- To facilitate meetings, determine the goals for the meeting, organize the meeting, manage the meeting, and provide follow-up communication.

There Are Five Common Types of Group Presentations: Oral Reports, Panel Discussions, Symposiums, Team Presentations, and Online Forums

- Oral reports are presentations given by one or two of the group members who present a group's findings, conclusions, or proposals to other members of the group or to a larger audience.
- A panel discussion is a structured discussion among group members facilitated by a moderator that takes place in front of an audience.

- A symposium is a public discussion in which several people each give speeches on different aspects of the same topic.
- A team presentation consists of several individual members of a group, with each one presenting a different speech on a single topic.
- Online forums occur when messages or topics are posted online and individuals have an opportunity to post their individual responses and ideas to those original messages.

Key Concepts

accommodation (202)

affective questions (207)

agenda (210)

authority rule (206)

avoidance (202)

brainstorming (199)

closed questions (207)

competition (202)

compromise (203)

consensus (204)

forums (215)

leading questions (208)

open questions (207)

oral reports (213)

panel discussion (213)

probing questions (207)

real time (210)

reciprocity (202)

reflective-thinking method (198)

relational stress (200)

symposium (214)

task stress (202)

team presentation (214)

virtual meetings (210)

workplace democracy (203)

Invitation to Human Communication Online

MindTap Speech includes an interactive MindTap Reader and interactive learning tools including National Geographic Explorer videos, student videos, quizzes, flash cards, and more. You can build your speech outline with Outline Builder and record, post, and watch videos with YouSeeU. Go to cengagebrain.com to access your MindTap for *Invitation to Human Communication* where these resources can be found.

MindTap®

Further Reflection and Discussion

1. Identify a group you are a member of now or have been in the past. Can you map out the stages that group went through: orientation, conflict, emergence, reinforcement, and dissolution?

2. If the group you identified in question 1 did not follow these stages or spend a good deal of time in one of the stages, was this productive or problematic for the group? How so?

3. Did this group from questions 1 and 2 manage participation and avoid pressures to conform? How so? Was this productive?

4. Consider your current workplace. How does it manage the information overload you read about in this chapter? Are these strategies effective? Why or why not?

5. Can you identify how your workplace might improve its approach to conflict? What suggestions could you make as people in your workplace work in groups with regard to conflict?

6. With a group of your classmates, identify a problem your campus faces. Work through the reflective-thinking model described in this chapter. What solutions might you come identify as a result of this process?

7. Imagine you are a member of a team. Some team members are from cultures that value working independently and looking out for their individual needs, while others are from cultures that value collaboration and looking out for the needs of the collective. How will you manage these different approaches to group work?

8. Imagine that your boss has asked you to conduct an online forum related to a project you are working on with a group of co-workers (launching a new product, for example). How will you structure this online forum to give as many individuals a possible a chance to be involved?

9. Now imagine that your boss has asked your group to give an oral report on this project and the information you gathered from the online forum in question 9. How will you organize the report? Who will speak about which aspects of the project and for how long?

10. Select one of the parts of the presentation you developed in question 9. Prepare a two-minute speech for this part of the presentation (for example, introducing the project, the results of the online forum, or future steps). Now give this presentation to your group.

Activities and Web Links

Visit cengagebrain.com to access the MindTap for *Invitation to Human Communication* where these activities and Web links can be found.

1. Read this National Coalition for Dialogue and Deliberation article on consensus, "Top Ten Most Common Mistakes in Consensus Process and How To Avoid Them." Now think of a disagreement in your family or at your workplace. How would you build consensus about the disagreement? How can you avoid the common mistakes? Be specific. Go to *Web link 9.1*.

2. Read "Eight Tips for Better Brainstorming." Which suggestions might work well for individualistic cultures? Which ones would work for collectivist cultures? Are there tips in the article that both types of cultures could learn to use to come up with effective ideas for solving a problem? Go to *Web link 9.2*.

10

IN THIS CHAPTER YOU WILL LEARN TO:

- Describe the public dialogue as an ethical and civil exchange of ideas.

- Explain what it means to be an audience-centered speaker.

- Select your speech topic.

- Distinguish between the general purpose and specific purpose of your speech.

- Develop a thesis statement and main points for your speech.

- Recognize the four parts of an introduction and the two goals of a conclusion.

Developing Your Speech Topic and Purpose

Christopher Furlong/Getty Images

More than any other time in our history, the issues facing us are global and central to the lives of each one of us. What issues do you feel concerned or even passionate about? Consider using these as a topic for your first speech.

When you speak publicly, you participate in a dialogue that can influence others. With every speech you give, you make choices about the kind of influence you will have in the dialogue. We are all familiar with the combative exchanges popular media present us, but you may also be familiar with the call for more civility in these public exchanges. Recall from Chapter 1 that the word *civility* comes from a root word meaning "to be a member of a household." Approaching public speaking as an act of civility means that we can think of the speeches we give as adding our views and voices to that household by way of a public dialogue or conversation. A **dialogue** is a *civil exchange of ideas and opinions between two people or a small group of people.* The **public dialogue** is the *ethical and civil exchange of ideas and opinions among communities about topics that affect the public.* To participate in the public dialogue is to offer perspectives, share facts, raise questions, and engage others publicly in thoughtful discussions. When we enter the public dialogue, we become active and ethical citizens who participate in our nation's democratic process and consider the needs of others in our communities as well as our own needs.

In this section of this book, you will learn about the power of public speaking and the ways it helps us enter this larger and sometimes global dialogue. As you engage with this power, strive to give speeches that help clarify issues and stimulate thinking as you inform, persuade, or invite others to consider a perspective. Although you may have strong views on issues, a civil and ethical approach to public speaking can be the most powerful way to present those views.

Why Enter the Public Dialogue?

People decide to participate in the public dialogue for three main reasons: they decide to speak, they are asked to speak, or they are required to speak.

Deciding to Speak

The most common reason to speak is because we find an issue so important or relevant that we decide to speak about it. Before the advent of television and radio, people used a variety of platforms to share their opinions and ideas. They spoke in churches and town halls, at street corners, and in town squares or centers. Today, people often view mass media as the voice of the public, forgetting we still can and do insert our own voices into public discussions. New technologies make it possible for us to share our views in a range of formats. And people still give real-time speeches so they can express their views. We give class presentations and participate in student government and student organizations debating issues and proposing solutions. In business and professional meetings, we discuss ideas, give presentations, and create new plans or programs. In

dialogue
civil exchange of ideas and opinions between two people or a small group of people.

public dialogue
ethical and civil exchange of ideas and opinions among communities about topics that affect the public.

Individuals often feel so strongly about an issue that they decide to speak out publicly. When you have listened to people speak out, what makes them effective or ineffective speakers?

community forums, we speak about issues that are important to us such as the environment, education, and social services.

Being Asked to Speak

When we are asked to speak, we are asked to share our knowledge, skills, experiences, and perspectives with others. In this setting, we are recognized as experts or as someone who has information others want. It can be exciting to think about sharing our experiences and knowledge with other people. As you move through life, you might find you are asked to speak in educational settings, at service clubs, or at formal or professional gatherings. If you are asked to speak publicly, it is because people want to hear your views and ideas. But remember that expertise in a particular subject area does not always guarantee you are an expert at giving speeches. Although you may be considered an expert on a topic or subject, you will be a more successful speaker if you follow the principles of speech preparation discussed in this book.

Being Required to Speak

Being required to speak can be a regular part of our lives. For example, you are now taking a communication course that requires you to give speeches. But outside your class, you may have a job that requires public speaking, such as in marketing or as a tour guide. Occasionally, you may have to fulfill a civic obligation such as speaking in front of a town council, at a public hearing, or even in a courtroom or for a legal investigation. National Geographic Explorer Wade Davis (2014) explains that in today's world, "being a public speaker is no longer an option, it's a necessity."

Although we may not like required public speaking, learning to give speeches in a communication course can be invaluable. If you view a classroom speaking requirement as an opportunity to prepare for other speaking contexts, then you can make the most of the time you spend in class.

Understanding how you become a public speaker is the first step in preparing a successful presentation. Once you recognize why you are speaking, you can turn your attention to who is in your audience, selecting and narrowing your speech topic and deciding on your purpose for speaking.

Your Audience

Your Audience Is a Group of Diverse People

People are unique for a variety of reasons related to combinations of culture, upbringing, experiences, personality, and even genetics (Wood, 2013). These differences are part of what causes speakers to want to be **audience centered**. An audience-centered speaker is one who *considers*

audience-centered speaker
speaker who considers the positions, beliefs, values, and needs of an audience.

How Much Public Speaking Will You Do?

According to Susan Ricker at AOL Jobs, at least sixteen different professions, or parts of that profession, make use of an employees' public speaking skills on a regular basis. Those occupations include the following:

1. fund-raisers who organize events and campaigns that raise money or awareness;
2. buyers, managers, and purchasing agents who review products, negotiate contracts, and evaluate materials;
3. training and development specialists who train others, conduct workshops, and plan programs;
4. health educators who teach people about appropriate wellness behaviors and share new information about healthy living with communities;
5. curators who manage art collections and exhibitions and engage in public service activities;
6. teachers who help prepare students for successful lives;
7. actors who work on television, in films, or at theme parks or other live events;
8. writers, producers, and directors who create entertainment and pitch ideas to others;
9. umpires, referees, and other sports officials who preside over sports events, maintain standards of conduct, and communicate those standards to others;
10. mediators who facilitate meetings, negotiations, and dialogue between individuals and parties who cannot reach decisions on their own;
11. judges who apply and communicate the law to others;
12. lawyers who advise and represent people in and out of court;
13. school principals who coordinate and manage school activities, curricula, and operations and communicate decisions and information to teachers, students, parents, school boards, and their communities;

dinozzaver/Shutterstock.com

14. announcers who share music, ideas, stories, and commentaries at public and private events;
15. journalists who communicate stories, important events, and breaking news to individuals as well as local and national communities; and
16. construction managers who coordinate and supervise projects from inception to completion.

The Bureau of Labor Statistics adds that those individuals who frequently use their public speaking skills also need to be good at listening, decision making, memorization, leadership, negotiating, and interpersonal relationships.

the positions, beliefs, values, and needs of an audience. As public speakers, how can we give a speech that considers audience members' differences as well as their similarities? To stay audience centered, review the material presented in Chapter 2 and try to consider how the members of your audience might view the world by analyzing their master statuses and their standpoints.

Master Statuses

Groups of people share common experiences, perspectives, and attitudes because they occupy certain master statuses. **Master statuses** are *significant positions a person occupies within society that affect that person's identity in almost all social situations* (Marshall, 1994). A person's master statuses might include race or ethnicity, gender, physical ability, sexual orientation, age, economic standing, religion or spirituality, and educational level. They could include positions in society such as being a

master statuses

significant positions a person occupies within society that affect that person's identity in almost all social situations.

parent, a child, or a sibling or being employed or unemployed and so on if those positions affect someone's identity in almost every social situation. Here is how one public-speaking student, Miranda, described her master statuses and how they influenced her life and speaking experiences:

> I have many master statuses. I am a daughter dedicated to her family and her family values. I am forever a student, always craving new knowledge. I am a first-generation student, boldly going where no one else in my family has gone before—college. I am a Mexican-American living life for my ancestors. Last but not least, I am curious, always searching for new adventures in life. All of this makes up who I am and affects every decision I make each day, from what clothes I choose to wear to the books I choose to read. It also affects what topics I choose to speak about and how effectively I listen to other speakers.

A status is a *master* status when it profoundly influences a person's identity and the way in which he or she is perceived by others. Whether we intend to or not, we often respond to other people based on one or more master statuses. For example, teenagers with rumpled and baggy clothes are often treated differently in a grocery store than neatly dressed adult mothers with children are. Whether or not our assumptions about these people are correct (teenagers will cause problems; mothers are responsible and will manage their children), we categorize and respond to people based on the positions they hold in society.

Master statuses affect our view of the world because we make judgments based on them, and hence, we see some as more valuable than others. For example, whether we are comfortable acknowledging such differences or not, U.S. American culture tends to rank people who are white, heterosexual, and male higher than people who are nonwhite, homosexual, and female. Because the first three statuses are considered more valuable, they are generally rewarded with higher salaries, more acceptance and protections, and more personal freedoms, whereas the last three, on average, receive lower salaries, less acceptance, fewer protections, and greater threats to physical safety (Bennett & Ellison, 2010; Browne & Williams, 1993; Buzawa, Austin, & Buzawa, 1995; Dobash, Dobash, Cavanagh, & Lewis, 1998; "Facts About Violence," 2010; Federal Bureau of Investigation, 1989, 1995; Lackie & de Man, 1997; National Coalition Against Domestic Violence, n.d.; National Organization for Women, n.d.; Timm, 2013; U.S. Bureau of Labor Statistics, 2010).

Master statuses affect our identity in most social situations. What are the master statuses of this young girl? What are your master statuses?

Standpoints, Attitudes, Beliefs, and Values The impact of different treatment because of master statuses can affect an individual's standpoint, the perspective from which a person views and evaluates society. Members of your audiences will have different standpoints. This is because they will have different master statuses and thus different experiences. For example, teenagers often see life as unfairly biased against them, and mothers often see the world as expecting them and their children to behave perfectly in all situations.

Note that although master statuses can have a powerful influence on a person's view of the world, master statuses do not *determine* a person's standpoint (see Chapter 2). For example, not all women believe they need to have children to fully experience womanhood, just as not all men believe their masculinity is weakened if they are not the primary breadwinners for their families. In addition, we all occupy numerous master statuses throughout our lives, and each one influences us in a different way. For example, although we maintain our ethnicity throughout our lives, if we move to a new country, adapt to a new culture, and learn a different language, our experience of our ethnic identity can evolve. Moreover, we all move from young to old and experience changing family and job roles, shifting from child to parent, unemployed to employed, and so on.

Our standpoints influence our attitudes, beliefs, and values. An **attitude** is *a general positive or negative feeling a person has about something*. Attitudes reflect our likes and dislikes and our approval or disapproval of events, people, or ideas (Eagly & Chaiken, 1998; Olson & Zanna, 1993). A **belief** is *a person's idea of what is real or true or not*. Beliefs are more conceptual than attitudes and reflect what we think we know about the world. A **value** is *a person's idea of what is good, worthy, or important*. Our values reflect what we think is an ideal world or state of being. Values help us determine whether we think a person, idea, or thing is acceptable in our worldview (Kidder, 1994; Rokeach, 1970, 1973; Schwartz & Blisky, 1990).

Conversations, debates, and arguments held as part of the public dialogue are heavily influenced by the different attitudes, beliefs, and values that result from our different standpoints and master statuses. In particular, attitudes, beliefs, and values are often influenced by our cultural backgrounds. All cultures have unique ways of explaining and organizing the world. Audience-centered speakers recognize these different worldviews and guard against ethnocentrism. Recall from Chapter 1 that **ethnocentrism** is the *belief that our own cultural perspectives, norms, and ways of organizing society are superior to others*. Speakers who let ethnocentric views come through in their speeches run the risk of alienating audience members who do not hold similar views.

To be audience centered, speakers must consider the significant influence of master statuses, standpoints, attitudes, beliefs, and values on audiences. When speakers take these factors into consideration, they increase their chances of giving effective speeches.

Choosing Your Speech Topic

Your **speech topic** is the *subject of your speech*. Selecting a topic for a speech can be a highly creative and energizing part of putting a speech together. The steps described in this section will help you find interesting and relevant speech topics for your required speeches, articulate your purpose, and narrow your topic.

attitude
general positive or negative feeling a person has about something.

belief
a person's idea of what is real or true or not.

value
a person's idea of what is good, worthy, or important.

ethnocentrism
belief that our own cultural perspectives, norms, and ways of organizing society are superior to others.

speech topic
subject of your speech.

NATIONAL GEOGRAPHIC EXPLORER TIP ↗

Courtesy of Chris Rainier

T. H. Culhane,
Explorer and Urban Planner

What beliefs or values are important to consider about your audience before you speak to them?

Well, I try to find out the expectations of the target audience. And some are really tough, so I do get very nervous. And I've had some failures. We were flown in after a very successful Cairo speech and asked to give one to some people in Abu Dhabi. The slides that I showed and the music that I played and experiences I related—they didn't resonate with the audience at all. And I could feel a misunderstanding and tension in the room, and it turned out it was because seeing slums and poverty, even though my messages are always hopeful and always about where we are going and how we are climbing up together, they didn't resonate. These very wealthy people, who were philanthropists, they didn't feel very motivated seeing what the other 90 percent go through and how they live. Many people actually felt threatened. So, I always try to get the message out that we human beings are part of something my dad introduced me to—part of the Great Conversation. We have been sharing stories for centuries that have helped us to progress, and because of that great conversation, I always say no human beings should be excluded from it. But that doesn't always work. I thought the idea that you can turn your waste into energy and fertilizer, and produce your own electricity from the available sunlight—doing it yourself—I thought it would have universal appeal, but it doesn't always.

The Classroom Setting

Before you can select an appropriate and interesting topic for your assigned speech, you must consider the requirements of your assignment:

- *Preselected purpose.* An instructor usually tells you to give a particular type of speech such as a speech that informs, invites, or persuades. You do not have the freedom to select your speech purpose, and you must select a topic that is compatible with the purpose.

- *Highly structured assignment.* You are usually asked to incorporate several specific speech components such as a specific number of outside sources, visual aids, or a specific style of language. You usually have strict time limits, so the structure of an assigned speech often influences topic selection.

- *Your audience.* You give your classroom speeches to an instructor, who is already a skilled public speaker, and your classmates. You must select a stimulating topic that both will appreciate and that is not commonly used.

So how do you select a manageable, interesting, and dynamic topic for your required speeches? The process takes a bit of planning and effort, but you will discover that you have a wealth of usable ideas once you organize your thoughts about who you are, what you know, and what issues and events capture your own attention.

Outline the Requirements for the Assignment The first step to selecting a topic is to outline the requirements of the speech assignment. Your assignment might look like this:

> Informative purpose; four minutes long; three to four sources; one statistic; one of the following: metaphor, analogy, narrative, or alliteration; inclusive language.

The second step is to match your interests or expertise to these requirements.

Matching Your Interests to the Speaking Assignment Before you can match your interests to a particular assignment, you must determine what they are. Divide your interests into the following categories: what you like to do, what you like to talk about, and what you would like to know more about.

Most people can identify many activities they like to participate in. Make a list of them, including those that seem serious as well as playful or silly. Try to be as detailed as possible. Krista, a twenty-three-year-old college senior, likes to do the following:

swim, run, cycle	spend time with friends
play soccer, volleyball, tennis, and Frisbee golf	coach children in sports during the summer
snowboard, skateboard, and hike	get good grades
watch television and movies	stay up late
Facebook	eat pizza, hamburgers, anything barbecued, and some vegetables

With a little adjustment and creativity, any of these interests could be turned into an interesting and engaging topic. Krista could inform her audience about any of the following:

the top ten medal-earning swimmers in the world

the history of marathon running

how to play Frisbee golf

who invented skateboards

the longest-running television sitcom

the first chat room on the Web

gender differences in friendship styles

the relationship between grades and annual income

medical research on optimal sleeping patterns

the origins of pizza

These are just a few of the many informative topics Krista could speak about, all relevant to her instructor, her classmates, and the public dialogue.

Issues, events, people, and ideas you are curious about also often make excellent speech topics. You could give a speech that informs others of a particular event, or you could persuade them to participate in that event.

Protecting Human Rights

J Tanner/Handout/Getty Images

daily global events I was not hearing about in the news. So I wanted to understand." Her belief in what the United Nations has always stood for—equality and the protection of human rights for all people—has resulted in her commitment to use her status as an A-list celebrity to learn as much as she can and speak out about the refugee crisis. For example, "When I read about the 20 million people under the care of UNHCR, I wanted to understand how in this day and age that many people could be displaced."

Jolie's focus is on the humanity and heroism of those who have been forced to leave their homes and live in overcrowded and dangerous refugee camps. "What was really shocking was that every individual person you meet will tell you that their immediate family was [affected]. Somebody's child was killed, somebody's husband. Someone was beaten. . . . You go to these places and you realize what life's really about and what people are really going through. . . . These people are my heroes" (Braun, 2009; UNHCR, n.d.).

A Google search for award-winning actor Angelina Jolie will show millions of hits, many of them highlighting her children, her relationships, her sexy image, her recent surgery, and her movies. However, many people beyond Hollywood know her primarily for her humanitarian work. Through her efforts as a goodwill ambassador for the United Nations High Commissioner for Refugees (UNHRC), she has help the United Nations provide relief to more than 20 million refugees displaced by violence, war, and poverty around the world. She not only engages directly with the men, women, and children who are affected but also assists in building shelters for refugees, visits U.S. detention centers so she can more effectively advocate for the reunion of families separated while escaping their home countries, and has released many journals that document her travels.

Jolie became interested in the plight of refugees after visiting Cambodia to film *Lara Croft: Tomb Raider.* "I started to travel and realized there was so much I was unaware of," she explains. "There were many things I hadn't been taught in school and

What Do You Think?

1. Are there issues you want to learn more about like Jolie did? What are those issues? Could you use them as possible speech topics?

2. Google "human rights" or "human rights violations." Make a list of the most serious violations listed. As a class, discuss how you would, ethically and civilly, develop a speech on one or more of these violations. Do you think you could give a speech on one of these? Why or why not?

3. Jolie is a powerful example of one person who uses her voice and takes action to make a difference in the lives of others. Can you think of other people who are using their time and energy to learn about issues and then speaking out about them ethically and with civility? Do you think celebrities and others who are in the public spotlight should engage in human rights work? Why or why not?

MindTap®

Go to cengagebrain.com to access the MindTap for *Invitation to Human Communication* to view a video about UNHRC.

If you are intrigued by a famous person, you could give a commemorative or informative speech about that person's life and accomplishments. If you are curious about a place, an idea, an object, or an animal, you could explore it with others in an informative or invitational speech. If you participate in an activity or have always wanted to do so, you could give a persuasive, informative, or invitational speech about it. Speeches that grow out of a speaker's curiosity often capture the attention, interest, and curiosity of an audience as well.

Matching Your Expertise to a Speech Assignment Whether we realize it or not, almost everyone is an expert in some area of life. Some people are experts in obvious ways, such as playing a musical instrument, painting, or computer programming. Others are experts in less obvious ways. They may have an unfailing sense of direction, know the right gift to buy for any occasion, or tell jokes that make people laugh. Dynamic speech topics can come from your own skills and talents. Consider the following examples:

- Tomás is an excellent cook. He decides to give an informative speech on the differences between traditional Bolivian and Spanish foods.

- April is fluent in American Sign Language. She decides to give a speech persuading her audience to learn a second language.

- Gardner is a mechanic. He decides to give a commemorative speech on nineteenth-century French inventor Gustave Trouvé, the creator of the first automobile powered by electricity.

These are interesting speech topics about activities or skills that may seem mundane to the person who has them. You can identify areas in which you may be considered an expert by asking yourself the questions in Practicing Human Communication. Your answers may reveal expertise that you have not thought much about.

Brainstorm Possible Topics Brainstorming is *the process of generating ideas randomly and uncritically, without attention to logic, connections, or relevance.* This process requires you to free associate rather than plan, and it is often used as a problem-solving strategy in business settings. Brainstorming can be an effective tool for coming up with speech topics in

istockphoto.com/Eva Katalin Kondoros

What are your areas of expertise? What topics could you teach your audience?

PRACTICING HUMAN COMMUNICATION
How Am I an Expert?

Answer the following questions to help identify areas in which you may be considered an expert.

- Does something come naturally to me?

- Does something run in my family?

- Do I often get compliments when I do a particular thing?

- Do others repeatedly ask me to take the lead, take care of some situation, or solve a problem for them?

- Have I ever had special training or lessons?

- Have I spent years studying, practicing, or doing something?

- Do I have degrees, certifications, licenses, or other markers of my accomplishments?

If you answered yes to any of these questions, you may be an expert in some area that would make an interesting topic for a required speech. A few final tips: As you translate your experiences into speech topics, be certain you can talk about them easily without getting upset or revealing more than you are comfortable with. And note that although you might know a lot about a topic, you should still research it to discover interesting aspects about which you might be unaware.

brainstorming
process of generating ideas randomly and uncritically without attention to logic, connections, or relevance.

required speaking situations, and you can use this technique by yourself, in pairs, or in groups. Here are some tips for successful brainstorming:

- Let your thoughts go where they will. Do not censor yourself or others. Allow all ideas, even those that seem trivial or odd.

- Write down your ideas quickly. Do not worry about spelling or punctuation, and abbreviate whenever you can.

- Keep your list handy over the course of several days, and add to it as new thoughts come to you.

You can approach brainstorming in several ways: by free association, by clustering, by categories, and by technology.

When you brainstorm using free association, you use a pencil and paper or your computer with a blank screen, and record all ideas that come to your mind (Rosa & Escholz, 1996). After only a minute, a typical free-association list might look like this:

hands, keyboard, letters, movement, running, wind, kites, children, play, laughter, skinned knees, Band-Aids, nurses, hospitals, sterile, feral cats, tiger, cougars, wilderness, encroachment, farming, ranching, cows, cowboys, rodeos, circus, clowns, entertainment, containment, buckets, garage, car, war, peace, hostility, conflict, harm, warm, cold, snow skiing, skis, lifts, chairs, dining rooms, meals, holidays, families, celebration, gifts

When you are trying to come up with a speech topic, try to spend at least several minutes brainstorming by free association to generate as many ideas as possible. Once you have compiled your list, explore it to determine if one of your ideas might be an appropriate speech topic. The free association list here could generate the following interesting speech topics:

- the inventor of the Band-Aid

- what to do when you encounter a feral cat

- different kinds of clowns

- how different countries celebrate holidays or the start of new seasons

You can also brainstorm by clustering. Using this method, you write down an idea in the center of a piece of paper and then draw four or five lines extending from it. At the ends of these lines, write down other ideas that relate to your first idea. Then extend lines from these new ideas to even more ideas.

Take a look at Jeret's clustering diagram. He began scuba diving at a young age, so he used this as his general idea and developed the cluster of ideas shown in Figure 10.1.

The figure shows that from his general idea of scuba diving, Jeret was able to branch out to many additional ideas. Brainstorming by clustering is a good way to generate speech topics because it gives structure to the brainstorming process without limiting your possibilities too much.

You can also brainstorm by listing items in various categories. Most speeches given in public-speaking classrooms are about concepts, events, natural phenomena, objects, people, places, plans and policies, problems,

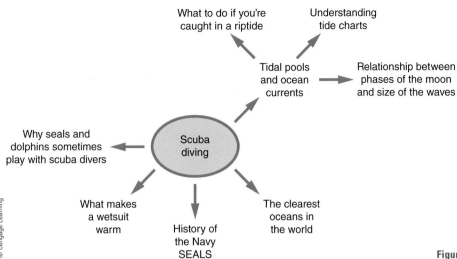

Figure 10.1 *Cluster diagram*

and processes. As you have probably noticed, these topics represent different categories. Brainstorming by generating ideas in these categories is an excellent way to select a speech topic, and it provides more structure than free association or clustering. To brainstorm using categories, list the following nine categories on your computer screen or a piece of paper and then list five or six different words under each heading. Two students working together came up with the list shown in Table 10.1.

TABLE 10.1 BRAINSTORMING BY CATEGORY

Concepts	Events	Natural Phenomena
Socialism	Haitian earthquake-relief efforts	Tornadoes
Tourism	Political elections	Eclipses
Sustainability	Walk for the Cure	Monsoons
Astrophysics	Mardi Gras	Geysers
Dieting	Inti Raymi	Mudslides
Relationships	Oktoberfest	Glaciers
Objects	**People**	**Places**
Cell phones	Barack Obama	My hometown
Guitars	Sarah Palin	Machu Picchu
Soda fountains	Tiger Woods	Germany
Books	Ellen Degeneres	China
Teapots	Kanye West	Tanzania
Mountains	Apollo Ohno	Stonehenge
Plans and Policies	**Problems**	**Processes**
Immigration reform	Terrorism	Brewing beer
Stimulus plan	Sexism	Building a house
No Child Left Behind	Racism	Preparing a meal
Sex education	Cancer	Debating, dialoguing
Censorship laws	Obesity	Making jewelry

If none of the words you write down immediately strikes you as a good speech topic, then select one or two and use free association or clustering to narrow your scope, generate new ideas, or frame the topic in a way that is interesting and fits the requirements of your assignment.

Similarly, if none of your brainstormed topics catches your interest, link several together. Can you find a connection among Mexico, India, and political elections? What about these locations and tsunamis or earthquakes? How about laptops, espresso machines, and theme dining? Linking any of these topics, randomly or with purpose, gives you additional opportunities to develop interesting speech topics.

Finally, you can brainstorm by using technology. If you have access to the Internet, you can discover possible topics by browsing a search engine's subject indexes. Using technology, you can explore an array of topics, click a general subject, and link to more and more specific Web sites until you find a topic that interests you and fits the requirements of your speech assignment.

Libraries also provide many online indexes for journals, newspapers, magazines, and the like. Browse through the *Reader's Guide to Periodical Literature,* InfoTrac College Edition, *The New York Times Index,* or subject-specific indexes about medicine, physics, science, or women's studies.

Stating Your Speaking Goals

Articulating Your Purpose

Once you have selected your speech topic, you will want to consider your *speaking goals,* which can be explained in terms of general purposes and specific purposes. The **general purpose** of a speech *is its broad goal: to inform, invite, or persuade.* The **specific purpose** is *a focused statement that identifies exactly what a speaker wants to accomplish with a speech.* Take a look at how you use each of these purposes to organize your thoughts about your speeches.

General Speaking Purposes Suppose you have decided to speak about organic farming. You could speak about many aspects of this topic. Without knowing your purpose for your speech, it can be difficult to know where to begin. Do you describe organic farming, what it is, and who practices it (informative)? Do you invite your audience to explore the impact of organic farming on the environment and the average family's grocery bills (invitational)? Do you attempt to convince your classmates that organic farming is the most efficient type of farming (persuasive)? Your first step toward answering these questions is to determine the overall goal for your speech or your general purpose:

> *to inform*—describe, clarify, explain, define;
>
> *to invite*—explore, discuss, exchange, understand; or
>
> *to persuade*—change, shape, influence, motivate.

Notice that each overall goal is quite different from the others. For example, the goal of describing is different from exploring, which is different from

general purpose
The broad goal of a speech—to inform, invite, or persuade.

specific purpose
focused statement that identifies exactly what a speaker wants to accomplish with a speech.

influencing. So by determining your general purpose, you begin to find a focus for your speech.

Specific Speaking Purposes Specific speaking purposes help you narrow the focus of your speech. A specific purpose states exactly what you want to accomplish in your speech. To understand the importance of specific purpose, consider Ashley's speaking situation.

Ashley tutored fourth graders in an after-school math homework program. This experience prompted her interest in several topics related to the public school system in her state, including possible gender bias in math education and the Pledge of Allegiance. She decided that she wanted to talk about the pledge and that her general speaking purpose was to persuade. But what did she want to persuade them to do or think? If she had not figured this out, she would have found herself going in circles as she prepared her speech. She would have researched supporting material she did not need, and she would have gotten frustrated as she lost sight of what she wanted to accomplish with her speech.

Ashley needed to develop a specific-purpose statement. How did she do this? First, she identified her **behavioral objectives**, *the actions she wanted her audience to take at the end of her speech*. After some thought, she decided she wanted her classmates to change their view of the pledge. She wrote on a piece of paper, "I want my classmates to believe a certain way about the Pledge of Allegiance." This speech purpose was still fairly broad, but it was more focused than her general purpose of persuading her classmates to change.

Ashley's next step was to narrow the focus of her behavioral objective even further. She defined what she meant by "believe a certain way." Based on her experiences in the public school and her research, she gained increased understanding of what the pledge means and why she thought it should be recited with the phrase "under God" by children in school. After some thought, Ashley realized that more specifically than wanting her classmates to believe a certain way, she wanted them to adopt her views about the pledge.

So even though Ashley generally wanted to persuade her audience to believe something, she specifically wanted to persuade them to support the pledge. Thus, her specific-purpose statement was "I want to persuade my audience that the pledge, with the phrase 'under God,' should be recited in schools." At this point, she had a focused idea of what she wanted to communicate to her audience. She then found it much easier to prepare a speech with a specific purpose than if she had stopped at her general purpose of wanting her audience to change.

Table 10.2 shows more examples of general and specific purposes. Notice the differences between the general and specific purposes. From the three general purposes, you could generate specific purposes for at least twelve distinctive speeches.

When you state your specific speaking purpose, state it clearly and remain audience centered. Consider the following tips.

Objects such as this automobile often make interesting subjects for a speech. Brainstorm as many different ways as you can to give a speech related to this image of a car.

Rob Wilson/Shutterstock.com

behavioral objectives
actions speaker wants audience to take at the end of a speech.

TABLE 10.2 GENERAL AND SPECIFIC SPEAKING PURPOSES

General Purpose	Specific Purpose
To inform	To inform my audience of the services offered by our campus counseling center.
	To inform my audience of the process of planting, harvesting, and preparing organic produce.
To invite	To invite my audience to explore the benefits of individual and group counseling.
	To invite my audience to explore the implications of turning part of our community park into organic gardening space.
To persuade	To persuade my audience to use the services offered by our campus counseling center.
	To persuade my audience to buy organic produce.

© Cengage Learning

State your specific speaking purpose clearly. Begin your specific-purpose statements with the infinitive phrases *to inform, to invite, or to persuade.* These phrases clearly indicate what your general purpose is and what you hope to accomplish with your speech. Compare the following correct and incorrect statements of purpose.

Correct	Incorrect
To inform my audience of the history of martial arts in the United States.	I'm going to talk about martial arts.
To invite my co-workers to explore ways we could support local community organic gardens.	Supporting community gardening.
To persuade my audience to participate in Walk for the Cure.	Walk for the Cure is a good event.

Notice that the incorrect statements are unfocused and do not indicate the overall goal of the speech. Although it may seem that the incorrect statements leave greater room for a speaker's creativity, they are too vague to be helpful when you prepare your speech.

Keep your audience in the forefront of your mind. Remember, you are speaking to and for a particular audience, and you research and organize your speech with this in mind. Your specific purpose should clearly reflect the presence of your audience. To this end, be sure your specific-purpose statement includes the words *my audience* or a more specific synonym.

Notice how the correct examples encourage you to reflect on the makeup of your audience in ways that the incorrect examples do not.

The phrases "my audience" and "my co-workers" encourage the speaker to focus not on some unspecified entity but on a specific group of people with particular traits and characteristics.

As you begin to organize your materials about your speech, write your general and specific statements of purpose at the top of all your research notes. Like any good road map, clear statements of purpose will help you select and navigate the path toward putting the final touches on your presentation.

Stating Your Thesis

So far in this chapter, you have explored how context affects your speaking goals, how to stay audience centered, how to select a speech topic, and what your general and specific purposes are. Now you are

NATIONAL GEOGRAPHIC SPEAKS

Syliva Earle, National Geographic Explorer and Oceanographer: Ocean Hero

Sylvia Earle, an oceanographer for more than fifty years, has written more than 175 publications, lectured in more than seventy countries, and led more than sixty diving expeditions worldwide. She is affectionately known as "Her Deepness" because she holds several world records for depth of diving. Earle has a profound commitment to civic engagement and communicating her insights and passions in as many ways as she can.

An explorer for National Geographic, Earle received the coveted TED Prize (TED stands for Technology, Entertainment, and Design) in 2009 for her proposal to establish Mission Blue, a global network of marine protected areas she dubbed "hope spots." Recipients of the TED Prize are known for their effective communication, commitment to civic engagement, and passion for the work they do. The prize includes $100,000, and the recipient is granted a "wish to change the world." Earle explained her wish as nothing short of saving our oceans. In her book *The World Is Blue: How Our Fate and the Ocean's Are One, she explains,* "My wish is a big wish, but if we can make it happen, it truly can change the world and help ensure the survival of what is actually my favorite species, human beings." She explains,

> Fifty years ago, when I began exploring the ocean, no one—not Jacques Perrin, not Jacques Cousteau, or Rachel Carson—imagined that we could do anything to harm the ocean by what we put into it or by what we took out of it. It seemed, at that time, to be a sea of Eden, but now we know, and now we are facing paradise lost. In fifty years, we've lost—actually, we've taken, we've eaten—more than 90 percent of the big fish in the sea; nearly half of the coral reefs have disappeared; and there has been a mysterious depletion of oxygen in large areas of the Pacific. It really should concern you. It does concern you.

When asked, "if you could have people do one thing to help the ocean, what would it be?" Earle replied,

> Hold up a mirror and ask yourself what you are capable of doing, and what you really care about. Then take the initiative—don't wait for someone else to ask you to act. . . . Everyone has power. But it doesn't help if you don't use it. Knowing is the key. Become informed! With knowing comes caring, and with caring there is hope that we will find an enduring place for ourselves within the natural—mostly blue—systems that sustain us.

Earle believes that becoming informed is the most important contribution to saving the ocean. And she has made it her mission to help inform people around from around the world (Earle, 2009a, 2009b, 2009c; National Geographic.com, n.d.; National Geographic.com, 2009).

Log on to http://www.ted.com/talks to watch Earl's TED Talks speech. As you listen, consider her speaking goals, how audience centered she is, and her introduction and conclusion.

WHAT DO YOU THINK?

1. Sylvia Earle was *asked to speak* at the TED2009 conference. What experiences or expertise does Earle possess that make her a good candidate to speak on changing the world? What are Earle's master statuses?

2. What are Earle's attitudes, beliefs, and values that influence her understanding of the ocean? Are they similar to yours or different? In what ways?

3. Based on the information presented in Earle's speech introduction, what would her specific purpose and thesis statement be?

Wangari Maathai, "I Had No Idea That Anyone Was Listening"

Wangari Maathai (1940–2011), the daughter of a sharecropper father and a farmer mother, was often considered something of a first lady. She is the first woman from East and Central Africa to earn a Ph.D. (in biological sciences); the first woman to become a department chair of the University of Nairobi; the first president of the African Union's Economic, Social, and Cultural Council; and the first African woman to earn a Nobel Peace Prize.

Maathai (2003) began her impressive career as an environmental and political activist in the 1970s. As part of her work with the National Council of Women of Kenya, Maathai established the Green Belt Movement in response to her conversations with rural women about their concerns over water, energy, and nutrition. Seeing the connections between the clear-cutting of forests and the diminished quality of life for many in Kenya, she began to lead high-profile campaigns to save Kenya's forests and protect its green spaces. Working with thousands of other women, she planted trees to replenish the soil, protect the watersheds, provide fuel, and enhance nutrition. "If you understand and you are disturbed,"

she said, "then you are moved to action. That's exactly what happened to me."

The government responded to the movement by harassing Maathai and many other women, holding them in jail and sending them death threats. At one point, Maathai was labeled a "madwoman" and beaten almost to death. However, these setbacks did not stop her. By the late 1990s, the government had abandoned its illegal deforestation and development plans and, to date, more than 30 million trees have been planted throughout Kenya. However, when Maathai received the Nobel Peace Prize in 2004 for her work with the Green Belt Movement, she was surprised. She said, "I had no idea that anyone was listening."

As the Green Belt Movement's official Web site states, the movement has evolved into "one of the most prominent women's civil society organizations, . . . advocating for human rights and supporting good governance and peaceful democratic change through the protection of the environment." Maathai explains this evolution by saying, "When you start working with the environment seriously, the whole arena comes:

human rights, women's rights, environmental rights, children's rights—you know, everybody's rights. Once you start making these linkages, you can no longer do just tree-planting."

What Do You Think?

1. Why do you think Maathai and other women were harassed for being involved in the Green Belt Movement? Are there examples of individuals being harassed for engaging in activism here in the United States? Why do you think this harassment occurs?
2. If you were to give a speech on the Green Belt Movement, and the work its members have done since Maathai's death, what would your specific purpose statement and thesis be?
3. What ethical issues would you want to raise for your audience if you were to give a speech on Maathai and the Green Belt Movement? How might you incorporate them into your speech?

ready to take the final step to complete this initial part of the speech preparation process. Every successful speech has a *thesis statement*, sometimes called a *central idea*. A **thesis statement** summarizes *in a single declarative sentence the main ideas, assumptions, or arguments you want to express in your speech*. It adds focus to your specific purpose because you state the exact content of your speech in a single sentence.

Note that the thesis statement is closely related to the specific purpose. Recall that the specific-purpose statement indicates what you want your audience to understand or do as a result of your speech. The thesis statement helps you identify the main ideas of your speech; these will become the main points for your speech.

Look again at some specific-purpose statements to see how they relate to thesis statements.

Specific purpose: To inform my audience of the different belts in the martial arts

With this statement, Oscar claims it is useful to understand the different belt levels in the martial arts. To focus his speech on a manageable aspect of this topic, he must determine exactly what he wants the audience to know about the systems of colored belts used in martial arts. He

thesis statement
single declarative sentence that summarizes the main ideas, assumptions, or arguments you want to express in your speech.

TABLE 10.3 GENERAL AND SPECIFIC PURPOSE AND THESIS STATEMENT

Informative Speech

General purpose	To inform.
Specific purpose	To inform my audience about where to seek shelter during a tornado.
Thesis statement	When a tornado strikes, seek shelter in a storm cellar, a fortified storm closet, or your bathtub.

Invitational Speech

General purpose	To invite.
Specific purpose	To invite my audience to explore the pros and cons of retaining the death penalty in the United States.
Thesis statement	I'd like to describe the benefits and drawbacks of retaining the death penalty in the United States and then explore with my audience whether this punishment is still appropriate for serious crimes.

Persuasive Speech

General purpose	To persuade.
Specific purpose	To persuade my audience to learn a second language.
Thesis statement	When we learn a second language, not only do we learn to appreciate the culture of the people who speak that language, but we also increase our understanding of our own culture.

© Cengage Learning

considers what he is asked most often about this topic. His thesis statement thus looks like this:

> *Thesis statement:* In the three most common schools of martial arts in the United States—judo, karate, and tae kwon do—the black belt is the most esteemed belt level among the slightly differing belt systems.

With his thesis statement, Oscar considers how much common knowledge there is about the martial arts as well as what people are most curious about. In addition, his thesis statement summarizes and previews two main points:

1. Judo, karate, and tae kwon do are the most common schools of martial arts in the United States.

2. Each school has a slightly different belt system, but the black belt is the most esteemed belt level in all the schools.

Table 10.3 shows the three different speech types as they evolve from the general purpose to the specific purpose and then into a thesis statement.

 ## Organizing Your Speech

You now are ready to begin organizing a speech. Start this process by identifying your **main points**, which are *the most important and comprehensive ideas you address in your speech.* They give your speech focus and help you decide what information to include and leave out.

main points
most important and comprehensive ideas you address in your speech.

Identify Your Main Points
If you have already written your thesis statement, then you should be able to find your main points within it. Notice in the following example about

PRACTICING HUMAN COMMUNICATION
Generating Purpose Statements

Look over the list of topics you generated in the previous Practicing Human Communication boxes. Select one or two topics and write a specific purpose and thesis statement for each. Consider which topics work best for informative, invitational, or persuasive speeches.

folding a flag that Cindy's thesis statement defines her main points: (1) the symbolism in the U.S. flag, (2) how a flag should be hung, (3) how it should be handled, and (4) how it should be folded. Without a thesis statement, a speaker's ideas are simply a random collection of points.

Specific purpose: To inform my audience about the rules and regulations for handling the U.S. flag.

Thesis statement: The flag, a symbol of much that is great about this nation, should be hung, handled, and folded in a specific manner.

Main points:
   I. Each part of the flag has a specific meaning or purpose dedicated to symbolizing patriotic ideas.
   II. Because of the symbolism of each of these parts, the flag should be hung in a specific manner.
   III. Flag etiquette, more than just stories told from generation to generation, tells us how to handle a flag properly.
   IV. Flags also should be folded in a specific way, with each fold representing important qualities of our country.

There are three keys to developing your main points. First, keep each main point separate and distinct—do not combine points. Second, word your points consistently. Finally, devote appropriate coverage to each main point. We will take a look at each key.

Tips for Preparing Main Points

Keep Each Main Point Separate and Distinct. Each main point should be a separate idea. Once you have identified your likely main points, double-check them to be sure you have not combined two ideas into one main point. We may be tempted to combine two ideas to cover as much information as we can. But notice what happened when Aaron combined two ideas into a single point.

Ineffective Main Points	More Effective Main Points
I. Electronic music is produced from a variety of machines that make noise electronically.	I. Electronic music is produced from a variety of machines that make noise electronically.
II. Electronic music has become more popular in recent years and is performed by many well-known artists.	II. Electronic music has become more popular in recent years.
	III. Electronic music is performed by many well-known artists.

Although both columns cover the same ground, the points in the right column are clearer because each addresses only one idea. By separating the two points, Aaron can avoid confusing or overwhelming his audience.

Word Your Main Points Consistently. Try to word your main points as consistently as possible. A parallel structure is easier to organize and remember. In the next example, Michael presented an informative speech on the reasons for stop signs. Notice how the parallel main points in the right column are clearer and more memorable than those in the left column.

Ineffective Main Points	More Effective Main Points
I. Drivers need to know who has the right of way, and a stop sign tells us that.	I. Stop signs assign the right of way to vehicles using an intersection.
II. Stop signs slow down drivers who are traveling at unsafe speeds.	II. Stop signs reduce the problem of speeding in certain areas.
III. Sometimes pedestrians need protection from vehicles, and stop signs give them that protection.	III. Stop signs protect pedestrians in busy intersections or near schools.

With a simple reworking of phrasing, Michael made his main points parallel: stop signs assign, stop signs reduce, stop signs protect. Although this kind of parallel structure is not always possible, your ideas will be clearer and more memorable when you can use it.

Devote the Appropriate Coverage to Each Main Point. Remember that your main points are your most important ideas. Therefore, each point should receive the same level of development and attention in your speech. On one hand, if you find yourself spending little time developing a particular point, then ask yourself whether it really is as important as you thought and whether it should be a main point in your speech. On the other hand, you find yourself putting a lot of development into one point, then consider whether you should divide it into two points. In preparing a speech on the art of batik, Martha discovered the following imbalance.

Specific purpose: To inform my audience about batik, a beautiful and diverse art form that has been practiced for centuries.

Thesis statement: The art of batik has an intriguing history as well as methods of production and designs that reflect the skill and politics of the artisan.

Main points:
    I. The history of batik (65 percent of the speech)
    II. The production of batik (15 percent of the speech)
    III. The designs of batik (15 percent of the speech)
    IV. Where to purchase batik (5 percent of the speech)

Martha realized she had spent so much time on her first point that she did not have time to cover her remaining points. Although the history of batik is important, it was not the only information she wanted to share with her audience. She also wanted to show them the production process and some of the designs she loved. After some consideration, Martha reduced the scope of her speech by dropping her fourth point (which was not really a part of her thesis statement), and she condensed

Batik is a complex process that results in beautiful designs and patterns. Can you think of other processes that are complex but still would make an interesting speech?

the details of her first point. She reworked her speech as follows, saving 20 percent of her time for her introduction and conclusion:

Specific purpose: To inform my audience about batik, a beautiful and diverse art form that has been practiced for centuries.

Thesis statement: The art of batik has an intriguing history as well as methods of production and designs that reflect the skill and politics of the artisan.

Main points: I. The history of batik (30 percent)
II. The production of batik (25 percent)
III. The designs of batik (25 percent)

Your goal, as Martha's revised main points suggest, is not necessarily to spend exactly the same amount of time on each point but to offer a balanced presentation of your ideas.

Connectives

Your main points are the heart of your speech. Once you have them on paper and supported with your research, you must find ways to connect them to enhance the audience's understanding. The *words and phrases we use to link ideas in a speech* are called **connectives**. They show audiences the relationship between ideas.

Before you read the descriptions of the four types of connectives, consider some of the connectives that speakers use unconsciously: "all right," "next," "now," "um," "and," "so," "so then," and "ah." These words are often called *fillers* because they are words or sounds that tell the audience almost nothing about the relationship between ideas. Fillers can be annoying, especially when the same one is repeated often in a speech.

connectives
words and phrases used to link ideas in a speech.

The following section offers four useful alternatives to these fillers: transitions, internal previews, internal summaries, and signposts. These will add meaning and help your audience remember your ideas.

Transitions

Transitions are *phrases that indicate you are finished with one idea and are moving to a new one.* Effective transitions restate the idea you are finishing and introduce your next one. In the following examples, the transitions are underlined:

> Now that you understand how our childhood memories influence our relationship to money, let's explore the relationship we have to money as adults.

> Once you've visited Manarola, you're ready to move to the final village, Riomaggiore, also known as "the village of love."

You can consciously insert transitions such as "let's turn to," "now that you understand," "in addition to," and "that brings me to my next point." But many will come naturally as you close one point or idea and begin a new one. Use transitions to link ideas within your main points and to guide your audience from point to point as you deliver your speech.

Internal Previews

An **internal preview** is *a statement in the body of your speech that details what you plan to discuss next.* Internal previews are used to introduce a new point in your speech. Internal previews focus on what comes next in the speech rather than linking two points as transitions do. In the next example, Martha introduces her second point, batik production, with an internal preview:

> In discussing the production of batik, I'll explain the four steps: the preparation of the cloth, the mixing of the dyes, the application of the dye, and the setting of the image in the cloth.

After hearing this preview, the audience is ready for four steps and begins to appreciate the intricacies of the batik process. Internal previews are often combined with transitions, as in Robert's discussion of theatrical lighting:

> As you can see, (*transition*) with the invention of the lightbulb came exciting and safer possibilities for theatrical lighting. And the now familiar lightbulb takes me to my third point, (*internal preview*) the invention of three instruments that revolutionized lighting in the theater: the ellipsoidal, the fresnel, and the intelabeam.

Not every main point requires an internal preview, but the unfamiliar terminology in Robert's third point lends itself to a preview. Introducing new concepts or terminology before offering the details enhances your audience's understanding of your topic.

Internal Summaries

An **internal summary** is *a statement in the body of your speech that summarizes a point you have already discussed.* If you have just finished an important or complicated point, add an internal summary to remind

transitions
phrases that indicate you are finished with one idea and are moving to a new one.

internal preview
statement in the body of your speech that details what you plan to discuss next.

internal summary
statement in the body of your speech that summarizes a point you have already discussed.

your audience of its highlights. In Jeremy's speech on sibling rivalry, he used an internal summary at the end of the first point:

> To summarize, the causes of sibling rivalry—birth order, sex, parental attitudes, and individual personality traits—can cause children to compete for their parents' affection and attention.

Like internal previews, internal summaries can be combined with transitions so you can move efficiently into your next point. Here is an example from Brandon's speech:

> <u>In short,</u> (*internal summary*) the lack of funding for before- and after-school meal programs leads to poor academic performance, increased absences, and behavioral problems. <u>But let's see</u> (*transition*) what this bond issue will do to remedy many of these problems.

Internal summaries are excellent tools to use when you want your audience to remember key points before you move on to a new idea. When combined with transitions, internal summaries can help audiences move smoothly from one idea to the next.

Signposts

A **signpost** is *a simple word or statement that indicates where you are in your speech or highlights an important idea*. Signposts tell your audience where you are in the presentation of your main points and help your listeners keep track of a detailed discussion or list of items. These tools add clarity to a speech and can make it flow.

Signposts can be numbers ("first," "second," "third"), phrases ("the most important thing to remember is," "you'll want to make note of this"), or questions you ask and then answer ("so how do we solve this dilemma?"). In Alex's speech on women in extreme sports, she asked questions to introduce each of her main points. For her first main point, she asked,

> How many of you know who Layne Beachley is?

For her second, Alex asked,

> So, you didn't know Layne Beachley. How about Cara Beth Burnside? Can anyone tell me her accomplishments?

And for her third, Alex asked,

> Okay, I'll give you one more try. Who knows Tara Dakides's contributions to the world of extreme sports?

Although you do not want to overuse these kinds of questions, they can be effective in getting an audience involved in your speech because audience members will try to answer the questions in their own heads before you do.

The final use of signposts is to mark the most important ideas in your speech. When you hear or use any of the following phrases, they are signposts that ask the audience to pay close attention:

> The most important thing to remember is . . .

> If you hear nothing else from today's speech, hear this . . .

Signposts give us important information about where we are in a speech. Be sure to include them in your main points.

FloridaStock/Shutterstock.com

signpost
simple word or statement that indicates where you are in your speech or highlights an important idea.

In a speech on adoption, Chad began with a simple quotation:

> Dennis Rainey, author of the book *One Home at a Time,* states, "I have a wife and six children, two of which are adopted—but I can't remember which ones."

In the next example, Jessica begins her speech with a poem to set the tone and reveal her topic:

> May your thoughts be as glad as the shamrocks.
> May your heart be as light as the song.
> May each day bring you bright happy hours,
> That stay with you all year long.
> For each petal on the shamrock,
> This brings a wish your way—
> Good health, good luck, and happiness
> For today and every day.

> My family has its roots in Ireland, and the shamrock has a long history of meaning . . .

Poems and quotations can be creative ways to begin a speech and reveal your topic. As you do your research for your speech, consider including something from a book, movie, song, or poem that matches your topic.

When you use a quotation or poem, be sure it relates directly to your topic or illustrates the importance of your subject. Like stories, there are many great quotations and poems, but you should only use one that sums up your topic and grabs your audience's attention.

Give a Demonstration. When you demonstrate some aspect of your topic, you can capture the interest of members of your audience and make them want to see or hear more. In the following example, Megan began by singing. After she had captured her audience's attention, she revealed the topic of her speech, the author of her song. In the second paragraph, she previewed her speech so her audience knew exactly what she was going to cover.

> (*Begin by singing "Amazing Grace."*) Comfort is what I feel when I hear this song. No matter if I am at a funeral service or singing it in a choir, this song overwhelms me with a sense of peace. I know it has the same effect on others as well. But who was the man behind this song? And isn't it, as some say, a bit overdone? Dr. Ralph F. Wilson states that he used to think "Amazing Grace" was just that—overdone. Wilson says, "'saved a wretch like me,' come on, really now. But the author really was a wretch, a moral pariah." Wilson is the author of *The Story of John Newton*, and John Newton is the author of America's most popular hymn, "Amazing Grace."

> But what happened to John Newton that made him a "moral pariah"? What happened in this man's life that it was only the "grace of God" that could save him? Well, today I'm going to share with you just how a "wretch" like John Newton wrote such a well-known hymn. I'll begin by telling you a little bit about his early life. Then, I'll tell you how he came to write "Amazing Grace." Finally, I'll conclude by discussing this hymn's legacy.

Make an Intriguing or Startling Statement. An intriguing or startling statement is an excellent way to draw in your audience with the unknown or the curious. As you read the following example, see if you can identify all four criteria for a strong introduction. Notice how Katy takes extra time in her introduction to relate the topic to her audience and to establish her credibility:

> 3.14159265358979323846264433832795. Most of you know the name of the number I just recited. It's a number found in rainbows, pupils of eyes, sound waves, ripples in the water, and DNA—a ratio that both nature and music understand but that the human mind cannot quite comprehend. This number has sparked curiosity in many minds over the past 4,000 years. I'm talking about pi—not the dessert, but the circle ratio.

> Now, a class of speech majors is probably wondering if they can survive a six-minute speech about math. My own interest came about when I was challenged to memorize more digits than a friend of mine could. As a result of that challenge, I have researched this topic, finding information not only technical and historical but also fanatical. Today, I plan to inform you of what pi is, the history of pi, and how pi has created an obsession in people's lives.

When you choose to introduce your speech with a startling statement, be careful. You want to startle rather than offend your audience. If you are thinking about using a statement that may be too graphic or inappropriate, find an acceptable alternative. Your startling statement should invite the audience to listen, not shut down communication.

State the Importance of the Topic. When you state the importance of the topic, you tell the audience why they should listen. Tina used this technique to introduce a speech on a topic that seemed fairly ordinary but was actually quite relevant to her audience:

> Okay. Everyone look down at your feet. How many of you have shoes on? Just as I thought. Each of us has a pair of shoes or sandals on our feet. But how many know where those shoes come from? And let's be honest. How many women in the audience have shoes with heels of an inch or more? Um-hmm. Don't answer. And for the men, do you steer the women in your lives toward the heels in the shoe stores? Maybe even some of you men own a pair of heels? Well, when I look in my closet, I see one pair of sneakers, two pairs of boots, and a dozen high-heeled shoes. But do I know where these shoes come from or how heels were invented? No. At least not until I did some research into my shoe fetish.

> Today, I'd like to share the story of shoes with you. I'd like to discuss the origination of shoes, the changes they've gone through, the invention of high heels (which originally were made for men, by the way), and the troubles those heels have caused.

Share Your Expertise. Although you know your qualifications for speaking on a subject, your audience may not. Establishing credibility does not mean boasting and bragging: it means sharing your expertise with your audience. Recall how Jessica, Katy, and Tina stated their credibility in their introductions:

> *Shamrocks.* My family has its roots in Ireland.

> *Why Pi?* As a result of that challenge, I have researched this topic, finding information not only technical and historical but also fanatical.

History of Shoes. Well, when I look in my closet, I see one pair of sneakers, two pairs of boots, and a dozen high-heeled shoes. But do I know where these shoes come from or how heels were invented? No. At least not until I did some research into my shoe fetish.

State What's to Come. Previewing your speech is a necessary component of your introduction. When you preview your speech, you give your audience an overview of your main points. The best previews are brief; they set the audience up for what is to come but do not go into too much detail. Here is how Nathan previewed his speech:

Appalachian Trail. First, I'll give you a brief history of the trail's formation. Then, I'll share some facts with you about the trail itself and how it's maintained. Finally, I'll tell you the stories from some of those who have hiked the trail.

The Conclusion

Your conclusion is your final contact with your audience. Just as the introduction represents the first impression you make on your audience, the conclusion represents your last impression. Take time to prepare and practice your conclusion so that you end your speech with as much care as you began it. When you deliver your conclusion, you have two primary goals: bring your speech to an end and reinforce your thesis statement.

End Your Speech When you end a speech, you are signaling to the audience that your presentation is over. This signal comes through your words as well as your style of delivery (Knapp, Hart, Friedrick, & Shulman, 1973). You can use simple words and phrases such as "in closing," "in summary," "in conclusion," "let me close by saying," and "my purpose today has been" to signal that you are finishing your speech. Although these transitions seem obvious, they alert your listeners that you are moving from the body of your speech to your conclusion.

Reinforce Your Thesis Statement The second function of your conclusion is to reinforce the thesis statement of your speech. When you restate or rephrase your thesis statement in your conclusion, you remind your audience of the core idea of your speech. Notice how this reinforcement can be very succinct as in Chad's speech on adoption or more elaborate as in Katy's on pi:

In my family, I have two parents, an older sister, and two younger brothers. One of them is adopted, but in my heart I could not tell you which one.

In conclusion, no one knows why pi has caused such a craze or why several books, movies, and fanatical Web pages have been produced on this subject. What inspired the Chudnovsky brothers to devote their lives to the search for pi? What inspired me to write a speech on a silly number? The answer lies in the mystery. Exploring pi is an adventure, which is why people do it. I want you to remember pi not only as the circle ratio, not only as the biggest influence on math over the course of history, but as a number that has an influence on everything we do.

Restating your thesis statement reinforces your arguments and encourages your audience to remember your speech.

Preparing a Compelling Conclusion There are several techniques for signaling the end of a speech and reinforcing your thesis statement. As you develop your conclusion, ask yourself, "What final ideas do I want to leave my audience with?"

Summarize Your Main Points An effective tool for ending your speech and restating your thesis statement is a summary of your main points. A **summary** is a *concise restatement of your main points at the end of your speech.* You use it to review your ideas and remind your audience of what is important in your speech. Review Katy's conclusion presented earlier and notice how she summarized each main point as she drew her speech to a close.

Answer Your Introductory Question If your speech begins with questions, answer them in the conclusion. This technique reminds the audience of what they have learned in the speech. Nathan began with questions about hiking the Appalachian Trail, so he now returns to those questions in his conclusion:

> So, now do you think you could walk from New York to Chicago or from Georgia to Maine? Well, even if you're not up for the hike, many others have been. As a result of the efforts to maintain the Appalachian Trail, individuals have hiked the 2,200-mile-long footpath to raise funds, overcome disabilities, and seek out spiritual insights. The next time someone asks you if you want to "take a hike," perhaps you'll say, "Why not?"

Refer Back to the Introduction Occasionally, a speaker opens with a word, phrase, or idea and then returns to it in the conclusion. Like answering introductory questions, this technique brings the speech full circle and provides a sense of completeness. This technique usually is combined with others such as summarizing the main points.

Reggie, who opened his speech with a story of a boy's battles with chronic health problems, finished the story in his conclusion. After restating his thesis, he said,

> And that boy I told you about in the opening of my speech? Well, I'm that boy. I'm now nineteen, doing fine, and in fact, I haven't set foot in a hospital for more than four years now.

Recite a Quotation When you conclude with a quotation, you rely on someone else's words to reinforce your thesis statement. A concluding quotation should come from someone you cited in your speech or from a famous person the audience will recognize. In the following example, Tina not only summarizes her main points but also returns to a source she had cited earlier in her speech:

> As we've heard today, shoes have gone through great changes over time. What started with animal skins and then lace transformed itself into the into the many types of heels worn by both men and women worn by both men and women and on to the modern look we know today. But as Dr. Rene Cailet says, "Shoes should protect the foot and not disturb it. Having sore feet is not normal. As in any body part, pain is a signal that something is wrong."

summary
concise restatement of your main points at the end of your speech.

Chapter Summary

When We Give a Speech, We Enter the Public Dialogue with Civility

- The word *civility* comes from a root word meaning "to be a member of a household."
- A dialogue is a civil exchange of ideas and opinions between two people or a small group of people.
- The public dialogue is the ethical and civil exchange of ideas and opinions among communities about topics that affect the public.
- People decide to participate in the public dialogue for three main reasons: they decide to speak, they are asked to speak, or they are required to speak.

To Be Audience Centered Is to Consider the Positions, Beliefs, Values, and Needs of an Audience

- Master statuses are significant positions a person occupies within society that affect that person's identity in almost all social situations and can affect an individual's standpoint or the perspective from which the person views and evaluates society.
- Our standpoints influence our attitudes, beliefs, and values.
- An attitude is a general positive or negative feeling a person has about something.
- A belief is a person's idea of what is real or true or not. A value is a person's idea of what is good, worthy, or important.
- Ethnocentrism is the belief that our own cultural perspectives, norms, and ways of organizing society are superior to others.

Your Speech Topic Is the Subject of Your Speech

- To select your topic, match your interests to the assignment, consider your expertise, and brainstorm.
- When you brainstorm, you generate ideas randomly and uncritically without attention to logic, connections, or relevance.

Keep in Mind the Goals of Your Speech

- The general purpose of a speech is its broad goal: to inform, invite, or persuade. The specific purpose is a focused statement that identifies exactly what a speaker wants to accomplish with a speech.
- To narrow your specific purpose, consider your behavioral objectives, which are the actions you want your audience to take at the end of your speech.

A Speech Is Organized Around the Thesis Statement, Which Is Sometimes Called *a Central Idea*

- A thesis statement summarizes in a single declarative sentence the main ideas, assumptions, or arguments you want to express in your speech.
- Main points are the most important, comprehensive ideas you address in your speech.
- Keep each main point separate and distinct, use parallel word structure, and devote appropriate coverage to each main point.
- The words and phrases we use to link ideas in a speech are called *connectives*.
- Connectives consist of transitions, internal previews, internal summaries, and signposts.

The Introduction of a Speech Has Four Parts: Catching the Audience's Attention, Revealing the Topic, Establishing Credibility, and Previewing the Speech

- Your conclusion signals the end of the speech and reinforces your thesis statement.
- Your conclusion should offer a summary, which is a concise restatement of your main points at the end of your speech.
- You can conclude your speech by answering your introductory question, referring back to your introduction, or reciting a quotation.

Key Concepts

attitude (223)
audience-centered speaker (220)
behavioral objectives (231)
belief (223)
brainstorming (227)

connectives (238)
credible (241)
dialogue (219)
ethnocentrism (223)
general purpose (230)

internal preview (239)
internal summary (239)
main points (235)
master statuses (221)
preview (241)

Invitation to Human Communication Online

MindTap Speech includes an interactive MindTap Reader and interactive learning tools including National Geographic Explorer videos, student videos, quizzes, flash cards, and more. You can build your speech outline with Outline Builder and record, post, and watch videos with YouSeeU. Go to cengagebrain.com to access your MindTap for *Invitation to Human Communication* where these resources can be found.

MindTap®

Further Reflection and Discussion

1. Use the strategies suggested in this chapter to make a list of four different speech topics you might like to speak about. How do you think the classroom setting would affect what you would say about these topics? What would you do to make these topics suitable for a classroom setting?

2. Rewrite the following incorrect specific-purpose statements so they are correct:
   a. To give five hours a month to a nonprofit organization.
   b. Isn't the level of water pollution in our local river too high?
   c. Improving literacy in our schools.
   d. Learning a second language.

3. Discuss how you might state a specific purpose for a speech on these topics: Olympic gold medals, natural disasters, giving 10 percent of your income to charity, and hybrid cars.

4. Think about the specific purpose of the topics listed in question 3. For each topic, discuss how your audience affects what you say about the topic.

5. Name the four parts of an introduction to a speech and the two parts of a conclusion of a speech. Discuss the strengths and importance of each component.

6. Why should speakers establish their credibility and preview the main points of a speech? Are these components of an introduction important? Why or why not?

7. Imagine that you have been asked to give a speech on the history of bubble gum. Brainstorm intriguing or startling introductions.

8. With a group of other students, select a speech topic that you would give to middle school students. Write a specific purpose and thesis statement for that speech. Now write out, in complete sentences, your main points. Finally, write a connective for each of your main points. Do you think your middle school audience would be interested in this speech? Why?

9. In class, write a possible speech topic on a slip of paper and trade that paper with another student. Now write an introduction and a conclusion for a speech on that topic using the techniques discussed in the chapter. Present your introduction and conclusion to the class for feedback on each of their components.

10. In this chapter, you have read about the prevalence of public speaking in the workplace. Do you agree with the findings and the importance of public speaking in the workplace? Can you identify occupations that do not need public speaking skills? What other kinds of communication skills do those professions need?

Activities and Web Links

Visit cengagebrain.com to access the MindTap for *Invitation to Human Communication* where these activities and Web links can be found.

1. Choose one fact listed on this Web page about violence and use it as an introduction to your speech. How would you need to consider your audience? What type of audience would respond well? What might you need to add or say to increase your credibility with the audience? Go to *Web link 10.1*.

2. Read the article "Tracking the Wage Gap: In Honor of Equal Pay Day; 12 Sobering Figures about Men, Women, and Work." Consider the issue of equal pay as a speech topic. Create a thesis statement and three main points you would cover in your speech. Go to *Web link 10.2*.

3. Watch this short video of Ken Banks talking about how an innovative idea for communication occurred to him while he was watching a soccer match on television. How does he establish credibility? Is his conclusion effective? Explain. Go to *Web link 10.3*.

4. Listen to the introduction to this speech by Robert Ballard on oceanography. What approach does he use in the introduction to his speech? How does he effectively engage the audience with his introduction? Go to *Web link 10.4*.

5. Watch Explorer Jimmy Chin tell his story about being trapped in an avalanche. How effective do you think climber and photographer Chin's story is? Why? Go to *Web link 10.5*.

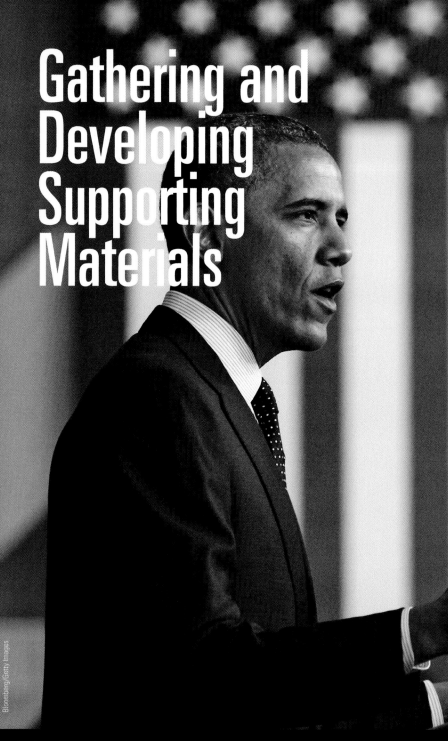

11

Use Your Personal Knowledge and Experience

Search for Materials

Conduct Research Interviews

Develop Your Supporting Materials

Understand the Patterns of Reasoning

Understand Emotion and Reasoning

Be Aware of Fallacies in Reasoning

IN THIS CHAPTER YOU WILL LEARN TO:

- Gather effective supporting material for your speech.

- Conduct research interviews.

- Develop the supporting material in your speech.

- Identify six patterns of reasoning.

- Explain the use of emotional appeals in your reasoning.

- Explain common types of fallacies in logical reasoning.

Gathering and Developing Supporting Materials

Bloomberg/Getty Images

Speakers often use the words of credible people as testimony, giving strength and credibility to the ideas being developed. If you could interview the President and use his testimony for your next speech, what questions might you ask him? What other supporting materials might you also include?

One of our primary responsibilities as public speakers is to provide audiences with accurate information. In addition to expressing our opinions on the topics we speak about, we must provide facts, examples, and evidence. We can find such *supporting material* by consulting our own experiences and knowledge, by doing research over the Internet and at the library, and by interviewing the right people. This chapter will help you collect the supporting materials you need and then develop them ethically and confidently so you can enter the public dialogue successfully.

Use Your Personal Knowledge and Experience

One excellent way to gather materials for your speech is from your personal, firsthand knowledge about a subject. After you have selected a topic, use your personal experience as a starting point for your research. Take a moment to consider what knowledge you already have about your topic. This knowledge can come from your own experiences and training, your family background, hobbies, job or profession, and even things you have read or observed.

Before you decide to use your own experiences as material for your speech, make sure it is appropriate and ethical to use that information. Ask yourself these questions:

- How much do I actually know about this topic?
- Does my knowledge fit with the purpose of the speech and the assignment?
- Would sharing my experiences harm others or violate their privacy?
- Will sharing my experiences help me build my arguments or develop a point?

If you have a solid background in or understanding of your topic (you have ridden horses since you were four years old, for example) and sharing that background is both ethical and appropriate, then you might consider how that knowledge and experiences can help you develop your ideas.

Search for Materials

For public-speaking students, the Internet and the library offer information on local, regional, national, and international events and issues and provide a truly staggering range of ideas to choose in selecting your supporting materials.

Find Materials on the Internet

Certain search techniques such as Google Scholar can help you with your research by taking you to relevant academic scholarship on your topic. Search engines such as LexisNexis can help you find popular press conversations about your subject. Using the Internet, you can also find government documents. These contain statistics; information on social, political, and historical issues; what Congress has been discussing or debating; what kind of research the government is sponsoring; and maps, charts, and other images you can download and use as visual aids for your speech. Most government information now is available on the Internet, and you can search by subject or by agency.

The Ethics of Internet Research Because the Internet is easy to access and open to anyone, less-than-accurate information from a variety of sources can be found all over the Internet. Although many Web sites are maintained and regularly updated by reputable people, companies, and institutions, just as many others are not. Web sites are regularly abandoned and thus never updated by operators who lose funding or simply lose interest. As a result, Web sites vary widely in accuracy, complexity, and usefulness. Many sites include information that is old, incomplete, or based on personal opinions and biases. In addition, identifying credible Internet sites can be difficult because many sites are well designed and look professional even if they are not.

Challenges like these place particular ethical responsibilities on anyone who uses the Internet to find supporting materials. To act in good faith with your audience, use only reliable and relevant information from the Internet and accurately credit the sources for this information in your speech. Knowing how to evaluate the quality of information you find on the Internet is crucial and ensures that you develop your speech ideas ethically and responsibly.

Evaluating Internet Information How do you know whether a source found on the Internet is usable in your speech? As with any other source of information, evaluate your data according to the criteria in Table 11.1.

If you keep the five criteria in Table 11.1 in mind as you research your speech topic on the Internet, you will be more likely to use supporting materials that are credible, reliable, authoritative, current, complete, relevant, and consistent. The Internet is certainly a source of much credible material, but it should be only one of many tools you use to gather materials for your speech.

Research Materials at the Library

The library gives you access to resources and materials you are unlikely to or cannot find on the Internet: librarians (to help you find materials); the most recent (or historical) copies of journals, magazines, and newspapers; books (old as well as new); databases and indexes; and hard copies of documents. Your librarian can help you with materials you might not be familiar with: databases, indexes, and reference works.

TABLE 11.1 HOW TO EVALUATE INFORMATION FROM THE INTERNET

Is the information reliable?	Check the domain in the uniform resource locator (URL). Is it *.com* (a commercial enterprise that might be trying to sell something), *.org* (a nonprofit organization that may be more interested in services and issues than in commerce), *.edu* (an educational institution), or *.gov* (a government agency)? What bias might those operating the site have about your topic?
Is the information authoritative?	URLs that include a tilde (~) often indicate that a single individual is responsible for the information on a Web site. Can you find the person's credentials posted on the site? Can you contact the person and ask for credentials? Can you find the person's credentials in any print sources, such as a *Who's Who* reference? And is the author an expert on the subject of the site?
How current is the information?	Many Web pages include a date that tells you when it was posted or last updated. If you do not see such a date, you may be able to find it in your browser's View or Document menu. If you determine that the Web site is current, is the time frame relevant to your subject or arguments?
Is the information consistent and unbiased?	Is the information you find consistent with information you find on other sites, from printed sources, or from interviews? Can you find other sources to support the statements, claims, and facts provided by a Web site? To guarantee a comprehensive picture of your topic, search several sites and be wary of outrageous or controversial claims that cannot be checked for accuracy or are not grounded in reasonable arguments or sources (Bolner & Poirier, 2002; Hult, 1996; Kennedy, 1998).

Bolner and Poirier, 2002; Kennedy, 1998

Angela Waye/Shutterstock.com

So much information is available on the Web that it can be difficult to determine which material and sources are the most ethical to use. How will you assess the ethical aspects of the research you find for your next speech?

Databases Databases store large collections of information electronically so they are easy to find and retrieve. You can search databases and indexes using keywords and subjects, and you can refine your search by indicating the time frame you want to limit your search to. Databases provide two types of information:

1. **full-text databases** give you the complete text of newspapers, periodicals, encyclopedias, research reports, court cases, books, and the like;

2. **abstracts** summarize the text in an article or publication and help you decide if the research is relevant to your speech.

Indexes Indexes are alphabetical listings of the topics discussed in a specific publication, along with the corresponding year, volume, and page numbers. You can find indexes from almost every academic discipline and area of interest. Table 11.2 presents a list of commonly used indexes.

It is always a good idea to cross-check information you find on the Internet (e.g., information found on Wikipedia), track down someone's credentials (something you read in a popular magazine), or find specific details of a person's life (something you heard on the news, for example). Your local library includes reference works such as almanacs, atlases, and encyclopedias to help you focus on a specific time frame (the worst storms in 2015), and they can give you ideas for other places to look for the materials you need.

Evaluate library sources by using the same strategies you use to assess Internet sources: check that the source is reliable, authoritative, current, complete, relevant, and consistent.

TABLE 11.2 LIST OF COMMONLY USED INDEXES

InfoTrac and InfoTrac College Edition	Citations, abstracts, and full-text articles from thousands of magazines, journals, and newspapers.
LexisNexis	Full-text database for legal, business, and current issues. Includes U.S. Supreme Court and lower court cases.
Academic Search Premier	Scholarly academic multidisciplinary database. Covers a broad range of disciplines, including general academic, business, social sciences, humanities, general sciences, education, and multicultural topics.
IngentaConnect	Indexes scholarly journals and delivers documents. A fee is charged for document delivery.
Readers' Guide to Periodical Literature	Indexes almost 300 popular and general-interest magazines, including *The New Yorker*, *Newsweek*, and *National Geographic Traveler*.
DataTimes	Online newspaper database, including *Washington Post*, *Dallas Morning News*, and *San Francisco Chronicle*.
Christian Science Monitor	Indexes the *Christian Science Monitor International Daily Newspaper*.
***New York Times* Index**	Indexes the *The New York Times* newspaper.
NewsBank	Microfiche collection covering current events from newspapers in more than 100 cities.
***The Times* Index (London)**	Index to *The Times* (daily), *The Sunday Times*, *The Times Literary Supplement*, *The Times Educational Supplement*, and *The Times Higher Education Supplement*.
***Wall Street Journal* Index**	Emphasizes financial news from the *Journal*. Includes *Barron's Index*, a subject and corporate index to *Barron's Business* and *Financial Weekly*.
***Washington Post* Newspaper**	Index of the newspaper from our nation's capital.

© Cengage Learning

Anti-Drug Campaigns and Persuasion

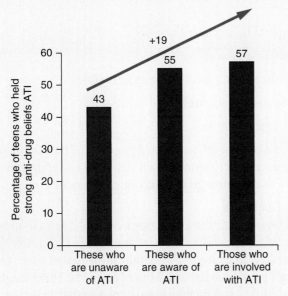

Above the Influence

Source: National Youth Anti-Drug Media Campaign Tracking Study from "Fact Sheet: Office of National Drug Control Poicy," www .WhiteHouseDrugPolicy.gov (http://www.whitehouse.gov/sites /default/files/ondcp/prevention/national_youth_anti_drug_page _media_campaign_fact_sheet_7-16-10.pdf).

In 2007, the U.S. Office of National Drug Policy Control (ONDCP) joined with news media and several states in a campaign to prevent methamphetamine use and raise awareness about the treatment of meth addiction. Two years later, the ONDCP launched an aggressive advertising campaign targeted at people ages eighteen to thirty-four in the sixteen states with the highest levels of reported meth use and lab seizures: Alaska, Washington, Oregon, Nevada, Wyoming, Arizona, New Mexico, Oklahoma, Arkansas, Missouri, Iowa, Minnesota, Illinois, Indiana, Kentucky, and Nebraska (Buddy T., 2009; Methresources.gov, 2009). The

ads for this campaign—created in conjunction with various state campaigns such as the Montana Meth Project's "Not Even Once" campaign and Alabama's "Zero Meth" campaign—are described as graphic and disturbing. They also seem to be effective in reducing meth use among young users (Life or Meth, 2002). The ONCDP also designed a second campaign, *Above the Influence*, to target youth between the ages of twelve and seventeen. The campaign includes broad media messages at the national level and promotes active engagement at the local community level. The campaign's in-market survey indicates that teens who are aware of the Above the Influence campaign "held significantly stronger anti-drug beliefs than those who were unaware of the campaign" (see chart to the left).

Much research suggests that if fear appeals are too graphic and cause an audience to feel immobilized, then speakers lose the support of the audience (Casey, Timmermann, Allen, Krahn, & Turkiewicz, 2009; Jessop & Wade, 2008; Nabi, Roskos-Ewoldsen, & Carpentier, 2008; Rippetoe & Rogers, 1987; Roser & Thompson, 1995; Schmitt & Blass, 2008; Wong & Capella, 2009). However, compared with appeals that cause an audience to shut down and dismiss the speaker, something unusual and effective is happening with the antimeth ads. The ads are appealing to fear by using fairly graphic and disturbing images with success.

What Do You Think?

1. Log on to http://trc.rmc.org/visual-aids and explore the images there. Do you find the images effective? Why or why not?

2. Do you think these images are ethical, credible, and appropriate? Why?

3. What sources will you use to search for visual images to support or clarify the claims you want to make in your speeches? How will you evaluate their credibility?

Conduct Research Interviews

An **interview** is *a planned interaction with another person that is organized around inquiry and response, with one person asking questions and the other person answering them* (Steward & Cash, 2006). Interviews require planning, so to make the most of an interview, decide whom you will interview and what questions to ask, and then schedule and conduct

interview
planned interaction with another person that is organized around inquiry and response, with one person asking questions and the other person answering them.

the interview in a professional and ethical manner. Remember to follow up with a thank-you letter.

Determine Whom to Interview

To determine whom you will interview for your speech, ask the following questions:

- Who are the experts on my speech topic?
- Who has personal experience with the topic?
- Who will my audience find interesting and credible?
- Who has time to speak with me?
- Who do I have time to contact?

A good interview subject might be a well-known expert or scholar, the head of an agency or company, someone on staff or in a support position, or a member of a community group, club, or organization.

Design the Interview Questions

Even seasoned interviewers plan their questions carefully, so take time with your interview questions because they are your guide (King, 1995). The goal of your interview questions is to obtain information that you could not find through your Internet and library research. Three kinds of questions are commonly used in interviews: open-ended questions, closed-ended questions, and probes.

- Open-ended questions invite a wide range of possible responses. They can be as broad as "How did you become an environmental activist?" and "What are your thoughts on this most recent form of legislation?" Open-ended questions are useful for several reasons. They are usually nonthreatening and so prompt interviewees to do most of the talking. They do not restrict the form or content of an answer, and they allow interviewees to offer information voluntarily. Finally, they encourage interviewees to pull together ideas, knowledge, and experiences in interesting ways.

- A closed-ended question invites a brief, focused answer and allows the interviewer to keep tighter control of the direction of the conversation. Closed-ended questions might be, "How long have you taught elementary school?" and "Do many of your students think about going to college?" Closed-ended questions are useful because they can be answered easily and quickly, encourage interviewees to give you specific information, and result in shorter answers for you to process.

- A probe is a question that fills out or follows up an answer to a previous question. Probes are useful for obtaining more far-reaching or comprehensive answers. They allow you to take an initial question further than you might have planned. A probe might be nonverbal (head nods and questioning eyes that indicate interest) minimal responses ("Really?" or "Um-hmm") or direct requests

Conducting Interviews

Media consultant and journalist Shel Israel has "conducted thousands of interviews, been interviewed hundreds of times," and "observed thousands of interviews from a neutral seat." In an article for *Forbes*, Israel offered nine tips for conducting interviews:

1. Start slow, safe, and personal. Begin with a question that will relax and focus the people you are interviewing. Ask them where they grew up or about their first job.
2. Coax rather than hammer. Although "shock jocks" might garner audiences, Israel suggests a softer approach is more likely to open someone up. He offers National Public Radio's Terry Gross as a model, advocating her highly personal style to interviewing.
3. Use open-ended questions. Even if you have views and opinions different from the person you are interviewing, keep them to yourself and ask open-ended questions. To Israel, the job of the interviewer is to get people to tell their stories "and let the readers decide what they think of [their] ideas."
4. Ask what you don't know. When we ask what we do not know, Israel says, we get surprises. "Surprises mean I have something that has not been previously reported," and that's great supporting material.
5. Let the interview subject wander, but not too much. Israel suggests that allowing the person you are interviewing to talk about what he or she sees as important rather than keeping the person focused on your questions can lead to interesting material. This is risky, Israel acknowledges. "Sometimes it works, sometimes it does not."
6. Interview in person rather than by e-mail. E-mail answers feel scripted and stilted, explains Israel. The format also prevents you from asking that important follow-up question or probe that often provides the best material.
7. Be prepared. Israel encourages interviewers to Google the name of the person they are interviewing and gather as much information about them as possible before the interview. Go three or four pages down into the results, he urges, to find forgotten information or "surprisingly interesting content that no one else has recently looked at."
8. Listen. Really listen. The most important information comes from what people say, Israel explains, not what we ask. So pay close attention to what your interviewee is saying and share that with your audience.
9. Yes, there are dumb questions. Ask about what is not on the person's bio or resume. Your goal, Israel states, is to get new information and insights, not to find out what you already know (Israel, 2012).

for clarification ("Could you explain those numbers a bit more?" Or, "Let see if I understand correctly . . .").

Most research on interviewing suggests that a combination of probes and open-ended and closed-ended questions yields the best results in an interview. Open-ended questions give you more stories and details than closed-ended questions, but when you just need facts, there is nothing like a closed-ended question to prompt the specific answer you need (Killenberg & Anderson, 1989). And probes allow you to explore ideas more carefully and comprehensively.

Schedule and Conduct the Interview

Many people are flattered to be asked for an interview. Take a moment to prepare your request and work through the following steps when you contact someone for an interview:

- Identify who you are. Provide your full name, where you are from (school, place of business), the course you are in, and your instructor's name.

- Specify the requirements of your assignment, including its purpose, length, and topic.

- Describe why you have chosen to contact the person (for example, she is an expert in the field; he is the head of an agency).

- Request the interview, letting the person know how much time it will take and what kinds of questions you will ask. You might even share two or three of your most important or engaging questions so your interviewee can prepare.

The guidelines for conducting interviews are essentially grounded in the rules of common courtesy, so they are not difficult to follow.

- Dress appropriately, show up on time for your interview (or phone in at the correct time if it will be a telephone interview), and begin by introducing yourself to your interviewee.

- Restate the purpose of the interview and your assignment and request permission to record the interview.

- Start with questions that will put the interviewee at ease and then follow those with your most important questions.

- At the end of your interview, ask your interviewee if she or he would like to add any information. (You may get a piece of information or a story you did not think to ask for directly but that fits into your speech perfectly.)

- Finally, thank the interviewee orally for his or her time and be sure you have recorded names, professional titles, and addresses correctly so you can cite them accurately and send a letter of thanks.

Ethical Interviews

Ethical interviewing means preparing, using quotations and information honestly, including only what was said and staying true to the intention of the speaker, and giving credit to interviewees for the words and ideas you include in your speech. If an interviewee provides information that seems inconsistent with what your other research supports, take the time to double-check your own research and the credentials of your interview subject. Ask your interviewee for documentation or sources that support unusual claims. If an individual shares something with you "off the record," that information should stay out of your speech and out of your conversations with others. In addition, if an interviewee provides information that is highly personal or would compromise the integrity or reputation of others, do not use that information in your speech.

Research interviews are an excellent way to gather materials for speeches. Consider the people you might interview for your next speech. What questions could you ask them?

Monkey Business Images/Shutterstock.com

Shakira, "I'm Going to Help These Kids"

Colombian singer Shakira may be one of the most driven people in the entertainment industry. Since 1995, she's released several best-selling albums (she's the highest-selling Colombian artist of all time), has won a couple of dozen major music awards (including two Grammy Awards), and collaborated with the South African group Freshlyground to sing the official song of the 2010 World Cup. Oh, and she also performed with superstars Stevie Wonder and Usher at President Obama's inaugural ceremonies in 2008.

But Shakira is also driven to succeed as a humanitarian. When she was eight years old, her father experienced some financial trouble and had to sell much of what her family owned. No longer were they living the comfortable middle-class life she was used to. "In my childish head, this was the end of the world." To help her see that their circumstances were not as dire as they could be, her father took her to the park to see the homeless kids who lived there. Many were addicted to sniffing glue. "From then on, I gained perspective, and realized that there were many underprivileged children in my country. The images of those kids, with their tattered clothes and bare feet, have stayed with me forever. I said to myself back then, one day I'm going to help these kids when I become a famous artist."

She has certainly made good on that promise to herself. With the money she made from her first successful album, she founded the Pies Descalzos (Barefoot) Foundation, a Colombian charity that provides education and meals for impoverished Colombian children. Shakira also founded the ALAS Foundation (Fundacion América Latina en Acción Solidaria), an organization dedicated to launching "a new social movement that will generate a collective commitment to comprehensive early childhood development programs for the children in Latin America." In 2007, she used her humanitarian clout and persuasive skills to secure commitments of an impressive $200 million for the ALAS Foundation from Mexican philanthropist Carlos Slim and U.S. philanthropist and conservationist Howard Buffett. In 2012, she asked her fans via YouTube to help her build a school in one of the most impoverished neighborhoods in Cartagena in her home country of Colombia by "buying a brick" ("Shakira Launches Buy-a-Brick Campaign," 2013). In 2013, she began to build that school. As a goodwill ambassador for UNICEF, in 2015 Shakira and her husband, Gerard Pique, threw a "charity baby shower for UNICEF ahead of the birth" of their second son and raised more than a million pounds for that charity.

Shakira decided to engage with her community because she wanted to help kids like those she saw in the park. But she also has a larger goal in mind, which she described in a 2008 speech to the Oxford Union about her humanitarian work in Latin America:

> Now I want to be clear about this, this isn't about charity. This is about investing in human potential. From an ethical point of view, from a moral point of view, it accomplishes a purpose. But also from an economic point of view,

Splash News/Newscom

this could bring enormous benefits to all mankind. Universal education is the key to global security and economic growth. (Kimpel, 2007; La Mala, 2008; Shakira, 2009; "Shakira's Charity Baby," 2015; Turner, 2009)

What Do You Think?

1. Shakira talks about human potential and the obligation we have to assist others. Do you agree with Shakira? Why or why not?
2. Could you give a speech related to your views on question 1? What kind of research would you conduct to gather materials for this speech?
3. Identify the three most successful charities in the United States. Do they match Shakira's humanitarian goals? Could you give a speech on one of these charities? What would your goals be as a speaker, if you did want to give a speech on one of these charities?

Now that you have explored what type of supporting material you need for your speech and how to obtain it, we can explore the types of supporting materials you will want to use in your speech.

When you give a speech to your classmates, you are speaking to a room of your peers. What kinds of examples do you think your classmates will find relevant and credible?

Develop Your Supporting Materials

The materials we gather from our research must be turned into **evidence**, the *information speakers use to develop and support their ideas*. Strong evidence helps you build your credibility. In this section, you will learn about five of the most common types of evidence: examples, narratives, statistics, testimony, and definitions.

Examples

Examples are *specific instances used to illustrate a concept, experience, issue, or problem*. Examples can be brief, only a word or a sentence or two, or they can be longer and more richly detailed. Examples can also be real or hypothetical. A **real example** is *an instance that has actually taken place*. A **hypothetical example** is *an instance that did not take place but could have*. Generally, real examples are more credible and convey a sense of immediacy. In her speech on binge drinking on college campuses nationwide, Eileen used a powerful example of a binge drinker by describing her friend who "consumed twelve to fifteen beers combined with shots of hard liquor, and stopped only because she ran out of alcohol, time, and money."

Occasionally, you can clarify a point with a hypothetical example. A hypothetical example usually begins with words and phrases such as *imagine*, *suppose*, or *let's say that*. For example, when Clara addressed a group of teenagers in an after-school program on proper eating, she could have simply said, "Skipping breakfast isn't good for you." Instead, she supported her claim with a hypothetical example:

> Suppose you skipped breakfast this morning. Let's see what that would do to your energy level by about 9 or 10 o'clock—that's during second period, right? If you haven't eaten by then, you'll probably feel bored or restless, and maybe sad or unmotivated. You might also feel angry or irritable, kind of grouchy and crabby. And maybe you'll feel a little lightheaded or dizzy if you stand up fast. You might have a headache. You'll definitely have trouble concentrating on your schoolwork because your blood sugar is low or because all you can think about is how hungry you are. Sound familiar to any of you?

Clara's hypothetical example, although not real, grew out of research that was grounded in real experience and helped her audience understand more clearly why skipping meals is not good for them.

evidence
information speakers use to develop and support their ideas.

examples
are specific instances used to illustrate a concept, experience, issue, or problem.

real example
an instance that has actually taken place.

hypothetical example
an instance that did not take place but could have.

Mireya Mayor,
Emerging Explorer, Primatologist, and Conservationist

How do you gather your supporting materials for your public speaking appearances? What is your process for gathering materials—where do you locate materials, how to you choose the best materials, how do you decide what not to use?

There are some audiences that lend themselves to more serious topics. For example, during my lectures I talk about the poaching that goes on in Congo with the gorillas, and I have some extremely graphic and powerful images of, well, slaughtered gorillas. They are very graphic, and I clearly wouldn't show that to an audience that's going to have kids or an audience where the venue is a more light-hearted. However, if I'm speaking to scientific audiences, or if I'm speaking to a more mature audience, and I feel that it is appropriate, then I would insert those pictures. If I feel that there is any question that somebody there might be offended, I won't use that kind of supporting material. I have to be very careful and I have learned to gauge who my audience is and who I am talking to.

Narratives

A **narrative** is *a story that recounts or foretells real or hypothetical events*. Narratives help us explain, interpret, and understand events in our lives or the lives of others (Fisher, 1987; Jamieson, 1988). Speakers can use *brief narratives*, sometimes called *vignettes*, to illustrate a specific point or *extended narratives* to make an evolving connection with a broader point. Josiah used this brief story, which he found as he gathered materials for his speech on the history of battles portrayed in theatrical productions:

> Planned stage combat reduces the level of danger that is part of any battle scene in a play. According to William Hobbs in *Fight Direction for the Stage and Screen*, in early sixteenth-century Stockholm, the actor who played the part of Longinus in *The Mystery of the Passion*, and who had to pierce the crucified Christ, was so carried away with the spirit of the action that he actually killed the other actor. The king, who was present, was so angry that he leapt onto the stage and cut off the head of Longinus. And the audience, who had been pleased with the actor's zeal, were so infuriated with the king that they turned upon him and slew him.

When used in speeches, stories can give historical context to events, make strong connections between ideas and experiences, add emotional depth to characterizations, and describe subjects, settings, and actions with sensory details that can captivate an audience.

narrative
a story that recounts or foretells real or hypothetical events; narratives can be brief or extended.

Class of admission

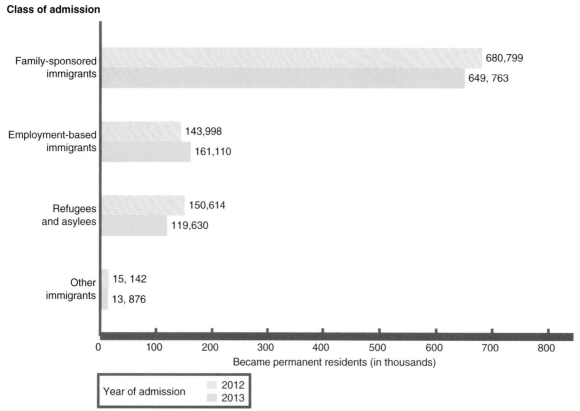

Figure 11.1 *Visual representation of statistics*

Visual representations of statistics help an audience understand complex or abstract information. This graph shows the numbers of immigrants to the United States who became permanent residents in 2012 and 2013 by class of admission.

Source: U.S. Department of Homeland Security, Office of Immigration Statistics, *2011 Yearbook of Immigration Statistics.* See also http://www.dhs.gov/ximgtn/statistics /publications/yearbook.shtm.

Statistics

Statistics are *numerical summaries of facts, figures, and research findings.* They help audiences understand amounts ("100 individuals participated"), proportions ("that's almost half the people in this organization"), and percentages ("fully 50 percent said they'd participate again"). Numbers summarize and help audiences make sense of large chunks of information ("eight glasses of water a day, every day of the year, is the equivalent of almost 3,000 glasses of water a year"), and they help people see where something is in relation to other things ("he's the third fastest runner in the world"). See Figure 11.1 for a visual representation of statistics that could help an audience understand how the U.S. government classifies people who immigrate to the United States.

Numbers and statistics may seem less glamorous than a story or a clever example, but relevant, surprising, or little-known statistics can grab an audience's attention (Best, 2001, 2008; Taylor, Rice, & Williams, 2000). In fact, according to Cynthia Crossen (1994), author of *Tainted Truth: The Manipulation of Fact in America,* 82 percent of people surveyed said statistics increase a story's credibility.

Common statistics include totals and amounts, costs, scales and ranges, ratios, rates, dates and times, measurements, and percentages. Other more technical statistics are the *mean,* the *median,* and the *mode.* The mean, the median, and the mode are numbers that summarize sets of numbers. The

statistics
numerical summaries of facts, figures, and research findings.

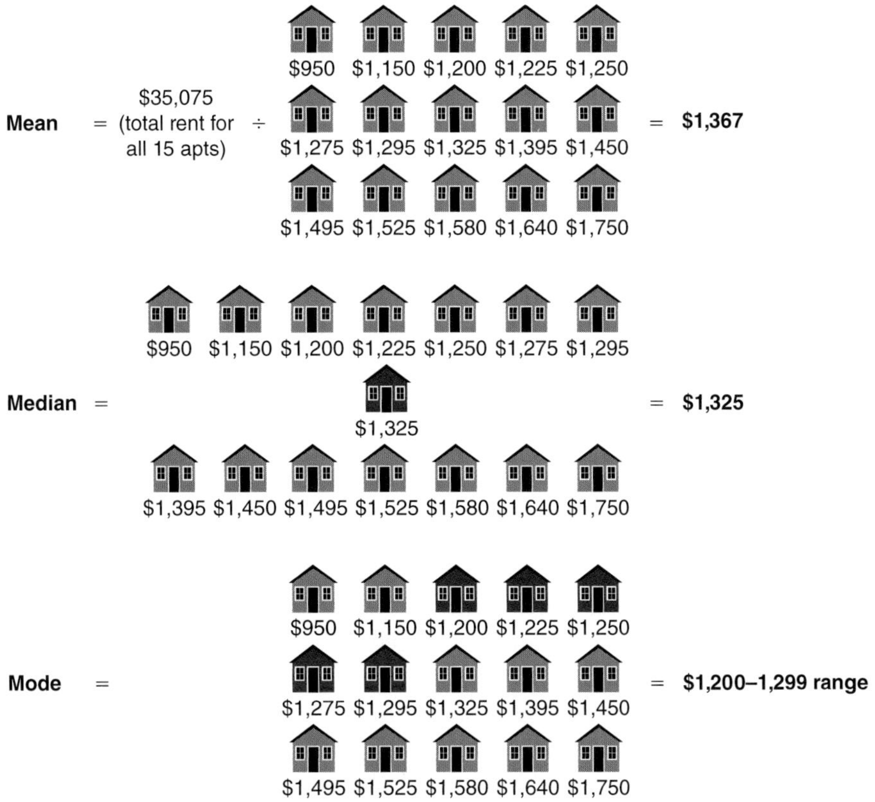

Figure 11.2 *Visual representation of mean, median, and mode*

The mean, median, and mode are numbers that summarize other groups of numbers. This figure shows the mean, the median, and the mode of the range of rents for fifteen one-bedroom apartments in the Boston area in September 2011.

Source: From GRIFFIN, *Invitation to Public Speaking,* 5E. © 2015 Cengage Learning.

descriptions that follow will help you determine the type of statistics you need in your speech. Also see Figure 11.2 for a visual representation of the differences between mean, the median, and the mode. The figure shows the mean, the median, and the mode of the range of rents for fifteen one-bedroom apartments in the Boston area in September 2011.

The **mean** shows *the average of a group of numbers*. Find it by adding all the numbers in your data set and then dividing by the total number of items. Use the mean when you want to describe averages, patterns, tendencies, generalizations, and trends, especially for large groups of data. For example, the mean is what you need if you want to find the average weight of a group of teenagers, as Clara did in her speech to the after-school youth in our previous example. To find her mean, Clara added together the weight in pounds of each of the teens in her audience (115, 121, 126, 132, 154, 159, 163, 167, and 170) and then divided that number by the total number of teens she had weighed (nine). This gave her the mean, 145 pounds, the average weight in her audience. She used that average, or mean, to compare her audience's average to the average weight of teenagers fifty years ago and then to teen athletes and nonathletes. She and her audience then entered into a discussion about average weights of teenagers in general.

When your data sets include extreme values, or what are called *outliers*, using the mean to generalize about the data is misleading (Fadei, 2000). A group of students speaking to county commissioners about affordable

mean

the average of a group of numbers.

housing illustrates why this is so. The students presented information about the average cost of housing in their area. Most of the houses rented for $900 to $1,500 a month, but one particular home rented for $2,250 a month. In this case, the students could not have used the mean because the outlier in this set of data ($2,250) would have distorted the picture of housing costs in their area. To provide a more accurate statistic, the students need to use the median or the mode or leave out the $2,250 rental and explain why.

The **median** is *the middle number in a series or set of numbers arranged in a ranked order*. A median shows the midpoint in your set of data. It shows that one-half of your observations will be smaller and one-half will be larger than the midpoint. Use the median when you want to identify the midpoint and make claims about its significance or about the items that fall above or below it. For example, the median weight of Clara's teens is 154 pounds. This means that half the teens weighed more than 154 and half weighed less. Both Clara and her audience now have more information than simply the average weight of teens (145 pounds) and, for example, can begin to explain weight in relation to body type or height (those below the median ranged in height from four feet eleven inches to five feet eight inches and those above the median ranged from five feet six inches to six feet one inch).

The **mode** is *the number that occurs most often in a set of numbers*. Use the mode when you want to illustrate the most frequent or typical item in your data set to establish the occurrence, availability, demand, or need for something. For example, if the students showed that the most common monthly income for people looking for rental homes was $1,500, they could use the mode to show that most of the homes for rent in their area were priced too high for these people. Thus, they could argue that Habitat for Humanity homes were crucial.

Testimony

When speakers use the *opinions or observations of others*, they are using **testimony** as a source of evidence. We usually think of testimony as coming from an authority, an expert, or a person who has professional knowledge about a subject. This is often true, but testimony can also come from average people who have relevant experience with your topic. Speakers sometimes also provide their own testimony—their own words and experiences as sources of evidence.

Testimony often takes the form of a **direct quotation**, *an exact word-for-word presentation of another's testimony*. At other times, speakers **paraphrase** the words or *provide a summary of another's testimony in the speaker's own words*. Direct quotations often seem more credible than paraphrasing, but sometimes a person's words or stories are too long, are too complex, or contain inappropriate language for a particular audience, making paraphrasing a better option. When you use the *testimony of someone considered an authority in a particular field*, you are using **expert testimony**. When you use the *testimony of someone who has firsthand knowledge of a topic*, you are using **peer testimony**, which is

---

median
the middle number in a series or set of numbers arranged in a ranked order.

mode
the number that occurs most often in a set of numbers.

testimony
opinions or observations of others.

direct quotation
an exact word-for-word presentation of another's testimony.

paraphrase
to provide a summary of another's testimony in the speaker's own words.

expert testimony
the testimony of someone considered an authority in a particular field.

peer testimony (lay testimony)
testimony of someone who has firsthand knowledge of a topic.

NATIONAL GEOGRAPHIC SPEAKS

Asher Jay, Creative Conservationist, Emerging Explorer: Channel Your Inner Mosquito

"I hope my creativity will inspire each individual to channel their inner mosquito and make an impact with every bite," states Asher Jay, "designer, artist, writer, and activist." Jay puts her artistic skills to use in a range of mediums: she sculpts, designs installations, makes films, advocacy advertising campaigns, and more, to "advance animal rights, sustainable development, and humanitarian causes." Jay, born in India, but "raised by the world," brings attention to the damage done by oil spills, dolphin slaughters, the illegal ivory trade, poaching, diminishing habitats for animals, and the seriousness of the loss of biodiversity. She explains, "The power of art is that it can transcend differences, connect with people on a visceral level, and compel action."

Jay organizes her efforts around two principles: compassion and coexistence. She explains that she chose to focus her efforts in this way because "without compassion and coexistence, we really don't accomplish what is in the best interest of the collective." We are all a part of this earth, and "only when we see things as being a true extension of our being," when we acknowledge there "are no separations," can we achieve empathy and compassion. We must stop "amputating ourselves from the bigger picture," Jay shares, "there is no way in which we can actually save that which we don't think is a part of us. The reason I do what I do is because I think of the world as an extension of who I am." Selfishness, she states, might be a "survival instinct," but we must expand our self-interests to the larger collective level: if we are to survive, we must "make ourselves large enough" to see the world as extensions of who we are.

Technology, Jay explains, creates dichotomies in our efforts toward compassion and coexistence. "I have a huge online tribe that has been of tremendous support to me . . . it's absolutely lovely how people can support you from across the world . . . there's something beautiful there." But, Jay's childhood, growing up without a computer, taking the time to handwrite letters, spending so much time in nature, causes her to reflect: "Now, people are always connected, we take it for granted, the connections don't matter anymore. My mum told me when I was really young, 'if you can do any activity more than once and have the same passion and enthusiasm for it, then do it. But if not, just stop.'" The repetition of this constant connection, she explains, "makes us lose the value of it, we're no longer truly engaged."

When Jay begins work on a new project, she does extensive research. She begins with newspapers and books, "you need to know how the world is in terms of politics and socioeconomics and the like." Then, she continues to research and read about the "particular ecosystem I am focusing on, the particular culture, popular culture references, and—just looking: I go for walks in the cities, to museum exhibits and galleries." Jay looks for shapes, colors, textures, parallels, and "references that could create interesting juxtapositions between what the lay person is comfortable with in their visual vocabulary and then what they need to know." Jay shares, that although she creates a visual story and even "restructures a problem," she does not give her audience the conclusion. She explains, "when they work out the argument behind my compositions, they have figured it out the way I figured it out—that's the moment of epiphany" (Jay, 2015; National Geographic Society, 2014).

WHAT DO YOU THINK?

1. Jay hopes that her work will inspire people make an impact (channel our inner mosquitoes) in this world. Do you think that art can be a source of such inspiration? Why or why not?

2. When Jay begins a project, she does extensive research in a range of places and from a variety of sources. Could you use some of her places and sources as possible sites for your own research on your next speech? Why or why not?

3. Jay suggests that when we separate ourselves and our thinking from others, we are failing to see that we all are connected and a part of the same planet. Do you agree with Jay? Why or why not?

sometimes called *lay testimony*. You also can *use your own testimony to convey your point*. This is called **personal testimony**. To use each type of testimony ethically, always give credit to the person you are quoting or paraphrasing, including his or her name and credentials.

Definitions

A **definition** is a *statement of the exact meaning of a word or phrase*. Definitions can make terms, whether simple or complex, clear and meaningful for your audiences. Every word has both a denotative and a connotative definition. Recall from Chapter 4 that the **denotative definition** is the *objective meaning you find in a dictionary*, the definition of a word on which most everyone can agree. In contrast, a **connotative definition** is the *subjective meaning of a word or a phrase based on personal experiences and beliefs*. Be aware that providing the dictionary definition of a word may not always be enough to get your point across—definitions come from personal experiences as well as from the dictionary.

Understand the Patterns of Reasoning

After you decide on the kinds of evidence to use in your speech, you must put that evidence into a pattern of reasoning. Although scholars have developed more than twenty-five different patterns of reasoning, we limit the discussion here to five of the most useful for beginning public speakers: reasoning by induction, deduction, cause, analogy, and sign (Gleason, 1999; Perelman & Tyteca, 1969; Toulmin, 1950; Toulmin, Rieke, & Januk, 1979; Walton, 1996). These patterns can help you develop logical arguments in all of your speeches. You probably are already familiar with most of these patterns because we use them every day without giving them much thought. What makes them unique in public speaking is that speakers consciously employ the patterns to arrange their evidence and develop the logic of their main points and subpoints.

Inductive Reasoning

Inductive reasoning is *a process of reasoning that uses specific instances, or examples, to make a claim about a general conclusion* (Faigley & Selzer, 2000; Kahane & Cavender, 1998; Toulmin, 1969). When we observe patterns or trends and then make a claim about something we expect to happen based on them, we are reasoning inductively. Inductive reasoning looks like this:

- James is an excellent basketball player.
- His brother Jeff is an excellent swimmer.
- Their sister Julia is the star of the track team.
- Therefore, Jenny, the youngest member of the family, will be a fine athlete, too.

Inductive reasoning, sometimes called *argument by example*, is best used when you can identify patterns in evidence that indicate something

personal testimony
one's own testimony used to convey a point.

definition
statement of the exact meaning of a word or phrase.

denotative definition
objective meaning of a word found in a dictionary.

connotative definition
subjective meaning of a word or a phrase based on personal experiences and beliefs.

inductive reasoning
a process of reasoning that uses specific instances, or examples, to make a claim about a general conclusion.

is expected to happen again or should hold true based on previous experience (Vancil, 1993; Zarefsky, 2002). Look at how inductive reasoning is used in the following speech. Ruby states her claim first and then provides specific instances:

> The amount of privacy we are allowed to keep is under siege every day [*claim*]. Beverly Dennis, an Ohio grandmother, completed a questionnaire to get free product samples. Instead, she got a sexually graphic and threatening letter from a convict in Texas who was assigned the task of entering product data into computers for the company [*specific instance*]. Similarly, the dean of the Harvard Divinity School was forced to resign after downloading pornography to his home computer. He asked a Harvard technician to install more memory to his computer at home, and in the process of transferring files, the technician discovered, and reported, the pornography [*specific instance*].

When you reason from specific instances, you can state your claim (general observation) first and then offer your supporting instances, or you can present the instances first and then make your claim.

Expressed as a formula, an inductive argument looks like this:

Specific instance A	or	Claim you want to establish
Specific instance B		Specific instance A
Specific instance C		Specific instance B
Specific instance D		Specific instance C
Claim based on the specific instances		Specific instance D

Guidelines for Inductive Reasoning   There are three guidelines for reasoning from specific instances:

1.   Make sure you have enough examples to make your claim.

2.   Make sure your generalizations are accurate.

3.   Support your inductive arguments with statistics or testimony.

Ethical Inductive Reasoning

There are three ways to be sure your reasoning is ethical. First, avoid **anomalies**, which are *exceptions to a rule and unique instances that do not represent the norm*. When a speaker relies on anomalies or uses too few examples to make a claim, she or he may be guilty of making a **hasty generalization** or *reaching a conclusion without enough evidence to support it*. To support your claim, find more than three instances before you make any inferences about larger patterns. However, your audience probably needs no more than four specific instances, even if you have identified many more.

Second, make sure your generalizations are accurate. Although it can be tempting to make a claim about something you see happening in one place, be careful not to overgeneralize. For example, if more and more people in your community are "going green," it is tempting to label this a "national trend." However, you cannot extend that prediction to other

anomalies
exceptions to a rule and unique instances that do not represent the norm.

hasty generalization
reaching a conclusion without enough evidence to support it.

parts of the country unless you have specific examples to support your claim. Do not be too hasty in extending examples from one area or group to another unless your data support that claim.

Third, support your inductive arguments with statistics or testimony. For example, if you want to explain that organic farms produce competitively priced, high-quality crops, then offer examples of two or three farms that do. Then strengthen your inductive process with statistics showing that organic farmers are successfully competing with nonorganic farms at a county, state, or national level. You also could support your examples with testimony from the head of the U.S. Department of Agriculture, validating the profitability of organic farming. Statistics and testimony help your audience better understand the validity of the larger trend you are describing.

Deductive Reasoning

When speakers reason from general principles to specific instances (the opposite of inductive reasoning), they reason deductively. **Deductive reasoning** is *a process of reasoning that uses a familiar and commonly accepted claim to establish the truth of a highly specific claim.* Deductive reasoning looks like this:

- All college students need to take an oral communication course.
- Jody is a college student.
- Jody needs to take an oral communication course.

The first statement, "All college students need to take an oral communication course," is called the **major premise** or the *general principle that states a familiar, commonly accepted belief.* The combination of the major premise with the second statement, "Jody is a college student," is called the **minor premise**, the *specific instance that helps establish the truth of the third statement,* "Jody needs to take an oral communication course," which is called the **conclusion**, or *the claim you are attempting to prove as true.*

Expressed as a formula, a deductive argument looks as follows:

- major premise, or general principle;
- minor premise, or specific instance of the general principle; and
- conclusion based on the combination of the major and minor premises.

Guidelines for Deductive Reasoning Reasoning from general principles to specific instances is an effective way to build a case for your claims. When your general principle is firmly established or commonly accepted, your reasoning should unfold smoothly. For example, some general principles that are clearly established and commonly accepted are that asbestos causes lung cancer, drunk driving is dangerous, and elected officials should act with integrity.

Sometimes, audiences will not accept your general principle. When they do not, you will need to strengthen it with additional evidence or

deductive reasoning
a process of reasoning that uses a familiar and commonly accepted claim to establish the truth of a highly specific claim.

major premise
the general principle that states a familiar and commonly accepted belief.

minor premise
specific instance that helps establish the truth of the conclusion.

conclusion
the claim you are attempting to prove as true.

reasoning. This process is called *establishing the validity of the major premise*. We often enter the public dialogue precisely *because* we want to establish the truth of a general principle. Consider how one famous speaker, Susan B. Anthony, worked from a controversial general principle. In the 1870s, Anthony spoke in favor of women's right to vote. She built her reasoning for women's right to vote on the premise that the U.S. Constitution guarantees all citizens the right to vote. Her full line of reasoning looked as follows:

Major premise:	The U.S. Constitution guarantees every citizen the right to vote.
Minor premise:	Women are U.S. citizens.
Conclusion:	The U.S. Constitution guarantees women the right to vote.

Although this deductive argument makes sense to us today, Anthony's major and minor premises were disputed more than 140 years ago. Not everyone agreed that the Constitution guaranteed all citizens the right to vote, and not all agreed about who was a citizen. Anthony and many other suffragists devoted much of their speeches to trying to convince their audiences of their major and minor premises. Despite their well-reasoned efforts, women did not get the right to vote in the United States until 1920 (Campbell, 1989; Fitch & Mandzuick, 1997).

Causal Reasoning

Causal reasoning is *a process of reasoning that supports a claim by establishing a cause-and-effect relationship*. Causal reasoning identifies an "if–then" relationship that suggests "if" one factor is present, "then" another is sure to follow (Faigley & Selzer, 2000; Inch & Warnick, 1998; Kahane & Cavender, 1998; Toulmin, 1969). Consider the following claims:

- If I don't study, then I'll do poorly on my exam.
- If I use recreational drugs, then I'll eventually turn to more addictive ones.
- If I study self-defense, then I'm less likely to be hurt if someone attacks me.

These statements are examples of causal relationships. Each establishes a cause-and-effect relationship: lack of preparation (the cause) results in poor grades (the effect); use of recreational drugs (the cause) leads to the use of addictive ones (the effect); and learning self-defense (the cause) lessens the risk of harm in the event of an attack (the effect).

Speakers often use causal reasoning to develop their ideas with great success. In the following example, Kameron uses causal reasoning to develop his argument that zebra mussels, a native species in the Caspian Sea in Europe but not in the waters of the United States, are seriously damaging the aquatic environment:

> Zebra mussels cause damage to every aspect of any aquatic ecosystem they encounter. They destroy the natural balance of the ecosystem by filtering the food from water at an insane rate of one

causal reasoning
a process of reasoning that supports a claim by establishing a cause-and-effect relationship.

liter of water each day. Not much you think? Well, these mollusks can live in colonies of up to 70,000 mussels. That's 70,000 liters of water cleared of all food each day. This means the zebra mussels consume all the food usually eaten by animals lower in the food chain. The result is catastrophic repercussions on down the line. For example, a body of water whose food is filtered away cannot support any kind of life. The larger fish then have nothing to eat, resulting in fewer fish for anglers.

Kameron's causal reasoning allows him to argue compellingly that zebra mussels (the cause) lead to aquatic devastation (the effect).

Guidelines for Causal Reasoning Causal reasoning is an effective form of reasoning because it allows you to link two events together. Causal relationships are sometimes difficult to prove, however, so consider the following three guidelines.

First, avoid false causes. A **false cause** is *an error in reasoning in which a speaker assumes that one event caused another simply because the first event happened before the second.* It can be easy to assume a false cause. You pick up your "lucky" pen from your desk and five minutes later you get a creative brainstorm for the project you are working on. Did the lucky pen cause the creative brainstorm? Perhaps, but it is hard to tell. Although it is tempting to assume direct causes when one event happens shortly after another, the two events may not be directly related. When one event happens immediately after another, there may be a link, but to stay ethical you would have to investigate further to be sure.

Second, avoid assuming that an event has only one cause. Events often have many causes, especially those that become topics in the public dialogue. For example, it is unrealistic to try to pin the cause of teen suicide on one factor. It is far more appropriate to address the multiple factors that contribute to teen suicide: the home and school environment, social pressures, individual personality traits, and the teen's support system and friendships.

Third, strengthen your cause-and-effect relationships by citing strong supporting evidence. For example, in his informative speech about zebra mussels, Kameron identified a strong connection between the overpopulation of zebra mussels and the damage done to boats, buoys, docks, and anchors. He supported his connection by providing testimony from local fishers who had seen buoys sink from the weight of too many mussels.

Analogical Reasoning

When we compare two similar things and suggest that what is true for the first will be true for the second, we are reasoning analogically. In an article on different approaches to assisting people who are homeless, the *Economist* uses an analogy involving a staircase and a hospital:

The standard way to help them has long been the "staircase" approach: requiring them to quit drink and drugs before shepherding them through emergency shelters and temporary lodging. . . . [but in] what has come to be know as "housing first". . . .

false cause

an error in reasoning in which a speaker assumes that one event caused another simply because the first event happened before the second.

Homeless people are triaged much like arrivals at a hospital emergency room: those deemed most at risk of dying on the street go to the top of the queue [for homes]. ("Rough Sleeping," 2014)

Analogical reasoning, or *reasoning by way of comparison and similarity*, implies that because two things resemble each other in one respect, they share similarities in another respect. So when *Economist* writers compare the "triage" approach to the "staircase" approach, they argue that "triage" and giving homeless individuals houses first, rather than requiring these individuals to climb "staircases" and get clean and sober before they receive homes, not only saves lives by treating the worst conditions first but also saves communities money.

Although they can be detailed, as in the previous example, analogies also can be simple. For example, when speaking to her audience about the importance of more than direct care, physician Deborah Prothrow-Stith used this simple and effective analogy: "We were just stitching them up and sending them back out on the streets, back to the domestic equivalent of a war zone" (Rogat Loeb, 1999).

Guidelines for Analogical Reasoning To increase the effectiveness of analogical reasoning, be sure the items or ideas you are comparing are truly alike. When you compare two things that do not share characteristics, your analogy is invalid and will seem illogical to your audience. Most of us have heard invalid analogies and thought to ourselves, "That's like comparing apples to oranges." For example, it is invalid to suggest that proposed nonsmoking ordinances will succeed in Kentucky, Tennessee, and North Carolina because they succeeded in California, Oregon, and Washington. This analogy is invalid because the public attitudes toward smoking in the three tobacco-growing southern states are different from those in the three western states whose economies do not depend on tobacco. If you make an analogy between two things, they must share true similarities for the analogy to be valid.

Reasoning by Sign

A **sign** is *something that represents something else*. It is one of the most common forms of reasoning we use in our daily lives: Dark clouds are a sign of a storm rolling in; a decrease in the number of applications for a certain academic program is a sign of declining interest; the bailiff's command "All rise" is a sign that the judge is about to enter the courtroom. Signs have an important function in the reasoning process because they prompt us to infer what is *likely* to be. They help speakers establish relationships and draw conclusions for their audiences based on those relationships.

Reasoning by sign *assumes something exists or will happen based on something else that exists or has happened*. Signs, like causal relationships, can have strong or weak relationships. Reasoning by sign is strengthened when you can point to the repetition of one example to build a case. For example, when the Richter scale registers above a certain level for an undersea earthquake, it is a sign that a tsunami can occur. Scientists have

analogical reasoning
reasoning by way of comparison and similarity.

sign
something that represents something else.

reasoning by sign
assumption that something exists or will happen based on something else that exists or has happened.

accurately predicted all five of the significant ocean-spanning tsunamis since 1950. But they also predicted fifteen that turned out to be false alarms, so note that few signs are infallible, and most are open to question (Alder & Carmichael, 2005).

Guidelines for Reasoning by Sign Because signs are fallible, consider three guidelines for using them:

- Think about whether an alternative explanation is more credible.
- Make sure a sign is not just an isolated instance.
- If you can find instances in which a sign does not indicate a particular event, you do not have a solid argument.

First, is an alternative explanation more credible? In a speech on the standards for licensing teachers, Seogwan suggested that the low test scores in the nation's public schools were a sign of poorly trained teachers. He reasoned that low scores represented, or signaled, poor teaching. However, when his audience questioned him, they raised several equally credible explanations. Could the lower scores be a sign of outdated or biased tests? Of overcrowded classrooms? Of the need to restructure our classrooms? Of poor testing skills? Each explanation is as likely as the one Seogwan offered, and much evidence supports each one. As a result, his audience thought Seogwan's reasoning was flawed. To avoid this pitfall, be sure that when you claim one thing is a sign of another, an alternative explanation is not equally valid or better.

Second, if you reason by sign, make sure the sign is not just an isolated instance. Speaking against the new no smoking ordinance in his town, Mark argued that all of his friends, even nonsmokers, had no problems with designated areas for smokers in public places. This, he claimed, was a sign that most people do not think a no-smoking ordinance is necessary. He ignored the many local and nationwide campaigns that favor establishing no-smoking ordinances in public places. He mistakenly assumed that one instance (his friends' support of smokers in public places) represented a larger pattern.

Third, if you reason by sign, you are suggesting the sign almost always indicates a particular event. If you can find instances in which the sign does not indicate that event, then you do not have a solid argument. In his speech on our ability to predict natural disasters, Tim offered the evidence that not every undersea earthquake of a certain magnitude results in a

Consider the reasoning you plan to use in your speech. If you share that reasoning with your friends or classmates, do you think they will find it credible? Why or why not?

Rich Legg/Vetta/Getty Images

tsunami, nor does every hurricane result in massive damage. Thus, he argued, blaming scientists for not notifying authorities before such natural disasters occur is unreasonable. However, Tim argued, the occurrence of the Sri Lanka tsunami and Hurricane Katrina and the tragedies left in their wake are signs that warning systems, regardless of their overprediction rates, are imperative.

Understand Emotion and Reasoning

Now that you have learned about the five most common patterns of reasoning used in speeches, we will consider appeals to emotion and how they can affect your reasoning. The use of emotional appeals can be one of the most challenging aspects of public speaking. On one hand, research suggests that effective speakers appeal to emotions because they encourage the audience to relate to an issue on an internal personal level. On the other hand, because emotions are so personal and powerful, research also suggests that an inappropriate appeal to emotions can cause an audience to shut down in an instant (Perloff, 1993; Stiff, 1994). Appeals to emotions can be complicated, so it is useful to understand what emotions are and which emotions people most commonly experience.

Emotions are *internal mental states that focus primarily on feelings* (Stiff, 1994). Communication research has identified six primary emotions that tend to be expressed similarly across cultures and four secondary emotions that are expressed differently depending on age, gender, and culture (Perloff, 1993). The primary emotions are

- *fear*, or an unpleasant feeling of apprehension or distress, the anticipation of danger or threat;
- *anger*, or a feeling of annoyance, irritation, or rage;
- *surprise*, or a feeling of sudden wonder or amazement, especially because of something unexpected;
- *sadness*, or a feeling of unhappiness, grief, or sorrow;
- *disgust*, or a feeling of horrified or sickened distaste for something; and
- *happiness*, or a feeling of pleasure, contentment, or joy.

The secondary emotions are

- *pride*, or an appropriate level of respect for a person, character trait, accomplishment, experience, or value; feeling pleased or delighted;
- *guilt*, or an awareness of having done wrong accompanied by feelings of shame and regret;
- *shame*, or a feeling of dishonor, unworthiness, and embarrassment; and
- *reverence*, or a feeling of deep respect, awe, or devotion.

In public speaking, you appeal to emotions to accomplish the following goals: gain attention and motivate listening, reinforce points, express personal commitment, and call people to action or conclude memorably.

emotions
internal mental states that focus primarily on feelings.

Gaining Attention and Motivating Listening You often catch an audience's attention and motivate listening by appealing to audience members' emotions with a compelling short story, testimony, or examples.

Reinforcing Points You can use emotional appeals to reinforce main points or subpoints. For example, when you support a point with a statistic and then reinforce the statistic with an example of how some aspect of the statistic has affected a specific person, an audience can understand your point on a more personal level.

Expressing Personal Commitment When you care deeply about an issue and want your audiences to recognize this depth of commitment, you may appeal to emotions by shifting your delivery to a more passionate or intense tone, or you may personalize your claims and arguments.

Calling to Action or Concluding Memorably You can often move an audience to action by asking members to envision the result of that action and how it could affect them personally. You might end your speech with a compelling story or quote and so conclude memorably.

Because emotional appeals engage an audience personally, you will want to consider three things to help you use them effectively: balancing emotion with reason, staying audience centered, and using vivid language carefully.

Balancing Emotion and Reason Overly emotional speeches may stimulate your audience, but without sound reasoning they are less likely to be effective. Balance emotional appeals with sound reasoning and your audience will see more than one dimension of your ideas and arguments.

Staying Audience Centered Consider your audience carefully before you decide what kinds of emotional appeals to use. Before incorporating any emotional appeal, ask yourself the following questions:

- *Is my appeal to emotion overly graphic or violent?* When a speaker's use of emotion provides extensive details about the horrors of a situation or injuries to a person, the audience may shut down or feel overwhelming revulsion.

- *Is my appeal to emotion overly frightening or threatening?* When a speaker describes something so frightening or threatening that the audience feels helpless or panicked, members may stop listening or feel immobilized.

- *Is my appeal to emotion overly manipulative?* When a speaker relies on theatrics, melodrama, and sensation rather than on fact and research, the audience can feel manipulated or reject the message or argument.

PRACTICING HUMAN COMMUNICATION
Test the Reasoning of Your Arguments

Bring one of your main arguments to your speech to class. Present this argument and determine which pattern of reasoning will help you develop this argument most fully (inductive, deductive, causal, analogical, or by sign). After each person has presented her or his argument and selected a pattern of reasoning to support it, discuss the strengths and weaknesses of each person's approach.

Using Vivid Language Vivid language helps audience members recall some of their most profound experiences and create images that are rich with feeling. Use vivid descriptions and examples that are not overly graphic or manipulative to help your audience members connect with those experiences.

Be Aware of Fallacies in Reasoning

Whether intentional or not, speakers sometimes make inaccurate arguments called *fallacies*. A **fallacy** is *an argument that seems valid but is flawed because of unsound evidence or reasoning*. Fallacies are a problem in speeches not only because they undermine speakers' arguments but also because, despite their factual or logical errors, they can be quite persuasive. Fallacies can seem reasonable and acceptable on the surface, but when we analyze them, we see that their logic is flawed. Although there are more than 125 different fallacies, we discuss the most common types for beginning public speakers: ad hominem, bandwagon, either–or, red herring, slippery slope, false cause, and hasty generalization (Kahane & Cavender, 1998; Van Eemeren & Gootendorst, 1992).

Ad Hominem: Against the Person

Ad hominem is a Latin term that means "against the person." One of the most familiar fallacies, the **ad hominem fallacy** is *an argument in which a speaker attacks a person rather than that person's arguments*. By portraying someone with an opposing position as incompetent, unreliable, stupid, or even evil, you effectively silence that person and discredit her or his arguments or ideas. Here are two examples of an ad hominem fallacy:

1. Certainly, Obama worked hard to pass the health-care bill. He's a liberal Democrat who only wants to make our country socialist.

2. Of course the commissioner would argue for cuts in social services. She's been an insensitive, money-grubbing Republican all her life.

Ad hominem fallacies turn the audience's attention away from the content of an argument and toward the character and credibility of the person who is offering that argument. This fallacy clouds an issue, making it hard for an audience to evaluate the ideas the speaker challenges.

Bandwagon: Everyone Else Agrees

When you fall prey to the **bandwagon fallacy**, you are *suggesting that something is correct or good because everyone else agrees with it or is doing it*. In public speaking, this translates to making statements like these:

- Many other communities are adopting this nonsmoking ordinance in restaurants. It is a perfect solution for us as well.

- Of course, this neighborhood should institute a pay-for-parking policy for its residents. Many of the surrounding neighborhoods have, so why should this one be exempt?

fallacy
an argument that seems valid but is flawed because of unsound evidence or reasoning.

ad hominem fallacy
an argument in which a speaker attacks a person rather than challenge that person's arguments.

bandwagon fallacy
a suggestion that something is correct or good because everyone else agrees with it or is doing it.

The bandwagon fallacy works a little like group pressure: It is hard to say no to something everyone else is doing. But the logic of the bandwagon is flawed for two reasons. First, even though a solution or a plan might work well for some, it might not be the best solution for your audience. You need to do more than argue "it will work for you because it worked for others." You need to explain exactly why a plan might work for a particular group of people, community, or organization. Second, just because "lots of others agree" does not make something "good." Large groups of people agree about many things, but those things are not necessarily appropriate for everyone. When you hear the bandwagon fallacy, ask yourself two questions: If it is good for them, is it good for *me* or *us*? Even if many others are doing something, is it something I or we support?

Either–Or: A False Dilemma

A dilemma is a situation that requires a choice from options that are equally unpleasant or mutually exclusive. When we face a dilemma, we feel we must make a choice even if it is not to our liking. In persuasive speeches, an **either–or fallacy**, sometimes called a "false dilemma," is *an argument in which a speaker claims our options are "either A or B," when actually more than two options exist*. To identify a false dilemma, listen for the words *either* and *or* as a speaker presents an argument. Consider these two examples:

> Either we increase access to our before- and after-school meal programs or our students will continue to fail.

> Either we increase our candidate's appeal to women or we don't get elected.

In both examples, the audience is presented with a false dilemma. Intuitively, we know there must be other options. In the first example, there are other ways to respond to poor student performance—better nutrition is only one part of the solution. In the second, there likely are other ways to increase a candidate's appeal and chances of success. Sometimes, it is hard to see the other options immediately, but they are usually there.

Either–or arguments are fallacious because they oversimplify complex issues. Usually, the speaker has created an atmosphere in which the audience feels pressured to select one of the two options presented. Even if those options may be good choices, an either–or argument prevents us from considering others that may be even better.

Red Herring: Raising an Irrelevant Issue

The term *red herring* comes from the fox-hunting tradition in England. Before a hunt began, farmers often dragged a smoked herring around the perimeter of their fields. The strong odor from the fish masked the scent of the fox and threw the hounds off its trail, keeping the hounds from trampling the farmers' crops. Although this worked well for the farmers, trailing the equivalent of a red herring around an argument is not such a good idea. When we make use of the **red herring fallacy**, we *introduce*

either–or fallacy (false dilemma)
an argument in which a speaker claims our options are "either A or B," when actually more than two options exist.

red herring fallacy
irrelevant information inserted into an argument to distract an audience from the real issue.

irrelevant information into an argument to distract an audience from the real issue. The following example illustrates the red herring fallacy:

> How can we worry about the few cases of AIDS in our town of only 50,000 when thousands and thousands of children are dying of AIDS and AIDS-related illnesses in other countries?

In this example, the speaker turns the argument away from her own community and toward the international problem of AIDS. The audience then becomes more concerned about AIDS in other countries. Undoubtedly, this is an important issue, but it is not the one under discussion, which is equally important. Because of the red herring, the audience is less inclined to move toward a solution for the local situation. This type of fallacy can be hard to spot because both issues usually are important, but the audience feels pulled toward the most recently raised issue. As an audience member, listen carefully when a speaker introduces a new and important topic in a persuasive speech; you might be hearing a red herring fallacy.

Slippery Slope: The Second Step Is Inevitable

A **slippery slope fallacy** is *an argument in which a speaker claims that taking a first step in one direction will inevitably lead to undesirable further steps.* Like a skier speeding down a hill without being able to stop, a slippery slope fallacy suggests the momentum of one decision or action will cause others to follow. Here is an example of a slippery slope fallacy:

> If we allow our children to dress in any way they want at school, they soon will be wearing more and more outrageous clothing. They'll start trying to outdress one another. Then it'll be increasingly outrageous behaviors inside and outside the classrooms. Soon they'll turn to violence as they try to top one another.

The speaker is making a slippery slope argument by suggesting that if one unwanted thing happens, others are certain to follow. The audience gets caught up in the momentum of this "snowball" argument. Slippery slope arguments can be persuasive because the speaker relates the first claim (for example, the dress codes) to a larger issue (violence) when the two may not even be linked. Before you accept the full claim made with a slippery slope argument, stop and consider whether the chain of events really is inevitable.

False Cause: Mistaking a Chronological Relationship

A **false cause fallacy** is *an argument mistaking a chronological relationship with a causal relationship.* There are two types of false cause fallacies. The first type occurs when a speaker assumes that one event *caused* the second to occur. Notice how the speaker in the following example mistakenly assumes that the first event caused the second:

> After the state passed legislation in favor of the death penalty, violent crimes decreased. The new legislation has deterred criminal activity.

slippery slope fallacy
an argument in which a speaker claims that taking a first step in one direction will inevitably lead to undesirable further steps.

false cause fallacy
an argument mistaking a chronological relationship with a causal relationship.

Criminal activity may have declined after the state implemented a new pro–death penalty policy; however, it does not prove that the legislation caused the decline. Other factors may have influenced the decline such as methods of reporting violent crimes, rehabilitation programs in prisons, and even educational opportunities for individuals at risk to commit violent crimes.

The second type of false cause fallacy is known as a **single cause fallacy**. This occurs *when speakers assume a particular effect only has one cause.* Many public problems are complex, resulting from multiple causes. Speakers want to avoid oversimplifying an effect to a single cause. Notice how the following example blames only one cause for childhood obesity:

> The number of obese children in the United States has significantly increased over the past decade. According to pediatric experts, approximately 30 percent of children under the age of thirteen are obese. This is because of the unhealthy school lunches being served in schools across the nation. We need legislation mandating more nutritious lunches in order to solve the obesity epidemic.

This example assumes that there is only one cause to the problem of childhood obesity—unhealthy school lunches. In fact, there are a number of reasons American children are obese: fast food, junk food, and trans fats consumed outside of school; lack of physical exercise inside and outside of school; and possibly genetic factors. Assuming only one cause exists for a complex problem is committing a false cause fallacy.

Hasty Generalization: Too Few Examples

A **hasty generalization fallacy** is *an argument based on too few cases or examples to support a conclusion.* When speakers rely only on personal experiences to draw conclusions, for example, they may fall into the trap of a hasty generalization because personal experiences are rarely enough to prove a claim true. Notice how the following student relies only on her personal experience to support a larger claim:

> The school of business and finance is the hardest program to be accepted into at our university. I have applied three times and still have not been admitted.

This student uses her personal experience of being rejected multiple times to support her argument on the overall difficulty of getting into the school of business and finance. Although this student may have been denied admission into the program, this does not prove that the program is the toughest one to enter for all students.

As you listen to speeches, and as you put your own arguments together, keep in mind that a fallacy is an error in logic. When we reason, we want to be sure our logic is sound and not based on error or deception.

Tips for Reasoning Ethically

Evidence, reasoning, logic, and arguments are powerful tools in the public dialogue. With them, we can share information, express our perspective, and invite dialogue on an issue. However, we also can

single cause fallacy
when speakers assume a particular effect only has one cause.

hasty generalization fallacy
an argument based on too few cases or examples to support a conclusion.

manipulate, confuse, and misrepresent with our reasoning. To ensure you reason ethically and effectively, follow these two tips: use accurate evidence and verify the structure of your reasoning.

Using Accurate Evidence As a speaker, you are ethically obligated to use accurate evidence in all of your reasoning. Although you may be able to present a fully developed argument based on fabricated evidence, that would be deceiving your audience and counterproductive to the public dialogue. To avoid this, use only evidence you are sure is from accurate and reliable sources.

Verifying the Structure of Your Reasoning When you give a speech, watch out for any fallacies that creep into your arguments and reasoning. Take time to assess each claim you make and be sure it is based on strong and credible inductive and deductive reasoning. When you spot a fallacy, take time to figure out what kind you are using and replace that fallacy with a sound example, bit of evidence, or statistic.

Chapter Summary

Gathering a Range of Materials for Your Speech Will Help You Enter the Public Dialogue Responsibly and Ethically and Deliver an Effective Speech

- Gather information from personal experiences and knowledge, the Internet, the library, and research interviews.
- Evaluate the strength of the materials you find on the Internet or in the library. Is the information reliable? authoritative? current? consistent and unbiased?

When You Conduct a Research Interview, Determine Whom to Interview, Design the Interview Questions Using Open- or Closed-Ended Questions and Probes, and Schedule and Conduct the Interview

The Material You Gather From Your Research Becomes the Evidence You Use to Develop and Support Your Ideas

- The five most common types of evidence are examples, narratives, statistics, testimony, and definitions.
- Examples can be real or hypothetical. Narratives can by brief or extended.
- Statistics can present the mean, median, and mode. Testimony consists of direct quotations or paraphrasing, as well as expert, peer, and personal testimony.
- Definitions can be either denotative or connotative.

Put the Evidence Into One of the Five Most Common Patterns of Reasoning: Induction, Deduction, Cause, Analogy, and Sign

- Inductive reasoning uses specific examples to make a claim about a general conclusion.
- To ensure your reasoning is ethical, avoid anomalies and hasty generalizations; make sure your generalizations are accurate; support your inductive arguments with statistics or testimony.
- Deductive reasoning includes the major premise (the general principle), a minor premise (the specific instance that helps establish the truth of the third statement), and a conclusion (the claim you are attempting to prove as true).
- Causal reasoning supports a claim by establishing a cause-and-effect relationship. Avoid false causes, avoid assuming an event has only one cause, and strengthen your causal reasoning by offering supporting evidence.
- Analogical reasoning compares two similar things and suggests that what is true for the first will be true for the second. To increase the effectiveness of analogical reasoning, be sure what you are comparing is truly alike.
- Reasoning by sign assumes something exists or will happen based on something else that exists or has happened. Because signs are fallible, consider whether an alternative explanation is more credible. Make sure

a sign is not just an isolated instance; if a sign does not indicate a particular event, then you do not have a solid argument.

- In public speaking, emotional appeals accomplish the following goals: gain attention and motivate listening, reinforce points, express personal commitment, and make a call to action or conclude memorably. When you use appeals to emotion, be sure to balance emotion with reason, stay audience centered, and use vivid but appropriate language.

Common Types of Fallacies for Beginning Public Speakers Are Ad Hominem, Bandwagon, Either–Or, Red Herring, Slippery Slope, False Cause, and Hasty Generalization

- Keep in mind that a fallacy is an error in logic. When we reason, we want to be sure our logic is sound and not based on error or deception.
- To be certain you are reasoning ethically, make sure your evidence is accurate and your reasoning does not rely on a fallacy of any sort.

Key Concepts

ad hominem fallacy (275)

analogical reasoning (271)

anomalies (267)

bandwagon fallacy (275)

causal reasoning (269)

conclusion (268)

connotative definition (266)

deductive reasoning (268)

definition (266)

denotative definition (266)

direct quotation (264)

either–or fallacy (false dilemma) (276)

emotions (273)

evidence (260)

examples (260)

expert testimony (264)

fallacy (275)

false cause fallacy (277)

false cause (270)

hasty generalization (267)

hasty generalization fallacy (278)

hypothetical example (260)

inductive reasoning (266)

interview (255)

major premise (268)

mean (263)

median (264)

minor premise (268)

mode (264)

narrative (261)

paraphrase (264)

peer testimony (lay testimony) (264)

personal testimony (266)

real example (260)

reasoning by sign (271)

red herring fallacy (276)

sign (271)

single cause fallacy (278)

slippery slope fallacy (277)

statistics (262)

testimony (264)

Invitation to Human Communication Online

MindTap Speech includes an interactive MindTap Reader and interactive learning tools including National Geographic Explorer videos, student videos, quizzes, flash cards, and more. You can build your speech outline with Outline Builder and record, post, and watch videos with YouSeeU. Go to cengagebrain.com to access your MindTap for *Invitation to Human Communication* where these resources can be found.

MindTap®

Further Reflection and Discussion

1. Bring the statistics you have gathered for your next speech to class. In groups, discuss what kind they are (mean, median, or mode, for example) and how you might work them into your speech so that you present them clearly and ethically. Discuss what each statistic illustrates and how to avoid misrepresenting your claims.

2. Bring a newspaper or news magazine to class. In groups, identify as many different types of reasoning as you can find in the text, photographs, and advertisements. Label each item as inductive reasoning, deductive reasoning, causal reasoning, analogical reasoning, or reasoning by sign and evaluate the strength of each type of reasoning according to the guidelines discussed in this chapter.

3. Using the same newspaper or magazine in question 2, find as many fallacies as you can. Label each fallacy you find. Now that you recognize these fallacies, evaluate the strength of the argument being advanced.

4. Log on to a shock jock's or other extreme personality's Web site, blog, or other posting. Review the arguments the person is making. Make a list of the different types of reasoning being used as well as any fallacies the person is advancing. Assess the strength of his or her arguments.

5. What sources do these newspapers, magazines, or media personalities use to support their ideas? Are their sources credible, ethical, and civil? Assess the strength of the arguments made and give the sources used.

6. Consider the examples and narratives you have found in your research and want to use in your speech. Are they real or hypothetical? Brief or extended? What do they contribute to your main points? Practice delivering one of the examples and one of the narratives aloud. Are your comfortable with your delivery?

7. Evaluate the strengths and weaknesses of the information you have gathered for your speech. Is it reliable, authoritative, current, complete, relevant, and consistent? Based on your assessment, identify information you might discard and consider whether you need to do more research for your speech.

8. Draft a list of questions you would like to ask a personal contact for your next speech. Keep in mind your speech goals, time limitations, and audience. Now organize that list so the most important questions are first and the least important are last. Next consider how you will begin your interview. Will you start with your most important questions or some warm-up questions? What questions will you use to close the interview?

9. Consider the sources that you gathered your research from. Did you use a wide range of materials? Did you consider the credibility of those sources? Did you evaluate the ethical nature of the sources and the information you plan to use in your speech? Are there any changes you might make to ensure your research is unbiased, appropriate, and ethical?

10. Consider the testimony and direct quotations you want to include in your speech. Read them aloud and consider whether your audience will be able to follow you and understand the ideas. Are they too complex and lengthy? Do you think paraphrasing might be clearer? Practice using the direct quotation and exact testimony as compared to paraphrasing. Which do you think is more audience centered?

Activities and Web Links

Visit cengagebrain.com to access the MindTap for *Invitation to Human Communication* where these activities and Web links can be found.

1. Visit the following databases and indexes and write brief notes about what type of information and sources you find there that could be helpful in gathering information for your speech: *New York Times* Index, *Wall Street Journal* Index, DataTimes, Academic Search Premier, IngentaConnect. Go to *Web link 11.1*.

12

IN THIS CHAPTER YOU WILL LEARN TO:

- Recognize the four different types of delivery methods for a speech.

- Explain the verbal and nonverbal components of your speech.

- Summarize the benefits of incorporating visual aids in your speech.

- Explain the importance of preparing for potential questions and managing the discussion during question-and-answer sessions.

- Identify ways to address feelings of nervousness that may accompany delivering a speech.

- Review the speeches of others to help you identify strengths and weaknesses in delivery.

Delivering Your Speech

Many celebrities are quite comfortable when they stand in front of an audience. What skills do you think most "every day" people need to deliver effective speeches?

When you deliver your speech, you connect with and share your ideas with an audience. Because of the importance of delivery, this chapter covers the methods of delivery and the verbal and nonverbal components that will help you present your ideas in the most effective way. It covers the most effective ways to incorporate visual aids into your speeches. It also addresses question-and-answer sessions and ways to control the nervousness many of us feel when we give speeches. In the first section, you will learn about four methods of delivery, the verbal and nonverbal components of delivery, using visual aids, and strategies for rehearsing your speech.

Methods of Delivery

The four types of delivery we can use for public speaking are extemporaneous, impromptu, manuscript, and memorized. We now look at each method of delivery and the reasons for using it.

Extemporaneous Delivery

Most of your speeches will be extemporaneous. When you give an **extemporaneous speech**, you present a *carefully prepared and practiced speech from brief notes rather than from memory or a written manuscript.* Because an extemporaneous delivery tends to be more natural than other deliveries, it is one of the more common methods. The advantages of extemporaneous deliveries are many. Your speaking outline or speaking notes prompt your ideas but do not allow you to read every word to your audience. Your eye contact and gestures are natural, and your tone is conversational. Finally, because extemporaneous deliveries encourage direct communication between the speaker and audience, it is easier to stay audience centered.

Delivery Tips Many beginning speakers worry they might forget their speeches if they use an extemporaneous delivery. However, the way to overcome this fear is not to write out every word of your speech but to add more keywords and phrases—not full sentences—to your outline. This you will give more cues to aid your memory. Next, practice your speech often before you give it so you will feel more confident about what you will remember and want to say. Your goal is not necessarily to eliminate your fear by reading your speech but to give yourself tools so you can "talk" your speech. National Geographic Explorer Wade Davis explains, "Public presentations demand a lot of work in advance. Giving my best presentation will never be off-the-cuff; it will just sound off-the-cuff" (Davis, 2014).

The differences between an extemporaneous delivery and a speech read aloud to an audience are striking. An extemporaneous delivery follows a **conversational style**, which is *more formal than everyday*

MindTap®

Go to MindTap to compare the differences between a speech delivered in a conversational style and one that is read. Watch the video of student speakers Shelley Weibel and Eric Daley. Which style of delivery do you think is more effective?

extemporaneous speech
carefully prepared and practiced speech from brief notes rather than from memory or a written manuscript.

conversational style
more formal than everyday conversation but it remains spontaneous and relaxed.

Language and the Music Industry

Cofounded by former head of Def Jam Recordings, Russell Simmons, and Dr. Benjamin Chavis, a civil rights leader, the Hip-Hop Summit Action Network (HSAN) is dedicated to using hip-hop as a catalyst for education and advocacy related to the well-being of at-risk youth. HSAN focuses on issues of community development, access to high-quality public education and literacy, freedom of speech, voter education, economic advancement, and youth leadership development.

Since its beginnings, HSAN has sponsored several civic events such as its Smackdown Your Vote! campaign, which sought to register 2 million additional voters in 2004; its 2008 get-out-the-vote campaign to register "50K in one day" (with the Hip-Hop Caucus); and the 2009 national Hip-Hop Summit on Financial Empowerment titled "Get Your Money Right." HSAN also works with the Recording Industry Association of America in support of the advisory labels that alert parents to explicit content in music. It has defended hip-hop culture before members of the U.S. Congress and such federal regulatory agencies as the Federal Trade Commission and the Federal Communications Commission. HSAN also offers support to the #EricGarner, #ICantBreath, and #BlackLivesMatter social media campaigns.

HSAN seeks to harness the immense popularity of hip-hop to educate others about hip-hop music and culture. "Once an underground, controversial style characterized by gangsta mythology and all-too-real turf wars," says Nelson George, author of *Hip-Hop America*, "rap music is now embraced across the radio dial and across the nation by a diverse, multiracial fan base. . . . Rappers are pop stars, pop stars rap, and the sound is as integral to the cultural landscape as country music or rock." HSAN's goal is to use this mainstream success to encourage the recording industry to establish mentoring programs and forums that will stimulate dialogue between artists, hip-hop fans, and industry leaders and promote understanding and positive change.

Recently, HSAN has been involved in a dialogue with the recording and broadcast industries about forming a coalition to recommend guidelines for lyrical and visual standards. In particular, it recommends that these industries "voluntarily remove/bleep/delete the misogynistic words *bitch* and *ho* and the racially offensive word *nigger*." They maintain that these words are utterly derogatory and show a complete lack of respect for the history of suffering and oppression that women, African Americans, and other people of color have experienced in the United States. They are not advocating censorship. Rather, "we are consistent in our strong affirmation, defense, and protection of the First Amendment right of free speech and artistic expression. . . . Our discussions are about the corporate social responsibility of the industry to voluntarily show respect to [African Americans, other people of color, and to all women]" (Bode, 2007; Gamboa, 2007; "Hip-Hop Setting the Beat," 2003; Simmons & Chavis, 2014; Smiley Group, 2006).

What Do You Think?

1. HSAN is recommending guidelines for the use of images and words in the entertainment industry. Are these efforts civil and ethical? Why or why not?
2. Have recording artists followed these guidelines? Why do you think they have followed them—or ignored them?
3. Will you monitor your language and the images you use in your speeches? How do you think this will affect your audience?

Photo credit: Rodrigo Varela/Getty Images

conversation but remains spontaneous and relaxed. In addition, with a conversational style, your posture and gestures are relaxed, and you make frequent eye contact with your audience (Branham & Pearce, 1996).

Impromptu Delivery

When you give an **impromptu speech**, you present a *speech that you have not planned or prepared in advance.* Although you may be wondering why anyone would do this—especially in light of the previous discussions about the importance of preparation, planning, and practice—impromptu speaking is quite common. It occurs in meetings or public gatherings when someone is asked to speak or feels the need to share her or his perspective. When you decide to speak, you have the advantage of having

impromptu speech
speech that you have not planned or prepared in advance.

a moment or two to organize your ideas. If you suddenly are asked to speak, you may not be able to jot down notes, but you still can organize your ideas. The following tips can help you do this.

Delivery Tips Although you never have much time to prepare an impromptu speech, you can practice impromptu deliveries. In fact, your speech instructor likely will ask you to give several impromptu speeches. When you deliver an impromptu speech, use the following guidelines:

1. Quickly and calmly decide on the main points you want to make.

2. Introduce your main points as you would in a speech you prepared in advance. Offer a preview such as "the three things I'd like to cover are" and use signposts such as "first."

3. Support your main points with subpoints and sub-subpoints.

4. Summarize your main points in a brief conclusion.

If you find yourself in an impromptu situation, stay calm. The skills you learn in your public-speaking course are invaluable for such situations. Even though you may be nervous, you have learned to organize ideas, relate them to the audience, and deliver various types of speeches. Remember, too, that when you give an impromptu speech, your audience does not expect elaborate source citations, fancy visual aids, or creative introductions. Members are looking for immediate clarity or guidance.

If you rely on the fundamental skills you have learned in your public-speaking course, then you can handle impromptu speeches successfully.

American writer and speaker Mark Twain joked, "It usually takes more than three weeks to prepare a good impromptu speech." This is not true, of course, but with a few minutes of thoughtful organization, you can make it seem as if you took three weeks to prepare.

Manuscript Delivery

When you give a **manuscript speech**, you *read to an audience from a written text*. Although most speeches are best delivered extemporaneously, some require a manuscript delivery such as the following occasions:

- when detailed and exact information must be reported carefully, such as to a professional board or a formal committee;

- when your speech will be scrutinized word by word, archived, and referred to later (for example, the president's address to the nation); and

- when your speech text will be used later for some other purpose (for example, a keynote address at a conference, which often is published).

PRACTICING HUMAN COMMUNICATION
Comparing Delivery Methods

In class, take an item out of your backpack or from your pocket. Turn to the person next to you and give an impromptu speech about this item. Now find an example of something written—a paragraph in this textbook, the newspaper, or something online. Give another sixty-second "speech" reading the written material. With your partner, discuss the differences between the delivery styles. Which did you prefer to deliver? Which did you prefer to listen to?

manuscript speech
speech that is read to an audience from a written text.

Consider the type of delivery you will use for your next speech. What steps will you take to ensure this is the most effective delivery you can use? Use the following tips to help you prepare for your speech.

A manuscript speech is one of the most challenging forms of delivery. Contrary to what most beginning public speakers think, speaking effectively from a manuscript requires more preparation and skill than extemporaneous or impromptu speaking (Hildebrandt & Stephens, 1963). Two problems are likely when a speaker reads from the full text. First, the speech often sounds like a written text and not an oral text, or a speech that "reads" well but does not "talk" well. Second, the speaker may be inclined to read to the audience rather than talk with them. There are solutions to these problems, and we explore those now.

Delivery Tips First, when you write your speech in manuscript format, talk the speech aloud as you write it so that it will not sound as if it was written. Working from your preparation outline, sit at your desk and speak the words as you write them on your computer or paper. If you find yourself thinking the speech rather than saying it aloud, go back and speak the part you have just written. You may well notice that you have slipped into a writer's style instead of a speaker's style. Change the language in these sections to reflect spoken ideas rather than written ideas. Remember, your goal is to write a speech, not an essay.

The second problem with using a manuscript is the temptation to read the text to your audience. This reduces your eye contact, and your words may sound wooden because you are reading. Finally, your delivery may be too fast because you are reading to rather than speaking with your audience.

The way to overcome the challenges associated with reading a speech is to practice speaking from the manuscript many times. If you become familiar with your manuscript during practice, you will find your natural rhythm and conversational style. You will figure out where you can easily make eye contact with your audience for extended periods. Like your extemporaneous speeches, you will be able to deliver full ideas or subpoints without reading. You also will discover that you will want to slow down because, even though the words are in front of you, you will feel more comfortable speaking the words with feeling rather than rushing through them.

Memorized Delivery

When you give a **memorized speech**, you present *a speech that has been written out, committed to memory, and given word for word*. With a memorized delivery, you give the speech without any notes. Orators 2,000 years ago prided themselves on their ability to memorize speeches that were hours long. Today, memorized speeches are usually used only for toasts, blessings, acceptance speeches, introductions, and sometimes in forensics. Use a memorized delivery in these situations:

- When your speech is extremely short,
- when you want to say things in a specific way, or
- when notes would be awkward or disruptive.

The trick to a memorized delivery is to speak as naturally and conversationally as possible. Rather than focusing on remembering your words, focus on communicating your words to your audience. When you deliver a memorized speech, do not recite it but deliver it as though you were talking to your audience.

Delivery Tips To commit a speech to memory, follow these steps:

1. Write a manuscript of the speech using an oral style, not a written one.

2. Commit each line of your speech to memory.

3. Every few lines, set the manuscript aside and practice delivering—not reading—them to an imaginary audience. Repeat until you can deliver your entire speech naturally and with confidence.

4. Once you have learned the full speech, practice it over and over, reminding yourself to listen to the meaning of your words. Remember, you want to bring the words to life and connect with your audience.

If you are delivering a long memorized speech, keep your manuscript nearby, if you can, so you can find your place if you get lost. If you cannot keep your manuscript near you, someone else may be able to hold it and prompt you if you lose your place. If you lose your place and have no one to prompt you, continue extemporaneously or pause, backtrack to the last line you remember, and repeat it in your head; you should be able to remember what comes next.

Table 12.1 reviews the advantages and disadvantages of the four delivery methods.

memorized speech
speech that has been written out, committed to memory, and given word for word.

TABLE 12.1   ADVANTAGES AND DISADVANTAGES OF THE FOUR DELIVERY METHODS

	Extemporaneous	Impromptu	Manuscript	Memorized
Definition	A speech that is carefully prepared and practiced from brief notes rather than from memory or a written manuscript.	A speech that is not planned or prepared in advance and uses few or no notes.	A speech that is completely written out and read word for word to an audience.	A speech that is written word for word, memorized, and given word for word.
Advantages	Combines a conversational style with a speaking outline. Encourages careful organization.	Allows for a conversational style with few or no notes.	Helps present detailed or specific information exactly as the speaker intends.	Frees the speaker to move about the room. No need for notes.
Disadvantages	Requires practice time. Speaker may be tempted to memorize the speech.	Requires thinking and organizing ideas quickly. No time for preparation.	Requires a conversational style that can be hard to achieve because the speaker reads from a full text.	Requires careful memorization. Speaker must remember important points and details without notes.

© Cengage Learning

Verbal Components of Delivery

A speech's success comes not only from its words but also from how they are delivered. Speakers known for their delivery—for example, John F. Kennedy, Barack Obama, Ann Richards, and Martin Luther King, Jr.—use **vocal variety**, or *changes in the volume, rate, and pitch of a speaker's voice that affect the meaning of the words delivered.* We achieve vocal variety by consciously using certain verbal components of delivery: volume, rate, pitch and inflection, and pauses. The proper articulation and pronunciation of words and a consideration of dialect are also important components of delivery.

Volume

Volume is *the loudness of a speaker's voice.* Common sense tells us that we want to speak loudly enough for our audiences to hear us but not so loudly that we make our listeners uncomfortable. Knowing just how loud to speak can be difficult because our own voice sounds louder to us than to the audience and because the appropriate volume varies with each situation. Culture also affects perceptions about appropriate speaking volume. For example, in some Mediterranean cultures, a loud voice signals sincerity and strength, whereas in parts of the United States, it may signal aggression or anger. In some Native American and Asian cultures, a soft voice signals education and good manners. However, in some European cultures, a soft voice may signal femininity, secrecy, or even fear (Andersen, Hecht, & Hoebler, 2002; Samovar & Porter, 1991).

Pay attention to nonverbal cues from your audience to help you adjust your volume. If you are speaking without a microphone, watch people in the back of the room as you begin to speak. If they are giving you cues that they cannot hear, you need to increase your volume. When you use a microphone, you still need to pay attention to your volume. Before you begin your speech, test your voice with the microphone and make sure

Chip Somodevilla/Getty Image

The late Ann Richards, then governor of Texas, gave the keynote address at the 1988 Democratic National Convention. This speech and many others she delivered were direct, humorous, gutsy, and memorable.

vocal variety
changes in the volume, rate, and pitch of a speaker's voice that affect the meaning of the words delivered.

volume
loudness of a speaker's voice.

Bil Zelman

Do you vary the tone and complexity of each talk geared toward your audience?

Absolutely. Sometimes I'm speaking to audiences that are already knowledgeable about environmental problems, so it's a matter of shaping the conversation on water issues and issuing a call to action. Sometimes, though, the audience is not as engaged on the environment or may have opposing views to mine. Those audiences need a softer approach. So, yes, I think knowing your audience is really important because it helps you choose the right stories. I find that picking my stories wisely gives me a little door into their heart or into their mind—that they open up more easily to what I have to say if my stories ones they can relate to (Cousteau, 2012).

you are the proper distance from it (neither too far nor too close) so the audience can listen comfortably.

Rate

Rate is the *speed at which we speak*. There is no formula for the proper rate at which to deliver a speech. For example, Dr. Martin Luther King, Jr., began his "I Have a Dream" speech at a rate of 92 words per minute and finished at a rate of 145 (Lucas, 2001). The rate at which we speak conveys different feelings. When we speak quickly, we project a sense of urgency, excitement, or even haste. When we speak slowly, we convey seriousness, heaviness, or even uncertainty. Both rapid and slow rates have their place in a speech. However, too much of one or the other strains audience members' attention and may cause them to stop listening. To check your rate, record yourself for several minutes. Play back the recording and assess your speed. Remember, rate is an audience-centered concern. We want to engage our audience, and our rate of speaking helps us in this effort by communicating certain emotions or energies.

Pitch and Inflection

Pitch refers not only to the position of tones on a musical scale but also to the *highness or lowness of a speaker's voice* in public speaking. **Inflection** is the *manipulation of pitch to create certain meanings or moods*. Together, pitch and inflection help us communicate more effectively with our audience. Consider the word *well* and its different meanings when used in spoken language. The control of pitch and inflection allows us to say "well" in ways that suggest joyful surprise or indecision or indignation or caution. All speakers manipulate their pitch to create meaning during their speeches. All of us alter our pitch to ask a question, express satisfaction or displeasure, convey confidence or confusion, or even communicate threats or aggression. Variations in pitch clarify meaning and help catch and maintain our audience's attention.

rate
speed at which we speak.

pitch
highness or lowness of a speaker's voice.

inflection
manipulation of pitch to create certain meanings or moods.

President Obama is an example of a speaker who varies his pitch and inflection to keep his audience engaged. Practice your delivery with someone you trust, and ask her or him to evaluate your pitch and inflection before the day of your speech.

Speakers who do not pay attention to their pitch and inflection risk losing their audience. *Speakers who do not alter their pitch* speak in a **monotone**. Other speakers may say everything in a pitch that is too low or too high. When a speaker never varies from a monotone or low pitch, the audience senses a lack of interest or energy. When the pitch is too high for too long, every word is communicated with equal enthusiasm, or "excessive zeal," and the audience begins to wonder which points are the most important (Soper, 1956).

You can monitor your voice by recording yourself so you can hear your pitch. If your pitch is too high, practice breathing more deeply (from the abdomen rather than the throat) and relaxing your throat muscles as you speak. Speak from your diaphragm rather than your throat, and read aloud regularly to practice this technique until you can get your pitch to drop naturally. (Note that proper breathing also helps you increase the volume of your voice and project your voice farther.) If you speak in a monotone or in too low a pitch, practice delivering your speech (or reading something aloud) in an overly dramatic way, using inflection, exclamations, and vocal variation as much as possible. With practice, vocal variation will come naturally and carry over into public-speaking situations.

Pauses

Pauses are *hesitations and brief silences in speech or conversation.* In speeches, they often are planned and serve several useful functions.

monotone
speaking without any change in pitch.

pauses
hesitations and brief silences in speech or conversation.

Pauses give us time to breathe fully and collect our thoughts during a speech or before we answer an audience question. Pauses also give audiences time to absorb and process information—they are like rest stops, giving the audience a breather before continuing. Finally, pauses before or after a climactic word or an important point reinforce that word or point.

Pauses can also add clarity. Read the passage here without stopping to pause after any of the words:

> The back of the eye on which an image of the outside world is thrown and which corresponds to the eye of a camera is composed of a mosaic of rods and cones whose diameter is little more than the length of an average light wave.

Without pauses, it is hard to understand what is being said here. Now read the passage again and note where you would naturally pause. Does the meaning of the passage become clearer?

> The back of the eye
> on which an image of the outside world is thrown
> and which corresponds to the eye of a camera
> is composed of a mosaic of rods and cones
> whose diameter is little more than the length of an average light wave

The four pauses that make this passage easier to understand are after *eye, thrown, camera,* and *cones* (Soper, 1956). These are places in written text where we would add commas to indicate meaning. In written text, pauses often are indicated by punctuation, but an audience cannot see punctuation in a speech. Pause to punctuate your words, as well as to establish mood, indicate a transition, take time to reflect, or emphasize a point. For example, in his speech on the pollution caused by using fossil fuels, Preston used a pause to make a particular impact: "In fact," Preston argued, "according to the Southern California Edison Electric Transportation Web site, updated only last month, running for half an hour in urban air pollution introduces as much carbon monoxide into your lungs as [pause] smoking a pack of cigarettes."

Learning the art of the pause takes time and practice. Before you become comfortable with the brief moments of silence necessary in a speech, you may have the urge to fill the silence. Avoid **vocalized pauses**, or *pauses that speakers fill with words or sounds like "um," "er," and "uh."* Vocalized pauses not only are irritating but also can create a negative

MCT/Getty Images

Senator Edward Kennedy was an inspiring speaker who was also known for a tendency to overuse pauses. If you are prone to using a lot of vocalized pauses, consider the four strategies noted in the text to help you eliminate some of them.

vocalized pauses
pauses that speakers fill with words or sounds such as "um," "er," and "uh."

impression of the speaker. When a speaker uses so many vocalized pauses that an audience becomes aware of them, listeners may begin to question the speaker's knowledge and speaking capabilities (Christenfeld, 1995). If you have a habit of vocalizing pauses, try the following process to eliminate them:

1. Listen for vocalized pauses in your daily speech.

2. When you hear one, anticipate the next one.

3. When you feel the urge to say "um" or "er" to fill space, gently bite your tongue and do not let the word escape.

4. Wait until your next word of substance is ready to come out and say that word instead.

It may take time to eliminate vocalized pauses from your speech, and you may feel awkward with the silence, but the results are worth the effort.

Articulation

Articulation is the *physical process of producing specific speech sounds to make language intelligible to our audiences.* Our clarity depends on our articulation—whether we say words distinctly or mumble and slur. Articulation depends on the accuracy of movement of our tongue, lips, jaws, and teeth. This movement produces either "Didjago?" or "Did you go?" In fact, scholars of performance and delivery argue that poor articulation is a trend across every sector of U.S. culture (Dowis, 2000; Gates, 2000; Martin & Darnley, 1996; Rodenburg, 2001).

Audiences expect public speaking to be more clearly articulated than private conversation. Speakers with an audience-centered focus care about clear articulation. Clearly articulated words communicate that you want your audience to understand you, which can add to your credibility. For your audience to understand your ideas, they must be able to decipher your words. To improve your articulation skills, try the following exercise:

1. Several days before your speech, select a part of your speech or a short written text you can read aloud.

2. Practice saying each word of your speech excerpt or text as slowly and clearly as possible, exaggerating the clarity of each word.

3. Repeat this exercise once or twice each day before you give your speech.

This exercise will help you recognize how much you slur or mumble and teach you to speak more clearly when you give your speech. Do not worry—you will not speak in this exaggerated way when you finally deliver your speech, but your words will be much clearer.

Pronunciation

Just as you would not turn in an essay you knew was filled with spelling errors, never deliver a speech filled with pronunciation errors. **Pronunciation** is the *act of saying words correctly according to the accepted standards of a language.* Pronunciation and articulation may seem

articulation
physical process of producing specific speech sounds to make language intelligible to our audiences.

pronunciation
act of saying words correctly according to the accepted standards of a language.

similar, but pronunciation refers to how *correctly* a word is said, whereas articulation refers to how *clearly* a word is said. For example, saying the word *nuclear* as "nu-cle-ar" (correct) rather than "nu-cu-lar" (incorrect) has to do with pronunciation, and mumbling either pronunciation rather than speaking it clearly has to do with articulation.

Pronouncing words correctly communicates to your audience that you have listened carefully to the public dialogue going on around you. You have taken care to learn the common language and pronounce it correctly. In addition, correct pronunciation of terms and names in a language other than your native one communicates your respect for that culture and enhances your credibility.

Dialect

A **dialect** is a *pattern of speech shared by an ethnic group or people from a specific geographical location*. Dialects include specific vocabulary that is unique to a group as well as styles of pronunciation shared by members of that group. All people have a dialect, and your own dialect comes from your ethnic heritage as well as the place you grew up. For example, do you say "wash" or "warsh" when you want something clean? How about "soda," "pop," or "coke" when you want a soft drink? Your choices reflect your dialect.

People who use a standard American dialect (the dialect most television newscasters use when they are on the air) often forget that they also have a dialect, and they sometimes view the dialect of others as inferior. For public speaking, dialect is important because speakers need to consider the effect their dialect has on those who are unfamiliar with it. Speakers may use words that are not familiar to their audience or may pronounce words in ways that sound odd or different.

If you know your dialect will be unfamiliar to your audience, try the following:

1. Acknowledge your region of birth or ethnic heritage.

2. Talk about how that shapes your use of language by giving examples of some of the differences you have encountered between your dialect and those of your audience.

3. Define terms that are unfamiliar to your audience.

4. Soften the accent associated with your dialect if that accent is fairly strong and might hinder understanding.

Nonverbal Components of Delivery

The nonverbal components of delivery are those aspects communicated through our bodies and faces. For public speakers, these include personal appearance, eye contact, facial expression, posture, gestures, and proxemics.

Scholars of interpersonal communication recognize that nonverbal communication has a powerful effect on the meanings exchanged between people. Researchers suggest that between sixty-five and ninety-three

dialect
pattern of speech shared by an ethnic group or people from a specific geographical location.

NATIONAL GEOGRAPHIC SPEAKS

Wade Davis, Explorer 2000–2015:
Unique Manifestations of the Human Spirit

MARK THIESSEN/National Geographic Creative

Wade Davis/National Geographic Creative

Anthropologist, ethnobotanist, ethnographer, author, filmmaker, and photographer, Wade Davis is described as "a rare combination of scientist, scholar, poet and passionate defender of life's diversity." His work has taken him to East Africa, Borneo, Nepal, Peru, Polynesia, Tibet, Mali, Benin, Togo, New Guinea, Australia, Colombia, Vanatu Mongolia, and the high Arctic of Nunuvut and Greenland. He has cataloged more than 6,000 botanical species; studied zombies and the plant preparations that accompany zombie practices; and has published more than a dozen books sharing his research and insights. He holds degrees in anthropology and biology, and a Ph.D. from Harvard in ethnobotany. Davis explains his perspective and one of the guiding principles behind his work: "The world in which you were born is just one model of reality. Other cultures are not failed attempts at being you. They are unique manifestations of the human spirit."

Davis urges students to become "entrepreneurs of knowledge" and skilled public speakers: our knowledge base can be "monetized," he says, if students "learn how to communicate." Davis suggests that one of the biggest challenges of the sciences is "the inability to communicate," in fact, the "disinclination to do so." One reason "climate change has not really captured the public imagination is, quite simply, that the narrative has not been properly communicated to the public."

He further notes that after the horrific events of September 11, 2001, anthropologists were not interviewed, yet anthropology may be the "one profession that actually could answer that question then on the lips of every American, why do they hate us?" So important are public speaking skills, in Davis's view, that individuals "literally have had their careers transformed by a single TED talk that turns up on line."

For Davis, the most important credential for being a communicator "is to have something important to say that the world needs to hear." He explains that before his association with National Geographic, he began speaking publicly about each book he wrote. Then his agent urged him to pull his experiences from his years of work with voodoo and in the Amazon to offer a "global perspective." As he did that, Davis recounts, "All that grew out of the process of communication, how the stories morphed" into larger perspectives. He adds, "[I]t's funny how it worked, I mean it kind of grew out of that one speech my agent asked me to do, this sort of greatest hits speech . . . that the Geographic Society heard at a film festival in Telluride . . . that led me to being recruited as an explorer in residence."

In the late 1990s, Davis discovered the work of Michael Krauss and Ken Hale, linguists who shared that of the "7,000 languages of the world, half weren't being taught to children," and added languages and linguistics to his long list of passions. Davis sees language as "not just grammar and vocabulary," but as "a flash of the human spirit, a vehicle to the soul of a culture." He finds the fact that we are losing so many languages so quickly horrifying. Languages communicate and organize ones culture, Davis explains, and cultures show us possibilities:

> The idea that the world in which you were born, it's just one model of reality, and the people of the world aren't failed attempts at being new or failed attempts at being modern. Each culture, by definition, is a unique answer to a fundamental question, what does it mean to be human and alive? When the people of the world answer that question, they do so in 7,000 different voices, which collectively become the human repertoire for dealing with the challenges that will confront us in the coming millennia. . . . every culture has something to say, and each one deserves to be heard. And the great curse of humanity is cultural myopia, the idea that my world is the real world and everybody else is a failed attempt of, of being me. (Davis, 2014; National Geographic Society, n.d.; TED, 2003, 2008, 2012)

WHAT DO YOU THINK?

1. Davis encourages students to become "skilled public speakers." How might communication apprehension affect a student's ability to initially accomplish this? What steps can a student take to become a skilled public speaker?

2. After 9/11, Davis says, anthropologists might have helped answer the question, "Why do they hate us?" What aspects about connecting with your audience would an anthropologist need to consider when helping to answer that question?

3. A speaker presenting a TED Talk usually uses technology such as PowerPoint slides or video to help present the speech. Watch several TED Talk presentations and assess their slides and videos. What makes them effective?

percent of the total meaning of a message comes to us through nonverbal signals (Birdwhistell, 1970; Mehrabian, 1981). In addition, when nonverbal signals contradict verbal signals (for example, you say you are glad to see someone but your facial expression and physical posture suggest you are not), people tend to believe the nonverbal signals over the verbal ones (McCroskey, Sallinen, Fayer, Richmond, & Barraclough, 1996; Mino, 1996; Trees & Manusov, 1998; Wood, 1999).

For public speakers, nonverbal communication is especially important because it conveys meaning and can either enhance or detract from the overall message. We now look at how the components of nonverbal communication affect a speech.

Personal Appearance

Personal appearance, or *the way you dress, groom, and present yourself physically*, is an important part of delivery. But how important? Consider the following sayings:

> You can't judge a book by its cover.
>
> Beauty is in the eye of the beholder.
>
> Looks are everything.
>
> Beauty is as beauty does.
>
> You can never be too rich or too thin.
>
> You can dress him up, but you still can't take him out.
>
> Good-looking lawyers make more money.

Which statements are true? Does physical appearance matter, or is it irrelevant? Studies show that personal appearance actually matters a lot. People deemed "more attractive" earn more money than their "less attractive" peers, and personal grooming plays a large part in our perception of a person's attractiveness to both men and women (Morris, Gorham, Cohen, & Huffman, 1996; Rozell, Kennedy, & Grabb, 1989; Weiss, 2008). Attractive characteristics are defined as "those characteristics that make one person appear pleasing to another" (Hartz, 1996, p. 683; Morrow, 1990). Even though we may say we should not judge people by their looks, we actually do just that.

Without a doubt, standards for attractiveness and beauty change with generations, as well as with cultures and subcultures. Despite these differences, though, there is a basic standard for acceptable personal grooming in public-speaking situations. That standard is that the speaker's dress should be appropriate to the occasion (Herman, Zanna, & Higgins, 1986; Rubinstein, 2001). If the occasion is formal, then the speaker is expected to dress formally. If the occasion is casual, the speaker's clothing should be less formal. A speaker who shows up at a formal occasion in a T-shirt and shorts not only displays a lack of audience awareness but also is unlikely to establish credibility. Similarly, wearing formal business attire to speak at a casual gathering is also inappropriate. In short, be sure your clothing matches the style and tone of the occasion.

personal appearance
the way someone dresses, grooms, and presents her- or himself physically.

Personal appearance is a complex combination of social norms, cultural and generational influences, and personal style. Your personal appearance should match your objective as a speaker, which is to have your words and ideas taken seriously in the public dialogue. Delivery begins the moment the audience sees you, so pay careful attention to your personal appearance and present yourself appropriately for the occasion at which you are speaking.

Eye Contact

The second essential component of nonverbal delivery is **eye contact**, or *visual contact with another person's eyes*. Like personal appearance, appropriate eye contact is affected by culture and gender. Most North Americans and Western Europeans expect a speaker to make extensive eye contact. However, in Native American cultures, in Japan, and in parts of Africa, extensive eye contact is considered invasive and disrespectful (Gudykunst & Moody, 2002). Gender, too, affects the meaning of eye contact. For men, direct and extended eye contact with another man may be perceived as a challenge or threat. For women, direct and extended eye contact with a man may be interpreted as an invitation to flirt. So knowing what to do with our eyes as we deliver a speech depends on knowing who is in our audience.

Even though the nuances of eye contact are complex, most cultures expect at least some eye contact during a speech. Eye contact has three functions. First, it is a way to greet and acknowledge the audience before the speech begins. Second, it is a way to gauge and keep our audience's interest. We use eye contact to monitor feedback from our audience and adjust our volume, rate, and pitch accordingly. Third, it is a way to communicate sincerity and honesty.

Audiences rate speakers who make eye contact for less than half their speech as tentative, uncomfortable, and even as insincere and dishonest (Palmer & Simmons, 1995). In contrast, speakers who make eye contact for more than half their speech are viewed as more credible and trustworthy (Beebe, 1974, 1979–1980; Cobin, 1963).

For eye contact to be effective, try to do two things as you look out at your audience. First, make eye contact with many people in the audience rather than just a few friendly faces. Make eye contact with people in all parts of the room, not just those immediately in front of you. Gather information about level of comprehension, interest, and agreement from as many people as you can.

Second, look with interest. Rather than scanning faces in the audience or looking over listeners' heads to the back of the room, really look at individual people in the audience. Slow down the movement of your eyes so you actually make a connection with people through your eye contact. Looking with interest communicates that you are pleased to be speaking to your audience and are interested in members' responses.

Facial Expression

Your face plays a central role in communicating with audience members, letting them know your attitudes, emotional states, and sometimes even

eye contact
visual contact with another person's eyes.

your inner thoughts. Your **facial expression** is the *movement of your eyes, eyebrows, and mouth to convey reactions and emotions.* Actors are highly skilled at using their faces to communicate, and audiences appreciate this talent. Although you do not need to be as skilled as an actor, you do need to consider your facial expressions as you deliver your speech. A poker face, although useful in a card game, will not help you communicate your ideas.

You can use your facial expressions to communicate your own interest in your topic, your agreement or disagreement with a point, your openness to an idea, and even your feelings about an issue. Take some time to decide which facial expressions might be useful to include in your speech. If these expressions do not come naturally to you, then practice them until you are comfortable delivering them.

Posture

Posture is *the way we position and carry our bodies,* and people assign meaning to our posture whether we realize it or not. We are perceived as confident and relaxed or tense and insecure based partly on our posture. A confident speaker is often called "poised," possessing assurance, dignity, and a sense of calm. Nervousness can affect our posture, making us feel awkward and act in ways we would never do in other situations: gripping the podium with both hands, slouching over our speaking notes, pacing back and forth, or standing in one spot. These nervous reactions detract from our delivery and communicate a message we probably do not want to send (Bull, 1987).

By paying attention during practice to the way we carry our bodies, we can eliminate some nervous postures. To become aware of your posture during a speech, practice your speech in the way you actually will give it. If you will deliver your speech standing, then practice it while standing. Consider devising a makeshift podium. If you are to sit while giving the speech, then practice while sitting, with chairs beside you and your notes on a table in front of you. Similarly, if you will use a handheld or attachable microphone, practice with something resembling it so you get the feel of speaking with a microphone.

By practicing the speech in the way you will actually give it, you can correct your nervous habits before you deliver the speech. For example, if you find that you pace or grip the podium tightly, you can replace the bad habit with a better one. If you discover you stand immobilized when you practice, then you can add cues to your speaking outline to remind you to move during your speech. If you slouch, you can practice sitting up straight and looking out at your audience. In sum, your posture during your speech should improve if you pay attention to your body during practice.

One final word about posture and delivery: Pay attention to the way you begin and end your speech. Wait until you are at the podium or have the microphone in your hand before you begin talking. Do not start speaking until you are facing your audience and have made eye contact. Similarly, do not walk off the stage until you have finished the last word of

facial expression
movement of eyes, eyebrows, and mouth to convey reactions and emotions.

posture
how speakers position and carry their bodies.

your conclusion. Finishing your conclusion or your final answer before you leave the spotlight communicates confidence and a willingness to give every word the attention it deserves. These guidelines will help you remain audience centered.

Gestures

Gestures are *movements, usually of the hands but sometimes of the entire body, that express meaning and emotion or offer clarity to a message.* Students of rhetoric in ancient Greece and Rome spent hours learning specific gestures to accompany specific parts of their speeches. For example, certain gestures were used with transitions, and others signaled specific kinds of main points or ideas. These choreographed gestures were used until the eighteenth century (Austin, 1806/1966; Bulwer, 1644/1974). Today, research on gestures in public speaking indicates they should be as natural as possible rather than memorized.

However, beginning public speakers do not always know what gestures will appear natural in a speech. With only minor variations, natural gestures in a speech are the same as those you normally use in personal conversations to complement your ideas and bring your words to life. The same is true for public speeches. Gestures make our delivery lively, offer emphasis and clarity, and convey our passion and interest. Use the following tips to help you with gestures:

gestures
movements, usually of the hands but sometimes of the entire body, that express meaning and emotion or offer clarity to a message.

The Dali Lama is known for his engaging and genuine delivery. Watch a video clip of him speaking and assess whether his gestures contribute to his appeal as a speaker.

360b/Shutterstock.com

1. **Vary your gestures.** Use different kinds of gestures rather than repeating only one gesture. Some gestures emphasize (a fist on the podium), clarify (counting first, second, third on your fingers), or illustrate (drawing a shape with your hands in the air). Incorporate a variety of these gestures into your speech.

2. **Use gestures that fit your message.** Sometimes, a point needs an extravagant gesture; at other times, a more subtle gesture is much more effective. For example, use a relaxed pattern of hand movement as you explain a point but a larger more vigorous movement when you are emphasizing something quite important.

3. **Stay relaxed.** Your gestures should flow with your words. Keep your movements comfortable and effortless. If you find a gesture makes you tense, drop it from the speech and replace it with something more casual and familiar.

You will find that as you relax and gain experience speaking, you will stop thinking about your gestures and simply use them as you normally do in conversation.

Proxemics

Effective speakers pay close attention to **proxemics**, the *use of space during communication*. Be mindful of how far away you are from your audience as well as how elevated you are from it (for example, on a platform or a podium). The farther away you are, the stronger the idea of separation. The higher up you are, the more the idea of power is communicated.

You can work with proxemics in your delivery. One strength of skilled speakers is their ability to move close to their audiences at key points during their speeches. Although you do not want to remain too close to your listeners throughout your speech, getting close to them at key points allows for greater connection and communicates a desire to be perceived as more of an equal. Try stepping from behind the lectern or down from the podium and moving closer to your audience. If you cannot do this because you need a microphone or a place to put your notes, then you might be able to move closer during a question-and-answer session. Doing so will help you communicate openness and a willingness to engage in conversation with your audience.

Technology and Delivery

Technology refers to the tools speakers use to help them deliver their message. Technology can be as elaborate as a computer and a liquid crystal display (LCD) panel or as simple as a pen and a flip chart. Table 12.2 lists technologies that speakers typically use. When you are thinking of using technology for your speech, stay audience centered by asking yourself the following questions:

- Have I asked what types of technology will be available for me to use?

- Do I have time to prepare the materials I need to use that technology?

- Do I have the time to practice using the technology? Have I worked out any glitches?

proxemics
use of space during communication.

TABLE 12.2 TECHNOLOGIES FOR SPEAKERS	
Traditional Technologies	**Electronic Technologies**
Podiums for notes	Microphones
Tables or easels for displays	Laptop computers and LCD projectors
Presentational aids such as posters	Overhead projectors and screens
Handouts	Slide projectors and screens
Chalk, chalkboards, and erasers	Presentational aids such as PowerPoint or Prezi slides
Ink markers, whiteboards, and erasers	Televisions, DVD players, and SMART Boards
Markers, pens, and flip charts	CD-ROM players
Tacks, pins, or tape	Audiocassette players

© Cengage Learning

- Am I prepared to speak if the technology fails?
- Does the technology help me communicate my messages clearly? Does it enhance my speech or detract from it?

When you decide to use technology, you want to be sure you can use it competently. Consider the importance of this competence in the following example.

Mike wanted to include several YouTube clips into his speech. He identified the ones he wanted two days before he spoke, and he figured he could pull them up during his speech. When he set up his computer on the day of his speech, he had trouble getting Internet access because the system was not running smoothly that day. After several tries, he was finally able to log on, but he could not locate his YouTube sites easily because he had searched for them by subject and failed to record the YouTube address. Then, because he was not familiar with the technology in the room, when he played his first clip, he discovered the volume on the projector had been turned off and no one could hear the clip.

Mike did what he could to recover, but after his speech, he felt he had not really created the kind of environment he wanted. He wanted people to get excited by his material, but he felt they simply were patient with him instead.

Remember, although technology is a tool that can help you give a more effective speech, it has its drawbacks. If your speech relies on technology to be effective but the technology you need is not available when you arrive to speak, your presentation will be negatively affected. That is why you need to take the time to consider how to present your speech without technology. Putting this time into your speech before you give it will help you stay audience centered by keeping your attention focused on delivering your message in a way your audience will appreciate.

Visual Aids

You probably will be asked to use visual aids in your speeches and presentations outside of this class, and you will likely want to incorporate them. But how do we compete with the sophisticated images we see on our computer screens, in magazines, in films, and on television? How do we decide what to include, and how do we effectively use the technology available to us? What does the research on visual aids tell us about their

Social Commentary, YouTube Style

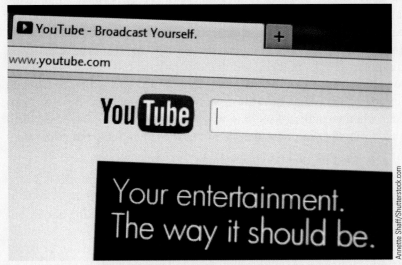

Annette Shaff/Shutterstock.com

angry letter to *The New York Times*. Instead, she remixed scenes from the TV and movie versions of *Sex and the City* into two pro-gay narratives and uploaded them to her blog, drawing 21,000 hits. "I wouldn't have done it if it was text-based," says Kreisinger. "Things are more easily communicated through video. . . . And there can be more powerful statements" (Aucion, 2010, p. A1).

The trend to use video to speak out about political and social issues has become immensely popular in the last few years, facilitated by Web 2.0 technology and in-spired by the entertaining and informative videos created by video bloggers and *The Daily Show*. "Making media now is a powerful way of participating in all kinds of life, including civic and political life," says Lee Rainie, director of the Pew Research Center's Internet and American Life Project. People in their teens and twenties "are now deeply connected to the political process in a way that their parents, at their age, could never be" (Aucion, 2010, p. A12).

Providing a forum for people to connect, inform, and inspire others across the globe, YouTube acts as a distribution platform for original content creators and advertisers large and small ("YouTube Fact Sheet," 2010). YouTube allows its users to create their own videos and upload and manipulate their favorite movie clips, TV clips, and music videos. Created in 2005 by former PayPal employees Chad Hurley, Steen Chen, and Jawed Karim, YouTube is now immensely popular. Over "300 hours of video are uploaded every minute" and YouTube "has more than a billion users" ("YouTube Statistics," 2014). In 2009, *Entertainment Weekly* magazine put YouTube on its end-of-the-decade best-of list, summing up its appeal by describing the site as "providing a safe home for piano-playing cats, celeb goof-ups, and overzealous lip-synchers since 2005" (Geier, Jensen, Jordan, Lyons, & Markovitz, 2009).

According to the *Boston Globe*, YouTube is also influencing a growing number of activists who use video imagery to speak their minds online. For example, when 23-year-old Elisa Kreisinger wanted to protest the lack of gay characters and story lines on television, she did not petition people to boycott HBO or write an

What Do You Think?

1. Compare the potential of a YouTube post to a celebrity's or politician's speech. Does one reach more individuals than another? Does one reach a different kind of audience as compared to the other? What are the advantages and disadvantages of each form of connecting with people?

2. How do you evaluate the credibility and accuracy of a YouTube post? Are there ways to identify which posts are accurate and which are not? What are those ways?

3. What ethical implications might be important to consider before posting something on YouTube? Do you think that those who post on YouTube consider the ethical implications of their videos?

benefits? Early research (Ayres, 1991; Bohn & Jabusch, 1982; Linkugel & Berg, 1970; Seiler, 1971; Zayas-Bazan, 1977–1978) tells us that visual aids do the following:

Visual aids help gain and maintain audience attention.

Visual aids help audiences recall information.

Visual aids help explain and clarify information.

Visual aids may increase persuasiveness and enhance credibility.

Visual aids may reduce nervousness.

More recent research confirms these findings (Garcia-Retamero & Cokley, 2011) and shows that visual aids help us accomplish a great deal as speakers.

By selecting the right visual aids for your speeches, you can help your audience stay focused and recall your ideas. You can add clarity, increase your credibility, and perhaps minimize nervousness. In this section, we explore how you might use different types of visual aids, ranging from simple to complex, to accomplish these goals. We also explore how you might use objects, models, and demonstrations; Internet or DVD clips; PowerPoint slides that include text, charts, and graphs; poster boards and flip charts; as well as drawings, paintings, photographs. We even consider whether putting lists on a whiteboard or SMART Board is worth considering for your next speech. Let us look at each type of visual aid.

Objects, Models, and Demonstrations

An **object** is *something that can be seen or touched*, and a **model** is *a copy of an object*. A **demonstration** is a *display of how something is done or works*. Objects help your audience see what you are talking about, but sometimes they are not practical because they are too large or too small. If this is the case, models can help because they can be smaller or larger than the thing you are talking about (a model of the Statue of Liberty or a hearing aid, for example). When neither an object or a model feels right, a demonstration might be what you need, allowing you to show your audience how to do something intricate (picking a lock, for example) or elaborate (assemble a first-aid kit). These three types of visual aids bring your ideas to life, showing people what you are talking about or describing. Objects, models, and demonstrations can help audience members understand unfamiliar ideas or processes because they can see what you are describing. Be sure to practice before using one of these visual aids in a speech and consider how much space you will have if you want to demonstrate a process.

Photographs, Maps, and Drawings

Photographs are *images produced with cameras or other forms of digital technology*. Photographs add clarity, color, and emotion to your speech and can be downloaded from the Internet or taken from your own collection. **Maps** are *visual representations of places*, and they help you show your audience geographical features and layouts (the nearest national park and its attractions, for example), where things are located in relation to one another (the most visited national parks in the United States, for example) and the best route to take from one place to another. Maps can be downloaded from the Internet or sketched by hand. **Drawings** are *diagrams and sketches of someone or something*. They add clarity to your presentation because they help you show your audience what something looks like (the alphabet used in a foreign language, for example, or different leaf patterns on trees). You can create your own drawings or download them from the Internet. If you use drawings, remember one important principle: simple drawings are best. According to many graphic arts texts, people seem to remember the outline of an

object
something that can be seen and touched.

model
copy of an object.

demonstration
display of how something is done or works.

photograph
image produced with a camera or other form of digital technology.

maps
visual representations of places.

drawings
diagrams and sketches of someone or something.

image more than its details (Kearny, 1996; Rabb, 1993; Wilder, 1994), so use line drawings, simple clip art, and even children's art to illustrate your images rather than elaborate sketches and presentations.

Internet and DVDs

You can use Internet technology to support your ideas and, if your audience is unfamiliar with your topic, an image or segment from the Internet or a DVD can help bring it to life. Although these types of visual aids can captivate your audience, you want to consider several guidelines to make sure the clips do not take over your speech. First, if you use this type of visual aid, keep your clip brief. Remember, your speech may be only four or five minutes long, so a clip should be less than a minute in length. The shorter clip ensures that you have time to make your points clear and provide an appropriate introduction and conclusion. Second, be sure the clip is appropriate for your audience. Analyze your audience carefully to determine whether the clip is too graphic, confusing, or contains offensive language or images. Third, download and cue your segment before your speech to make certain it plays smoothly and without delay. Internet and DVD clips can add drama and interest, but they do take preparation and forethought.

PowerPoint Slides and Presentational Technologies

PowerPoint slides as well as other technologies, like Prezi, allow speakers to display text, as well as important images such as charts and graphs. Let us consider what might be appropriate for this type of visual aid.

Text Including text on a PowerPoint or presentational slide allows speakers to display an outline of their ideas, important quotations, definitions, statistics, and even questions for their audience on a large screen behind them. Although these are the strengths of this type of visual aid, many audiences are bored with this technology because the material presented does not enhance or add clarity to ideas, add interest or help with recall—it simply is a repetition of what the speaker is saying. When you use slides, share information that will help your audience with clarity and recall rather than just duplicate what you are saying. Be sure to include a heading on each slide and try to follow the six-word and six-line rule, which suggests you use no more that six words per line and no more than six items per list (Davidson & Klein, 1999). If you are displaying a list of items or concepts, try to balance that list so that each item is parallel and contains similar amounts of words and balanced phrasing.

Charts and Graphs Charts show steps in a process or parts of a concept. They can help speakers illustrate the relationship between the steps or parts and how each relates to the whole process or concept. The two most common charts used as visual aids are the flowchart and the organizational chart. A **flowchart** illustrates *direction or motion*—for example, the unfolding of a process or the steps to a goal. An **organizational chart** *illustrates the structure of groups*, such as organizations, businesses, or departments. Use a chart as a visual aid when you want to represent the parts of a whole or to simplify a complex process.

flowchart
illustrates direction or motion.

organizational chart
illustrates the structure of groups.

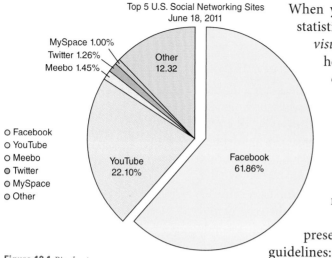

Top 5 U.S. Social Networking Sites
June 18, 2011

MySpace 1.00%
Twitter 1.26%
Meebo 1.45%

Other 12.32

YouTube 22.10%

Facebook 61.86%

○ Facebook
○ YouTube
○ Meebo
◉ Twitter
○ MySpace
○ Other

Figure 12.1 *Pie chart*
Source: Hitwise

When you want to compare numbers, quantities, or statistics, graphs are excellent visual aids. A **graph** is a *visual comparison of amounts or quantities*. Graphs help audiences see growth, size, proportions, or relationships. You can use different kinds of graphs for different purposes. **Bar graphs** *compare quantities at a specific moment in time*. **Line graphs** *show trends over time*. **Pie graphs** *show the relative proportions of parts of a whole*. **Picture graphs** *present information in pictures or images*. Figure 12.1 shows how data related to social media could be represented.

When you decide to display the figures you present in a chart or graph, consider the following guidelines:

- emphasize the visual image;
- use lines, arrows, shading, and color to show relationships and direction;
- use clear and consistent labels; or
- use a computer to design your chart or graph.

Emphasizing the Visual Image When you create a chart or graph, use single words or short labels for titles and positions and as few words as possible to describe the steps of a process or progression of data. Help your audience visualize the process and its parts quickly and clearly by keeping it simple. Figures 12.2 and 12.3 are examples of a bar graph and a flowchart, respectively, that emphasize the visual aspect of the message.

Use Lines, Arrows, Shading, and Color to Show Relationships and Direction To keep audience members' attention moving in the direction you want, use lines, arrows, shading, and color to help them follow your points as you explain the steps in a process or the structure of an organization. Notice how Figure 12.1 uses color to emphasize size and percentages.

graph
a visual comparison of amounts or quantities

bar graph
compares quantities at a specific moment in time

line graph
shows trends over time

pie graph
shows relative proportions of parts of a whole.

picture graph
presents information in pictures or images.

Growth (in millions) of U.S. Population: 1950–1960 to 2000–2010

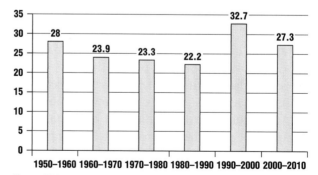

Figure 12.2 *Bar graph*
Source: U.S. Census Bureau

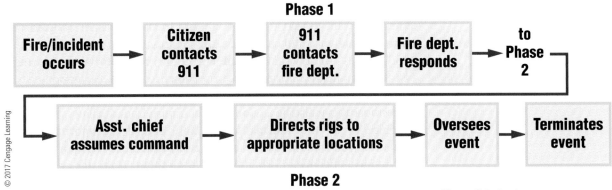

Phase 1

Fire/incident occurs → Citizen contacts 911 → 911 contacts fire dept. → Fire dept. responds → to Phase 2

Asst. chief assumes command → Directs rigs to appropriate locations → Oversees event → Terminates event

Phase 2

© 2017 Cengage Learning

Figure 12.3 *Flowchart*

Use Clear and Consistent Labels Use descriptive headings for graphs that contain horizontal and vertical axes—for example, "Year" and "Percentage." For line graphs, mark equal intervals in the graph's grid—for example, numbers by tens, hundreds, or thousands and dates by decades or centuries. Show the numbers of those intervals on the horizontal and vertical axes. Notice how Figure 12.4 uses clear and consistent labels to help the audience track complex information.

Use a Computer to Design Your Chart or Graph Because charts and graphs display amounts, relationships, and proportions, presenting this information accurately is important. A computer can help you represent this information cleanly and precisely, drawing images to scale and clearly marking points on a graph. Using software such as Microsoft Excel (or an equivalent), simply enter the numbers and labels into the program's data table and select the type of graph you want to depict. You can even experiment with different kinds of graphs to see how each one shows your information.

Figure 12.4 *Organizational chart*

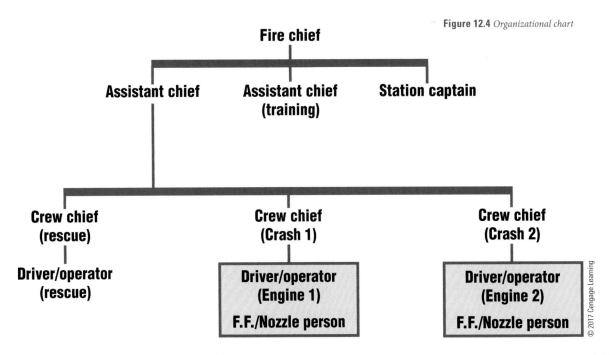

Fire chief

Assistant chief — Assistant chief (training) — Station captain

Crew chief (rescue) — Crew chief (Crash 1) — Crew chief (Crash 2)

Driver/operator (rescue)

Driver/operator (Engine 1) — F.F./Nozzle person

Driver/operator (Engine 2) — F.F./Nozzle person

© 2017 Cengage Learning

Flip Charts, Whiteboards or SMART Boards, and Poster Boards

When you want to lead a discussion, keep track of ideas, or brainstorm with your audience, flip charts, SMART Boards, and whiteboards can be good choices. These visual aids allow you to record information during your speech, and the information can be shown to audiences electronically. If you do not have access to computer technology, or the group is small, poster boards can also be a good choice. A poster board allows a smaller audience to see the information up close and, if the information is something you will use again, it can be easily stored and transported.

The most effective information to put on these visual aids are lists of ideas. A **list** is *series of words or phrases that organize ideas one after the other.* Use lists when you are brainstorming or when your material is easily organized into groups (names, key features, or procedures, for example). Lists also help audiences keep track of material and identify the main points of a complex speech or discussion. Use the following principles to record ideas:

- Make your list brief and balanced.
- Use keywords or phrases.
- Avoid full sentences.
- Write neatly and legibly.
- Include headings (Rabb, 1993).

 ## Question-and-Answer Sessions

Speeches often involve question-and-answer sessions. These sessions provide an opportunity for audience members to explore an idea or proposal in more detail, ask for clarity, and share their own perspectives. Even though you will not know for sure what to expect during question-and-answer sessions, there are ways you can prepare for them, and advanced preparation can make the difference between a mediocre question-and-answer session and a stimulating one. Ensuring a good question-and-answer session has two steps: preparing for potential questions beforehand and managing the discussion during the session.

Preparing for Questions

You can do several things to prepare for the question-and-answer session. First, take time to identify the questions you think might be asked. Then prepare your answers to the questions.

Identify Potential Questions As you think about the topic under discussion, keep a log of the questions your audience might ask. Pay attention to the controversies or disagreements raised by the issue you are discussing to help you identify potential questions. If you can discuss the topic with others before the session, they can help you identify likely questions. Add these to your log of questions.

Formulate and Practice Answers After you have identified the questions you might be asked, prepare your answers as thoroughly as you can.

Nerves and Public Speaking

If you fear public speaking, you are not alone. Speaking in front of others is one of the most common fears of people in the workplace. Some individuals are so fearful, explains anxietycoach.com, that they turn down promotions or change jobs if the position will require giving speeches. Others might not take such extreme measures, but they may try to avoid giving even the smallest of speeches by arriving late to a meeting or a function so that they can avoid self-introductions. If they cannot avoid these small presentations, they cope by rushing through them, which gives others a less than desirable first impression. When speaking is required, fearful individuals often try several unproductive measures, such as skipping parts of their speech, rushing or reading, pretending to be sick so they can shorten their presentation or excuse their delivery, or using too many slides and images to avoid speaking. Although this may not seem like much of a problem, these behaviors can get in the way of our work performance. Imagine a coworker who avoids, stumbles, rushes, or omits information—it does not bode well for the company or the individual. Many Web sites offer a range of solutions. Most of them use the relaxation techniques discussed in this chapter, including visualization, breathing, and staying positive. Others involve writing, exercising, reframing, and working with a therapist (CalmClinic, 2014; Carbonell, 2014; Tartakivsky, n.d.).

Our nervousness before a speech is often called **communication apprehension**; it is *the level of fear or anxiety associated with either real or anticipated communication with another person or persons* (Finn, Sawyer, & Schrodt, 2009; McCroskey, 1977; Winters et al., 2007; Witt, Roberts, & Behnke, 2008). Communication apprehension can take two forms. People who are *apprehensive about communicating with others in any situation* are said to have **trait anxiety**. People who are *apprehensive about communicating with others in a particular situation* are said to have **state, or situational, anxiety**. To help reduce your nervousness, take a moment to consider whether you are trait anxious or state anxious in communication situations. Do you fear all kinds of interactions or only certain kinds? Most of us experience some level of state anxiety about some communication events, such as asking a boss for a raise, verbally evaluating another's performance, or introducing ourselves to a group of strangers. This is quite normal.

Most people also experience some level of state anxiety about public speaking. This is called *public-speaking anxiety* (PSA), the anxiety we feel when we learn we have to give a speech or take a public-speaking course (Behnke & Sawyer, 1999; Bippus & Daly, 1999; Robinson, 1997). You can build your confidence and reduce some of your PSA by following the tips in this section. However, if you are extraordinarily nervous about giving speeches, see your instructor for special help with your fears.

Knowing why we become nervous before a speech can help us build our confidence. Research suggests that most people's state anxiety about public speaking exists for six reasons. Many people are state anxious because public speaking is

1. **novel**—we do not do it regularly and thus lack necessary skills;
2. **done in formal settings**—our behaviors when giving a speech are more prescribed and rigid than usual;
3. **often done from a subordinate position**—an instructor or boss sets the rules for giving a speech and the audience acts as a critic;
4. **conspicuous or obvious**—the speaker stands apart from the audience;
5. **done in front of an audience that is unfamiliar**—most people are more comfortable talking with people they know, and we also fear that an audience will not be interested in what we have to say; and
6. **a unique situation in which the degree of attention paid to the speaker is quite noticeable**—audience members either stare at us or ignore us, so we become unusually self-focused (Beatty, 1988; Bippus & Daly, 1999).

The suggestions offered here should help you build your confidence and turn your nervous energy to your advantage.

Do Your Research

One way to build your confidence before giving a speech is to prepare as well as you can (Daly, Vangelisti, & Webber, 1995). Careful preparation will help you feel more confident about what you will say (and what others will think) and ease fears about drawing a blank or not being able to answer a question. Speakers who research their topics thoroughly before they speak feel prepared. As a result, they tend to be much more relaxed and effective during their presentations.

Practice Your Speech

You can build your confidence and reduce the nervousness associated with the formality of a speech by practicing. The more times you practice, the more confident you can become. The following example shows how this can be done.

communication apprehension
the level of fear or anxiety associated with either real or anticipated communication with another person or persons.

trait anxiety
apprehension about communicating with others in any situation.

state, or situational, anxiety
apprehension about communicating with others in a particular situation.

PRACTICING HUMAN COMMUNICATION
Building Your Confidence

With another member of your class, make a list of what makes each of you feel nervous about public speaking. Now sort this list into categories that reflect your view of yourselves as speakers, your audience, the process of developing your speech and presentational aids, and delivering your speeches. Identify which aspect or aspects of the public-speaking process generate the most anxiety for each of you. Discuss which techniques for easing public-speaking anxiety presented in this chapter might work best for you.

Randy was terrified to give his first speech. His instructor suggested a solution he reluctantly agreed to try. When no one else was home, Randy began to present his speech aloud and alone in his room. He then stood in front of a mirror and delivered his speech to his own reflection. After several horrifying attempts, he began to feel more comfortable.

Soon after, he began to trust his speaking ability enough to deliver his speech to his older sister, whom he trusted to be kind and constructive. After doing this a few times, he asked her to give him honest feedback. Finally, he practiced once more in the clothing he planned to wear and delivered his speech in his kitchen, which he arranged so it resembled his classroom as much as possible.

When speakers practice their speeches before they give them, they become more familiar with the process of speaking and the formality of the situation. As they gain comfort by practicing alone, they can move to rehearsals before an audience. They also have time to make changes in their presentation and smooth out the rough spots before they actually speak. This practice is part of a process known as **systematic desensitization**, a *technique for reducing anxiety that involves teaching your body to feel calm and relaxed rather than fearful during your speeches*. This technique can help you give successful speeches and build your confidence, thus breaking the cycle of fear associated with public speaking. Talk to your instructor if you would like to learn more about this technique (Kangas Dwyer, 1998, 2000; McCroskey, 1972; Smith & Frymier, 2006).

Have Realistic Expectations

A third way to build your confidence is to set realistic expectations about your delivery. Few speakers sound or look like professional performers. When real people give real speeches, they sound like real people who are invested in their topic and speech. So rather than worry about delivering a flawless performance, adjust your expectations to a more realistic level.

Remember, speakers pause, cough, rely on their notes for prompts, occasionally say "um," and even exhibit physical signs of nervousness such as blushing or sweating. As we give more speeches, these "flaws" either go away or become less noticeable or we learn to manage them effectively. Here are a few realistic expectations for beginning speakers:

- Take a calming breath before you begin your speech.
- Remember your introduction.
- Strike a balance between using your notes and making eye contact with your audience.
- Make eye contact with more than one person.

systematic desensitization
technique for reducing anxiety that involves teaching your body to feel calm and relaxed rather than fearful during your speeches.

- Gesture naturally rather than hold on to the podium.
- Deliver your conclusion the way you practiced it.

Practice Visualization and Affirmations

Sometimes, we increase our nervousness by imagining a worst-case scenario for the speech, and these images often stay in our minds. This can set up a *self-fulfilling prophecy*: if you see yourself doing poorly in your mind before your speech, you set yourself up to do so in the speech. There are two ways to turn this negative dynamic around and build your confidence as a speaker: visualization and affirmations.

Visualization **Visualization** is *a process in which you construct a mental image of yourself giving a successful speech.* Research on the benefits of visualization suggests that one session of visualization (about fifteen minutes) has a significant positive effect on communication apprehension (Ayres & Hopf, 1985, 1989, 1990; Ayres, Hopf, & Ayres, 1994; McGarvey, 1990). The techniques of visualization are used by a wide range of people—athletes, performers, and executives—and can range from elaborate to quite simple processes. For public speakers, the most effective process works like this.

Find a quiet, comfortable place where you can sit in a relaxed position for approximately fifteen minutes. Close your eyes and breathe slowly and deeply through your nose, feeling relaxation flow through your body. In great detail, visualize the morning of the day you are to give your speech.

You become filled with confidence and energy, and you wear the perfect clothing for your speech. You drive, walk, or ride to campus filled with this same positive and confident energy. As you enter the classroom, you see yourself relaxed, interacting with your classmates, full of confidence because you have thoroughly prepared for your speech. Your classmates are friendly and cordial in their greetings and conversations with you. You are *absolutely* sure of your material and your ability to present that material in the way you would like.

Next, visualize yourself beginning your speech. You see yourself approaching the place in your classroom from which you will speak. You are sure of yourself, eager to begin, and positive in your abilities as a speaker. You know you are organized and ready to use all your visual aids with ease. Now you see yourself presenting your speech. Your introduction is wonderful. Your transitions are smooth and interesting. Your main points are articulated brilliantly. Your evidence is presented elegantly. Your organization is perfect. Take as much time as you can in visualizing this part of your process. Be as specific and positive as you can.

Visualize the end of the speech: it could not have gone better. You are relaxed and confident, the audience is eager to ask questions, and you respond with ease and poise. As you return to your seat, you are filled with energy and appreciation for the job well done. You are ready for the next events of your day, and you accomplish them with success and confidence.

Now take a deep breath and return to the present. Breathe in, hold it—and release. Do this several times as you return to the present. Take as much time as you need to make this transition (Ayres & Hopf, 1989).

visualization
a process in which you construct a mental image of yourself giving a successful speech.

Research on visualization for public speakers suggests that the more detail we give to our visualizations (what shoes we wear, exactly how we feel as we see ourselves, imagining the specifics of our speech), the more effective the technique is in building our confidence and reducing apprehension. Visualization has a significant effect on building our confidence because it systematically replaces negative images with positive images.

Affirmations Speakers sometimes undermine their confidence through negative self-talk; they listen to the harsh judgments that many of us carry within ourselves. When we think, "I'm no good at this," "I know I'll embarrass myself," or "Other people are far more talented than I am," we engage in negative self-talk. We judge ourselves as inferior or less competent than others. Although it is natural to evaluate our own performances critically (that is how we motivate ourselves to improve), negative self-talk in public-speaking situations often is never helpful. When our internal voices tell us we cannot succeed, our communication apprehension only increases (Ayres, 1988).

To build your confidence and counter the negative self-talk that might be going on in your head before a speech, use **affirmations**, *positive statements that assert that what we wish to be true is already happening*. To replace the negative self-talk with affirmations, try the following technique. For every negative assessment you hear yourself give, replace it with an honest assessment that you reframe to make positive. This technique, sometimes called **cognitive restructuring**, is a *process that builds confidence because it replaces negative thoughts with positive thoughts called affirmations* (Fremouw & Scott, 1979). Affirmations are positive, motivating statements. They are helpful in

Negative	Positive
I don't know how to organize this material.	I can find a way to present this effectively. I have a good sense of organization. I can get help if I need it.
I know I'll get up there and make a fool of myself.	I am capable of giving a wonderful speech. I know lots of strategies to do so.
I'll forget what I want to say.	I'll remember what I want to say, and I'll have notes to help me.
I'm too scared to look at my audience.	I'll make eye contact with at least five people in the audience.
I'm scared to death!	I care about my performance and will do very well.
I'll be the worst in the class!	I'll give my speech well and am looking forward to a fine presentation. We are all learning how to do this.

affirmations
positive statements that assert that what we wish to be true is already happening.

cognitive restructuring
process that builds confidence because it replaces negative thoughts with positive thoughts called affirmations.

turning our immobilizing self-doubts into realistic assessments and options. Consider the following examples.

Positive affirmations build confidence because they reframe negative energy and evaluations and shed light on your anxieties. To say you are terrified is immobilizing, but to say you care about your performance gives you room to continue to develop your speech. It is also a more accurate description of what is going on inside. Affirmations can help you minimize the effects of your internal judgments; with visualization, they can help build your confidence about public speaking.

Connect With Your Audience

A final way to build your confidence is to connect with your audience—getting to know members in class or gathering information about them before a more formal speaking situation. As you prepare your speech, identify what you know about them, the ways you are similar to audience members, and the ways you might be different. The similarities may be as general as living in the same town or working for the same company or as specific as sharing the same views on issues. Whatever the level of comparison, finding out about your audience reminds you that we all share many aspects of our daily lives. This helps you see that we share similar views and experiences even if we have differences.

You can also build your confidence by being a good member of the audience when others are speaking. Although this might seem unusual, ask yourself the following questions: When you are listening to a speech, do you make eye contact with the speaker? Do you sit with an attentive and alert posture, taking notes or showing interest in the presentation? Do you ask relevant questions of the speaker when the speech is over or offer constructive comments if you have the opportunity to evaluate his or her performance? Speakers who fail to behave as engaged and interested audience members often fear the same responses to their speeches.

One way to overcome this fear of disrespectful audiences is to behave as an audience member as you would want others to behave when you speak. Doing so helps establish rapport (if you are kind to a speaker, she or he likely will respond similarly to you). It also helps you learn about how to put together and deliver an effective speech.

The solutions offered in this section may help you reduce the speech anxiety so common to beginning public speakers. Preparing, practicing, being realistic, visualizing and affirming, finding connections, and modeling appropriate audience behavior are options that even experienced public speakers use to build their confidence. Learning to relax while giving speeches enhances your ability to contribute to the public dialogue.

PRACTICING HUMAN COMMUNICATION
Writing Affirmations

In one column, write down a list of negative statements you typically tell yourself about giving a speech. Create a second column and make each negative statement positive. Now identify which statements pertain to aspects of speech preparation, delivery, and audience feedback. Discuss as a class how speakers can build their confidence and how listeners can help speakers build confidence.

MindTap®

Sample Speeches
Go to the MindTap for *Invitation to Human Communication*. To view a speech about self-introduction, watch Tiffany Brisco's speech. To view an informative speech, watch Cindy Gardner's "U.S. Flag Etiquette." To view an introduction using a narrative, watch Brandi Lafferty's opening story in her speech "Feeding the Wildlife: Don't Do It!"

Chapter Summary

The Four Methods of Delivery Used by Public Speakers Are Extemporaneous, Impromptu, Manuscript, and Memorized

- Effective speakers use vocal variety in their delivery—changes in the volume, rate, and pitch of a speaker's voice that affect the meaning of the words delivered.
- Vocal variety is achieved when speakers adjust the volume, rate, pitch and inflection, pauses, articulation, pronunciation, and dialect throughout their speeches.

The Nonverbal Components of Delivery Are Those Aspects Communicated Through Our Bodies and Faces

- For public speakers, these include personal appearance, eye contact, facial expression, posture, gestures, and proxemics.
- *Technology* refers to the tools speakers use to help them deliver their message. Speakers use both traditional and electronic technologies in their speeches.
- **When you use visual aids, remember that they have five purposes:** gain and maintain audience attention, help audiences recall information, help explain and clarify information, increase persuasiveness and enhance credibility, and reduce nervousness
- You can choose from a variety of visual aids, such as Objects, Models and Demonstrations; Photographs, Drawings and Maps; Internet and DVDs; PowerPoint Slides and Presentational technologies; and Flip Charts, Whiteboards or Smartboards, and Poster Boards
- **When you use visual images, follow several important principles**: Emphasize the Visual Image; Use Lines, Arrows, Shading, and Color to Show Relationships and Direction; Use Clear and Consistent Labels; and Use a Computer to Design Your Chart or Graph

Speeches Often Involve Question-and-Answer Sessions

- Ensuring a good question-and-answer session has two steps: preparing for potential questions beforehand and managing the discussion during the session.
- When you prepare for the question-and-answer session, you do two things: identify potential questions and formulate and practice answers to those questions.
- When you manage the discussion, you explain the format before the session begins, listen thoughtfully and clarify any potential misunderstandings, keep a positive mind-set, address the full audience when you offer answers, answer with honesty, and keep the session focused.

Our Nervousness Before a Speech Is Often Called *Communication Apprehension*, and Speakers Can Have Trait Anxiety or Situational Anxiety

- Tips for managing speech apprehension are do your research, practice your speech, have realistic expectations, practice visualization and affirmations, and connect with your audience.
- Speakers sometimes undermine their confidence through negative self-talk. To replace the negative self-talk, use affirmations—positive statements that assert that what we wish to be true is already happening.

Key Concepts

affirmations (314)

articulation (292)

bar graph (304)

cognitive restructuring (314)

communication apprehension (310)

conversational style (283)

demonstration (302)

dialect (293)

drawings (302)

extemporaneous speech (283)

eye contact (296)

facial expression (297)

flowchart (303)

gestures (298)

graph (304)

impromptu speech (284)

inflection (289)

line graph (304)

list (306)

manuscript speech (285)

maps (302)

memorized speech (287)

model (302)

monotone (290)

object (302)

organizational chart (303)

pauses (290)

personal appearance (295)

photograph (302)

picture graph (304)

Invitation to Human Communication Online

MindTap Speech includes an interactive MindTap Reader and interactive learning tools including National Geographic Explorer videos, student videos, quizzes, flash cards, and more. You can build your speech outline with Outline Builder and record, post, and watch videos with YouSeeU. Go to cengagebrain.com to access your MindTap for *Invitation to Human Communication* where these resources can be found.

MindTap®

Further Reflection and Discussion

1. Identify speakers you think have good delivery. What characteristics make their delivery strong? How many of these characteristics might you incorporate into your style of delivery?

2. Identify the differences among extemporaneous, impromptu, manuscript, and memorized deliveries. What are the strengths and weaknesses of each type of delivery?

3. Write a quick speech and exchange the speeches among classmates. In groups, give that speech as though it were a tragedy, a surprise, or a hilarious story—or choose some other approach that will allow you to work on vocal variety. How well are you able to match the verbal aspects of your delivery to the mood you have selected?

4. Bring a dictionary to class. Look up the following commonly confused pairs of words:

accept/except	stationery/stationary
adverse/averse	uninterested/disinterested
affect/effect	who/whom
fewer/less	nauseated/nauseous
healthy/healthful	principal/principle
imply/infer	anxious/eager
lay/lie	appraise/apprise
compose/comprise	between/among
explicit/implicit	compliment/complement
poured/pored	insure/ensure
reign/rein	

   How many of these words did you have confused before you began this exercise?

5. Look up the dictionary definitions of five to ten key-words you will use in your next speech. Do they mean what you thought they meant? Have you been pronouncing them correctly? If you were using an incorrect word, replace it with a correct one.

6. Bring an object or a model to class and practice describing it to your classmates. Try holding it, displaying it, and passing it around, which techniques work well for you and which do not? Why and why not?

7. Many students believe computer-generated visual aids are superior to other types of visual aids. In addition, many employers want employees to be familiar with this technology. What kind of material is best suited to this form of presentation?

8. Either alone or with a friend, discuss the negative self-talk you use to describe your ability to give a speech. Identify the specific negative phrases you use and turn them into positive affirmations. Be realistic in reframing your negative self-talk into positive self-talk using the examples in this chapter as a guide.

9. Set aside fifteen minutes of alone time the day before your first speech. Take time to visualize that speech as the process is described in this chapter. Go through each step carefully and in detail. Do not rush or overlook any aspect of the speech process. After you give your speech, compare having visualized the speech and your level of nervousness to a situation in which you were nervous but did not visualize. Was the visualization helpful in reducing your nervousness? Why or why not?

10. Make a list of issues you find interesting and have followed for some time (or would like to begin following). Spend time on researching who has spoken or written publicly about these issues. See if you can find their speeches on line. After you watch them, consider how these speeches have influenced your views on these issues. Could you add your voice to this public dialogue and unending conversation (from Chapters 1 and 10)? Why or why not? Consider one of these issues as possible topics for your first speech.

Activities and Web Links

Visit cengagebrain.com to access the MindTap for *Invitation to Human Communication* where these activities and web links can be found.

1. Listen to a brief portion of Randy Pausch's famous last lecture. How would you describe his delivery? What is most compelling about his delivery? Go to *Web link 12.1.*

2. Read or listen to Ann Richards's speech at the Democratic National Convention in 1988. What makes her delivery unique? How does she maintain her audience's attention? Go to *Web link 12.2.*

3. Read this article about Senator Edward Kennedy's speeches and delivery. Did his delivery hinder the effectiveness of his speeches? Why or why not? Go to *Web link 12.3.*

4. Read this article about Chicano dialect. What advice would you give to a classmate about what to tell the audience about his or her dialect? Go to *Web link 12.4.*

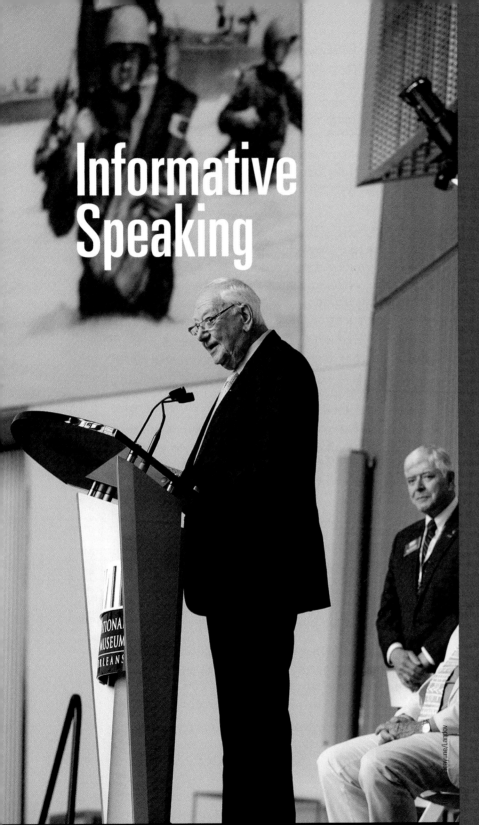

Informative Speaking

13

IN THIS CHAPTER YOU WILL LEARN TO:

- Describe the five types of informative speeches.

- Apply the four most common patterns of organization for informative speeches.

- Employ language that is clear and unbiased in your informative speech.

- Conduct careful research, use unbiased information, and present your information honestly as you give ethical informative speeches.

As you read in an earlier chapter, most of our days are spent listening to others. If you could select three informative speech topics you would like to listen to, what would those topics be? Why would you select those topics?

When we need information on what a new health-care plan will mean, how to fix a flat tire, or which bottled water is the highest quality, we need complete and accurate information. To meet that need, speakers in the workplace, in the classroom, and in our communities often speak informatively. An **informative speech** *communicates knowledge and understanding about a process, an event, a place or person, an object, or a concept.* Informative speakers share what they know or have researched to familiarize an audience with a topic its members want or need to understand.

Informative speakers create **informative speaking environments**, *environments in which a speaker has expertise or knowledge that an audience needs but does not already have.* Informative speakers attempt to enhance an audience's understanding of how some part of the world works.

As you enter the public dialogue, you will give many informative speeches (Johnson & Szczupakiewicz, 1987). In fact, across professions, demand is growing for employees with strong public communication skills and an ability to share information with others in a wide range of settings (Dannels, 2001; Morreal, Osborn, & Pearson, 2000; National Association of Colleges and Employers, 2012; Wolvin, 1989). We often give informative speeches because we need information every day—for example, to understand how a new medication will affect us, to learn how to parallel park, to deliberate over the governor's proposal for spending a budget surplus, or to complete the complex assignment our boss just gave us.

 Types of Informative Speeches

The five types of informative speeches most common in classes that teach public speaking and in the workplace are speeches about processes, events, places and people, objects, and concepts. Each type of speech has a different focus, and each is suited to a different occasion.

Speeches About Processes

Commonly called a how-to or a demonstration speech, **speeches about processes** *describe how something is done, how something comes to be*

---

informative speech
speech that communicates knowledge and understanding about a process, an event, a place or person, an object, or a concept.

informative speaking environments
environments in which a speaker has expertise or knowledge that an audience needs but does not already have.

speeches about processes
informative speech that describes how something is done, how something comes to be what it is, or how something works.

what it is, or how something works. Process speeches help an audience learn how to complete a task, understand how something develops over time, or comprehend how a process unfolds. The fundamental goal of a process speech is to show your audience how to *perform* a process or how to better *understand* a process. Sample topics for process speeches include the following:

How to get a passport

How coal is mined in the United States

How a solar panel converts the sun's heat into our energy

How to protect yourself from harmful sunburns

How to decide how much to tip a server in a restaurant

Process speeches are common because people are constantly learning how to perform new tasks. For example, your boss may ask you to explain to a colleague how to fill out and submit an expense report. Or you may be asked to explain to new staff how an employee incentive program came to be implemented, especially if you have a history with that particular program. In the classroom, you may be required to speak about a process that your classmates will benefit from learning more about.

The following two examples illustrate process speeches about a familiar topic: coffee. In the first example, Tracee describes how coffee came to be a popular drink in North America.

Specific purpose:	To inform my audience how coffee became one of the most popular drinks in North America.
Thesis statement:	Through a series of historical events beginning in the 1500s, coffee replaced tea as one of the most popular drinks in North America.
Main points:	I. Coffee found its way to North America in the 1500s when trade routes opened between coffee-growing countries and Europe, then expanded to North America.
	II. Coffee began to gain in popularity as tensions with England accelerated in the 1700s and imports of tea decreased.
	III. By the 1900s, international commerce, marketing techniques, and individual lifestyles made coffee one of the most popular drinks in North America.

In the second example, Wynton describes how the process of growing and harvesting a particular kind of coffee works.

MARK THIESSEN/National Geographic

Mireya Mayor,
Emerging Explorer, Primatologist, and Conservationist

When giving an informative speech, what types of visual aids have you used, and which have been most effective?

My most popular presentation is based on my life, so the materials come from me and my experiences. What I really like to bring to those presentations are visuals. I start telling stories about my childhood and being an NFL cheerleader and going to these wild and remote places and the animals there. I try to support that with visuals.

I think it's really important to use visual aids to connect people to what I'm talking about. They might not be able to visualize what a tropical rainforest in Madagascar looks like, so I show them, or the amazing array of species there, so I show them. I also try to find timely references that relate to, say, the science that I'm talking about or things that have inspired me. For example, there was an article in *Time* magazine entitled "Death Row," and it showed these critically endangered primates. And that's what really captured my attention and was actually the motivating factor in me going into this field. And years later I dug that article up, scanned it, and I use that as one of the pictures in my PowerPoint. It's so important to show them, to really show them what you are talking about.

Specific purpose:	To inform my audience how shade-grown coffee is grown and harvested.
Thesis statement:	The process of growing and harvesting shade-grown coffee differs from the process used by coffee plantations in three significant ways.
Main points:	I. Shade-grown coffee is grown in small plots, quite unlike the more familiar coffee plantation method.
	II. As the plants grow, these plots provide non-chemical forms of fertilizer and pest control.
	III. When the coffee beans are mature, they are harvested and stored in ecologically friendly ways.

Notice how each speech follows a progression of steps from first to second to third. Because process speeches describe step-by-step progressions, they are almost always organized chronologically. A chronological pattern of organization allows you to develop your speech from the first step to the last or from the earliest signs to the most recent examples. (Later in this chapter, you will explore organizational patterns for informative speeches more fully.)

Speeches About Events

Speeches about events *describe or explain significant, interesting, or unusual occurrences.* These speeches help an audience understand what happened, why it happened, and what effect the event had. Just as we

speeches about events
informative speeches that describe or explain significant, interesting, or unusual occurrences.

often describe what happens in our personal lives so we can better understand how events influence our lives, public speakers share what happens with audiences to help them understand a significant event in the context of history or society or community. In some ways, speeches about events are mini history lessons that educate audiences about key moments. Sample topics for speeches about events would be

the resignation of Egyptian President Hosni Mubarak

the radioactive leaks at Japan's Fukushima nuclear power plant

the origins of the Occupy movement

large-scale food recalls

Speakers are often asked to speak about events, usually in professional settings. Consider Sophia, whose boss asked her to speak to her fellow employees about the latest recall of beef in their region.

Specific purpose:	To inform our staff of the most recent recall of beef and products that contain beef.
Thesis statement:	This most recent recall of beef from our stores requires that we identify all beef purchased within the last three months, identify all products containing beef purchased within the last three months, and remove and dispose of these products in specific ways.

In a community setting, people may decide to speak about local events as a way to inform councils, planning boards, or community service agencies and perhaps assist them with the decisions they make.

Specific purpose:	To inform the city council about the high rate of accidents at the corner of College and Elm Streets.
Thesis statement:	The intersection of College and Elm is the site of an unusually high rate of accidents during certain hours of the day.

When you are required to speak about an event, select a topic your audience will find interesting and relevant. For example, inform your classmates of an event that affects your own campus (a public hearing to improve public transportation to the campus), the community that houses your campus (an annual jazz festival that showcases successful musicians from the community), or your state or region (a recognition ceremony for local volunteers who helped elect a candidate to Congress).

Most speeches about events, especially historical events, are arranged chronologically. However, if the way an event unfolds is not the focus of your speech, then you can organize your speech topically. Or if you want to analyze why an event occurred and what effect it had, you can use a causal pattern. (These and other patterns of organization are examined later in the chapter.)

Speeches About Places and People

Speeches about places and people *describe significant, interesting, or unusual places or people.* These speeches can be fun to give in a classroom because you can share your experiences with places and people you have visited or have found fascinating. In the workplace or the community, speeches about places and people help audiences understand the importance, nature, appeal, charm, or integrity of a particular place or person or the contributions a particular person has made to an organization or a community. Sample topics for speeches about places and people might be

top ten nightlife cities

Jason Collins

New Orleans

Nelson Mandela

Haiti

Jane Goodall

Because you will not have time in a speech to discuss all there is to know about a place or a person, the goal of this type of speech is to capture the *spirit* of that place or person. You want audience members to understand why this place or person is important or useful to them or their community, important historically, or just interesting and worth learning about. Look at this example of a speech that Adrianna gave in her public-speaking course.

Specific purpose:	To inform my audience about the history and features of the Freedom Trail in Boston, Massachusetts.
Thesis statement:	The Freedom Trail, which originated in the late 1950s, is a pedestrian path through downtown Boston that links sites of historical importance to the United States, such as our first public school and the site of the Boston Massacre.

In the next example, Garrett informs his classmates about Captain Nicole Malachowski, the first woman selected to join the Thunderbirds, the air force's most elite team of pilots.

Specific purpose:	To inform my classmates of Lieutenant Colonel Nicole Malachowski, the first woman selected to fly with the Thunderbirds.
Thesis statement:	In 2005, the Thunderbirds, a small elite team of the best pilots in the air force, selected its first woman pilot, Nicole Malachowski, to join them, opening the doors for other talented female pilots to fly the most advanced aircraft in the world.

speeches about places and people
speeches that describe significant, interesting, or unusual places or people.

Unheard Voices to the Rescue

Benny's sight." Her interactions with Josephs and Iron Head inspired her to found Downtown Dog Rescue in 1996. Since then, this organization has rescued and adopted out more than 3,000 dogs, provided resources for homeless people and their pets, and raised awareness in the Los Angeles area about animal cruelty. Lori is a tireless advocate for healthy and responsible pet ownership, using many channels to get the word out, including community events, letter-writing campaigns, speeches at conferences, and Twitter.

Luigi "Shorty" Rossi, also from Los Angeles, credits pit bulls with saving his life when he was young and providing loyal companionship during the hardest times of his life, including a stint in prison for gang-related activity. In 2001, after having made a successful career for himself as an entertainer and talent manager, he founded Shorty's Pit Bull Rescue. Just as Downtown Dog Rescue does, Shorty's Rescue rescues, rehabilitates, and adopts out neglected and abused pit bulls. The organization also promotes a positive view of this misunderstood breed, using education and activism to help prevent animal cruelty. Shorty's forums for speaking out include short films, public service commercials, and *Pit Boss*, Animal Planet's reality show about his endeavors ("Meet Shorty Rossi," 2010).

People often join the public dialogue to speak for those who cannot speak for themselves. Sometimes these unheard voices belong to other people, such as children, or to entities such as the environment. Many times, these voices belong to animals (LeBeau, 2008; Weise, 2009).

Dog owner Lori Weise, a manager at a furniture store in Los Angeles, crossed paths one day with a homeless man named Benny Josephs and his pit bull, Iron Head. The bond between this man and his dog had a profound impact on Weise. "I was so impressed with how the two were really one," she says. "Iron Head was never on a leash and never strayed too far from

What Do You Think?

1. If you wanted to give an informative speech about someone who might be considered as being a member of "unheard voices," what individuals or groups could you speak about?
2. What about these individuals or groups would be interesting to share with your audience?
3. What ethical issues you might need to consider and address if you were to give a speech about one of these individuals or groups?

Speeches about places or people can be organized topically (how the Freedom Trail was conceived, the importance of the historical sites to which the trail leads), chronologically (events in Captain Malachowski's life that led to her selection), or spatially (Big Bend National Park in Texas features recreational areas in the mountains and desert and along the Rio Grande River).

Speeches About Objects
Speeches about objects are about *anything that is tangible—that is, can be perceived by the senses.* When we speak informatively about objects, we describe the components or characteristics of something so an audience

speeches about objects
informative speeches about anything that is tangible—that is, can be perceived by the senses.

Art often makes an interesting topic for a speech. Make a list of your favorite photos, paintings, music, or other art forms. Could you give a speech on one of these topics?

can better understand it and why it might be important or valued. Sample topics for speeches about objects include

credit cards

honeybees

hybrid automobiles

poisonous frogs

Speeches about objects are common in the working world. For example, a product-development coordinator might speak regularly to her colleagues about new products that come across her desk, describing their qualities, uses, and appeal. Similarly, tour guides often speak about local objects of importance or interest, describing buildings, sculptures, and pieces of art. For a required classroom speech about an object, you might describe something useful, rare, or interesting to a speech class audience. For example, Jun Lee gave a speech about *Mona Lisa*'s mysterious smile.

Specific purpose: To inform my audience about the *Mona Lisa* and the many theories about her famous smile.

Thesis statement: One of the most famous paintings of all time, the *Mona Lisa* has inspired several theories about why she has such a mysterious smile.

A popular topic for speeches about *animate* objects is animals and their behaviors, habitats, and ways of interacting with humans and other animals. Here is a sample specific purpose and a thesis statement for Shana's speech about the African serval.

Specific purpose:	To inform my audience about keeping the African serval as a house pet.
Thesis statement:	Although the African serval's legs, ears, and coloration aid in its survival in the wild, these same adaptations have a whole new meaning in the context of keeping a serval as an exotic house pet.

Many speeches about objects are organized topically (the characteristics of the poisonous frog). Others are organized using a causal pattern (possible causes of the colony collapse disorder plaguing our honeybees) and sometimes, a speech about an object can be organized chronologically (hybrid automobile, from the first to the latest model) or spatially (the different features of a hybrid car). Be sure to select the pattern that helps you express your ideas clearly and efficiently.

Speeches About Concepts

Speeches about concepts are *about abstractions, things you cannot perceive with your senses—such as ideas, theories, principles, worldviews, or beliefs.* The goal of a speech about a concept is to help your audience understand your subject, its history, its characteristics, and its effect on society or individuals. Some sample topics for speeches about concepts are

the new frugality

sustainability

adult literacy

theories of adolescent development

global citizenship

When you give speeches about concepts, you help audiences more fully understand or appreciate issues, principles, systems, and the like. Consider Tory's speech about the new frugality, sometimes described as "less is more."

Specific purpose:	To inform my audience about the new frugality, which is sometimes called "less is more."
Thesis statement:	In times of economic crisis, many people embrace the values of frugality, which involve owning fewer material possessions, being less "possession-identified" and more "self-identified," and, of course, spending less money.

speeches about concepts
informative speeches about abstractions, things you cannot perceive with your senses—such as ideas, theories, principles, worldviews, or beliefs.

PRACTICING HUMAN COMMUNICATION

Select an Informative Speech Topic and Type

As a class, brainstorm as many different informative speech topics as you can. Next, group the topics according to the five types of informative speeches you have just read about. Some might fit into several groups, depending on how you phrase your thesis statement for a particular topic. Discuss which of these topics you find most interesting and why. Save this list for the next Practicing Human Communication activity.

Speeches about concepts can be challenging because it might be difficult to explain an abstraction clearly. However, this type of speech is also very helpful because sometimes audiences need to understand concepts before they can understand how something works or why a person is significant. Speeches about concepts are often organized topically (the principles behind sustainability) or chronologically (early theories of adolescent development to the most recent theories). Sometimes, a speech about a concept can be organized causally (the causes of the idea of global citizenship).

 ## Organizational Patterns for Informative Speeches

Informative speeches can be organized in a variety of ways, and you will probably use a wide range of organizational patterns as you become a proficient public speaker. These organizational patterns are chronological, spatial, causal, and topical. Using these patterns, you can organize your main points logically.

Chronological Pattern

With a **chronological pattern**, you can *organize your main points to illustrate how a topic has developed over time or what sequential steps an audience must take to complete a task*. Most of us are familiar with the chronological pattern because most stories we tell or hear progress from start to finish chronologically. Chronological patterns are especially effective for process speeches, but as you learned earlier in this chapter, they also are well suited for other kinds of informative speeches. In the following example, Alan gives a speech to explain to his audience how the Ford Mustang set the standard for the so-called muscle cars of the 1960s.

Specific purpose:	To inform my audience of the history of the Ford Mustang.
Thesis statement:	The Ford Mustang, which quickly became the muscle car to beat in 1964 with its combination of high performance and low cost, continues to be the most popular car of that decade.
Main points:	I. Pontiac's GTO—which stands for "gas, tires, oil"—is credited as the first of the muscle cars of the 1960s.
	II. Ford quickly took the top spot among muscle cars, releasing the high-performance, low-cost Mustang to the public on April 17, 1964.

chronological pattern
a pattern of organization in which you illustrate how a topic has developed over time or what sequential steps an audience must take to complete a task.

Sol Guy, New Media Cultural Story Teller, Emerging Explorer: "Apathetic Is Pathetic"

HALE REBECCA/National Geographic Creative

Courtesy of 4REAL

As an artist, social entrepreneur committed to ethical business practices, former manager of some of today's highest-profile hip-hop artists, and a film and TV producer, Canadian-born Sol Guy was "[r]iding the wave of the hip-hop music explosion" and "on track to becoming a top recording industry executive." However, "at the height of his success, he grew disillusioned with the North American hip-hop scene's increasing emphasis on violence and materialism." In 2000, he travelled to Africa to be a part of the award-winning documentary *Musicians in the War Zone*. The trip, Guy states, changed his life: "I can't really explain why that happened, but it was this thing where I saw something that I couldn't look away from. And then, in fact, I saw there was a way I could influence it. And then I saw the power of storytelling." Returning from the trip, Guy "adopted a new focus." He explains, "Acknowledging my success and experience in the music industry I began to realize the power I possessed in creating media. I decided that I wanted to create a new hybrid that connects the worlds of entertainment and activism." He and long-time friend Josh Thome coproduced *4REAL*, a television series that introduces celebrities, such as Cameron Diaz, Joaquin Phoenix, and others, to young people "creating real social change using music, art, and culture to propel communities forward. They've been through some of the most horrible experiences imaginable, yet have come out shining with phenomenal passion and power."

What makes these young people so exceptional, Guy explains, is "their desire to radically change their community and their inability to see any obstacle as an obstacle." What some of us might see as "insurmountable odds," these young leaders see as something to be pushed through. What is missing, he says, is "the can't, the idea of cannot. Instead, it's just, like 'well, why not?' And that's a really interesting thing because the only barriers to any entry to radically changing something are the thoughts you have and what you believe yourself to be capable of." He continues, "The people, the things they've seen, the world," don't stop them; instead, these young leaders from some of the harshest conditions imaginable "are just like . . . well, why not? And I know that feeling because I share it with them. You see something that you want to do, and you're passionate about it, you go for it. And that's how you create things. That's how you create change. That's how new things come about."

Guy has delivered speeches and presentations "from boardrooms to primary schools, community centers, jails, reservations, wherever I am invited." We all have stories to tell, he says; what we must do is "create space for important stories to be told . . . and whatever the medium is, if the story is told and the storyteller is good, it'll find its way." He continues, "apathetic is pathetic"; people have to stop blaming one another and take action. He sees all of us living in a "time of urgency" and believes there is no time to "play it safe." Guy concludes, humans are "an extraordinary animal, you know? And we stifle ourselves and our potential only because we forget that we created everything that we are living in. These are all ideas. Our thoughts created reality. And that's our power of manifestation. And, wow, imagine when we all recognize that collective power" (Guy, 2014a; Guy & Thome, n.d.).

WHAT DO YOU THINK?

1. Sol Guy suggests that "apathetic is pathetic." As a class, discuss what you think he means by this. How might this influence your informative speech topic?

2. Guy urges young people to say "Why not?" rather than "I can't." Reflect on times you have said, "I can't." What would change if you had said "Why not?" instead?

3. Log on to TEDx Toronto and watch Guy's presentation and delivery. What are the strengths of his presentation? In what ways can you incorporate some of these strengths into your own speech?

III. Ford then added new makes with increasingly attractive features and options to maintain its popularity—among them the Fastback, the Grande, the Mach I, the Boss 302, and the Boss 429.

IV. The muscle cars of the 1960s remain some of the most popular cars of that decade, and the newer Mustangs give us a glimpse into why this is so.

Alan takes his audience through the evolution of muscle cars in the 1960s, beginning with the Pontiac GTO; moving on to Ford's first Mustangs and the company's release of newer makes, features, and options; and then showing the current influence of those features on today's cars. By using this pattern, Alan provides his listeners with basic information they can build on as he progresses through his speech.

Spatial Pattern

The **spatial pattern** allows you to *address topics logically in terms of location or direction*. With this pattern, you can arrange your main points by the position they represent within a physical space. You also can use this pattern to inform your audience of the places that relate to your topic, the activities that occur in those places, or the activities that are necessary to the functioning of your topic. In the following example, Scott uses a spatial pattern to describe the different parts of a guitar and how each part works to produce sound.

Specific purpose:	To inform my audience of how the different parts of the guitar work together to produce sound.
Thesis statement:	The guitar has three main parts—the head, neck, and body—and each works with the others in intricate ways to produce the sounds we call music.
Main points:	I. The top of the guitar is the head, which houses the nut and the tuning pegs.
	II. The next part is the neck, which contains three essential parts: the frets, the truss rod, and the fingerboard.
	III. The bottom part is the body, which is made of a reinforced front, back and side panels, a sound hole, and the bridge and saddle.

The spatial pattern is a clear and effective way to describe the different parts of an object.

Causal Pattern

Causal patterns *highlight cause-and-effect relationships*. A cause is an event that makes something happen, and an effect is the response, impression, or change that results from that cause. When you use causal

spatial pattern
a pattern of organization that allows you to address topics logically in terms of location or direction.

causal patterns
a pattern of organization that allows you to highlight cause-and-effect relationships.

patterns, you inform your audience about what causes certain events, places, objects, or concepts to come into being.

In the following example, Kelsey describes the causes of the onion's tearful effect as well as methods to prevent tears when cutting an onion.

Specific purpose:	To inform my audience about the cause of an onion's tearful effect and methods used to prevent tears when cutting an onion.
Thesis statement:	The internal chemistry of the onion is the cause of its tearful effect when being chopped, but various methods may be used to prevent this occurrence.
Main points:	I. The onion's chemical makeup combines with the physiology of the human eye to induce tears.
	II. The first method to prevent tears is chilling the onion.
	III. The second method involves using an open flame during onion preparation
	IV. Using water around the onion is a helpful technique to reduce tears as well.
	V. The last method involves cutting the core from an onion, where most tear-producing compounds—lachrymators—are thought to be stored.

Kelsey's use of the causal pattern helped her explain what caused the tears and then show certain ways of cutting an onion to reduce tear production.

Topical Pattern

The **topical organizational pattern** *allows a speaker to address different aspects of a topic.* For example, in Shana's speech on the African serval, she organized her ideas topically to address the physical characteristics that make the animal so suited to life in the wild and then the consequences of bringing it into a domestic setting.

Topical patterns work well in informative speeches with topics that can be easily and logically divided into subtopics. Using a topical pattern, you can highlight the aspects of a topic that are most useful and important for an audience to understand. In Lauren's speech about nursery rhymes, she used a topical pattern to discuss their dark history.

PRACTICING HUMAN COMMUNICATION
Select an Organizational Pattern for Your Informative Speech

Return to the list of possible informative speech topics you prepared in Practicing Human Communication earlier in this chapter. In groups, select a single topic and see if you can create a rough thesis statement and main points for four different informative speeches on this topic, using each of the organizational patterns you have just read about. As a class, discuss which of these speeches you would find most interesting and why. As you discuss your favorite topic and organizational pattern, consider the tips for giving effective informative speeches in the next section.

topical organizational pattern
a pattern of organization that allows a speaker to address different aspects of a topic.

Specific purpose:	To inform the audience about the dark history of the origin of nursery rhymes.
Thesis statement:	Nursery rhymes are seen as innocent and light-hearted tales because they are always associated with children, but the truth is that stories such as "Ring Around the Rosie," "Peter Peter Pumpkin Eater," and "Mary, Mary, Quite Contrary" may have dark and often gruesome origins that would seem anything but appropriate for children.
Main points:	I. The rhyme "Ring Around the Rosie" goes all the way back to the year 1350 Europe when the Black Plague was at its peak.
	II. The rhyme "Peter, Peter Pumpkin Eater" is actually a rhyme about a man who forced his mistress to wear a chastity belt.
	III. "Mary, Mary, Quite Contrary" is actually the most gruesome rhyme of the three.

By using this organizational pattern, Lauren was able to inform her audience of the dark origins of many of their favorite childhood nursery rhymes.

 ## Tips for Giving Effective Informative Speeches

In an informative speaking environment, you contribute to the public dialogue by sharing your knowledge with your audience, illustrating with clarity and detail the relevance of that knowledge to your listeners. Three tips that will help you create informative speaking environments and give effective informative speeches are (1) bring your topic to life, (2) tailor your information to your audience, and (3) use language that is clear and unbiased.

Bring Your Topic to Life

When you give an informative speech, you want your audience to understand your topic in a detailed and dynamic way. Effective informative speakers bring a subject to life for an audience, engaging their listeners so they appreciate the information they receive. Take careful stock of your topic and your audience so you can be sure to share information that is both *engaging* and *relevant*. Engaging material draws audience members in and excites or interests them. Listeners find material relevant if it is useful or something they must know to do their jobs, live in a community, or make informed decisions.

One way to bring a topic to life is to stay audience centered. As you craft your speech, continually ask yourself how your overall topic, main points, and subpoints relate to your audience:

What do audience members need to know?

How will they use the information you present?

How can you make the information clear? If you keep these questions in mind throughout your preparation process, you will be more likely to present your material in an engaging and relevant way. For example, in the speech about school violence, Erin brought her second point—manipulation by other students—to life by asking her audience a rhetorical question: "Think back to high school. How many examples of manipulative behavior can you think of? Probably too many. In my junior year, I remember one group of students who constantly picked on my friends and me. It felt like no matter what we did, we were the brunt of their jokes and the focus of their hostility." By sharing her own experience of manipulation, she touched on an experience common to many members of her audience.

Demonstration speeches are often engaging because they provide audiences with especially relevant and useful information. If you give this type of speech, avoid overwhelming your audience with too much information. Consider a demonstration speech you might like to give. What is the most important information you think your audience would need?

Another way to bring your topic to life is to share the human side of your topic. If you are presenting technical information, explaining intricate details, or carefully outlining a process, try to use examples, images, and descriptions that help your audience connect to your topic personally. If you are presenting numbers or statistics, give the figures a human face. As one student asked after hearing an informative speech about how to avoid the kinds of sunburns that lead to skin cancer, "What do all those SPF factors and fancy names mean for me and my skin tone personally?" As you prepare your speech, anticipate this kind of question and look for opportunities to relate your information to the human experience. For example, in a speech on modern art, you might personalize different techniques and styles by drawing parallels to skills learned in art classes or by asking your audience to attempt the techniques on their own as you describe them.

Tailor Your Information to Your Audience

Just as you can feel overwhelmed by the abundance of information you find in your research, your audiences can be equally overwhelmed by the information you share with them in your speech—no matter how engaging and relevant you make that information. As an informative speaker, one of your most challenging tasks is to decide how much information to include in a speech and how much to leave out. Here are a few reasons why:

- When you present too much information, you run the risk of overwhelming an audience.

- When you present too little information, you run the risk of leaving them unclear or confused about your topic.

- If you present material that is too technical, detailed, and complicated, your audience will have a hard time following it.

- If the information in your speech is too simple, audience members will become bored or feel that you are talking down to them.

Given these dilemmas, the best way to tailor your information to your audience is to *stay audience centered* throughout the speech process. As

Managing Rumors

When people work together, they talk and share information. When talking and sharing of information is comprehensive, clear, and accurate, the activities of workplace flow fairly smoothly and workplace creativity and productivity often are enhanced. But when talking and sharing of information is incomplete, misleading, or speculative, rumors circulate and problems can begin. When information is absent or inadequate in the workplace, people begin to worry and often share those worries with others. We wonder who will be fired, who will get a promotion, who will get credit on a project, why are two individuals working so closely together, and what exactly is going on? People talk with one another because they are trying to make sense of what is going on around them (Mind Tools, n.d.). When they do not have enough information, they speculate; when they have inaccurate information, they share it; when they hear something, true or not, they tell others. This is the recipe for rumors, and rumors can lead to hurt feelings, mistakes, and even bullying in the workplace.

But you can manage rumors, according to Mind Tools Essential Skills for a Successful Career, and here's how:

1. Keep people informed. Tell your employees, team members, office staff, and co-workers what is going on. Share information accurately, openly, and as often as possible.
2. Communicate. When tough times happen, which they will, keep the lines of communication open and honest. During a crisis, when distress is high, keep your staff updated regularly (even if simply to say, "I have no new information").
3. Share what you can. When you cannot give employees all the information, share what you can with them. Be honest that you cannot tell them everything but you are sharing what you can.
4. Create transparent procedures. Create and share how individuals get promoted, what leads to termination, how raises happen, who supervises whom, and the like. Create

documents for these processes and procedures and make them easily available to employees.
5. Get to know people. Establish relationships with your employees, staff, co-workers, and so on. Spend time learning about them and developing healthy relationships with them. This is the first step toward setting the stage for trust, and trust goes a long way when workplace environments become hectic, tense, or even conflicted.
6. Support collaboration and cooperation. Workplaces that encourage competition and pit workers against one another usually have the most rumors circulating, and some of those are among the worst rumors to fill any workplace. Workplaces that reward cooperation, collaboration, kindness, and honesty are more productive and with healthier employees. Deal with rumors immediately and reward individuals who are supportive and collaborative with one another.

you develop and present your speech, continually reflect on the needs and interests of your audience. Include information that you think would be of the greatest educational value for your audience, and then adjust your presentation of this information so that it matches your audience's level of knowledge, expertise, and experience.

Use Language That Is Clear and Unbiased

Because informative speeches focus on describing, defining, and explaining, use language that is descriptive and instructive. To ensure your audience can follow you, define all new terminology, break complicated processes into steps, and explain language specific to a particular field or activity. For example, when Wynton spoke about shade-grown coffee, he explained what the terms *shade grown*, *fair trade*, *organic*, and *sustainable* mean. Similarly, when Sophia spoke to her colleagues about the beef recall affecting their company, she made sure her audience understood the specific dates and the exact methods of disposal. You can also make a point of explaining familiar words you use in new ways. For example, Lauren took time to link what her audience thought were lighthearted phrases and words from the nursery rhymes to their darker historical origins.

Informative language should be as objective as you can make it. Focus on presenting your information as clearly and accurately as you can and avoid expressing your own views (as in invitational speaking) or trying to sway your audience (as in persuasive speaking). Remember that the goal of informative speaking is to pass along information your audience needs or wants. Make sure the language of your speech is fair and unbiased. Use phrases like "My research indicates that" or "According to the experts" rather than "I hope I've convinced you that this is the best way."

Similarly, when you incorporate personal knowledge into an informative speech, which is common when you describe or explain something you have experience with, make sure the language you use reflects your *experience*, not your biases or preferences. For example, phrases like "After seven years with these machines, I'd recommend the following steps" and "I've been involved in four food recalls since I began in this industry, so I can give you some background and details" are more informative than persuasive.

 ## Ethical Informative Speaking

Ethical informative speakers make sure their speeches are based on careful research, unbiased information, and the honest presentation of information. Take a look at each of these components of ethical informative speaking.

First, our audiences expect that we have taken the time to find information that is accurate and complete, so we must carefully research the

Robert Kyncl, vice president of global content partnerships at YouTube, delivered the keynote speech at the Entertainment Matters 2012 International Consumer Electronics Show. What would you listen for to evaluate whether this speech was an ethical informative speech?

Ethan Miller/Getty Images

When Must We Speak?

In 2003, as part of a federal case against the Bay Area Laboratory Co-Operative (BALCO) for distributing illegal "designer steroids" to professional athletes, baseball great Barry Bonds told a grand jury that he had not taken steroids during his career. Bonds provided this information because he and other athletes were offered immunity if they testified in the case, which targeted Victor Conte, the founder of BALCO, and Greg Anderson, Bond's trainer and longtime friend. Bonds explained that he trusted Anderson and used the creams and gels Anderson supplied because he thought they were simply flax seed oil and arthritis pain relievers. His testimony, which was supposed to be secret, was leaked to outside sources. Believing that Bonds had lied under oath, prosecutors began a perjury investigation. Bond's attorney, Mike Raines, responded by claiming that the federal government was persecuting Bonds and "going after his client because of his name and notoriety, not the allegations leveled against him." He said, "You offer immunity and you get him in there and then you ask them questions and you get them on lying to federal officers. That's the trap. That's exactly what they got Martha [Stewart] for." In 2011, however, "a federal court jury found [Bonds] guilty of obstruction of justice," for "giving an evasive answer under oath" in 2003. Although Bonds was acquitted on three other charges of making false statements, he was convicted on the obstruction of justice charges, and he received a sentence of two years of probation and 30 days of house arrest (Martinez & Simon, 2011; Quinn, 2007; Rosynsky, 2007; Rowlands, 2006; Williams & Fainaru-Wada, 2004).

What Do You Think?

1. Both Barry Bonds and Martha Stewart were required to speak in a court of law about cases that were not about them specifically. Do you think people should be required to speak in this way? Why or why not?

2. Lance Armstrong, another superstar athlete, did eventually share information about illegal drug use during his Tour de France reign. Discuss the consequences of his sharing that information publicly. What are the benefits and costs, to Armstrong and the cycling community, of his disclosure?

3. What are the ethical implications of asking individuals to speak when what they share might incriminate themselves or do harm to others? When might it be important to share information that might put someone in an unfavorable light or reveal something illegal?

Barry Bonds of the San Francisco Giants hits career home-run number 723 in a game against the Colorado Rockies on August 4, 2006, in San Francisco.

Daniel M. Silva/Shutterstock.com

details of our topic and share the full story with our audiences. If we have not done this, then we may wind up giving our audiences inaccurate or incomplete information.

Second, as an informative speaker, you want to present unbiased information to your audience. Although we all hold biases, we can take steps to minimize them. You can minimize your biases by presenting examples, statistics, testimony, and other materials as fairly and as neutrally as possible, regardless of your personal positions. Save your preferences for your persuasive speeches; use your informative speeches to help your audiences gain a full understanding of your topic.

Finally, present your information honestly. Do not distort your evidence or make up supporting material as you need it. A healthy public dialogue depends on accuracy. If you misrepresent your speech topic, your audience will come away with an inaccurate view of important issues and situations. Ethical informative speaking relies on the honest and accurate distribution of information, which can happen only if speakers present that information truthfully.

MindTap®

Go to your MindTap for *Invitation to Human Communication* to view a video about Rachel Roto giving her speech.

PREPARATION OUTLINE WITH COMMENTARY

Tap
by Rachel Rota

Specific Purpose: To inform my audience about the art of tap dancing.

Thesis Statement: Tap dancing, one of the oldest forms of dance, is based on just a few basic steps and was popularized in modern times in part by the great tap dancer and choreographer Gregory Hines.

You may have already given an informative speech in your class. Whether you have or whether this is the first time you have spoken informatively, you can use the following outline as a model.

Rachel gave this speech in an introductory public-speaking class in 2006. The assignment was to give a four- to six-minute speech, citing a minimum of four sources. Students were also asked to create a preparation outline that included a Works Cited section and to use at least one visual aid in their speech. (Remember that you can go to your CourseMate to access videos of several other informative speeches, including Chung-yan Man's "Chinese Fortune Telling," Elizabeth Lopez's "The Three C's of Down Syndrome," and Josh Valentine's "The Dun Dun Drum.")

INTRODUCTION

(Begin by doing a short tap routine) (*catch attention*)

I. Tap dancing is a vibrant art that is popular around the world and continues to appeal to people. (*reveal topic*)

   A. According to performingarts.net, tap artist Gregory Hines once said, "Tap is here, now."

Commentary

Rachel begins her speech with a demonstration and a quotation pertaining to her speech topic, and she cites the source of the quotation.

B. The art of tap dancing can be found all around our nation, with style variations around the world.

C. Public interest in tap is growing, and tap can be seen in many forms of entertainment, such as films and theatrical Broadway shows.

II. Still alive today, tap is one of the oldest styles of dance.

A. Many may think tap went out with performers like Gene Kelly and Fred Astaire, but it is still thriving.

B. Have you encountered tap dancing? (*connect to the audience*)

III. I am interested in this topic because I have been dancing since the age of four and have found tap quite enjoyable. (*establish credibility*)

A. Not only have I been a student of tap, but I have also taught tap to young dancers.

B. I also enjoy watching entertainment that includes tap dancing.

IV. Today I will tell you about the beginnings of tap dancing, some basic techniques of tap, and I will also discuss a tap great, the late Gregory Hines. (*reveal thesis statement and preview main points*)

BODY

I. According to performingarts.net, tap is a combination of elements of African drumming and dancing and European clog and step dancing.

A. The core of all forms of tap is percussive footwork, but the unique rhythms of jazz distinguish American tap dance from other types of tap.

B. From the 1600s to the early 1800s, tap evolved from European step dances (for example, clog and jig) and African religious dances (for example, juba and ring shout).

C. These dances were performed mostly by African slaves.

1. Around 1828 the juba and the jig evolved to dances performed on the minstrel stage.

2. Later these dances were polished into what is now American tap dance.

D. The article "The History of Tap" from performingarts.net outlines the evolution of modern tap.

1. Vaudeville talents like Bill "Bojangles" Robinson and John Bubbles helped define the rhythm of tap dance.

2. Hollywood popularized tap in films starring Fred Astaire and the Nicholas Brothers.

After Rachel reveals the topic of her speech, she proceeds by asking her audience to think about their experiences with her speech topic. Notice how Rachel uses this strategy to connect the audience to her topic.

Rachel clearly establishes her credibility as a speaker by revealing her personal experience as both a student and a teacher of tap.

Rachel briefly previews the main points of her speech, revealing her topical organizational pattern. Notice how she will elaborate on each main point in the same order provided in this internal preview statement.

Rachel's first main point discusses the evolution of tap to provide her audience a brief overview of the history of her topic. Within her explanation of how tap evolved, Rachel cites the Web sites that contain the information provided in her speech. Notice that she cites them in her speech as well as in her outline.

3. According to offjazz.com, Gene Kelly became a star in the 1950s and created his own style of tap by adding movements from ballet and modern dance.

4. Although tap lost some popularity in the 1950s, it became known as an art form as well as a form of entertainment in the 1960s.

5. In the 1970s tap returned to film, the concert stage, and the theater in the United States, Europe, and Japan.

6. Tap still flourishes in the entertainment industry today and can be seen on stage, TV, and in the movies.

Transition: In light of the early beginnings of tap, the steps that created the history are just as important.

II. Tapdance.org lists a few basic movements and steps in tap dance.

A. The shuffle, flap, heel drop, brush, tip, step, stomp, and stamp create the basis of all the steps and sounds of tap.

B. These basics create steps like the cramp role, time steps, Maxi-ford, and the rolling pullback.

C. To successfully create these sounds, tap shoes have hard leather soles with metal "taps" screwed into them.

D. Although there are many variations of tap shoes, the sounds and steps of American tap dancing remain the same.

Transition: We've heard about the history and the basics of tap. Now, let's take a deeper look into the life of a tap dancing great.

III. According to an article at the Web site cigaraficionado.com, one famous modern tap dancer, Gregory Hines, led an interesting life and became a highly acclaimed dancer and choreographer.

A. When he was five years old, he was in a tap group called the Hines Kids with his older brother, Jake.

1. When the boys reached adolescence, they were called the Hines Brothers, and they spent much of their time performing at the Apollo Theatre.

2. In 1954, Gregory debuted on Broadway at the age of eight in the musical *The Girl in Pink Tights*.

3. In 1963, the family group became Hines, Hines, and Dad, and they performed in New York nightclubs and on television.

4. In 1992, Gregory was awarded a Tony for his role in *Jelly's Last Jam*.

5. He showcased his dancing talent in movies such as *The History of the World*, *The Cotton Club*, and *White Nights*.

> Rachel provides a clear transition from her first to her second main point to signal that she has finished discussing the history of tap and will move on to discuss tap steps. She also performs the steps she describes in her first subpoint. This demonstration adds clarity to her speech.

> Again, between Rachel's second and third main points, she provides a short internal summary and transitions to her third point.

> Notice how her three main points are fairly balanced, providing approximately the same amount of information in each. Also notice how each of her points, subpoints, and sub-subpoints includes only one complete sentence.

B. Gregory has left his mark on the world of tap, and his technique and style continue to be studied.

C. His untimely death in August 2003 from liver cancer has been a great loss not only for the tap community but also for the entire entertainment industry.

CONCLUSION

Rachel signals that she is concluding her speech by saying, "As we have seen today." She provides a clear internal summary, briefly recapping her three main points. Her conclusion is short, and she ends memorably.

I. As we have seen today, tap is a very old form of dance, and the steps and sounds of tap have been performed by many talented people throughout its history. (*reinforce thesis and summarize main points*)

A. The basic steps of tap remain about the same as they have throughout tap's history.

B. The work of Gregory Hines contributed greatly to tap.

II. If any of you desire to be a tap dancer, I hope I have equipped you with enough information to get you started.

III. Just go and screw some metal taps into the bottom of your shoes and start tapping! (*end memorably*)

WORKS CITED

"The History of Tap." Accessed April 30, 2005. http://www. performingarts.net.
Rothstein, Mervyn. "The Man in the Dancing Shoes: Gregory Hines Scores Big on Broadway with *Jelly's Last Jam*." *Cigar Aficionado*. Autumn 1992. Accessed April 30, 2005. http://www.cigaraficionado.com/Cigar/CA _Archives/CA_Show_Article/0,2322,863,00.html.
"Tap Steps." Accessed April 30, 2005. http://www.tapdance.org/tap/steps /index.html.
"Top of the Taps." Accessed March 19, 2005. http://www.offjazz.com/tap -stars.htm.

Chapter Summary

To Speak Informatively Is to Share Knowledge with an Audience to Increase Their Understanding of a Particular Topic

- To create an informative speaking environment is to bring a topic to life for an audience and to illustrate its relevance so audience members better understand its impact on their world.

The Five Types of Informative Speeches Are About Processes, Events, Places and People, Objects, and Concepts

- Process speeches describe how something is done, how something comes to be what it is, or how something works.
- Speeches about events describe or explain a significant, interesting, or unusual occurrence.

- Speeches about places and people describe something significant, interesting, or unusual about places and people.
- Speeches about objects inform your audiences about anything that can be perceived by the senses.
- Speeches about concepts describe or explain abstractions, or things you cannot perceive with your senses, such as ideas, theories, principles, worldviews, or beliefs.

The Five Different Types of Informative Speeches Can Be Organized Chronologically, Spatially, Causally, or Topically

- Chronological patterns illustrate the development of an event or a concept or describe the steps necessary for completing a task.
- Spatial patterns reveal how various locations relate to a topic or how activities related to a topic occur in specific locations.
- Causal patterns are useful when you want to show important cause-and-effect relationships or clarify how ideas or behaviors relate to one another.

- Topical patterns allow you to highlight the different facets or characteristics of a topic for an audience.
- Three tips that can help you give an effective a speech are (1) bring your topic to life, (2) tailor your information to your audience, and (3) use language that is clear and unbiased.

When You Bring Your Subjects to Life, You Relate Your Topic to Your Audience by Sharing the Human Side of That Topic with Engaging and Relevant Details

- When you tailor your information to your audience, you remain audience centered so you can determine how much an audience knows about a topic and thus how much information to present.
- Use language that focuses on descriptions, definitions, and explanations so audiences can more easily learn new information.

Key Concepts

causal patterns (330)

chronological pattern (328)

informative speaking environments (320)

informative speech (320)

spatial pattern (330)

speeches about concepts (327)

speeches about events (322)

speeches about objects (325)

speeches about places and people (324)

speeches about processes (320)

topical organizational pattern (331)

Invitation to Human Communication Online

MindTap Speech includes an interactive MindTap Reader and interactive learning tools including National Geographic Explorer videos, student videos, quizzes, flash cards, and more. You can build your speech outline with Outline Builder and record, post, and watch videos with YouSeeU. Go to cengagebrain.com to access your MindTap for *Invitation to Human Communication* where these resources can be found.

MindTap®

Further Reflection and Discussion

1. Consider the following subjects as possible informative speaking topics for your next assigned speech:

   carpets
   making pizza
   graffiti
   religion
   Nicki Minaj
   subways

   How many different kinds of informative speeches could you give on each topic? What would be the strengths or advantages of choosing one type of speech over another for these topics?

2. Consider your list of possible speeches from question 1. Even with the frivolous nature of some of these topics, can you think of ways you could make these speeches be relevant to the public dialogue? Consider giving one

of these more lighthearted but relevant speeches as your informative speech.

3. Create a preparation outline for an informative speech on the topic of the U.S. response to natural disasters. How many different organizational patterns could you use for this topic? How would each pattern highlight a different aspect of this topic? How would you reduce the scope of your speech to make it manageable for your public-speaking course?

4. In groups or as a class, identify five or six of the most commonly used but poorly defined terms you hear regularly. Use informative language to define those terms for your classmates. Some terms to define might be include the following:

democracy
socialism
religion
free speech
hate speech
gun control
conservation

5. Select one of the topics from question 4 and write a specific purpose and thesis statement for a speech about that topic. Next, choose your organizational pattern and develop the main points for this speech. How might you bring this topic to life and manage the information you have about this topic so it is relevant to the audience?

6. Imaging that your instructor assigned the topic of "boxes" as your next informative speech. How could you bring this seemingly uninteresting topic to life for your audience? How are boxes relevant to your classmates, the public dialogue, and our way of living?

7. Log on to TED Talks and consider the 10 most popular TED Talks. What about these topics makes them so popular, relevant, and related to the issues people are interested in today?

8. Watch one or two of these most popular TED Talks. How did these speakers bring these topics to life? Are there ethical issues they had to address? What ideas and speaking strategies can you borrow from these speakers for your next speech?

9. In her National Geographic Explorer Tip, Mireya Mayor discusses visual aids and the importance of selecting the best visual aid possible. Consider the topic you have selected or are thinking about selecting for your informative speech. What visual aids would be inspiring, appropriate, and engaging for your audience? Consider incorporating them into your speech.

10. What do you love to do? Whose music do you love to listen to? What athletes inspire you? What places do you want to visit? What is the most important principle that guides your life? Consider your answers to each question. Could you give an informative speech on one of them? Why or why not?

Activities and Web Links

Visit cengagebrain.com to access the MindTap for *Invitation to Human Communication* where these activities and Web links can be found.

1. Choose one of the speeches from the list at this Web site. As you listen to the speech, write down which pattern of organization is used for this speech, which parts of the speech are information, and which parts might be persuasive. Go to *Web link 13.1*.

2. Look online for resources that will provide information on organic farming, laser surgery, or alternative fuels for automobiles. Create a speech outline for a process speech on one of these topics.

Persuasive Speaking

14

IN THIS CHAPTER
YOU WILL LEARN TO:

- Describe the three types
  of persuasive speeches.

- Apply the chronological, spatial,
  topical, and problem–solution
  patterns of organization for
  persuasive speeches.

- Discuss the importance of the
  elaboration likelihood model
  (ELM).

- Explain the importance of
  being realistic, using evidence
  fairly and strategically, and
  using language to respectfully
  motivate your audience when
  giving effective persuasive
  speeches.

- Weigh the complexity of
  audiences and issues and
  the effect of the changes
  you request in giving ethical
  persuasive speeches.

Xinhua/Landov

*Actress Li Bingbing is a United Nations Environment Programme Ambassador. At a press
conference in Nairobi, Kenya, she spoke in favor of greater protections for wildlife and
increased efforts to stop illegal wildlife trade. What might make her, and others like her,
successful at persuasive speaking?*

Throughout history, people have given persuasive speeches in political arenas, courtrooms, workplaces, community settings, social gatherings, and classrooms. Just as our ancestors did, we use persuasive speech in today's public dialogue to influence and alter the perspectives, positions, and even lives of others. When you understand the principles of persuasive speaking, you also can add your voice to the public dialogue as a persuasive speaker whether you decide to speak, are asked to speak, or are required to speak.

A **persuasive speech** is one *whose message attempts to change or reinforce an audience's thoughts, feelings, or actions.* When we speak to persuade, we ask an audience to think as we do about a topic, to adopt our position, or to support our actions and beliefs. In that sense, we act as advocates for a particular issue, belief, or course of action.

This chapter examines several aspects of speaking that are central to persuasion. You will explore the three major types of persuasive speeches, the organizational patterns best suited to persuasive speeches, some strategies for gaining audience support, and some of the common challenges and ethical considerations that persuasive speaking presents.

Types of Persuasive Speeches

Attempts at persuasion generally address questions of fact, questions of value, or questions of policy. Each category concerns a different type of change sought from an audience. Knowing which type of change you want to request from audience members helps you develop a listenable message for them.

Questions of Fact

When we want to persuade an audience about debatable points, we are speaking about questions of fact. A **question of fact** addresses *whether something is verifiably true or not.* For example, we can determine with certainty who won last summer's Boston Marathon by consulting a yearbook or looking up marathon records online, and so the facts concerning this topic are not open to debate. But we cannot absolutely determine the training schedule that will produce the fastest marathon runners in the future. Any claim to such knowledge is speculative and open to dispute. An audience, however, can be persuaded to accept one

persuasive speech
speech whose message attempts to change or reinforce an audience's thoughts, feelings, or actions.

question of fact
question that addresses whether something is verifiably true or not.

opinion or another about the best training method by a speaker's use of arguments, evidence, and reasoning.

Our understanding of many topics today derives from theories that have not yet been conclusively proved. Whether it is the reason dinosaurs became extinct, the original purpose of Stonehenge, the techniques used to construct the Egyptian pyramids, the way to end hunger and poverty, or the most effective methods to improve students' reading skills, the facts about these issues are not absolute and leave room for competing theories. Therefore, they make excellent topics for speeches in which you try to persuade audiences that you have the correct answers.

Questions of Value

When we want to persuade an audience about what is good or bad, right or wrong, we are speaking about questions of value. A **question of value** *addresses the merit or morality of an object, action, or belief.* Is it right to continue offshore drilling or to support nuclear power, even though both present risks to the environment and to humans? Is it moral to punish certain crimes with death? Is it ethical to require all children to say the pledge of allegiance in school or to pause for a moment of prayer? These are questions of value, as are debates over what constitutes "good" and "bad" art, music, poetry, and theater.

question of value
question that addresses the merit or morality of an object, action, or belief.

Questions of value are often complex yet important to discuss. Here a woman is speaking as part of a British May Day demonstration against the government's spending cuts.

Clive Chilvers/Shutterstock.com

When you attempt to persuade your audiences about questions of value, you move from asserting that something is true or false to advocating that one thing is better or worse than another. Questions of value cannot be answered simply by analyzing facts. Rather, they are grounded in what people believe is right, good, appropriate, worthy, and ethically sound. Thus, it can be difficult to persuade audiences about questions of value. This is because when we speak on questions of value, we must *justify* our claims. We must provide suitable reasons for accepting a particular action or view. When we justify a claim, we set *standards*, and we argue that our view satisfies certain principles or values generally regarded as correct and valid by most people. So when we try to persuade an audience that drilling for oil is worth the risk to the environment, we justify that claim by arguing that the oil from offshore drilling meets a certain standard of necessity that warrants risks to the environment. Or when we attempt to persuade our audience that it is moral to punish certain crimes with death, we try to justify our claim on the basis of a particular standard: that certain actions fall into a specific category that warrants this kind of punishment.

Questions of Policy

When we want to persuade an audience about the best way to act or solve a problem, we are speaking about questions of policy. A **question of policy** *addresses the best course of action or solution to a problem*. What form of support should employers provide for veterans with disabilities? How should the federal government implement mandatory drug testing? How many credits for graduation should the university require? At what age should people be allowed to legally drink alcoholic beverages? Each question focuses on an issue that cannot be resolved solely by answering a question of absolute fact or debating the morality of an issue.

Although questions of policy might address the facts about the contributions veterans make in the workplace or the morality of mandatory drug testing, they go beyond these questions to offer solutions and plans of action. In sum, speeches about questions of policy present audience members with a specific solution or plan to a problem and try to persuade them that the solution or plan will eliminate the problem satisfactorily.

Because each type of persuasive speech—questions of fact, value, or policy—focuses on different issues and goals for change, each requires a different type of organizational pattern to be most effective. Many persuasive speeches can be organized according to the patterns discussed in Chapter 13, particularly speeches about questions of fact and value. However, because speeches about questions of policy often call on an audience to take a specific action, they sometimes require unique organizational patterns.

question of policy
question that addresses the best course of action or solution to a problem.

PRACTICING HUMAN COMMUNICATION
Select a Persuasive Speech Type

As a class, brainstorm as many different persuasive speech topics as you can. Next, group the topics according to the three types of persuasive speeches you have just read about. Some might fit into more than one group, depending on how you phrase your thesis statement for a particular topic. Discuss the topics you find most interesting and why. Save this list for the next Practicing Human Communication activity.

A Few Citizen Activists With Buckets

When activist Erin Brockovich and attorney Edward Masry—both made famous by the movie *Erin Brockovich*—became ill in 1995 from fumes emitted by an oil refinery that Masry was suing, the bucket brigade movement was born. Bucket brigades are community-based groups that use specially designed buckets, commissioned by Masry, to gather and test air samples in neighborhoods near oil refineries, chemical plants, and similar facilities that emit toxins into the environment. When people in these neighborhoods experience health problems they suspect are caused by pollution, they form bucket brigades to help crack down on facilities that are violating environmental laws.

The bucket brigade movement achieved one of its most important successes in 1999 when a Louisiana brigade successfully monitored emissions from more than fifty industrial facilities around Mossville, Louisiana, including vinyl plastic manufacturers, chemical-production facilities, oil refineries, and a coal-fired power plant. Mossville residents had long complained of numerous illnesses but were repeatedly told by industry representatives that the facilities' emissions were not harmful. "I've asked [the refinery officials] to solve their problems, but they deny, deny, deny," explained Ken Ford, president of St. Bernard Citizens for Environmental Quality.

Fed up with the companies' lack of responsiveness to their complaints, the community decided to make its problem a "national issue," says Anne Rolfes, director of the Louisiana Bucket Brigade. Mossville residents formed their own bucket brigade and began taking samples of air around the facilities, which revealed extraordinarily high levels of contaminants. Those levels were verified by the federal Environmental Protection Agency, and offending companies were forced to pay fines and upgrade to state-of-the-art monitoring equipment. In addition, other towns in Louisiana's "cancer alley" took Mossville's cue and formed their own bucket brigades, leading to the establishment of the Louisiana Bucket Brigade. As a result, the Louisiana Bucket Brigade's Web site reports that pollution "has been significantly reduced, all of which stemmed from a few citizen activists with their buckets."

The brigade now is partnered with Grassroots Mapping, a group of Gulf Coast residents and activist mappers who are documenting the effects of the BP oil spill in the Gulf Coast. Their goal is to collect data that will assist in the federal government's assessment and response to the disaster,

Courtesy of labucketbrigade

as well as in the coming litigation over the spill (Cannizaro, 2003, 2004; Louisiana Bucket Brigade, n.d.; Sine, 2000; Smiley, 2006; Swerczek, 2002; "Watchdog Group to Protest Refinery," 2005).

What Do You Think?

1. Is there an event or issue in your community that could be addressed at the local level, by citizens like those in the Bucket Brigade? What might that issue or event be?

2. Could you give a persuasive speech about the issue or event you identified in the first question? What might you try to persuade your audience to do or think?

3. What other movies or large events call attention to problems created by industries, governments, or local businesses exist? Are these attempts at persuading people that there are serious problems that need to be addressed effective? Why or why not?

Organization of Speeches on Questions of Fact

Speeches on questions of fact can be organized chronologically, spatially, and topically. To help you decide which organizational pattern is best, ask yourself the following question: Can you achieve your goals best by describing the issue as it developed over time, by describing a spatial arrangement, or by covering distinct topics?

Thomas used the spatial pattern to organize his speech about the lack of sufficient lighting at night on the college campus. He traced the layout of the campus from its center to its perimeter to make the case that it is not adequately lit for safety.

Specific purpose:	To persuade my audience that the lighting on campus is not adequate.
Thesis statement:	From the library to the farthest parking lot, the lighting on campus is not adequate to ensure safety after dark.
Main points:	I. Lighting near the center of the campus casts many shadows in which someone can hide.
	II. Around the perimeter of this center, the lighting is spaced too far apart to offer adequate protection.
	III. The lighting in the parking lots that border the campus should be much brighter than it currently is.

This spatial pattern of organization helped Thomas highlight the key spots on his campus where lighting was inadequate.

Organization of Speeches on Questions of Value

Like speeches on questions of fact, speeches on questions of value can be organized chronologically, spatially, or topically. In the following example, Eiji used the chronological pattern to develop her speech about the value of encouraging girls to participate in the sciences.

Specific purpose:	To persuade my audience that encouraging girls to participate in the sciences is of value to us all.
Thesis statement:	Throughout history, when women have been encouraged to participate in the traditionally male-dominated world of science, they have made significant contributions that have benefited all of us.
Main points:	I. In the late 1700s, Caroline Lucretia Hershel's father and brother encouraged her interest in astronomy, and she developed the modern mathematical approach to astronomy.
	II. In the late 1800s, with the support of her husband and colleagues, botanist Elizabeth Knight Britton built impressive botanical collections and is said to be the first person to suggest the establishment of the New York Botanical Gardens.
	III. In the early 1900s, Maria Goeppert-Mayer was encouraged by her university professors to pursue her interest in science, which led to her winning the 1963 Nobel Prize in physics for her groundbreaking work in modeling the nuclei of atoms.

When we give persuasive speeches on questions of fact or value, we may ask audience members to change their view or agree on what is right or wrong, but we do not ask them to do anything. Therefore, the chronological, spatial, and topical patterns work well for these types of speeches. However, for persuasive speeches about questions of policy, we also ask our audience to agree on what must be done to solve a problem. Thus, we must rely on different types of organizational patterns.

Organization of Speeches on Questions of Policy

Persuasive speeches about questions of policy usually require organizational patterns that clearly define a problem and then offer a well-developed solution. Determining the best pattern for your speech depends on the kind of change you are hoping to get from your audience: *immediate action or passive agreement*. The differences between the two are simple, yet the effects they have on a speech are significant.

When you attempt to gain **immediate action**, *your goal is to encourage an audience to engage in a specific behavior or take a specific action.* You want to move beyond simply asking your audience to alter a belief. When you seek immediate action, you want to be as specific as possible in stating what you want your audience to do. You need a clear **call to action**, *an explicit request that an audience engage in some clearly stated behavior.* For example, rather than asking audience members to simply agree with you that the lighting on campus is inadequate, you ask them to contact the school administration and urge its staff to provide the funds needed to improve campus lighting in next year's budget.

In contrast, when you want to gain **passive agreement**, *your goal is to ask audience members to adopt a new position without asking them to act in support of that position.* When you seek passive agreement, you still advocate a solution to a problem, but you do not call your audience to action. Instead, you simply encourage listeners to adopt a new position or perspective. Consider the differences between requesting immediate action and passive agreement in the following specific purpose statements.

Immediate Action

> To persuade my audience to vote against placing vending machines in our public schools.

> To persuade my audience to adopt my aerobics training program.

Passive Agreement

> To persuade my audience that open space in a city benefits that city and its residents by making it more attractive and livable.

> To persuade my audience that childhood obesity is a serious problem.

Notice how the requests for immediate action focus on asking an audience to do something specific, whereas the requests for passive agreement simply ask an audience to alter a belief. We now look at some organizational patterns that will help you meet your speech goals whether you request immediate action or passive agreement.

immediate action
when the speaker's goal is to encourage an audience to engage in a specific behavior or take a specific action.

call to action
an explicit request that an audience engage in some clearly stated behavior.

passive agreement
when the speaker's goal is to ask audience members to adopt a new position without asking them to act in support of that position.

Becca Skinner, Young Explorer, Social Work Student, Photographer: How A Community Recovers

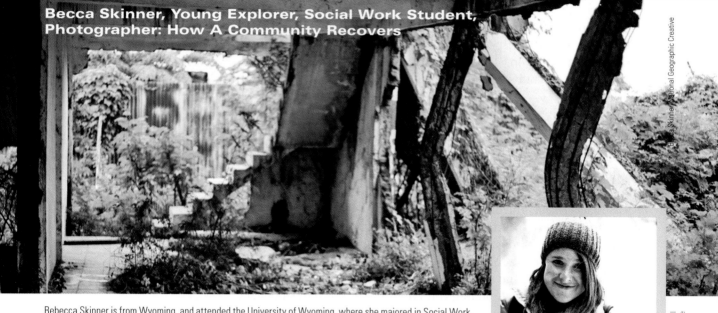

Becca Skinner/National Geographic Creative

John Lloyd/National Geographic Creative

Rebecca Skinner is from Wyoming, and attended the University of Wyoming, where she majored in Social Work. For Skinner, photography became more than a hobby when, in the fall of 2010, she won a grant from her university to travel to New Orleans to photograph the rebuilding after Hurricane Katrina. Then, as a National Geographic Young Explorer, she traveled to Banda Aceh, Indonesia, to photograph rebuilding efforts after the 2004 tsunami in the Indian Ocean. In Indonesia, she found it "most challenging" to try to document seven years of rebuilding in one short month on location. Since then, she has spoken about her expeditions to varied audiences, from small groups of third graders to large audiences of potential Young Explorer candidates.

Her talks feature her photographs, which she selects to suit the particular group or occasion. As someone who majored in social work, she is concerned about people's lives, and she realized that, through her photography, she could tell the personal stories of people whose lives were affected by natural disasters. She says,

> Studying social work in school has made me really passionate about giving a voice to people who feel they cannot be heard. Through both my tsunami and Hurricane Katrina photo projects, I've realized that post-natural disaster communities are often forgotten about or pushed aside in the wake of more recent news stories. I strongly believe that how a community recovers (or does not recover) is just as important as the disaster itself. Photographically documenting these communities and individuals seems to give personal stories and experiences a voice through an artistic and tangible venue.

Skinner says she is a "really visual person," and she selects her photographs to tell particular stories that are tailored to her audience. For example, when she gave a presentation to a group of third graders, her talk focused not on natural disasters, but about the process of photography; she selected both "good" and "bad" photographs, and engaged the students in a discussion of what they liked or didn't like about the photos. For older audiences, she talks about the people she meet and tries to convey both individual and community stories of disaster and rebuilding; her stories also describe how she makes connections across cultures through her photography. In Indonesia, she photographed the top of a mosque that had been carried nine miles from a village and landed in the middle of a rice paddy. She said, "I went that night and all the stars were out, and so I have a picture of the top of this mosque in a rice field with all of the stars overhead, and that picture to me was very special," because it reminds her of the people she met, their stories, and their resilience (Skinner, n.d.).

WHAT DO YOU THINK?

1. Skinner turned her hobby, photography, into a way to raise awareness, advocate for change, and stimulate public discussion and dialogue. What interests of your own, or your classmates, could be used in a similar way to stimulate the public dialogue on important issues?

2. The severity of recent natural disasters has made this phenomenon a common topic in our public deliberations. What are the different aspects of natural disasters that you might consider developing into a speech, and what would try to persuade your audience to think or do if you were to give a speech on natural disasters?

3. Skinner relies on her photographs to help her persuade her audiences. As she photographs natural disasters, and their effects, what ethical issues do you think she needs to consider?

Problem–Solution Organization

Speeches that follow a **problem–solution organization** *focus on persuading an audience that a specific problem exists and can be solved or minimized by a specific solution.* These types of persuasive speeches are generally organized into two main points. The first point specifies a problem, and the second proposes a solution to that problem. In the problem component of your speech, you must define a problem clearly, and the problem must be relevant to your audience. In the solution component, you must offer a solution that really does help solve the problem and that an audience can reasonably support and implement.

Consider the following example of a problem–solution speech given by Sheri. Notice how she used her thesis statement to state a problem clearly and then how she communicated that problem to her audience in her first main points. Also notice how she related the problem to her audience directly and personally.

Specific purpose:	To persuade my audience that although light pollution is a problem that increasingly affects us every day, we can implement simple solutions to reduce the effects of this pollution.
Thesis statement:	Light pollution disrupts ground-based astronomy, is a costly energy waste, and affects our health and safety, but there are simple solutions to the problem of light pollution.
Main points:	I. Light pollution poses three significant problems.

       A. In cities, light pollution causes urban sky glow, which disrupts ground-based telescopes.

       B. Light pollution represents an extreme waste of energy, and that waste is costly to all of us.

       C. Light pollution causes mild to severe medical conditions and so is unsafe for our communities.

    II. The problem of light pollution can be alleviated in two ways.

       A. Light pollution can be controlled through government regulations, such as light codes, which are similar to noise codes.

       B. Light pollution can be reduced through personal actions, such as using less unnecessary light and purchasing equipment that reduces light directed toward the sky.

Notice how Sheri's first main point clearly defines the specific problems created by light pollution and how her second main point offers reasonable solutions. Also note that she requests both passive agreement and immediate action. She asks for passive agreement when she states that supporting

problem–solution organization
pattern of organization that focuses on persuading an audience that a specific problem exists and can be solved or minimized by a specific solution.

government regulations is a good idea, and she asks for immediate action when she suggests her audience modify the lights in their homes.

Because problem–solution speeches pose a problem while simultaneously offering a solution, they are excellent vehicles for persuading an audience to support a cause or take an action.

Problem–Cause–Solution Organization

The problem–cause–solution pattern of organization is a slight variation of the problem–solution pattern. Speeches that follow a **problem–cause–solution organization** *focus on identifying a specific problem, the causes of that problem, and a solution to the problem.* This type of speech is especially effective when you think you will be more persuasive if you explain how a problem came about. Explaining the causes of a problem can help your audience better see the merits of a proposed solution. Describing causes also allows you to explain how audience members came to believe what they do and to clarify any misconceptions they may have about a topic. In either case, you are sometimes more persuasive if you provide an audience with more information about a problem.

Problem–cause–solution speeches generally have three main points. The first identifies a clear and relevant problem, the second identifies the relevant causes of that problem, and the third details a clear and appropriate solution to the problem. The next example illustrates this pattern of organization.

Specific purpose:	To persuade my audience that the problems caused by feeding big-game wildlife can be easily solved.
Thesis statement:	The problems of wildlife overpopulation, the spread of disease, and other negative consequences caused by feeding big-game wildlife can be solved by keeping food away from wild animals.
Main points:	I. In many areas where people and big-game wildlife live near each other, there is overpopulation in certain species, outbreaks of disease, and a decrease in our acceptance of hunters and hunting.
	II. These problems are caused by well-meaning people leaving food out for wildlife in the winter and by campers who are not careful about keeping their food and food smells away from wild animals.
	III. These problems can be solved by simply not feeding wildlife; by protecting our food, washing our dishes, and washing our faces and hands when camping; and by putting our garbage in sealed containers.

problem–cause–solution organization

pattern of organization that focuses on identifying a specific problem, the causes of that problem, and a solution to the problem.

Notice how Brandi was able to make a stronger case for her solution by identifying the specific causes of wildlife overpopulation, the spread of disease, and other wildlife-related problems. Once her listeners knew the reasons for the problems, they could see the merits of a solution that might have seemed too simple to be effective.

Problem–cause–solution organizational patterns are useful when you think that providing information about the cause of a problem will help persuade audience members to change their views or beliefs.

Causal Organization

When *a problem is based on a cause-and-effect relationship*, a **causal organization** will work well to persuade an audience. There are two possible ways to arrange a speech using a causal pattern: moving from cause to effect or from effect to cause. For example, Eli wanted to discuss the effects of reintroducing wolves in several western states. He first described the process of reintroducing the wolves (cause) and then focused on the decline in wildlife population (effect).

Specific purpose:	To persuade my audience that the reintroduction of the gray wolf has significantly decreased the elk population in Idaho, Montana, and Wyoming.
Thesis statement:	Since the reintroduction of wolves in Western regions, the elk population has declined dramatically, and farmers' cattle, sheep, and dogs have been killed.
Main points:	I. In 1995, gray wolves were reintroduced to Yellowstone National Park and the surrounding states of Montana and Idaho.
	II. Since the reintroduction of wolves in Western regions, the elk population has declined dramatically, forcing some regions to ban elk hunting.
	III. Other animals, including cattle, sheep, and dogs, have also been affected by the reintroduction of wolves.

A cause-to-effect pattern worked well for Eli's topic because it emphasized that the wolves were the main reason for the decline in elk populations. In contrast, Rupa chose to arrange her speech using a contrasting pattern of organization: effect to cause. She wanted to make her point by first capturing her audience's attention with a real story of five girls who died in a car accident (effect) and then explaining the events leading to the horrific accident (cause).

Specific purpose:	To persuade my audience that texting while driving can lead to fatal accidents.
Thesis statement:	When drivers text while driving, they are putting their lives, and their passengers' lives, in danger.

causal organization
pattern of organization used when a problem is based on a cause-and-effect relationship.

| Main points: | I. In 2007, five high school graduates from Rochester, New York, died when their vehicle swerved into oncoming traffic and hit a tractor trailer. |
| | II. Authorities believe the driver became distracted while she was sending text messages, which caused the head-on collision. |

In this speaking situation, Rupa's audience were members of the western New York community and had heard about the accident (the effect) weeks before learning of the cause. Rupa believed that reminding the audience members of the deadly outcome of the accident before revealing its cause would help persuade them that texting while driving is a serious issue.

Narrative Organization

Speeches can also be organized using a **narrative organizational** pattern, or *one or more stories to construct an argument*. Depending on the topic, a speaker may share an extended narrative to help personalize an argument that may seem difficult for some audience members to fully comprehend. In the example that follows, Razz implemented this strategy in his speech on the problem of children being abducted and forced to work as child soldiers in countries such as Sierra Leone in western Africa. Razz wanted to share Ishmael Beah's story as an extended narrative to reveal the thoughts, reactions, and experiences of one boy's journey from abduction to rehabilitation.

Specific purpose:	To convince my audience that rehabilitation programs work to change child soldiers' lives for the better.
Thesis statement:	Ishmael Beah is a former child soldier from Sierra Leone in western Africa, and his story teaches us that rehabilitation programs can work to give child soldiers a new life.
Main points:	I. Ishmael Beah was a young boy when his village was attacked and burned, forcing him and several other children to wander from place to place to survive.
	II. At the age of twelve, Beah was captured by the Revolutionary United Front and forced to become a child soldier.
	III. Beah was rescued by UNICEF, was given counseling and rehabilitation services, and received the opportunity to start a new life in the United States.

By using Beah's story to personalize the problem of child soldiers, Razz made his topic more accessible for his audience. This strategy helped him convince his audience that rehabilitation programs sponsored by UNICEF can work to provide these young children with a better life.

narrative organization
organizational pattern that uses one or more stories to construct an argument.

Comparative Advantages Organization

When your audience agrees with you about a problem but feels the solution is up for debate, a comparative advantages speech is often an excellent choice. Speeches that follow a **comparative advantages organization** illustrate *the advantages of one solution over others*. In this type of speech, use each main point to explain why your solution is preferable to other possible solutions. If you must criticize alternative solutions to strengthen your explanations, then simply explain why the alternatives will not work, taking care not to degrade or belittle them.

Consider Angela's situation. Her co-workers and bosses already knew a problem existed: sales were down, and they were beginning to lose what had once been faithful customers. Therefore, Angela chose to give a comparative advantages speech so she could focus on illustrating the strengths of her proposed training program.

JACK GUEZ/Getty Images

Forced to serve as a child soldier in his native Sierra Leone, Ishmael Beah, frequently speaks to audiences about his experiences. He also is the author of *A Long Way Gone: Memoirs of a Boy Soldier*. If you were to give a persuasive speech about Beah, his book, Sierra Leone, or kidnapping and forcing young children to become soldiers, what might your specific purpose be?

Specific purpose: To persuade my co-workers that my new training program will increase our sales and enhance our public profile.

Thesis statement: My proposed training program—which includes a longer initial training period, a more detailed assessment and understanding of the strengths of our products, and a stronger mentoring component than our current program—will turn our sales around.

Main points:

I. A longer initial training program will give our staff more time than our current program allows to develop a working knowledge and appreciation of the company and its mission.

II. A more detailed knowledge of our products and their value will enable our staff to work with our clientele more expertly than our current training allows.

III. A stronger mentoring program will improve the communication style of our new sales staff and help them respond to unfamiliar situations more effectively than our current mentoring program does.

Angela did not spend time outlining the problem because her audience already knew the training program needed improvement. Instead, she compared the advantages of her program to the weaknesses of the company's current program. She was careful to avoid criticizing the current program too heavily because her boss had been instrumental in bringing that model to the company. Rather, she simply said, "Our current program no longer is meeting our needs. If we make these changes, we'll be back on top."

comparative advantages organization

an organizational pattern in which the speaker illustrates the advantages of one solution over others.

Monroe's Motivated Sequence

Monroe's motivated sequence is an organizational pattern that helps you address an audience's motives and how those motives could translate into action. Developed in 1935 by Alan Monroe, **Monroe's motivated sequence** is a *step-by-step process used to persuade audiences by gaining attention, demonstrating a need, satisfying that need, visualizing beneficial results and calling for action.* Monroe maintained that this pattern satisfies an audience's desire for order and helps a speaker focus on what motivates an audience to action. Monroe's motivated sequence organizes the entire speech, not just the body, and takes listeners through a step-by-step process of identifying a problem and helping to solve that problem (Gronbeck, McKerrow, Ehninger, & Monroe, 1990).

1. **Attention**. In this step, you catch audience members' interest so they take notice of an issue. Your goal is to motivate the audience members to listen and see the personal connection they have to a topic. Using statistics or a story can accomplish this task. For example, Sierra began her speech by telling a story to capture her audience's attention. She began by saying, "I was only ten years old when I found my mother sitting on her bed crying. Not knowing how to react, I sat down beside her and grabbed her hand. When I asked her what was wrong, she replied, 'I am sick and hope that I can hold your hand for many, many more years.' I soon learned my mother had breast cancer and that she would not be able to hold my hand much longer."

2. **Need.** In this step, you identify the need for a change—that is, the problem can be solved. You define the problem and how it directly or indirectly affects the audience. Your goal is to encourage your audience to become invested in the problem, feel affected by it, and want to find a solution. Sierra began the need section by proving the severity of the problem. She stated, "The latest study on breast cancer indicates that one in eight women will be diagnosed with breast cancer in her lifetime! That means two of you in this room will be directly affected, and almost everyone else will likely know someone affected by breast cancer."

3. **Satisfaction**. In this step, you define what the specific solution is and why it solves the problem. In doing so, you show audience members how their "need" is "satisfied." Sierra argued in her speech that the Susan G. Komen Breast Cancer Foundation was making important strides in finding a cure for breast cancer and needed more national, state, and local funding to support its research efforts.

4. **Visualization**. In this step, you describe the benefits that will result from the audience's need being satisfied. You can describe what life will be like once the solution is in place, or you can remind the audience what it would be like if the solution were not implemented. Either way, you help audience members visualize how the solution will benefit them. Sierra achieved the visualization step by asking her audience to imagine life without the fear of breast cancer. "Imagine one day you're standing in your bedroom and your

Monroe's motivated sequence
step-by-step process used to persuade audiences by gaining attention, demonstrating a need, satisfying that need, visualizing beneficial results, and calling for action.

daughter walks in and takes your hand. Now imagine being able to tell her that you want to be able to hold her hand for many years in the future, and this time, you can. Reducing the rates of breast cancer will ensure longer, healthier lives for women."

5. **Action**. In this final step, you outline exactly what the audience should do. This is your call to action, the plea for the audience to take immediate action or make a personal commitment to support the changes you are advocating. Sierra asked her class to join her for a breast cancer walk being held in the community. "This Saturday at 9 A.M., a walk to raise money for breast cancer research will take place right here on campus. I ask that you join me in this fight and join me on the walk."

PRACTICING HUMAN COMMUNICATION
Select an Organizational Pattern for Your Persuasive Speech

Return to the list of possible persuasive speech topics that you prepared for the Practicing Human Communication earlier in the chapter, select a single topic and determine whether you want to work on a question of fact, value, or policy. See if you can create a rough thesis statement and main points for a persuasive speech on this topic using one of the organizational patterns you have just read about. Select the pattern that would best help you persuade your audience to take action or modify its thinking about a topic. As you discuss your organizational pattern, consider how you might also incorporate the tips for giving effective persuasive speeches in the next section.

 ## Connecting With Your Audience

Petty and Cacioppo's (1986) **elaboration likelihood model (ELM)** explains that *receivers process persuasive messages in either a central processing* or a *peripheral processing* route, depending on how motivated the audience is to think critically about a message. The more a speaker encourages listeners to become consciously engaged to think about a persuasive message, the more likely they are processing information in the central route. This means listeners are evaluating the overall quality of the argument, evidence and supporting material included, and any call for action presented in the speech. In this situation, listeners may research additional information on the topic after they listen to the speech because they want more details before deciding if they will support the speaker's argument.

When listeners lack motivation to think critically about a topic, they move toward using the peripheral route. In this situation, listeners consume messages passively. They may focus on parts of the speech without thinking critically about the message in its entirety. In addition, listeners may be influenced by the speaker's style of dress or delivery, not the quality of speech structure and content.

To encourage listeners to process information in the central route, speakers should connect their topic to their audience, explain the reasons that the audience should be concerned about the speech topic, and continually work toward keeping the audience actively and critically thinking about the speech information. Listeners using the central processing route tend to be more heavily influenced by a speaker than those using the peripheral route.

elaboration likelihood model (ELM)
model that explains an audience's motivation for processing persuasive messages in either a central processing or a peripheral processing route.

What Motivates Employees?

Although persuasion might seem the obvious answer to the question, "What motivates employees to produce good work?" it's not that straightforward. What makes the "Leslies" of the hit television show *Parks and Recreation* "Leslies," and the "Aprils," well, "Aprils"? *Forbes* and its "Data Freaks," working with guest writer Robert Bullock, asked this question. Bullock explains that not only do we have, and need, the Aprils and the Leslies in our workplaces, if we are not careful, we can demotivate the worker who would do anything for us (Leslie) as well as motivate the "disengaged employee with the toxic attitude" (April). But how? *Forbes* and Bullock (and others before them) knew that employees are the most motivated when they felt ownership of their organization. This type of ownership is called

psychological ownership, and it refers to the "*extent to which an employee feels as though their organization or their job is 'theirs'* (i.e., 'this is *my* company!')." Psychological ownership isn't the same as owning stocks in a company—it is, rather, feeling like the company is a part of the employees' own identity.

Managers and supervisors are central to this ownership process, and there are two parts to consider. First, managers need to create *autonomy* for their employees. Autonomy refers to the "extent to which an employee can use their own judgments in making decisions and carrying out their work." Second, they need to foster *task identity*, which is the "extent to which a job allows someone to be involved from the beginning to the end of a project." When both of these

are high, employees, whether they be "Aprils" or "Leslies," are highly motivated. To create autonomy and task identity, Bullock suggests the following communication practices:

1. Involve your staff in decision making.
2. Encourage staff members to solve problems.
3. Avoid "excessive monitoring," "directive styles," and "practices and processes that constrain autonomy."
4. Involve staff members in "planning, reporting," and evaluating projects, "rather than just the 'doing.'"
5. Communicate to staff members how their contributions to a project matter.
6. Give employees an opportunity to finish projects they start (Bullock, 2014).

 ## Tips for Giving Effective Persuasive Speeches

Consider the many times you wanted to convince others to join with you, think like you, or support you. You may have wanted them to do something as simple as go to a movie or eat a new kind of food or to do something as complicated as join a particular organization or share your passionate social views. Most people are deeply committed to certain things in life such as spiritual or political beliefs. Or because of deeply held convictions, they feel a strong sense of right and wrong about certain issues, such as whether women should participate in active military combat. It is natural to want others to share our commitments and beliefs, and most of us can think of many times we wanted to convince others to think, feel, and act as we do.

To help you give persuasive speeches, remember the following tips to increase your chances for successful persuasion:

- Be realistic about changing audience members' views.
- Use your evidence fairly and strategically for the best results.
- Use language that respectfully motivates your audience to change.

Be Realistic About Changing Your Audience's Views

Researchers generally agree that for persuasion to succeed, an audience must be open to change. If an audience is not open to change, then even your best persuasive efforts are likely to fail. This means you must consider your audience's perspectives carefully and frame your persuasive attempts around issues that your audience will be open to considering. If you know your audience believes something quite strongly and is not open to change (views on religion often fall into this category), you probably

psychological ownership
refers to how much employees feel that their jobs or organizations are theirs.

will not be successful in convincing its members to change that view no matter how well reasoned or researched your speech is. However, if the audience is open to considering an alternative perspective (for example, that there is a place in our society for different religious practices), then your persuasive efforts are more likely to be successful.

This means you must think carefully about the positions your audience members hold and choose a realistic argument before you attempt to change their views. It is often tempting to ask audience members to change their views completely, especially if you do not agree with those views. However, successful persuasion involves advocating a position, or some *aspect* of a position, that your audience can be open about. For example, it may be unrealistic to think you can change audience members' views on legalizing certain drugs if they have had bad experiences with drugs or people who use drugs. But you may be able to persuade them to see the benefits that some drugs offer in medical treatments. In other words, you might persuade them to reconsider some part of their position rather than undertake a radical change (Miller & Roloff, 1980; Reardon, 1991; Stiff, 1994). Your attempts at persuasion will likely be more successful if you take a realistic, audience-centered approach to changing others. Rather than asking for radical changes, approach your speech goals and your audience with some restraint.

Remember, audiences hold particular beliefs and positions because of their experiences and worldviews. If you respect those positions and experiences as you ask your audience to change, you will be more likely to give a successful speech.

Use Evidence Fairly and Strategically

Research on evidence and persuasion suggests that besides carefully researching, organizing, and delivering your speech, there are some strategies you can use to help construct effective persuasive arguments. These strategies involve two-sided messages, counterarguments, and fear appeals.

Because persuasive speakers advocate one position over others, they often frame an issue as two-sided, even if there are multiple perspectives on the issue (Chapter 15). A **two-sided message** *addresses two sides of an issue, refuting one side to prove the other is better*. Research suggests that when speakers discuss two sides of an issue, they are more persuasive if they actively refute the side they oppose rather than simply describe it without providing evidence for why the audience should share the speaker's views (Stiff, 1994).

Similarly, addressing **counterarguments**, *arguments against the speaker's own position*, enhances a speaker's credibility. For example, when Tony advocated a policy of controlled burns to prevent forest fires, he increased his believability when he also discussed the argument that controlled burns can get out of control and cause major damage. By acknowledging this counterargument, Tony illustrated why the concerns it raises are unfounded, strengthening his position that controlled burns prevent other fires from burning out of control.

Use two-sided messages and counterarguments with care. In persuasion, credibility is important, and you must take care that your opposing comments are not too judgmental or inflammatory. If you unfairly attack

two-sided message
message that addresses two sides of an issue, refuting one side to prove the other is better.

counterarguments
addressing the arguments against the speaker's own position.

Ribbon Campaigns and Awareness Bracelets

A woman walks past a work of art by Athina Robie inside an Athens metro station that depicts AIDS awareness ribbons at an exhibition marking World AIDS Day.

Are you wearing a ribbon or bracelet to show your support for a cause you believe in? This trend has been popular with military families who display yellow ribbons to communicate support for military troops and their families. However, the meaning of this visual symbol has changed over time. Four hundred years ago, the reference to the ribbon originated in a song about a woman wearing a yellow ribbon to signal that she was waiting for the return of her beloved. In the late 1800s and early 1900s, the yellow ribbon became associated with waiting for the return of a soldier. And in the 1970s, Irwin Levine and L. Russell Brown wrote "Tie a Yellow Ribbon Round the Ole Oak Tree," a song about a convict returning home. In the song, if the convict's lover tied a yellow ribbon around the oak tree near a certain bus stop, she was telling him "Welcome home."

In addition to communicating support for our soldiers, today's yellow ribbons also communicate our awareness of and desire to prevent teen suicide. Other ribbon colors communicate commitments to other causes. Red symbolizes AIDS awareness as well as a drug-free lifestyle; pink expresses breast cancer awareness; white symbolizes ending men's violence against women; blue supports free speech; and green supports open adoption records.

Similar to ribbons, gel bracelets have become a way to communicate one's feelings about a cause. A well-known example is the yellow Livestrong band established by Lance Armstrong to promote support for cancer research. Other examples include a white gel bracelet that speaks out against poverty and a half-blue and half-red gel bracelet that speaks for epilepsy awareness.

Gel bracelets also make statements, and what they are suggesting is important to consider. Popularized by Madonna in the 1980s, gel bracelets were once just an inexpensive form of teen fashion. But in recent years, "some teens and pre-adolescents, including elementary school students, know gel bracelets as sex bracelets. Sex bracelets are a coded form of communication among teens and young people where wearing different colored jelly bracelets indicate what sexual acts the teen is supposedly willing to perform" (Gargaro, n.d.; Livestrong, n.d.; Martell, n.d.; TeenHelp.com, n.d.; Yellow Ribbon America, n.d.).

When people convey their messages through ribbons and bracelets, they expect their audiences to respond on different levels (Lester, 2004). First, the audience must respond personally to the object. For example, listeners might be curious ("What is it about?") or annoyed ("I don't like all these useless ribbons and bracelets!"). Second, the audience places the object into a historical framework, responding with "I know (or don't know) the history of this cause or issue." At this level, the audience relies on mythos and a cultural memory of the issues the object supports and the circumstances that prompted its creation. Finally, the audience responds ethically, assessing the "rightness" of the object's visual communication and the wearer's explanation of it. As a result of the audience's own ethical framework and the arguments and evidence that back up the meaning of the object, the audience responds with "I support (or don't support) this cause" (Lester, 2004).

What Do You Think?

1. Are you or someone near you wearing a gel bracelet or ribbon? What is the history of that issue or argument?

2. If you do not know its history, should you try to learn something about the issue or argument? Why or why not?

3. What persuasive argument are you or they attempting to make with that ribbon or bracelet? Is that persuasive argument consistent with the history of that bracelet, or does it contradict it? How does this affect the argument made by this ribbon or bracelet?

someone else's view or refute an opposing position too harshly, audiences may perceive you as less likable—and audiences find unlikable speakers less persuasive. In addition, audience members will focus their attention on assessing the merit of your judgmental claim rather than attending to your message (Whaley & Wagner, 2000). When Tony advocated for controlled burns, he avoided saying, "That's stupid. Anyone knows that the fear of out-of-control prescribed burns is as ridiculous as fearing you'll burn down your house by lighting your barbecue!" Instead, he clearly and directly illustrated why the fear is unfounded—but not stupid—and why his policy is preferable.

Speakers can also use fear appeals to persuade audiences to change or take action. A **fear appeal** is *the threat of something undesirable happening if change does not occur.* In political ads, politicians frequently employ fear appeals as a way to motivate voters. Research suggests that fear appeals may motivate audiences who are not initially invested in your topic to *become* invested (Roser & Thompson, 1995). A fear appeal causes audience members to take notice of an issue and see how it relates to them personally. When audiences already feel connected to the topic, fear appeals simply reinforce that connection. However, if a fear appeal is so extreme that audience members feel immobilized, imagining that there is nothing they can do to solve the problem, then they may simply avoid or deny the problem (Casey, Timmermann, Allen, Krahn, & Turkiewicz, 2009; Jessop & Wade, 2008; Nabi, Roskos-Ewoldsen, & Carpentier, 2008; Rippetoe & Rogers, 1987: Roser & Thompson, 1995; Schmitt & Blass, 2008; Wong & Cappella, 2009). Thus, if you use fear appeals, temper them so your audience feels there is a solution to the problem that will actually work. For example, if your speech is about the risk of violent crime in your community, speak honestly about it but do not exaggerate it, and then offer practical steps that audience members can take to reduce their risk so they feel hopeful and empowered rather than defeated.

Use Language That Encourages an Audience to Change

Just as informative speaking relies on language that is clear and unbiased, persuasive speaking relies on language that will motivate an audience to think or act differently. The most obvious examples of persuasive language are words and phrases that indicate what an audience "should do," what the "best" solution would be, or how something is "better than" something else. Persuasive language often appeals to emotions as in "Wouldn't it be tragic if we failed to respond appropriately to this situation?" In addition, audiences should hear strong calls to action such as "I'm asking each one of you to attend the rally tonight" or appeals such as "Imagine what our national park would look like with power lines running through it." However, research indicates that the more invested people are in a position, the less effective are such phrases as "Today, I'll persuade you that" or "I'm here to convince you that" especially in your introduction (Chen, Reardon, Rea, & More, 1992). When you tell audience members you will persuade them, they tend to hold more firmly to their positions.

Research on persuasion in conversations suggests that speakers who use words and phrases that show they understand the feelings and motivations of others are generally more persuasive than speakers who do

fear appeal
threat of something undesirable happening if change does not occur.

Aziz Abu Sarah,
Emerging Explorer and Cultural Educator

Tell us about a persuasive speech you gave and how you used evidence fairly and ethically without compromising the power of persuasion. Was the speech about a statement of "fact" that you questioned, proved, or disproved; a speech based on a question of value(s); or an issue of policy?

I always start with the personal level; then I move to a value that people agree on. The main thing is to understand who you're speaking to and to understand your crowd and what statistics and what facts would speak to them. In every situation, it's not always useful to just recount multiple facts. I try to show many studies to prove a point. And even if you are successful, sometimes facts alone don't always move people and their ideals. There are also values. Let me give you an example. If I'm speaking to a religious Jewish group, what I try to do is to understand that their values have a lot to do with the Torah and their Holy Bible. So I try to relate to that as much as possible. I try to use stories from the Torah as much as possible. I will share with them the story of the burning tree, for example, one of the things that I happen to know, and I'll share the scripture that they relate to. Then the fact becomes related to their value. That's my strategy for connecting these two—fact and value—together.

not (Waldron & Applegate, 1998). This means your language should reflect an appreciation for the positions audience members hold. Use language that helps you clarify your position and its merits without casting a negative light on the views of others. Although persuasive speeches are sometimes used to attack or argue, avoid this tactic when you enter the public dialogue by using respectful language, even if you and your audience disagree.

Using respectful language does not mean you should not try to motivate your audiences to change. On the contrary, the goal of persuasive speaking is to encourage an audience to think or act differently, and your language should reflect this challenge. Phrases like "Perhaps you've never thought about the impact of," "I encourage you to consider this evidence carefully," and "How can we let this kind of damage continue?" do not attack or demand but instead urge audiences to reevaluate their positions. Some of our best efforts at persuasion have resulted in speeches that respectfully challenge an audience to think in new ways.

Ethical Persuasive Speaking

You may have noticed that sometimes when you try to change someone, that person regularly resists your attempts (Brehm, 1996; Kearney, Plax, & Burroughs, 1991). Can you recall when your parents tried to persuade you to do (or not do) something such as dress a certain way, date a certain kind of person, or attend a certain function? For many people, as soon as the persuasion began, so does the resistance. Why did this happen when your parents likely had your best interests at heart?

Research and personal experience tell us that when others try to persuade us, we feel our freedom to choose our own path is threatened. In the United States especially, the freedom to choose is often basic to our sense of self. When someone tries to convince us to think, feel, or do something new or different, many of us dig in our heels and hold onto our positions even more firmly. The issues we try to persuade others about are often complicated, making the process of persuasion even more challenging. Questions of fact, value, and policy are rarely simple or clear-cut. When beliefs, preferences, experiences, and habits come into play, these questions can get clouded and emotional, and people often invest in particular outcomes.

Given these characteristics of persuasion, be sure you request change ethically. To persuade ethically is to persuade others without threatening or challenging their sense of freedom to choose what is best for them. Remember, when you persuade, you act as an advocate for a particular position, not as a bully who tries to force or threaten an audience to see things your way. Ethical persuasion also requires you to recognize the complexity of the issues you speak about and the possible effects of your proposed solutions on your audience. As you prepare your persuasive speech, keep the following four questions in mind. The first three address the complexity of audiences and issues, and the fourth helps you consider the effect of the changes you request:

1. What is my position on this topic, and why do I hold this position?

2. What are audience members' positions on this topic, and why do they hold these positions?

3. Why am I qualified to try to persuade my audience on this issue?

4. Is my request reasonable for my listeners, and how will they be affected by the change?

As an ethical persuasive speaker, you must understand your own position and the positions of your audience. Acknowledge your own master statuses, standpoints, and unique experiences as well as those of each member of your audience.

Similarly, ethical persuasive speaking requires you to present information in an ethical way. This means you must tell the truth, avoid distorting or manipulating evidence, and present information accurately and completely. Audiences dislike being manipulated and mislead. Even if a speaker gains support through the unethical manipulation of evidence or ideas, that support is usually lost when the audience discovers the deceit. Gaining support through ethical means will only increase your credibility.

Anadolu Agency/Getty Images

In her role as a UN Women Global Goodwill Ambassador, Emma Watson founded #HeforShe, a campaign designed to bring greater gender equality and awareness to the fashion industry. In her VogueUK video, Watson brings leaders in the fashion industry together to speak about the need for gender equality in fashion. What about Watson makes her credible in her campaign?

No Child Left Behind: Addressing the School Dropout Rate Among Latinos
by Dana Barker

Specific purpose: To persuade my audience that our nation must address the high dropout rate among Latinos

Thesis statement: The dropout rate among Latinos in high schools and colleges, caused by low economic status and lack of family support, is too high, and this problem must be addressed with increased funding and teacher training.

Commentary

Dana created and gave this speech in 2008 to her public speaking class. She begins her speech by sharing an inspiring story about Mabel, a young Latina high school dropout. With this story, she reveals the topic and problem of her speech: Latino dropout rates.

She then establishes her credibility by explaining that she has conducted extensive research on her topic. She completes her introduction by previewing the main points of her speech.

Dana begins the body of her speech by clearly stating her argument: The dropout rate for Latinos in secondary schools must be addressed.

She supports her proposition by citing recent statistics about the North Carolina school system. In addition, she uses peer testimony to explain why Latino students are dropping out of high school and thus establishes pathos.

INTRODUCTION

I. I'll begin with a story from the Santa Fe New Mexican about Mabel Arellanes. (catch attention)

   A. After becoming pregnant and dropping out of school at sixteen, Mabel has reenrolled in high school and is the junior class president.

   B. Her change in attitude has led her to the hope of becoming a lawyer.

   C. But Mabel's story is not representative of the current trends among Latinos.

II. I have researched trends in Latino socioeconomic status, graduation rate, and population in the U.S. (establish credibility)

III. Today I will discuss the problem of a high Latino dropout rate and suggest a solution. (preview main points)

Transition: Let me begin by discussing the problem.

BODY

I. The dropout rate among Latinos in secondary schools and colleges is too high and must be addressed.

   A. The dropout rate is excessive.

      1. Statistics and firsthand accounts attest to the high dropout rate.

         a. According to the *News & Observer*, one in twelve Latino students dropped out of high school in North Carolina during the 2003–2004 school year.

         b. This statistic does not account for the 47.5 percent of Latino students who have not graduated in four years since the beginning of the 1999–2000 academic year.

c. Gamaliel Fuentes, who dropped out of school at fifteen, said, "We have no money; that's why I dropped out of school. [My father] asked me, but I decided. Now, if I could go back in time, I would stay still in school."

2. The tendency for Latinos to drop out is triggered by low socioeconomic status and a lack of family support.

   a. The *Hispanic Outlook in Higher Education* explains that students coming from families of lower socioeconomic status are less likely to succeed in college because high schools do not prepare them well.

   b. Latino families expect their young people to contribute economically, and work schedules often conflict with studies.

Transition: Next, I will discuss the importance of addressing the Latino dropout rate.

B. Addressing the dropout rate will keep Latinos from remaining at a generally low economic status.

1. Income is heavily dependent on education level.

   a. According to the *Daily Evergreen* newspaper, a person with a bachelor's degree can earn almost one million dollars more over the course of their lifetime than someone with no college education.

   b. A census report in the *San Antonio Express-News* found that Latinos earned merely 6.2 percent of the bachelor's degrees awarded in 2001.

   c. Yet, the U.S. Census Bureau found that Latinos made up 12 percent of the national population in 2000 and 13.3 percent in 2002.

   d. In her essay "Canto, Locura, y Poesia," Olivia Castellano of California State University, Sacramento, writes, "They [Latinos] carry a deeply ingrained sense of inferiority, a firm conviction that they are not worthy of success."

2. Ultimately, all who hold the belief that our country is the "land of opportunity" are affected by the Latino dropout rate.

   a. The U.S. Census Bureau states that in 2001 two out of ten Hispanics lived below the poverty line, while only one out of four earned a yearly salary of $35,000 or more.

   b. Comparatively, around 50 percent of non-Hispanic whites earned $35,000 or more that year.

   c. These figures are far from exemplifying opportunity for Latinos.

To support her point that dropout rates contribute to the generally low economic status of U.S. Latinos, Dana provides a source that describes the discrepancy of income levels between high school dropouts and university graduates. Again, the sources reflect the most current statistics she could find in 2008. She also provides statistics to highlight the low number of Latinos graduating from college.

Next, Dana uses expert testimony to explain why such low graduation rates exist for the Latino population.

Dana also provides statistics from a highly credible source to illustrate the typical disparity between the income level of Hispanics and non-Hispanic whites.

Dana's transition between her points I.B. and I.C. tells her audience that she is about to explain the consequences of not addressing the problem of Latino dropout rates.

Before moving to her solution, Dana draws audience members in personally by asking them to consider the urgency of the problem. Then Dana presents her solution, explaining that teacher training and educational success programs will help Latinos succeed in school and will help change the Latino mind-set about education.

She uses an example of a successful program, AVID, to support her claim. Note how with this example Dana uses analogical reasoning (Chapter 11) to convince her audience that her solution will be successful, suggesting that the success of this program could be repeated with similar programs. In addition, in point II.B., she succinctly states how her solution could be implemented.

Dana explains the potential results of implementing her plan. She informs her audience that the results will take time, but the plan could produce a newfound sense of accomplishment and pride among the U.S. Latino community.

Transition: But what will happen if the problem is not solved?

C. Since the percentage of Latinos in our population is still climbing, ignoring this issue will lead to a greater gap between the life of the typical American and the life of the Latino American.

Transition: As I proceed to discuss the solutions for this problem, are you beginning to sense the urgency of this situation?

II. To solve the problem of a high dropout rate, we must fund teacher sensitivity training and programs that help Latinos succeed in education, and Latinos must change their perspective on the importance of education and their ability to succeed.

A. Programs that educate teachers about Latino culture and beliefs and that help Latino students succeed in education will have the most impact on the dropout rate.

1. Properly educated teachers will become aware of how they are able to meet the needs of Latino students.

2. The Santa Fe New Mexican reported on the success of a program called AVID, which boasts a 95 percent college entrance rate among its Latino students.

Transition: What can we expect from this solution?

B. This solution, which can be implemented at the national, state, and local levels, is dependent on increased funding and the efforts of educators with experience in Latino culture.

1. Increased funding will help reform educational budgets for Latino communities and fund college success programs like AVID.

2. This solution also requires the collective efforts of highly knowledgeable professionals with experience in education and Latino culture who can train other educators.

C. Given proper attention and execution, the plan to address the Latino dropout rate will help the dropout rate begin to fall and will instill pride in the Latino community.

1. Although it will take at least a decade before results are fully apparent, perhaps even a generation, ideally the plan will result in an increase in Latinos earning bachelor's, master's, and doctoral degrees.

2. The sense of accomplishment gained by furthering education will change the typical Latino mind-set regarding education and instill an overall sense of pride in the U.S. Latino community.

CONCLUSION

I. I have discussed the problem of high dropout rate among Latinos, and I have discussed a possible solution for addressing the issue. (summarize main points)

II. Hopefully, you can clearly see that the high Latino dropout rate is an issue of great concern, one that requires prompt and thorough attention. (reinforce thesis)

Dana completes her speech with a brief conclusion that summarizes her main points and reinforces her thesis.

WORKS CITED

Castellano, Olivia. "Canto, Locura, y Poesia." *Race, Class, and Gender: An Anthology*. Compiled by Margaret L. Andersen. Edited by Patricia Hill Collins. Belmont, CA: Wadsworth, 1997.

Economics and Statistics Administration. The Hispanic Population in the United States, 2002. United States Department of Commerce. Accessed March 14, 2005. http://www.census.gov/population/

Ferry, Barbara. "High School Program Gives Students a Fighting Chance." *Santa Fe New Mexican*. February 15, 2005: p. B-1.

Hannah-Jones, Nikole. "School an Elusive Dream: For Latino Students, Desire for Diploma Often Clashes with Needs of Families." *News & Observer*. February 18, 2005: p. A1.

McGlynn, Angela Provitera. "Improving Completion Rates for Hispanic Students: 'Best Practices' for Community Colleges." *Hispanic Outlook in Higher Education* 14.4 (2003): pp. 21–25.

Silva, Elda. "Latino Grad Rate Still Lags across U.S.: Finances Often Hinder Earning a Four-Year Degree." *San Antonio Express-News*. June 6, 2004: p. 1K.

Turner, Drew. "Four Year Degree Worth the Wait." *Daily Evergreen*. January 10, 2005.

Dana's bibliography of the specific research she references in her speech shows the currency of her sources. (She created the speech in 2008.) She relies on a variety of sources, including books, newspapers, and the Internet.

Chapter Summary

Persuasive Speaking Often Addresses Questions That Are Complex and Not Easily Resolved

- The goal of a persuasive speech is to alter or influence an audience's thoughts, feelings, or actions about issues that are not easily resolved.

Persuasive Speeches Generally Fall into Three Categories

- Questions of fact address the verifiable truth of an issue.
- Questions of value refer to the merit or morality of an action or belief.

- Questions of policy focus on the best solution to a problem.

Several Organizational Patterns Can Be Used for Persuasive Speeches

- Persuasive speeches on questions of fact and value can be organized with the chronological, spatial, and topical patterns.
- Persuasive speeches on questions of policy can be organized with the problem–solution, problem–cause–solution, causal, narrative, comparative advantages, and Monroe's motivated sequence patterns.

- All of these organizational patterns provide different ways to present information about a problem and proposed solutions. Which pattern you select depends on your audience and your speech goals.

Policy Speeches Request Immediate Action or Passive Agreement

- When you seek to gain immediate action, you attempt to encourage an audience to engage in a specific behavior or take a specific action.
- When you seek to gain passive agreement, you try to persuade audience members to adopt a new position without asking them to act in support of that position.

Remember Three Important Tips for an Effective Persuasive Speech

- Use persuasion realistically. Do not ask for radical changes if an audience is not likely to support your proposals. Adapt your request for change to your audience's ability to change.

- Use evidence fairly and strategically to strengthen your arguments and increase your chances for audience support. Address complex issues with two-sided messages and counterarguments so you can refute opposing positions and appear more credible to your audience.
- Similarly, use fear appeals to motivate your audience to change, but do not overuse this strategy to the point of immobilizing your audience with fear.
- Use language that will motivate your audience to change but will not threaten or insult it.

Elements of Ethical Persuasive Speeches Include the Following Actions:

- Request change without threatening or manipulating your audience.
- Make an effort to understand your audience members' positions on an issue as well as you understand it.
- Present information that is honest, accurate, and fair.

Key Concepts

Invitation to Human Communication Online

MindTap Speech includes an interactive MindTap Reader and interactive learning tools including National Geographic Explorer videos, student videos, quizzes, flash cards, and more. You can build your speech outline with Outline Builder and record, post, and watch videos with YouSeeU. Go to cengagebrain.com to access your MindTap for *Invitation to Human Communication* where these resources are located.

MindTap®

Further Reflection and Discussion

1. With other members of your class, develop a speech to persuade lawmakers to lower the voting age to sixteen. As you develop this speech, consider the implications of the requested change for as many constituencies as possible: sixteen-year-olds, parents, lawmakers, voter-registration workers, voting sites, mail ballots, candidates, teachers, the structure of education, and the like. What are the implications of this persuasive request?

2. You have just been informed you have only five minutes of the legislator's time to present your persuasive appeal

developed in question 1. How will you revise your speech to account for this time frame? How will you determine what information to keep in and what to leave out?

3. Consider the speeches you have heard that changed your mind or actions regarding an issue. How were you persuaded to change? Can you incorporate any techniques from these speeches into your own persuasive speeches?

4. Your topic is public transportation. Develop a specific purpose statement, thesis statement, and main points for the following three types of persuasive speeches: a question of fact, a question of value, and a question of policy.

5. Use the discussion of organizational patterns in this chapter to help organize the speech you are developing in question 4. Which organizational pattern do you prefer? Why?

6. Write an outline for a persuasive speech on the subject of physical education in schools. Organize this speech according to Monroe's motivated sequence. Pay careful attention to each step in this organizational pattern. What are the advantages of this pattern over, say, a comparative advantages pattern or a problem–solution pattern? What are the disadvantages?

7. Search for a graphic antismoking ad online. Are the fear appeals used in antismoking campaigns legitimate? Do they motivate an audience to action, or are they so strong that they immobilize an audience? Why?

8. Imagine that the area in which you live is experiencing the most serious drought in recorded history. You have been asked to give a persuasive speech on rationing water. Who must you consider as you develop your persuasive arguments? What are the pragmatic implications of rationing water for each group? What ethical issues must you consider?

9. Identify an issue in which you hold firm beliefs that are not likely to be affected by someone's attempts at persuasion. Now imagine that someone in your class gives (or wants to give) a speech persuading you to change your position on this issue. What would this speaker need to consider in order for you to feel like the speech is audience centered, respectful, and ethical?

10. Make a list of language and phrases that are disrespectful, insulting, and even inaccurate around the issue you identified in question 9. Rewrite this language and these phrases so that they are respectful, fair, and accurate. Would this rewritten language make it easier for you to listen to a persuasive speech on this topic that urges you to change your views? Why or why not?

Activities and Web Links

Visit cengagebrain.com to access the MindTap for *Invitation to Human Communication* where these activities and web links can be found.

1. Read this article on fear appeals. Write down three ideas or pieces of information that interested you in this article. Share these with the class and discuss how they affect whether you would use a fear appeal in a persuasive speech. Go to *Web link 14.1*.

2. Read this speech given by then-president Ronald Reagan in Berlin, in which he asked the leader of the Soviet Union and the East German government to tear down the wall that divided the city. Write down the sentences that you find most persuasive. Identify any of the tips for persuasive speaking that are covered in this chapter. What makes this speech effective persuasion? What would have made it less effective? Go to *Web link 14.2*.

15

IN THIS CHAPTER YOU WILL LEARN TO:

- Explain the relationship between communication, civility, and ethics.

- Describe public deliberation.

- Identify the three conditions for an invitational speaking environment.

- Describe the invitational speech.

- Apply the chronological, spatial, topical, and multiple perspectives patterns of organization for invitational speeches.

- Discuss the importance of using invitational language, allowing time, and showing respect for diverse positions when giving effective invitational speeches.

- Weigh the ability to reach mutual understanding and whether this is a topic that your audience is open to discussing when giving ethical invitational speeches.

Invitational Speaking

Stephen Simpson/Getty Images

Invitational speeches are designed to help you explore complex issues that have no easy answers. What complex issues do you want to know more about and think are worth exploring?

We all have encountered people whose positions on social and political issues are nothing like ours. In these cases, we are not likely to change their views and they are not likely to change ours no matter how hard both parties try. In fact, in many situations, such as business meetings or community forums, trying to persuade someone that our view is the best not only is unrealistic but also sometimes inappropriate, especially when mutual problem solving is the goal. Trying to persuade other people to change their views about something can also be inappropriate when we do not know enough about what is best for them or when their positions are so personal that it is not our place to ask them to change. For example, issues such as the death penalty, animal rights, and stem-cell research are tied to deeply held personal beliefs about politics, economics, and religion that are far beyond any one speaker's area of expertise.

As public speakers, what should we do in these types of situations? Do we simply give up when our audience sees things differently than we do? Or do we forge ahead with our attempts to persuade them even though we do not really understand their perspectives? In this chapter, you will learn a different approach, one that encourages us to explore the many sides of an issue.

You will learn that even though you may not be able to change audience attitudes—or even want to change them—you can still enter the public dialogue. You will learn to engage in **invitational speaking**, a *type of public speaking in which a speaker enters into a dialogue with an audience to clarify positions, explore issues and ideas, or articulate beliefs and values* (Foss & Griffin, 1995). To speak invitationally is to do something other than inform or persuade. To speak invitationally is to continue the public dialogue and seek mutual recognition despite firm differences in opinions, values, and beliefs (Bone, Griffin, & Scholz, 2008; Foss & Griffin, 1995).

Inviting Public Deliberation

Invitational speaking is an important component of what scholars now call **public deliberation**. To deliberate publicly is to *engage in a process that "involves the careful weighing of information and views."* Deliberation combines "an egalitarian" process that gives people ample time to speak and to listen to others, with "dialogue that bridges differences among participants" (Burkhalter, Gastil, & Kelshaw, 2002). When we speak invitationally and deliberate with others, we are speaking because we are well informed or want to be well informed, open to different ideas and positions, and respectful of others, even if they hold different views and positions.

invitational speaking
type of public speaking in which a speaker enters into a dialogue with an audience to clarify positions, explore issues and ideas, or articulate beliefs and values.

public deliberation
to engage in a process that "involves the careful weighing of information and views."

Consider the following example that illustrates the difference between informative, invitational, and persuasive speaking. In a speech proposing that a school district cut its school week down from five days to four days, an informative speaker might describe the proposal and stop there. In a persuasive speech, the speaker might ask the audience to support the cuts to a four-day school week and possibly take a course of action such as supporting a local initiative to make the change. However, recognizing that this issue is complex and contentious, an invitational speaker would give an invitational speech on the four-day school week that explores the implications of schools changing to a four-day week and then invite the audience to discuss the topic. An invitational speaker engages the audience in a civil and open investigation of a topic and explores its complexities without trying to persuade the audience of the "right" decision.

The Invitational Speaking Environment

How does a speaker move away from persuading and go beyond informing in a speech? To speak invitationally, you must create an **invitational environment**. In this environment, your highest priorities are to

- understand the issue fully;
- respect diverse views;
- appreciate the range of possible positions on an issue, even if those positions are quite different from your own;
- engage in a dialogue with your audience; and
- create a space in which your audience can express its views just as you can express your own.

Although all speakers want to create an environment of respect, doing so is especially important in invitational speaking because the speaker and the audience members engage in a dialogue. Because invitational speaking allows for a dialogue, it is best suited for situations in which speakers have enough time with an audience to allow the full expression of a variety of positions on the subject.

An Invitational Environment

Invitational deliberations occur at almost every level of our society: local, state, and national. When members of a community gather to examine questions, plans, issues, and policies that affect diverse individuals, they often deliberate on (rather than debate) the impacts of those questions, plans, issues, and policies. Topics range from the quality of our lives (parking, housing, transportation, services, and resources) to the impact on our finances (tuition, taxes, zoning ordinances, and city or government services). At the local and state levels, the dilemmas we deliberate over are extensive and complex. However, as a nation, we also deliberate over matters of national concern.

invitational environment
environment in which the speaker's highest priorities are to understand, respect, and appreciate the range of possible positions on an issue, even if those positions are quite different from his or her own.

If you recall the events of September 11, 2001, then you may also recall the lengthy deliberations that the Lower Manhattan Development Corporation (LMDC) and the Port Authority of New York and New Jersey undertook as they solicited ideas for rebuilding on the World Trade Center site (Bone et al., 2008). The attacks on New York City and Washington, D.C., and the failed attack that led to the plane crash in Pennsylvania seemed unimaginable to many people in the United States and created an atmosphere of chaos and conflict. When discussion began about replacing the fallen World Trade Center towers and providing memorials to the victims of the attacks, many people could not imagine what the new site would look like. Both the LMDC and the Port Authority recognized the need for public input about the project, and they created an invitational environment in which people could express their thoughts and ideas. The LMDC twice held public meetings linking Long Island and New York City's five boroughs through videoconferencing to explore the issue of redeveloping the World Trade Center and Lower Manhattan. Furthermore, an LMDC Web site invited thousands of citizens to observe and participate in additional meetings and participate in a dialogue (LMDC, 2004).

Some of our most hotly debated issues are perfect topics for an invitational approach. Rather than persuade your audience of the "right" view, how might you create an invitational environment around immigration, such that your audience members feel comfortable and open not only to express their views but also to hear views they might disagree with or have not heard before?

When the first round of designs for the memorial failed to inspire New York's citizens, officials started a second design competition and received 5,201 entries from forty-nine U.S. states and sixty-three nations. Further public forums solicited input from the community, and a thirteen-member jury reviewed the submissions. When the jury—which included, among others, a family member of one of the attack victims, architects, public officials, and a historian—reached its final decision, its statement illustrated the invitational approach taken to selecting the finalists: "We understand the obligation we have to the victims, to their families, to society—indeed, to history—to serve the mission given to us; to remember and honor those who died, to recognize the endurance of those who survived, the courage of those who risked their lives to save the lives of others, and the compassion of all those who supported

SeanPavonePhoto/Shutterstock.com

Onlookers view the World Trade Center building under construction on April 29, 2011, in New York City. Using an invitational approach, how might you build a speech related to the attacks, the U.S response to them, or even our views of different religions?

the victims' families in their darkest hours" ("World Trade Center Site Memorial Competition Jury Statement," 2003).

The jury admitted the task was not easy. Coming to a consensus "entailed hours of frank discussions, agreements, and disagreements, always with the goal of arriving at common ground." When selecting the finalists, the jury consulted with many members of the community, including New York City mayor Michael Bloomberg, New York governor George Pataki, people who lived and worked in Lower Manhattan, and representatives of the victims' families. In a final invitational move, the jury exhibited all 5,201 submissions, allowing the public to consider the meaning of each one. When the final design, *Reflecting Absence*, was displayed, the jury avoided suggesting how the audience should think, feel, or react to the memorial. Instead, the jury acknowledged "that memory belongs primarily to the individual."

As the jury noted, "*Reflecting Absence* . . . evolved through months of conversation between the jury and its creators" (LMDC, 2003), making the process of selecting a memorial to the victims of the September 11 attacks on the World Trade Center a truly invitational one. As Port Authority executive director Joseph J. Seymour stated, "The rebuilding of Lower Manhattan has been the most open and accessible process in history" (LMDC, 2003).

This example illustrates one of the keys to creating a successful invitational environment: A speaker must alter the traditional roles of the speaker and the audience. Rather than taking on the role of the "expert" and assigning the role of the "listener" to the audience, invitational speakers consider themselves and the audience as both the experts and the listeners. They not only express their views but also listen carefully to their audience's views. They then facilitate a discussion of ideas, and the speaking environment becomes more than a speech given by one person to an audience. As the example about the World Trade Center memorial shows, the traditional relationship between the speaker and the audience is replaced with one that encourages the exchange of views without risk of attack or ridicule.

To build this invitational environment, you must create three conditions: equality, value, and self-determination. These conditions allow you and your audience to see one another as knowledgeable and capable, although perhaps in different ways. These three conditions are interrelated, but they are presented separately here to clarify each condition and its goal. However, all of these conditions help you create an atmosphere of mutual respect, understanding, and exploration. They help you communicate effectively with people who hold positions quite different from your own (Barrett, 1991; Benhabib, 1992; Ellinor & Gerard, 1998; Isaacs, 1999; Loeb, 2010; Peck, 1987; Radcliff, 2005; Rogers, 1962; Walker, 1989).

The Condition of Equality

When you create the **condition of equality**, you acknowledge that *all audience members hold valid perspectives worthy of exploration*. Your language, delivery, and presentation of ideas let audience members know that you recognize them as people whose knowledge, experiences, and perspectives are as valid for them as yours are for you. Because you and your audience are equal participants in a dialogue (although you still give the speech and lead the discussion), your audience members are able to offer their perspectives, share their experiences, and even question you—in the same way you do with them. A condition of equality creates a sense of safety and welcome that encourages audience members to share their perspectives. The jury who selected the World Trade Center memorial created the condition of equality by making every effort to recognize all community members as equals and to solicit their input.

The Condition of Value

When you create the **condition of value**, you recognize the *inherent value of your audience's views, although those views might be different from your views* as a speaker. In creating the condition of value, you let your audience know that when members express differing views and opinions, those differences will be explored in a spirit of mutual understanding and without judgment or any effort to change them. In fact, in creating the condition of value, you communicate that you will step outside your own standpoint (Chapter 2) to understand another perspective and see the world as your audience sees it. So when disagreement on an issue arises, you and the other participants in the dialogue try to understand the opposing positions and the reasons that people hold their views. The fact that jury members reopened the process after their first attempt is a reflection of the condition of value and their willingness to step outside their own standpoints.

condition of equality
acknowledging that all audience members hold valid perspectives worthy of exploration.

condition of value
recognizing the inherent value of your audience's views, although those views might be different from yours.

The Condition of Self-Determination

As a speaker, you can create a **condition of self-determination** by *recognizing that the members of your audience are experts in their own lives—* that they know what is best for them and have the right to make choices about their lives based on this knowledge. Although their choices may not be the ones you would make, the members of your audience are free to decide for themselves how to think, feel, and act. The condition of self-determination means you will not close off conversation or try to persuade your audience to do something its members may not feel inclined to do. Rather, you create an atmosphere in which the people in your audience feel in control of their choices and are respected for their ability to make them. Once again, in the previous example, the jury displayed all 5,201 entries and allowed people to view each submission as well as the final selection, determining for themselves the meaning of each.

In our increasingly diverse and complicated world, invitational speaking is a useful tool in some of the most difficult public conversations and exchanges. When you choose to speak invitationally, you are seeking a full and open exchange of ideas and positions. Creating these three conditions—equality, value, and self-determination—helps you succeed in this exchange. Remember, the goal of invitational speaking is to go beyond informing and to avoid any effort to persuade. Instead, when you speak invitationally, you try to explore issues in a spirit of acceptance and openness.

 ## The Invitational Speech

Although there are several ways to approach the invitational speech, we will explore the most common used by beginning public speakers: the speech to explore an issue.

Speeches to Explore an Issue

When you give an invitational **speech to explore an issue**, you *attempt to engage your audience in a discussion about an idea, concern, topic, or plan of action*. Your goal is to present an overview of the issue and to gather different perspectives from your audience so you can understand the subject more fully. Quite often, you use what you have learned from your audience to solve problems or plan courses of action that appeal to a broad range of perspectives.

Begin this type of speech by stating your intention to explore the issue. Then lay out as many positions as possible, trying to go beyond presenting just two sides. By presenting three or more perspectives, you help your audience understand the issue's complexity and why making a decision might be difficult. You might also share your opinions about the issue, even if they are tentative, but only to help the dialogue and not for the intent of persuading your audience to agree with you. As a speaker, you are laying the groundwork for an open dialogue, one rooted in equality, value, and self-determination and one in which people feel heard and respected by one another.

condition of self-determination
recognizing that the members of your audience are experts in their own lives.

speech to explore an issue
a speaker attempts to engage an audience in a discussion about an idea, concern, topic, or plan of action.

The following examples illustrate invitational speeches to explore an issue. In the first, David spoke invitationally about the issue of the federal minimum wage. His goal was to get his audience thinking about the amount of money someone earning the minimum wage actually makes, the way of life of the working poor, and possible ways to address this issue.

Specific purpose:	To invite my audience to explore along with me the federal minimum wage and whether there are better approaches to assisting the working poor.
Thesis statement:	A federal minimum wage of $7.25 per hour leaves many working people dependent on public assistance agencies like our county's food bank, but raising the minimum wage creates many problems and may not be the best approach to helping the working poor.
Main points:	I. The minimum wage of 25 cents per hour set in 1938 has risen to $7.25 per hour, providing a full-time worker a little over $16,200 annually.
	II. In recent years, food banks and other public assistance agencies have seen huge growth in the number of working families seeking their aid.
	III. Experts suggest that raising the minimum wage may decrease employment opportunities for entry-level employees.
	IV. Other options exist, but all have their own limitations.
	V. An open discussion about the minimum wage can help us gain more insight into this complex issue.

In this speech, David provides some history regarding the federal minimum wage, debunks some of the myths about the working poor, and presents a few of the existing approaches to this issue. He then opens the discussion, knowing that his audience will have strong views. However, throughout his speech, he set the stage for an invitational discussion so that audience members felt free to share their own views.

In the next example, Amanda explores the issue of funding HIV/AIDS research and support in both Africa and the United States. She compares and contrasts the AIDS epidemic in both regions, inviting her audience to explore the topic of prioritizing funding and support efforts when there is too little money to fully assist research and support in both parts of the world.

Specific purpose: To invite my audience to explore with me the issues involved in funding HIV/AIDS research and support in Africa and the United States.

Thesis statement: The HIV/AIDS epidemic significantly affects our local communities as well as communities in Africa, funding is a problem and people are divided over where federal funding should go. But exploring with my audience possible ways to prioritize relief efforts in both regions could give us insight into how to solve this dilemma.

Main points:

I. Both Africa and the United States are dealing with an AIDS epidemic.
   A. Sub-Saharan Africa has less than 11 percent of the world's population but is home to 70 percent of those living with HIV.
   B. Approximately 1 million people currently living in the United States have HIV/AIDS.

II. Funding is inadequate for both Africa and the United States.
   A. The budget the U.S. Agency for International Development (USAID) set aside for Africa is $15 billion for the next five years, but that barely scratches the surface of the HIV/AIDS problems in Africa's fifteen most affected countries.
   B. The federal HIV/AIDS budget for the United States is $11 billion this year, but that also falls short of the goal of adequate assistance.

III. People are conflicted over where funds to alleviate the HIV/AIDS crisis should go.
   A. Some argue that our money is being wasted on Africa and we should just support the United States.
   B. Others believe that we should give more money to Africa because the problem there is so large.
   C. Yet others believe that we are spending just the right amount of money in both regions.
   D. And some believe that not enough is being spent in either region.

IV. Prioritizing relief funding for HIV/AIDS in Africa and the United States requires careful discussion, and I'd like to now open up the floor to my audience so we can discuss this important issue.

Today's new technologies are quickly leading to advances in a number of fields. However, the ethical implications raised by some advances, such as cloning and stem-cell therapies, are not always clear. Invitational speeches are well suited to exploring the pros and cons of issues such as these. As an audience member, how might you express your concerns about an issue such as stem-cell research in an invitational way?

Yuri Arcurs/Shutterstock.com

Alexandra Cousteau
Explorer and Social Environment Advocate

Please share a situation in which you spoke to an audience of peers and they held positions of equal merit to you but different than yours. What specific approaches did you use to invite expression of a variety of perspectives?

Because we drink clean water, we can all agree we want the water resources in our own backyard to be unpolluted; we can all agree on certain number of things no matter who we are. And that aspect of water transcends both politics and religion. I had an experience working with groups in the Middle East made up of Israelis and Arabs, where students from both sides of the conflict would get together and study together and work together and talk together and tell each other their stories. And they realized through this process that they have the same stories. They had a story of conflict, a story of lost loved ones, and a story of fear of others. And because they told each other these stories from their own perspectives, when there was conflict in Gaza, they protested that conflict together and they grieved for each others' losses even though the other was traditionally considered the enemy. So I think we can overcome a lot of those barriers to mutual understanding through effective communication in an unbiased and open way that focuses on our own experiences rather than what we've been taught to believe.

In this example, Amanda presented the controversy fairly and openly. She asked audience members to share their views with her, and she kept a tone of equality and respect to help them explore the issue. Using an invitational approach, she created an environment in which both she and her audience felt free to express their views openly.

Speaking invitationally, like any form of speaking, has its challenges and rewards. Remember, people are more likely to feel free to share their positions when the conditions of equality, value, and self-determination are met, and

How necessary and effective are random searches at airport security checkpoints? This is a frequently debated topic. What are some of the benefits and drawbacks of these types of searches? How would you explore this topic in an invitational way speech to your classmates?

these conditions can take time to develop, especially among strangers or when issues are hotly contested. You can create the conditions from the beginning of your speech and maintain them through your delivery. You also create them through the organizational patterns you choose for your invitational speech, which are discussed next.

Trespassers Welcome

The life story of Australian aboriginal philosopher and educator Jack Beetson reads like a rags-to-riches story. The son of a Wongaibon mother and an Ngemba father, he was kicked out of school at age thirteen and got into trouble with the police. After spending a few years working in various unfulfilling jobs, he became a street kid in Sydney, Australia. As he neared thirty, he decided to continue his education and started attending Tranby Aboriginal College, an alternative learning environment for adult aboriginal students. He stuck around and several years later became the school's executive director. In 2001, the Year of Dialogue among Civilizations, he was awarded the Unsung Hero Award by the United Nations, one of only twelve people in the world to receive this award.

Today Beetson lives on his farm, the Linga Longa Philosophy Farm, in New South Wales, Australia. A product of Beetson's lifelong efforts to bring indigenous and nonindigenous people together, the farm's workshops and forums provide a rare opportunity for people of all cultures to come together to explore their identities and differences in a friendly, informal environment. He and his wife, Shani, began the farm "so that nonindigenous Australia wouldn't have the excuse that 'there is no-where we can go to find out'"

Courtesy of University of New England (Australia)

about indigenous culture. Beetson is so welcoming that he has said he'd like to put up a "Trespassers Welcome" sign on the front gate in the hopes that people will feel free to stop by for a conversation.

Beetson is a well-respected community leader who also travels extensively, speaking out about compassion, justice, and self-determination for aboriginal and indigenous peoples. He encourages other aboriginal people to share their culture and experiences with others in an effort to come to a mutual understanding. One of his latest endeavors is to use aboriginal culture, philosophy, and ceremony to help at-risk young people embrace their indigenous heritage and reconcile with nonindigenous people. Summing up his philosophy and approach, he says, "I share this particularly with young people who come out here who are living on the street. . . . There's not a person on the planet who's better than you are, but always remember you're no better than anybody else either. That's how I've tried to live my life." ("Jack Beetson Spoke with Tony Jones," n.d.; "The Unsung Heroes of Dialogue," n.d.).

What Do You Think?

1. In what ways does Beetson's philosophy of "Trespassers Welcome" match the goals of invitational rhetoric?
2. Beetson suggests that no one is better than any other person. How might you engage your classmates invitationally on this claim?
3. Beetson suggests that we need to share our cultural backgrounds and experiences with others to increase our understanding of our differences. What cultural backgrounds or experiences might you share in an invitational speech, and how would you listen respectfully and openly to the background and experiences of others?

 ## Organizational Patterns for Invitational Speeches

Many organizational patterns are suitable for invitational speaking. The easiest for beginning speakers are the familiar chronological, spatial, and topical, as well as a new pattern called *multiple perspectives*. As your skill at invitational speaking develops, you can modify these patterns and adapt to your audiences and speaking situations as needed.

Chronological Pattern

A chronological pattern of organization allows you to trace a sequence of events or ideas. In the next example, Jenni uses this pattern to explore the issue of bilingual education. She develops the issue and explores how various thoughts on that issue have changed over time.

Specific purpose:	To invite my audience to explore the issues involved in implementing bilingual education in public schools across the United States.
Thesis statement:	Bilingual education has a long and controversial history in the United States, and understanding the complexity of this history helps us understand today's framing of the issue.
Main points:	I. Historically, bilingual education was designed to provide a better education for children who immigrated from a variety of countries.
	II. After World War I, legislation changed in many states, reducing the support for bilingual education.
	III. Today's debates over bilingual education reflect the cost of this kind of education as well as the right for children whose first language is not English to a quality education.
	IV. Now that we see the complex history, changing views, benefits, and costs of bilingual education, I'd like to explore this issue with my audience.

Jenni used the chronological pattern and traced the evolution of bilingual education to help her audience understand the issue more fully. In the discussion with her audience, she explored this history, listened to members' personal experiences and views, and raised questions of her own. Jenni's audience learned about the complexity of the issue and went beyond the "for" and "against" perspectives so commonly offered. Together, they explored issues and solutions that could work for a whole school rather than just one group of individuals.

A chronological pattern allows you to share history and offer background information that may help audience members enter a discussion. By tracing your perspective on an issue over time, you establish common ground and openness for seeing how the perspective or issue might continue to evolve.

Spatial Pattern

The spatial pattern of organization can help you organize your ideas according to location or geography. This pattern is helpful when you want to discuss what a topic has in common or how it differs across countries,

---

PRACTICING HUMAN COMMUNICATION
Select an Invitational Speech Topic

In class, identify some of the most controversial issues our society faces today. List these issues on the board. How many of these issues do you have strong feelings about? Which issues do you wish you could learn more about in an invitational way? Select two topics from the list and, with a partner, discuss the ways you could frame speeches about these topics invitationally. How would you use equality, value, and self-determination to create an invitational speaking environment? Save this list for the next Practicing Human Communication activity.

nations, states, or cities. Riley used a spatial pattern to describe the ways communities have responded to hate crimes and to explore how his community might begin to heal from such a crime.

Specific purpose:	To invite my audience to visit the scene of several hate crimes committed across the country so we might know how to begin to heal from what happened in our own town.
Thesis statement:	Trying to understand the response to the many hate crimes that have been committed in other communities across the United States might help my own community heal from our recent tragedy.
Main points:	I. The response of a Texas community to the hate crime against James Byrd Jr. involved both public and private actions.
	II. Similarly, the response of a Wyoming community to the hate crime against Matthew Shepard was both private and public, bringing in the surrounding areas as well.
	III. The response of a California community to the hate crime against a church with a largely Middle Eastern congregation was far more public in nature.
	IV. With these responses in mind, I'd like to invite the audience to discuss ways in which we might respond to our own recent tragedy.

By describing how other communities responded to hate crimes, Riley stimulated and encouraged discussion with his audience about the needs of the community and how listeners felt they might respond to their own tragedy. By exploring this issue, both he and his audience began to formulate a plan of action that helped the community come to terms with a painful event.

You can use a spatial pattern to invite your audience to see how other localities have dealt with many types of public issues, such as transportation, health, poverty, crime, education, and pollution. You can also use this pattern in business speeches to compare how other businesses have approached a problem. This pattern allows you to connect your position to others or help your audience explore an issue using information from other places.

Topical Pattern
This pattern allows you discuss the aspects of your topic point by point. Here is an example of the topical pattern from Phillip's speech exploring the implications of sentencing people who commit serious crimes to death or to life in prison.

Specific purpose: To invite my audience to explore whether the death penalty is as just and efficient as keeping an inmate in prison for life.

Thesis statement: Although the death penalty is commonly accepted as a just form of punishment, keeping inmates in prison without the possibility of parole may be a better solution, but both approaches present ethical dilemmas.

Main points:

I. Life sentences may be a better option than the death penalty, primarily because there have been cases of innocent people being placed on death row and subsequently executed.

II. The death penalty does not seem to deter people from committing murder—the United States is one of the few first-world countries to practice corporal punishment, yet it still has the highest rate of murder.

III. Surprisingly, a life sentence is cheaper for tax-payers than an execution.

IV. However, the suffering caused by a lifetime spent in prison cannot be overlooked.

V. Because each approach presents moral dilemmas, I'd like to invite my audience to explore the implications of sentencing people who commit serious crimes to life in prison as compared with sentencing them to death.

Using the topical pattern, Phillip shared what he had learned from his research about corporal punishment and life sentencing. However, he did more than inform his audience about these aspects of our penal system; he shared the ethical dilemmas of each and remained open to alternatives, new information, and concerns from his audience.

Multiple Perspectives Pattern

Although you can use this organizational pattern in other types of speeches, it is particularly well suited for invitational speeches. The **multiple perspectives pattern** allows you to *systematically address the many sides and positions of an issue before opening up the speech for dialogue, exploration, and deliberation with the audience.* You go beyond dividing an issue into only two opposing sides and illustrate multiple perspectives. This approach respects a diversity of opinions and also invites your audience to consider even more views than those you covered and makes room for additional perspectives from your audience.

This organizational pattern works well when you want to speak to explore an issue with an audience. In the next example, Cara invited her audience to explore what U.S. schools should teach about the creation of the universe. She used the multiple perspectives pattern for her speech,

multiple perspectives pattern
pattern that allows the speaker to systematically address the many sides and positions of an issue before opening up the speech for dialogue, exploration, and deliberation with the audience.

Raghava KK, Explorer: Sensitivity Towards Others

Raghava K.K./National Geographic

JAIN MIMISH/National Geographic Creative

"My art looks at issues from multiple perspectives to help open minds, inspire tolerance, and engender empathy. You can appreciate other viewpoints even if you don't accept them," explains internationally acclaimed artist Raghava KK. "Everyone has a bias. What can be transformational is creative expression that allows many different biased perspectives to coexist simultaneously. When you see the world through other people's eyes, you have a richer understanding of who you are and why people do what they do."

Raghava was born in India and left school at age sixteen. His life as a professional artist began in the world of cartooning and later expanded to include painting, sculpture, film, performance, and installations. He explains, "I like to question the way information is delivered"; we have to view "knowledge as an active process," and we have to engage that process. To help him accomplish this questioning and engaging and to continue to communicate multiple perspectives through his art, he has again expanded and entered into the realm of interactive technology. Raghava creates picture frames that turn his paintings into touch screens. People can "touch" his paintings by pressing or tapping on the frames. Each touch changes the image; through a process of digital projection, the painting is "reinvented by each person who interacts with it." To Raghava, "it's fascinating to see how people step out of their own inhibitions and start moving in the way they think that character would move."

Another of Raghava's recent projects is an iPad picture book for children and a new genre he calls "shaken stories." The picture book, which children and parents "read" on their iPads, takes up notions of family. He explains how every time children and their parents "shake the screen, a new definition of 'family' appears. Mom, dad, and child; two dads and kids; two moms and kids; single parents," and so on. Raghava explains why: "I created this book because I wanted to expose my own children to many perspectives at an early age." As Raghava says, "I grew up in the bubble of a very traditional Indian family and only saw one point of view. It was only when I started to travel that I was exposed to different realities. And I realized that there is no one truth, there are many truths, and . . . it's important for me to contextualize what is true and real for me but also to be willing to question the most basic assumptions that I have."

As he says, "life is mysterious and we are constantly learning." Communication, effective communication, requires "empathy," "responsibility," "acknowledging bias," and "sensitivity toward others," and the question is "are we getting better and better" at these things? (Raghava KK, 2010, 2015, n.d.)

WHAT DO YOU THINK?

1. Raghava KK suggests we can view the world from the perspectives of others. Do you think it is possible to appreciate the views of others with whom you do not agree? How might (or do) you do this?

2. Raghava creates a "shaken story" around ideas of the structure of a family. What other constructs, beliefs, and practices might make interesting shaken stories? What could people learn from these stories?

3. Raghava calls for empathy, responsibility, acknowledging bias, and sensitivity toward others. How do these communication skills fit into an invitational environment?

inviting her audience to consider how views from different cultures might fit into an elementary or high school education. The following is the basic outline of her speech.

Specific purpose: To invite my audience to explore the many theories of creation and their role in U.S. education.

Thesis statement: Schools in the United States could consider teaching some of the many theories throughout time and across cultures that explain how the universe was created—particularly creationism, the Big Bang theory, intelligent design, ancient Egyptian and African theories, and Native American theories.

Main points:

I. One of the modern theories of how the universe was created, that God created the universe, comes from the Judeo-Christian tradition.

II. A second theory, proposed by the Greek philosopher Democritus in 400 B.C., set the stage for the Big Bang theory of creation proposed by most scientists today.

III. A third theory, known as the intelligent design theory, accounts for the origins of RNA and DNA.

IV. A fourth theory, offered by ancient Egyptian and African civilizations, presents a holistic view of existence in which many deities are worshiped as different aspects of God.

V. A theory advocated by many Native American peoples suggests that the creator of all, sometimes known as Thought Woman, has both female and male aspects and "thinks" all things into being.

VI. I'd like to discuss with my audience the possibility that all of these creation theories be taught in U.S. schools to create a more inclusive curriculum.

To use a multiple perspectives organizational pattern, follow these three guidelines:

1. Do your research so you can explain the various perspectives on the topic to your audience.

2. Present each perspective fairly so audience members can make their own assessments.

3. Make room for even more points of view to be offered from the audience when you open your speech up for dialogue.

If you were in the audience for an invitational speech on the death penalty, what concerns or points might you bring up for discussion? How would you communicate your ideas to keep the discussion open and nonjudgmental?

Robert J. Daveant/Shutterstock.com

In this diverse world, invitational speaking is an option that allows you to continue the public dialogue, even about the most controversial issues. With effort and respect, you can establish the conditions of equality, value, and self-determination even when you disagree with someone. These three conditions become increasingly important because, as cultural critic bell hooks explains, if "a person makes a unilateral decision that does not account for me, then I feel exploited by that decision because my needs haven't been considered. But if that person is willing to pause, then at that moment of pause there is an opportunity for mutual recognition because they have at least listened to and considered, honestly, my position" (1994, p. 241).

Tips for Giving Effective Invitational Speeches

Like informative and persuasive speaking, invitational speaking has specific guidelines to follow so you can give a more effective speech. Three tips will help you give effective invitational speeches and create a speaking environment of equality, value, and self-determination: (1) use invitational language, (2) allow time for discussion, and (3) know your position.

Use Invitational Language

One way to create an effective invitational speaking environment and encourage deliberation is to use invitational language. Phrases such as "You should . . . ," "The correct position is . . . ," and "Anyone can see . . ." advocate one position over others and only reduce your chances of creating

Are There Advantages to Diversity?

Although we regularly hear the words and phrases *diversity*, *accepting diversity*, and *appreciating diversity* in our workplaces, classrooms, communities, and media, what does the word *diversity* actually mean? Diversity in the workplace can be defined as "differences among people with respect to age, class, ethnicity, gender, physical and mental ability, race, sexual orientation, spiritual practice, and public assistance status" as well as primary languages spoken (Etsy, Griffin, & Schorr-Hirsh 1995; Green, Lopez, Wysocki, & Kepner, 2012; Ingram, 2015). However, diversity also includes "a wide variety of other differences, including work experience, parental status, educational background, geographic location, and much more" (University of California San Francisco Human Resources [UCSF]. n.d.). When we "accept" or "embrace" diversity, we acknowledge, understand, accept, value, and celebrate "the variety of experiences and perspectives that arise" from these differences (UCSF, n.d.; Green et al., 2012). In short, a diverse workplace encompasses the range of social positions, identities, and abilities and makes the most of these diverse elements.

What does the valuing of diversity add to a workplace? Numerous studies show that the more diversity a business or organization has, the better off its workplace and its workers. According to Kim Abreu, a recruiting trends analyst at Glassdoor, and Sophia Kerby and Crosby Burns, researchers at the Center for American Progress, the benefits derived from diverse workplaces include the following (Abreu, 2014; Kerby & Burns, 2012):

1. **A more qualified workforce.** Recruiting from the "best of the best" means that companies are "more likely to hire the best and brightest in the labor market." Where talent is crucial, hiring from "the largest and most diverse set of candidates" only makes sense (Abreu, 2014; Kerby & Burns, 2012).

2. **Lower employee turnover.** When companies lack diversity, their environments are often hostile and unpleasant (even if unintentional) and drive away talented people who feel like they do not fit in. In fact, businesses with little or no diversity see higher turnover rates than those with diverse employees.

3. **More creativity and innovation.** Workplace teams that include individuals from different backgrounds and experiences often "come up with more creative ideas and methods of solving problems" (Abreu, 2014).

4. **A larger share of the market.** Workers with diverse "backgrounds and experiences . . . can more effectively market to consumers from different racial and ethnic backgrounds, women, and consumers" from different sexual orientations and identities. "Diversifying the workplace helps businesses increase their market share" (Kerby & Burns, 2012).

5. **More competitive in our globalized world.** When businesses and organizations welcome diverse employees, they become more competitive in our "global economy by capitalizing on the unique talents and contributions that diverse communities bring to the table" (Kerby & Burns, 2012).

the condition of equality. Equality means that all positions have merit; they are viable for the people who hold them, even if they may not be for you. Invitational language offers your view as one possible view but not as the "best" view. When you present many perspectives, use fair and unbiased adjectives and a respectful tone of voice that showcases the range of ideas and does not belittle or minimize the potential of any of them.

During the dialogue and deliberative parts of your speech, you can use phrases such as "I came to this view because . . . " or "Because of that experience, I began to see this issue as . . . " to help identify your views as your own. Use questions and phrases such as "What other views or positions do we need to consider?" "Who haven't we heard from yet?" and "That's a new perspective. Let's explore that more." These communicate to your audience that you value them and encourage people to offer views different from yours or even ones already up for discussion. Encourage those views and dialogue about those differences and disagreement rather than silencing or censoring them. Offer positive reinforcement to the ideas of others so the dialogue and deliberation can develop openly and freely. Respond with questions and phrases such as "Can you elaborate on that idea?" "How might that work?" "Why do you think so?" "Can you explain why you prefer that solution?" and "What benefits do you see with that position?" As you engage audience members in the exploration of an issue, draw them out and get them to elaborate on their views. If the discussion becomes heated, keep track of ideas you want to return to later by writing notes on a whiteboard or flip chart.

Finally, if you encounter a hostile audience member, your language can help manage and even reduce some of that hostility (consider Aziz Abu Sarah in Chapter 7). When audience members respond with anger, the reason usually is that the speaker has touched a sensitive nerve. But your language can defuse the situation and reestablish value. Use words and phrases that acknowledge your audience member's position, express your desire to understand that position more fully, and even apologize for upsetting that person. Rather than responding with angry words or denying that the person has reason to be angry, use language that communicates your respect for him or her as someone with views that may be different from yours.

Allow Time for Discussion

Exploring ideas and deliberating with an audience take time. This means you must be patient and not rush through your presentation or hurry the discussion with your audience. If we want to create the conditions of equality, value, and self-determination and make space for others in the public dialogue, then we must be willing to take the time required to do that. Sometimes this can seem inefficient. Western culture encourages us to get things done quickly and to make decisions without delay. Efficient presentations are often seen as brief, to the point, and tightly organized. However, in invitational speaking, brevity and efficiency may work against you if you become controlling and unwilling to explore someone's position. Invitational speakers must allow time for the dialogue about ideas.

When the time is limited, finding the time for invitational speeches can be challenging. If you are required or choose to speak invitationally, there is a solution to these time constraints. Begin by considering your time frame carefully. If you have only a small amount of time, reduce the scope of your presentation. Decide what you can address in a shorter amount of time and restructure your invitation. For example, instead of covering five different cultural views of creation, Cara could have named as many different theories of creation as she had been able to discover and then explained two of those views in detail. With this reduced scope, Cara still could have offered an invitation but with less detail than the presentation she first chose. By reducing the scope of your presentation, you respect the opinions of the audience and make it possible to engage in a discussion of the larger issue.

Respect Diverse Positions

One of the most important aspects of invitational speaking is to show respect for a diverse range of positions. This means you must research an invitational speech as thoroughly as you would any other type of speech. You must support each of your main ideas with evidence to the fullest extent possible. Fully exploring an issue does not mean you can ramble on about different perspectives. You must take time to understand what

What Are Good Reasons?

In 2010, the New York City Department of Health and Mental Hygiene angered some New York City residents after publishing a pamphlet for drug users. Because accidental drug overdose is reportedly the fourth leading cause of early adult death in New York City, the agency hoped the pamphlet would help save lives. The pamphlet consisted of ten tips to help users reduce the harms associated with injecting drugs. These tips included information about how to "prepare drugs carefully" and advised people to use new syringes every time and to make sure to find a vein before injecting drugs. This detailed advice left some NYC residents questioning whether the pamphlet was actually helpful or just a how-to guide.

John P. Gilbride, a Drug Enforcement Administration official, "expressed his concern that the pamphlet could send a message that leads individuals to believe they can use heroin in a safe manner" and that "heroin can never be safe." Similarly, New York City Council Representative Peter F. Vallone, Jr., said he was unhappy that taxpayer money was used to produce the pamphlet and asked the health commissioner to stop circulating it.

Don Des Jarlais, a research director for the Chemical Dependency Institute, offered a different view of the pamphlet. He believed the pamphlet information could save lives. Des Jarlais claimed that after the city implemented a needle-exchange program, there was an 80 percent reduction in HIV cases among new drug users. He also believed the advice could reduce the number of deaths associated with heroin overdoses.

What Do You Think?

1. Are there good reasons to try to prevent HIV infections or deaths among drug users, even though users engage in an illegal activity? What are those reasons?

2. Do you think the pamphlet is unethical and a misuse of taxpayer money? Why or why not?

3. In what ways could an invitational exchange help the health department collect ideas on how best to help reduce drug-related deaths? Whose ideas and opinions should be heard?

each position is, why people have those views, and why those views are correct for them. You will discover that your attempts to create conditions of value and self-determination will be enhanced if you speak with accuracy, clarity, and detail about the various views and their strengths as well as their weaknesses.

Ethical Invitational Speaking

Ethical invitational speakers must be sure their purpose is mutual understanding and that they are speaking on a topic that they are open to discussing. Let us look at these two components of ethical invitational speaking.

Stay True to Your Purpose

It is tempting to attempt an invitational speech while having the underlying goal of persuading them that your view is best. To speak ethically, you truly must have invitation as your goal. Although you can create the conditions of equality, value, and self-determination in other types of speaking, in invitational speaking you create these conditions because your fundamental goal is the exchange and appreciation of perspectives, not persuasion. Invitational speeches are the heart of deliberation and mutual exploration. If you really want to change your audience, do not pretend you are offering an invitational approach. Save that topic for a persuasive speech instead.

Share Your Perspective and Listen Fully to the Perspectives of Others

If you are not able to listen to perspectives that are incompatible with your own or to grant them value, then it would be unethical for you to give an invitational speech. Ethical speakers stay true to their beliefs and values, and they do not pretend they are open to views when they are not. Thus, your topic in an invitational speech must be one about which you truly are open. This does not mean you have to be willing to change your view, but it does mean you have to be willing to listen with respect to other views. If you cannot grant value and self-determination to someone who disagrees with you on a topic, then give an informative or a persuasive speech on that topic. Religion, sexuality, and instances of oppression are three topics that may be especially difficult for invitational speeches because people have such strong beliefs about them.

STUDENT SPEECH WITH COMMENTARY

Four-Day School Week: An Invitational Dialogue
by Courtney Felton

Are you ready to give an invitational speech? You can use the following speech as a model. Courtney Felton gave this speech in an introductory public speaking class. The assignment was to give a five- to seven-minute invitational speech, manage a five- to seven-minute dialogue with the audience, and wrap up with a one-minute conclusion. Courtney was also asked to provide at least four sources, meet the objectives of an effective introduction and conclusion, and provide relevant information. Notice how she created the conditions of equality, value, and self-determination and remained invitational throughout her dialogue with the audience. Access your MindTap for Invitation to Human Communication *to watch a video clip of this speech, see the accompanying outline, and read the discussion that followed the speech. (In the video, Eric Rollins delivered Courtney's speech.) Remember that you can use your MindTap to access videos of other invitational speeches, including David Barworth's "Federal Minimum Wage" and Cara Buckley-Ott's "Creationism versus the Big Bang Theory."*

Specific Purpose: To explore with my audience the idea of changing the five-day high school week to a four-day week.

Thesis Statement: Today I want to explore with you the idea of high schools changing from a regular five-day-week schedule to a four-day schedule with longer days.

Seven hours! That's almost enough sleep for a night. Or perhaps a solid day's worth of skiing. Or the time it takes to travel by plane across the country. Seven hours is also roughly the amount of time high school students spend in school in one school day. Take a second to imagine what it would have been like not having school on Fridays when you were in high school. This would have you with an extra seven hours you hadn't had before! That would have been seven hours to do countless activities.

The National Conference of State Legislatures states, "Supporters of the shortened week also boast of improved morale and increased attendance (by both students and teachers), open Fridays for sporting events and doctor appointments, and more time to spend with loved ones."

This idea of having a shorter high school week has been a topic of interest for me. Since all of us go to school—even though now it's college—I have a feeling it may be a topic that you might want to explore as well. Today I want to explore with you the idea of schools changing from the normal schedule of a five-day week to a four-day week with longer school days. Since I don't have a solid opinion on whether or not this would be beneficial to all schools, I'd like to share two of the many perspectives on this issue, one for and one against. I'd also like to hear your feedback on the issue.

I'd like to start by addressing the pros of a four-day school week. Perhaps the most significant issue right now in education is the idea of budget cuts. Cutting back on one day of school per week saves on expenses such as transportation, utilities such as heat for the school, food expenses, and the other costs to keep a school open.

Another advantage to having only four days of school is the option to hold sporting events on Fridays. And if students are free on Fridays, the attendance at games could increase. A March 12, 2009, Associated Press article from FoxNews.com, accessed on March 9, 2010, explains that "about 85 percent of the district's athletic events are scheduled on Fridays, so a Monday-to-Thursday school week means fewer Friday absences as students and teachers prepare for or travel to games."

A third advantage to the shortened schedule is the idea of having more time to spend with family or friends, taking care of doctor appointments, or being able to schedule any other weekday activity that one may not have time for on a five-day school schedule.

Exactly how many schools are actually doing this, though? An article from the *Wall Street Journal*, accessed on March 9, 2010, states, "Of the nearly 15,000-plus districts nationwide, more than 100 in at least 17 states currently use the four-day system, according to data culled from the Education Commission of the States."

While, in my opinion, all of these aspects seem appealing, I want to address another side of the issue and consider the views of those opposing the

Commentary

Courtney begins her speech with two simple words and a series of intriguing possibilities for what might take seven hours to do. In this way, she draws her audience into her topic and relates it to their lives.

Courtney cites a credible source (National Conference of State Legislatures) and uses a quotation that begins to introduce her topic. She then shares her own interest in the topic, relates her topic to her audience again, and reveals her specific purpose.

Courtney openly shares that she has no firm position and that she is interested in her audience's feedback. Although she offers only two positions on her subject, she is clear that there are many more. In doing so, she begins to establish an invitational environment for her audience.

Courtney shares the advantages and disadvantages of the shorter week in a fair and unbiased way. She cites her sources, is open about the pros and cons, and uses statistics and examples to explain some of the advantages of the shorter week.

Courtney continues to establish an invitational environment by clearly pointing out the exact number of schools that are adopting this plan.

Because she is exploring the issue with her audience, she then shares the disadvantages of the four-day week, presenting her evidence clearly and fairly.

She presents the cons of the four-day week invitationally, being open and nonjudgmental so that her audience can hear the evidence and make their own decisions about it. Notice that her language is unbiased.

Using a signpost ("Finally, it is important to consider"), Courtney addresses one final point before she opens the speech up to dialogue with her audience. In this point, she cites experts to enhance her credibility and to illustrate that she has done her research. She then closes with an invitation to her audience to explore the issue with her openly.

Just in case her audience was hesitant to participate, she prepared a list of questions she could use to encourage dialogue. Preparing like this helped her feel more confident and gave her a wide platform from which to begin the invitational dialogue.

Although she didn't need the questions, they reminded her to remain neutral during the discussion and address the many aspects of her topic.

change. Each of the articles I looked at on FoxNews.com as well as the NCSL site discussed the following issues.

While the shorter week appears to be helpful in saving money, it may cause parents to take on the cost burden. With their children home during a normal workday, parents have to find extra child care.

Another important problem opponents of the four-day schedule discuss is the increased length of the school day. As current students, some of us may feel like the school day is already long enough. Adding to the length may make high school students even more tired, less able to concentrate, and could hinder their learning time while at school. And extending school further into the day cuts into students' time for extracurricular activities on days other than Friday.

In addition, while an extra day off leaves time for family time and other activities, some parents—and even students—are afraid of how students will actually use this time off.

Finally, it is important to consider the current school reform movement. A research brief prepared by The Principles Partnership of the Union Pacific Foundation explains, "Some educators are concerned that the four-day week may appear to be inconsistent with the new emphasis for more time in school."

Now that we have explored both sides of the issue, as well as opinions of students, teachers, and parents, I think it is important to hear your opinions as well as ideas that I may not have addressed yet.

Courtney and her audience discussed the issues related to moving from a five-day to a four-day week in high schools. To encourage audience members to share their views, she prepared the following questions in advance:

To begin, by a show of hands, who would like the keep the current school schedule?

And who would want to change the high school week to four longer days rather than five?

For those of you who want to change, what aspect of changing is most appealing to you?

For those of you who think the current schedule should stay, what isn't appealing about changing for you?

For those of you who were athletes in high school, how do you think changing this schedule would have affected your athletic schedule? Practice time, game time, et cetera?

As a high school student, would you personally have been able to concentrate and work at the level you did on a five-day week for a longer amount of time at school?

If you had had one extra free day, do you feel like you would have worked
better as a student?

What types of things would you have done with an extra day?

What aspects of the four days of the week would have been hindered by
your longer day at school?

Are there any other drawbacks or benefits you want to share that I
didn't cover?

When the discussion was over, Courtney concluded her speech.

Thanks for sharing your ideas and opinions. I think that really helped shed
some more light on the situation and how students really feel about the issue.

We've heard today some of the views in favor of and some against changing
the current five-day high school week to a four-day week with longer days.
For students, perhaps a shorter week would allow for more time outside
school, but it could also cut into sports practice time and extracurricular
activities. For parents, finding day care could be an issue, but for the schools, it
could be a way to save money.

On the whole, though, I think there are multiple perspectives to consider,
and I've enjoyed being able to talk about some of them with you.

— From GRIFFIN, *Invitation to Public Speaking, Fifth Edition* © 2015 Cengage Learning.

> Courtney closes her invitational speech by expressing her appreciation to her audience members for sharing their views. She summarizes the dialogue in a fair and neutral way, restates that there are many ways to think about her topic, and ends in a respectful tone.

Chapter Summary

When You Speak Invitationally, You Are Inviting Others to Deliberate with You

- You set the stage for an open dialogue, despite differences in beliefs or values.
- You explore many sides of an issue and continue the public dialogue, even when seemingly insurmountable differences of opinion, value, and belief exist.
- Invitational speakers must be ethical and choose topics about which they truly want to invite an exchange of perspectives, rather than inform or persuade their audience.

When Speaking Invitationally, It Is Important to Create an Invitational Speaking Environment

- In an invitational environment, the speaker gives top priority to understanding, respecting, and appreciating the range of positions possible on an issue.
- You create this environment by developing conditions of equality, value, and self-determination in your speeches.

- The condition of equality entails recognizing that both you and your audience hold equally valid perspectives that are important to explore.
- The condition of value involves recognizing that audience members' positions have merit, even if they differ from your own.
- The condition of self-determination involves recognizing that your audience members have the right to choose what is best for them, even if those choices are not the ones you would make.

The Invitational Speech Engages Your Audience in an Exploration of an Idea, Concern, Topic, or Plan of Action

- Your goal is to lay the groundwork for an open dialogue and deliberation rooted in equality, value, and self-determination.
- You want people to feel valued, heard and respected by one another.

The Four Most Common Organizational Patterns for Invitational Speeches Are

- chronological,
- spatial,
- topical, and
- multiple perspectives.

Three Tips Are Useful for Invitational Speakers

- Use invitational language that encourages the respect and expression of different views and that helps you have an open discussion of those views.
- Allow time for dialogue and discussion in your speeches.
- Show respect for the diverse range of positions.

Key Concepts

condition of equality (375)

condition of self-determination (376)

condition of value (375)

invitational environment (372)

invitational speaking (371)

multiple perspectives pattern (383)

public deliberation (371)

speech to explore an issue (376)

Invitation to Human Communication Online

MindTap Speech includes an interactive MindTap Reader and interactive learning tools including National Geographic Explorer videos, student videos, quizzes, flash cards, and more. You can build your speech outline with Outline Builder and record, post, and watch videos with YouSeeU. Go to cengagebrain.com to access your MindTap for *Invitation to Human Communication* where these resources can be found.

MindTap®

Further Reflection and Discussion

1. Do you think the idea of deliberating invitationally about complex issues is a useful one? Why or why not?

2. Make a list of five controversial issues people in the United States face today. Consider an invitational speech, persuasive speech, and informative speech on each topic. What would be the strengths and weaknesses of each speech?

3. Can you identify situations in which you might have preferred giving an invitational speech but gave another type instead? What might have been different if you had given an invitational speech rather than the type of speech you actually gave?

4. Imagine you are giving an invitational speech on the implications of the Don't Ask, Don't Tell Repeal Act of 2010, which ended restrictions on military service for gay, lesbian, and bisexual individuals. How might you create conditions of equality, value, and self-determination in this speech?

5. Identify a person or a group with whom you strongly disagree. Consider whether you might speak invitationally with that person or group and what benefits or disadvantages might result from such an interaction.

6. In a small group, select a complex topic or issue to discuss among your selves. Make a list of the questions you have about this issue or topic. Write a thesis statement for an invitational speech that would allow you to address many of these questions. Would you consider giving an invitational speech on this topic? Why or why not?

7. Suppose that while you are giving the speech you developed in question 6, a member of your audience strongly disagrees with the position you articulate. What kind of language could you use to acknowledge his anger and frustration but also continue to have a productive dialogue with him and other members of the audience? (You might role-play this scenario with members of your class.)

8. This chapter introduces you to the idea of an invitational environment, which includes creating equality, value, and self-determination for your audience. Make a list of topics you think you might be able to successfully create such an environment for an audience. Why do you think you could create this environment successfully? What would that environment look like?

9. Now make a list of topics you believe you would not be able to create an invitational environment for. Why would you be unsuccessful in creating equality, value, and self-determination? What would this "noninvitational environment" look like?

10. Generate a list of noninvitational language, as described in the section on invitational language in this chapter. Translate those noninvitational words and phrases into invitational ones. Which do you prefer to use and to hear in your speeches and the speeches of your classmates? Explain why.

Activities and Web Links

Visit cengagebrain.com to access the MindTap for *Invitation to Human Communication* where these activities and web links can be found.

1. Read this speech on animal rights. The speaker is presenting to a group that already holds the same opinion as he does. What position does the speaker take on the issue? Research additional viewpoints that you would need to add for this to be an invitational speech. What are the views on using animals for research testing? Are there words or phrases in this speech that you might not use in an invitational speech? *Go to Web link 15.1.*

2. Create an outline for a chronological invitational speech on the issue of equal pay for equal work. What did women get paid for their work during World War II? What do they get paid now in comparison to men's wages? What are the laws about equal pay, and where do those laws fit into the chronology? Do women receive equal pay for work equal to men's? What should be done? Is current legislation effective? Should the government introduce more legislation? If so, what should the legislation require? These Web sites will provide information for you to use. *Go to Web link 15.2.*

Chapter 1

Association of American Colleges and Universities. (2007). Top ten things employers look for in new college graduates. Accessed November 18, 2014, from http://www.aacu.org/leap/students/employers-top-ten.

Bieri, J. (1955). Cognitive complexity–simplicity and predictive behavior. *Journal of Abnormal Psychology, 51*, 263–268.

Burke, K. (1973). *The philosophy of literary form: Studies in symbolic action* (3rd ed., pp. 110–111). Berkeley: University of California Press. (Original work published 1941)

Carter, S. L. (1998). *Civility: Manners, morals, and the etiquette of democracy* (pp. 15, 23). New York: Basic Books.

Culhane, T. T. R. (2011a). *The great conversation: Solar CITIES.* Speech prepared for Abu Dhabi Media Company, March 2011. Retrieved December 27, 2011, from http://solarcities.blogspot.com/2011/03/great-conversation-solar-cities.html.

Culhane, T. T . R. (2011b). Urban planner [December]. Retrieved December 27, 2011, from http://www.nationalgeographic.com/explorers/bios/culhane-thomas/.

Dennis G. (2014). Fifty most popular tattoo designs. Rankmytattoo. Accessed November 18, 2014, from http://mag.rankmytattoos.com/top-50-most-popular-tattoo-designs.html.

Domangue, B. B. (1978). Decoding effects of cognitive complexity, tolerance of ambiguity, and verbal–nonverbal consistency. *Journal of Personality, 46*, 519–535.

Emanuel, R., Adams, J., Baer, K., Daufin, E. K., Ellington, C., Fitts, E., et al. (2008). How college students spend their time communicating. *International Journal of Listening, 22*, 13–28.

Ferreira da Cruz, M. R. D. (2008). Intercultural cybercommunication: Negotiation of representations of languages and cultures in multilingual chat rooms. *Journal of Multicultural Discourses, 3*, 98–113.

hooks, b. (1994). *Outlaw culture: Resisting representations* (pp. 241–242). New York: Routledge.

Jantsh, J. (2012). Ten on-line marketing terms you need to know. Accessed November 18, 2014, from Openforum.com/articles/marketing (https://www.americanexpress.com/us/small-business/openforum/articles/10-online-marketing-terms-you-need-to-know-now/).

Kelgdord, M. (2014). Most popular tattoos of 2014: Cutest tattoo ideas of the year. YouQueen. Accessed November 18, 2014, from http://youqueen.com/beauty/most-popular-tattoos-2014/.

Klemmer, E. T., & Snyder, F. W. (1972). Measurement of time spent communicating. *Journal of Communication, 22*, 142–158.

Kline, S., & Clinton, B. (1998). Development in children's persuasive message practices. *Communication Education, 47*, 120–126.

Lindeberry, C. (2007a). Tattoos: The ancient and the mysterious history. Retrieved June 24, 2010, from http://www.smithsonianmag.com/istory-archeology/1002306.html#ixzz0pX08ZUVx.

Lindberry C. (2007b). Today's tattoos. Retrieved from http://www.smithsonianmag.com/peole-places/tattoo_modern.html.

Martin, J., & Nakayama, T. (2008). *Experiencing intercultural communication: An introduction* (2nd ed., pp. 27, 28). Boston: McGraw-Hill.

Martin, M. M., & Anderson, C. M. (1998). The cognitive flexibility scale: Three validity studies. *Communication Reports, 11*(1), 1–9.

Martin, M. M., Staggers, S. M., & Anderson, C.M. (2011). The relationships between cognitive flexibility with dogmatism, intellectual flexibility, preference for consistency, and self-compassion, *Communication Research Reports, 28*(3), 275–280.

Merriam-Webster. (2014). A sample of words for 2014. Accessed November 15, 2014, from http://merriam-webster.com/new-words/2014-update.htm.

Mill, J. (1984). High and low self-monitoring individuals: Their decoding skills and empathic expression. *Journal of Personality, 52*, 372–388.

Ogden, C. K., & Richards, I. A. (1923). *The meaning of meaning: A study of the influence of language upon thought and of the science of symbolism.* New York: Harcourt, Brace.

Reiss, J. (Director). (2007). *Bomb It* [Documentary film]. New York: Antidote Films (http://www.bombit-themovie.com).

Snyder, M. (1974). Self-monitoring of expressive behavior. *Journal of Personality and Social Psychology, 30*, 526–537.

Spitzberg, B. H., & Cupach, W. R. (Eds.). (2007). *The dark side of interpersonal communication* (2nd ed.). Hillsdale, NJ: Erlbaum.

Statistic Brain. (2013). Tattoos. Accessed November 18, 2014, from http://www.statisticbrain.com/tattoo-statistics.

Tannen, D. (1998). *The argument culture: Stopping America's war of words.* New York: Ballantine Books.

Tutu, D. M. (1994). Agents of transformation. In J. Allen (Ed.), *Rainbow people of God: The making of a peaceful revolution* (p. 125). New York: Doubleday.

Chapter 2

ALS Association. (n.d.). What is ALS? Retrieved December 1, 2014, from http://www.alsa.org/about-als/what-is-als.html.

Attree, P., French, B., Milton, B., Poval, S., Whitehead, M., & Popay, J. (2011, May). The experience of community engagement for individuals: A rapid review of evidence, heath, and social care in the community. *Health in and Social Care in the Community, 19*(3), 250–260.

Bahk, C. M., & Jandt, F. E. (2004). Being White in America: Development of a scale. *Howard Journal of Communcations*, 15, 57–68.

Barlett, C. P., Vowels, C. L., & Saucier, D. A. (2008). Meta-analysis of the effects of media images on 11 men's body-image concerns. *Journal of Social and Clinical Psychology, 27*(3), 279–310. Retrieved March 6, 2012, from http://www.public.iastate.edu/~cpb6666/pubs/Barlett%20Vowels%20%26%20Saucier.pdf.

Barton, J., & Pretty, J. (2010, May 15) What is the best dose of Nature and green exercise for increasing mental health? A multistudy analysis. *Environmental Science and Technology, 10*, 3947–3955.

Bechtoldt, M. N., Carsten, K. W., Dreu, D., Nijstad, B. A., & Zapf, D. (April 2010). Self-concept clarity and the management of social conflict. *Journal of Personality, 78*(2), 539–574.

Borzekowski, D., Schenk, S., Wilson, J. L., & Peebles, R. (2010). e-Ana and e-Mia: A content analysis of pro–eating disorder Web sites. *American Journal of Public Health, 8, 100* 1526–1534.

Brand-Williams, O. (2011). CAIR says Muslin-Americans harassed when crossing borders. *Detroit News*. Retrieved March 16, 2011, from http://detnews.com/article/20110325/METRO/103250392/CAIR-says-Muslim-Americans-harassed-when-crossing-border.

Bulanda, R. E., & Majumdar, D. (2009). Perceived parent–child relations and adolescent self-esteem. *Journal of Child and Family Studies, 18*, 203–212.

Caunt, J. (2003). *Boost your self-esteem*. London: Kogan Page.

Cooley, C. H. (1968). The social self: On the meanings of I. In C. Gordon & K. J. Gergen (Eds.), *The self in social interactions. Vol. 1: Classic and contemporary perspectives* (pp. 87–91). New York: Wiley.

Cousteau, A. (2012, January 18). Telephone communication.

DeVito, J. A. (1986). *The communication handbook: A dictionary*, (p. 269). New York: Harper & Row.

Fox31 News. (2013, September 22). Firefighter, father of 5, dies after Ice Bucket Challenge goes wrong. Retrieved December 1, 2014, from http://kdvr.com/2014/09/22/firefighter-father-of-5-dies-after-ice-bucket-challenge-goes-wrong/.

France begins ban on niquab and burqa: Women wearing a face veil in public could now be fined or given lessons in French citizenship. (2011, April 11). *The Guardian*. Retrieved from http://www.guardian.co.uk/world/2011/apr/11/france-begins-burqa-niqab-ban.

Hartstock, N. (1999). *Feminist standpoint theory revisited and other essays*. New York: Basic Books.

Holland, A., & Andre, T. (1994). Athletic participation and the social status of adolescent males and females. *Youth and Society, 25*, 388–407.

Hormouth, S. E. (1990). *The ecology of the self: Relocation and self-concept change*. New York: Cambridge University Press.

Huckshorn, K. (2009). The next generation makes history. *ESPN Her Story*. Retrieved November 11, 2014, from http://sports.espn.go.com/espn/womenshistory2009/columns/story?id=3940730.

Jhally, S., & Kilbourne, J. (Directors). (2010). *Killing us softly IV: Advertising's image of women*. [Documentary film]. Northampton, MA: Media Education Foundation.

Kilbourne, J. (1999). *Deadly persuasion: Why women and girls must fight the addictive power of advertising*. New York: Free Press.

Kimmell, M. (2008). *Guyland: The perilous world where boys become men*. New York: Macmillan.

Kuhlberg, J. A., Peña, J. B., & Zayas, L. H. (2011, August). Familism, parent–adolescent conflict, self-esteem, internalizing behaviors, and suicide attempts among adolescent Latinas. *Child Psychiatry and Human Development, 4*, 425–440.

Loden, M., & Rosener, J. B. (1991). *Workforce America: Managing workforce diversity as a vital resource*. Homewood, IL: Business One Irwin.

Lovett, I. (2011). UCLA student's video rant against Asians fuels firestorm. *The New York Times*. Retrieved January 21, 2012, from http://www.nytimes.com/2011/03/16/us/16ucla.html.

MacDonald, K., & Greggans, A. (2010, September). "Cool Friends": An evaluation of a community befriending program for young people with cystic fibrosis. *Journal of Clinical Nursing, 17/18*, 2406–2414.

Mead, G. H. (1934). *Mind, self, and society*. Chicago: University of Chicago Press.

Mehra, A., Kilduff, M., & Brass, D. J. (2001, March). The social networks of high and low self-monitors: Implications for workplace performance. *Administrative Science Quarterly, 1*, 121–146.

Mruk, C. (1999). *Self-esteem research, theory, and practice*. London: Free Association Books.

Muhindi, M. M., & Nyakato, K. (2002). Integration of the Sudanese Lost Boys in Boston, Massachusetts USA. Retrieved November 10, 2011, from http://web.mit.edu/cis/www/migration/pubs/Mahindi.pdf.

National Geographic Video. (n.d.). God grew tired of us: Cultural differences. Retrieved January 21, 2012, from http://education.nationalgeographic.com/education/multimedia/cultural-differences/.

Nisbett, R. E. (2000). *The geography of thought*. London: Nicholas Brealey.

Orbe, M. P., & Drummond, D. K. (2009). Negotiations of the complicitous nature of U.S. racial/ethnic categorization: Exploring rhetorical strategies. *Western Journal of Communication, 73*(4), 437–455.

Paterson, C. H., Buser, T. J., & Westburg, N. G. (2010). Effects of familial attachment, social support, involvement, and self-esteem on youth substance use and sexual risk taking. *Family Journal, 18*(4), 369–376.

Phinney, J. S., Cantu, C. L., & Kurtz, D. A. (1997). Ethnic and American identity as predictors of self-esteem among African American, Latino, and White adolescents. *Journal of Youth and Adolescence, 2*, 165–185.

Piers, E. V., & Harris, D. B. (1996). *Piers-Harris Children's Self-Concept Scale, 2*. Los Angeles: Western Psychological Services.

Robins, R. W., Tracy, J. L., Trzesniewski, K. H., Gosling, S. D., & Potter, J. (2001). Personality correlates of self-esteem. *Journal of Research in Personality, 35*, 463–482.

Rose, B. (2004). Lost boys of Sudan in Chicago. Retrieved November 10, 2011, from http://www.lostboyschicago.com/Writings/JacobDing.htm.

Rowley, M. (2014, Oct. 31). The water bucket challenge. Retrieved November 7, 2014, from http://www.broomfieldumcblog.blogspot.com/2014/10/the-water-bucket-challenge.html.

Salamon, M. (2011). For college students, praise may trump sex and money, *Bloomberg BusinessWeek*. Retrieved January 11, 2011, from http://www.businessweek.com/lifestyle/content/healthday/648705.html.

Samenow, J. (2014, Aug. 18). How much water has been used in the Ice Bucket Challenge? Retrieved November 7, 2014, from http://www.washingtonpost.com/blogs/capital-weather-gang/wp/2014/08/18/how-much-water-has-been-used-in-the-ice-bucket-challenge.

Singer, M. R. (1982). Culture: A perceptual approach. In L. A. Samovar & R. E. Porter (Eds.), *Intercultural communication: A reader* (3rd ed., pp. 54–61). Belmont, CA: Wadsworth.

Snyder, M. (1979). Self-monitoring processes. In L. Berkowitz (Ed.), *Advances in experimental social psychology* (Vol. 12, pp. 85–128). New York: Academic Press.

Sterling, M. (2006). Do you make your first impression your best impression? Retrieved January 20, 2012, from http://entrepreneurs.about.com/cs/marketing/a/uc051603a.htm.

Story, L. (2007). Anywhere an eye can see, it's likely to see an ad. *The New York Times*. Retrieved January 15, 2007, from http://www.nytimes.com/2007/01/15/business/media/15everywhere.html.

Sunnafrank, M., & Ramirez, A., Jr. (2004, June). At first sight: Persistent relational effects of get-acquainted conversations. *Journal of Social and Personal Relationships, 3*, 361–379.

Tantleff-Dunn, S. (2001). Breast and chest size: Ideals and stereotypes through the 1990s. *Sex Roles, 3 & 4*, 231–242.

Taylor, D. L. (1995). A comparison of college athletic participants and nonparticipants on self esteem. *Journal of College Student Development, 36*, 444–451.

Thomas, J. J., & Daubman, K. A. (2001). The relationship between friendship quality and self-esteem in adolescent girls and boys. *Sex Roles, 1 & 2*, 53–65.

Ting-Toomey, S. (1999). *Communicating across cultures*. New York: Guilford.

Toegel, G., Anand, N., & Kilduff, M. (2007). Emotion helpers: The role of high positive affectivity and high self-monitoring managers. *Personnel Psychology, 2*, 337–365.

Trevino, J. (2003). *Goffman's legacy*. Oxford, UK: Rowman & Littlefield.

Umaña-Taylor, A. (2004, April). Ethnic identity and self-esteem: Examining the role of social context. *Journal of Youth and Adolescence, 2*, 139–146.

Wilkins, J. A., Boland, F. J., & Albinson, J. (1991). A comparison of male and female university athletes and nonathletes on eating disorder indices: Are athletes protected? *Sport Behavior, 14*, 129–143.

Willis, J., & Todorov, A. (2006). First impressions. *Psychological Science*. Retrieved January 20, 2012, from http://www.psychologicalscience.org.

Wilson, G. A., Zeng, Q., & Blackburn, D. G. (2011, January–March). An examination of parental attachments, parental detachments and self-esteem across hetero-, bi-, and homosexual individuals. *Journal of Bisexuality, 1*, 85–96.

Zaslow, J. (2009, September 2). Girls dieting, then and now. *The Wall Street Journal Online*. Retrieved November 11, 2011, from http://online.wsj.com/article/SB10001424052970204731804574386822245731710.html.

Chapter 3

Afifi, W. A. (2007). Nonverbal communication. In B. B. Whaley & W. Samter (Eds.), *Explaining communication: Contemporary theories and exemplars* (pp. 39–60). Mahwah, NJ: Erlbaum.

Andersen, P. A. (2003). In different dimensions: Nonverbal communication and culture. In L. A. Samovar & R. E. Porter (Eds.), *Intercultural communication: A reader* (pp. 239–252). Belmont, CA: Wadsworth.

Andersen, P. A., & Guerrero, L. K. (1994). Patterns of matching and initiation: Tough behavior and touch avoidance across romantic relationship stages. *Journal of Nonverbal Behavior, 16*, 55–63.

Axtell, R. E. (2007). *Essential do's and taboos: The complete guide to international business and leisure travel*. Hoboken, NJ: Wiley.

Birdwhistell, R. (1970). *Kinesics and context*. Philadelphia: University of Pennsylvania Press.

Boone, R. T., & Sunningham, J. G. (1998). Children's decoding of emotion in expressive body movement: The development of cue attunement. *Developmental Psychology, 34*, 1007–1016.

British Monarchy. (2014). The official website of the British Monarch. Retrieved December 10, 2014, from http://www.royal.gov.uk/ThecurrentRoyalFamily/Greetingamemberof TheRoyalFamily/Overview.aspx.

Burgoon, J. K., & Bacue, A. E. (2003). Nonverbal communication skills. In J. O. Greene & B. R. Burleson (Eds.), *Handbook of communication and social interaction skills*, (pp. 179–220). Mahwah, NJ: Lawrence Erlbaum.

Burgoon, J. K., Guerrero, L., & Floyd, K. (2010). *Nonverbal communication*. Boston: Allyn & Bacon.

Chartrand, T. L., & Bargh, J. A. (1999). The chameleon effect: The perception–behavior link and social interaction. *Journal of Personality and Social Psychology, 76*, 893–910.

Davitz, J. R. (1964). *The communication of emotional meaning*. New York: Macmillan.

Derks, D., Bos, A. E., & von Grumbkow, J. (2008). Emoticons and online message interpretation. *Social Science Computer Review, 26*, 379–388.

Derlega, V. J., Lewis, R. J., Harrison, S., Winstead, B. A., & Costanza, T. (1989). Gender differences in the initiation and attribution of tactile intimacy. *Journal of Nonverbal Behavior, 13*, 3–14.

DiNardo, M. L. (2011, October 21). If you're happy and you know it, must I know, too? Retrieved January 21, 2012, from http://www.nytimes.com/2011/10/23/fashion/emoticons-move-to-the-business-world-cultural-studies.html.

Dresser, N. (1996). *Multicultural manners*. New York: Wiley.

Dresser, N. (2005). *Multicultural manners: Essential rules of etiquette in the 21st century* (Rev. ed.). New York: Wiley.

Eakins, B. W., & Eakins, R. G. (1988). Sex differences in nonverbal communication. In L. A. Samovar & R. Porter (Eds.), *Intercultural communication: A reader* (pp. 292–309). Belmont, CA: Wadsworth.

Ekman, P., & Friesen, W. (1967). Head and body cues in the judgment of emotion: A reformulation. *Perceptual and Motor Skills, 24*, 711–724.

Ekman, P., & Friesen, W. (1969). The repertoire of nonverbal behavior: Categories, origins, usage, and coding. *Semoitica, 1*, 49–98.

Ekman, P., Sorenson, E. R., & Friesen, W. V. (1969). Pan-cultural elements in facial displays of emotions. *Science, 164*, 86–88.

Feldman, R., Singer, M., & Zagoory, O. (2009). Touch attenuates infants' psychological reactivity to stress. *Developmental Science, 13*(2), 271–278.

Field, T. (2002). Infants need for touch. *Human Development, 45*, 100–104.

Fox, K. (2010, November 20). *The smell report*. Social Issues Research Centre. Retrieved September 20, 2010, from http://www.sirc.org/publik/smell.pdf.

Givens, D. B. (2005). *The nonverbal dictionary of gestures, signs, and body language cues*. Spokane, WA: Center for Nonverbal Studies Press.

Graham, J. A., & Jauhar, A. J. (1982). *The effects of cosmetics on self perception: How we see ourselves*. Unpublished manuscript, University of Pennsylvania.

Halberstadt, A. G., & Saitta, M. B. (1987). Gender, nonverbal behavior, and perceived dominance: A test of the theory. Journal of Personality and Social Psychology, 53, 257–272.

Hall, E. (1969). *The hidden dimension*. Garden City, NY: Anchor Books.

Hall, E. T. (1959). *The silent language*. New York: Doubleday.

Hall, E. T., & Hall, M. R. (1990). *Understanding cultural differences*. Yarmouth, ME: Intercultural Press.

Hall, J. A. (1984). *Nonverbal sex differences: Communication accuracy and expressive style*. Baltimore: The John Hopkins University Press.

Hammermesh, D. S., & Biddle, J. F. (1994). Beauty and labor market. *American Economic Review, 84*(5), 1175–1194.

Harrigan, J. A. (1984). The effects of task order on children's identification of facial expression. *Motivation and Emotion*, *8*, 157–169.

Havlicek, J., Saxton, T. K., Roberts, S. C., Jozifkova, E., Lhota, S., Valentova, J., & Fleger, J. (2008). He sees, she smells? Male and female reports of sensory reliance in mate choice and non-mate choice contexts [Electronic version]. *Personality and Individual Differences*, *45*, 565–570.

Heslin, R., & Alper, T. (1983). Touch: The bonding gesture. In J. M. Wiemann & R. P Harrison (Eds.), *Nonverbal interaction*, 47–75. Beverly Hills, CA: Sage.

Hickson, M., Stacks, D. W., & Moore, N.-J. (2004). *Nonverbal communication: Studies and applications*. Los Angeles: Roxbury.

Hummert, M. L., Mazloff, D., & Henry, C. (1999). Vocal characteristics of older adults and stereotyping. *Journal of Nonverbal Behavior*, *23*, 111–132.

Keeley, M. P., & Hart, A. J. (1994). Nonverbal behavior in dyadic interaction. In S. W. Duck (Ed.), *Understanding Relationship Processes: Vol. 4. Dynamics of relationships* (pp. 135–162). Thousand Oaks, CA: Sage.

Kido, M. (2000). Bio-psychological effect of color. *Journal of International Society of Life Information Science*, *1*, 254–262.

Kramer, E. (1963). The judgment of personal characteristics and emotions from nonverbal properties of speech. *Psychological Bulletin*, *60*, 408–420.

Lawrence, E. D. (2010, January 6). Hundreds attend Dearborn meeting about Twin Towers shirts. *Detroit Free Press*. Retrieved September 10, 2010, from http://www.pocketfives.com/.

Leathers, D. (1997). *Successful nonverbal communication: Principles and applications* (3rd ed.). Boston: Allyn & Bacon.

Leathers, D. G. (1986). *Successful nonverbal communication: Principles and applications*. New York: Macmillan.

Lewis, R. D. (1999). *When cultures collide: Managing successfully across cultures*. London: Nicholas Brealey.

Lieberman, D. A., Rigo, T. G., & Campain, R. F. (1988). Age-related differences in nonverbal decoding ability. *Communication Quarterly*, *36*, 290–297.

Loureiro, P. R. A., Sachsida, A., & Cardoso de Mendonça, M. J. (2011). Links between physical appearance and wage discrimination: Further evidence. *International Review of Social Sciences and Humanities*, *2*(1), 249–260.

Markhan, R., & Adams, K. (1992). The effect of type of task on children's identification of facial expressions. *Journal of Nonverbal Behavior*, *16*, 21–39.

Maslow, A., & Mintz, N. L. (1956). Effects of esthetic surroundings. I: Initial effects of three esthetic conditions upon perceiving "energy" and "well-being" in faces. *Journal of Psychology*, *41*, 247–254.

Matsumoto, D. (1989). Cultural influences of the perception of emotion. *Journal of Cross-Cultural Psychology*, *20*, 92–105.

Mayor, M. (2011). *Pink boots and a machete: My journey from NFL cheerleader to National Geographic explorer* (pp. 297, 298). Washington, DC: National Geographic Society.

McClure, E. B. (2000). A meta-analytic review of sex differences in facial expression processing and their development in infants, children, and adolescents. *Psychological Bulletin*, *126*, 424–453.

Mehrabian, A. (1981). *Silent messages: Implicit communication of emotion and attitudes*. Belmont, CA: Wadsworth.

Montpare, J., Koff, E., Zaitchik, D., & Albert, M. (1999). The use of body movements and gestures as cues to emotion in younger and older adults. *Journal of Nonverbal Behavior*, *23*, 133–152.

Morrin, M., Krishna, A., & Lwin, M. O. (2001). Is scent-enhanced memory immune to retroactive interference? *Journal of Consumer Psychology*, 21, 354–361.

Niedenthal, P., Halberstadt, J. B., Margolin, J., & Innes-Ker, A. H. (2000). Emotional state and the detection of change in facial expression of emotion. *European Journal of Social Psychology*, *30*, 211–222.

Nowicki, S., Jr., & Duke, M. P. (1994). Individual differences in the nonverbal communication of affect: The diagnostic analysis of nonverbal accuracy scale. *Journal of Nonverbal Behavior*, *18*, 9–35.

Pittman, J., & Scherer, K. S. (1993). Vocal expression and communication of emotion. In M. Lewis & J. M. Haviland (Eds.), *Handbook of emotions*, 185–97. New York: Guilford.

Prochnik, G. (2010). *In pursuit of silence: Listening for meaning in a world of noise*. New York: Anchor Books.

Reid, A., Lancuba, V., & Murrow, B. (1997). Clothing style and formation of first impressions. *Perceptual and Motor Skills*, *84*, 237–238.

Safdar, S., Friedlmeier, W., Matsumoto, D., Yoo, S. H., Kwantes, C. T., Kakai, H., et al. (2009). Variations of emotional display rules within and across cultures: A comparison between Canada, USA, and Japan. *Canadian Journal of Behaviour Science, 41*, 1–10.

Singh, S. (2006). The impact of color on marketing, management decisions. *Management Decision*, *44*, 783–789.

Smith, J. (2013, March 11). Ten nonverbal cues that convey confidence at work. *Forbes* online. Accessed October 28, 2014, at http://www.forbes.com/sites

/jacquelynsmith/2013/03/11/10-nonverbal-cues-that
-convey-confidence-at-work/.

Smith, P. B., & Bond, M. H. (1994). *Social psychology across cultures: Analysis and perspectives*. Boston: Allyn & Bacon.

Thompson, L. A., Aidinejad, M. R., & Ponte, J. (2001). Aging and the effects of facial and prosodic cues on emotional intensity ratings and memory reconstructions. *Journal of Nonverbal Behavior, 25*, 101–125.

Ting-Toomey, S. (1997). Managing intercultural conflicts effectively. In L. A. Samovar & R. E. Porter (Eds.), *Intercultural communication: A reader* (8th ed., pp. 392–404). Belmont, CA: Wadsworth.

Van Lancker, D., Kreiman, J., & Emmorey, K. (1985). Familiar voice recognition: Patterns and parameters—Precognition of backward voices. *Journal of Phonetics, 13,* 19–38.

Villaros, L. (1994, January). Dangerous eating. *Essence*, pp. 12–21.

Waskul, D. D., & Vannini, P. (2008). Smell, odor, and somatic work: Sense-making and sensory management [Electronic version]. *Social Psychology Quarterly*, 71, 53–71.

Wood. J. (2013). *Gendered lives: communication, gender, and culture.* Boston: Cengage Learning.

Yarrow, L. J. (1963). Research in dimension of early maternal care. *Merrill-Palmer Quarterly, 9*, 101–122.

Chapter 4

Anderson, G. (2010–2013). Explorers/bio. National Geographic. Retrieved January 27, 2015, from http://www.nationalgeographic.com/explorers/bios/gregory-anderson/.

Anderson, G. (2015, January). Personal interview.

Austin, I., & Robins, L. (2009, December 23). BlackBerry breakdown puts users in uproar. *The New York Times*. Retrieved September 7, 2010, from http://www.nytimes.com/2009/12/24/technology/companies/24blackberry.html.

Blake, A. (2013, November 4). Paul Rand's plagiarism allegations and why they matter. *Washington Post*. Retrieved January 5, 2015, from http://www.washingtonpost.com/blogs/the-fix/wp/2013/11/04/rand-pauls-plagiarism-allegations-and-why-they-matter.

Boyle, C. (2010). Hot 97 DJ suspended indefinitely after on-air Haiti HIV crack that sparked protests among listeners. *Daily News*. Retrieved January 12, 2011, from http://www.nydailynews.com/ny_local/bronx/2010/12/26/2010-12-6_hot_97_dj_suspended_for_haiti_slur.html.

Burke, D. (2010, November 2). Supreme Court torn over speech rights, private rites. *Christian Century*, p. 17.

Canary, D. J., & Hause, K. S. (1993). Is there any reason to research sex difference in communication? *Communication Quarterly, 41*, 129–144.

Congressional Digest Corp. (2010, November). Does the Constitution protect the right of protestors to demonstrate during a private citizen's military funeral? *Supreme Court Debates: A Pro & Con Monthly, 13*(8), 17–27.

Enduring Voices. (2009). Western North America trip. *National Geographic*. Retrieved January 27, 2015, from http://www.nationalgeographic.com/mission/enduringvoices/pdfs/Wintu_final_email.pdf.

Gardner, A. (2011a, November 1). David Simpson loses Oklahoma Cartoonist Hall of Fame honor. *Daily Cartoonist*. Retrieved January 5, 2015, from http://dailycartoonist.com/index.php/2011/11/01/david-simpson-loses-oklahoma-cartoonist-hall-of-fame-honor/.

Gardner, A. (2011b, November 1). David Simpson resigns from the Urban Tulsa (Updated). *Daily Cartoonist*. Retrieved January 5, 2015, from http://dailycartoonist.com/index.php/2011/11/01/david-simpson-resigns-from-urban-tulsa/.

Goleman, D. (2007). E-mail is easy to write (and to misread). *The New York Times*. Retrieved December 10, 2010, from http://www.nytimes.com/2007/10/07/jobs/07pre.html.

Guffey, M. E., & Loewy, D. (2011). *Business communication: Process and product* (7th ed.). Mason, OH: Cengage Learning.

Harper, J. (2006, March 24). Riders shield mourners: Patriot Guard offers "corridor of honor" for troops. *Washington Times*, p. A9.

Harris, F. (2006, March 9). Bikers on guard at war funerals; Volunteer army of patriots shields grieving relatives from anti-gay pickets. *Daily Telegraph* (London), p. 8. Retrieved November 11, 2011, from www.patriotguard.org.

Holmes, J. (2006). *Gendered talk at work: Constructing gender identity through workplace discourse*. New York: Blackwell.

Howard, R. (2010, October 29). "The Dilemma's" gay joke: It stays in the movie. Los Angeles Times [online]. Retrieved November 11, 2011, from http://latimesblogs.latimes.com/the_big_picture/2010/10/ron-howard-on-the-dilemmas-gay-joke-it-stays-in-the-movie.html.

Hughes, S. A. (2011, October 10). Tracy Morgan on homophobic comments: It was all a misunderstanding. *Washington Post* [online]. Retrieved October 30, 2011, from http://www.washingtonpost.com/blogs/celebritology/post/tracy-morgan-on-homophobic-comments-it-was-a-misunderstanding-video/2011/10/11/gIQAsmkVcL_blog.html.

Johnson, S. K., Bettenhausen, K., & Gibbons, E. (2009). Realities of working in virtual teams: Affective and attitudinal outcomes of using computer-mediated communication, *Small Group Research, 6*, 623–649.

Kanawattanachai, P., & Yoo, T. (2002). Dynamic nature of trust in virtual teams. *Journal of Strategic Information Systems, 11*, 187–213.

Krulwich, R. (2009, April 6). Shakespeare has roses all wrong. National Public Radio. Retrieved November 29, 2010, from http://www.npr.org/templates/story/story.php?storyId=102518565.

Leaper, C. (1996). The relationship of play activity and gender to parent and child sex-typed communication. *International Journal of Behavioral Development, 19*, 689–703.

Leaper, C., & Ayres, M. M. (2007). A meta-analytic review of gender variations in adults' language use: Talkativeness, affiliative speech, and assertive speech. *Personality and Social Psychology Review, 4*, 328–363.

Maltz, D. C., & Borker, R. (1982). A cultural approach to male–female miscommunication. In J. J. Gumperz (Ed.), *Language and social identity* (pp. 196–216). Cambridge, UK: Cambridge University Press.

Martin, C., Fabes, R., Evans, S., & Wyman, H. (2000). Social cognition on the playground: Children's beliefs about playing with girls versus boys and their relationship to sex segregated play. *Journal of Social and Personal Relationships, 17*, 751–771.

McLaughlin, E. C. (2015). "Disgraceful" University of Oklahoma fraternity shuttered after racist chant. CNN. Retrieved March 30, 2015, from http://www.cnn.com/2015/03/09/us/oklahoma-fraternity-chant/index.html.

Merolla, A. J. (2010). Relational maintenance during military deployment: Perspectives of wives of deployed U.S. Soldiers. *Journal of Applied Communication Research, 1*, 4–26.

Mulac, A., Bradac, J. J., & Gibbons, P. (2001). Empirical support for the gender-as-culture hypothesis: An intercultural analysis of male/female language differences. *Human Communication Research, 27*, 121–152.

Mulac, A. J., Wiemann, J. M., Widenmann, S. J., & Gibson, T. W. (1988). Male/female language differences and effects in same-sex and mixed-sex dyads: The gender-linked language effect. *Communication Monographs, 55*, 315–335.

New words in the OED. (n.d.). Retrieved October 27, 2010, from http://newsfeed.time.com/new-words-in-the-ode/.

Ogden, C. K., & Richards, I. A. (1923). *The meaning of meaning: A study of the influence of language upon thought and of the science of symbolism.* New York: Harcourt Brace & World.

Oxford Dictionaries: Language Matters. (2013, August 28). Oxford Dictionaries Online Quarterly Update: New words added to oxforddictonaries.com today. Retrieved January 6, 2014, from http://blog.oxforddictionaries.com/august-2013-update/.

Oxford English Dictionary. (2013). Recent Updates to the OED. Retrieved January 6, 2014, from http://public.oed.com/the-oed-today/recent-updates-to-the-oed/.

pearanalytics. (2009, August). Twitter study. Retrieved October 27, 2010, from http://www.pearanalytics.com/blog/wp-content/uploads/2010/05/Twitter-Study-August-2009.pdf.

Pennebaker, J. W., Mehl, M. R., & Niederhoffer, K. G. (2003). Psychological aspects of natural language use: Our words, our selves. *Annual Review of Psychology, 54*, 547–577.

Petrow, S. (2009, February 9). "That's so gay" is not so funny. Huffington Post. Retrieved November 16, 2010, from http://www.huffingtonpost.com/steven-petrow/thats-so-gay-is-not-so-fu_b_165109.html.

Roth Walsh, M. (Ed.). (1997). *Women, men, and gender: Ongoing debates* (p. 87). Rensselaer, NY: Hamilton.

Shepard, J. (2010, October 2). Judy Shepard on gay suicides. *Advocate* [online].Retrieved November 11, 2011, from http://www.advocate.com/News/Daily_News/2010/10/02/Judy_Shepard_on_Gay_Suicides/.

Simmons, A. M. (2007, October 1). Biker groups escorts fallen troops; Patriot Guard riders, an informal organization of motorcyclists, attends funerals to pay tribute to military personnel. *Los Angeles Times*, p. 1B. Retrieved November 11, 2011, from http://articles.latimes.com/2007/oct/01/local/me-bikers1.

Sisters reunite after 18 years in checkout line. (1983, September 29). Retrieved January 21, 2012, from http://news.google.com/newspapers?nid=1876&dat=19830928&id=iWEsAAAAIBAJ&sjid=2c4EAAAAIBAJ&pg=6778,6962937

Spanos, B. (2015). Marvin Gaye's children: What our father would say about lawsuit. *RollingStone*. Retrieved March 30, 2015, from http://www.rollingstone.com/music/news/marvin-gayes-children-what-our-father-would-say-about-lawsuit-20150318.

Spurgeon, T. (2011, October 26). David Simpson accused of plagiarizing Jeff MacNelly cartoon [blog]. Retrieved October 30, 2011, from http://www.comicsreporter.com/index.php/david_simpson_accused_of_plagiarizing_jeff_macnelly_cartoon/.

Tannen, D. (2001). *You just don't understand: Women and men in conversation.* New York: Morrow.

Tannen, D. (2007, July 15). Who does the talking here? *Washington Post.* Retrieved September 7, 2010, from http://www.washingtonpost.com/wp-dyn/content/article/2007/07/13/AR2007071301815_pf.html.

"That's so gay" prompts a lawsuit. (2007, February 28). Retrieved November 16, 2010, from http://www.msnbc.msn .com/id/17388702/.

Vitchers, T. (2011, November 14). Violent hate speech incident at Williams college. *Huffington Post*. Retrieved January 5, 2015, from http://www.huffingtonpost.com/tracey-e-vitchers/violent -hate-speech-incid_b_1093846.html.

Watzlawick, P., Beavin, J. H., & Jackson, D. D. (1967). Some tentative axioms of communication. In P. Watzlawick, J. H. Beavin, & D. D. Jackson (Eds.), *Pragmatics of human communication: A study of interactional patterns, pathologies, and paradoxes* (pp. 48–71). New York: W. W. Norton.

Westboro Baptist Church. (2010, December 8). News release. Retrieved November 11, 2011, from http://www.godhatesfags .com/fliers/20101220_God-Hates-The-Media-Launch.pdf.

Wood, J. T. (2000). He says/she says: Misunderstandings in communication between women and men. In D. O. Braithwaite & J. T. Wood (Eds.), *Case studies in interpersonal communication* (pp. 93–100). Belmont, CA: Wadsworth.

Wood, J. T. (2011). *Gendered lives: Communication, gender, and culture*. (9th ed.). Boston: Wadsworth Cengage Learning.

Wood, J. T. (2013). *Gendered lives: Communication, gender, and culture*. (10th ed.). Boston: Wadsworth Cengage Learning.

Chapter 5

Belkin, L. (2007, July 26). Life's work: When whippersnappers and geezers collide. *The New York Times*. Retrieved November 3, 2011, from https://www.marycrane.com /press/26-07-26-07_NYT_When%20Whippersnappers%20 and%20Geezers%20Collide%20-%20New%20York%20 Times.pdf.

Bentley, S. C. (2000). Listening in the 21st century. *International Journal of Listening*, *14*, 129–142.

Brookfield, S. (1995). *Becoming a critically reflective teacher* (p. 115). San Francisco: Jossey-Bass.

Burns, S. M., & Lohenry, K. (2010, September). Cellular phone use in class: Implications for teaching and learning a pilot study. *College Student Journal*, *44*, 805–810.

Chesebro, J. L. (1999). The relationship between listening styles and conversational sensitivity. *Communication Research Reports*, *16*, 223–238.

Emanuel, R., Adams, J., Baker, K., Daufin, E. K., Ellington, C., Fitts, E., et al. (2008). How college students spend their time communicating, *International Journal of Listening*, *22,* 13–28.

Grognet, A., & Van Duzer, C. (2002–2003). Listening skills in the workplace. Retrieved December 21, 2014, from http:// www.springinstitute.org/Files/listeningwkplc.pdf.

Harrison, K. D. (2010, February 5). The tragedy of dying language. BBC. Retrieved December 21, 2014, from http:// news.bbc.co.uk/2/hi/8500108.stm.

Harrison, K. D. (2015a). Explorers/bio. *National Geographic* Retrieved January 6, 2015, from http://www.nationalgeographic .com/explorers/bios/david-harrison/.

Harrison, K. D. (2015b). Personal interview.

Harrison, L. H. (n.d.). *Managing today's multigenerational workforce*. Retrieved November 3, 2011, from http://www .lhh.com/knowledgecenter/Pages/Managingtodays multigenerationalworkforce.aspx.

Johnson, M. K., Weaver, J. B., III, Watson, K. W., & Barker, L. B. (2000). Listening styles: Biological or psychological differences? *International Journal of Listening*, *14*, 32–46.

Johnstone, A. H., & Percival, F. (1976). Attention breaks in lectures. *Education in Chemistry*, *13*, 49–50.

Klemmer, E. T., & Snyder, F. W. (1972), Measurement of time spent communicating. *Journal of Communication*, *22*, 142–158.

Kolb, D.A. (1984). *Experiential learning: Experience as the source of learning and development*. Englewood Cliffs, NJ: Prentice Hall.

Middendork, J., & Kalish, A. (1996). The "change-up" lectures. *The National Teaching and Learning Forum*, *5*(2).

Nichols, M. P. (2009). *The lost art of listening*. (2nd ed.) New York: Guilford Press.

Reavy, P. (2008, May 27). Cell phone use is creating new problems in schools. *Salt Lake City Deseret News*. Retrieved November 11, 2011 , from http://www.deseretnews.com/article/700229338 /Cell-phone-use-is-creating-new-problems-in-schools.html.

Sargent, S. L., Weaver, J. B., III, & Kiewitz, C. (1997). Correlates between communication apprehension and listening style preferences. *Communication Research Reports*, *14*, 74–78.

Sims, R. R., & Sims, S. J. (1995). *The importance of learning styles: Understanding the implications for learning, course design, and education*. Westport, CT: Greenwood.

Steil, L. K., Barker, L. L., & Watson, K. W. (1993). *Effective listening: Key to your success* (p. 51). New York: McGraw-Hill.

Understanding scientific jargon. (n.d.). Retrieved November 3, 2011, from http://science.discovery.com/quizzes /science-jargon/science-jargon-quiz.html.

Villeneuve, M. (2012, April 17). Report: Men still out-earning women. *Burlington Free Press* [online]. Retrieved April 18, 2012, from http://www.9to5.org/media/press/report-men -still-out-earning-women.

Wallis, C. (2006, March 27). The multitasking generation. *Time*, pp. 48–55.

White House. (2012, April). Equal pay task force accomplishments: Fighting for fair pay in the workplace [online]. Retrieved April 18, 2012, from http://www.whitehouse.gov /sites/default/files/equal_pay_task_force.pdf.

Wolvin, A., & Coakley, C. G. (1996). *Listening* (5th ed., p. 232). Madison, WI: Brown & Benchmark.

Wolvin, A., & Coakley, C. G. (2000). Listening education in the 21st century. *International Journal of Listening, 14*, 143–152.

Chapter 6

Alberts, J. K., Yoshimura, C., Rabby, M., & Loschiavo, R. (2005). Mapping the topography of couples' conversation. *Journal of Social and Personal Relationships, 22*, 299–322.

Allen, K. R., & Walker, A. J. (2000). Constructing gender in families. In R. M. Milardo & S. Duck (Eds.), *Families as relationships* (pp. 1–17). Chichester, UK: Wiley & Sons.

Altman, I., & Taylor, D. (1973). *Social penetration: The development of interpersonal relationships*. New York: Holt, Rinehart & Winston.

Biblarz, T. K., & Savci, E. (2010, June). Lesbian, gay, bisexual, and transgender families. *Journal of Marriage and Family, 72*, 480–497.

Canary, D., & Wahba, J. (2006). Do women work harder than men at maintaining relationships? In K. Dindia & D. Canary (Eds.), *Sex differences and similarities in communication* (2nd ed., pp. 359–377). Mahwah, NJ: Erlbaum.

Canary, D. J., & Stafford, L. (1994). Maintaining relationships through strategic and routine interaction. In D. Canary & L. Stafford (Eds.), *Communication and relational maintenance* (pp. 3–22). San Diego: Academic Press.

Cancian, F. M., & Oliker, S. J. (2000). *Caring and gender*. Thousand Oaks, CA: Pine Forge Press.

Collins, H. (2010, August 19). "Teacher quits after Facebook post, diss parents, kids" Retrieved April 23, 2012 from http:// www.aolnews.com/2010/08/19/teacher-quits-after -facebook-posts-diss-parents-kids/.

DeFrancisco, V. P., & Palczewski, C. H. (2007). *Communicating gender diversity*. Thousand Oaks, CA: Sage.

Downing, J. B., & Goldberg, A. E. (2010). Lesbian mothers' constructions of the division of paid and unpaid labor. *Feminism & Psychology, 21*, 100–120.

Eiler, S. (2010, July 30). Content management: Does an age divide exist? *PRWeb*. Retrieved from http://www.prweb.com /releases/Eiler-Communications/social-media.

Ellison, N. B., Steinfield, C., & Lampe, C. (2007). The benefits of Facebook friends: Social capital and college students' use of online social network sites. *Journal of Computer-Mediated Communication, 12*, 1143–1168.

Facebook post prompts prison probe. (2010, February 25). KETV 7 [television broadcast]. Omaha, NE. Retrieved November 16, 2011, from http://www.ketv.com/r/22675556 /detail.html.

Facebook Statistics (2015). Retrieved February 6, 2015, from http://www.statisticbrain.com/facebook-statistics/

Finholt, T., & Sproull, L. (1990). A social influence model of technology use. In J. Fulk & C. Steinfield (Eds.), *Organizations and communication technology* (pp. 117–140). Newbury Park, CA: Sage.

Fitzpatrick, M. A. (2003). *Between husbands and wives: Communication in marriage*. Newbury Park, CA: Sage.

Fry, R., & Cohn, D'V. (2010, July 19). *New economics of marriage: The rise of wives. Pew Research Center Publications.* Retrieved July 28, 2010, from http://pewresearch.org /pubs/1466/economics-marriage-rise-of-wives.

Galvin, K. M., Bylund, C. L., & Brommel, B. J. (2003). *Family communication: Cohesion and change* (6th ed., p. 5). Boston: Allyn & Bacon.

Gershon, I. (2010). *The breakup 2.0: Disconnecting over new media*. Ithaca, NY: Cornell University Press.

Goldberg, A. E., & Perry-Jenkins, M. (2007). The division of labor and perceptions of parental roles: Lesbian couples across the transition to parenthood. *Journal of Social and Personal Relationships, 24*, 297–318.

Guy, S., & Thome, J. (2015). New media culture storytellers. *National Geographic*. Retrieved February 8, 2015, from http:// www.nationalgeographic.com/explorers/bios/guy-thome/.

Haas, S. M., & Stafford, L. (1998). An initial examination of relationships maintenance behaviors in gay and lesbian relationships. *Journal of Social and Personal Relationships, 15*, 846–855.

H. S. teacher loses job over Facebook posting (2010, August 18). Retrieved November 3, 2011, from http://www .thebostonchannel.com/r/24670937/detail .html.

Knapp, M. L. (1978). *Social intercourse: From greeting to goodbye*. Boston: Allyn & Bacon.

Knapp, M. L. (1984). *Interpersonal communication and human relationships*. Boston: Allyn & Bacon.

Knapp, M. L., & Daly, J. A. (2010). *Interpersonal communication* (Sage Benchmarks in Communication, 4 vols.). London: Sage.

Kurdek, L. A. (2005). The allocation of household labor by partners in gay and lesbian relationships. *Journal of Family Issues, 28*, 132-148.

Laner, R., & Ventrone, N. A. (2000). Dating scripts revisited. *Journal of Family Issues*, *21*, 488–500.

Madden, M., Lenhart, A., Cortesi S., Gasser U., Duggan, M., Smith A., & Beaton, M. (2013, May 13). Teens, Social Media, and Privacy. *Pew Research Center*. Retrieved Feburary 6, 2015, from http://www.pewinternet.org/2013/05/21/teens-social-media-and-privacy/

Martin, J., & Nakayama, T. (2004). *Experiencing intercultural communication: An introduction* (2nd ed., pp. 27–28).

Military life. (n.d.). National Geographic [Online]. Retrieved from http://video.nationalgeographic.com/video/national-geographic-channel/specials-1/bin-laden-1/ngc-military-life/.

Mongeau, P. A., & Henningsen, M. L. M. (2008). Stage theories of relationship development. In Engaging theories in interpersonal communication: Multiple perspectives (pp. 363-375), L. A. Baxter & D. O. Braaithwaite (eds.). Los Angeles, CA: Sage.

Monsour, M. (2002). *Women and men as friends: Relationships across the lifespan in the twenty-first century*. Mahwah, NJ: Lawrence Erlbaum Associates.

National Public Radio. (2009, November 25). 2010 census will count same-sex couples. Retrieved July 10, 2010, from http://www.npr.org/templates/story/story.php?storyId=120816467&sc=emaf.

Nie, N., & Hillygus, D. S. (2002). The impact of Internet use on sociability: Time-diary findings. *IT & Society*, *1*, 1–20.

Peplau, L. A., & Beals, K. P. (2004). The family lives of lesbians and gay men. In A. L. Vangelisti (Ed.), *Handbook of family communication* (pp. 233–248). Mahwah, NJ: Erlbaum.

Petronio, S. (2002). *Boundaries of privacy: Dialectics of disclosure*. Albany: SUNY Press.

Pettigrew, J. (2009). Text messaging and connectedness within close interpersonal relationships. *Marriage & Family Review*, *45*(6–8), 697–716.

Pew Research Internet Project. (2015). Social networking fact sheet. Retrieved January 5, 2015, from http://www.pewinternet.org/fact-sheets/social-networking-fact-sheet/.

Putnam, R. D. (1995). Bowling alone: America's declining social capital. *Journal of Democracy*, *6*(1), 65–78.

Rainie, J. L. (2010, January 5). Report: Internet, broadband, and cell phone statistics. Pew Research Center Internet and American Life Project. Retrieved July 22, 2010, from http://www.pewinternet.org/Reports/2010/Internet-broadband-and-cell-phone-statistics/Report.aspx?r=1.

Rawlins, W. K. (1981). *Friendship as a communicative achievement: A theory and an interpretive analysis of verbal reports* (Unpublished doctoral dissertation). Temple University, Philadelphia.

Recruit Yuri Wright Expelled for Tweets. (2012, January 20). *ESPN*. Retrieved January 6, 2015, from http://espn.go.com/college-sports/recruiting/football/story/_/id/7484495/yuri-wright-twitter-posts-cost-college-scholarship)

Schwartz, M. J. (2010, June 22). Teens engage in risky online behavior. *InformationWeek*. Retrieved July 22, 2010, from http://www.informationweek.com/news/.

Shah, D. V., McLeod, J. M., & Yoon, S. (2001). Communication, context, and community: An exploration of print, broadcast, and Internet influences. *Communication Research*, *28*, 464–506.

Spence, J. T., & Buckner, C. E. (2000). Instrumental and expressive traits, trait stereotypes, and sexist attitudes: What do they signify? *Psychology of Women Quarterly*, *24*, 44–63.

Sproull, L., & Kiesler, S. (1986). Reducing social context cues: Electronic mail in organizational communication. *Management Science*, *32*, 1492–1512.

Stevens, B. (2011, June 21). Social media and divorces: Examining the impact of Facebook and Twitter on relationships. Retrieved November 16, 2011, from http://www.scfamilylaw.com/2011/06/articles/divorce/guest-post-social-media-and-divorces-examining-the-impact-of-facebook-and-twitter-on-relationships/.

Thirty-Eight Percent of Workers Have Dated a Co-Worker, Finds CareerBuilder Survey (2014, February 12). *Careerbuilder*. Retrieved February 8, 2015, from http://www.careerbuilder.com/share/aboutus/pressreleasesdetail.aspx?sd=2%2f13%2f2014&id=pr803&ed=12%2f31%2f2014

Thome, J. (2015, February 10). Personal communication.

Tom Tong, S., Van Der Heide, B., Langwell, L., & Walther, J. B. (2008). Too much of a good thing? The relationship between number of friends and interpersonal impressions on Facebook. *Journal of Computer-Mediated Communication*, *13*, 531–549.

"United Nations Millennium Development Goals Report 2014" retrieved February 10, 2015 from http://www.un.org/millenniumgoals/2014%20MDG%20report/MDG%202014%20English%20web.pdf.

U.S. Census Bureau. (2013a). America's families and living arrangements, 2013. Retrieved January 5, 2015, from http://www.census.gov/hhes/families/data/cps2013C.html.

U.S. Census Bureau. (2013b). Characteristics of same sex couple households, 2013. Census Bureau releases estimates of same-sex married couples. Retrieved January 6, 2015, from http://www.census.gov/hhes/samesex/.

USC Annenberg School for Communication and Journalism, Center for the Digital Future (2011, June 3). 2010 digital future report. Retrieved November 16, 2011, from http://www.digitalcenter.org/pdf/2011_digital_future_final_release.pdf.

Vlahakis, G. (2010, July 22). "The breakup 2.0": A look at how new media is used to end relationships. Retrieved November 16, 2011, from http://www.eurekalert.org/pub_releases/2010-07/iu-b2072110.php.

Wood, J. (2013). *Gendered lives: Communication, gender, and culture* (10th ed., pp. 20–21). Boston: Cengage Learning.

Wright, P. H. (1982). Men's friendships, women's friendships, and the alleged inferiority of the latter. *Sex Roles, 8*, 1–20.

Chapter 7

Addo, D. (2014, January 16). Social media, Malala, and changing the world. Retrieved April 3, 2015, from http://blog.flvs.net/social-media-malala-and-changing-the-world/.

BBC News. (2009, January 19). Diary of a Pakistani schoolgirl. Retrieved April 3, 2015, from http://news.bbc.co.uk/2/hi/south_asia/7834402.stm.

Bern, S. L., & Lenney, E. (1976). Sex-typing and the avoidance of psychological androgyny. *Journal of Personality and Social Psychological*: *International Journal of Conflict Management, 31*, 634–643.

Bone, J. E., Griffin, C. L., & Scholz, T. M. L. (2008). Beyond traditional conceptualizations of rhetoric: Invitational rhetoric and a move toward civility. *Western Journal of Communication, 72*(4), 434–462.

Brooks, C. (2012, December 2). How to be a good mentor. Retrieved April 15, 2015, from http://www.businessnewsdaily.com/3504-how-to-mentor.html.

Brower, N., Mitchell, P., & Weber, N. (2002). Gender role, organizational status, and conflict management styles. *International Journal of Conflict Management, 13*(4), 78–94.

Carter, S. L. (1998). *Civility: Manners, morals and the etiquette of democracy*. New York: Basic Books.

Clark, L. S. (2009, April). Digital media and the generation gap: Qualitative research on U.S. teens and their parents. *Information, Communication & Society, 12*(3), 388–407, 403.

Dainton, M., & Aylor, B. (2001). A relational uncertainty analysis of jealousy, trust, and maintenance in long-distance versus geographically close relationships. *Communication Quarterly, 49*, 172–188.

Denetdale, J. R. (2013, November 22). "Nava-hos" frat party sparks outrage. Retrieved April 3, 2015, from http://indiancountrytodaymedianetwork.com/2013/11/22/outrage-over-nava-hos-frat-party-cal-poly-san-luis-obispo-152384.

Domestic Violence Statistics. (n.d.). Retrieved June 7, 2011, from http://domesticviolencestatistics.org/domestic-violence-statistics//.

Dries, K. (2013, November 22). Cal Poly frat holds classic "Colonial bros and Nava-hos" party. Retrieved April 3, 2013, from http://jezebel.com/cal-poly-frats-hold-classic-colonial-bros-and-nava-hos-1469271171.

Fallon, N. (2014, April 16). Need a mentor? Here's how to ask. Retrieved April 15, 2015, from http://www.businessnewsdaily.com/6248-how-to-find-mentor.html.

Ferber, A., Jimenez, C.M., Herrera, A. O., & Samuels, D. R. (2008). *The matrix reader: Examining the dynamics of oppression and privilege*. Boston: McGraw-Hill Higher Education.

Fox, Z. (2013, October 31). Is anonymous social media the answer to cyberbullying? Retrieved April 3, 2015, from http://mashable.com/2013/10/31/whisper/.

Gerstel, N., & Gross, H. (1984). *Commuter marriage: A study of work and family*. New York: Guilford.

Hall, E. T., & Hall, M. R. (1989). *Understanding cultural differences*. Yarmouth, ME: Intercultural Press.

Hoffman, L. (2015, April 1). Yik Yak: The age of destructive anonymity. Retrieved April 3, 2015, from http://www.huffingtonpost.com/lindsay-hoffman/yik-yak-the-age-of-destru_b_6979836.html.

Hofstede, G. (1986). Cultural differences in teaching and learning. *International Journal of Intercultural Relations, 10*, 301–320.

Holstrom, A. J. (2009). Sex and gender similarities and differences in communication values in same-sex and cross-sex friendships. *Communication Quarterly, 57*(2), 224–238.

Holt, J. L., & DeVore, C. J. (2005). Culture, gender, organizational role, and styles of conflict resolution: A meta-analysis. *International Journal of Intercultural Relations, 29*, 165–196.

hooks, b. (2004). *The will to change: Men, masculinity, and love*. New York: Washington Square Press.

Johnson, A. J., Becker, J., Craig, E. A., Gilchrist, E. S., & Haigh, M. M. (2009). Changes in Friendship commitment: Comparing geographically close and long-distance young-adult friendships. *Communication Quarterly, 57*(4), 395–415.

Johnson, A. J., Wittenberg, E., Haigh, M., Wigley, S., Becker, J., Brown, K., et al. (2004). The process of relationship development and deterioration: Turning points in friendships that have terminated. *Communication Quarterly, 52*, 54–67.

Kaushal, R., & Kwantes, C. T. (2006). The role and personality in choice of conflict management strategy. *International Journal of Intercultural Relations, 30*, 580, 581.

Kayany, J. M. (1998). Contexts of uninhibited online behavior: Flaming in social newsgroups on Usenet. *Journal of the American Society for Information Science*, 49(12), 1135–1141.

Kimmel, M. (2011). *The gendered society* (4th ed.). London: Oxford University Press.

Kostucki, N., & Chen, L. (2014). *Seek to keep: How to find the best mentors and keep them*. CreateSpace Independent Publishing Platform.

Kunkel, A. W., & Burleson, B. R. (1998). Social support and the emotional lives of men and women: An assessment of the different cultures perspective. In D. Canary & K. Dindia (Eds.), *Sex differences and similarities in communication: Critical essays and empirical investigations of sex and gender in interaction* (pp. 101–125). Mahwah, NJ: Lawrence Erlbaum Associates.

Leung, K., & Lind, E. A. (1986). Procedural justice and culture: Effects of culture, gender, and investigator status on procedural preferences. *Journal of Personality and Social Psychology*, 50(6), 1134–1140.

Lloyd, S. A., & Cate, R. M. (1985). The developmental course of conflict in dissolution or premarital relationships. *Journal of Social and Personal Relationships*, 2, 179–194.

Merolla, A. J. (2010). Relational maintenance and noncopresence reconsidered: Conceptualizing geographic separation in close relationships. *Communication Theory*, 20(2), 169–193.

National Coalition Against Domestic Violence. (n.d.). Domestic violence facts. Retrieved November 16, 2011, from http://www.ncadv.org/files/DomesticViolenceFactSheet (National) .pdf.

Putnam, L. (2010). Communication as changing the negotiation game. *Journal of Applied Communication Research*, 38(4), 325–335.

Ratcliff, K. (2005). *Rhetorical listening: Identification, gender, whiteness*. Carbondale: Southern Illinois University Press.

Sarah, A. A. (2009, May 6). A conflict close to home. Retrieved November 29, 2011, from http://azizabusarah.wordpress .com/2009/05/06/a-conflict-close-to-home/.

Seo, K. K., Miller, P. C., Schmidt, C., & Sowa, P. C. (2008). Patience, creating synergy between collectivism and individualism in cyberspace: A comparison of online communication patterns between Hong Kong and U.S. students. *Journal of Intercultural Communication*, no. 18. Retrieved November 29, 2011, from http://www.immi.se/jicc /index.php/jicc/article/view/55/28.

Stafford, L., & Merolla, A. J. (2007). Idealization, reunions, and stability in long-distance dating relationships. *Journal of Social and Personal Relationships*, 24, 37–54.

Stafford, L., Merolla, A. J., & Castle, J. D. (2006). When long-distance dating partners become geographically close. *Journal of Social and Personal Relationships*, 23(6), 901–919.

Statistic Brain. (2015, March 18). Long distance relationship statistics. Retrieved April 3, 2015, from http://www .statisticbrain.com/long-distance-relationship-statistics/.

Taylor, M., & Segrin, C. (2010). Perceptions of parental gender roles and conflict style and their association with young adults' relational and psychological well-being. *Communication Research Reports*, 27(3), 230–242.

Thomas, K. W., & Kilmann, R. H. (2007). Thomas-Kilmann conflict mode instrument: Profile and interpretative report. Retrieved April 24, 2012, from http://www.opp.eu.com /SiteCollectionDocuments/pdfs/reports/tki_profile_and _interpretive_sample_report_sample.pdf.

Warech, M. A., Smither, J. W., Reilly, R. R., Millsap, R. E., & Reilly, S. P. (1998). Self-monitoring and 360-degree ratings. *Leadership Quarterly*, 9, 449–473.

Zhang, S., Merolla, A., & Lin, S.-F. (2009, November). *The nature and consequences of topic avoidance in Chinese and Taiwanese close relationships*. Paper presented at annual meeting of National Communication Association, 95th Annual Convention, Chicago. Available at http://www.allacademic .com/meta/p367288_index.html.

Chapter 8

Albrecht, L. B., & Brewer, R. M. (1990). *Bridges of power: Women's multicultural alliances*. Philadelphia: New Society.

Alsever, J. (2009, February 17). How to handle a workplace bully. Retrieved April 24, 2015, from http://www.cbsnews .com/news/how-to-handle-a-workplace-bully/.

Ashcraft, K. (2001). Feminist organizing and the construction of "alternative" community. In G. J. Shepherd & E. W. Rothenbuhler (Eds.), *Communication and community* (pp. 79–110). Mahwah, NJ: Lawrence Erlbaum.

Bakhtin, M. M. (1993). *Toward a philosophy of the act* (V. Liapunov & M. Holquist, Eds.; V, Liapunov, Trans.). Austin: University of Texas Press. (Original work published 1979)

Barbuto, J. E., Fritz, S. M., Matkin, G. S., & Marx, D. B. (2007). Effects of gender, education, and age upon leaders' use of influence tactics and full range leadership behaviors. *Sex Roles*, 56, 71–83.

Bass, B. M. (1985). *Leadership and performance*. New York: Free Press.

Batra, N. D. (2008). *Digital freedom: How much can you handle?* New York: Rowman & Littlefield.

Boyes, S. (2011). Crossing the Okavango Delta for world heritage status: Celebrating Botswana's wetland wilderness. Retrieved December 27, 2011 from http://newswatch.nationalgeographic.com/2011/12/22/crossing-the-okavango-delta-for-world-heritage-status-celebrating-botswanas-wetland-wilderness.

Burns, J. M. (1978). *Leadership*. New York: Harper & Row.

Castells, M. (2009). *Communication power*. London: Oxford University Press.

Cherry, K. (n.d.). What is laissez-faire leadership? Retrieved June 9, 2011, from http://psychology.about.com/od/leadership/f/laissez-faire-leadership.html.

Cohen, A. (2010, July 21). New laws target workplace bullying. *Time*. Retrieved June 9, 2011, from http://www.time.com/time/nation/article/0,8599,2005358,00.html.

Cousteau, A. (2009). Alexandra Cousteau's Blue Planet. Retrieved December 27, 2011 from http://newswatch.nationalgeographic.com/tag/blue-planet/.

Cousteau, A. (2011). Blue legacy. Retrieved December 27, 2011 from http://www.alexandracousteau.org/blue-legacy-overview.

Cousteau, A. (2012, January 18). Telephone communication.

Darlington, P. S. E., & Mulvaney, B. M. (2002). Gender, rhetoric, and power: Toward a model of reciprocal empowerment. *Women's Studies in Communication*, 25, 139–172.

Davenport, N., Schwartz, R. D., & Elliott, G. P. (2005). *Mobbing: Emotional abuse in the American workplace*. Collins, IA: Civil Society Publishing.

Davison, K. P., Pennebaker, J. W., & Dickerson, S. S. (2000). Who talks? The social psychology of illness support groups. *American Psychologist*, 55(2), 205–217.

Dewey, J. (1910). *How we think*. Boston: D.C. Heath.

Druskat, V. U. (1994). Gender and leadership style: Transformational and transactional leadership in the Roman Catholic Church. *Leadership Quarterly*, 5, 99–119.

Duggan, M., Ellison, N. B., Lampe, C., Lenhart, A., & Madden, M. (2015, January 9). Demographics of key social networking platforms. PewResearch Center. Retrieved March 26, 2015, from http://www.pewinternet.org/2015/01/09/demographics-of-key-social-networking-platforms-2/.

Eagly, A. H., Johannesen-Schmidt, M. C., & van Engen, M. L. (2003, July). Transformational, transactional, and laissez-faire leadership styles: A meta-analysis comparing women and men. *Psychological Bulletin*, 129(4), 569–591.

Everest Peace Project. (2009). Retrieved November 11, 2011 from www.everestpeaceproject.com/about/everest-peace-climbers/everest-peace-climbers.html.

Fahmy, M. (2010, May 11). Face-to-face time makes us happier than Facebook. Retrieved November 11, 2011, from www.reuters.com.

Fairhurst, G. T. (2001). Dualisms in leadership research. In F. M. Jablin & L. L. Putnam (Eds.), *The new handbook of organizational communication: Advances in theory, research, and methods* (pp. 379–439). Thousand Oaks, CA: Sage.

Foucault, M. (1972). *The archaeology of knowledge and the discourse on language*. (A. M. S. Smith, Trans.). New York: Pantheon.

French, J. R., & Raven, B. (1968). The basis of social power. In D. Cartright & A. Zander (Eds.), *Group dynamics* (pp. 259–269). New York: Harper & Row.

Frey, L. R. (Ed.). (1999). *The handbook of group communication theory and research*. Thousand Oaks, CA: Sage.

Frey, L. R. (Ed.). (2003). *Group communication in context: Studies of bona fide groups* (2nd ed.). Mahwah, NJ: Lawrence Erlbaum.

Gastil, J. (1994). A definition and illustration of democratic leadership. *Human Relations*, 47, 953–975.

Goodwin, P. J., Leszcz, M., Ennis, M., Koopmans, J., Vincent, L., Guther, H., et al. (2001). The effect of group psychosocial support on survival in metastatic breast cancer. *New England Journal of Medicine*, 345, 1719–1726.

Green, D. A. (2011, March). Twitter is more than just a fad, so don't miss the boat. The Lawyer. Retrieved November 8, 2011, from www.thelawyer.com.

Halverson, S., Murphy, S. E., & Riggio, R. E. (2004). Charismatic leadership in crisis situations: A laboratory investigation of stress and crisis. *Small Group Research*, 35, 495–514.

House, R. J., Hanges, P. J., Javidan, M., Drofman, P. W., & Gupta, V. (Eds.). (2004). *Culture, leadership, and organizations: The GLOBE study of 62 societies*. Thousand Oaks, CA: Sage.

House, R. J., Hanges, P. J., Ruiz-Quintanilla, S. A., Dorfman, P. W., Javidan, M., Dickson, M., et al. (n.d.). *Cultural influences on leadership and organizations: Project GLOBE*. Retrieved June 9, 2011, from http://www.thunderbird.edu/wwwfiles/sites/globe/pdf/process.pdf.

Jamieson, K. H. (1995). *Beyond the double bind: Women and leadership*. London: Oxford University Press.

Janis, I. L. (1972). *Victims of groupthink* (p. 9). Boston: Houghton Mifflin.

Johnson, C. E. (2009). *Meeting the ethical of leadership: Casting light or shadow* (p. 8). Newbury Park, CA: Sage.

Kelly, J. A., Murphy, D. A., Bahr, G. R., Kalichman, S. C., Morgan, M. G., Stevenson, L. Y., et al. (1993). Outcome of cognitive-behavioral and support group brief therapies for depressed, HIV-infected persons. *American Journal of Psychiatry*, *150*, 1679–1686.

Kets de Vries, M. F. R. (2001). *Struggling with the demon: Perspectives on individual and organizational irrationality* (p. 189). Madison, Connecticut. Psychosocial Press.

Kiesler, S., & Sproull, L. (1992). Group decision making and communication technology. *Organizational Behavior and Human Decision Processes*, *52*, 96–123.

Lewin, K., Lippitt, R., & White, R. (1939). Patterns of aggressive behavior in experimentally created "social climates." *Journal of Social Psychology*, *10*, 271–299.

Littlejohn, S. W., & Foss, K. A. (2007). *Theories of human communication* (8th ed., p. 232). Boston: Wadsworth/ Cengage.

Mesterhazy, L. (2008, September 23). Two Israelis and a Palestinian: Conquering Everest together. Retrieved November 17, 2011, from http://www.haaretz.com/news/two-israelis-and-a -palestinian-conquering-everest-together-1.254383.

Minors, Z. (2010, August 16). Twitter goes to college, Retrieved November 8, 2011, from http://www.usnews.com.

Namie, G., & Namie, R. (2011). *The bully-free workplace: Stop jerks, weasels, and snakes from killing your organization*. New York: Wiley.

Namie, G., & Namie, R. (2014). From bullied to bullyproof: The WBI-3-step target action plan. Retrieved April 24, 2015, from http://www.workplacebullying.org/individuals/solutions /wbi-action-plan/.

O'Sullivan, P. B., & Flanagin, A. J. (n.d.). An interactional reconceptualization of "flaming" and other problematic messages. Retrieved November 17, 2011, from http://my .ilstu.edu/~posull/flaming.htm.

Popper, M. (2005). *Leaders who transform society: What drives them and why we are attracted to them* (pp. 18–21, 27–28). Westport, CT: Praeger.

Putnam, L. L., & Stohl, C. (1990). Bona fide groups: A reconceptualization of groups in context. *Communication Studies*, *41*, 248–265.

Reid, M., & Hammersley, R. (2000). *Communicating successfully in groups: A practical guide for the workplace* (pp. 82–92, 92–99). Philadelphia: Routledge.

Sargent, C. (2006). *From buddy to boss: Effective fire service leadership*. Tulsa, OK: PennWell Corp.

Skogstad, A., Ståle, E., Torsheim, T., Aasland, M. S., & Hetland, H. (2007, January). The destructiveness of laissez-faire leadership behavior. *Journal of Occupational Health Psychology*, *12*(1), 80–92.

Starhawk. (1990). *Truth or dare: Encounters with power, authority, and mystery*. San Francisco: Harper & Row.

Washington State Department of Labor and Industries. (2011, April). *Workplace bullying and disruptive behavior: What everyone needs to know*. Report no. 87-2-2011. Olympia: Author. Retrieved June 9, 2011, from http://www.lni.wa.gov /safety/research/files/bullying.pdf.

Western, S. (2008). *Leadership: A critical text* (pp. 23, 35). Thousand Oaks, CA: Sage.

Wilson, G., & Hanna, M. (1986). *Groups in context: Leadership and participation in decision making groups*. New York: McGraw-Hill.

Workplace Bullying Institute. (2011). Work shouldn't hurt. Retrieved June 9, 2011, from http://www.workplacebullying .org/targets/starthere.html.

Chapter 9

Alderton, S. M., & Frey, L. R. (1986). Argumentation in small group decision-making. In R. Y. Hirokawa & M. S. Poole (Eds.), *Communication and group decision making* (pp. 157–173). Beverly Hills, CA: Sage.

Basij-Rasikh, S. (2012). Dare to educate Afghan girls. TEDx Women2012. Retrieved April 9, 2015, from https://www.ted .com/talks/shabana_basij_rasikh_dare_to_educate_afghan _girls/transcript?language=en.

Bulletin Community Forum FAQ. (n.d.). Retrieved November 2011 from https://www.vbulletin.com/forum/faq .php?faq=vb3_board_usage#faq_vb3_forums_threads _posts.

Chappell, B. (2015, March 13). Athletes help cheerleader with Down Syndrome defy bullies. The Two Way, NPR. Retrieved April 3, 2015, from http://www.npr.org/blogs/thetwo -way/2015/03/13/392782830/athletes-help-cheerleader -with-down-syndrome-defy-bullies.

Cong, G., Wang, L., Lin, C.-Y., Song, Y.-I., & Sun, Y. (2008). Finding question-answer pairs from online forums. In T.-S. Chua & M.-K. Leong (General Chairs), *Proceedings of the 31st Annual International ACM SIGIR Conference on Research and Development in Information Retrieval* (pp. 467–474). New York: Association for Computer Machinery.

Creative Group. (n.d.). New job? Avoid those rookie mistakes. PRSA jobcenter. Retrieved April 2, 2015, from http://www .prsa.org/jobcenter/career_resources/issues_and_trends /careerarticleemployment120507.

Dowd, K. E. (2015). Basketball team banned from playoffs for wrong uniforms is reinstated, panel rules. *People*. Retrieved April 3, 2015, from http://www.people.com/article/girls -basketball-team-uniform-ban-breast-cancer-reinstated.

Fisher, B. A. (1970). Decision emergence: Phases in group decision making. *Speech Monographs*, *37*, 53–66.

Food Not Bombs. (n.d.). The story of Food Not Bombs. Retrieved January 15, 2012, from http://www.foodnotbombs .net/story.html.

Forsyth, D. R. (1990). *Group dynamics* (2nd ed., p. 369). Pacific Grove, CA: Brooks/Cole Publishing.

Frey, L. R. (Ed.). (2003). *Group communication in context: Studies of bona fide groups* (2nd ed.). Mahwah, NJ: Lawrence Erlbaum.

Hirokawa, R. Y., & Salazar, A. J. (1999). Task group communication and decision making performance. In L. R. Frey, D. S. Gouran, & M. S. Poole (Eds.), *The handbook of group communication theory and research* (pp. 167–191). Thousand Oaks, CA: Sage.

Hofstede, G. (2010). *Cultures and organizations: Software of the mind* (p. 158). New York: McGraw-Hill.

Internet and Environmental Education. (2010, June 23). Environmental panel. YouTube Harvard Extension. Retrieved December 27, 2011, from http://www.youtube.com /watch?v=lekNrH9edaM.

Jansenn, D., & Kies, R. (2005, September). Online forums and deliberative democracy. *Acta Politica*, *40*(3), 317–335.

Keyton, J., & Stallworth, V. (2003). On the verge of collaboration: Interaction processes versus group outcomes. In L. R. Frey (Ed.), *Group communication in context: Studies of bona fide groups* (2nd ed., pp. 235–260). Mahwah, NJ: Lawrence Erlbaum.

Miller, K. (2006). *Organizational communication: Approaches and processes* (4th ed., p. 184). Belmont, CA: Thomson/ Wadsworth.

National Coalition for Dialogue and Deliberation. (n.d.). Retrieved February 11, 2012, from http://www.ncdd.org.

National Geographic Society. (2014). Explorers Bio: Shabana Basij-Rasikh. Retrieved April 2, 2015, from http://www .nationalgeographic.com/explorers/bios/shabana-basij -rasikh/.

Oetzel, J. G., & Ting-Toomey, S. (Eds.). (2006). *The Sage handbook of conflict communication: Integrating theory, research, and practice*. Thousand Oaks, CA: Sage.

Poole, M. S., & Garner, J. T. (2006). Perspectives on workgroup conflict and communication. In J. G. Oetzel & S. Ting-Toomey (Eds.), *The Sage handbook of conflict communication: Integrating theory, research, and practice* (pp. 267–292). Thousand Oaks, CA: Sage.

Reagan, M. (2015). Boy Scout troop kicks gay mom from Converse out of meeting. *San Antonio Current*. Retrieved April 3, 2015, from http://www.sacurrent.com/Blogs /archives/2015/04/01/boy-scout-troop-kicks-gay-mom -from-converse-out-of-meeting.

Reid, M., & Hammersley, R. (2000). *Communicating successfully in groups: A practical guide for the workplace* (pp. 36–37). Philadelphia: Routledge.

Salazar, A. J. , Hirokawa, R. Y., Propp, K. M., Julian, K. M., & Leatham, G. B. (1994, June). In search of true causes: Examination of the effect of group potential and group interaction on decision performance. *Human Communication Research*, *20*(4), 529–599.

Seibold, D. R., & Meyers, R. A. (1986). Communication and influence in group decision-making. In R. Y. Hirokawa & M. S. Poole (Eds.), *Communication and group decision making* (pp. 133–156). Beverly Hills, CA: Sage.

Stohl, C. (2001). Globalizing organizational communication. In F. M. Jablin & L. L. Putnam (Eds.), *The new handbook of organizational communication: Advances in theory, research, and methods* (pp. 323–375). Thousand Oaks, CA: Sage.

What Is an "Internet Forum"? (n.d.). Videojug Corporation Limited. Retrieved November 17, 2011, from http://www .videojug.com/expertanswer/internet-communities-and -forums-2/what-is-an-internet-forum.

Chapter 10

Andeweg, B. A., de Jong, J. C., & Hoeken, H. (1998). "May I have your attention?" Exordial techniques in informative oral presentations. *Technical Communication Quarterly*, *7*(3), 281.

Bennett, J., & Ellison, J. (2010, April 10). Tracking the wage gap: In honor of equal pay day, 12 sobering figures about men, women, and work. *Newsweek*. Retrieved from http: //www .newsweek.com/2010/04/19/tracking-the-wage-gap.html.

Braun, D. (2009, June 18). Angelina Jolie has a heartfelt message for World Refugee Day. National Geographic. Retrieved from http://newswatch.nationalgeographic .com/2009/06/18/angelina_jolie_world_refugee_day.

Browne, A., & Williams, K. R. (1993). Gender, intimacy, and lethal violence: Trends from 1976–1987. *Gender & Society*, *7*(1), 78–98.

Buzawa, E., Austin, T. L., & Buzawa, G. G. (1995). Responding to crimes of violence against women: Gender differences versus organizational imperatives. *Crime and Delinquency*, *41*(4), 443–466.

Davis, W. (2014, December 15). Personal interview. December 15, 2014.

Dobash, R. P., Dobash, R. E., Cavanagh, K., & Lewis, R. (1998). Separate and intersecting realities: A comparison of men's and women's accounts of violence against women. *Violence Against Women*, 4(4), 382–414.

Eagly, A. H., & Chaiken, S. (1998). Attitude structure and function. In D. T. Gilbert, S. T. Fiske, & G. Lindzey (Eds.), *Handbook of social psychology* (4th ed., pp. 323–390). Boston: McGraw-Hill.

Earle, S. (2009a). *The world is blue: How our fate and the ocean's are one.* Washington, DC: National Geographic Books.

Earle, S. (2009b). My wish: Protect our oceans. TED2009. Retrieved December 28, 2011, from http://www.ted.com/talks/lang/en/sylvia_earle_s_ted_prize_wish_to_protect_our_oceans.html.

Earle, S. (2009c). National Geographic Explorer-in-Residence Sylvia Earle spotlights crisis facing our seas. Ocean Zone News Blog. Retrieved December 2011 from http://ocean.nationalgeographic.com/ocean/take-action/ocean-hero-sylvia-earle.

Facts about violence. (2010). Retrieved January 7, 2012, from http://feminist.com/antiviolence/facts.html.

Federal Bureau of Investigation. (1989). *Crime in the United States. Uniform crime reports.* Washington, DC: U.S. Department of Justice.

Federal Bureau of Investigation. (1995, August). Violence against women: Estimates from the redesigned survey. Available from http://www.ojp.usdoj.gov.

Kidder, R. M. (1994). *Shared values for a troubled world.* San Francisco: Jossey-Bass.

Knapp, M. L., Hart, R. P., Friedrick, G. W., & Shulman, G. M. (1973). The rhetoric of goodbye: Verbal and nonverbal correlates of human leave-taking. *Speech Monographs*, 40(3), 182–198.

Lackie, L., & de Man, A. F. (1997). Correlates of sexual aggression among male university students. *Sex Roles*, 37(5–6), 451–457.

Maathai, W. (2003). The Green Belt movement: Sharing the approach and the experience. (New York: Lantern Books, 2003). Maathai, W. M. Unbowed. New York: Knopf, 2006.

Marshall, G. (Ed.). (1994). *The concise Oxford dictionary of sociology* (p. 315). New York: Oxford University Press.

National Coalition Against Domestic Violence. (n.d.). Domestic violence facts. Retrieved January 7, 2012, from http://www.ncadv.org/files/DomesticViolenceFactSheet(National).pdf.

National Geographic.com. (n.d.). Ocean hero: Sylvia Earle. Retrieved December 27, 2011, from http://ocean.nationalgeographic.com/ocean/take-action/ocean-hero-sylvia-earle/.

National Geographic.com. (2009, October 10). National Geographic explorer-in-residence Sylvia Earle spots crisis facing our seas. Retrieved December 27, 2011, from http://www.thecre.com/zoning-news/?p=382.

National Organization for Women. (n.d.). Violence against women in the United States: Statistics. Retrieved January 7, 2012, from http://www.now.org/issues/violence/stats.html.

Olson, J. M., & Zanna, M. P. (1993). Attitudes and attitude change. *Annual Review of Psychology*, 44, 117–154.

Ricker, S. (2014). Skills spotlight: Public speaking and 16 related jobs. Retrieved December 29, 2014, from www.jobs.aol.com/articles/2014/08/10/skills-spotlight-public-speaking-jobs/.

Rokeach, M. (1970). *Beliefs, attitudes, and values: A theory of organization and change.* San Francisco: Jossey-Bass.

Rokeach, M. (1973). *The nature of human values.* New York: Free Press.

Rosa, A., & Escholz, P. (1996). *The writer's brief handbook* (2nd ed., p. 7). Scarborough, Ontario, Canada: Allyn & Bacon.

Schwartz, S. H., & Blisky, W. (1990). Toward a theory of the universal content and structure of values: Extensions and cross-cultural replications. *Journal of Personality and Social Psychology*, 58(5), 878–891.

Timm, J. C. (2013). VAWA passes house, with full protections for LGBT and Native Americans. MSNBC. Accessed December 29, 2014, from www.msnbc.com/morning-joe/vawa-passes-house-full-protections.

UNHCR. (n.d.). Goodwill ambassadors. Retrieved February 17, 2012, from http://www.unhcr.org/pages/49c3646c3e.html.

U.S. Bureau of Labor Statistics. (2010). Labor force statistics from the current population survey 2010. Retrieved January 7, 2012, from http://www.bls.gov/cps/demographisc.hem#women.

Wood, J. T. (2013). *Gendered lives: Communication, gender, and culture* (10th ed.). Boston: Wadsworth/Cengage.

Chapter 11

Alder, J., & Carmichael, M. (2005, January 20). The tsunami threat. *Newsweek*, p. 42.

Best, J. (2001). *Damned lies and statistics: Untangling numbers from the media, politicians, and activists.* Berkeley: University of California Press.

Best, J. (2008). *Stat-spotting: A field guide to identifying dubious data.* Berkeley: University of California Press.

Bolner, M. S., & Poirier, G. A. (2002). *The research process: Books and beyond* (2nd ed., pp. 144–145, 168, 248). Dubuque, IA: Kendall/Hunt.

Buddy T. (2009, October 15). White House launches anti-meth campaign. Retrieved from http://alcoholism.about.com/b/2009/10/15/white-house-launches-anti-meth-campaign.htm.

Campbell, K. K. (Ed.). (1989). *Man cannot speak for her: Key texts of the early feminists*. New York: Praeger.

Casey, M. K., Timmermann, L., Allen, M., Krahn, S., & Turkiewicz, K. L. (2009). Response and self-efficacy of condom use: A meta-analysis of this important element of AIDS education and prevention. *Southern Communication Journal*, *74*(1), 57–78.

Crossen, C. (1994). *Tainted truth: The manipulation of fact in America* (p. 42). New York: Simon & Schuster.

Fadei, R. (Ed.). (2000). *Applied algebra and statistics* (pp. 544, 545). Needham Heights, MA: Simon & Schuster.

Faigley, L., & Selzer, J. (2000). *Good reasons*. Needham Heights, MA: Allyn & Bacon.

Fisher, W. R. (1987). *Human communication as narration: Toward a philosophy of reason, value, and action* (p. 58). Columbia: University of South Carolina Press.

Fitch, S. P., & Mandziuk, R. M. (1997). *Sojourner Truth as orator: Wit, story, and song*. Westport, CT: Greenwood Press.

Gleason, M. M. (1999). The role of evidence in argumentative writing. *Reading & Writing Quarterly*, *14*, 81–106.

Hult, C. A. (1996). *Researching and writing across the curriculum* (pp. 28–29). Boston: Allyn & Bacon.

Inch, E. S., & Warnick, B. (1998). *Critical thinking and communication: The use of reason in argument* (3rd ed., pp. 194–197). Boston: Allyn & Bacon.

Israel, S. (2012). Nine tips on conducting great interviews. *Forbes*. Retrieved February 4, 2015, from www.forbes.com/sites/shelisrael/2012/04/8-tips-on-conducting-great-interviews/2/.

Jamieson, K. H. (1988). *Eloquence in the electronic age: The transformation of political speechmaking* (p. 140). New York: Oxford University Press.

Jay, A. (2015, March 25). Personal interview.

Jessop, D. C., & Wade, J. (2008, November). Fear appeals and binge drinking: A terror management theory perspective. *British Journal of Health Psychology* [serial online], *13*(4), 773–788. Retrieved May 27, 2010, from Academic Search Premier, Ipswich, MA.

Kahane, H., & Cavender, N. (1998). *Logic and contemporary rhetoric: The use of reason in everyday life* (8th ed.). Belmont, CA: Wadsworth.

Kennedy, S. D. (1998). *Best bet Internet: Reference and research when you don't have time to mess around* (pp. 144–145). Chicago: American Library Association.

Killenberg, G., & Anderson, R. (1989). *Before the story: Interviewing and communication skills for journalists*. New York: St. Martin's Press.

Kimpel, D. (2007, July 30). Shakira's songs are the heart of her success. BMI.com. Retrieved February 7, 2013, from http://www.bmi.com/news/entry/535199.

King, L. (1995). *The best of Larry King Live: The greatest interviews*. Atlanta: Times.

La Mala, M. (2008, May 16). Slim and Buffett donate to Shakira's ALAS. VivirLatino.com. Retrieved February 7, 2013, from from http://vivirlatino.com/2008;05/16/slim-and-buffett-donate-to-shakiras-alas.php.

Life or Meth. (2002). Australia's Life or Meth organization reports a 45 percent reduction of meth use in teens and a 75 percent reduction in adults. Retrieved May, 27, 2010, from http://www.lifeormeth.com/.

Methresources.gov. (2009). Anti-meth ad campaign. Retrieved May 27, 2010, from http://www.methresources.gov/2009antimeth.html.

Nabi, R. L., Roskos-Ewoldsen, D., & Carpentier, F. D. (2008). Subjective knowledge and fear appeal effectiveness: Implications for message design. *Health Communication*, *23*(2), 191–201. Retrieved May 27, 2010, from Academic Search Premier, EBSCOhost.

National Geographic Society. (2014). Explorers bio: Asher Jay, creative conservationist, emerging explorer. Retrieved April 10, 2015, from http://www.nationalgeographic.com/explorers/bios/asher-jay/ accessed.

Perelman, C., & Tyteca, L. O. (1969). *The new rhetoric: A treatise on argumentation* (J. Wilkinson & P. Weaver, Trans.; pp. 31–35). South Bend, IN: University of Notre Dame Press.

Perloff, R. M. (1993). *The dynamics of persuasion* (pp. 136–155, 170–179). Hillsdale NJ: Erlbaum.

Rippetoe, P. A., & Rogers, R. W. (1987). Effects of components of protection-motivation theory on adaptive and maladaptive coping with a health threat. *Journal of Personality and Social Psychology*, *52*(3), 596–604.

Rogat Loeb, P. (1999). *Soul of a citizen: Living with conviction in a cynical time* (pp. 68–69). New York: St. Martin's Griffin.

Roser, C., & Thompson, M. (1995). Fear appeals and the formation of active publics. *Journal of Communication*, *45*, 103–121.

Rough sleeping: One home at a time, How to cut the number of street dwellers—and save money too. (2014, November 15). *Economist*, p. 64.

Schmnitt, C. L., & Blass, T. (2008). Fear appeals revisited: Testing a unique antismoking film. *Current Psychology*, *27*(2),

145–151. Retrieved May 27, 2010, from Academic Search Premier, EBSCOhost.

Shakira. (2009, December 8). The democratization of education. Speech to the Oxford Union. Retrieved February 7, 2013, from http://www.shakira.com/news.title/the-democratication-of-education.

Shakira launches buy-a-brick campaign for charity. (2013, February 1). Look to the Stars. Retrieved April 9, 2015, https://www.looktothestars.org/news/9644-shakira-launches-buy-a-brick-campaign-for-charity.

Shakira's charity baby shower raises thousands and hailed "her biggest hit." (2015, April 9). Retrieved from http://us.hellomagazine.com/celebrities/2015040924508/shakira-charity-baby-shower-success/.

Steward, C. J., & Cash, W. B., Jr. (2006). *Interviewing: Principles and practices* (11th ed., p. 1). Boston: McGraw-Hill, 2006.

Stiff, J. B. (1994). *Persuasive communication* (pp. 89–106, 102–104), New York: Guilford Press.

Taylor, P. H., Rice, P. F., & Williams, R. H. (2000). *Basic statistics* (chap. 2, pp. 1–4). Cincinnati: Thompson Learning.

Toulmin, S. (1950). *The place of reason in ethics* (p. 72). Chicago: University of Chicago Press.

Toulmin, S. (1969). *The uses of argument*. London: Cambridge University Press.

Toulmin, S., Rieke, R., & Janik, A. (1979). *An introduction to reasoning*. New York: Macmillan.

Turner, A. (2009, March 1). Shakira: Every little think she does is magic. *Sunday Times* [London]. Retrieved February 4, 2013, from http://entertainment.timesonline.co.uk/tol/arts_and_entertainment/music/article5802815.ece.

Vancil, D. (1993). *Rhetoric and argumentation* (p. 134). Boston: Allyn & Bacon.

Van Eemeren, F. H., & Gootendorst, R. (1992). *Argumentation, communication, and fallacies: A pragma-dialectical perspective*. Hillsdale, NJ: Erlbaum.

Walton, D. N. (1996). *Argumentation schemes for presumptive reasoning*. Mahwah, NJ: Erlbaum.

Wong, N. C. H., & Cappella. J. N. (2009, February). Antismoking threat and efficacy appeals: Effects on smoking cessation intentions for smokers with low and high readiness to quit. *Journal of Applied Communication Research* [serial online], *37*(1), 1–20. Retried May 27, 2010, from Academic Search Premier, Ipswich, MA.

Zarefsky, D. (2002). *Public speaking: Strategies for success* (pp. 153–154). Needham Heights, MA: Allyn & Bacon.

Chapter 12

Andersen, P. A., Hecht, M. L., & Hoebler, G. D. (2002). The cultural dimension of nonverbal communication. In W. B. Gudykunst & B. Moody (Eds.), *Handbook of international and intercultural communication* (pp. 89–106). Thousand Oaks, CA: Sage.

Aucion, D. (2010, March 5). For young activists, video is their voice. *Boston Globe*, pp. A1–A12.

Austin, G. (1966). In M. M. Robb & L. Thonssen (Eds.), *Chironomia or a treatise on rhetorical delivery*. Carbondale: Southern Illinois University Press. (Original work published 1806)

Ayres, J. (1988, October). Coping with speech anxiety: The power of positive thinking. *Communication Education, 37*(4), 289–296.

Ayres, J. (1991). Using visual aids to reduce speech anxiety. *Communication Research Reports, 8*(1) 73–79.

Ayres, J., & Hopf, T. S. (1985). Visualization: A means of reducing speech anxiety. *Communication Education, 34*(4) 318–323.

Ayres, J., & Hopf, T. S. (1989). Visualization: Is it more than extra attention? *Communication Education, 38*(1), 1–5.

Ayres , J., & Hopf, T. S. (1990). The long-term effect of visualization in the classroom: A brief research report. *Communication Education, 39*(1), 75–78.

Ayres, J., Hopf, T., & Ayres, D. M. (1994). An examination of whether imaging ability enhances the effectiveness of an intervention designed to reduce speech anxiety. *Communication Education, 43*(3), 252–258.

Beatty, M. J. (1988, January). Situational and predispositional correlates of public speaking anxiety. *Communication Education, 37*(1), 29–30.

Beebe, S. A. (1974). Eye contact: A nonverbal determinant of speaker credibility. *Speech Teacher, 23*(1), 21–25.

Beebe, S. A. (1979–1980). Effects of eye contact, posture, and vocal inflection upon credibility and comprehension. *Australian Scan Journal of Nonverbal Communication, 7–8*, 57–70.

Behnke, R. R., & Sawyer, C. R. (1999). Milestones of anticipatory public speaking anxiety. *Communication Education, 48*(2), 164–172.

Bippus, A. M., & Daly, J. A. (1999). What do people think causes stage fright? Naïve attributions about the reasons for public speaking anxiety. *Communication Education, 48*(1), 63–72.

Birdwhistell, R. (1970). *Kinesics and context*. Philadelphia: University of Pennsylvania Press.

Bode, N. (2007, April 24). Zip un-hip lyrics: Rap bigs say industry should "bleep" out three dirty words. *Daily News* (New York), p. 4.

Bohn, E. & Jabusch, D. (1982). The effect of four methods of instruction on the use of visual aids in speeches. *Western Journal of Communication, 46*(3) 253–265.

Branham, R. J., & Pearce, W. B. (1996). The conversational frame in public address. *Communication Quarterly, 44*(4), 423.

Bull, P. E. (1987). *Posture and gesture*. New York: Pergamon.

Bulwer, J. (1974). *Chirologia: Or the natural language of the hand, and chiromomia: Or the art of manual rhetoric* (J. W. Cleary, Ed.). Carbondale: Southern Illinois University Press. (Original work published 1644).

CalmClinic. (2014). How to stop feeling nervous from anxiety. Retrieved January 2, 2015, from http://www.calmclinic.com/anxiety/symptoms/nervous.

Carbonell, D. (2014). The anxiety trick. Retrieved January 2, 2015, from http://www.anxietycoach.com/anxietytrick.html.

Christenfeld, N. (1995, Fall). Does it hurt to say um? *Journal of Nonverbal Behavior, 19*(3), 171–186.

Cobin, M. (1963). Response to eye contact. *Quarterly Journal of Speech, 48*(4), 415–419.

Cousteau, A. (2012, January 18). Telephone communication.

Daly, J. A., Vangelisti, A. L., & Weber, D. J. (1995, December). Speech anxiety affects how people prepare speeches: A protocol analysis of the preparation processes of speakers. *Communication Monographs, 62*(4), 383–397.

Davidson, W., & Klein, S. (1999). Ace your presentation. *Journal of Accountancy, 187*, 61–63.

Davis, W. (2014, December 15). Personal interview.

Dowis, R. (2000). *The lost art of the great speech: How to write one, how to deliver it*. New York: American Management Association.

Finn, A. N., Sawyer, C. R., & Schrodt, P. (2009, January). Speech anxiety affects how people prepare speeches: *Communication Education, 58*(1), 92–109.

Fremouw, W. J., & Scott, M. D. (1979). Cognitive restructuring: An alternative method for the treatment of communication apprehension. *Communication Education, 28*(2), 129–133.

Gamboa, G. (2007, April 25). Industry insiders call for limits on rap lyrics: Group seeks voluntary standards for language. *Houston Chronicle*, p. 2.

Garcia-Retamero, R., & Cokely, E. T. (2011). Effective communication of risks to young adults: Using message framing and visual aids to increase condom use and STD screening. *Journal of Experimental Psychology: Applied, 17*, 270–287.

Gates, L. (2000). *Voice for performance*. New York: Applause.

Geier, T., Jensen, J., Jordan, T., Lyons, M., & Markovitz, A. (2009, December 11). The 100 greatest movies, TV shows, albums, books, characters, scenes, episodes songs, dresses, music videos, and trends that entertained us over the past 10 years. *Entertainment Weekly, 1079/1080,* 74–84.

Gudykunst, W. B., & Moody, B. (Eds.). (2002). *Handbook of international and intercultural communication*. Thousand Oaks, CA: Sage.

Hartz, A. J. (1996). Psycho-socionomics: Attractiveness research from a societal perspective. *Journal of Social Behavior and Personality, 11*, 683.

Herman, C. P., Zanna, M. P., & Higgins, E. T. (1986). *Physical appearance, stigma, and social behavior: The Ontario Symposium, Vol. 3*. Hillsdale, NJ: Erlbaum.

Hildebrandt, H. W., & Stevens, W. W. (1963). Manuscript and extemporaneous delivery in communicating information. *Speech Monographs, 30*(4), 369–372.

Hip-hop setting the beat in first: Black artists hold billboard's top 10. (2003, October 4). *Boston Globe*. Retrieved December 31, 2014, from http://www.hsan.org.

Kangas Dwyer, K. (1998). *Conquer your speechfright: Learn how to overcome the nervousness of public speaking*. Fort Worth, TX: Harcourt.

Kangas Dwyer, K. (2000). The multidimensional model: Teaching students to self-manage high communication apprehension by self-selecting treatments. *Communication Education, 49*(1), 72–81.

Kearny, L. (1996). *Graphics for Presenters: Getting your ideas across*. Menlo Park, CA: Crisp.

Linkugel, W., & Berg, D. (1970). *A time to speak*. Belmont, CA: Wadsworth.

Lucas, S. E. (2001). *The art of public speaking* (7th ed., p. 290). New York: McGraw-Hill.

Martin, S., & Darnley, L. (1996). *The teaching voice* (p. 60). San Diego: Singular Publishing Group.

McCroskey, J. C. (1972). The implementation of a large scale program of systematic desensitization for communication apprehension. *Speech Teacher 21*(4), 255–264.

McCroskey, J. C. (1977). Oral communication apprehension: A summary of recent theory and research. *Human Communication Research, 4*(1), 78.

McCroskey, J. C., Sallinen, A., Fayer, J. M., Richmond, V. P., & Barraclough, R. A. (1996). Nonverbal immediacy and cognitive learning: A cross-cultural investigation. *Communication Education, 45*(3), 200–211.

McCullough, S. C., Russell, S. G., Behnke, R. R., Sawyer, C. R., & Witt, P. L. (2006, February). Anticipatory public speaking state anxiety as a function of body sensations and state of mind. *Communication Quarterly, 54*(1), 101–109.

McGarvey, R. (1990, January–February). Rehearsing for success: Tap the power of the mind through visualization. *Executive Female*, pp. 34–37.

Mehrabian, A. (1981). *Silent messages: Implicit communication of emotion and attitudes* (2nd ed.). Belmont, CA: Wadsworth.

Mino, M. (1996). The relative effects of content and vocal delivery during a simulated employment interview. *Communication Research Reports, 13*(2), 225–238.

Morris, T. L., Gorham, J., Cohen, S. H., & Huffman, D. (1996). Fashion in the classroom: Effects of attire on student perceptions of instructors in college classes. *Communication Education, 45*(2), 135–148.

Morrow, P. (1990). Physical attractiveness and selection decision making. *Journal of Management, 16*(1), 45–60.

National Geographic Society. (n.d.). Explorers/bio: Wade Davis, anthropologist/ethnobotanist. Retrieved March 2, 2015, from http://www.nationalgeographic.com/explorers/bios/wade-davis/.

Palmer, M. T., & Simmons, K. B. (1995). Communicating intentions through nonverbal behaviors. *Human Communication Research, 22*(1), 128–160.

Rabb, M. Y. (1993). *The presentation design book: Tips, techniques and advice for creating effective, attractive slides, overheads, multimedia presentations, screen shows, and more.* Chapel Hill, NC: Ventana.

Robinson, T. E., II. (1997). Communication apprehension and the basic public speaking course: A national survey of in-class treatment techniques. *Communication Education, 46*(3), 190–197.

Rodenburg, P. (2001). *The need for words: Voice and the text.* New York: Routledge.

Rozell, P., Kennedy, D., & Grabb, E. (1989). Physical attractiveness and income attainment among Canadians. *Journal of Psychology, 123*(6), 547–559.

Rubinstein, R. P. (2001). Dress codes: *Meanings and messages in American culture* (2nd ed.). Boulder, CO: Westview.

Samovar, L. A., & Porter, R. E. (1991). *Communication between cultures* (pp. 205–206). Belmont, CA: Wadsworth.

Seiler, W. J. (1971). The effects of visual materials on attitudes, credibility, and retention. *Speech Monographs, 38*(4), 331–334.

Simmons, R., & Chavis, B. (2014). Hip-hop summit action network (HSAN). Retrieved December 31, 2014, from https://www.facebook.com/hiphopsummit?fref=nf.

Smiley Group. (2006). *The covenant with black America.* Chicago: Third World Press.

Smith, T. E., & Frymier, A. B. (2006, February). Get "real": Does practicing speeches before an audience improve performance? *Communication Quarterly, 54*(1), 111–125.

Soper, P. L. (1956). *Basic public speaking* (2nd ed., pp. 143, 150, 151). New York: Oxford University Press.

Stein, M. B., Walker, J. R., & Forde, D. R. (1996). Public-speaking fears in a community sample: Prevalence, impact on functioning, and diagnostic classification. *Archives of General Psychiatry, 53*(2), 169–174.

Tartakivsky, M. (n.d.). Nine ways to reduce anxiety right here, right now. Retrieved January 2, 2015, from PsychCentral, http://psychcentral.com/lib/9-ways-to-reduce-anxiety-right-here-right-now/00017762.

TED. (2003, February). Wade Davis: Dreams from endangered cultures. Accessed March 2, 2015, from https://www.ted.com/talks/wade_davis_on_endangered_cultures accessed.

TED. (2008, February). Wade Davis: The worldwide web of belief and ritual. Accessed March 2, 2015, from https://www.ted.com/talks/wade_davis_on_the_worldwide_web_of_belief_and_ritual.

TED (2012, February). Wade Davis: Gorgeous photos of a backyard worth saving. Accessed March 2, 2015, from https://www.ted.com/talks/wade_davis_gorgeous_photos_of_a_backyard_wilderness_worth_saving.

Trees, A. R., & Manusov, V. (1998). Managing face concerns in critics: Integrating nonverbal behaviors as a dimension of politeness in female friendship dyads. *Human Communication Research, 24*(4), 564–583.

Weiss, C. D. (2008, January 2). Good-looking lawyers make more money, researcher says. *ABA Journal.* Retrieved August 3, 2015, from www.abajournal.com/news/article/good_looking_lawyers_make_more_money_researcher_says.

Wilder, C. (1994). *The presentations kit: Ten steps for spelling out your ideas.* New York: Wiley.

Winters, J. J., Horvath, N. R., Moss, M., Yarhouse, K., Sawyer, C. R., & Behnke, R. R. (2007, Winter). Affect intensity of student speakers as a predictor of anticipatory public speaking anxiety. *Texas Speech Communication Journal, 31*, 44–48.

Witt, P. L., & Behnke, R. R. (2006, April). Anticipatory speech anxiety as a function of public speaking assignment type. *Communication Education, 55*(2), 167–177.

Witt, P. L., Roberts, M. L., & Behnke, R. R. (2008, Summer). Comparative patterns of anxiety and depression in a public speaking context. *Human Communication, 11*(1), 219–230.

Wood, J. T. (1999). *Interpersonal communication: Everyday encounters* (2nd ed., p. 148). Belmont, CA: Wadsworth.

YouTube Statistics. (2014, October 10). Retrieved April 17, 2015, from https://www.youtube.com/yt/press/statistics.html.

Zayas-Bazan, E. P. (1977–1978). Instructional media in the total language picture. *International Journal of Instructional Media, 5,* 145–150.

Chapter 13

Dannels, D. P. (2001). Time to speak up: A theoretical framework of situated pedagogy and practice for communication across the curriculum. *Communication Education, 50*(2), 144–158.

Guy, S. (2014a, March 3). Personal interview.

Guy, S. (2014b, October 2). Sol Buy. TEDx Toronto. Retrieved March 25, 2015, from http://www.tedxtoronto.com/speakers /sol-guy/.

Guy, S., & Thome, J. (n.d.). New media cultural story tellers, emerging explorers. Retrieved March 24, 2015, from http:// www.nationalgeographic.com/explorers/bios/guy-thome/.

Johnson, J. R., & Szczupakiewicz, N. (1987). The public speaking course: Is it preparing students with work-related public speaking skills? *Communication Education, 36*(2), 131–137.

LeBeau, D. (2008). Saving America's dog. Retrieved June 10, 2010, from http://network.bestfriends.org/groups/conferences /news/archive/2008/10/29/saving-americas-dog-aspx.

Martinez , M., & Simon, D. (2011, December 16). Barry Bonds gets probation, house arrest for obstruction of justice. Retrieved January 9, 2012, from http://www.cnn .com/2011/12/16/justice/barry-bonds-sentencing/index .html?iref=allsearch.

Meet Shorty Rossi. (2010). *Pit boss* [Television series]. Animal Planet. Retrieved October 28, 2010, from http://animal .discovery.com/tv/pit-boss/bios/shorty-rossi.html.

Mind Tools. (n.d.). Rumors in the workplace: Managing and preventing them. Retrieved February 4, 2015, from www .mindtools.com/pages/article/newTMM_25.htm.

Morreal, S., Osborn, M., & Pearson, J. (2000). Why communication is important: Rationale for the centrality of the study of communication. *Journal of the Association for Communication Administration, 29*(2), 1–25.

National Association of Colleges and Employers. (2012). Job outlook 2012 survey. Retrieved March 7, 2012, from http:// www.naceweb.org/Research/Job_Outlook/Job_Outlook .aspx accessed.

Quinn, T. J. (2007, July 21). Jury's in on Bonds: Feds eye fall indictment. *New York Daily News.* Retrieved June 10, 2010, from http://www.nydailynews.com/sprots/baseball/2007/07.

Rosynsky, P. T. (2007, August 13). Bonds threatens to sue detractors. *Mercury News* (San Jose, CA). Retrieved August 22, 2007, from http://www.mercurynews.com.

Rowlands, T. (2006, April 14). Sources: Grand jury looking at whether Bonds lied about steroid use. CNN Justice. Retrieved June 10, 2010, from http://articles.cnn.com/2006-04-14 /justice/bonds_1_grand-jury-bay-area-laboratory-bonds -and-other-athletes?_s=PM:LAW.

Weise, L. (2009). Downtown dog rescue needs your support—letter writing camp. Retrieved December 27, 2009, from Ashleyandhobie.com, Animal Rescue for Southern California Message Boards: http://ashleyandhobie.com /board/viewtopic.php?f=26&t=15481&p=66869.

Williams, L., & Fainaru-Wada, M. (2004, December 3). What Bonds told BALCO grand jury. *San Francisco Chronicle.* Retrieved June 10, 2010 from http:/sfgate.com/chi-bin /article.cgi?file.

Wolvin, A. D. (1989). The basic course and the future of the workplace. *Basic Communication Course Annual, 10,* 1–6.

Chapter 14

Brehm, J. W. (1996). *A theory of psychological reactance.* New York: Academic Press.

Bullock, R. (2014, September 25). Motivating employees has everything to do with giving them feelings of ownership. *Forbes.* Retrieved February 10, 2015, from http://www.forbes .com/sites/datafreaks/2014/09/25/motivating-employees -has-almost-nothing-to-do-with-their-attitude-and-almost -everything-to-do-with-feelings-of-ownership/.

Cannizaro, S. (2003, December 5). Group plans to file suit against refinery: They allege pollution violations. *Times-Picayune* (New Orleans), p. 1.

Cannizaro, S. (2004, February 13). Two groups suing refinery: They claim plant violates Clean Air Act. *Times-Picayune* (New Orleans), p. 1.

Casey, M. K., Timmermann, L., Allen, M., Krahn, S., & Turkiewicz, K. L. (2009, January). Response and self-efficacy of condom use: A meta-analysis of this important element of AIDS education and prevention. *Southern Communication Journal* [serial online], *74*(1), 57–78.

Chen, H. C., Reardon, R., Rea, C., & More, D. J. (1992). Forewarning of content and involvement: Consequences for persuasion and resistance to persuasion. *Journal of Experimental Social Psychology, 28*(6), 523–541.

Gargaro, C. C. (n.d.). Ribbon campaigns: The most comprehensive ribbon list on the "net." Retrieved March 7, 2012, from http://www.gargaro.com/ribbons.html.

Gronbeck, B. E., McKerrow, R. E., Ehninger, D., & Monroe, A. H. (1990). *Principles and types of speech communication* (11th ed., pp. 180–205). Glenview, IL: Scott, Foresman/Little, Brown Higher Education.

Jessop, D. C., & Wade, J. (2008, November). Fear appeals and binge drinking: A terror management theory perspective. British *Journal of Health Psychology* [serial online], *13*(4), 773–788.

Kearney, P., Plax, T. G., & Burroughs, N. F. (1991). An attributional analysis of college students' resistance decisions. *Communication Education, 40*(4), 325–342.

Lester, P. M. (2004). *Visual communication: Images with messages* (4th ed., pp. 111–118), Boston: Wadsworth/Cengage.

Livestrong. (n.d.). Retrieved March 21, 2012 from www.livestrong.org.

Louisiana Bucket Brigade. (n.d.). Clean air. Justice. Sustainability. Campaigns/Programs. Retrieved March 7, 2012, from http://www.labucketbrigade.org.

Martell, A. (n.d.). Call for Canadian government to hold Rituximab clinical trials for ME/CFS patients. Retrieved March 7, 2012, from http://www.blueribboncampaignforme.org/.

Miller, G. R., & Roloff, M. E. (Eds.). (1980). *Persuasion: New directions in theory and research*. Beverly Hills, CA: Sage.

Nabi, R. L., Roskos-Ewoldsen, D., & Carpentier, F. D. (2008). Subjective knowledge and fear appeal effectiveness: Implications for message design. *Health Communication, 23*(2), 191–201.

Petty, R. E., & Cacioppo, J. T. (1986). *Communication and persuasion: Central and peripheral routes to attitude change*. New York: Springer-Verlag.

Reardon, K. K. (1991). *Persuasion in practice*. Newbury Park, CA: Sage.

Rippetoe, P. A., & Rogers, R. W. (1987). Effects of components of protection-motivation theory on adaptive and maladaptive coping with a health threat. *Journal of Personality and Social Psychology, 52*(3), 596–604.

Roser, C., & Thompson, M. (1995). Fear appeals and the formation of active publics. *Journal of Communication, 45*(1), 103–121.

Schmitt, C. L., & Blass, T. (2008). Fear appeals revisited: Testing a unique anti-smoking film. *Current Psychology, 27*(2), 145–151.

Sine, R. (2000, July 20). Neighbors seeking proof of pollution. *Times-Picayune* (New Orleans), p. 1.

Skinner, B. (n.d.) Explorer Bios. Photographer, Young Explorers Grantee. Retrieved May 27, 2013, from http://www.nationalgeographic.com/explorers/bios/becca-skinner/.

Smiley, T. (Ed.). (2006). *The covenant with Black America*. Chicago: Third World Press.

Stiff, J. B. (1994). *Persuasive communication* (pp. 117–119). New York: Guilford Press.

Swerczek, M. (2002, October 18). Residents to learn to test air quality: Devices to check for chemicals on display. *Times-Picayune* (New Orleans), p. 1.

TeenHelp.com. (n.d.). Jelly bracelets and their meaning. Retrieved March 7, 2012, from http://www.teenhelp.com/teen-sexuality/jelly-bracelets.html.

Waldron, V. R., & Applegate, J. L. (1998). Person-centered tactics during verbal disagreements: Effects on student perceptions of persuasiveness and social attraction. *Communication Education, 47*(1), 55–56.

Watchdog group to protest refinery: Activists to mix with Exxon stockholders. (2005, May 24). *Times-Picayune* (New Orleans), p. 1.

Whaley, B. B., & Wagner, L. S. (2000). Rebuttal analogy in persuasive messages: Communicator likability and cognitive responses. *Journal of Language and Social Psychology, 19*(1), 66–84.

Wong, N. C. H., & Cappella, J. N. (2009, February). Antismoking threat and efficacy appeals: Effects on smoking cessation intentions for smokers with low and high readiness to quit. *Journal of Applied Communication Research* [serial online], *37*(1), 1–20.

Yellow Ribbon America. (n.d.). Helping our nation's military and their families in their local communities. Retrieved March 7, 2012, from http://www.yellowribbonamerica.org/.

Chapter 15

Abreu, K. (2014). The myriad benefits of diversity in the workplace. Entrepreneur. Retrieved February 10, 2015, from http://www.entrepreneur.com/article/240550.

Barrett, H. (1991). *Rhetoric and civility: Human development, narcissism, and the good audience*. Albany: State University of New York Press.

Benhabib, S. (1992). *Situating the self: Gender, community, and postmodernism in contemporary ethics*. New York: Routledge.

Bone, J. E., Griffin, C. L., & Scholz, T. M. L. (2008). Beyond traditional conceptualizations of rhetoric: Invitational rhetoric and a move toward civility. *Western Journal of Communication, 72*(4), 434–462.

Burkhalter, S., Gastil, J., & Kelshaw, T. (2002). A conceptual definition and theoretical model of public deliberation in small face-to-face groups. *Communication Theory, 12*, 418.

Ellinor, L., & Gerard, G. (1998). *Dialogue: Creating and sustaining collaborative partnerships at work*. New York: Wiley.

Etsy, K., Griffin, R., & Schorr-Hirsh, M. (1995). *Workplace diversity: A manager's guide to solving problems and turning diversity into a competitive advantage*. Avon, MA: Adams Media Corporation

Foss, S. K., & Griffin, C. L. (1995). Beyond persuasion: A proposal for an invitational rhetoric. *Communication Monographs, 62*(1), 1–18.

Green, K. A., Lopez, M., Wysocki, A., & Kepner, K. (2015). *Diversity in the workplace: Benefits, challenges, and the required managerial tools*. EDIS, University of Florida, IFAS Extension, Publication HR022.

hooks, b. (1994). *Outlaw culture: Resisting representations*. New York: Routledge.

Ingram, D. (2015). Advantages and disadvantages of diversity in the workplace. Chron: Small Businesses. Retrieved February 10, 2015 from http://smallbusiness.chron.com/advantages-disadvantages-diversity-workplace-3041.html.

Isaacs, W. (1999). *Dialogue and the art of thinking together*. New York: Currency.

Jack Beetson spoke with Tony Jones. (n.d.). Television program transcript, Australian Broadcasting Corporation. Retrieved May 22, 2006, from http://www.abc.net/au/lateling/content/2006/s1644688.htm

Kerby, S., & Burns, C. (2012). Top10 economic facts of diversity in the workplace: A diverse workforce is integral to a strong economy. Center for American Progress. Retrieved February 10, 2015, from https://www.americanprogress.org/issues/labor/news/2012/07/12/11900/the-top-10-economic-facts-of-diversity-in-the-workplace/.

Loeb, P. R. (2010). *Soul of a citizen*. New York: St. Martins's Griffin.

Lower Manhattan Development Corporation. (2003, January 2). Renew NYC. [Online]. Retrieved June 16, 2004, from http://www.renewnyc.com.

Lower Manhattan Development Corporation. (2004, January 13). Memorial-reflecting absence: WTC memorial jury statement for winning design. [Online]. Retrieved June 16, 2004, from http://www.renewnyc.com.

Peck,. M. S. (1987). *The different drum: Community—making and peace*. New York: Simon & Schuster.

Radcliff, K. (2005). *Rhetorical listening: Identification, gender, whiteness*. Carbondale: Southern Illinois Press.

Raghava KK. (2010). My 5 lives as an artist. TED2010. Retrieved February 4, 2015, from www.ted.com/talks/raghava_kk_five_lives_of_an_artist.

Raghava KK. (2015, January 13). Personal interview.

Raghava KK. (n.d.). Explorers Bio: Artist, emerging explorer. Retrieved February 4, 2015, from www.nationalgeographic.com/explorers/bios/raghava-kk.

Rogers, C. R. (1962). The interpersonal relationship: The core of guidance. *Harvard Educational Review, 32*(4), 416–429.

University of California San Francisco Human Resources. (n.d.). Chapter 12: Managing diversity in the workplace. Retrieved February 10, 2015, from http://ucsfhr.ucsf.edu/index.php/pubs/hrguidearticle/chapter-12-managing-diversity-in-the-workplace/.

Unsung Heroes of Dialogue, The. (n.d.). Retrieved March 7, 2012, from http://www.un.org/Dialogue/heroes.htm.

Walker, M. U. (1989). Moral understandings: Alternative "epistemology" for a feminist ethics. *Hypatia, 4*(2), 15–28.

World Trade Center Site Memorial Competition Jury Statement. (2003, November 19). *The New York Times*. Retrieved June 16, 2004, from http://www.nytimes.com/2003/11/19/nyregion/19WTC-JURY-TEXT.html.

accommodation: a conflict style in which individuals do what they are asked in order to "resolve" the conflict (9)

acronym: the first letters or initials of terms that form a word (4)

action-oriented listener: listener who wants speakers to provide clear, detailed, and straight-to-the-point information (5)

ad hominem fallacy: an argument in which a speaker attacks a person rather than challenge that person's arguments (11)

adaptors: gestures we use to manage our emotions (3)

affect displays: nonverbal movements that indicate how we feel (3)

affective questions: questions that acknowledge that people have feelings as well as ideas that are important to share (9)

affirmations: positive statements that assert that what we wish to be true is already happening (12)

agenda: formal and organized outline of items to address in order to meet the goals of a meeting (9)

ambushing: listening carefully to information in order to attack what the speaker has to say (5)

analogical reasoning: reasoning by way of comparison and similarity (11)

androgynous: displaying both masculine and feminine traits or behaviors (7)

androgynous communicators: individuals who are adept at using different speech styles, depending on the situation (4)

anomalies: exceptions to a rule and unique instances that do not represent the norm (11)

articulation: physical process of producing specific speech sounds to make language intelligible to our audiences (12)

artifacts: the personal objects we use to communicate something about ourselves (3)

asynchronous: message that is sent but not received at the same time (6)

attitude: general positive or negative feeling a person has about something (10)

audience-centered speaker: speaker who considers the positions, beliefs, values, and needs of an audience (10)

auditory communication system: paralanguage (3)

auditory listener: listener who needs to hear verbal descriptions and explanations (5)

authoritarian leader: leader who tells others what to do, gives orders, and makes the final decisions regarding how to act or what to do next (8)

authority rule: allowing the leader or head of a group to make the final choice (9)

avoidance: a conflict style in which individuals will not address or acknowledge its existence (9)

avoiding step: when couples attempt to stay away from each other (6)

bandwagon fallacy: a suggestion that something is correct or good because everyone else agrees with it or is doing it (11)

bar graph: compares quantities at a specific moment in time (12)

behavioral objectives: actions speaker wants audience to take at the end of a speech (10)

belief: a person's idea of what is real or true or not (10)

blind window: information that others know about you but that you are not aware of (6)

bonding step: step that occurs when a couple commits to their relationship (6)

brainstorming: process of generating ideas randomly and uncritically without attention to logic, connections, or relevance (9, 10)

breadth: the range of topics discussed in self-disclosure (6)

bullying: repeated unreasonable actions of individuals or a group directed toward an individual or another group that are intended to intimidate, degrade, humiliate, or undermine; actions that threaten the health or safety of individuals or group (8)

call to action: an explicit request that an audience engage in some clearly stated behavior (14)

careful listener: listener who overcomes listener interference in order to listen effectively to another person's message (5)

causal organization: pattern of organization used when a problem is based on a cause-and-effect relationship (14)

causal patterns: a pattern of organization that allows you to highlight cause-and-effect relationships (13)

causal reasoning: a process of reasoning that supports a claim by establishing a cause-and-effect relationship (11)

channel: means by which ideas are communicated (1)

chronemics: how humans organize and structure time and the messages conveyed as a result of this organization (3)

chronological pattern: a pattern of organization in which you illustrate how a topic has developed over time or what sequential steps an audience must take to complete a task (13)

circumscribing step: when couples begin communicating less frequently, share less personal information, and spend shorter amounts of time together (6)

civic engagement: individual and collective actions designed to identify and address issues of public concern (1)

civil listener: listener who is open to hearing different views and perspectives, even when there is disagreement (5)

civility: expressing care and concern for others, the thoughtful use of words and language, and the flexibility to see the many sides of an issue (1)

closed questions: yes or no questions that limit the kind of answers a person can give (9)

coercive power: ability to punish those who do not meet demands or follow the rules set by the group (8)

cognitive complexity: capacity to make sense of social behavior in a multidimensional way (1)

cognitive restructuring: process that builds confidence because it replaces negative thoughts with positive thoughts called affirmations (12)

cohesiveness: degree of mutual interest among members of a group (8)

collectivism: degree to which organizational, societal, and family practices encourage and reward collective distribution of resources and collective action as well as the degree to which they express pride and loyalty (8)

collectivist culture: culture that values relationships and harmony with others (6)

colloquialism: words and phrases used in relaxed, informal conversations (4)

communicating civilly: making a decision to be open to hearing different views and perspectives, even though we may not agree with them (1)

communicating ethically: considering the moral impact of our words, ideas, and views on other people when we communicate (1)

communication: the use of symbols by humans to create messages for other humans (1)

communication apprehension: anxiety about speaking in any number of situations (interviews, speeches, etc); the level of fear or anxiety associated with either real or anticipated communication with another person or persons (1, 12)

communication climates: climates that set the tone for interpersonal relationships (7)

comparative advantages organization: an organizational pattern in which the speaker illustrates the advantages of one solution over others (14)

competition: a style of managing conflict in which one individual makes sure his or her needs are met, with disregard for the needs of others (9)

complementation: when the nonverbal signal elaborates or expands the meaning of the verbal message (3)

compromise: a style of managing conflict in which the needs of every member of the group are considered and met (9)

computer-mediated communication (CMC): the exchange of messages transmitted between two or more people using a digital electronic device (6)

concern for others: when individuals attempt to get along with and satisfy another's needs using cooperative communication (7)

concern for self: when individuals seek to satisfy their own desires and needs through direct and assertive communication (7)

conclusion: the claim you are attempting to prove as true (11)

condition of equality: acknowledging that all audience members hold valid perspectives worthy of exploration (15)

condition of self-determination: recognizing that the members of your audience are experts in their own lives (15)

condition of value: recognizing the inherent value of your audience's views, although those views might be different from yours (15)

confirming: listening in order to recognize, acknowledge, and express value for another person (5)

confirming statements: statements that validate other people by recognizing them, acknowledging their ideas and feelings, and approving or supporting their ideas (7)

connectives: words and phrases used to link ideas in a speech (10)

connotative definition: subjective meaning of a word or a phrase based on personal experiences and beliefs (11)

connotative meanings: the meanings we associate with particular words based on our experiences, understanding, or opinions of the word (4)

consensus: general or widespread agreement among all the members of a group (9)

content messages: the actual things we say (1)

content-oriented listener: listener who pays close attention to the facts and details of a message (5)

contradiction: when verbal and nonverbal forms of communication conflict with one another (3)

conversational style: more formal than everyday conversation but it remains spontaneous and relaxed (12)

counterarguments: addressing the arguments against the speaker's own position (14)

credible: to gain the trust of your audience and to communicate that you have considerable knowledge of your topic (10)

critical listener: listener who listens for accuracy of content and the implications of a message (5)

cultural competence: the ability to relate appropriately to members from a different culture (4)

culture: learned patterns of perception, values, and behaviors shared by a group of people (1, 6)

decode: interpreting or trying to understand what the sender is communicating (1)

deductive reasoning: a process of reasoning that uses a familiar and commonly accepted claim to establish the truth of a highly specific claim (11)

defensive listener: listener who perceives a message as a personal attack or a form of criticism (5)

definition: statement of the exact meaning of a word or phrase (11)

democratic leader: one who distributes responsibility among the group members and shows a desire to empower all members of the group and a willingness to assist in decision making (8)

demonstration: display of how something is done or works (12)

denotative definition: objective meaning of a word found in a dictionary (11)

denotative meanings: the literal or commonly accepted meaning of a word (4)

depth: how personal the information is in self-disclosure (6)

dialect: pattern of speech shared by an ethnic group or people from a specific geographical location (12)

dialogue: civil exchange of ideas and opinions between two people or a small group of people (10)

differentiating step: when individuals in a couple begin to spend time on their own interests in order to express their individuality and separate from their partner (6)

direct quotation: an exact word-for-word presentation of another's testimony (11)

disconfirming statement: statement that rejects or invalidates another person's statements (7)

doublespeak: language used to purposefully disguise the actual meaning of something (4)

drawings: diagrams and sketches of someone or something (12)

either–or fallacy (false dilemma): an argument in which a speaker claims our options are "either A or B," when actually more than two options exist (11)

elaboration likelihood model (ELM): model that explains an audience's motivation for processing persuasive messages in either a central processing or a peripheral processing route (14)

emblems: gestures that can be translated into words (3)

emoticons: typed characters used to convey feelings (3)

emotions: internal mental states that focus primarily on feelings (11)

empathy: ability to see the world through another person's eyes and to understand his or her feelings and perspectives (1)

emphasis: using nonverbal cues that strengthen what is stated verbally (3)

encode: putting ideas, thoughts, and meanings into a message (1)

environment: cultural backgrounds and experiences that people bring to the exchange (1)

environmental factors: surroundings that influence how we think, feel, and behave as we communicate with others (3)

equivocal words: words that have more than one meaning (4)

ethics: moral standards behind decisions and how they affect others (8)

ethnocentrism: belief that our own cultural perspectives, norms, and ways of organizing society are superior to other cultures (1, 10)

euphemism: polite terms or more socially acceptable ways to describe something that someone may find unpleasant (4)

evidence: information speakers use to develop and support their ideas (11)

examples: are specific instances used to illustrate a concept, experience, issue, or problem (11)

experiential listener: listener who learns best by touching, exploring, and participating in what is being described (5)

experimenting step: step when small talk is used to learn more about the other person and to help present a likable self-image (6)

expert power: ability to influence others because of some skill, knowledge base, or set of experience (8)

expert testimony: the testimony of someone considered an authority in a particular field (11)

extemporaneous speech: carefully prepared and practiced speech from brief notes rather than from memory or a written manuscript (12)

external noises: distractions that exist around you—like sights and sounds that take your attention away from the message (1)

eye contact: visual contact with another person's eyes (12)

facework: verbal and nonverbal strategies used to present different faces to others (2)

facial expression: movement of eyes, eyebrows, and mouth to convey reactions and emotions (12)

fallacy: an argument that seems valid but is flawed because of unsound evidence or reasoning (11)

false cause fallacy: an argument mistaking a chronological relationship with a causal relationship (11)

false cause: an error in reasoning in which a speaker assumes that one event caused another simply because the first event happened before the second (11)

family: network of people who live together over long periods of time bound by ties of marriage, blood, or commitment, legal or otherwise, who consider themselves as family and share a significant history and anticipated future of functioning in a family relationship (6)

fear appeal: threat of something undesirable happening if change does not occur (14)

feedback: verbal and nonverbal signals we give to one another while we communicate (1)

flaming: uninhibited expression of hostility such as swearing, name-calling, ridicule, and insults directed toward another person, his or her character, religion, race, intelligence, and physical or mental ability (7)

flowchart: illustrates direction or motion (12)

formal role: role that is clearly defined and assigned (8)

forums: occur when messages or topics are posted online and individuals have an opportunity to post their individual responses and ideas to those original messages (9)

framing: the way people use language to define a conflict situation (7)

friendly relations: situation that allows each person to determine whether common interests exist (6)

friendship or warmth touch: a sense of closeness and caring between individuals (3)

functional or professional touch: the least intimate touch, including touch by others according to their professional position (3)

gender: society's use of verbal and nonverbal symbols to express masculinity and femininity (6)

gender egalitarianism: extent to which an organization or society minimizes gender-role differences (8)

gender role: used to refer to feminine and masculine social expectations in a family based on a person's sex; the social expectations for how males and females should behave (6, 7)

general purpose: The broad goal of a speech—to inform, invite, or persuade (10)

gestures: movements, usually of the hands but sometimes of the entire body, that express meaning and emotion or offer clarity to a message (12)

globalization: processes through which local and regional ideas, products, and practices are transformed into worldwide ideas, products, and practices (1)

graph: a visual comparison of amounts or quantities (12)

group: small number of people who belong together, share something in common, or are assigned to a similar task (8)

group communication: interacting with a small but organized collection of people (1)

groupthink: mode of thinking that people engage in when they are deeply involved in a cohesive in-group, when the members' striving for unanimity override their motivation to realistically appraise alternative courses of action (8)

growth group: group whose goals are to help individuals cope with issues, recover from a crisis or trauma, or resolve personal concerns; also known as a *therapy group* (8)

haptics: the study of communicating via touch (3)

hasty generalization fallacy: an argument based on too few cases or examples to support a conclusion (11)

hasty generalization: reaching a conclusion without enough evidence to support it (11)

hearing: vibrations of sound waves on our eardrums; the impulses then travel to the brain (5)

hidden agendas: unspoken goals and visions for the group that a can get in the way of progress or take a group in a direction other than the one it has explicitly stated (8)

hidden window: information that you understand about yourself but are not willing to share with others (6)

high self-monitors: individuals who are acutely aware of their self-expressions and identity management behavior (2)

high-context culture: culture in which people use less straightforward and more indirect communication (6)

humane orientation: degree to which individuals in organizations or societies encourage and reward individuals for being fair, altruistic, friendly, generous, caring, and kind to others (8)

hyperpersonal communication: communication that occurs when individuals express themselves more freely in a mediated channel than in a face-to-face interaction (6)

hypothetical example: an instance that did not take place but could have (11)

identity: social categories that we and others identify as important characteristics of who we are (2)

identity management: process of altering our own behaviors in order to shape others' impressions of who we are (2)

illustrator: nonverbal behavior that reinforces spoken words (3)

immediate action: when the speaker's goal is to encourage an audience to engage in a specific behavior or take a specific action (14)

impromptu speech: speech that you have not planned or prepared in advance (12)

independent couple: couple who holds less traditional views of family roles and expectations (6)

individualistic culture: culture in which individuals make their own decisions, take responsibility for their actions, and are self-sufficient (6)

inductive reasoning: a process of reasoning that uses specific instances, or examples, to make a claim about a general conclusion (11)

inflection: manipulation of pitch to create certain meanings or moods (12)

informal role: role that is not formally assigned to individuals in the group (8)

informative speaking environments: environments in which a speaker has expertise or knowledge that an audience needs but does not already have (13)

informative speech: speech that communicates knowledge and understanding about a process, an event, a place or person, an object, or a concept (13)

initiation step: step involving the first set of interactions made between people (6)

insensitive listener: listener who pays attention to the content or literal meaning of the message but not the relationship level of the meaning (5)

insulated listener: listener who purposefully avoids listening to specific pieces of information (5)

integrating step: step consisting of two individuals merging their social circles and organizing their daily activities around each other (6)

intensifying step: step when there is an increase in communication, intimacy, and connectedness (6)

interdependent couple: couple who shares traditional views of marriage and family life, activities , and interests (6)

internal noises: thoughts and feelings we are experiencing (1)

internal preview: statement in the body of your speech that details what you plan to discuss next (10)

internal summary: statement in the body of your speech that summarizes a point you have already discussed (10)

interpersonal communication: communication with other people that ranges from highly personal to highly impersonal (1)

interpersonal conflict: when two interdependent parties express different opinions, goals, or interests (7)

interpersonal relationship: relationship that involves the establishment of a personal connection with another person through the intentional use of communication (6)

interview: planned interaction with another person that is organized around inquiry and response, with one person asking questions and the other person answering them (11)

intimate partner violence: willful intimidation, physical assault, battery, sexual assault, or other abusive behavior perpetrated by an intimate partner against another (7)

intrapersonal communication: when people communicate internally with their own selves (1)

invisible communication system: chronemics, olfactics, and haptics (3)

invitational environment: environment in which the speaker's highest priorities are to understand, respect, and appreciate the range of possible positions on an issue, even if those positions are quite different from his or her own (15)

invitational speaking: type of public speaking in which a speaker enters into a dialogue with an audience to clarify positions, explore issues and ideas, or articulate beliefs and values (15)

jargon: technical language used by professional groups (4)

kinesics: the study of bodily movements such as gestures, posture, eye contact, and facial expressions (3)

labels: words used to describe ourselves and others (2)

laissez-faire leader: one who offers little or no guidance and allows individuals to make all decisions themselves, giving them as much freedom as possible (8)

language: a collection of symbols or words used to communicate with others (4)

leader: someone who guides or directs a group or activity with vision, charisma, and care (8)

leading questions: questions that urge people to respond in a particular way (9)

learning groups: groups that offer members a new skill or provide members with new information (8)

legitimate power: ability to control or influence others because of the formal position one holds in the group (8)

liking: using our body orientation, facial expression, use of touch, or proximity to communicate our feelings about another person (3)

line graph: shows trends over time (12)

list: series of words or phrases that organize ideas one after the other (12)

listening interference: anything that stops or hinders a listener from receiving a message (5)

listening style: preferred approach to understanding a message (5)

listening: process of giving thoughtful attention to another person's words and understanding what you hear (5)

logic: system, principles, and arguments that make up a person's worldview (1)

looking-glass self: the way other people's perceptions of us define our own perceptions of ourselves (2)

love or intimacy touch: touch between family members or romantic partners (3)

low self-monitors: people who communicate without paying much attention to how others are responding to their messages (2)

low-context culture: culture in which people emphasize direct and literal communication (6)

main points: most important and comprehensive ideas you address in your speech (10)

major premise: the general principle that states a familiar and commonly accepted belief (11)

manuscript speech: speech that is read to an audience from a written text (12)

maps: visual representations of places (12)

mass communication: communication designed and generated by media organizations to reach large audiences (1)

master statuses: significant positions a person occupies within society that affect that person's identity in almost all social situations (10)

mean: the average of a group of numbers (11)

median: the middle number in a series or set of numbers arranged in a ranked order (11)

memorized speech: speech that has been written out, committed to memory, and given word for word (12)

minor premise: specific instance that helps establish the truth of the conclusion (11)

mode: the number that occurs most often in a set of numbers (11)

model: copy of an object (12)

monochronic cultures: cultures in which people carefully schedule tasks, complete them one by one, and follow strict agendas (3)

monotone: lack of variation in a speaker's rate, pitch, and volume; speaking without any change in pitch (3, 12)

Monroe's motivated sequence: step-by-step process used to persuade audiences by gaining attention, demonstrating a need, satisfying that need, visualizing beneficial results, and calling for action (14)

moves toward friendship: when people begin to self-disclose in small amounts (6)

multiple perspectives pattern: pattern that allows the speaker to systematically address the many sides and positions of an issue before opening up the speech for dialogue, exploration, and deliberation with the audience (15)

narrative: a story that recounts or foretells real or hypothetical events; narratives can be brief or extended (11)

narrative organization: organizational pattern that uses one or more stories to construct an argument (14)

nascent friendship: time when people interact on a personal level, choose to participate in a range of activities with another, and let down their guard in communication (6)

noise: things that interfere with the transmission and reception of a message (1)

nonverbal communication: the process of conveying meaning without using the spoken word (3)

norms: patterns of behavior that are expected of individuals and seen as correct or even necessary in specific situations (8)

object: something that can be seen and touched (12)

olfactics: use of our sense of smell to gather information (3)

open questions: questions that give people the freedom to answer in a range of ways (9)

open window: information about yourself that is already known by you and others (6)

oral reports: presentations given by one or two of the group members who present a group's findings, conclusions, or proposals to other members of the group or to a larger audience (9)

organizational chart: illustrates the structure of groups (12)

panel discussion: structured discussion among group members and facilitated by a moderator that takes place in front of an audience (9)

paralinguistics: the vocal aspects of nonverbal communication, such as rate, volume, pitch, and emphasis (3)

paraphrase: to provide a summary of another's testimony in the speaker's own words (11)

paraphrasing: restating the essence , or summary, of a person's message in your own words (11)

passive agreement: when the speaker's goal is to ask audience members to adopt a new position without asking them to act in support of that position (14)

pauses: hesitations and brief silences in speech or conversation (12)

peer testimony (lay testimony): testimony of someone who has firsthand knowledge of a topic (11)

people-oriented listener: listener who is concerned about the feelings and emotions of other people as well as the quality of interpersonal relationships (5)

perception checking: when we consider a series of statements or questions to confirm (or challenge) our perceptions of others and their behaviors (2)

perception: process of acquiring and interpreting information from sensory data (2)

personal appearance: specific aspects of our appearance including facial features; skin color; hair color, length, and style; and body type; the way someone dresses, grooms, and presents her- or himself physically (3, 12)

personal testimony: one's own testimony used to convey a point (11)

persuasive speech: speech whose message attempts to change or reinforce an audience's thoughts, feelings, or actions (14)

phonology: the study of how sounds are used to communicate meaning (4)

photograph: image produced with a camera or other form of digital technology (12)

picture graph: presents information in pictures or images (12)

pie graph: shows relative proportions of parts of a whole (12)

pitch: highness or lowness of a speaker's voice (12)

polychronic cultures: cultures in which people take on several tasks at once and view time as flexible (3)

posture: how speakers position and carry their bodies (12)

power and assertiveness: measure of the degree to which members of an organization or society expect and agree that power should be unequally shared or that individual assertiveness is valued (8)

power over: ability to control others and dictate the course of events (8)

power with: power of a strong individual in a group of equals, the power not to command, but to suggest and be listened to, to begin something and see it happen (8)

preview: brief overview of each of the main points in your speech (10)

primary dimensions: identity traits that we are born with and are significant parts of who we are (2)

probing questions: questions that help people talk more about an idea or feeling (9)

problem–cause–solution organization: pattern of organization that focuses on identifying a specific problem, the causes of that problem, and a solution to the problem (14)

problem–solution organization: pattern of organization that focuses on persuading an audience that a specific problem exists and can be solved or minimized by a specific solution (14)

pronunciation: act of saying words correctly according to the accepted standards of a language (12)

proxemics: the use of space; use of space during communication (3, 12)

pseudolistening: when listeners act like they are listening or pretend to be paying close attention to the message (5)

psychological ownership: refers to how much employees feel that their jobs or organizations are theirs (14)

public deliberation: to engage in a process that "involves the careful weighing of information and views" (15)

public dialogue: ethical and civil exchange of ideas and opinions among communities about topics that affect the public (10)

public or presentational communication: when one person gives a speech to other people, most often in a public setting (1)

question of fact: question that addresses whether something is verifiably true or not (14)

question of policy: question that addresses the best course of action or solution to a problem (14)

question of value: question that addresses the merit or morality of an object, action, or belief (14)

rate: speed at which we speak (12)

real example: an instance that has actually taken place (11)

real time: when people in a room together can speak and hear one another in the moment without needing computers, phones, or the like (9)

reasoning by sign: assumption that something exists or will happen based on something else that exists or has happened (11)

reciprocity: the mutual exchange of symbols and meanings; actions of interdependence or mutual respect;

when people who help you later need help, you return the favor (1, 9)

red herring fallacy: irrelevant information inserted into an argument to distract an audience from the real issue (11)

referent: concept or thing the symbol represents (1)

referent power: ability to influence others because of an association with or respect for the people who hold power in the group (8)

reflected appraisal: the process of developing an image of who we are based on the way others describe us (2)

reflective-thinking method: six-step method for structuring a problem-solving and decision-making discussion (9)

regionalism: words or phrases common to particular geographical regions (4)

regulation: the process of controlling conversations and interactions with others (3)

relational maintenance: process of keeping a relationship together through the use of mundane activities (6)

relational messages: the parts of the communication that give us information about how we are or are not connected to another person (1)

relational stress: stress that occurs when there are interpersonal incompatibilities among group members based on differences in their personalities, communication styles, attitudes, and preferences (9)

repetition: using the nonverbal signals that reproduce what is said verbally (3)

responsiveness: displaying positive facial expressions, posture, and gestures (3)

reward power: ability to give others what they seek or will benefit from for meeting the demands of the group or following the rules set by the group (8)

rhetorical question: question used for effect that audience members are not supposed to answer out loud but rather in their own minds (10)

role: expected and defined pattern of behavior carried out by an individual or individuals (8)

role-limited interaction: engaging in small talk and sharing only minimal amounts of information (6)

secondary dimensions: identities that we acquire, develop, or discard throughout our lives (2)

selective attention: process of consciously or unconsciously selecting sensory data to maintain our focus (2)

selective listening: when listeners only pay attention to particular parts or sections of a message (5)

self-concept: perception of who we are and what makes us unique as well as similar to others (2)

self-disclosure: intentional sharing of personal information that would not otherwise be known to others (6)

self-efficacy: a person's belief that she or he can be flexible (1)

self-esteem: how we feel about ourselves based on perceptions of our own strengths and weaknesses (2)

self-fulfilling prophecy: to act in accordance with expectations (2)

self-monitoring: ability to observe one's own behaviors and communication and to see how they are affecting others (1)

semantic noise: interference that occurs when a speaker uses a word or phrase that is unfamiliar, confusing, offensive, or contradictory (1)

semantic triangle of meaning: ways people use or hear a symbol or word and attach a meaning to it (1)

semantics: the meaning of specific words (4)

separate couple: couple who is extremely autonomous (6)

sex: biological and genetic characteristics (6)

sexual arousal touch: the type of touching that conveys sexual meaning and stimulation (3)

sign: something that represents something else (11)

signpost: simple word or statement that indicates where you are in your speech or highlights an important idea (10)

silence: the lack of vocal sound (3)

single cause fallacy: when speakers assume a particular effect only has one cause (11)

slang: informal nonstandard vocabulary used by members of a co-culture or group who have similar interests, goals, or life experiences (4)

slippery slope fallacy: an argument in which a speaker claims that taking a first step in one direction will inevitably lead to undesirable further steps (11)

social comparison: comparing ourselves with another in order to determine our value or worth in relationship to that other person (2)

social groups: formal or informal groups of individuals who gather to meet the personal, communal, and collective needs of people (8)

social or polite touch: part of an initial interaction, greeting, or informal ritual (3)

social-penetration theory: describes the variation in breadth and depth of self-disclosure in a relationship (6)

spatial pattern: a pattern of organization that allows you to address topics logically in terms of location or direction (13)

specific purpose: focused statement that identifies exactly what a speaker wants to accomplish with a speech (10)

speech to explore an issue: a speaker attempts to engage an audience in a discussion about an idea, concern, topic, or plan of action (15)

speech topic: subject of your speech (10)

speeches about concepts: informative speeches about abstractions, things you cannot perceive with your senses—such as ideas, theories, principles, worldviews, or beliefs (13)

speeches about events: informative speeches that describe or explain significant, interesting, or unusual occurrences (13)

speeches about objects: informative speeches about anything that is tangible—that is, can be perceived by the senses (13)

speeches about places and people: speeches that describe significant, interesting, or unusual places or people (13)

speeches about processes: informative speech that describes how something is done, how something comes to be what it is, or how something works (13)

spotlighting: practice of highlighting a person's race, ethnicity, sex, sexual orientation, or physical disability (5)

stabilized friendship: when trust has been established, allowing friends to communicate fully, share private information, and establish additional relationship rules (6)

stage hogging: when people make the conversation about themselves instead of showing interest in the person who is talking (5)

stagnating step: when couples have minimal interaction or shared activities (6)

standpoint: the perspectives from which a person views and evaluates society (2)

state, or situational, anxiety: apprehension about communicating with others in a particular situation (12)

statistics: numerical summaries of facts, figures, and research findings (11)

stereotype: broad generalization about a group of people based on limited exposure to an individual or small number of members of that particular group (2)

substitution: when we rely on nonverbal codes instead of verbal ones (3)

summary: concise restatement of your main points at the end of your speech (10)

symbol: word, gesture, sound, image, or object that stands for or represents something else (1)

symbolic interactionism: process of understanding our sense of self based on other's observations, judgments, and evaluations of our behavior (2)

sympathy: feeling sorry for or pitying another (1)

symposium: public discussion in which several people each give speeches on different aspects of the same topic (9)

synchronous: message that is received in real time (6)

syntax: the rules that govern word order (4)

systematic desensitization: technique for reducing anxiety that involves teaching your body to feel calm and relaxed rather than fearful during your speeches (12)

task groups: problem-solving groups formed when individuals want to take on a job or solve an issue that is affecting them or those around them (8)

task stress: stress that consists of contrasting views and opinions among group members regarding the tasks at hand (9)

team: collections of individuals who come together to attempt to win something, to set a record, or be the best at some task or event (8)

team presentation: when several individual members of a group each present a different speech on a single topic (9)

terminating step: when individuals in a couple make their separation final (6)

testimony: opinions or observations of others (11)

thesis statement: single declarative sentence that summarizes the main ideas, assumptions, or arguments you want to express in your speech (10)

thought or reference: memory or past experiences people have with the words being communicated (1)

time-oriented listener: listener who views time as a commodity and does not want to have it wasted and wants speakers to be clear, succinct, and to the point (5)

topical organizational pattern: a pattern of organization that allows a speaker to address different aspects of a topic (13)

trait anxiety: apprehension about communicating with others in any situation (12)

transformative leader: one who creates significant change in the life of people and organizations (8)

transitions: phrases that indicate you are finished with one idea and are moving to a new one (10)

two-sided message: message that addresses two sides of an issue, refuting one side to prove the other is better (14)

uncertainty avoidance: extent to which members of an organization or society strive to avoid uncertainty by relying on social norms, rituals, and bureaucratic practices to alleviate the unpredictability of future events (8)

understand: to gain knowledge of a view or an idea (1)

unknown window: information about yourself that is yet to be discovered by you and others (6)

value: a person's idea of what is good, worthy, or important (10)

verbal clutter: extra words in sentences that do not add meaning (5)

virtual group: group of individuals who have never met one another in person but who communicate regularly through electronic means (8)

virtual meetings: meetings that take place via electronic means such as Skype or teleconferencing or other electronic media that can bring people together across distances (9)

visual communication system: includes the codes of kinesics, proxemics, and artifacts (3)

visual listener: listener who needs to see something in order to understand it (5)

visualization: a process in which you construct a mental image of yourself giving a successful speech (12)

vocal cues: aspects of the human voice that create rhythm or musical flow (3)

vocal variety: changes in the volume, rate, and pitch of a speaker's voice that affect the meaning of the words delivered (12)

vocalized pauses: the use of filler words or sounds such as *"er," "um,"* and *"uh";* pauses that speakers fill with words or sounds such as "um," "er," and "uh" (3, 12)

volume: loudness of a speaker's voice (12)

waning friendship: friendship that experiences a breach in trust, less quality or quantity of time spent together, or a violation in relational expectations (6)

workplace democracy: system of governance that truly values individuals' goals and feelings (9)

INDEX

A

Abreu, Kim, 387
abstracts, 254
accommodation, 144, 202
acronym, 80
action, 357
action-oriented listening, 106
adaptors, 60
Addo, Darcy, 151
ad hominem fallacy, 275
affect displays, 60
affection, 87
affective questions, 207
affiliative speech, 84
affirmations, 314–315
African Americans, self-concept and, 34–35
agenda, for meetings, 210–211
ALS Ice Bucket Challenge, 47
ambiguity
   in language, 77–80
   of nonverbal communication, 56–58, 64
ambushing, 102
American Life Project, 130–134
analogical reasoning, 270–271
Anderson, Carolyn, 18
Anderson, Gregory D. S., 82, 88, 111
androgynous communication, 84
androgyny, 145
anomalies, 267
anonymous posting, 151
appearance, listening and, 110
Arab Americans, harassment of, 48
argument by example, 266–267
argument culture, 6
   nonverbal communication, 64
Armstrong, Jeffrey, 148
articulation, 292
artifacts, nonverbal communication
   and, 62, 64
Ashcraft, Karen, 169
assertiveness, 184
asynchronous communication, 131–134
attention, getting, 274
   Monroe's motivated sequence, 356
attitudes, 222–223
audience
   catching attention of, 241
   connecting with, 315, 357–358
   focus on, 274–275
   informative speeches and, 333–334
   realistic attitudes concerning, 358–359, 361
   speaking to, 220–223, 232
audience-centered speaker, 220–221
auditory codes, nonverbal communication,
   64–66
auditory communication system, 59
auditory listening, 104–105
authoritarian leader, 179–181
authority rule, 206

B

avoidance, 144, 147
   in groups and teams, 202
avoiding step, romantic relationships, 127

background, listening and, 110
bandwagon fallacy, 275–276
bar graphs, 304
Barton, Jo, 40
Basij-Rasikh, Shabana, 201
Bass, Barnard M., 182
Bates, Lisa M., 71
Batra, Narian, 187
Bay Area Laboratory Co-Operative (BALCO), 336
Beetson, Jack, 380
behavioral objectives, 231–232
beliefs, 222–223
Bezos, Jeff, 180
bias, in language, 334–335
Bieri, Joseph, 19–20
BlackBerry, 86
blame shifting, 153
blind window, self-disclosure and, 128
"Blurred Lines" (song), 90
body movements, nonverbal communication, 60
body orientation, nonverbal communication
   and, 56
Bomb It (film), 17
bonding, romantic relationships, 124
Bonds, Barry, 336
brainstorming, 199–200, 227–230
breadth, 127
The Breakup 2.0: Disconnecting over New Media
   (Gershon), 127
Brockovich, Erin, 347
Brommel, Bernard, 119
bucket brigades, 347
bullying, 185–188
Burke, Kenneth, 5
Burns, James MacGregor, 182
burqas, French law banning, 48
Bylund, Carma, 119

C

call to action, 349
careers, communication and, 23
careful listener, 110, 112–113
Carter, Stephen, 15–16, 24, 156
casual language, 108
categorization, 228–230
Caunt, John, 39
causal organization, 353
causal pattern in speeches, 330–331
causal reasoning, 269–270
change, in groups, 209
channels, linear communication model, 10
charts, 303–304
Chavis, Dr. Benjamin, 284
chronemics, 66–67

chronological pattern for speeches, 328, 330,
   380–381
Chukchi language, 84
circumscribing, romantic relationships, 126–127
C.I.T.I.E.S organization, 22
civic communication, 3
   listening and, 98
civic engagement, 24
civility
   communication and, 15–17
   conflict and, 156–158
   in groups, 195–196
   language and, 92–93
   perception and, 46–48
   technology and, 189–190
clarification, 112
   of questions, 308–309
classroom setting, speaking in, 224
Clinton, Barbara, 19
closed questions, 207, 256
clustering, 228–230
coercive power, 168
cognitive complexity, 19–20
cognitive restructuring, 314–315
cohesion of groups or teams, 167
collaboration, 144
collectivist culture, 137, 208
   leadership and, 185
college students, communication by, 3, 3f
colloquialisms, 81
color, nonverbal communication and, 69–70
commitment
   in interpersonal relationships, 118–119
   romantic relationships, 123–126
communication. *See also* nonverbal
   communication
   androgynous communication, 84
   civic communication, 3
   climate for, 154–155
   competence and, 17–20
   culture and, 6–7, 9
   dark side of, 16
   defined, 3
   ethical communication, 3
   gender and, 82–83
   in groups or teams, 196, 208–210
   models for, 9–17
   process, 5–7
   self-concept and, 35–36
   small group communication, 87, 89
   study of, 21–24
   as symbol, 4
   types of, 7–9
communication apprehension, 23–24, 311
comparative advantages organization, 355
competence, communication and, 17–20
competition, 144
   in groups and teams, 202–203
complementation, 58

compromise, 144, 153
in groups and teams, 203
computer-mediated communication (CMC), 130–134, 150–151, 159
charts and graphs, 305
concepts, speeches about, 327–328
concern
for others, 143
for self, 143
conclusions
deductive reasoning, 268
in speeches, 245–246
condition of equality, 375
condition of self-determination, 376
condition of value, 375
confidence, during speeches, 310–315
confirming
listening and, 97
statements, 154–155
conflict
civility and, 156–158
culture and, 147–148
gender and, 144–145
in groups and teams, 196, 202–204
international conflict, 150–151
interpersonal relationships and, 142–143
management of, 152–155
naming of, 153
nature of, 143–155
technology and, 148–151
conformity, avoidance in groups and teams, 197–198
connectives, in speech, 238–239
connotative definitions, 77, 266
consensus, 204–206
Conte, Victor, 336
content messages, 23
content-oriented listening, 105
contradiction, 58
contrast, 30
conversation, gender and, 84
conversion rate optimization (CRO), 10–11
"Cool Friends" (MacDonald and Greggins), 39–40
counterarguments, 359
Cousteau, Alexandre, 44, 172, 199, 289, 379
credibility, in public speaking, 242
critical listening, 112–113
Crossen, Cynthia, 262
Culhane, Thomas Taha Rassam, 22, 78, 131, 224
cultural competence, 81–82
culture
communication and, 6–7, 9, 13
conflict and, 147–148
defined, 6
in groups and teams, 208–210
interpersonal relationships and, 136–137, 161
language and, 80–82, 108–110
leadership and, 183–185
linear communication model, 11
listening and, 100
monochronic cultures, 67
nonverbal communication and, 53–55
polychronic cultures, 67
self and, 31–32
self-concept and, 34–35

self-esteem and, 38–39
speaking volume and, 288–289
stereotypes, 148
technology and, 149–150
touch and, 67–69
Cupach, William, 16

D

The Daily Cartoonist, 90
Dalai Lama, 298
databases, 254
Daubman, Kimberly, 40
Davis, Wade, 294
debriefing talk, 87
decision making
by consensus, 205
in groups and teams, 198–202
decoding, linear communication model, 10
deductive reasoning, 268–269
defensive listening, 101–102
definitions, 266
delivery methods, 283–288
extemporaneous delivery, 283–284
impromptu delivery, 284–285
manuscript delivery, 285–287
memorized delivery, 287–288
nonverbal components, 293–300
technology and, 299–300
verbal components, 288–293
democratic leadership, 181
in workplace, 203–204
demonstrations, 302
in speeches, 243
Denetdale, Jennifer Rose, 148
denotative definitions, 4, 77, 266
depth, 127–128
Des Jarlais, Don, 389
deterioration, romantic relationships, 126
Dewey, John, 198–199
dialect, 293
dialogic power, 168
dialogue, 219
differences
interference from, 109–110
in interpersonal relationships, 160–161
Digital Freedom: How Much Can You Handle?
(Batra), 187
Ding, Jacob Deng, 28
direct quotations, 264
disconfirming statement, 154–155
discussions
gender and, 83–84
time for, 388
dissolution stage, in groups and teams, 197
distance in relationships, 158
distractions, listening and, 110, 112
diversity
advantages to, 387
in audience, 220–221
respect for, 388–389
DJ Cipha Sounds, 90, 92
domestic violence, 161–162
doublespeak, 80
Downey, Raymond, 180–181
drawings, 302–303

Druskat, Vanessa Urch, 183
DVDs, as visual aid, 303

E

Earle, Sylvia, 233
effective communication, 112
either-or fallacy, 276
Ekman, Paul, 61
elaboration likelihood model (ELM), 357–358
electronically medicated communication (EMC), group dynamics and, 202
Ellison, Nicole, 132
e-mail, language in, 85–86, 89
emblems, nonverbal communication, 58
emergence stage, in groups and teams, 197
emoticons, 70–71
emotions, reasoning and, 273–275
empathy, 20
emphasis, 58
encoding, linear communication model, 10
endangered languages, 88, 111
Enduring Voices project, 88, 111
engagement
in informative speeches, 332–333
listening and, 98
self-esteem and, 39–40
environment
awareness campaign, 47
interactive communication, 11–13, 13f
invitational speaking, 372–376
linear communication, 11
nonverbal communication and, 69–70
equality, 208–209, 375–376
equivocal words, 78–79
ethical communication, 3
anonymous posting, 151
anti-drug campaigns and persuasion, 255
death with dignity, 113
in groups and teams, 203
human rights protection and, 226
inductive reasoning, 267–268
informative speeches, 335–337
Internet research, 252
interviews, 258–259
invitational speeches, 389–390
maneuvers in, 169
nonverbal communications, 64
persuasive speaking, 362–363
reasoning ethically, 278–279
ribbon campaigns and awareness
bracelets, 360
social commentary on YouTube, 301
task groups and, 174
ethnicity
communication and, 6–7, 9, 13
nonverbal communication and, 53–55, 60
self-concept and, 34–35
self-esteem and, 38–39
stereotypes, 44–45
ethnocentrism, 7, 222
euphemisms, 80
events, speeches about, 322–323
Everest Peace Project, 174
evidence, 261, 279, 359
evolution of communications, 21–22